T0214557

Lecture Notes in Computer Science 11487

Commenced Publication in 1973
Founding and Former Series Editors:
Gerhard Goos, Juris Hartmanis, and Jan van Leeuwen

More information about this series at http://www.springer.com/series/7407

José Manuel Ferrández Vicente ·
José Ramón Álvarez-Sánchez ·
Félix de la Paz López ·
Javier Toledo Moreo ·
Hojjat Adeli (Eds.)

From Bioinspired Systems and Biomedical Applications to Machine Learning

8th International Work-Conference on the Interplay
Between Natural and Artificial Computation, IWINAC 2019
Almería, Spain, June 3–7, 2019
Proceedings, Part II

Springer

Editors
José Manuel Ferrández Vicente
Universidad Politécnica de Cartagena
Cartagena, Spain

José Ramón Álvarez-Sánchez
Universidad Nacional de Educación
a Distancia
Madrid, Spain

Félix de la Paz López
Universidad Nacional de Educación
a Distancia
Madrid, Madrid, Spain

Javier Toledo Moreo
Universidad Politécnica de Cartagena
Cartagena, Spain

Hojjat Adeli
The Ohio State University
Columbus, OH, USA

ISSN 0302-9743   ISSN 1611-3349 (electronic)
Lecture Notes in Computer Science
ISBN 978-3-030-19650-9   ISBN 978-3-030-19651-6 (eBook)
https://doi.org/10.1007/978-3-030-19651-6

LNCS Sublibrary: SL1 – Theoretical Computer Science and General Issues

This Springer imprint is published by the registered company Springer Nature Switzerland AG
The registered company address is: Gewerbestrasse 11, 6330 Cham, Switzerland

Preface

Bio-inspired computing methods take inspiration from nature to develop optimization and search algorithms or metaheuristics, typically in order to tackle the search for optimal solutions of complex problems in science and engineering, which usually imply a high dimensionality of the search space. The interplay between natural and artificial computation creates new paradigms not only in computer science but also in medicine and biology. The hybridization between social sciences and social behaviors with robotics, between neurobiology and computing, between ethics and neuroprosthetics, between cognitive sciences and neurocomputing, and between neurophysiology and marketing, will give rise to new concepts and tools that can be applied to ICT systems, as well as to natural science fields. Through IWINAC, we provide a forum in which research in different fields can converge to create new computational paradigms that are on the frontier between neural and biomedical sciences and information technologies.

As a multidisciplinary forum, IWINAC is open to any established institutions and research laboratories actively working in the field of natural or neural technologies. But beyond achieving cooperation between different research realms, we wish to actively encourage cooperation with the private sector, particularly SMEs, as a way of bridging the gap between frontier science and societal impact. In this edition, four main themes outline the conference topics: Affective Computing, Machine Learning Applied to NeuroScience, Deep Learning, and Biomedical Applications.

Emotions are essential in human–human communication, cognition, learning and rational decision-making processes. However, human–machine interfaces (HMIs) are still not able to understand human feelings and react accordingly. With the aim of endowing HMIs with the emotional intelligence they lack, affective computing science focuses on the development of artificial intelligence by means of the analysis of affects and emotions, such that systems and devices may be able to recognize, interpret, process and simulate human feelings.

Today, the evaluation of electrophysiological signals plays a key role in the advancement toward that purpose since they are an objective representation of the emotional state of an individual. Hence, the interest in physiological variables like electroencephalogram, electrocardiogram, or electrodermal activity, among many others, has notably grown in the field of affective states detection. Furthermore, emotions have also been widely identified by means of the assessment of speech characteristics and facial gestures of people under different sentimental conditions. It is also worth noting that the development of algorithms for the classification of affective states in social media has experienced a notable boost in the last years. In this sense, language of posts included in social networks, such as Facebook or Twitter, is evaluated with the aim of detecting the sentiments of the users of these media tools. Affective computing and sentiment analysis is intended to be a meeting point for researchers that are interested in any of those areas of expertise related to sentiment analysis and who want to initiate their studies or are currently working on these topics. Hence, manuscripts introducing new proposals based on the analysis of physiological measures, facial recognition, speech recognition, or natural language processing in social media are examples on affective computing and sentiment analysis.

Currently, machine learning holds great promise in the development of new models and theories in the field of neuroscience, in conjunction with classic statistical hypothesis testing. Machine learning algorithms have the potential to reveal interactions, hidden patterns of abnormal activity, brain structure and connectivity, and physiological mechanisms of the brain and behavior. In addition, several approaches for testing the significance of the machine learning outcomes have been successfully proposed to avoid "the dangers of spurious findings or explanations void of mechanism" by means of proper replication, validation, and hypothesis-driven confirmation. Therefore, machine learning can effectively provide relevant information to take great strides toward understanding how the brain works. The main goal of this field is to build a bridge between two scientific communities, the machine learning community, including lead scientists in deep learning and related areas in pattern recognition and artificial intelligence, and the neuroscience community.

Deep learning has represented a breakthrough for the artificial intelligence community. The best performances attained so far in many fields, such as computer vision or natural language processing, have been overtaken by these novel paradigms up to a point that only ten years ago was just science fiction. In addition, this technology has been open sourced by the main AI companies, hence making it quite straightforward to design, train, and integrate deep-learning based systems. Moreover, the amount of data available every day is not only enormous, but growing at an exponential rate. Over the past few years there has been increasing interest in using machine learning methods to analyze and visualize massive data generated from very different sources and with many different features: social networks, surveillance systems, smart cities, medical diagnosis, business, cyberphysical systems or media digital data. This topic is designed to serve researchers and developers to publish original, innovative, and state-of-the art machine learning algorithms and architectures to analyze and visualize large amounts of data.

Finally, biomedical applications are essential in IWINAC meetings. For instance, brain–computer interfaces (BCI) implement a new paradigm in communication networks, namely, brain area networks. In this paradigm, our brain receives input data (external stimuli), performs multiple media-access controls by means of cognitive tasks (selective attention), processes the information (perception), takes a decision (cognition) and, eventually, transmits data back to the source (by means of a BCI), thus closing the communication loop. Image understanding is a research area involving both feature extraction and object identification within images from a scene, and a posterior treatment of this information in order to establish relationships between these objects with a specific goal. In biomedical and industrial scenarios, the main purpose of this discipline is, given a visual problem, to manage all aspects of prior knowledge, from study start-up and initiation through data collection, quality control, expert independent interpretation, to design and development of systems involving image processing capable of tackle with these tasks. These areas are clear examples of innovative applications in biology or medicine.

The wider view of the computational paradigm gives us more elbow room to accommodate the results of the interplay between nature and computation. The IWINAC forum thus becomes a methodological approximation (set of intentions, questions, experiments, models, algorithms, mechanisms, explanation procedures, and engineering and computational methods) to the natural and artificial perspectives of the mind embodiment problem, both in humans and in artifacts. This is the philosophy that continues in IWINAC meetings, the "interplay" movement between the natural and the artificial, facing this same problem every two years. This synergistic approach will permit us not only to build new computational systems based on the natural measurable phenomena, but also to understand many of the observable behaviors inherent to natural systems.

The difficulty of building bridges between natural and artificial computation is one of the main motivations for the organization of IWINAC 2019. The IWINAC 2019 proceedings contain the works selected by the Scientific Committee from nearly 200 submissions, after the refereeing process. The first volume, entitled *Understanding the Brain Function and Emotions*, includes all the contributions mainly related to the new tools for analyzing neural data, or detecting emotional states, or interfacing with physical systems. The second volume, entitled *From Bioinspired Systems and Biomedical Applications to Machine Learning*, contains the papers related to bioinspired programming strategies and all the contributions oriented to the computational solutions to engineering problems in different application domains, as biomedical systems, or big data solutions.

An event of the nature of IWINAC 2019 cannot be organized without the collaboration of a group of institutions and people whom we would like to thank now, starting with Universidad Nacional de Educación a Distancia (UNED) and Universidad Politécnica de Cartagena. The collaboration of the Universidad de Granada and Universidad de Almeria was crucial, as was the efficient work of the local Organizing Committee, chaired by Juan Manuel Gorriz Sáez with the close collaboration of Manuel Cantón Garbín, Manuel Berenguel Soria, Javier Ramírez Pérez de Inestrosa, Andrés Ortiz García, Francisco Jesús Martínez Murcia, Diego Salas González, Ignacio Álvarez Illán, Fermín Segovia Román, and Diego Castillo Barnés. In addition to our universities, we received financial support from the Spanish CYTED, Red Nacional en Computación Natural y Artificial, Programa de Grupos de Excelencia de la Fundación Séneca and Apliquem Microones 21 s.l.

We want to express our gratitude to our invited speakers, Prof. Hojjat Adeli (Ohio State University, USA), Prof. Francisco Herrera (Universidad de Málaga, Spain), Prof. John Suckling (University of Cambridge, UK), and Prof. Hiroaki Wagatsuma (Kyushu Institute of Technology, Japan), for accepting our invitation and for their magnificent plenary talks. We would also like to thank the authors for their interest in our call and the effort in preparing the papers, condition sine qua non for these proceedings. We thank the Scientific and Organizing Committees, in particular the members of these committees who acted as effective and efficient referees and as promoters and managers of preorganized sessions on autonomous and relevant topics under the IWINAC global scope. Our sincere gratitude also goes to Springer and to Alfred Hofmann and his colleagues, Anna Kramer and Elke Werner, for the continuous receptivity, help efforts, and collaboration in all our joint editorial ventures on the interplay between neuroscience and computation. Finally, we want to express our special thanks to Viajes Hispania, our technical secretariat, and to Chari García and Beatriz Baeza, for making this meeting possible, and for arranging all the details that comprise the organization of this kind of event.

Last year, in 2018, was 10 years without Professor Mira, without his close and friendly presence. We want to dedicate these two volumes of the IWINAC proceedings to Professor Mira's memory.

June 2019

José Manuel Ferrández Vicente
José Ramón Álvarez-Sánchez
Félix de la Paz López
Javier Toledo Moreo
Hojjat Adeli

Organization

General Chair

José Manuel Ferrández Vicente, Spain

Organizing Committee

José Ramón Álvarez-Sánchez, Spain
Félix de la Paz López, Spain
Javier Toledo Moreo, Spain

Honorary Chairs

Hojjat Adeli, USA
Zhou Changjiu, Singapore
Rodolfo Llinás, USA

Local Organizing Committee

Ignacio Álvarez Illán, Spain
Manuel Berenguel Soria, Spain
Manuel Cantón Garbín, Spain
Diego Castillo Barnés, Spain
Juan Manuel Górriz Sáez, Spain

Francisco Jesús Martínez Murcia, Spain
Andrés Ortiz García, Spain
Javier Ramírez Pérez de Inestrosa, Spain
Diego Salas González, Spain
Fermín Segovia Román, Spain

Invited Speakers

Hojjat Adeli, USA
Francisco Herrera, Spain

John Suckling, UK
Hiroaki Wagatsuma, Japan

Field Editors

Jose Santos Reyes, Spain
Ramiro Varela Arias, Spain
Arturo Martínez-Rodrigo, Spain
Antonio Fernández-Caballero, Spain
Jose García-Rodríguez, Spain
Enrique Domínguez, Spain
David Tomás, Spain

Jaime Oswaldo Salvador Meneses,
   Ecuador
Zoila Ruiz, Ecuador
Rafael Verdú Monedero, Spain
José Luis Sancho Gómez, Spain
Rafael Martínez Tomás, Spain
Mariano Rincón Zamorano, Spain

Javier de Lope Asiain, Spain
Manuel Graña, Spain
Alfredo Cuesta Infante, Spain
Juan José Pantrigo, Spain

Antonio S. Montemayor, Spain
Juan Manuel Górriz Sáez, Spain
Javier Ramirez Pérez de Inestrosa, Spain

International Scientific Committee

Ajith Abraham, Norway
Michael Affenzeller, Austria
Peter Ahnelt, Austria
Boris Almonacid, Chile
Amparo Alonso Betanzos, Spain
Antonio Anaya, Spain
Davide Anguita, Italy
Manuel Arias Calleja, Spain
Jose Luis Aznarte Mellado, Spain
José M. Azorín, Spain
Jorge Azorin Lopez, Spain
Margarita Bachiller Mayoral, Spain
Antonio Bahamonde, Spain
Emilia I. Barakova, The Netherlands
Alvaro Barreiro, Spain
Senén Barro Ameneiro, Spain
María Consuelo Bastida Jumilla, Spain
Francisco Bellas, Spain
Rafael Berenguer Vidal, Spain
Guido Bologna, Italy
Maria Bonomini, Argentina
Juan Carlos Burguillo Rial, Spain
Enrique J. Carmona Suarez, Spain
Juan Castellanos, Spain
German Castellanos Dominguez,
    Colombia
José Carlos Castillo, Spain
Miguel Cazorla, Spain
Joaquin Cerda Boluda, Spain
Alexander Cerquera, USA
Santi Chillemi, Italy
Carlos Colodro Conde, Spain
Ricardo Contreras, Chile
Carlos Cotta, Spain
José Manuel Cuadra Troncoso, Spain
Adriana Dapena, Spain
Angel P. del Pobil, Spain
Ana E. Delgado García, Spain
Jose Dorronsoro, Spain

Richard Duro, Spain
Patrizia Fattori, Italy
Paulo Félix Lamas, Spain
Eduardo Fernandez, Spain
Manuel Fernández Delgado, Spain
Miguel A. Fernandez Graciani, Spain
Jose Luis Fernández Vindel, Spain
Cipriano Galindo, Spain
Vicente Garceran Hernandez, Spain
Francisco Javier Garrigos Guerrero,
    Spain
Elena Gaudioso, Spain
Pedro Gomez Vilda, Spain
Pascual González, Spain
Francisco Guil Reyes, Spain
Juan Carlos Herrero, Spain
Cesar Hervas Martinez, Spain
Tom Heskes, The Netherlands
Eduardo Iáñez, Spain
Roberto Iglesias, Spain
Fernando Jimenez Barrionuevo, Spain
Jose M. Juarez, Spain
Joost N. Kok, The Netherlands
Elka Korutcheva, Spain
Ryo Kurazume, Japan
Jorge Larrey Ruiz, Spain
Jerome Leboeuf, Mexico
Álvar-Ginés Legaz Aparicio, Spain
Emilio Leton Molina, Spain
Maria Teresa Lopez Bonal, Spain
Mguel Angel Lopez Gordo, Spain
Tino Lourens, The Netherlands
Manuel Luque, Spain
Saturnino Maldonado, Spain
Ángeles Manjarrés, Spain
Dario Maravall, Spain
Jose Javier Martinez Alvarez, Spain
Antonio Martínez Álvarez, Spain
Rosa-María Menchón Lara, Spain

Contents – Part II

Applications

Bioinspired Systems

Machine Learning for Big Data and Visualization

Biomedical Applications

Deep Learning

Contents – Part I

Affective Computing

Neuroethology

Machine Learning in Neuroscience

Models

Towards a General Method for Logical Rule Extraction from Time Series

Guido Sciavicco[1]([✉])[iD], Ionel Eduard Stan[2][iD], and Alessandro Vaccari[1][iD]

[1] Department of Mathematics and Computer Science,
University of Ferrara, Ferrara, Italy
guido.sciavicco@unife.it, alessandr.vaccari@student.unife.it
[2] Department of Mathematics, Computer Science, and Physics,
University of Udine, Udine, Italy
stan.ioneleduard@spes.uniud.it

Abstract. Extracting rules from temporal series is a well-established temporal data mining technique. The current literature contains a number of different algorithms and experiments that allow one to abstract temporal series and, later, extract meaningful rules from them. In this paper, we approach this problem in a rather general way, without resorting, as many other methods, to expert knowledge and ad-hoc solutions. Our very simple temporal abstraction method allows us to transform time series into timelines, which can be then used for logical temporal rule extraction using an already existing temporal adaptation of the algorithm APRIORI. We have tested this approach on real data, obtaining promising results.

Keywords: Rule extraction · Time series · Timelines

1 Introduction

Rule-based methods are a popular class of techniques in machine learning and data mining [8]. They share the goal of finding regularities in data that can be expressed in the form of *if-then* rules. Depending on the type of rules, we can discriminate between *descriptive rules* discovery, which aims at describing significant patterns in the given data set in terms of rules, and *predictive rules* discovery, which is focused on learning a collection of the rules that collectively cover the instance space and can make a prediction for every possible instance. In this paper, we are interested in descriptive (or *association*) rules, for which there are three popular approaches: *inductive logic programming*, which uses logic programming as a uniform representation for examples, background knowledge and hypotheses, and aims at deriving a hypothesised logic program (that is, a set of rules) which entails all the positive and none of the negative examples (see, e.g., [18,19]); *rule induction via metaheuristics*, typically driven by evolutionary algorithms; and APRIORI [1] and its subsequent developments. These approaches have been extensively compared in the literature (see, e.g., [9] and

© Springer Nature Switzerland AG 2019
J. M. Ferrández Vicente et al. (Eds.): IWINAC 2019, LNCS 11487, pp. 3–12, 2019.
https://doi.org/10.1007/978-3-030-19651-6_1

references therein); apparently, although APRIORI is probably the first technology for rule extraction that gained some acknowledgment in the community, its main ideas are still widely used, since no negative examples are needed (in contrast to inductive logic programming), and since it is considered reliable and fast (in contrast to metaheuristic approaches, which are computationally expensive).

Time series are largely used to describe a wide range of data. Their use is ubiquitous; among others, they are commonly used in *environmental sciences* [22], where data describing the quality of air, water, soil, food most often include multi-variate time series, in *industry* [21], where time series are used to describe the working parameters of machines, in *medical sciences* [14], where complex medical exams are normally described by multi-variate series, and in *smart homes* [13], where sensors that help the intelligent systems in taking decisions usually generate data in form of series. As a consequence, extracting rules from time series can be very important, and the literature on this topic is relatively large, ranging from primitive approaches [6,7], to generalizations of APRIORI to take into account the temporal component [2], to more general and modern methodologies [20]. A survey on temporal abstraction methods is given by Höppner in [12]. There exist several abstraction methods, which can be roughly separated into *adimensional*, that is, methods that do not consider the temporal dimension, and *dimensional*, which do consider the temporal dimension. Examples of the first category include: *(i) Equal Width Discretization* (EWD), *(ii) Equal Frequency Discretization* (EFD), and *(iii) k-means clustering*. Examples of dimensional methods, include: *(iv) Symbolic Aggregate approXimation* (SAX) [15], which does not explicitly consider the temporal order of the values and *(v) Persist* [16], which maximizes the duration of the resulting time intervals and which explicitly considers the temporal order. Moreover, in [17], a classification-driven discretization method, namely *Temporal Discretization for Classification* (TD4C), is presented. A comparative study on various *pattern languages* (i.e. approaches to represent the temporal interval patterns) is presented in [11], where the authors point out the strengths and weaknesses for each of them, based on four well-known problems in the literature: preservation of qualitative relationship, preservation of quantitative durations, concurrency and robustness; many of such languages are Allen-based, but none of them have a logical approach.

Upon examining the current literature on temporal series extraction, one can see that most of the proposed solutions share common characteristics: *(i)* temporal abstraction, that is, the segmentation and (possibly) aggregation of time series into symbolic time intervals is often based on external knowledge and/or specific to the rule extraction algorithm; *(ii)* rule extraction algorithm are mostly ad-hoc, and *(iii)* the extracted rules are usually existential, often limited to being binary rules, in which the temporal (Allen's) relations between intervals are used in a very limited way. In this paper, we present a general technique, structured into the two, classical steps of temporal abstraction and rule extraction, that addresses the above issues. Our temporal abstraction step is completely general and domain-independent, and separated from the rule extraction phase, which,

HS	Allen's relations	Graphical representation
$\langle A \rangle$	$[x,y]R_A[x',y'] \Leftrightarrow y = x'$	
$\langle L \rangle$	$[x,y]R_L[x',y'] \Leftrightarrow y < x'$	
$\langle B \rangle$	$[x,y]R_B[x',y'] \Leftrightarrow x = x', y' < y$	
$\langle E \rangle$	$[x,y]R_E[x',y'] \Leftrightarrow y = y', x < x'$	
$\langle D \rangle$	$[x,y]R_D[x',y'] \Leftrightarrow x < x', y' < y$	
$\langle O \rangle$	$[x,y]R_O[x',y'] \Leftrightarrow x < x' < y < y'$	

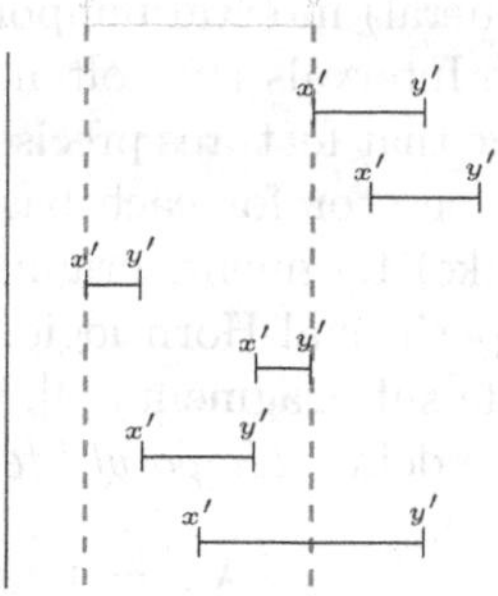

Fig. 1. Allen's interval relations and HS modalities.

in turn, is based on a general tool known as Temporal APRIORI [3]. The main characteristics of our approach are: *(i)* rules are written in a well-known logical language, that is, Halpern and Shoham's interval-based temporal logic HS [10], *(ii)* every Allen's relation may have a role in the extracted rules, and the (sub)set of relations that are actually used is completely customizable, and *(iii)* rules are logic formulas, that is, they generalize classical, static, APRIORI rules. Temporal APRIORI is a rule extraction algorithm to extract interval temporal logic rules from timelines; the cornerstone of this method is, therefore, consistently transforming multi-variate time series into timelines.

2   Temporal APRIORI

Temporal APRIORI is a rule extraction algorithm that generalizes APRIORI to cope with instances with a temporal component, and it has been presented in [3]. The starting point of Temporal APRIORI is the observation that non-temporal rules can be thought as implications written in propositional logic, even though they are not interpreted as implications in strict logical terms. On the one hand, rules represent positive information only: instances where the implication is trivially satisfied by the absence of the antecedent are not relevant in this setting. On the other hand, rules express a likelihood information, such as *if these items are present, it is very likely that this other item will be present, too*, rather than a deterministic Boolean value. Classical static rules (such as rules extracted from frequent item sets, to use APRIORI terminology) have the form of propositional Horn logic rules:

$$\rho : p_1 \wedge p_2 \wedge \ldots \wedge p_k \Rightarrow p \tag{1}$$

where $p_1, \ldots, p_k, p$ are propositional letters associated to the items of the instances in the data set (*literals*). Since in many application domains temporal information is stored in form of intervals, extracting interval-based temporal rules is the natural generalization of the above idea. The most representative (and general) interval temporal language is Halpern and Shoham's Modal Logic of Time Intervals [10], often referred to as HS, and it is a modal propositional language that features precisely one existential modal operator and one universal modal operator for each basic relation between two intervals. Its sub-Boolean (Horn-like) fragment, originally studied in [5] naturally generalizes the classical propositional Horn logic, and, at the same time, it has some decidable and tractable sub-fragments [4]. The Horn fragment of HS has a simple grammar. First, we define *temporal literals*:

$$\lambda :: = \top \mid \bot \mid p \mid \langle X \rangle \lambda \mid [X] \lambda \mid \langle \overline{X} \rangle \lambda \mid [\overline{X}] \lambda,$$

where $\langle X \rangle$ (resp., $\langle \overline{X} \rangle$) is a modal operator that existentially ranges over the Allen's relation R_X (see Fig. 1), that is, $X \in \{A, B, E, D, O, L\}$ (resp., the inverse of Allen's relation R_X), $[X]$ (resp., $[\overline{X}]$) is its universal version, and p is a propositional letter, and then, we define *rules*:

$$\varphi :: = \lambda \mid [G](\lambda_1 \wedge \ldots \wedge \lambda_k \rightarrow \lambda) \mid \varphi_1 \wedge \varphi_2.$$

The semantics of Horn HS formulas is given in terms of *interval models* (or *timelines*) of the type $T = \langle D, V \rangle$, where $(D, \leq)$ is a linearly ordered set and $V : \mathcal{AP} \rightarrow 2^{I(D)}$ is a *valuation function* which assigns to each atomic proposition $p \in \mathcal{AP}$ the set of intervals $V(p)$ on which p holds, being $I(D)$ the set of all intervals (that is, pairs of the type $[x, y]$, where $x < y$) that can be formed on D. The *truth* of a formula φ on a given interval $[x, y]$ in a timeline T is defined by structural induction on formulas as follows:

- $T, [x, y] \Vdash \top$ and $T, [x, y] \not\Vdash \bot$ for every $[x, y] \in I(D)$;
- $T, [x, y] \Vdash p$ if $[x, y] \in V(p)$;
- $T, [x, y] \Vdash \langle X \rangle \psi$ if there is a $[w, z]$ such that $[x, y] R_X [w, z]$ and $T, [w, z] \Vdash \psi$;
- $T, [x, y] \Vdash [X] \psi$ if, for all $[w, z]$ such that $[x, y] R_X [w, z]$, $T, [w, z] \Vdash \psi$;
- $T, [x, y] \Vdash [G](\lambda_1 \wedge \ldots \wedge \lambda_k \rightarrow \lambda)$ if, for all $[w, z]$ such that $T, [w, z] \Vdash \lambda_1 \wedge \cdots \wedge \lambda_k$, $T, [w, z] \Vdash \lambda$;
- $T, [x, y] \Vdash \psi_1 \wedge \psi_2$ if $T, [x, y] \Vdash \psi_1$ and $T, [x, y] \Vdash \psi_2$.

Timelines generalize static instances. Consider, for example, the medical history of a patient. While during a interesting period of observation, we may *statically* describe the set of its symptoms, the (suitably discretized) values of his/her tests, and the therapies to which he/she has undergone, and extract static rules in the form of (1), if we take into account the temporal component, we may, instead, describe the same medical histories by associating every interesting information to the temporal interval in which it holds. The rules that may be extracted take, therefore, the form:

$$\rho : \lambda_1 \wedge \lambda_2 \wedge \ldots \wedge \lambda_k \Rightarrow \lambda, \tag{2}$$

where $\lambda_1, \ldots, \lambda_k, \lambda$ are temporal literal. As we have already recalled, rules are not implications in the strict logical sense. As much as static rules are concerned, the validity of a rule such as (1) in a static data set depends on two parameters, known as support and confidence: the *support* of a rule is the minimum fraction of instances of the data set in which every one satisfies both the antecedent $(p_1 \wedge p_2 \wedge \ldots \wedge p_k)$ and the consequent (p) should hold, and the *confidence* is the minimum fraction of the support of the antecedent only in which both the antecedent and the consequent should hold in order to consider a rule such as (1) as true on a data set. So, for example, we say that $p_1 \wedge p_2 \Rightarrow p$ *holds on a data set with support* 0.75 *and confidence* 0.95 if at least three quarters of the instances satisfy p_1, p_2 and p and, of those instances which satisfy p_1 and p_2, ninety-five percent satisfy also p. Temporal rules require a similar treatment, with the additional problem that instances are not static, and thus evaluating a rule on single instance is not immediate. The concepts of support and confidence naturally generalize along two directions. First, we use the *temporal support* and *temporal confidence* to evaluate a single temporal literal λ on a single timeline T: the former establishes which is the minimal fraction of all intervals of T that must be captured by the relation R_X over the interval $[x, y]$ in order to the temporal literal λ to make sense on it, and the latter establishes the minimal fraction of those that must satisfy the argument of λ in order for λ to be considered true. In this, way, for example, we do not evaluate $[D]p$ on a too short interval, or $[A]p$ on an interval too close to the rightmost point of a timeline, and we do evaluate as true $[L]p$ on an interval $[x, y]$ when the number of intervals of the type $[z, t]$ $(z > y)$ with $\neg p$ are less than a certain fraction. Observe that temporal support and confidence may depend on the specific relation R_X and on the fact that λ is existential or universal. Second, we use the *global support* and *global confidence* to set, respectively, the minimum fractions of intervals of T in which both the antecedent and the consequent of a rule such as (2) should hold and the minimum fraction of the support of the antecedent only in which also the consequent should hold in order to evaluate as true the entire rule. Finally, to evaluate a rule on a temporal data set, one applies a generalized version of the standard support, defined as the minimum fraction of timelines in which at least one intervals satisfies both the antecedent and the consequent of the body of the rule (so that the rule is significant in the temporal data set).

A prototypal implementation of Temporal APRIORI is described in [3] that implements most of the above concepts, and has been used to run the experiments described in this paper.

3   Temporal Abstraction of Time Series

As we have already recalled, temporal abstraction has been widely studied in the recent literature. Our proposal is driven by two objectives: first, generalizing and systematizing the other approaches with a simple, domain-independent algorithm, and, second, transforming time series into timelines from which rules such as those described in the previous section can be extracted.

Let $\bar{F}(t) = (f_1(t), \ldots, f_m(t))$ be a multi-variate time series. Each $f_j(t)$ is referred to as *variable* (or *attribute*, to use the standard terminology for static data). A data set of multi-variate time series has the form $\bar{F}_1(t), \bar{F}_2(t), \ldots, \bar{F}_n(t)$. Although time series that describe real-life data may have any codomain (typically, the reals), since a data set is always finite and extensively described we can always assume that each $f_j(t)$ is a function of the type:

$$f_j : D \to \mathbb{N},$$

where D is a finite temporal domain. As for example, in a medical domain temporal data set, each instance $\bar{F}(t) = (f_1(t), f_2(t))$ may be the description of the medical history of a patient that includes his/her *fever* ($f_1(t)$) and his/her level of *blood pressure* ($f_2(t)$). Our purpose is to convert $\bar{F}(t)$ into a timeline T in which every interval is suitably labelled to carry the same information (in abstract form). Time series are often abstracted in different ways with different aims; in some cases, an interval is labelled with the *state* of some variable $f_j(t)$, that is, with the average value of $f_j(t)$ in that intervals; in some other cases, a label represents the *trend* of some variable. In order to generalize and systematize such a labelling process, we introduce the concept of *z-th degree of timeline*, in analogy with the z-th degree of *discrete derivative*. As a matter of fact, states are simply averages of the values of some $f_j(t)$, while trends are averages of the values of $f_j^1(t)$. In general, therefore, one may be interested to abstract a time series at any degree of derivative, to obtain a timeline from which rules can be extracted. In the following, we use the symbol $\bar{F}^z(t)$ for $(f_1^z(t), f_2^z(t), \ldots, f_m^z(t))$.

Since at each degree of derivative the finite domain of the resulting function contains one less point, we denote by D^z the domains obtained from D at the z-th degree of derivative. Fixed a degree z, the abstraction process consists of producing a timeline $T_{\bar{F}^z(t)}$ from $\bar{F}^z(t)$:

$$T_{\bar{F}^z(t)} = \langle D^z, V \rangle,$$

and we have to specify the valuation function V. To this end, we first consider the mean (denoted by μ_j) and the standard deviation (denoted by σ_j) of the j-th component entire series (at the z-th derivative), and, for a specific interval $[x, y] \in I(D)$, we define:

$$\mu_j^{xy} = \frac{\Sigma_{x \leq t \leq y} f_j^z(t)}{y - x},$$

that is, the mean of the values of $f_j^z(t)$ between x and y, and we use them to build a set of propositional letters to define the valuation function V. In classical solutions for temporal abstraction labels are often domain-dependent. In order to avoid the use of domain-related knowledge, we introduce two parameters, that is, $l > 1, l \in \mathbb{N}$ (*number of labels*, assumed to be odd) and $k \in [0,1] \subset \mathbb{R}$ (*displacement*), and define the set of propositional letters:

$$\{L_p^j \mid 1 \leq p \leq l, 1 \leq j \leq m\},$$

```
proc Abstract (F, z, l, k)
  T = ∅
  for (i = 1 to n)
    Ti = Abs(F̄i(t), z, l, k)
    T = T ∪ {Ti}
  return T
```

Fig. 2. A general, domain-independent, temporal abstraction algorithm.

and, finally, define:

$$[x, y] \in V(L_p^j) \text{ iff } \begin{cases} \mu_j^{xy} < \mu_j - \lfloor \frac{l}{2} \rfloor k\sigma_j & \text{if } p = 1 \\ \mu_j - (\lceil \frac{l}{2} \rceil - p + 1)k\sigma_j \le \mu_j^{xy} < (\lceil \frac{l}{2} \rceil - p)k\sigma_j & \text{if } 1 < p < \lceil \frac{l}{2} \rceil \\ \mu_j - k\sigma_j \le \mu_j^{xy} \le \mu_j + k\sigma_j & \text{if } p = \lceil \frac{l}{2} \rceil \\ \mu_j - (p - \lceil \frac{l}{2} \rceil)k\sigma_j < \mu_j^{xy} \le (p - \lceil \frac{l}{2} \rceil + 1)k\sigma_j & \text{if } \lceil \frac{l}{2} \rceil < p < l \\ \mu_j^{xy} > \mu_j + \lfloor \frac{l}{2} \rfloor k\sigma_j & \text{if } p = l \end{cases}$$

So, for example, if $z = 0$, $l = 3$ and $k = 0.5$, then L_1 (resp., L_2, L_3) can be read as *low* (resp., *average*, *high*), and an interval $[x, y]$ is labelled with *low* if its mean value is less than the mean value of the entire series (on the same component) minus half of its standard deviation. As another example, if $z = 1$, $l = 3$, and $k = 0.25$, then an interval $[x, y]$ is labelled with *increasing* (corresponding to L_3 on the first derivative, that is, the series of the trends) if the mean value of the differences in $[x, y]$ exceeds the mean value of all differences plus one fourth of the standard deviations of all differences. In this way, we can temporally abstract any multi-variate time series at any level of derivative, so that rules can be discovered that link the states, or the trends, or the accelerations, and so on, in a consistent, simple, and general way.

Given a time series $\bar{F}(t)$, we say that the *abstracted z-th degree timeline* $T_{\bar{F}^z(t)}$, with l labels and displacement k is:

$$T_{\bar{F}^z(t)} = Abs(\bar{F}(t), z, l, k),$$

where *Abs* is a procedure that applies the above labelling strategy. Given a set of n time series $\mathcal{F} = (\bar{F}_1(t), \bar{F}_2(t), \ldots, \bar{F}_n(t))$, we convert it into a temporal data set (a set of n timelines) $T = (T_1, T_2, \ldots, T_n)$ by simply applying the procedure *Abstract* in Fig. 2.

4   Application Example

In this example we use a set of time series that emerges from collecting physical-chemical data from underground water of a very specific area in the North-East of Italy. Such samples were collected as a part of a ongoing investigation commissioned by the local Regional Agency for Environment and Prevention to the University of Ferrara, with the purpose of exploring the causes of a sudden,

Table 1. Examples of rules extracted from the temporal data set at the 0-th degree of derivative.

$\langle A \rangle$ *C.E.* is average $\Rightarrow \langle L \rangle$ *Na* is high
$\langle A \rangle$ *Cl* is average $\Rightarrow \langle L \rangle$ *Na* is high
$\langle A \rangle$ *Na* is low $\Rightarrow \langle L \rangle$ *C.E.* is average
$\langle L \rangle$ *C.E.* is high $\Rightarrow \langle L \rangle$ *Na* is high
C.E. is average $\wedge$ *HCO3* is average $\Rightarrow \langle L \rangle Na$ is high

Table 2. Examples of rules extracted from the temporal data set at the 1-th degree of derivative.

$\langle A \rangle$ *Cl* decreaes $\Rightarrow \langle A \rangle$ *C.E.* is stable
$\langle A \rangle$ *Cl* decreaes $\Rightarrow \langle A \rangle$ *I* is stable
$\langle D \rangle$ *C.E.* is stable $\wedge \langle A \rangle$ *I* is stable $\Rightarrow [O]$ *Cl* does not increase
$\langle D \rangle$ *C.E.* is stable $\wedge [A]$ *I* is not stable $\Rightarrow [O]$ *Cl* does not decrease

unexpected spike of certain polluting agents in the underground water. Such data are being used to perform several physical-chemical researches; since they have the form of multi-variate time series, we can also use them to test our rule extraction method.

In the relevant area, 92 sampling points (underground water wells) were chosen for this analysis. Samples have been collected from 2012 to 2018, in a periodic way, on most of such points. Each sample has been analyzed from the physical-chemical point of view, and several indicators have been registered: *Br* (*Bromine*), *Ca* (*Calcium*), *Cl* (*Chlorine*), *Fe* (*Iron*), *HCO3* (*Bicarbonate*), *I* (*Iodine*), *K* (*Potassium*), *Mg* (*Magnesium*), *NH4* (*Ammonium cation*), *NO3* (*Nitrate*), *Na* (*Sodium*), *SO4* (*Sulfate*), *Hg* (*Mercury*), *T* (*Temperature*), *Eh* (*Reduction potential*), *DO* (*Chemical oxygen demand*), and *C.E.* (*Electric conductivity*). After re-normalization, such data have been temporally ordered, obtaining 92 17-variate time series. These have been abstracted using the algorithm explained in the previous section, at the 0-th, and the 1-st degree, with 3 labels (per variable), and $k = 0.5$, to obtain two temporal data sets. Of the 92 series, only 43 meaningful timelines could be extracted: the remaining ones where too short (they have less than 3 observations). Moreover, for this particular exercise, the function *Abs* has been implemented in such a way that intervals that contain too long gaps (more than 150 consecutive days without observations) have not been labelled. The following parameters have been set for both experiments: minimum support 0.8, minimum confidence 0.85, minimum global confidence 0.85. For a better understanding of the underlying problem, the three labels have been paired with the labels corresponding to their negation, during the abstraction process. So, for example, for the 1-st degree of derivative and the value of Magnesium, we have used the letters *decreasing, stable, increasing* (corresponding to the three possible values of the derivative) and *not decreasing, not stable, not increasing*.

As it happens with classical, static APRIORI, a rule extraction generally produces many results. We have limited ourselves to analyze rules with unary or binary antecedent, and modal depth 1. Also, in this particular context, at the 0-th derivative degree rules that relate in time average situations with average situation are probably meaningless, as well as, at the 1-th degree, are rules that relate stable situations with stable situations. Examples of extracted rules are in Tables 1 and 2. The first two rules predict a future period of high Sodium in the sample, provided that the observation is made immediately before a period in which conductivity or Chlorine is stable. By means of the fourth rule we are able to foresee that a future period of high conductivity will be associated with a future period of high Sodium. The last two rules of the second group, corresponding to the 1-st degree of derivative, are particularly interesting. The first one allows us to say that if we are in a period in which, at some point, the conductivity is stable, and right before a period in which the Iodine level is also stable, then, the level of Chlorine will be stable or it will decrease for a while. But the second one says that if we are in a period in which, at some point, the conductivity is stable (as before), and never in future the Iodine level will be stable, then, the level of Chlorine will be stable or it will increase for a while.

5 Conclusions

It is well-recognized that extracting rules from time series is an important task. In this paper we approached the problem in a general way, and with a novel technique. We made use of a temporal logic language with a very high expressive power (at least at the qualitative level), and we have designed a temporal abstraction algorithm that transforms time series into timelines, so that temporal rules can be extracted with an already existing temporal generalization of APRIORI.

Acknowledgements. G. Sciavicco acknowledges the partial support by the Italian INDAM GNCS project *Formal methods for techniques for combined verification.*

References

1. Agrawal, R., Imieliński, T., Swami, A.N.: Mining association rules between sets of items in large databases. In: Proceedings of the 1993 ACM SIGMOD International Conference on Management of Data, pp. 207–216 (1993)
2. Agrawal, R., Srikant, R.: Mining sequential patterns. In: Proceedings of the 11th International Conference on Data Engineering, pp. 3–14 (1995)
3. Bresolin, D., Cominato, E., Gnani, S., Muñoz-Velasco, E., Sciavicco, G.: Extracting interval temporal logic rules: a first approach. In: Proceedings of the 25th International Symposium on Temporal Representation and Reasoning. Leibniz International Proceedings in Informatics, vol. 120, pp. 7:1–7:15 (2018)
4. Bresolin, D., Kurucz, A., Muñoz-Velasco, E., Ryzhikov, V., Sciavicco, G., Zakharyaschev, M.: Horn fragments of the Halpern-Shoham interval temporal logic. ACM Trans. Comput. Logic **18**(3), 22:1–22:39 (2017)

5. Bresolin, D., Muñoz-Velasco, E., Sciavicco, G.: Sub-propositional fragments of the interval temporal logic of Allen's relations. In: Fermé, E., Leite, J. (eds.) JELIA 2014. LNCS (LNAI), vol. 8761, pp. 122–136. Springer, Cham (2014). https://doi.org/10.1007/978-3-319-11558-0_9

6. Cotofrei, P., Stoffel, K.: Rule extraction from time series databases using classification trees. In: Proceedings of the IASTED International Conference on Applied Informatics, pp. 327–332 (2002)

7. Das, G., Lin, K., Mannila, H., Renganathan, G., Smyth, P.: Rule discovery from time series. In: Proceedings of the 4th International Conference on Knowledge Discovery and Data Mining, pp. 16–22 (1998)

8. Fürnkranz, J., Gamberger, D., Lavrac, N.: Foundations of Rule Learning. Cognitive Technologies. Springer, Heidelberg (2012). https://doi.org/10.1007/978-3-540-75197-7

9. Fürnkranz, J., Kliegr, T.: A brief overview of rule learning. In: Bassiliades, N., Gottlob, G., Sadri, F., Paschke, A., Roman, D. (eds.) RuleML 2015. LNCS, vol. 9202, pp. 54–69. Springer, Cham (2015). https://doi.org/10.1007/978-3-319-21542-6_4

10. Halpern, J., Shoham, Y.: A propositional modal logic of time intervals. J. ACM **38**(4), 935–962 (1991)

11. Höppner, F., Peter, S.: Temporal interval pattern languages to characterize time flow. Wiley Interdisc. Rev. Data Mining Knowl. Discov. **4**(3), 196–212 (2014)

12. Höppner, F.: Time series abstraction methods - a survey. In: Proceedings of the 32nd Annual Meeting of the Society for Informatics, pp. 777–786 (2002)

13. Jakkula, V., Cook, D., Jain, G.: Prediction models for a smart home based health care system. In: Proceedings of the 21st International Conference on Advanced Information Networking and Applications, pp. 761–765 (2007)

14. Kurbalija, V., et al.: Time-series analysis in the medical domain: a study of tacrolimus administration and influence on kidney graft function. Comput. Biol. Med. **50**, 19–31 (2014)

15. Lin, J., Keogh, E., Wei, L., Lonardi, S.: Experiencing SAX: a novel symbolic representation of time series. Data Mining Knowl. Discov. **15**(2), 107–144 (2007)

16. Mörchen, F., Ultsch, A.: Optimizing time series discretization for knowledge discovery. In: Proceedings of the 11th ACM SIGKDD International Conference on Knowledge Discovery and Data Mining, pp. 660–665. ACM (2005)

17. Moskovitch, R., Shahar, Y.: Classification-driven temporal discretization of multivariate time series. Data Mining Knowl. Discov. **29**(4), 871–913 (2015)

18. Muggleton, S.: Inductive logic programming: issues, results and the challenge of learning language in logic. Artif. Intell. **114**(1–2), 283–296 (1999)

19. Raedt, L.D.: Logical and Relational Learning. Cognitive Technologies. Springer, Heidelberg (2008). https://doi.org/10.1007/978-3-540-68856-3

20. Sacchi, L., Larizza, C., Combi, C., Bellazzi, R.: Data mining with temporal abstractions: learning rules from time series. Data Mining Knowl. Discov. **15**(2), 217–247 (2007)

21. Sheremetov, L., González-Sánchez, A., López-Yáñez, I., Ponomarev, A.: Time series forecasting: applications to the upstream oil and gas supply chain. In: Proceedings of the 7th IFAC Conference on Manufacturing Modelling, Management, and Control. IFAC Proc. Vol. **46**, 957–962 (2013)

22. Vito, S.D., Piga, M., Martinotto, L., Francia, G.D.: CO, NO2 and NOx urban pollution monitoring with on-field calibrated electronic nose by automatic Bayesian regularization. Sens. Actuators B: Chem. **143**, 182–191 (2009)

A Principled Two-Step Method
for Example-Dependent Cost Binary
Classification

Javier Mediavilla-Relaño[✉], Aitor Gutiérrez-López[✉], Marcelino Lázaro[✉],
and Aníbal R. Figueiras-Vidal[✉]

Department of Signal Theory and Communications,
Carlos III University of Madrid, 28911 Leganés, Spain
{javiermedia,aitorgl,mlazaro,anibalrfv}@tsc.uc3m.es

Abstract. This paper presents a principled two-step method for example-dependent cost binary classification problems. The first step obtains a consistent estimate of the posterior probabilities by training a Multi-Layer Perceptron with a Bregman surrogate cost. The second step uses the provided estimates in a Bayesian decision rule. When working with imbalanced datasets, neutral re-balancing allows getting better estimates of the posterior probabilities. Experiments with real datasets show the good performance of the proposed method in comparison with other procedures.

Keywords: Bregman divergences · Classification ·
Example-dependent cost · Imbalanced data · Neural networks

1 Introduction

Processing raw data and representing a given pattern to assign it to a category or class, which is called classification or pattern recognition [1], is a task that appears recurrently in many fields of application. If enough statistical knowledge is available, statistical decision theory [2] can solve the problem. If the solution has to be learned from an available labeled dataset containing samples of the objects to be classified along with their corresponding class labels, discriminative machine learning methods [3] can be used to solve the problem. Specifically, neural networks can be designed for classification purposes [4], and they have been extensively used to solve this kind of problems in industry, business, and science [5].

In many classical classification problems, the goal is to minimize the probability of an erroneous decision. Humans do them at least as a first approach. This is appropriate in applications where the costs of an error are equal for all

This work has been partially supported by Research Grant MacroADOBE (TEC2015-67719-P, MINECO/FEDER, EU) and by Research Project 2-BARBAS (Fundación BBVA).

J. M. Ferrández Vicente et al. (Eds.): IWINAC 2019, LNCS 11487, pp. 13–22, 2019.
https://doi.org/10.1007/978-3-030-19651-6_2

patterns and the classes are balanced. However, in many applications, the costs of erroneous decisions can depend on the class, such as in medical diagnosis, where the cost of an error in the diagnostic is higher if the patient is sick. It is also frequent that the classes are imbalanced, which means that the number of instances of the classes is very different [6]. Humans are sensitive to cost problems but not enough to imbalance situations. Yet there are also problems where the costs can depend on each pattern, such as in fraud detection [7,8], credit scoring [9,10], or direct marketing [11,12], just to mention some relevant examples. These are called example-dependent cost (EDC) classification problems. Despite their relevance in real-world applications, the number of works on this topic is still relatively low, although it is receiving more attention in the last years.

The first works using discriminative machines to solve EDC problems were based on proportional re-sampling [13,14], with the idea of training the machines with data distributions that are proportional to the costs of the examples. However, these methods suffer the typical problems of sampling techniques, which can modify the problem by reducing the influence of critical samples and/or emphasizing unimportant instances [15]. The SVM formulation was also analyzed for EDC problems [16]. Although it asymptotically minimizes the Bayes cost, for training sets of finite size SVMs only establish a bound of the classification costs [17].

The Bayesian theory allows an appropriate formulation for EDC problems. Some machines can be used to estimate statistical information from the available training data, to be used later in a Bayesian decision rule. Bahnsen and his colleagues [10,18–21] proposed a two-step procedure:

1. The posterior probabilities for each class are estimated with some machine.
2. The EDC classification is solved with a Bayesian decision rule using these estimates.

The main drawback of the proposed solutions is that the methods that these works employ in the first step are not guaranteed to provide consistent estimates of the posterior probabilities. The practical implication is that although each method is able to provide good results in some problems, all of them also provide very poor results in others.

In this paper, we propose a two-step procedure where a principled method is used in the first step to obtain consistent estimates of the posterior probabilities, which will provide robustness to the classification method.

The rest of the paper is organized as follows. Section 2 states the problem of EDC classification and presents the principled approach. In Sect. 3, some experiments are shown to test the proposed method, comparing its performance with that of other methods. Section 4 closes the contribution remarking its main conclusions and suggesting some directions for further research.

2   Proposed Method

In this contribution, we will consider binary problems. The extension of this method to multiclass cases is not difficult.

In binary EDC classification problems, the cost for attributing a class i pattern to class j, $c_{ji}(\mathbf{x})$, depends on i, j and the corresponding observation vector $\mathbf{x}$. Solving an EDC problem is to minimize the average classification cost. From Bayes theory, the decision which minimizes the statistical average cost can be written

$$j^* = \arg \max_j \left\{ \sum_i c_{ji}(\mathbf{x}) Pr(C_j|\mathbf{x}) \right\}, \tag{1}$$

where C_j are the classes, $\mathbf{x}$ the observation, and $Pr(C_i|\mathbf{x})$ the "a posteriori" class probabilities. Alternative forms for binary problems are

$$\frac{Pr(C_1|\mathbf{x})}{Pr(C_0|\mathbf{x})} \underset{C_0}{\overset{C_1}{\gtrless}} \frac{c_{10}(\mathbf{x}) - c_{00}(\mathbf{x})}{c_{01}(\mathbf{x}) - c_{11}(\mathbf{x})} = Q_c(\mathbf{x}), \tag{2a}$$

or

$$q_L(\mathbf{x}) = \frac{p(\mathbf{x}|C_1)}{p(\mathbf{x}|C_0)} \underset{C_0}{\overset{C_1}{\gtrless}} \frac{c_{10}(\mathbf{x}) - c_{00}(\mathbf{x})}{c_{01}(\mathbf{x}) - c_{11}(\mathbf{x})} \frac{P_0}{P_1} = Q_c(\mathbf{x})Q_P = Q(\mathbf{x}). \tag{2b}$$

The likelihood ratio for the pattern, $q_L(\mathbf{x})$, is compared with a threshold $Q(\mathbf{x})$ that is obtained by the product of two terms: $Q_P = P_0/P_1$, which defines the ratio between the a priori class probabilities, and $Q_c(\mathbf{x})$, which depends on the classification costs for pattern $\mathbf{x}$. Or, equivalently, the ratio between the posterior probabilities for the pattern, $Pr(C_i|\mathbf{x})$, is directly compared with $Q_c(\mathbf{x})$.

From (1) or (2a), it is obvious that to find reasonable estimates of $Pr(C_i|\mathbf{x})$ serves to design a (good) classifier. In many real applications this statistical information has to be obtained from a labeled train set

$$\left\{ \left(\mathbf{x}^{(n)}, t^{(n)}, c_{ji}(\mathbf{x}^{(n)}) \right) : i, j \in \{0, 1\}, n \in 0, 1, ..., N \right\}, \tag{3}$$

composed by the patterns, $\mathbf{x}^{(n)}$, the class labels, $t^{(n)}$, and the cost policy for each decision, $c_{ji}(\mathbf{x}^{(n)})$.

In this work we propose to use a learning machine, specifically a neural network, to obtain estimates of the posterior probabilities $Pr(C_i|\mathbf{x})$. One approach that has been used to solve EDC classification problems is minimizing some surrogate cost $c(t^{(n)}, \mathbf{x}^{(n)})$ weighting the instances with the corresponding classification costs, but in general this does not approximate the Bayes solution. The proposed algorithm applies a two step strategy to obtain better results:

- The first step is to train a Multi-Layer Perceptron (MLP) to estimate $Pr(C_i|\mathbf{x})$ by using a Bregman divergence [22] as surrogate cost, which provides a consistent estimate of the posterior probabilities.
- The second step applies (1) or (2a) with the above estimates and the EDCs.

Bregman divergences are cost functions that satisfy

$$\frac{\partial c(t, o)}{\partial o} = -g(o)(t - o), \tag{4}$$

with $g(o) > 0$. Consequently, the output of a machine that minimizes this surrogate cost provides a consistent estimate of $E\{C_i|\mathbf{x}\}$ –the proof is easy–, and this expected value is related with the posterior probabilities. In a binary problem with $t = \pm 1$

$$E\{C_1|\mathbf{x}\} = 2Pr(C_1|\mathbf{x}) - 1. \tag{5a}$$

If Bregman divergences are included, $o(\mathbf{x}) = \widetilde{E}\{C_1|\mathbf{x}\}$, so

$$\widetilde{Pr}(C_1|\mathbf{x}) = [1 + o(\mathbf{x})]/2, \tag{5b}$$

where $o(\mathbf{x})$ is the output of the learning machine. Further discussions about Bregman divergences and their capacity to estimate posterior probabilities can be found in [23, 24].

Then, a method that offers a consistent solution for the EDC problem can be found by applying (5b) to obtain estimates of the posterior probabilities from the machine output, and then to use these estimates on (2a), which leads to the decision rule

$$\frac{1 + o(\mathbf{x})}{1 - o(\mathbf{x})} \underset{C_0}{\overset{C_1}{\gtrless}} Q_c(\mathbf{x}). \tag{6}$$

Although this solution is theoretically consistent, in practice the estimation $\widetilde{Pr}(C_i|\mathbf{x})$ loses quality if the training set is imbalanced, decreasing the detection of the minority class instances. To solve this difficulty it is possible to apply "neutral" re-balancing procedures, i.e, those which do not modify the form of the class likelihoods $p(\mathbf{x}|C_i)$ and, therefore, the likelihood ratio. These "neutral" re-balancing methods are uniform re-sampling and/or generation processes and/or (constant) classification costs modifications. Then, we will obtain an estimate $p(\mathbf{x}|C_i)$ which does not correspond to the original problem, but if we consider

$$Pr(C_1|\mathbf{x}) = \frac{p(\mathbf{x}|C_1)P_1}{p(\mathbf{x}|C_1)P_1 + p(\mathbf{x}|C_0)P_0} = \frac{1}{1 + Q_P/q_L(\mathbf{x})} \tag{7}$$

it is easy to prove that we can recover a consistent estimate $\widehat{Pr}(C_1|\mathbf{x})$ from the re-balanced machine output by obtaining $\widehat{q_L}(\mathbf{x})$ (for the re-balanced problem) from (7), and applying (7) again for the real problem:

$$\widehat{Pr}(C_1|\mathbf{x}) = \frac{\widetilde{Q}\widetilde{Pr}(C_1|\mathbf{x})}{\widetilde{Q}\widetilde{Pr}(C_1|\mathbf{x}) + Q_P\left[1 - \widetilde{Pr}(C_1|\mathbf{x})\right]}, \tag{8}$$

where $\widetilde{Q}$ [1] (a constant) is the threshold value for the re-balanced machine, and Q_p corresponds to the real situation. After it, applying (5b) and (2a) to (8)

$$\frac{1 + \widetilde{o}(\mathbf{x})}{1 - \widetilde{o}(\mathbf{x})} \underset{C_0}{\overset{C_1}{\gtrless}} \frac{Q_p}{\widetilde{Q}} Q_c(\mathbf{x}) \tag{9}$$

---

[1] $\widetilde{Q}$ can be interpreted as $\widetilde{Q}_P$.

where $\tilde{o}(\mathbf{x})$ is the output of the "neutral" re-balanced machine. (9) is the solution for the EDC IB problem. In this contribution, the first step trains an MLP that minimizes the mean squared error (MSE), a Bregman divergence, and we consider full re-balancing: $\tilde{Q} = 1$. Re-balancing is carried out by class weighting during the training phase.

3 Experiments

3.1 Figure of Merit

The classical figure of merit for EDC problems, 'savings', represents the percentage of cost reduction with respect to the best trivial decision (the best average cost between deciding all patterns in class 0 or deciding all patterns in class 1). Assuming zero costs for correct decisions, the average decision cost for a classification is

$$Cost_D = \sum_{\mathbf{x}_n \in C_0} \hat{y}_n c_{10}(\mathbf{x}_n) + \sum_{\mathbf{x}_n \in C_1} (1 - \hat{y}_n) c_{01}(\mathbf{x}_n), \tag{10}$$

where $\mathbf{x}_n, n \in \{1, 2, ..., N\}$, are the samples, and $\hat{y}_n$ the corresponding $(0, 1)$ decisions. The savings measure the relative cost reduction provided by a given decision rule with respect to the best trivial decision rule

$$Sav_D = \frac{Cost_T - Cost_D}{Cost_T}. \tag{11}$$

where

$$Cost_T = \min\{Cost_{T0}, Cost_{T1}\} \tag{12}$$

is the minimum of the costs of the two trivial decision rules and $Cost_{Ti} = Cost(\hat{y}_l = i), \forall l$.

3.2 Datasets

We will work with two real databases. The first database is Creditscoring1 (CS1) from Kaggle competition 'Give Me Some Credit', an EDC database with an imbalance ratio (IB) of 13.8:1 and 112915 10-dimensional samples. The cost policy for CS1 is $c_{01} = 0.75cl(\mathbf{x})$ and $c_{10} = r(\mathbf{x} + c_a)$, where $cl(\mathbf{x})$ is the credit line (amount of the credit) for $\mathbf{x}$, $r(\mathbf{x})$ the operation benefit, and $c_a = 0.75 P_1 \overline{cl} - P_0 \overline{r}$, where $^-$ indicates average. This dataset was obtained from Cost-Sensitive Classification (Costcla) Python module repository [25].

The second is a home equity loans dataset, HMEQ[2] [26], which reports characteristics and delinquency information for 5,960 home equity loans in an observation space of 34 dimensions, with an imbalance ratio of approximately 4:1. The cost policy is 75% of the loan amount for false negative and the loss of profit for the false positives, in this case, 15% of the loan amount.

---

[2] Dataset available at http://www.creditriskanalytics.net.

3.3   Benchmark Methods

Several methods that have been used for EDC classification will be applied for comparison purposes:

– One step methods: Logistic Regression (LR) and Random Forest (RF).
– One step cost-sensitive methods: Cost-Sensitive Logistic Regression (CSLR) [10] and Cost-Sensitive Decision Tree (CSDT) [21], which are trained considering the example-dependent costs.
– Two step cost-sensitive methods: The second step is the Bayes Minimum Risk (BMR) [18] (1), with several different methods to estimate the posterior probabilities, LR, RF, CSLR, and CSDT. The methods will be denoted BMR (RF), BMR (LR), BMR (CSLR), and BMR (CSDT).

The Python implementation provided in the *Scikit-learn*[3] software [27] has been employed for LR and RF. The Python implementation of the *Costcla*[4] module [25] has been used for CSLR, CSDT, and BMR. The parameters for each method are those recommended in [10]. To improve performance, these methods are sometimes combined with some re-sampling techniques. Therefore, the training phase of these methods will be performed with 3 different data sets: The training set, and two additional sets obtained using cost-proportional over-sampling (OS) [13] and cost-proportional rejection sampling (RS) [14] techniques.

A linear classifier fitted to minimize an estimate of the Bayes risk (extending the linear method presented in [28] to deal with EDC) will also be used as a benchmark. Since this classifier uses the information about the a priori probabilities of the two classes along with the cost policy, it is not used in combination with the re-sampling techniques, but only with the original train set.

We apply full rebalancing by means of sample weighting, i.e., $\tilde{Q} = 1$.

3.4   Results

In all the experiments, data is randomly split into 75% train and 25% test subsets for each realization (keeping the IB ratio of the original database). The average results obtained in 100 independent realizations are presented, including the standard deviation.

Experiments with CS1. Table 1 presents the average savings ± standard desviations obtained with the Proposed Method (PM) and the benchmark methods. For the proposed method, an MLP with a single hidden layer with ReLU activation functions and a single neuron output layer with tanh activation is used. For the number of neurons in the hidden layer, 5, 7, 9, 11, 13, 15, 17, 19, 21, and 30 neurons were explored by 5-fold cross-validation in the training subset of each realization. The mini-bach size and number of epochs were selected to guarantee the convergence in each realization.

---

[3] http://scikit-learn.org.
[4] http://pypi.org/project/costcla/.

Table 1. Test Savings (average ± standard deviation, in %) for the CS1 dataset. Results for 100 independent realizations.

Method	Train set	Re-sampling (OS)	Re-sampling (RS)
LR	2.97 ± 0.4	32.97 ± 1.0	40.07 ± 2.6
RF	13.17 ± 0.7	18.43 ± 0.8	45.79 ± 1.2
CSLR	0.02 ± 2.4	1.46 ± 2.8	2.01 ± 2.8
CSDT	47.90 ± 1.2	−7.97 ± 1.0	−8.66 ± 1.1
BMR (LR)	28.66 ± 1.3	40.70 ± 1.3	43.06 ± 3.0
BMR (RF)	32.37 ± 1.5	18.91 ± 1.5	45.29 ± 1.2
BMR (CSLR)	17.55 ± 11.0	−1.49 ± 2.4	−1.07 ± 2.2
BMR (CSDT)	**48.04 ± 1.1**	−5.12 ± 1.6	−0.94 ± 2.0
Linear (Bayes)	46.72 ± 1.1		
PM	**48.35 ± 1.0**		

The methods that do not include the costs in their formulation, as LR or RF, obtain a clear benefit from re-sampling. CSDT includes the costs in its formulation, and therefore it is able to obtain satisfactory results working with the original dataset. The best benchmark method for this dataset is BMR (CSDT), and the proposed method obtains results at least as good. Looking at the results obtained with the linear classifier, it appears that CS1 is not far from linearly separable, and therefore the advantages that an MLP can provide in non-linear problems are limited.

Experiments with HMEQ. For the proposed method, an MLP with a single hidden layer with ReLU activations and an output layer with a single neuron and tanh activation is used again. For the hidden layer, 70, 80, 90, 100, 110, 120, 130, 140, and 150 neurons were explored by 5-fold cross-validation in the training subset of each realization. Once more, the mini-batch size and number of epochs were selected to guarantee the convergence in each realization. Table 2 shows the average savings obtained with the Proposed and the benchmark methods.

Again, as expected, LR and RF obtain a clear benefit from re-sampling. Now, looking at the results obtained with the linear method, HMEQ seems to be clearly non-linear. The best results are now provided by BMR (RF) working with the original train set. Interestingly, although the performance of RF is better using re-sampling techniques, when combined with BMR it provides better estimates of the posterior probabilities if trained with the original train set. This is because RF, although an excellent classifier in many applications, in general, does not provide consistent estimates of the posterior probabilities. This can be seen again in the results obtained for CS1, where BMR (RF) only provided 17.55% savings when RF was trained with the original dataset, a very poor result.

Table 2. Test Savings (average ± standard deviation, in %) for the HMEQ dataset. Average results for 100 independent realizations.

Method	Train set	Re-sampling (OS)	Re-sampling (RS)
LR	40.12 ± 4.2	52.90 ± 3.6	52.86 ± 4.0
RF	57.52 ± 4.4	61.54 ± 3.9	67.57 ± 3.0
CSLR	16.33 ± 4.5	13.51 ± 3.8	13.90 ± 4.2
CSDT	65.72 ± 2.7	2.10 ± 1.1	1.79 ± 1.4
BMR (LR)	−0.00 ± 0.0	−0.00 ± 0.1	−0.01 ± 0.1
BMR (RF)	**75.19 ± 4.0**	58.87 ± 9.9	5.78 ± 10.8
BMR (CSLR)	−0.00 ± 0.1	−0.00 ± 0.1	−0.00 ± 0.1
BMR (CSDT)	0.37 ± 0.8	2.02 ± 1.5	1.34 ± 2.5
Linear (Bayes)	54.66 ± 3.9		
PM	**72.87 ± 3.0**		

The proposed method also provides competitive results in this dataset. Although slightly worse than BMR (RF), they are much better than the remaining benchmark methods.

4 Conclusions

In this work, a principled two-step method for example-dependent cost classification problems has been proposed. In the first step, an MLP is trained to provide consistent estimates of the posterior probabilities of the classes. To do this, the surrogate cost function for the MLP is a Bregman divergence, and "neutral" re-sampling has been used to fully rebalance the training set when imbalanced. The second step is applying a Bayesian decision.

We have tested the proposed method in two real datasets for EDC problems. Looking at the results provided by the linear classifier, CS1 seems to be slightly non-linear, while HMEQ seems to be clearly non-linear. The proposed method obtained competitive results in both datasets, while the benchmark methods achieve very diverse results. Although some of them are able to obtain satisfactory results in one of the datasets, the same methods provide very poor results in the other (for instance, BMR (CSDT), which is the best benchmark method for CS1, is only able of obtaining 0.37% savings in HMEQ. Or BMR (RF), which is the best benchmark method for HMEQ, only achieves 32.37% of saving in CS1, a poor result). The proposed method is a principled method, designed to provide consistent estimates of the posterior probabilities, which is an important advantage with respect to most of the current state-of-the-art methods.

We emphasize that the proposed method provides to the user very useful information. On the one hand, consistent estimates of the a posteriori class probabilities. On other hand, a classification decision for each sample, which includes the comparison of the estimated probability with a threshold. So, the user can separate the effects of the population statistics from the effects of the cost policy. Additionally, changes in the cost policy can be included in the algorithm introducing minor modifications. Undoubtedly, these facts are important for gaining a better understanding of the problem under study.

Further work will explore the results of optimizing the re-balance, of employing more powerful machines, such as Deep NNs, of applying other Bregman divergences, and of using principled informed re-balancing mechanisms. Extensions to multi-class problems will also be studied.

References

1. Duda, R.O., Hart, P.E., Stork, D.G.: Pattern Classification, 2nd edn. Wiley, New York (2001)
2. Van Trees, H.L.: Detection, Estimation, and Modulation Theory: Part I. Wiley, New York (1968)
3. Bishop, C.M.: Pattern Recognition and Machine Learning. Springer, New York (2006)
4. Zhang, G.P.: Neural networks for classification: a survey. IEEE Trans. Syst. Man Cybern. **30**(4), 451–462 (2000)
5. Widrow, B., Rumelhart, D.E., Lehr, M.A.: Neural networks: applications in industry, business and science. Commun. ACM **37**(3), 93–105 (1994)
6. He, H., Garcia, E.A.: Learning from imbalanced data. IEEE Trans. Knowl. Data Eng. **21**(9), 1263–1284 (2009)
7. Panigrahi, S., Kundu, A., Surai, S., Majumdar, A.K.: Credit card fraud detection: a fusion approach using Dempster-Shafer theory and Bayesian learning. Inf. Fusion **10**(4), 354–363 (2009)
8. Bhattacharyya, S., Jha, S., Tharakunnel, K., Westland, J.C.: Data mining for credit card fraud: a comparative study. Decis. Support Syst. **50**(3), 602–613 (2011)
9. Verbraken, T., Bravo, C., Webber, R., Baesens, B.: Development and application of consumer credit scoring models using profit-based classification measures. Eur. J. Oper. Res. **238**(2), 505–513 (2014)
10. Bahnsen, A.C., Aouada, D., Ottersten, B.: Example-dependent cost-sensitive logistic regression for credit scoring. In: Proceedings of 13th International Conference on Machine Learning and Applications, pp. 263–269. IEEE Computer Society (2014)
11. Ngai, E.W.T., Xiu, L., Chau, D.C.K.: Application of data mining techniques in customer relationship management: a literature review and classification. Expert Syst. Appl. **36**(2), 2592–2602 (2009)
12. Moro, S., Laureano, R.M.S., Cortez, P.: Using data mining for bank direct marketing: an application of the CRISP-DM methodology. In: Proceedings of European Simulation and Modeling Conference, Guimaraes (Portugal), pp. 117–121 (2011)
13. Elkan, C.: The foundations of cost-sensitive learning. In: Proceedings of 17th International Joint Conference on Artificial Intelligence, vol. 2, pp. 973–978 (2001)
14. Zadrozny, B., Langford, J., Abe, N.: Cost-sensitive learning by cost-proportionate example weighting. In: Proceedings of Third International Conference on Data Mining, pp. 435–442 (2003)
15. Branco, P., Torgo, L., Ribeiro, R.P.: A survey of predictive modeling on imbalanced domains. ACM Comput. Surv. **49**(2), 31:1–31:50 (2016)

16. Brefeld, U., Geibel, P., Wysotzki, F.: Support vector machines with example dependent costs. In: Lavrač, N., Gamberger, D., Blockeel, H., Todorovski, L. (eds.) ECML 2003. LNCS (LNAI), vol. 2837, pp. 23–34. Springer, Heidelberg (2003). https://doi.org/10.1007/978-3-540-39857-8_5

17. González, P., et al.: Multiclass support vector machines with example dependent costs applied to plankton biomass estimation. IEEE Trans. Neural Netw. Learn. Syst. **24**(11), 1901–1905 (2013)

18. Bahnsen, A.C., Stojanovic, A., Aouada, D., Ottersten, B.: Cost sensitive credit card fraud detection using Bayes minimization risk. In: Proceedings of 12th International Conference on Machine Learning and Applications, pp. 333–338. IEEE Computer Society (2013)

19. Bahnsen, A.C., Stojanovic, A., Aouada, D., Ottersten, B.: Improving credit card fraud detection with calibrated probabilities. In: Proceedings of 14th International Conference on Data Mining, Philadelphia, USA, pp. 677–685. SIAM (2014)

20. Bahnsen, A.C., Aouada, D., Ottersten, B.: A novel cost-sensitive framework for customer churn predictive modeling. Decis. Anal. **2**(5), 1–15 (2015)

21. Bahnsen, A.C., Aouada, D., Ottersten, B.: Example-dependent cost-sensitive decision trees. Expert Syst. Appl. **42**(19), 6609–6619 (2015)

22. Bregman, L.M.: The relaxation method of finding the common point of convex sets and its application to the solution of problems in convex programming. USSR Comput. Math. Math. Phys. **7**, 200–217 (1967)

23. Cid-Sueiro, J., Arribas, J.I., Urbán-Muñoz, S., Figueiras-Vidal, A.R.: Cost functions to estimate a posteriori probabilities in multiclass problems. IEEE Trans. Neural Netw. **10**(3), 645–656 (1999)

24. Cid-Sueiro, J., Figueiras-Vidal, A.R.: On the structure of strict sense Bayesian cost functions and its applications. IEEE Trans. Neural Netw. **12**(3), 445–455 (2001)

25. Bahnsen, A.C.: Cost Sensitive Classification (COSTCLA) Python module for cost-sensitive machine learning (classification), Version 0.5 (1996). https://pypi.org/project/costcla/

26. Baesens, B., Roesch, D., Scheule, H.: Credit Risk Analytics: Measurement Techniques, Applications, and Examples in SAS. Wiley, New York (2016)

27. Pedregosa, F., et al.: Scikit-learn: machine learning in python. J. Mach. Learn. Res. **12**, 2825–2830 (2011)

28. Lázaro, M., Hayes, M.H., Figueiras-Vidal, A.R.: Training neural network classifiers through Bayes risk minimization applying unidimensional Parzen windows. Pattern Recognit. **77**, 204–215 (2018)

Symbiotic Autonomous Systems with Consciousness Using Digital Twins

Felipe Fernández[1], Ángel Sánchez[2(✉)], José F. Vélez[2], and A. Belén Moreno[2]

[1] ETSIINF, UPM, 28660 Boadilla del Monte, Madrid, Spain
`felipefernandez@fi.upm.es`
[2] ETSII, URJC, 28933 Móstoles, Madrid, Spain
{`angel.sanchez,jose.velez,belen.moreno`}`@urjc.es`

Abstract. The IEEE work-group for *Symbiotic Autonomous Systems* defined a *Digital Twin* as a digital representation or virtual model of any characteristics of a real entity (system, process or service), including human beings. Described characteristics are a subset of the overall characteristics of the real entity. The choice of which characteristics are considered depends on the purpose of the digital twin. This paper introduces the concept of *Associative Cognitive Digital Twin*, as a real time goal-oriented augmented virtual description, which explicitly includes the associated external relationships of the considered entity for the considered purpose. The corresponding graph data model, of the involved world, supports artificial consciousness, and allows an efficient understanding of involved ecosystems and related higher-level cognitive activities. The defined cognitive architecture for Symbiotic Autonomous Systems is mainly based on the consciousness framework developed. As a specific application example, an architecture for critical safety systems is shown.

Keywords: Consciousness · Symbiotic Autonomous Systems ·
Cognitive architectures · Digital Twin · Industrial Internet of Things ·
Industry 4.0

1 Introduction

Advanced *cognitive systems* dealing with human-like intelligent activities, have multiple partially overlapping process areas, such as: perception, data fusion, information integration, recognition, discernment, understanding, insight, awareness, *consciousness*, estimation, heuristic, learning, model building, structured knowledge, associative knowledge, reasoning, working and long-term memory, multimodal interactions, augmented reality and decision-making.

The corresponding hybrid human-machine cognitive systems will be used in different applications, which include: driving autonomous vehicles, monitoring nuclear power plants, supervising advanced manufacturing systems or smart cities management; or in sectors such as: industry, plant automation, intelligent

© Springer Nature Switzerland AG 2019
J. M. Ferrández Vicente et al. (Eds.): IWINAC 2019, LNCS 11487, pp. 23–32, 2019.
https://doi.org/10.1007/978-3-030-19651-6_3

transport systems, automotive, aircraft, monitoring and surveillance, medical services, homeland security, cybersecurity, defense, public safety, marketing or education.

Mature goal-oriented hybrid human-machine situation awareness systems usually define five basic cognitive layers [12]: perception of the system, environment, context and their state; comprehension; prediction and estimation of consequences; decisions; and actions.

In the near future, highly cooperative hybrid human-machine cognitive systems in real-time environments, will be certainly crucial for improving the capability, reliability, robustness, agility, adaptability, safety and security of involved platforms.

Additionally, new trends in artificial intelligence has a renewed interest in building systems that think and learn like humans, suggesting that human-like thinking and learning machines will have to reach beyond current engineering practices, in what and how they think, learn, and model; and knowing about knowing [13].

A flexible roadmap for reverse engineering of human intelligence should be considered as a continuous process, to inspire some aspects of artificial cognitive frameworks, especially for the types of domains and tasks that humans excel at. New derived approaches should support semantic cognitive knowledge, integrate context and historical knowledge, learning and decision support [17].

Cognitive agents should continuously build goal-oriented dynamic holistic models of the involved world, to support efficient domain understanding and general learning, rather than merely solving pattern recognition problems. A holistic model of the considered scene would require the composition of individual object models, glued together by associated relationships, helping to connect different object model views to support open and scalable scenarios.

Additionally, if the systems include complex cooperative interactions between humans and machines, it will be nearly impossible to efficiently manage communications and actions without considering their involved mental models and states, and especially their goals, objectives, purposes and intentions.

Complementary, in many industrial applications, it will be relevant to use efficient information models, such as augmented reality principles [7] to improve the corresponding HMI, to efficiently communicate associated relevant information to other cognitive agents, and to create more complete insights.

In this whole context, this paper presents the developed consciousness architecture framework that is mainly based on a network of associative cognitive digital twins, to support cognitive activities of symbiotic autonomous systems.

The paper is organized as follows. Section 2 reviews symbiotic human-machine autonomous systems. In Sect. 3, we introduce associative cognitive digital twin networks. Section 4, describes the consciousness associative layer defined. Section 5, presents a general conscious associative architecture framework. Section 6 summarizes a specific architecture for critical safety systems, using the previous framework. Finally, Sect. 7 discusses the conclusions and further research.

2 Symbiotic Autonomous Systems

The IEEE Future Direction. Symbiotic Autonomous Systems (SAS) Initiative fosters studies and applications focused on the cooperation, and convergence of human and machine augmentation, with increasing intelligence and consciousness, leading towards a continuous symbiosis of humans and machines [3].

A basic description of a SAS can be defined by the following expression:

$$SAS = \{Humans,\ Machines,\ Cooperation\text{-}relationships\}$$

SAS frameworks of hybrid human-machine systems usually should have varying levels of autonomy, decision capabilities, augmented human-machine characteristics, cooperative support, and multimodal human-machine communication. It is estimating that SAS orientation will have a profound impact in the corresponding societal, economic, legal and ethical factors, and in the fields of education, healthcare, manufacturing, maintenance and transportation [2,3] (Fig. 1).

Fig. 1. SAS human-machine cognitive cooperation.

A practical example is an advanced smart city, with a strong interplay of several autonomous systems, including its authorities and citizens, platforms and services, and with several technologies, ecosystems, and associated goals and objectives.

SAS technology implies: an increasing robotization, computerization and digitalization of objects and processes, mature relationships between humans and machines, renewable human-machine agreements, and suitable legislation.

In the future SAS should be able: to become aware and conscious, to self-adapting, to self-diagnosis, to self-repair, and to look for necessary information and means, to reach the defined goals and cooperatively manage the corresponding world.

3   Associative Cognitive Digital Twin Network

Digital Twin (DT) basically refers as a real time digital replica of a physical asset [2]. In this paper, we redefine a DT as a suitable digital description, representation, view or model, of a physical or abstract entity (object, system, structure; asset; process, service, etc) for an intended purpose. An entity can have multiple DT (views). A DT can be described by the function:

$$DT = Model\ (Entity, Purpose)$$

General internal dimensions of a DT are: complexity, knowledge level, abstraction level, granularity, cardinality, description types, life cycle, purpose, etc.

DT technology aggregates data, collects real-time models of the assets, integrates necessary services; and it is a key enabling concept in business digitalization efforts. Gartner named digital twins as a top trend for 2018, saying that digital twins will exist for billions of things in the near future [15].

Presently, DT technology [DT technology] has moved beyond the original manufacturing field to the ecosystems of the Internet of Things, cloud computing, data analytics and artificial intelligence. The technology behind DT has expanded to include larger items such as buildings, factories, cities, enterprise processes, and even persons, groups and societies, expanding the original concept, with increasing practical interest in the Internet of Things (IoT) and Industrial IoT (IIoT) ecosystems. Product-DT and Process-DT are also additional levels of *Digital Transformation*. The collection of data across the lifecycle is called *Digital Thread*, which defines the traceability of a product, system or process. Common use cases of Digital Threads include, real time machine monitoring, predictive maintenance, and digitalized product and process lifecycle, real-time system management and root cause analysis.

DT applications include: manufacturing, energy, construction, transport, aircraft engines, vehicles, trains, roads, railways, healthcare, etc. These applications also require integrated information systems that permit a continuous exchange of information. But DT also implies different concerns about cost, security and privacy.

A DT can be used for a wide variety of *purposes*: integration, control, analysis, visualization, interfacing, simulation, monitorization, prediction, optimization, etc.

A DT that represents an entity in real-time, can be applied in situational awareness and augmented reality applications, to improve observability, controllability and decision-making.

A *Cognitive Digital Twin* (C-DT) can be defined as a digital representation and augmentation of an entity across its lifecycle to optimize cognitive activities [14]. It can be considered as a digital expert or copilot, which can learn and evolve, and that integrates different sources of information for the considered purpose. A C-DT can be described by the following functional description:

$$C\text{-}DT = Model\ (Entity,\ Cognitive\text{-}Purpose)$$

The structure of a C-DT partially emulates the structure of the corresponding human mental models, which are very efficient, optimized and adapted structures, through millions of years of evolution.

To enhance C-DTs, our framework considers an explicit connectivity model: *Associative C-DT* (AC-DT), which is a contextual augmented description that explicitly includes the relevant associated relationships, connections or information channels of the considered entity with the other entities, for the considered application and purpose. An AC-DT can be described by the following functional description:

$$AC\text{-}DT = Model\ (Entity,\ Associated\ Relationships,\ Cognitive\text{-}Purpose)$$

An AC-DT can use diverse information channels, such as: HMI and augmented reality information, contextual information, related data, historical data, associated knowledge, voice interface, management, guidance and control instructions, legislation, regulation checking, binary large objects (blobs), etc.

Example. An AC-DT of a speed controller of a train can include the reference data of the railway route and an autonomous real-time situational awareness system to analyze the corresponding data. It can have channels-connections-relationships with railway signaling (visual signs, balises-transponders, etc.), automatic train protection systems, train state variables, safety driving regulations, video cameras, GPS, etc.; to alarm the train operator and remote command and control, and manage train speed.

The main building blocks of an AC-DT technology are: cognitive digital models, real time databases, hierarchical relationships, and associated analytics, simulation and predictive tools, to better understand the behavior and performance of the systems or services, and for decision-making.

To leverage the full cognitive potential of AC-DT of SAS, these systems in the future do not just need to be networked with each other; they also need to develop the ability to understand, learn and act, autonomously and cooperatively, especially in complex digital ecosystems, such as IoT and IIoT.

We conclude this section with a general observation: an AC-DT is not really a new concept. These virtual models were also created, developed and used in our cognitive minds. Today these virtual network models can also exist and evolve within the corresponding digital spaces.

4 Consciousness Associative Layer

A relevant aim of present cognitive engineering is the transposition of high-level core brain activities in artificial cognitive digital systems and processes. For diverse automation and autonomous fields, a crucial objective is the development of artificial consciousness systems, which generate suitable real-time models of the involved world for the considered purpose and provide convenient support tools.

Today there is a wide consensus that the main element of basic human consciousness is having a *mental model* of a specific world (mental possession of something according to Graziano [9]) and involved *attention schema*. This real-time goal-oriented and efficient virtual model, with a defined owner, scope and purpose, gradually simplifies, integrates and structures, diverse data, information and knowledge.

Consciousness content is a matter of *perspective* or cognitive purpose. It is a matter of *association*, with a hierarchical multilevel and multiphase structure (Damasio [8]). Consciousness content is also a matter of connection, with global broadcast channels (Global Workspace Theory Theater of Consciousness according to Baars [5,6]). Consciousness content is also a matter of integration and degree (Integrated Information Theory by Tononi [11]).

The core support of artificial consciousness, a mental model (MM) of the considered world, is a real-time integrated adaptive goal-oriented associative description of the involved entity and context, for the intended purpose. MMs should support perception, comprehension predictions, decision, action; learning, adaptation and evolution. An MM of a specific world can be basically described by the following functional expression:

$$MM = Model\ (World\ Entities,\ Associated\ Relationships,\ Cognitive\text{-}Purpose)$$

Therefore, considering this basic perspective, artificial mental models can be implemented using the ICT resources of DTs infrastructure. This way, we practically align the application fields of Artificial Consciousness and Digital Twin technologies.

In this paper, a MM is represented by an Object Graph Database [16] using MS Azure Digital Twins [4]: The corresponding *Consciousness Associative Graph Database* (CAGDB) explicitly represents the relevant entities-objects and connectivity of the object data model (See basic example in Fig. 2), to support artificial consciousness structure and higher-level cognitive activities. This dynamic goal-oriented graph of nodes-vertices (entities) and edge-arcs (relationships), provides a copilot map layer, which is a constructive description of associated facts, data, information and knowledge; rules and events; history, objectives, context, etc.

In cloud ecosystems, artificial *Consciousness as a Service* (CaaS) model can be defined, to construct and share real-time dynamic descriptions of the corresponding world, and to provide suitable modeling tools for the intended purpose.

As a general application conclusion of this section, we think that the considered AC-DT technology can be very useful for the development of industrial conscious systems and platforms, and for conscious IoT and IIoT ecosystems.

5   Conscious Associative Cognitive Architecture Framework

A *Conscious Associative Cognitive Architecture Framework* (CACAF) for SAS, to guide the development of the corresponding architectures, is sketched in this section. It is summarized, the main general process areas necessary to develop

Consciousness Object Graph. DT: Digital Twin

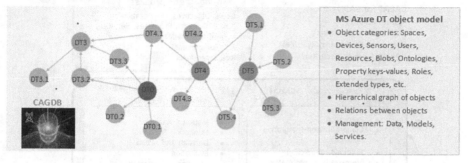

Fig. 2. Example of a consciousness associative graph database using DT technology.

cognitive human-machine agent architectures that have consciousness, to realize basic cognitive tasks such as: signal, data, information and knowledge processing; and accomplish consciousness related activities such as: perception, comprehension, prediction, decision making, planning, learning, adapting and evolving.

The main components of CACAF are outlined in Fig. 3, which consider the necessary human-machine cooperation, through common goals and objectives, suitable information channels and HMI, and optimal assignments of human and machines roles, to really improve the performance of these hybrid systems.

The main innovation aspect of this cognitive architecture framework is the use of interoperable mental models between humans and machines, to improve goals and objectives alignment, and for better communication between the involved agents, allowing a better human-machine cooperation, understanding and empathy.

6   A Conscious Architecture for Critical Safety SAS

Risk and uncertainty management is inherent complex in large systems, infrastructures and services, such as: railways, airports, nuclear plants, big cities, etc. The corresponding complexity has different dimensions: system, context, environment, economy, investment, society, management, governance, HMI, stakeholder communication and participation, human factors, organizational factors, historical factors, evolution, etc.

Presently several mature risk management methods are available such as: FMEA, FMECA, Root Cause Analysis, Fault Tree Analysis, etc. The basic rationale and viewpoint underlying these techniques is the integration of risk management into a structured and controlled process to reduce the involved risks to an acceptable level.

A recurrent lesson learned, from many extremely destructive disasters such as: Chernobyl and Fukushima nuclear accidents, Catrina hurricane category 5, Santiago de Compostela derailment, etc., is that the main common root cause is

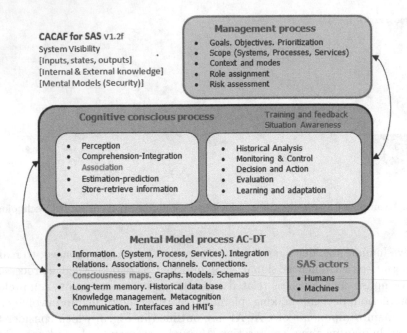

CACAF for SAS v1.2f
System Visibility
[Inputs, states, outputs]
[Internal & External knowledge]
[Mental Models (Security)]

Management process
- Goals. Objectives. Prioritization
- Scope (Systems, Processes, Services)
- Context and modes
- Role assignment
- Risk assessment

Cognitive conscious process   Training and feedback
Situation Awareness

- Perception
- Comprehension-Integration
- Association
- Estimation-prediction
- Store-retrieve information

- Historical Analysis
- Monitoring & Control
- Decision and Action
- Evaluation
- Learning and adaptation

Mental Model process AC-DT
- Information. (System, Process, Services). Integration
- Relations. Associations. Channels. Connections.
- Consciousness maps. Graphs. Models. Schemas
- Long-term memory. Historical data base
- Knowledge management. Metacognition
- Communication. Interfaces and HMI's

SAS actors
- Humans
- Machines

Fig. 3. Architecture framework for conscious associative cognitive agents.

the *insufficient level of common collaborative understanding of the whole system and its environment* [10].

In many practical cases, it is usually observed insufficient: management support, preparedness, adaptive safety regulations and updated knowledge; due to a deficient consciousness (integrated, dynamic and global) of the involved systems, context and environment.

In order to improve the safety and security services of critical infrastructures, this section proposed an architecture based in CACAF for SAS, which explicitly includes the connected automation services, and the risk, alarm, cybersecurity and knowledge management modules. The necessary cooperation and interplay between these systems and the consciousness layer, provide a better knowledge integration, and an increased robustness, reliability and agility.

Figure 4 summarizes the corresponding architecture model for critical safety SAS, which includes different collaborative human-machine processes. To end this section, we briefly summarize some implementation details of the corresponding cognitive real-time services based on a network of DTs and using the proposed CACAF methodology.

For the mental map description, we chose Neo4j Graph Database [1] to create comprehensive consciousness data graphs, which represent the relevant relationships and connections between humans, machines, infrastructure, locations, assets, systems, processes, services, regulations, instructions, etc. The graph relationship perspective adopted is oriented to efficiently capture the crucial high connectivity of practical mental models.

For implementation, we have selected Microsoft Azure Digital Twins Azure IoT Services [4] to define the corresponding systems, environment and context.

SAS application services for critical safety infrastructures. v1.2d			
Connected Automation Services	**Alarm Management. ANSI / ISA 18.2**		**Cybersecurity Management**
A. OT+IT Cobotics Services	A. Philosophy	H. Change Management	A. Architecture
Co: human-robot collaboration	B. Identification	I. Monitoring and Assess.	B. Control access
B. CACAF for SAS	C. Rationalization	J. Audit	C. Authentication
Consciousness as a Service	D. Detailed design	K. Co-alarm management	D. Data Encryption
C. Digital Twin + Digital Threads	E. Implementation		E. Layer defences
Analytics + Simulation + Prediction	F. Operation		F. Threat detection
D. Cloud-Fog-Edge Computing	G. Maintenance		G. Co-security
Communication + Computation			
E. Edge Devices	**Risk Management**		**Quality Management**
Plant location. RFID. RTLS	A. RCA. FTA. FMEA. FMECA ...		A. KPI's
	B. RT automated methods. Co-risk methods		B. Co-quality

Fig. 4. A conscious architecture for critical safety SAS.

7 Conclusions

This paper has shown that consciousness maps can be efficiently implemented by networks of digital twins. It has presented a conscious associative cognitive architecture framework for SAS to develop novel architectures of hybrid human-machine agents, mainly based on the application of digital twin technology, to support the involved mental models. A particular architecture for critical safety SAS was considered, to emphasize some specific and practical characteristics of the digital consciousness networks defined.

To conclude, we add some general suggested guidelines for SAS development: Humans shall decisively cooperate with the machines, as partners, to achieve their goals and objectives. Humans should delegate to the machines those tasks they can perform best. Humans and machines shall especially supervise the execution of critical tasks. *Intelligent machines should learn, reason, have experience and shall be conscious of the systems, situations, processes and services they handle.* Finally, we hypothesize that regular interactions with conscious machines would probably make humans more intelligent, by improving their consciousness of the corresponding world.

In the future, we plan to enhance the considered artificial consciousness framework to develop more applications in different scenarios and contexts.

Acknowledgements. The authors gratefully acknowledge the financial support of the CYTED Network "Ibero-American Thematic Network on ICT Applications for Smart Cities" (Ref: 518RT0559) and also the Spanish MICINN RTI Project (Ref: RTI2018-098019-B-100).

References

1. Neo4j Graph Platform. Sandbox v2. https://neo4j.com/sandbox-v2
2. IEEE Future Directions: IEEE Symbiotic Autonomous Systems White Paper II (2018). https://symbiotic-autonomous-systems.ieee.org/white-paper/white-paper-ii
3. IEEE Future Directions Initiative, Symbiotic Autonomous Systems (2018). https://symbiotic-autonomous-systems.ieee.org
4. Microsoft Azure: Understand Digital Twins object models and spatial intelligence graph (2018). https://docs.microsoft.com/nb-no/azure/digital-twins/concepts-objectmodel-spatialgraph
5. Baars, B.: Metaphors of consciousness and attention in the brain. Trends Neurosci. **21**(2), 58–62 (1998)
6. Baars, B.: In the Theater of Consciousness: The Workspace of the Mind. Oxford University Press, Oxford (2008)
7. Biron, J., Lang, J.: Unlocking the Value of Augmented Reality Data. MIT Sloan Management Review. Frontiers Blog (2018). https://sloanreview.mit.edu/article/unlocking-the-value-of-augmented-reality-data
8. Damasio, A.: The Neurology of Consciousness. Cognitive Neuroscience and Neuropathology. Elsevier (2008)
9. Graziano, M.: Consciousness engineered. J. Conscious. Stud. **23**(11–12), 98–115 (2016)
10. Horii, H.: Root causes of Fukushima nuclear power station accident and lessons to be learned. In: Proceedings of the World Engineering Conference and Convention (WECC 2015) (2015)
11. Koch, C., Tononi, G.: Can we quantify machine consciousness? IEEE Spectrum (2017). https://spectrum.ieee.org/computing/hardware/can-we-quantify-machine-consciousness
12. Kokar, M., Endsley, M.: Situation awareness and cognitive modeling. IEEE Intell. Syst. **27**(3), 91–96 (2008)
13. Lake, B., Ullman, T., Tenenbaum, J., Gershman, S.: Building machines that learn and think like people. Behav. Brain Sci. **40**, e253 (2017)
14. Matthews, S.: Designing better machines: the evolution of a cognitive Digital Twin explained (2018). https://www.ibm.com/blogs/internet-of-things/iot-evolution-of-a-cognitive-digital-twin/
15. Panetta, C.: Gartner Top 10 Strategic Technology Trends for 2018 (2017). https://www.gartner.com/smarterwithgartner/gartner-top-10-strategic-technology-trends-for-2018
16. Robinson, I., Webber, J., Eifrem, E.: Graph Databases. O'Reilly Media, Newton (2015)
17. Wolf, T.: From zero to research. An introduction to Meta-learning (2018). https://medium.com/huggingface/from-zero-to-research-an-introduction-to-meta-learning-8e16e677f78a

Deep Support Vector Classification and Regression

David Díaz-Vico[1,2](✉), Jesús Prada[1], Adil Omari[3], and José R. Dorronsoro[1,2]

[1] Dpto. Ing. Informática, Universidad Autónoma de Madrid, Madrid, Spain
david.diazv@estudiante.uam.es
[2] Instituto de Ingeniería del Conocimiento,
Universidad Autónoma de Madrid, Madrid, Spain
[3] Signal Theory and Communications Department,
Universidad Carlos III, Madrid, Spain

Abstract. Support Vector Machines, SVM, are one of the most popular machine learning models for supervised problems and have proved to achieve great performance in a wide broad of predicting tasks. However, they can suffer from scalability issues when working with large sample sizes, a common situation in the big data era. On the other hand, Deep Neural Networks (DNNs) can handle large datasets with greater ease and in this paper we propose Deep SVM models that combine the highly non-linear feature processing of DNNs with SVM loss functions. As we will show, these models can achieve performances similar to those of standard SVM while having a greater sample scalability.

1 Introduction

Support Vector Machines (SVM; [17]) are one of the state of the art methods for supervised classification and regression and, as such, widely used. One key fact for this is their ability to work implicitly with kernels such as the Gaussian one, which map the initial features to a possibly infinite dimensional reproducing kernel Hilbert space. But, on the other hand, this capability also hinders their ability to cope with large datasets, as the handling of the kernel matrix becomes too costly or, sometimes, unfeasible and, even if a model is finally built, the so called "kernelization curse", i.e., the fact that the number of Support Vectors grows linearly with sample size, implies that the model may be too costly in memory or time to exploit.

Many proposals have appeared in the literature to overcome these problems, usually for Support Vector classification (SVC) problems. Among them we can mention the incremental learning of SVMs [1], ensemble learning of SVMs [6] or cutting planes [15] but, nevertheless, it can be said that, unless substantial hardware resources are committed, current kernel SVM training methods are not competitive for datasets with more than about 100,000 patterns.

A. Omari—Currently at Telefónica.

© Springer Nature Switzerland AG 2019
J. M. Ferrández Vicente et al. (Eds.): IWINAC 2019, LNCS 11487, pp. 33–43, 2019.
https://doi.org/10.1007/978-3-030-19651-6_4

These problems are largely mitigated when working with linear SVMs [21] for which efficient algorithms, such as Pegasos [19] or dual coordinate descent [14], exist. However, efficient linear SVM models can only be expected when the original features have very large dimension so that projections are no longer needed. When sample dimension is just moderate, linear SVM models are usually less powerful that their Gaussian counterparts.

In principle, the main difficulty when working with SVMs is the non differentiable nature of the SVC hinge loss that, at first sight, forces a dual probem to be solved. However, its non differentiability is rather mild and subgradient descent is used, for instance, in the Pegasos algorithm. In fact, the SVM losses have the same non-differentiable behavior of the ReLU loss [11] routinely used in Deep Neural Networks (DNN) to compute gradients by backpropagation and which are easily handled automatically by DNN backends such as TensorFlow [12]. In fact, the hinge loss is already predefined in the Keras wrapper [5] for Tensor-Flow. Also, and although not predefined in Keras, the ϵ-insensitive loss used in Support Vector regression (SVR) has the same nondifferentiable behavior.

This suggests to consider an alternative to non linear SVMs by means of DNNs for which the standard cross entropy for classification or squared error for regression are replaced by the hinge and ϵ-insensitive losses respectively. This approach has been already applied in [20], where it is compared with standard softmax DNNs on classification problems, and by [22] in speech recognition. Here we will also extend it to Deep Support Vector Regression models and we will compare these Deep SV Classifiers and Regressors with their standard Gaussian SVC and SVR counterparts in a number of medium to large classification and regression problems.

The paper is organized as follows. In Sect. 2 we will briefly review standard kernel based SVC and SVR models while their deep counterparts are explained in Sect. 3. Numerical experiments are presented in Sect. 4 and the paper ends with a discussion, conclusions and pointers to further work.

2 Support Vector Machines

Given a sample $S = \{(x^p, y^p), p = 1, \ldots, N, y^p = \pm 1\}$, if we have a linear model $\xi = f(x) = w \cdot x + b$ and h denotes the hinge loss

$$h(y, f(x)) = \max\{0, 1 - yf(x)\} = \max\{0, 1 - y\xi\} = h(y, \xi),$$

the optimization problem to be solved for a linear SVC is

$$\arg\min_{w,b} \frac{1}{2}\|w\|^2 + C \sum_{1}^{N} h(y^p, w \cdot x^p + b)$$

$$\equiv \arg\min_{w,b} \left(\frac{1}{2CN}\|w\|^2 + \frac{1}{N} \sum_{1}^{N} h(y^p, w \cdot x^p + b) \right)$$

$$\equiv \arg\min_{w,b} \left(\frac{1}{N} \sum_{1}^{N} h(y^p, w \cdot x^p + b) + \alpha\|w\|^2 \right) \tag{1}$$

with $\alpha = \frac{1}{2CN}$. In general, SVCs are usually built solving the dual problem of (1), namely

$$\max_{\alpha_i} \sum_{i=1}^{N} \alpha_i - \frac{1}{2} \sum_{i=1}^{N} \sum_{j=1}^{N} \alpha_i \alpha_j y_i y_j x_i^T x_j \tag{2}$$

subject to $0 \leq \alpha_i \leq C$, $i = 1, \ldots, N$, $\sum_{i=1}^{N} \alpha_i y_i = 0$.

Notice that problems (1) and (2) only involve dot products; this is also the case of the final SVM model. As a consequence, all can be written as just done but replacing x with a kernel-related projection $\Phi(x)$. The map Φ can be implicit, as is the case with standard kernel SVCs, where the dot product only enters through some kernel, or it can be an explicit one, as it will be the case here, where $\Phi(x) = F(x, \mathcal{W}_h)$ will be the vector of last hidden layer values of a MLP with input to last hidden layer weighs $\mathcal{W}_h$. Moreover, if the kernel representation $\Phi(x^p)$ is known explicitly, the primal problem (1) can be directly solved, as done by the Pegasos algorithm [19] (see also [3], where the primal problem is solved for the squared hinge loss). We will also exploit the explicit kernel knowledge in the Deep SVC approach that we describe in the next section.

Given now a sample $S = \{(x^p, y^p), p = 1, \ldots, N\}$ with the y^p here being numerical targets, and a linear model $\xi = f(x) = w \cdot x + b$, the ϵ-insensitive loss, $\epsilon > 0$, would now be

$$\ell_\epsilon(y, f(x)) = \ell_\epsilon(y, \xi) = \max\{0, |\xi| - \epsilon\}.$$

The optimization problem to be solved now for linear SV Regression (SVR) is

$$\arg\min_{w,b} \frac{1}{N} \sum_{1}^{N} \ell_\epsilon(y^p, w \cdot x^p + b) + \alpha \|w\|^2. \tag{3}$$

As it was the case in SVC, the ϵ-insensitive loss is convex but only piecewise differentiable and because of this, here again, the task solved in practice is the following dual problem derived through the Lagrangian formalism

$$\max_{\alpha_i, \alpha_i^*} \sum_{i=1}^{N} y_i(\alpha_i^* - \alpha_i) - \frac{1}{2} \sum_{i=1}^{N} \sum_{j=1}^{N} (\alpha_i^* - \alpha_i)(\alpha_j^* - \alpha_j) x_i \cdot x_j -$$

$$\epsilon \sum_{i=1}^{N} (\alpha_i^* + \alpha_i) \tag{4}$$

subject now to $0 \leq \alpha_i, \alpha_i^* \leq \frac{1}{2\alpha N}, i = 1, \ldots, N$, $\sum_{i=1}^{N} (\alpha_i^* - \alpha_i) = 0$.

The kernel trick can also be applied here and, if it is known explicitly, gradient or subgradient descent can be used. We describe next how to exploit this for Deep SVR.

3 Deep Support Vector Machines

3.1 Deep Learning

Artificial Neural Networks (ANNs) can be seen as an extension of the classical linear and logistic regression models. They can generate an arbitrarily good latent representation of the data [8,13] that can be efficiently used to build powerful models. Starting with the multi layer perceptrons (MLPs), whose basic theory was already well established in the 80s, and the backpropagation algorithm for gradient computation during ANN training, they can be considered as the first example of modern machine learning algorithms that could be applied to both regression and classification problems with minimal conceptual variations. However, technical difficulties, essentially due to knowledge gaps about their training plus the lack of computing power at the time, led to their relative decline in the late 90's and the rise of competing methods, particularly SVMs, for classification and regression.

But about 2010, the wide availability of powerful computing facilities, advances on the theoretical underpinnings of MLPs, many refinement of their training procedures and a better understanding of the difficulties related to many layered architectures [10] have produced a spectacular expansion under the deep neural network (DNN) paradigm. To all this we can add the appearance of several development frameworks such as TensorFlow [12], CNTK [18], MXNET [4] or Torch [7], as well as wrappers for them such as Keras [5], that have allowed the practitioners to experiment with different architectures, non-differentiable activations and, even, non-differentiable loss functions. Last, but not least, the iterative nature of backpropagation and its linear cost growth with respect to sample size imply that DNNs are much less affected from the bad scalability of kernel methods, and can be applied with relative ease to datasets with hundreds of thousands of patterns. As mentioned, mildly non-differentiable functions such as ReLUs or the hinge loss, can be handled within the DNN framework and are relatively simple to incorporate into DNN tools. We discuss next how the hinge and ϵ-insensitive loss can be introduced in a DNN set up.

3.2 Deep SVC and SVR

Consider a more or less standard DNN architecture where an input layer is followed by a number of hidden layers that can be either convolutional or fully connected or of any other type, and, finally, linear output activations. The transformation of such a network can be thus written as

$$f(x, w, b, \mathcal{W}_h) = w \cdot F(x, \mathcal{W}_h) + b = w \cdot \Phi(x) + b,$$

where $\mathcal{W}_h$ denotes the set of weights and biases up to the last hidden layer, w, b denote the linear weights and bias acting on this last hidden layer, and $F(x, \mathcal{W}_h)$ the last hidden layer outputs. We also denote these outputs as $\Phi(x)$ when we want to emphasize a kernel perspective.

Considering first SVCs, the hinge loss is differentiable, as mentioned, everywhere except at $\xi = 0$; the same is true for the ReLU activations commonly used in deep networks. As it is the case of ReLUs, the hinge loss can be implemented using the primitives of backends such as TensorFlow, and loss gradients are derived automatically when network models are compiled. Here, the optimal weights are to be obtained minimizing the following regularized cost

$$J(w, b, \mathcal{W}_h) = \frac{1}{N} \sum_1^N h\left(y^p, w \cdot F(x^p, \mathcal{W}_h) + b\right) + \alpha_S \|w\|^2 + \alpha_H \mathcal{R}(\mathcal{W}_h); \quad (5)$$

here $\|w\|^2$ is the squared norm of the linear output weights and $\mathcal{R}(\mathcal{W}_h)$ can be any regularizer function acting on the weights of the hidden layers. The preceding formulation points for instance to the regularization given by the Frobenius norm of the weights of fully connected or convolutional layers. Notice that, as explained below, we would keep in principle different weight penalties α_S and α_H for the linear output weights and for the hidden layer ones; if dropout was to be used, α_H would be the dropout probability.

The minimization of (5) can be achieved by standard DNN solvers such as stochastic gradient descent, Adam [16], Adagrad [9] or others. The regularization parameters α_S, α_H are to be selected by some form of cross validation (as well as the DNN architecture, if desired). If we work with a predefined DNN architecture, we will have to optimize here two hyperparameters, α_S, α_H, the same number than in Gaussian SVC, where the C penalty and γ kernel width have to be adjusted.

Notice that after optimization, the w^*, b^* weights correspond to a linear SVC acting on the hidden layer outputs $F(x^p, \mathcal{W}_h^*)$, for they must solve

$$\arg\min_{w,b} \frac{1}{N} \sum_1^N h(y^p, w \cdot z^p + b) + \alpha_S \|w\|^2 \quad (6)$$

with $z^p = F(x^p, \mathcal{W}_h^*)$. This is just the problem solved by a linear SVC on the z^p patterns; in particular, its margin is given by $\frac{1}{\|w^*\|}$. Since $\|w^*\|$ will be controlled by α_S while the other layers have different goals, this seems to point to the convenience of working with separate penalties α_S and α_H. Observe also that although the network's outputs $\xi = w^* \cdot F(x, \mathcal{W}_h^*) + b^*$ are continuous real numbers, the class prediction $\widehat{y}$ is obtained as $\widehat{y} = \text{sign}(\xi)$. Therefore, it is straightforward to obtain discrete classification scores such as accuracy, precision or recall, but some further work would be needed to achieve a more fine-grained prediction that makes possible to compute, for instance, ROC curves or their AUC. Possible ways of doing so would be to consider moving classification thresholds or to have a predict_proba method where the raw outputs of the Deep SVC were calibrated in some way.

Turning our attention to SVR, we again consider a more or less standard DNN architecture with linear outputs that defines a nonlinear transformation $f(x, w, b, \mathcal{W}_h) = w \cdot F(x, \mathcal{W}_h) + b = w \cdot \Phi(x) + b$ and a loss

$$J_\epsilon(w, b, \mathcal{W}_h) = \frac{1}{N} \sum_1^N \ell_\epsilon \left(y^p, w \cdot F(x^p, \mathcal{W}_h) + b \right) + \alpha_S \|w\|^2 + \alpha_H \mathcal{R}(\mathcal{W}_h) \quad (7)$$

where the regularization parameters α_S, α_H (and, if desired, the DNN architecture) are selected again by some form of cross validation. The optimal w^*, b^* will now coincide with those obtained by a linear SVR model acting on the last hidden layer outputs $z^p = F(x^p, \mathcal{W}_h^*)$. In Deep SVR we will have to optimize now three hyperparameters, α_S, α_H and the ϵ-insensitivity value, again the same number than in Gaussian SVRs.

In summary, essentially the same network structure is used for Deep SVC and SVR and the only differences are in the targets (± 1 for classification, real numbers for regression) and the loss used in each situation. In principle, we could expect classification accuracies or regression errors to be more or less the same when standard Gaussian or Deep SVC/SVR models are used, although the greater flexibility of the Deep SVC/SVR architectures should also result in a better performance in some problems, such as for instance, those dealing with images. In any case, the main advantage of the Deep SVC/SVR networks is likely to be manageable training times and, perhaps, more importantly, the ability to build models over large samples. Current kernel SV models have substantial difficulties with sample sizes above 100,000 and sizes above 500,000 are often outside their present reach unless really substantial computing resources are available. On the other hand, Deep SV models will be costly but still possible to be trained on those sample sizes. Moreover, prediction times will certainly be much faster for Deep SV models than for kernel based ones.

4   Experiments

4.1   Classification Experiments

We compare the performance of Kernel and Deep SVC over the datasets a4a, a8a, australian, cod-rna, diabetes, german.numer, ijcnn1, w7a and w8a from the LibSVM repository [2]. Their training and, when available, test sample sizes and dimensions are given in Table 1. In the Deep SVC (DSVC) models we will use ReLU hidden layer activations and Adam over minibatches as the loss optimizer. To lighten the hyper-parameterization costs we will use the default values in the Keras implementation of Adam for the initial learning rate (0.001) and the β_1 (0.9) and β_2 (0.999) parameteres. We shall also use in all cases a minibatch size of 200. Notice that network architecture, i.e., the number of hidden layers and of their units, could also be considered as hyper-parameters to be optimized. However we will work with DSVC models with 1 to 5 hidden layers and 100 units in all layers but the last one, which will have $0.1 \times |S|$ units, with $|S|$ denoting sample size, with a lower bound of 100 and an upper bound of 1000. The rationale for this is to enlarge the dimension of the last hidden layer projections of the sample patterns, so that the linear SVC models that act on them can have a large enough representation power.

Table 1. Number of train and test patterns and dimensions in the two-class problems.

	No. patterns train	No. patterns test	Dimension
a4a	4781	27780	123
a8a	22696	9865	123
australian	690		14
cod-rna	59535	271617	8
diabetes	768		8
german.numer	1000		24
ijcnn1	49990	91701	22
w7a	24692	25057	300
w8a	49749	14951	300

Table 2. Accuracies in the two-class problems.

	SVC	DSVC1	DSVC2	DSVC3	DSVC4	DSVC5	Best DSVC
a4a	**84.32 (1)**	84.19 (5.5)	84.20 (4)	84.19 (5.5)	84.29 (2)	84.27 (3)	84.29
a8a	84.92 (6)	**85.18 (1)**	84.95 (5)	85.14 (2.5)	85.08 (4)	85.14 (2.5)	**85.18**
australian	85.50 (5)	85.51 (4)	**87.09 (1)**	86.82 (2)	86.09 (3)	85.21 (6)	**87.09**
cod-rna	96.58 (5)	**96.66 (1)**	96.62 (2)	96.61 (3)	96.60 (4)	96.45 (6)	**96.66**
diabetes	**77.60 (1)**	76.95 (4)	77.47 (2)	76.43 (5)	76.43 (6)	77.21 (3)	77.47
german.numer	76.10 (2)	75.80 (3.5)	75.20 (5)	75.10 (6)	**76.60 (1)**	75.80 (3.5)	**76.60**
ijcnn1	97.93 (6)	98.88 (4)	99.03 (2)	**99.07 (1)**	98.84 (5)	98.99 (3)	**99.07**
w7a	**98.87 (1)**	98.82 (5)	98.85 (2)	98.83 (3.5)	98.79 (6)	98.83 (3.5)	98.85
w8a	99.04 (2)	98.99 (5)	98.92 (6)	**99.16 (1)**	99.04 (3)	99.03 (4)	**99.16**
rank mean	3.2222	3.6667	3.2222	3.2778	3.7778	3.8333	

We thus will hyperparameterize the L_2 (or Tikhonov) regularization penalties. We will consider two different such penalties one α_S, for the output weights and another one α_H which is the same for all the hidden layer weights. In both cases we will explore 5 values evenly spaced on a log scale in the interval $[2^{-30}, 2^{10}]$ selecting the optimal one by 4-fold cross validation as described below. As customary with neural networks, the Deep SVC inputs have been normalized feature-wise to 0 mean and 1 standard deviation.

The SVC models require two hyperparameters, the C regularization term and the width γ of the Gaussian kernels $\exp\left(-\gamma\|x - x'\|^2\right)$. For C we will explore 5 values in the interval $[10^{-3}, 10^6]$. In order to select the Gaussian kernel width γ, we scale feature-wise the SVC inputs to a $[0, 1]$ range; the rationale for this is that after this normalization, we have $\|x - x'\|^2 \leq d$ with d pattern dimension. Because of this we will explore γ values of the form $\frac{2^k}{d}$, with k in the $[-3, 6]$ range.

Table 3. Number of patterns and dimensions in the regression problems.

	No. patterns	Dimension
abalone	4177	8
bodyfat	252	14
cpusmall	8192	12
housing	506	13
mg	1385	6
mpg	392	7
pyrim	74	27
space_ga	3107	6

Turning now to the cross validation (CV) procedure, when there is a separate test set, we find model hyperparameters by 4-fold stratified CV over the train set and then report the performance of the best hyperparameter model over the test set. When there is only one dataset, we use a nested two loop CV approach in order to assess model performance. More precisely, we apply stratified 4-fold CV on both loops. In the outer loop each one of the four outer folds is set apart for testing and the dataset made of the other three folds is passed to the inner loop, where again 4 fold CV is applied to determine the best hyperparameters, which are then tested on the test fold set apart. Model performance is measured as the average over these 4 test folds. Notice that while in the first case a single best parameter set is found, in the nested procedure optimal model hyperparameters may be different for each one of the outer test folds. In all cases the score used is model accuracy.

We report in Table 2 the accuracies of the Gaussian SVCs (SVC) and of Deep SVCs with 1 (DSVC1) to 5 (DSVC5) layers. For a better reading the table also gives in parenthesis the ranking of these accuracies. Similarly, we also give in the last column the accuracy of the best performing deep SVC model. This is done on a descriptive basis, as we have not performed a statistical analysis of the accuracy table, given the relatively small number of datasets considered. Gaussian SVCs give the largest accuracies on four datasets, a4a, cod-rna, diabetes and w7a. For the other five datasets the highest accuracy is achieved by a Deep SVC model. The row at the bottom of the table gives the average rankings. The better performing models appear to be SVC, DSVC2 and DSVC3. But, in any case, notice that all accuracy values are quite similar; this seems to imply that a statistical analysis of these accuracies would show them to be essentially the same. As mentioned before, the difference would lie in training and, particularly, test times, much lower for the deep models over the larger datasets.

4.2 Regression Experiments

Turning our attention to the regression problems, the datasets used to assess the performance of Kernel SVR and Deep SVR are abalone, bodyfat, cpusmall, housing, mg,

Table 4. MAEs in the regression problems.

	SVR	DSVR1	DSVR2	DSVR3	DSVR4	DSVR5	Best DSVR
abalone	1.48 (2)	1.49 (4)	1.49 (3)	1.50 (5)	**1.48 (1)**	1.51 (6)	**1.48**
bodyfat (×100)	**0.05 (1)**	0.42 (4)	0.31 (3)	0.51 (5)	0.53 (6)	0.28 (2)	0.28
cpusmall	2.13 (2)	2.21 (4)	**2.12 (1)**	2.19 (3)	2.31 (5)	2.40 (6)	**2.12**
housing	**2.28 (1)**	2.58 (6)	2.51 (4)	2.34 (3)	2.30 (2)	2.57 (5)	2.30
mg (×100)	9.26 (2)	9.68 (6)	9.65 (5)	**9.13 (1)**	9.36 (3)	9.58 (4)	**9.13**
mpg	**1.91 (1)**	2.39 (4)	2.28 (2)	2.49 (6)	2.42 (5)	2.36 (3)	2.28
pyrim (×100)	**5.62 (1)**	6.78 (3)	8.39 (5)	6.45 (2)	8.81 (6)	8.02 (4)	6.45
space_ga (×100)	9.67 (6)	9.14 (4)	9.22 (5)	**8.63 (1)**	8.70 (2)	8.86 (3)	**8.63**
rank mean	2	4.375	3.5	3.25	3.75	4.125	

mpg, pyrim and space_ga, again taken from the LibSVM repository [2]. Their sample sizes and dimensions are given in Table 3; notice that in this case there are no test sets.

The experimental setup is now exactly the same as in the classification setting, with the exception of the extra hyper-parameter needed for the ϵ-insensitive loss used in regression. This hyper-parameter ϵ is searched in a grid of 5 values distributed in a log scale between $2^{-10} \times std(y)$ and $2^{-1} \times std(y)$. Since there are no separate test sets, model performance in all cases is estimated by nested 4 fold CV.

We report now in Table 4 the mean absolute errors (MAEs) of the Gaussian SVRs (SVR) and of Deep SVRs with 1 (DSVR1) to 5 (DSVR5) layers. Again, the table also gives in parenthesis the ranking of these MAEs for a better reading; no statistical analysis has been performed here, again because of the relatively small number of datasets involved. We also give here the MAE of the best performing deep SVR model in the last column. Gaussian SVRs give the smallest MAE on the four smaller datasets, bodyfat, housing, mpg and pyrim, and give the second smallest MAE in three others. A Deep SVR model gives the smallest MAE for the other four datasets. Looking at the bottom row of the table, which has the average rankings, the SVR is clearly in the first place but, nevertheless, here again all MAE values are quite similar, something that a statistical test would probably confirm.

5   Conclusions and Further Work

In this paper we have shown that Deep SVC or SVR models, i.e., more or less standard DNNs with linear outputs and either hinge or ϵ-insensitive losses can give classification accuracies or mean absolute errors similar or even slightly better than those of Gaussian SVC or SVR models, but with much more manageable computational training and, particularly, test costs.

However, our experimental results open the way to more questions. A first one is which margin structure arises on the last hidden layer representations of the sample patterns. Moreover, we have also seen that each problem seems to have its own optimal DNN architecture. Notice that Gaussian (or other kernel) SVMs also define a particular kind of architecture in terms of the kernel width hyper-parameter γ and the concrete support vectors found during training. This suggests that possible Deep SVM architectures should also be considered as hyperparameters to be adequately found. If this is done, it is likely that we would find a tie between the SVC/SVR performance and that of the best deep counterpart. Finally, when used for classification, DNNs with softmax outputs and cross entropy loss automatically yield posterior probabilities. However, this is not the case with standard SVC and, thus, neither with the deep SVMs proposed here. These and other related questions are currently under study.

Acknowledgments. With partial support from Spain's grants TIN2016-76406-P and S2013/ICE-2845 CASI-CAM-CM. Work partially supported also by project FACIL-Ayudas Fundación BBVA a Equipos de Investigación Científica 2016, and the UAM-ADIC Chair for Data Science and Machine Learning. We also gratefully acknowledge the use of the facilities of Centro de Computación Científica (CCC) at UAM.

References

1. Bordes, A., Ertekin, S., Weston, J., Bottou, L.: Fast kernel classifiers with online and active learning. J. Mach. Learn. Res. **6**, 1579–1619 (2005)
2. Chang, C.C., Lin, C.J.: LIBSVM: a library for support vector machines. ACM Trans. Intell. Syst. Technol. **2**(3), 27:1–27:27 (2011). http://www.csie.ntu.edu.tw/~cjlin/libsvm
3. Chang, K., Hsieh, C., Lin, C.: Coordinate descent method for large-scale L2-loss linear support vector machines. J. Mach. Learn. Res. **9**, 1369–1398 (2008)
4. Chen, T., et al.: MXNet: a flexible and efficient machine learning library for heterogeneous distributed systems. CoRR abs/1512.01274 (2015)
5. Chollet, F.: Keras: deep learning library for Theano and TensorFlow (2015). https://github.com/fchollet/keras
6. Claesen, M., Smet, F.D., Suykens, J.A.K., Moor, B.D.: Ensemblesvm: a library for ensemble learning using support vector machines. J. Mach. Learn. Res. **15**(1), 141–145 (2014)
7. Collobert, R., Kavukcuoglu, K.: Torch7: a matlab-like environment for machine learning. In: BigLearn, NIPS Workshop (2011)
8. Cybenko, G.: Approximation by superpositions of a sigmoidal function. Math. Control Sig. Syst. (MCSS) **2**(4), 303–314 (1989)
9. Duchi, J.C., Hazan, E., Singer, Y.: Adaptive subgradient methods for online learning and stochastic optimization. J. Mach. Learn. Res. **12**, 2121–2159 (2011)
10. Glorot, X., Bengio, Y.: Understanding the difficulty of training deep feedforward neural networks. In: JMLR W&CP: Proceedings of the Thirteenth International Conference on Artificial Intelligence and Statistics (AISTATS 2010), vol. 9, pp. 249–256, May 2010
11. Glorot, X., Bordes, A., Bengio, Y.: Deep sparse rectifier neural networks. In: JMLR W&CP: Proceedings of the Fourteenth International Conference on Artificial Intelligence and Statistics (AISTATS 2011), April 2011

12. Google: Tensorflow, an open source software library for machine intelligence. https://www.tensorflow.org/
13. Hornik, K.: Approximation capabilities of multilayer feedforward networks. Neural Netw. **4**(2), 251–257 (1991)
14. Hsieh, C., Chang, K., Lin, C., Keerthi, S.S., Sundararajan, S.: A dual coordinate descent method for large-scale linear SVM. In: Machine Learning, Proceedings of the Twenty-Fifth International Conference (ICML 2008), Helsinki, Finland, 5–9 June 2008, pp. 408–415 (2008)
15. Joachims, T., Yu, C.J.: Sparse kernel SVMs via cutting-plane training. Mach. Learn. **76**(2–3), 179–193 (2009)
16. Kingma, D.P., Ba, J.: Adam: A method for stochastic optimization. CoRR abs/1412.6980 (2014)
17. Schölkopf, B., Smola, A.J.: Learning with Kernels: Support Vector Machines, Regularization, Optimization, and Beyond. Adaptive Computation and Machine Learning Series. MIT Press, Cambridge (2002)
18. Seide, F., Agarwal, A.: CNTK: Microsoft's open-source deep-learning toolkit. In: Proceedings of the 22nd ACM SIGKDD International Conference on Knowledge Discovery and Data Mining, San Francisco, CA, USA, 13–17 August 2016, p. 2135 (2016)
19. Shalev-Shwartz, S., Singer, Y., Srebro, N., Cotter, A.: Pegasos: primal estimated sub-gradient solver for SVM. Math. Program. **127**(1), 3–30 (2011)
20. Tang, Y.: Deep learning using support vector machines. CoRR abs/1306.0239 (2013). http://arxiv.org/abs/1306.0239
21. Yu, H., Hsieh, C., Chang, K., Lin, C.: Large linear classification when data cannot fit in memory. TKDD **5**(4), 23:1–23:23 (2012)
22. Zhang, S., Liu, C., Yao, K., Gong, Y.: Deep neural support vector machines for speech recognition. In: 2015 IEEE International Conference on Acoustics, Speech and Signal Processing, ICASSP 2015, South Brisbane, Queensland, Australia, 19–24 April 2015, pp. 4275–4279 (2015)

An Experimental Study on the Relationships Among Neural Codes and the Computational Properties of Neural Networks

Sergio Miguel-Tomé[✉] (iD)

CITAI (Cluster de Invetigación en Tecnologías Aplicadas a la Innovación), Universidad Isabel I, Calle Fernán González, 76, 09003 Burgos, Spain
sergio.miguel@ui1.es

Abstract. Biological neural networks (BNNs) have inspired the creation of artificial neural networks (ANNs) [19]. One of the properties of BNNs is computational robustness, but this property is often overlooked in computer science because ANNs are usually virtualizations executed in a physical machine that lacks computational robustness. However, it was recently proposed that computational robustness could be a key feature that drives the selection of the computational model in the evolution of animals [20]. Until now, only energetic cost and processing time had been considered as the features that drove the evolution of the nervous system. The new standpoint leads us to consider whether computational robustness could have driven the evolution of not only the computational model but also other nervous system traits in animals through the process of natural selection. Because an important feature of an animal's nervous system is its neural code, we tested the relationship among the computational properties of feed-forward neural networks and the neural codes through *in silico* experiments. We found two main results: There is a relationship between the number of epochs needed to train a feed-forward neural network using back-propagation and the neural code of the neural network, and a relationship exists between the computational robustness and the neural code of a feed-forward neural network. The first result is important to ANNs and the second to BNNs.

Keywords: Computational robustness · Neural code · Neural network · Back-propagation

1 Introduction

Biological neural networks (BNNs) have inspired the creation of artificial neural networks (ANNs) [19], which are quite successful at executing tasks of pattern

---

This research was supported by Universidad Isabel I. I would like to thank Lori-Ann Tuscan for proofreading this paper.

J. M. Ferrández Vicente et al. (Eds.): IWINAC 2019, LNCS 11487, pp. 44–57, 2019.
https://doi.org/10.1007/978-3-030-19651-6_5

recognition. Neural networks can learn patterns (or classes) quickly and support noise or variation in input. Another feature of BNNs is computational robustness to damage, which prevents the failure of a unit from affecting the performance of the computational process. Computational robustness to damage is an established feature of nervous systems, and degenerative brain diseases (e.g., spongiform encephalopathy, Alzheimer's disease) have shown that the brain can withstand considerable damage before function is seriously altered or lost. For example, amyloidosis, a condition that occurs in Alzheimer's disease, provokes acutely inhibited synaptic transmission [21], but the process begins 10 to 15 years before the first cognitive symptoms appear. Also, computational experiments have shown that the deterioration of the output is small, even when a large number of nodes or links are damaged [7]. Neural networks are computationally robust not only in processing information but also generating signals. Although ANNs are usually modeled in a simple way without intrinsic electrophysiological properties, biological neurons confer robustness because they have intrinsic properties that allow them to self-synchronize [17]. This capacity provides computational robustness to damage because the system can re-synchronize itself when the organism loses part of its neurons or even some of its articulations, generating a new pattern that permits the maintenance of a useful function [12]. However, unlike BNNs, ANNs usually do not have physical computational robustness. This lack is found in ANNs that are virtual machines simulated by physical machines that lack computational robustness, but it does not occur in ANNs that are physical machines. Because ANNs are usually executed on register-architecture machines (e.g., PCs, laptops), which are not computationally robust to physical damage, the machine will fail if there is a failure in one of the units of the register-machine. This fact has led to computational robustness being overlooked in computer science.

Recently, it has been proposed that the selection of the neural network model against other computational models in Eumetazoa (a clade containing most animal groups) is a consequence of neural networks possessing computational robustness, which leads to longer survival and greater reproduction performance when compared to computational models that lack this trait [20]. Until now, only energetic cost and processing time had been considered as the features that had drove the evolution of the nervous system [5, 6, 14]. But if computational robustness can affect Eumetazoa's evolutionary direction in determining which computational model is used to process environmental information and make motility decisions, then maybe the evolution of other computational features in the nervous system, such as the neural code, could have been driven by computational robustness.

The neural code refers to the set of responses from a population of neurons that represents a set of stimuli. The channel coding theory studies codes and their features for transmitting information in networks [25]. However, it does not cover the differences among codes in a neural network and how they affect computational processes carried out by a neural network.

Also, in artificial intelligence, although the problem of identifying what class an input belongs to requires encoding the classes in the output neurons when a method of supervised learning is being applied in an ANN, the neural code of ANNs has not been studied. When applying an ANN in supervised learning to a problem that requires classifying the input configurations in k-classes, the rule is to directly use k output neurons, so each output neuron represents a class [1]. In neuroscience, researchers have studied how the neural code is related to the energetic cost of the computational processes of a BNN, and although it has recently been proposed that BNNs use error-correcting codes [3] and that human neural code is more efficient transmitting information but less robust against error than other species [22], the author is not aware of any proposal or experimental research on how neural code features affect computational features of neural networks.

In this investigation, we posed a new question: Do neural codes affect the computational features of a neural network? Finding any effect caused by the neural codes on any computational feature of a neural network would show that the answer to this question is yes. We used an experimental approach to address this question and examine how the computational processes of a neural network were affected by different neural codes. The investigation focused on two features: computational robustness and the number of epochs of training. Section 2 describes the design, configurations, and methods of the experiments. Section 3 presents the results of the series of experiments, Sect. 4 discusses the results, and Sect. 5 presents our conclusions.

2   Materials and Methods

We implemented a program using Delphi XE 10.3 that allows different feed-forward topologies to be built for ANNs. The program trains them using back propagation, damages the network neurons, and tests the networks by classifying a batch of images. All the experiments were performed with this program, which implements a classical feed-forward architecture in which each layer is connected only to the next layer. The implementation permits the modification of the following: the number of neurons in the input layer, the number of neurons in the hidden layers, the number of hidden layers (all hidden layers always have the same number of neurons), and the number of the output layers. The implementation takes 24-bit bitmap images in color with a resolution of 200×200. The input layer of the implementation can be modified, but it is fixed at $120,000$ neurons, with one neuron per pixel and color channel. Each topology of the hidden layers can differ in the number of layers and neurons per layer, but each topology has the same number of neurons in all its hidden layers. We created five different topologies whose features are in Table 1. The output layer of each ANN differs in the number of neurons according to the number of classes considered in each experiment. Each neuron is modeled by the classical sigmoid function, and each neuron takes one input from each of the neurons of the previous layer.

We performed two series of experiments: one measured the required number of training epochs needed to achieve a maximum value or error under a given

Table 1. This table shows the topologies of the ANN used in the experiments. i.p. = input layer, h.l. = hidden layers, o.l. = output layer.

Topology	No. neurons i.l.	No. of h..l	No. of neurons per hidden layer	No. neurons o.l.
1	120000	2	50	3
2	120000	2	50	2
3	120000	2	50	7
4	120000	2	50	3
5	120000	2	50	4

value and the second tested if a relationship exists between neural codes and a neural network's computational robustness. Computational robustness must not be confused with robustness of transmitting signals [2,11] or navigability [10]. Quantifying computational robustness requires studying a neural network's computational process and performance; examining only signal transmission does not reveal anything about computational robustness. We need to know what computation an undamaged neural network is performing to be able to study how damage affects its computational process and to determine its level of computational robustness.

We organized the second series of experiments as two phases of the research. The first phase studied the required minimum number of training epochs needed to achieve a maximum error for each training example. This phase generated a set of neural networks with known computational processes that we used in the second series of experiments about computational robustness and neural codes.

All the results of the experiments have been analyzed using XLSTAT Premium 2019.1.2 and Excel.

2.1 Methods of First Series of Experiments

The first series of experiments focused on testing the relationship between the neural code and the number of epochs of training and used the classical method of back-propagation (BP) [23,24]. We did not apply momentum, and the rate of learning was 0.3. The loss function used to calculate the error of each output neuron was the classical function:

$$e_j = \frac{1}{2}(y_i - o_i)^2 \tag{1}$$

We calculated the total error of the output layer to an input as:

$$E_p = \frac{1}{n}(\sum_{j=1}^{n}(e_j)) \tag{2}$$

We did not use the mean squared error to determine the degree of learning relative to the batch of examples of the neural network. Instead, the training process through BP was not stopped until all the training samples had an error less than a certain value, called maximum error, which we set at 0.01. To assess that the goal was achieved, the program first executed an epoch of training, and then calculated the error with each training sample of the batch without executing BP. When all training examples of the batch had an error less than the maximum error allowed, the training finished.

Each hidden topology of the ANN was confronted with several different problems, all of which were focused on recognizing letters. The problems were variants of recognizing 3 letters from the English alphabet. To create the neural networks, random values were used for the initial weights. Thus, all the neural networks that were trained to resolve a specific problem were considered one population. We used $P_{\{a,b,c\}}$ to denote the population of neural networks that learned the letters "a", "b", and "c", and we denoted $P_{\{c,d,e\}}$ as the population that learned the letters "c", "d", "e", and so on.

In the experiments, three different neural codes were considered: unary, binary, and Lucal code. Unary codification uses one output neuron per class, binary codification uses n output neurons to classify $2^n - 1$ classes, and Lucal code uses $n + 1$ output neurons to codify $2^n - 1$ classes. Lucal code was chosen because it has error detection properties [16]. Table 2a and b show two examples of how the classes were codified. In addition to the classes that learn a population of neural networks, a population is also defined by the neural code that it uses. We denote the kind of code used by adding capital letters in the subindex after the set of classes. Thus, a population that uses unary code and is trained to learn "a", "b", and "c" is denoted by $P_{\{a,b,c\}|U}$. Also, if all the neural networks of the population have the same topology, it is denoted by adding a superindex that identifies the topology between the parentheses, e.g., $P_{\{a,b,c\}|U}^{(n)}$, where n identifies the topology of the neural networks. We denote a sample of a population with a capitalized "S" and the subindex of the population, and a superindex with the size of the sample and the identifier of the topology between parentheses, e.g., $S_{\{a,b,c\}|U}^{30(1)}$ is a sample of 30 subjects of topology 1 from the population $P_{\{a,b,c\}|U}^{(1)}$. A brave over the P or S denote when a population or sample has already been trained to identified the classes specified by the subindex e.g. $\check{S}_{\{a,b,c\}|U}^{30(1)}$.

There were 40 pictures for each letter used as training examples, and the training batch size for the 3 letters was 120 images.

The training process through BP did not stopped until all the training samples had an error less than a certain value. The value chosen was been 0.001. To assess that the goal was achieved, the program first executed an epoch of training and after the epoch, the program calculated the error with each training sample of the batch without executing BP. If all training examples of the batch had an error less than the maximum error allowed the training finish.

2.2   Methods of the Second Series of Experiments

The second series of experiments evaluated the computational robustness of ANNs with different neural codes. To evaluate computational damage, we need to know what a neural network knows, so we used neural networks that had learned

Table 2. Two codifications of the three classes in output layer used in the experiments. No. ONs: Number of output neurons.

(a)				(b)			
Class	Neural code	No. ONs	Code	Class	Neural code	No. ONs	Code
a	Unary code	3	001	c	Unary code	3	001
b	Unary code	3	010	d	Unary code	3	010
c	Unary code	3	100	e	Unary code	3	100
a	Binary code	2	01	c	Binary code	2	01
b	Binary code	2	10	d	Binary code	2	10
c	Binary code	2	11	e	Binary code	2	11
a	Lucal code	3	011	c	Lucal code	3	011
b	Lucal code	3	110	d	Lucal code	3	110
c	Lucal code	3	101	e	Lucal code	3	101

to classify 120 images of different tree classes correctly using BP. The ANNs were trained until they achieved a maximum error of 0.001 for each training example. Damage to each ANN was produced by destroying a specific number of neurons in random positions in the ANN's hidden layers. This method simulates the kind of damage that a brain suffers during aging.

The experiment for each neural network consisted of two phases at each level of damage:

1. A fixed number of neurons were damaged.
2. A batch of images was given as input to the ANN and the number of mis-classified images is measured.

The destroyed neurons always belonged to the hidden layers, and 5 new neurons were destroyed in each damaging phase. We selected this number because there were 100 neurons in the ANN's hidden layers, so destroying 5 neurons damaged 5% of the ANN. The batch of images given to the ANN in the second phase was the same as that used for the training. This procedure allowed us to know exactly how much of a loss the ANN's performance suffered from the damage.

Determining the image's class from the ANN's output after the feed-forward process required binarizing the output of each neuron. Once the ANN did a feed-forward process, the value of each output neuron was compared with a threshold. If the value of the output neuron was equal to or greater than the threshold value, it was transformed into a 1, and if it was lower than the threshold it was transformed into a 0. The threshold assigned to the ANNs was 0.84.

3   Results

The objective for each series of experiments was to study a null hypothesis. The null hypotheses are the following:

- HME$_0$ (Null hypothesis of the maximum error): The neural code of a neural network does not affect the back-propagation process required to achieve a maximum error.
- HCR$_0$ (Null hypothesis of computational robustness): The neural code of a neural network does not affect the computational robustness of the neural network.

If the results of the experiments showed that we could reasonably reject either of the two null hypotheses, the answer to our question posed in Sect. 1 would be affirmative.

3.1 Results of the First Series of Experiments

The first series of experiments measured the number of epochs needed to achieve the maximum error for a batch of training examples. We performed three experiments with a total of 120 neural networks that were divided into three groups of 40 using the same neural code. Table 3 shows the average number of epochs each sample needed to fulfil the maximum error.

Table 3. Average number of epochs needed to achieve a maximum error for the batch.

Experiment	Sample	Topology	Maximum error	Epochs needed ($\bar{X} \pm SD$)
1	$S_{\{a,b,c\}|U}^{1(40)}$	1	0.01	16.33 ± 0.90
1	$S_{\{a,b,c\}|B}^{2(40)}$	2	0.01	18.63 ± 0.91
1	$S_{\{a,b,c\}|L}^{1(40)}$	1	0.01	16.5 ± 0.87
2	$S_{\{c,d,e\}|U}^{1(40)}$	1	0.01	15.83 ± 2.12
2	$S_{\{c,d,e\}|B}^{2(40)}$	2	0.01	18.45 ± 2.32
2	$S_{\{c,d,e\}|L}^{1(40)}$	1	0.01	16.18 ± 0.83
3	$S_{\{e,f,g\}|U}^{1(40)}$	1	0.01	15.65 ± 1.97
3	$S_{\{e,f,g\}|B}^{2(40)}$	2	0.01	19.43 ± 2.37
3	$S_{\{e,f,g\}|L}^{1(40)}$	1	0.01	15.7 ± 1.94

To use a statistical test to decide on the HME$_0$, we first applied the Shapiro–Wilk test to each sample to examine normality. Because none of the samples followed a normal distribution, we then used the Kruskal–Wallis test to set the null hypothesis HME$_0$. The results are shown in Table 4.

Thus, the result of test implies that the hypothesis HME$_0$ can be rejected, but we also wanted to study the samples in further detail. We used the Mann-Whitney U test to address HME$_0$ two by two. The results of the test are shown in Table 5.

Table 4. Results of the Kruskal–Wallis test for the three samples.

Samples	Alpha	p-value	H_0 decision
$S_{\{a,b,c\}|U}^{1(40)}$, $S_{\{a,b,c\}|B}^{2(40)}$, $S_{\{a,b,c\}|L}^{1(40)}$	0.05	<0.0001	Rejected
$S_{\{c,d,e\}|U}^{1(40)}$, $S_{\{c,d,e\}|B}^{2(40)}$, $S_{\{c,d,e\}|L}^{1(40)}$	0.05	<0.0001	Rejected
$S_{\{e,f,g\}|U}^{1(40)}$, $S_{\{e,f,g\}|B}^{2(40)}$, $S_{\{e,f,g\}|L}^{1(40)}$	0.05	<0.0001	Rejected

Table 5. Results of the Mann–Whitney test for the samples two by two.

Samples	Alpha	p-value	H_0 decision
$S_{\{a,b,c\}|U}^{1(40)}$, $S_{\{a,b,c\}|B}^{2(40)}$	0.05	<0.0001	Rejected
$S_{\{a,b,c\}|L}^{1(40)}$, $S_{\{a,b,c\}|B}^{2(40)}$	0.05	<0.0001	Rejected
$S_{\{a,b,c\}|U}^{1(40)}$, $S_{\{a,b,c\}|L}^{2(40)}$	0.05	0.305	Not rejected
$S_{\{c,d,e\}|U}^{1(40)}$, $S_{\{c,d,e\}|B}^{2(40)}$	0.05	<0.0001	Rejected
$S_{\{c,d,e\}|L}^{1(40)}$, $S_{\{c,d,e\}|B}^{2(40)}$	0.05	<0.0001	Rejected
$S_{\{c,d,e\}|U}^{1(40)}$, $S_{\{c,d,e\}|L}^{2(40)}$	0.05	0.333	Not rejected
$S_{\{e,f,g\}|U}^{1(40)}$, $S_{\{e,f,g\}|B}^{2(40)}$	0.05	<0.0001	Rejected
$S_{\{e,f,g\}|L}^{1(40)}$, $S_{\{e,f,g\}|B}^{2(40)}$	0.05	<0.0001	Rejected
$S_{\{e,f,g\}|U}^{1(40)}$, $S_{\{e,f,g\}|L}^{2(40)}$	0.05	0.294	Not rejected

3.2 Results of the Second Series of Experiments

The second series of experiments used ANNs that had learned to classify 120 images of the letters "a", "b" and "c" correctly. The ANNs were trained until they achieved a maximum error of 0.001. There were three kinds of ANNs according to the neural code used: unary, binary, and Lucal. The ANNs were damaged, and each neural network's performance was evaluated by testing how many of the 120 images were classified correctly after the damage. Because each neuron's role could be different, chance could lead the random damaging process to cause a difference in performance between one neural code and another. Thus, for each experiment we took a sample of 40 neural networks that carried out the same computational function.

The statistical results of the experiments are given in Table 6.

We applied the Kruskal–Wallis test to each damage level for the samples of ANNs. The results obtained are in Table 7.

We also applied the Mann–Whitney test to each damage level for the samples of ANNs. The results are in Table 8.

Table 6. Statistical results of the computational robustness of each sample of ANNs. The table shows the average and the standard deviation $(\bar{X} \pm SD)$ in % of images failed from the total of images learned to recognize with a maximum error of 0.001 of each respective sample.

% Neurons damaged	$\breve{S}^{1(40)}_{\{a,b,c\}|U}$	$\breve{S}^{2(40)}_{\{a,b,c\}|B}$	$\breve{S}^{2(40)}_{\{a,b,c\}|L}$
5%	0 ± 0	0 ± 0	0.54 ± 2.43
10%	0.31 ± 0.01	0.08 ± 0.36	4.17 ± 7.11
15%	1.31 ± 0.02	0.19 ± 0.76	12.71 ± 12.36
20%	4.56 ± 3.76	0.125 ± 0.35	28.21 ± 18.71
25%	10.81 ± 5.83	0.29 ± 0.69	41.79 ± 17.85
30%	17.23 ± 7.51	0.5 ± 1.05	52.79 ± 13.82
35%	25.17 ± 8.47	1.1 ± 3.5	61.60 ± 7.77
40%	32.98 ± 8.78	3.06 ± 5.09	65.83 ± 2.45
45%	39.88 ± 8.33	7.60 ± 8.65	66.35 ± 1.39
50%	47.77 ± 8.69	18.35 ± 14.57	66.67 ± 0
55%	53.58 ± 7.09	34.43 ± 14.94	66.67 ± 0
60%	58.42 ± 6.03	51.46 ± 13.64	66.67 ± 0
65%	61.56 ± 4.94	62.20 ± 8.29	66.67 ± 0
70%	63.48 ± 3.89	66.20 ± 1.9	66.67 ± 0

Table 7. Kruskal–Wallis test results for $\breve{S}^{1(40)}_{\{a,b,c\}|U}$, $\breve{S}^{2(40)}_{\{a,b,c\}|B}$ and $\breve{S}^{2(40)}_{\{a,b,c\}|L}$. The value of alpha is 0.0005.

Damaging stage	p-value	HCR_0
5%	0.133	Not rejected
10%	<0.0001	Rejected
15%	<0.0001	Rejected
20%	<0.0001	Rejected
25%	<0.0001	Rejected
30%	<0.0001	Rejected
35%	<0.0001	Rejected
40%	<0.0001	Rejected
45%	<0.0001	Rejected
50%	<0.0001	Rejected
55%	<0.0001	Rejected
60%	<0.0001	Rejected
65%	<0.0001	Rejected
70%	<0.0001	Rejected

Table 8. This table shows the p-value of Mann–Whitney test of the null hypothesis HCR_0 using the results of the computational robustness experiments of the samples two by two. The value of alpha is 0.05.

Damaging stage	$\check{S}^{1(40)}_{\{a,b,c\}|U}$ vs $\check{S}^{2(40)}_{\{a,b,c\}|B}$	$\check{S}^{2(40)}_{\{a,b,c\}|B}$ vs $\check{S}^{2(40)}_{\{a,b,c\}|L}$	$\check{S}^{2(40)}_{\{a,b,c\}|L}$ vs $\check{S}^{1(40)}_{\{a,b,c\}|U}$
5%	0.494/Not rejected	Not rejected	Not rejected
10%	0.123/Not rejected	< 0.0001/Rejected	0.0051/Rejected
15%	<0.0001/Rejected	<0.0001/Rejected	<0.0001/Rejected
20%	<0.0001/Rejected	<0.0001/Rejected	<0.0001/Rejected
25%	<0.0001/Rejected	<0.0001/Rejected	<0.0001/Rejected
30%	<0.0001/Rejected	<0.0001/Rejected	<0.0001/Rejected
35%	<0.0001/Rejected	<0.0001/Rejected	<0.0001/Rejected
40%	<0.0001/Rejected	<0.0001/Rejected	<0.0001/Rejected
45%	<0.0001/Rejected	<0.0001/Rejected	<0.0001/Rejected
50%	<0.0001/Rejected	<0.0001/Rejected	<0.0001/Rejected
55%	<0.0001/Rejected	<0.0001/Rejected	<0.0001/Rejected
60%	0.078/Not rejected	<0.0001/Rejected	<0.0001/Rejected
65%	0.019/Rejected	<0.0001/Rejected	<0.0001/Rejected
70%	<0.0001/Rejected	0.24/Not rejected	<0.0001/Rejected

4 Discussion

The neural code of the nervous systems is a hot topic in neuroscience, and we lack of a full understanding of it [3, 26]. We know there are multiple kinds of neural codes. We know that neurons communicate information through frequency of their spikes, by a precise timing of individual spikes, sniffing or spatial codes [3]. Until now, the research about the neural codes has been focused on how the transportation of information is affected by the neural code [3, 18] and the energy cost of the neural codes [13, 15]. Although this line of research has provided much information about these issues, examining only these topics provides an incomplete view of the processes of the nervous system. The nervous system contains a network that not only transmits information but also processes it; however, research has only studied how neural codes affect information transmission. This asymmetry may be due to our powerful mathematical tools, such as information theory and channel coding theory, that can be used to study these processes. However, if we want to fully understand neural codes, we need to know how neural codes affect the computational processes and properties of neural networks. To address this limitation, we performed two series of experiments, each of which focused on testing whether a neural network's neural code can affect its computational features and processes.

The first series of experiments focused on checking if the neural code affects the BP method of learning used in an ANN. We did not use the mean squared error to determine the degree of learning relative to the batch of examples of the neural network, but instead we fixed a maximum error, and each training example had to have less than or equal to that maximum error. We selected this option so we could assess if the error was less than or equal to the maximum error allowed for all the training examples in the second series of experiments.

The results of the Kruskal–Wallis test show that the neural code affected the BP process by modifying the number of epochs needed for the training to achieve a maximum error. Also, we performed the Mann–Whitney U test using groups of samples, two by two. The results show that there is a difference between the number of epochs needed caused by the binary and unary codes and between the binary and Lucal codes. However, the results were not statistically significant between unary and Lucal codes. It is possible that the effect is real but the test failed to show it because the experimental setup did not show the effect. The statistical descriptions show that binary codification caused the need for more training epochs on average to achieve the maximum error allowed for all the batches. Also, in the three experiments, the Lucal code needed on average a smaller number of epochs to achieve the maximum error than the unary code did, but we do not know if these results occurred by chance. Therefore, additional experiments with different topologies and maximum error values and can shed light on whether there are differences between unary and binary codes.

The results regarding the effect of the neural code on the BP process could be important also for BNNs. It was recently shown that segregated dendritic compartments allow deep learning [9], and that kind of compartment has been found in human neurons [4].

The second series of experiments focused on checking if the computational robustness was affected by the neural code. For the experiments, neither input neurons nor output layers were damaged. We did not damage the input neurons because we wanted to ensure that all information was arriving to the hidden neural network. Also, the input neurons do not realize any kind of computation, so they do not contribute to the computational robustness. With regard to the output neurons, we did not damage the output neurons for the experiments because each was not really an output neuron, but a population of neurons electrically coupled and synchronized. Thus, we supposed that, even if some of the neurons of the population were damaged, the response of the population would not be affected, and the response would only depend on the input from the last hidden layer.

The reader can observe that the classifying error never overcome the 66.67%. The classification error did not overcome 66.67% because there were only three classes, one of which the undamaged neurons activated. This effect can be explained with the proverb "Even a broken clock is right twice a day." The classification, although correct, was not caused by the neural network's knowledge but because the network always activated that output neuron.

The results of the experiments show that at 5% damage, the performance of the ANNs was barely affected independently of the neural code. The disrupted performance started when the number of damaged neurons was equal to or greater than 10%. Another conclusion that can be extracted from the second series of experiments is that there were key neurons in the ANNs. If the performance of a network markedly decreased when certain neurons were damaged, then those neurons were considered to be key neurons. We came to this conclusion by comparing the performance of the ANNs of the same sample in 10%, 15%, and 20% of damage level. We found ANNs with very low performance and others that lost no or very little performance. In the sample with Lucal code, we found a range: 49 images failed at 15% neuronal damage and 58 at 20% neuronal damage. This shows that the BP training process generates key neurons because we found a very high difference in performance with the same number of damaged neurons. Also, high standard deviations indicated the presence of key neurons. Given that the neural networks of the samples had key neurons, the performance difference in the same sample at different damaging stages depended on how lucky or unlucky the ANN was regarding the randomly selected neurons to be damaged. In the first phase of damage, there was a low probability that key neurons were damaged, and in last phase of damage there was a low probability that key neurons were not damaged.

The Kruskal–Wallis and Mann–Whitney U tests provide strong evidence against the hypothesis HCR_0, indicating that the neural code affected the computational robustness of the neural networks. One unexpected fact we observed in the second series of experiments is how computational robustness varied with the damage level. While the binary code clearly demonstrated greater computational robustness than the unary code for the first and middle stages of damage, the performance of ANNs with binary code fell drastically in subsequent stages and even began to perform worse than the neural networks with the unary code.

Another fact we observed is that the Lucal code provided the worst computational robustness to the ANN among the three codes. The Lucal code has important error detection properties [16], but it does not positively affect the computational robustness of the neural network. In fact, we could say it has a negative effect. Therefore, transmitting information and processing information appear to diverge in their requirements regarding the codes they need to give their best performance.

The computational model of neurons used in the experiments is far from including the complexity of biological neurons and BNN topology. However, the computational process carried out by any neural network originates from the same principle, and the outcome is generated through the combination of simple computations done by all the units of the neural network. If, in a simple topology with a simple neuron model, the neural code affects the computational properties of the neural network, relationships must exist between neural codes and the computational properties of all neural networks.

5   Conclusions

From a computational point of view, few studies have examined the function of an ANN when its nodes or links are damaged [7,8]. The most probable cause of this situation is that the results are not relevant to ANNs because they are executed as virtual machines on physical machines that lack computational robustness. However, the recent proposal that the computational model of the neural network was selected in Eumetazoa because of its computational robustness [20] brings attention to this feature and increases our knowledge about the evolution of nervous systems. This issue has led to the question of whether neural codes affect the computational features and processes of neural networks. Channel coding theory explains how information transmission in a network depends on the code and shows, among other results, that adding extra data bits to a code makes data transmission more robust to disturbances on the transmission channel because we can detect errors and apply error correction. However, channel coding theory does not address relationships between neural codes and the computational properties of neural networks; it only studies information transmission through channels, and neural networks do not transmit signals but process information to generate a codification. Because no prior knowledge allowed us to answer the question posed in this paper, we performed an experimental study on the relationships between neural codes and the computational processes and features of neural networks.

To discover if neural codes affect the computational features of neural networks, we performed experiments using a feed-forward ANN to investigate two features: the number of training epochs and computational robustness. The results show that the neural code affects the process of training through BP and the computational robustness of neural networks. Thus, we can conclude that the initial question posed in this paper can be answered affirmatively: the neural code affects the computational process and properties of a neural network. Until now, the effects of the neural code on the computational properties and processes of neural networks had been not considered, but this study highlights the effects of the neural code on neural networks and further studies should be done. Also, these effects can be key to understand the evolution of some features of nervous system.

Finally, it must be noted that the results of this study indicated that a neural network code theory exists, and the results presented here are part of this theory. Developing the neural network code theory can be a key to advancing our understanding of the BNN and its evolution in natural history and improving the methods of our ANNs.

References

1. Aggarwal, C.: Neural Networks and Deep Learning: A Textbook. Springer, Cham (2018). https://doi.org/10.1007/978-3-319-94463-0
2. Albert, R., et al.: Error and attack tolerance of complex networks. Nature **406**, 378–382 (2000)
3. Antonopoulos, C., et al.: Evaluating performance of neural codes in model neural communication networks. Neural Netw. **109**, 90–102 (2019)
4. Beaulieu-Laroche, L., et al.: Enhanced dendritic compartmentalization in human cortical neurons. Cell **175**(3), 643–651 (2018)
5. Bullmore, E., Sporns, O.: The economy of brain network organization. Nat. Rev. Neurosci. **12**, 336–349 (2012)
6. Cherniak, C.: Component placement optimization in the brain. J. Neurosci. **14**(4), 2418–2427 (1994)

7. Ghosh, A., Pal, N., Pal, S.: Modeling of component failure in neural networks for robustness evaluation: an application to object extraction. IEEE Trans. Neural Netw. **6**(3), 648–656 (1995)
8. Ghosh, A., Tanaka, H.: On making neural network based learning systems robust. IETE J. Res. **44**(4–5), 219–225 (1998)
9. Guerguiev, J., et al.: Towards deep learning with segregated dendrites. eLife **6**, e22901 (2017)
10. Gulyás, A.E.A.: Navigable networks as nash equilibria of navigation games. Nat. Commun. **6**(7651), 1–10 (2015)
11. Kalampokis, A., et al.: Robustness in biological neural networks. Physica A: Stat. Mech. Appl. **317**(3–4), 581–590 (2003)
12. Kazantsev, V.B., et al.: Self-referential phase reset based on inferior olive oscillator dynamics. Proc. Nat. Acad. Sci. **101**(52), 18183–18188 (2004)
13. Kong, Q., et al.: Efficient coding matters in the organization of the early visual system. Neural Netw. **105**, 218–226 (2018)
14. Laughlin, S.B., Sejnowski, T.J.: Communication in neural networks. Science **301**(5641), 1870–1874 (2003)
15. Lianchun, Y., Yuguo, Y.: Energy-efficient neural information processing in individual neurons and neuronal networks. J. Neurosci. Res. **95**(11), 2253–2266 (2017)
16. Lucal, H.M.: Arithmetic operations for digital computers using a modified reflected binary code. IRE Trans. Electron. Comput. **EC-8**(4), 449–458 (1959)
17. Makarenko, V., Llinás, R.: Experimentally determined chaotic phase synchronization in a neuronal system. Proc. Nat. Acad. Sci. **95**(26), 15747–15752 (1998)
18. Manin, Y.I.: Error-correcting codes and neural networks. Sel. Math. **24**(1), 521–530 (2018)
19. McCulloch, W., Pitts, W.: A logical calculus of the ideas immanent in nervous activity. Bull. Math. Biophys. **5**, 115–133 (1943)
20. Miguel-Tomé, S.: The influence of computational traits on the natural selection of the nervous system. Natural Comput. **17**(2), 403–425 (2018)
21. Moreno, H., et al.: Synaptic transmission block by presynaptic injection of oligomeric amyloid beta. Proc. Nat. Acad. Sci. **106**(14), 5901–5906 (2009)
22. Pryluk, R., et al.: A tradeoff in the neural code across regions and species. Cell **176**(3), 597–609.e18 (2019)
23. Rumelhart, D.E., Hinton, G.E., Williams, R.J.: Learning internal representations by error propagation. In: Parallel Distributed Processing: Explorations in the Microstructure of Cognition, vol. 1, pp. 318–362. MIT Press (1986)
24. Werbos, P.: Beyond regression: new tools for prediction and analysis in the behavior sciences. Doctor in philosophy, Harvard University (1974)
25. Yeung, R.: Information Theory and Network Coding. Springer, Boston (2008). https://doi.org/10.1007/978-0-387-79234-7
26. Yuste, R.: From the neuron doctrine to neural networks. Nat. Rev. Neurosci. **16**, 487–497 (2015)

Uninformed Methods to Build Optimal Choice-Based Ensembles

Ameed Almomani and Eduardo Sánchez[(✉)]

CITIUS, University of Santiago de Compostela, Santiago, Spain
{ameed.aliahmad,eduardo.sanchez.vila}@usc.es

Abstract. The paper explores uninformed methods to build ensembles using aggregations of single choice models. The research aims at developing new models to combine the performance of ensembles with the transparency of choice models. The dataset used to fit the models included rational, emotional and attentional features that were used as explanatory variables of user's choice. The results point out the superior performance of bagging methods to build optimal choice-based ensembles.

Keywords: Recommender systems · Ensembles · Choice models · Decision-making

1 Introduction

Ensembles are widely used to assist the decision-making processes in many areas such as tourism, marketing and health. In ensemble learning a number of weak learners are aggregated to produce a more accurate prediction than the one provided by a single learner [1]. Different methods have been proposed to come up with an efficient aggregation of learner predictions. The most popular ones are: bagging, boosting, and random forest [2]. In the field of recommender systems, ensemble models have become the dominant paradigm after the success of the Bellkor team in the Netflix prize [3]. The appeal of the approach has been reinforced with further empirical evidences [4]. However, in spite of their current success, ensemble algorithms might show important limitations in terms of transparency. People may perceive explicit recommendations negatively if they feel them as a tool of the advertising industry. As a result, there is an increasing demand to explain the outcomes offered by recommendation engines to the final user.

With the aim of providing a trade-off between interpretability and performance our lab developed choice-based models [5]. They are grounded on sound decision-making principles in order to explain and predict human choice. Under this approach, the recommendation problem is faced as a choice prediction task in which the key elements are: (1) the learning of user's preferences from user's choices, (2) the consideration of the choice set as an important explanatory variable, and (3) the inclusion of unobserved factors that may affect decision-making as random variables.

J. M. Ferrández Vicente et al. (Eds.): IWINAC 2019, LNCS 11487, pp. 58–65, 2019.
https://doi.org/10.1007/978-3-030-19651-6_6

The estimation of choice models require the identification of the relevant processes and variables underlying human behavior. The Dual Process Theory proposes two major sources [6]: the first one is fast, unconscious and effortless; the second one is slow, conscious and energy-consuming. These processes were associated to cognitive systems that were labelled as System I and System II [7]. System I is the fast system, which is related to intuition and driven by emotional factors, while System II is the slow one, linked to reasoning and rational outcomes. According to previous results reported from our lab [8], choice models (emotional and attentional) derived from System I features yielded better prediction performance than the ones obtained with System II features. Moreover, the attentional models in general, and the Fixations model in particular, they both made a better job than emotional models.

This work is aimed at developing new models to combine the high performance of ensembles with the transparency and interpretability of choice models. Specifically, we wonder about the optimal methods to build choice-based ensembles. In this paper, we explore the possibilities of uninformed or blind methods focusing on two aspects of the ensemble building process: the data sampling strategy and the aggregation technique. In the following sections, the questions and hypotheses are presented, the methods are described, and the main results and contributions are discussed.

2   Questions and Hypotheses

The work focuses on uninformed or blind methods to build the choice-based ensembles. Therefore, it is assumed that no prior information about the performance of the learners of the ensemble is available. The specific questions and hypotheses that have guided this work are briefly described:

1. Question 1: which method is better to build ensembles? Two sample strategies (bagging and boosting) as well as two aggregation techniques (average and majority vote) were tested. H1: No prior hypothesis was stated on that point.
2. Question 2: will choice-based ensembles outperform single choice models? H2: We expect the best choice-based ensembles to perform better than the corresponding single models.
3. Question 3: how good are choice-based ensembles compared to ensembles built with other models? As the baseline model we have resorted to Decision Trees (DT), which provide transparency and intrepretability. H3: We predict that choice-based ensembles will show better performance than DT-based ensembles.

3   Methods

3.1   Dataset

The dataset was collected during a choice experiment designed in collaboration with two Business partners: Neurologyca and Movistar. The subjects were presented a Web interface (Fig. 1) and asked to choose a movie from a set of four alternatives across 20 trials or choice situations. The movies were labeled with three attributes (see Table 1): Genre, Novelty and Price. During the experiment both neural and gaze activity were recorded in order to find the explanatory variables of human decision-making. Two main types of variables were recorded as described in Table 2.

Data were collected from 39 subjects (20 females, 19 males, age range = 18–51 years). All subjects had prior experience using Internet and Web applications and had normal or corrected-to-normal vision.

Table 1. Characterization of movies: attributes and values.

Feature	Values
Genre	Action, Comedy, Science Fiction, Drama
Novelty	Release, Catalog
Price	4,99 euros (Release), 0 euros (Catalog)

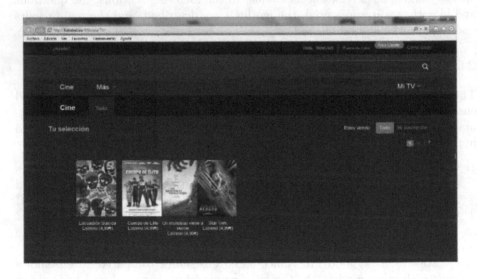

Fig. 1. Web interface.

3.2   Models

Choice Models. This paradigm considers that a decision-maker c_n will choose the alternative a_i from a choice set A by estimating the probability P_{ni} of utility U_{ni} of a_i being higher than utility U_{nj} of the other alternatives a_j in A. The process is formally represented as a choice rule (CR):

$$CR(A, \geq) = \{a_i \in A \,\|\, \mathbb{P}_{ni} \geq \mathbb{P}_{nj}, \forall a_j \in A\} \tag{1}$$

Table 2. Devices and recorded variables.

Devices	Variables	Variable type
EEG	Frustration, Excitement and Engagement	Emotional
Facial Coding (FACET)	Joy, Anger, Fear, Surprise, Contempt, Disgust, Sadness, Neutral, Positive and Negative	Emotional
Eye-Tracking	TimeSpend and Fixations	Attentional

The most popular form of the probability is the standard logit model [9], which is obtained under the assumption that the unobserved portion of utility U_{ni} is distributed independently, and identically. In this case, P_{ni} becomes:

$$\mathbb{P}_{ni} = \frac{e^{V_{ni}}}{\sum_j e^{V_{nj}}}. \tag{2}$$

This model estimates the probability on the basis of the observed utilities V_{ni} and all V_{nj}. These values are specified to be linear in the set of the features used to label the alternatives: $V_{nj} = \beta_{nj} \cdot x_j$, where x_j is the vector of observed features, and β_{nj} the vector of preferences of decision-maker c_n on the features of the alternatives a_j. The preferences β_{nj} are model coefficients that need to be estimated by fitting Eq. 2 to a dataset of choices. When a matching exist between the observed features and the preferences of the decision maker, V_{ni} rises and the probability $\mathbb{P}_{ni}$ approaches to one.

Observed Features. The data gathered in the experiment were aggregated in the Neurologyca-Movistar Dataset. Each choice situation was characterized with the choice set (4 movies), the chosen movie, and a set of features describing the process. These features included both the attributes of the movies and the subject's variables recorded during the experiment. Three different set of features were considered (Table 3): rational, emotional and attentional. Each set was used to fit a different model.

Table 3. Observed features.

Models	Features
Rational	Action, Comedy, Science Fiction, Drama, Release and Catalog
Emotional	Frustration, Excitement, Engagement, Joy, Anger, Fear, Surprise, Contempt, Disgust, Sadness, Neutral, Positive and Negative
Attentional	TimeSpend and Fixations

Ensemble Methods. Ensembles are aggregations of simple learners and the final prediction is estimated by combining the outcomes. Two data sampling strategies were implemented:

- *Boosting* builds the ensemble by using an iterative procedure over the same learner. This means that a single learner improves its accuracy on the basis of the performance of previous versions of himself.
- *Bagging* estimates different versions of the same learner on M different boot-strapped training data set.

Moreover, two aggregation techniques were tested under the bagging app-roach to estimate the final outcome:

- *Probability Average* For a decision-maker c_n, each learner of the ensemble estimates the choice probability for each item and then the average of prob-abilities is computed. The final prediction corresponds with the item with higher probability average.

$$a' = \arg\max_{a_i \in A} \overline{\mathbb{P}_{ni}} \tag{3}$$

- *Majority Vote* The prediction using this technique is the most often pre-dicted outcome by the set of K C_k learners:

$$a' = \arg\max_{a_i \in A} \sum_{k:C_k(x_j)=a_i} 1 \tag{4}$$

Model Estimation. To preserve individual preferences, we built choice models for every single user. As a number of observations per user is required to learn a model, we set to 12 the minimum threshold (the maximum number of obser-vations were 20). It determined that the total number of available users for the experiment was 18.

3.3   Evaluation

We applied the Accuracy metrics to measure the performance of models. Accu-racy is just the ratio between the correct and all prediction results:

$$Accuracy = \frac{T_{CorrectPrediction}}{T_{AllPrediction}} \tag{5}$$

10 trials of each training-evaluation cycle were carried out for each model. Thereafter, the average of the 10 Accuracy values was estimated.

3.4   Software

The main tool used was R, free software environment for statistical computing. Specifically, we used the mlogit package for estimation the multinomial logit model (see [9] for further details).

4   Results

4.1   Best Method to Build Ensembles

First, we compared the performance of aggregation techniques in terms of the accuracy of predictions. Table 4 shows the results for emotional, attentional and rational choice-based ensembles. The figures illustrate that performance is quite similar on using the two schemes. As a result, we choose the probability average (PA) as the aggregation techniques for the rest of experiments carried out in this work. Second, we tested the performance of bagging and boosting sampling strategies. The comparison shown in Table 5 points out that the bagging strategy outperforms the boosting one in all three models. The difference is significant in all cases, so bagging seems to be the best candidate as to build choice-based models.

Table 4. Comparison of aggregation techniques: Probability Average and Majority Vote. Three choice-based ensembles were built using the bagging sampling method. The average of accuracy over all users is shown.

Models	Accuracy Aggregation Technique: Probability Average	Accuracy Aggregation Technique: Majority Vote
Emotion-Choice-Bagging	0.38	0.37
Attention-Choice-Bagging	0.55	0.55
Rational-Choice-Bagging	0.46	0.46

Table 5. Comparison of sampling strategies: bagging and boosting. Three choice-based ensembles were built using the probability average (PA) as the aggregation technique. The average of accuracy over all users is shown.

Models	Accuracy Sample Strategy: Bagging	Accuracy Sample Strategy: Boosting
Emotion-Choice-PA	**0.38**	0.25
Attention-Choice-PA	**0.55**	0.34
Rational-Choice-PA	**0.46**	0.26

4.2   Comparison with Single Learners and Random Predictions

Three choice-based ensembles were built using the bagging sampling method as well as the probability average (PA) as aggregation technique. Table 6 illustrates their performance when compared with their corresponding single choice models.

The results are slightly better in two cases (emotional and attentional) but worse in the case of the rational model. The figures illustrate that the single choice models seems to be strong rather than weak learners. This probably explains the superior performance of single models against boosting-based ensembles (See Table 5). Finally, we confirmed that all models worked better than a random scheme.

Table 6. Comparison of choice-based ensembles with single choice models. The average of accuracy over all users is shown.

Models	Accuracy Ensemble: Bagging-PA	Accuracy Single Learner
Emotion-Choice	**0.38**	0.35
Attention-Choice	**0.55**	0.52
Rational-Choice	**0.46**	0.47
Random Pediction	0.21	

4.3 Comparison with Ensembles Built with Decision Trees

Three choice-based ensembles were built using the bagging sampling method, and other three using the boosting one. Both implemented the probability average (PA) as aggregation technique They were compared with ensembles built with decision-trees as single learners and the majority vote as aggregation technique (decision trees do not estimate probabilities). Table 7 shows the superior performance of choice-based ensembles using the bagging method. However, DT-based ensembles offer better results when compared under the boosting approach. Boosting seems to deepen the performance of single choice models, which seems to confirm their classification as strong single learners.

Table 7. Comparison of learner types: choice and decision-trees (DT). The average of accuracy over all users is shown.

Models	Accuracy Learner: Choice	Accuracy Learner: DT
Emotion-Bagging	**0.38**	0.34
Attention-Bagging	**0.55**	0.39
Rational-Bagging	**0.46**	0.34
Emotion-Boosting	0.25	**0.33**
Attention-Boosting	0.34	**0.34**
Rational-Boosting	0.26	**0.33**

5 Discussion

The results shown in this paper provide evidences to confirm hypothesis H2 and H3. The bagging sampling method combined with the PA aggregation technique allowed to build choice-based models that outperformed their corresponding single choice models as well as DT-based ensembles. The surprisingly good results of single choice models when compared with boosting-based ensembles might indicate that they would be better considered as strong learners. This finding probably explains why boosting is able to improve the performance of ensembles of decision-trees while reducing the accuracy obtained with choice-based ensembles. Overall, the results are promising and motivate the future exploration of elaborated methods to build better choice-based ensembles.

Acknowledgments. We want to acknowledge the collaboration of Movistar and Neurologyca on building the dataset used in this paper.

References

1. Polikar, R.: Ensemble based systems in decision making. IEEE Circuits Syst. Mag. **6**(3), 21–45 (2006)
2. Friedman, J., Hastie, T., Tibshirani, R.: The Elements of Statistical Learning: Data Mining, Inference, and Prediction. Springer Series in Statistics. Springer, New York (2009). https://doi.org/10.1007/978-0-387-84858-7
3. Koren, Y.: The Bellkor solution to the netflix grand prize. Netflix Prize Doc. **81**(2009), 1–10 (2009)
4. Bar, A., Rokach, L., Shani, G., Shapira, B., Schclar, A.: Improving simple collaborative filtering models using ensemble methods. In: Zhou, Z.-H., Roli, F., Kittler, J. (eds.) MCS 2013. LNCS, vol. 7872, pp. 1–12. Springer, Heidelberg (2013). https://doi.org/10.1007/978-3-642-38067-9_1
5. Saavedra, P., Barreiro, P., Duran, R., Crujeiras, R., Loureiro, M., Vila, E.S.: Choice-based recommender systems. In: RecTour@ RecSys, pp. 38–46 (2016)
6. Vaisey, S.: Motivation and justification: a dual-process model of culture in action. Am. J. Sociol. **114**(6), 1675–1715 (2009)
7. Kahneman, D.: Think Fast, Think Slow. Farrar, Straus and Giroux, New York (2011)
8. Almomani, A., Monreal, C., Sieira, J., Graña, J., Sánchez, E.: Rational, emotional and attentional choice models for recommender systems. In: Rocha, Á., Adeli, H., Reis, L., Costanzo, S. (eds.) WorldCIST 2019. AISC, vol. 931, pp. 557–566. Springer, Cham (2019). https://doi.org/10.1007/978-3-030-16184-2_53
9. Croissant, Y.: Estimation of multinomial logit models in R: the mlogit packages. R package version 02-2 (2012)

Robotics

Design and Implementation of a Robotics Learning Environment to Teach Physics in Secondary Schools

Samantha Orlando, Félix de la Paz López, and Elena Gaudioso[✉]

Artificial Intelligence Department, National Distance Education University (UNED),
28040 Madrid, Spain
sorlando1@alumno.uned.es, {delapaz,elena}@dia.uned.es

Abstract. Robotics have proved to be a very attractive tool for students specially in STEM areas that involve active exploration. Nevertheless, learning activities with robotics kits are usually isolated from official curriculum and no evaluation about the learning outcomes of students are provided. In this paper, we present IDEE, an integrated learning environment which uses robotics as a learning tool for a physics laboratory. Experiments in IDEE are proposed following a scientific experimental procedure. Students in IDEE have to achieve certain learning goals or skills when solving physics problems. The skills accomplished by a student while using IDEE are stored in students models. To this end, students' performance data is stored in a database. On the basis of students' skills, IDEE shows certain hints to help students. This information can be also bee shown to teachers to help them in supporting students' learning process.

1 Introduction

The learning of physics in secondary school demands the students to participate in laboratories to solve certain practical exercises. One of the main challenge of teachers is to plan creative and inspiring experiments taking into account the available equipment and to face equipment failures.

Virtual and remote labs [4,6] are used to make lab experiments available almost at any time and everywhere without restrictions on time and equipment. Nevertheless, remote labs require students certain skills in order to guide their own experiment. Especially in lower secondary education, students benefit from hands-on laboratories [2]. However, these laboratories should be redesigned to overcome new requirements in STEM (Science, Technology, Engineering and Mathematics) area. Educational robotics has been proved as useful learning tools that offer interesting teaching and learning opportunities at various levels and school subjects [1,9].

In fact, the low cost and highly accessible educational robots kits have gained popularity in schools [7]. Nevertheless, educational robotics is currently used predominantly in extracurricular classes and the activities usually done with

J. M. Ferrández Vicente et al. (Eds.): IWINAC 2019, LNCS 11487, pp. 69–76, 2019.
https://doi.org/10.1007/978-3-030-19651-6_7

robotics are isolated from the main curriculum. In this way, students do not establish the cognitive relationships between the theory concepts and the concepts involved in the activities done with robotics [5].

To overcome this limitation, in this paper we present IDEE (Integrated Didactic Educational Environment) a learning environment which integrates in an unique environment, learning activities and interaction with robotics [7,8].

IDEE is a visual programming tool that together with a robotic kit, provide experiments following a scientific experimental method while tracking students interactions with the learning environment. Moreover, students are asked to use robotics as laboratory artifacts in order to test their hypothesis about the solution of a problem. Thus, students can visualize their proposed solutions as often as they wish to observe what happens with the robot. IDEE allows the introduction of a real robotics laboratory into a physic class for secondary school students. In IDEE the learning activities are designed to guide the students to understand the physic concepts involved in each experiment. In addition, the data about the performance of the students in IDEE is stored in order to maintain certain students' profiles. On the basis of these profiles, IDEE can adapt the problem statement to each student's skills and can provide some hints to help students in problem solving.

The rest of the paper is organized as follows: Sect. 2 describes an overview of IDEE. In Sect. 3 the implementation of IDEE is described. Section 4 presents an example of an inclined plane experiment in IDEE. Finally, Sect. 5 concludes the paper and describes some lines of future work.

2 IDEE Overview

IDEE is a learning environment that provides a framework to solve learning activities in physics through the use of robotics. Students have to manipulate robotics as laboratory artifacts in order to test their hypothesis about the solution of an activity. Through the use of the robot, students can visualize their proposed solutions as often as they wish while observing the behavior of the robot.

Experiments in IDEE are based on the scientific procedure approach. For each experiment, IDEE provides the following learning activities: (i) presentation of the phenomenon to be observed in the experiment through exercises guided by the teachers (short problems, test, ...); (ii) testing the elements of the robot that are going to be used in the experiment (students should know the elements presented in the robot, such as, motors, sensors, ...); (iii) experimental testing of the hypothesis (students program the robot through IDEE and collect the data they obtain from the interaction with the robot); (iv) students should make at least two tests to evaluate their knowledge level about the concepts involved in the experiment; (v) mathematical study of the phenomenon (students make an exercise without using the robot; this exercise is adapted taking into account the level of competence of each student).

In IDEE students solve the activities and manipulate the robot using programming blocks. Each learning activity in IDEE is composed by the following elements: statement of the problem, blocks that will be necessary for its resolution, solution and students' profiles to which it is recommended.

Students interact with IDEE through a web-based interface. This interface provides the problem statement and a student working area. In this area, students solve the problem using the visual programming editor that is based on drag-and-drop blocks. When students finished the problem, they submit the solution and IDEE evaluate it. In addition, IDEE can show the correct answer if the student experiences difficulties (Fig. 1 depicts a screen-shot of IDEE learning environment).

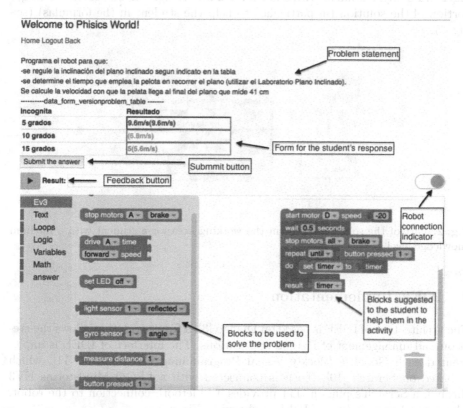

Fig. 1. General interface of IDEE. Notice that robot connection indicator changes from red to green to acknowledge the student when the robot is connected with IDEE. (Color figure online)

In order to guide the students, the set of blocks proposed in the working area is adapted to each problem, showing only the blocks that should be used in the solution. In addition, the progress of each student is stored in a database. IDEE stores for each student and for each exercise the student's answer, the right answer, the number of attempts in the tests and the time spent in each

72   S. Orlando et al.

exercise. From these data, IDEE can manage and update the skills acquired by each student. Each learning activity in IDEE is related to the skills the student has to work on.

Depending on the student's skills, part of the solution can be shown in the working area or not. Thus, a student who has achieved the necessary competences, will not be offered any part of the solution since it is not supposed that the student would need it. A student with a medium level of knowledge will be provided organizational and logical help (since it is supposed that the student needs to be guided in the logical steps necessary to solve the problem (see Fig. 2)). Finally, a student with a low level of knowledge will be provided a larger portion of the solution (in particular, to help the student in the formulas) (see Fig. 3).

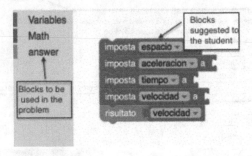

Fig. 2. Part of the solution shown in the working area for a student with a medium knowledge level

3   IDEE Implementation

The architecture of IDEE is based on Django [3], a framework that allows the creation and management of Python applications. The interface of IDEE is implemented with Google's Blockly Visual Programming Environment [11], which is based on Scratch [10]. IDEE is connected with a LEGO Mindstorms EV3 through a Scratch's plug-in that provides a bluetooth connection to the robot. The general architecture of IDEE is shown in Fig. 4.

Apart from the blocks available in the Blockly library, several additional blocks have been implemented for the interface of IDEE. Thus, it has been implemented:

- A complete set of blocks to control a LEGO Mindstorms EV3 kit.
- A set of composed blocks to help the students to manipulate the robotics kit. The goal of these composed blocks is to wrapper several actions with the robot in an unique block (see Fig. 5). For example, the composed block shown in Fig. 6 makes the robot to rise a plane to an established angle. In EV3 this operation should be done using all the blocks shown in Fig. 7.

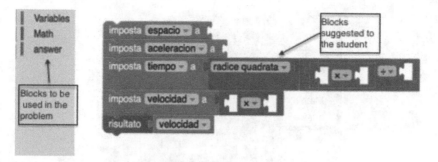

Fig. 3. Part of the solution shown in the working area for a student with a low knowledge level

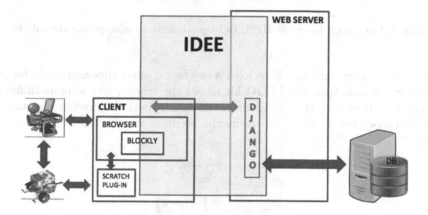

Fig. 4. General architecture of IDEE

The interaction data generated from the students working on IDEE is stored in the database. In addition, the data from the robot is also stored in the database, i.e., data from sensors and control variables are sent through bluetooth to IDEE and stored in the database to be further checked.

In order to manage the skills in IDEE, its database includes a *profile* table which includes a field to store the knowledge level of each student for each skill. This field can take three different values: *low*, *medium* and *high*.

As it has been describe above, the interface of IDEE is adapted to the knowledge level of a student in a skill.

Moreover, this information could be used to provide to the teachers information about the students' learning progress, such as for example: learning progress of the whole group of students, concepts that are difficult for a group of students or group of students with no learning gains.

IDEE uses the EV3 LEGO Mindstorms educational kit as the robotic component. It offers several advantages in the context of secondary education. (i) most students are familiar with programming blocks; (ii) the kit is robust and it

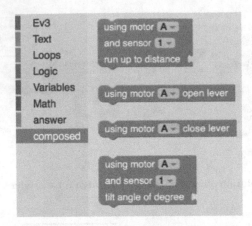

Fig. 5. Composed blocks in IDEE to help students to manipulate the robot

is quite inexpensive (in fact, the price is a key factor when choosing a tool for the classroom). In addition, the LEGO kit allows the teacher to configure different experiments. However, the configuration of each robotic laboratory instrument must be carried out carefully to ensure the accuracy required in a physics laboratory.

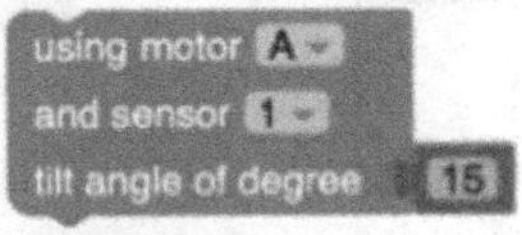

Fig. 6. Composed block to rise a plane to an established angle

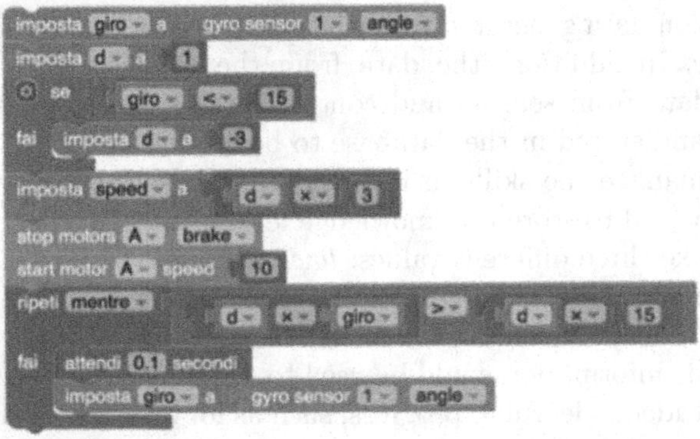

Fig. 7. EV3 blocks to rise a plane to an established angle

4 The Inclined Plane in IDEE

The goal of the inclined plane experiment is to show the students the theory behind the phenomenon where an object placed on a tilted surface slides down the surface. Students should understand that the speed at which the object slides down the surface is dependent upon how tilted the surface is. With this experiment, students are able to visualize experimentally the invariance of the velocity of fall as a function of the mass of the object, how the velocity does not change if the object has a free fall or if the object moves along the tilted surface, starting from the same point and visualize how the friction with the tilted surface affects the motion.

The robotics involved in this experiment is shown in Fig. 8. A EV3 Large Motor is used to raise and lower the plane by adjusting the angle of inclination with respect to the horizontal. This angle is measured by the EV3 Gyro Sensor. An EV3 Medium motor is used to change the state of the contact sensor to drop the ball. A contact sensor which changes its state when the ball contacts with it, gives the necessary information to measure the time of fall of the ball along the plane.

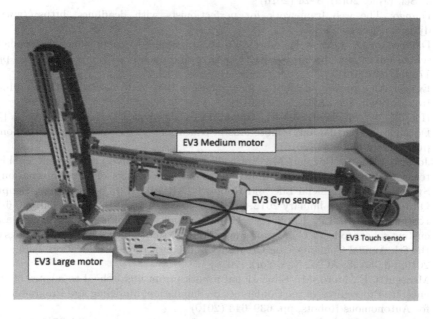

Fig. 8. The EV3 robot designed for the inclined plane experiment

In this experiment the following skills in physics are involved: relate magnitudes, operation maths, uniformly accelerated movement, definition of an inclined plane, velocity, friction. In addition, a skill about competences on the robotics involved in this experiment is also measured in IDEE.

5   Conclusions and Future Work

This paper describes IDEE a learning environment to support hands-on laboratory activities with robotics. IDEE monitors performance data of the students to adapt the working area of the students and to provide support to teachers in the evaluation of the learning process.

At this moment, thanks to an agreement with the Scuola Italiana in Madrid and the Santa Francisca Cabrini school, IDEE has been used in real class settings to prove its usefulness. Our main line for future work is the design and development of a teacher module to help teachers in the assessment of the learning process from the analysis of the data gathered while students are working in IDEE.

References

1. Barreto, F., Benitti, V.: Exploring the educational potential of robotics in schools: a systematic review. Comput. Educ. **58**(3), 978–988 (2012)
2. Burkett, V., Smith, C.: Simulated vs. hands-on laboratory position paper. Electron. J. Sci. Educ. **20**(9), 8–24 (2016)
3. Diango: The web framework for perfectionists with deadlines. https://www.djangoproject.com/
4. Dziabenko, O., Ordua, P., García-Zubia, J.: Remote experiments in secondary school education. In: 2013 IEEE Frontiers in Education Conference (FIE), pp. 1760–1764 (2013)
5. Eguchi, A.: Educational robotics for promoting 21st century skills. J. Autom. Mob. Robot. Intell. Syst. **8**(1), 5–11 (2014)
6. Heradio, R., de la Torre, L., Galan, D., Cabrerizo, F., Herrera-Viedma, E., Dormido, S.: Virtual and remote labs in education: a bibliometric analysis. Comput. Educ. **98**, 14–38 (2016)
7. Jormanainen, I., Beynon, M., Sutinen, E.: An abductive environment enables teacher's intervention in a robotics class. In: Proceedings of 17th International Symposium on Artificial Life and Robotics (AROB 2012), B-Con Plaza, Beppu, Oita, Japan, 19–21 January 2012, pp. 1075–1078 (2012). ISBN 978-4-9902880-6-8
8. Krishnamoorthy, S.P., Kapila, V.: Using a visual programming environment and custom robots to learn C programming and K-12 stem concepts. In: Proceedings of the 6th Annual Conference on Creativity and Fabrication in Education, FabLearn 2016, pp. 41–48. ACM, New York (2016)
9. Menegatti, E., Moro, M.: Educational robotics from high-school to master of science. In: Proceedings of the Conference on Simulation, Modeling and Programming for Autonomous Robots, pp. 639–648 (2010)
10. Resnick, M., et al.: Scratch: programming for all. Commun. ACM **52**(11), 60–67 (2009)
11. Trower, J., Gray, J.: Blockly language creation and applications: visual programming for media computation and bluetooth robotics control. In: Proceedings of the 46th ACM Technical Symposium on Computer Science Education, SIGCSE 2015, p. 5. ACM (2015)

Multi-robot User Interface for Cooperative Transportation Tasks

Majd Kassawat$^{(\boxtimes)}$, Enric Cervera, and Angel P. del Pobil

Universidad Jaume I, Castellon, Spain
{majd,ecervera,pobil}@uji.es

Abstract. In this research we attempt to build a user interface for controlling a group of omnidirectional robots to realize the transportation of convex shape edge objects. Our method establishes a manual guidance to the robots initial positions, initializes the collective grasping/lifting process and finally, provides the user with a high level control over the velocity of the load during transportation to the required destination. The hardware and software structure of the system are described and a simulation is performed to convey the data from the robots sensors.

Keywords: Multi-robot control · Load sharing · Hybrid teleoperation

1 Introduction

The need for manipulating large scale bodies has been spreading to multiple areas of the industry. While a lot of the current enterprises still use single agent to handle these problems, the necessity for a robust distributed system has inspired many researching teams to design and implement a variety of systems supporting the concept of load sharing [1,9,13]. Considered three main types of transportation methods which are grasping, pushing and caging. Each one of those approaches brings its own advantage towards solving the final problem. Grasping forms physical links between the agents and the targeted body, which connects all agents as well. This secures the target load in place providing stable movement of the sum [3–5,7]. Several researchers have proposed the possibility of accomplishing the task by constraining the body by applying forces surrounding the edge known as caging [2,10,11]. Systems using caging and grasping techniques afford resistance against external forces applied to the object compared to the pushing. Industrial solutions have already become available such as KUKA's OmniMove [8] which provides the users with an expandable system for massive item manipulation such as caravans or aircraft sections. The use of omnidirectional platforms facilitate the motion planning of complex trajectories and permits applying torques and forces whenever needed [7,11,12]. In this research we will study a simplified simulation for multi-robot load manipulation. A teleoperation work flow is proposed to control the elements of the system separately and as a unit as they advance in the task.

© Springer Nature Switzerland AG 2019
J. M. Ferrández Vicente et al. (Eds.): IWINAC 2019, LNCS 11487, pp. 77–81, 2019.
https://doi.org/10.1007/978-3-030-19651-6_8

2   System Design

2.1   Hardware

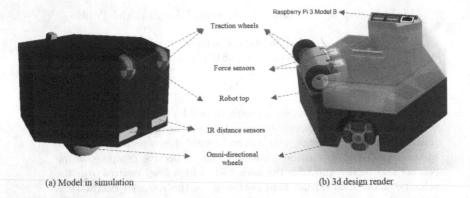

(a) Model in simulation   (b) 3d design render

Fig. 1. Hardware description of the model in simulation (left) and a render of the 3d model (right)

The developed model consists of a hexagonal shaped body which sustain the ability of joining multiple robots to harvest more power. The platform actuating system is based on 3 dynamixel servo motors driving an omnidirectional wheel each, Fig. 1. To simplify the model in the simulation, the wheels are represented by a sphere having 2 DOF (only one of them is actively actuated). Two IR distance sensors are fixed at the lower part of the model making an 80° angle with the horizon to measure the distance to the load. The robots can manipulate the load by means of a simple actuating module which contains two sets of wheel, servo motor and a force sensor to control the pressure exerted on the load by each robot. The actuating wheels in the simulated model are modeled as spheres to ensure a single stable contact point with the load. The model is also equipped with a compass sensor which is used to guide the robots in right required global direction. A Raspberry Pi3 Model B along with an Arduino nano are used for control.

2.2   Software

The control of the group is achieved using joystick commands. ROS (Robotic Operating System) handles the commands and receives the data collected by the ROS nodes launched on the Raspberry Pi in each robot. The sum of all data defines the state of the group Fig. 2. The low level control of the omnidirectional system is described in [12] and is implemented in the on-board micro controller. This simple architecture allows the user to send high level commands to the individual robots to reach the initial position as well as permitting the execution of more programmed complex procedures in sync with all other agents Fig. 3.

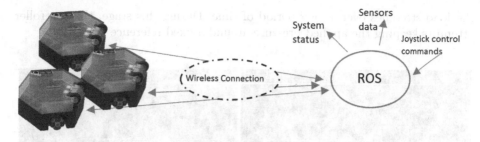

Fig. 2. Data/commands flow

3 Our Approach and Results

3.1 Approach

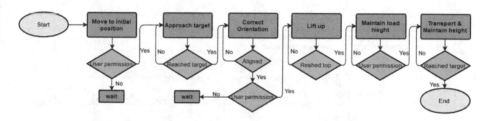

Fig. 3. Transportation flow chart

The transportation task can be divided into several stages as in Fig. 3. First, the robots are guided manually to their starting positions which is expected to secure a good grasp of the object. With the user permission, robots approach the target and align the traction wheels to a 90° angle with the local load surface for maximum friction. Once all agents have faced the load, the user initiates the lifting procedure. The load is kept at a defined height and then transported using global velocity commands transmitted by the user. Certain pressure on the load is defined and maintained throughout the task to obtain enough friction and ensure a stable transportation.

3.2 Results

Figure 4 shows the initial and final positions of the target load along with 3 transportation agents and the paths provoked of transporting the load counter the z axis direction. The simulation is performed using Webots 2019 [6]. The values of both force sensors of robot 1 are plotted in Fig. 5. It is worth noting a few points; the first contact with the target object could be only by one sensor (in this case "TouchSensor2"). The traction module speed is limited and therefore, lifting up the load stretches over a long period of time. During this stage, the controller attempts keeping the applied pressure around a fixed reference value (20).

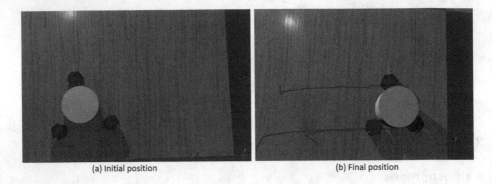

(a) Initial position   (b) Final position

Fig. 4. Transportation task in simulation

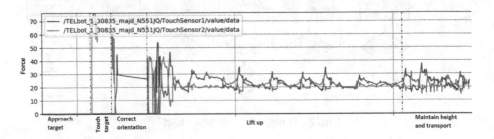

Fig. 5. Force sensors readings for robot 1

4 Conclusion

An omni-directional platform is modeled along with a traction module for cooperative lifting and transportation purposes. A simulation model of the platform is implemented using Webots 2019. A controller is implemented to perform a cooperative transportation task. A simplified user interface is realized to enable the user to control the group of robots all along the task.

References

1. Bayındır, L.: A review of swarm robotics tasks. Neurocomputing **172**, 292–321 (2015). https://doi.org/10.1016/j.neucom.2015.05.116
2. Dai, Y., Kim, Y., Wee, S., Lee, D., Lee, S.: Symmetric caging formation for convex polygonal object transportation by multiple mobile robots based on fuzzy sliding mode control. ISA Trans. **60**, 321–332 (2016). https://doi.org/10.1016/j. isatra.2015.11.017

3. Farivarnejad, H., Wilson, S., Berman, S.: Decentralized sliding mode control for autonomous collective transport by multi-robot systems. In: 2016 IEEE 55th Conference on Decision and Control, CDC 2016, pp. 1826–1833. IEEE, December 2016. https://doi.org/10.1109/CDC.2016.7798530
4. Groß, R., Mondada, F., Dorigo, M.: Transport of an object by six pre-attached robots interacting via physical links. In: 2006 Proceedings of IEEE International Conference on Robotics and Automation, pp. 1317–1323 (2006). https://doi.org/10.1109/ROBOT.2006.1641891
5. Groß, R., Tuci, E., Dorigo, M., Bonani, M., Mondada, F.: Object transport by modular robots that self-assemble. In: 2006 Proceedings of IEEE International Conference on Robotics and Automation, pp. 2558–2564 (2006)
6. Michel, O.: Cyberbotics Ltd. webots^{TM}: professional mobile robot simulation. Int. J. Adv. Robot. Syst. **1**(1), 39–42 (2004). https://doi.org/10.5772/5618
7. Ponce-Hinestroza, A.N., Castro-Castro, J.A., Guerrero-Reyes, H.I., Parra-Vega, V., Olguin-Diaz, E.: Cooperative redundant omnidirectional mobile manipulators: model-free decentralized integral sliding modes and passive velocity fields. In: 2016 Proceedings of IEEE International Conference on Robotics and Automation, vol. 2016-June, pp. 2375–2380. IEEE (2016). https://doi.org/10.1109/ICRA.2016.7487387
8. Shepherd, S., Buchstab, A.: KUKA robots on-site. In: McGee, W., de Ponce Leon, M. (eds.) Robotic Fabrication in Architecture, Art and Design 2014, pp. 373–380. Springer, Cham (2014). https://doi.org/10.1007/978-3-319-04663-1_26
9. Tuci, E., Alkilabi, M.H.M., Akanyeti, O.: Cooperative object transport in multi-robot systems: a review of the state-of-the-art. Front. Robot. AI **5**, 59 (2018)
10. Wan, W., Shi, B., Wang, Z., Fukui, R.: Multirobot object transport via robust caging (2017). https://doi.org/10.1109/TSMC.2017.2733552
11. Wang, Z., Yang, G., Su, X., Schwager, M.: OuijaBots: omnidirectional robots for cooperative object transport with rotation control using no communication. In: Groß, R., et al. (eds.) Distributed Autonomous Robotic Systems. SPAR, vol. 6, pp. 117–131. Springer, Cham (2018). https://doi.org/10.1007/978-3-319-73008-0_9
12. Watanabe, K.: Control of an omnidirectional mobile robot. In: Proceedings of the 2nd International Conference on Knowledge-Based Intelligent Electronic Systems, pp. 51–60 (2002). https://doi.org/10.1109/kes.1998.725827. http://mate.tue.nl/mate/pdfs/7566.pdf
13. Yogeswaran, M., Ponnambalam, S.: Swarm robotics: an extensive research review. In: Advanced Knowledge Application in Practice, pp. 259–278. InTech/Sciyo, November 2010. https://doi.org/10.5772/10361

Precise Positioning and Heading for Autonomous Scouting Robots in a Harsh Environment

David Obregón[1]([✉]), Raúl Arnau[1], María Campo-Cossio[1],
Juan G. Arroyo-Parras[1], Michael Pattinson[2], Smita Tiwari[2], Iker Lluvia[3],
Oscar Rey[4], Jeroen Verschoore[5], Libor Lenza[6], and Joaquin Reyes[7]

[1] Centro Tecnológico CTC, Santander, Spain
dobregon@centrotecnologicoctc.com
[2] Nottingham Scientific Limited, Nottingham, UK
[3] Fundación Tekniker, Eibar, Spain
[4] Inkoa Sistemas, Erandio, Spain
[5] Aerovision BV, Amersfoort, The Netherlands
[6] Mendelova Univerzita v Brně, Brno, Czech Republic
[7] European GNSS Agency (GSA), Prague, Czech Republic

Abstract. This document describes the design and verification of the GreenPatrol localization subsystem. Greenpatrol is an autonomous robot system intended to operate in light indoor environments, such as greenhouses, detecting and treating pests in high-value crops such as tomato and pepper. High accuracy positioning is required for performing this in a trustable and safety manner. The proposed localization solution is described hereafter. Test have been carried out in the real greenhouse environment. The proposed localization subsystem consists of two differentiate parts: (1) an absolute localization module which uses precise positioning GNSS techniques in combination with the robot proprioceptive sensors (i.e. inertial sensors and odometry) with an estimated position error lower than 30 cm, and (2) a relative localization module that takes the absolute solution as input and combines it with the robot range readings to generate a model of the environment and to estimate the robot position and heading inside it. From the analysis of the tests results it follows that the absolute localization is able to provide a heading solution with accuracy 5° more than a 85% of the time. The relative localization algorithm, on the other hand, gives an estimation of the robot position inside the map which does not improve significantly the absolute solution, but it is able to refine the heading estimation and to absorb transitory error peaks.

This paper is organized as follows: first an introduction describing the robot localization system purposed and the state of the art of the involved technologies, second a description of the main subsystems involved and the problems associated, then the tests carried out in a real scenario and the obtained results for check its behavior for each one of the subsystems, and finally conclusions and future work.

Supported by European GNSS Agency (GSA).

J. M. Ferrández Vicente et al. (Eds.): IWINAC 2019, LNCS 11487, pp. 82–96, 2019.
https://doi.org/10.1007/978-3-030-19651-6_9

Keywords: GNSS · SLAM · Galileo · Precise Point Positioning · AMCL · Precision farming · Integrated pest monitoring · Greenhouse · ROS

1   Introduction

Precise localization is a fundamental capability for GreenPatrol [14]. It enables autonomous navigation of the robot inside the greenhouse and also makes it possible to register accurately the position of detected pests. One of the main features of the GreenPatrol robot, is its ability to apply treatment only in the affected areas, reducing the use of pesticides and guarantee the early control of the plagues. Given that the use of pesticides is subject to regulation, the robot has two working modes: detection and treatment. During the detection mode, the detected pests must registered in the generated map with enough accuracy to guarantee that the robot will be able to come back to the issued areas when working in treatment mode. To perform the mentioned tasks, it has been stated that the localization modules should prove an accuracy of 30 cm in position and 5° in heading at least the 95% of time.

Greenhouse is a light indoor environment where traditional GNSS solutions have trouble generating precise consistent solutions due to the effects of high multi-path presence caused by ceiling reinforcements and plants that can exceed 2 m high, and other sources of signal blockage and obstruction (for example pipes or columns) as shown in Fig. 2. The localization subsystem is the core component in charge of providing a positioning and heading solution with enough quality (in terms of precision, accuracy, repeatability, periodicity, etc.) for the robotic system to carry out its mission. In order to manage the mentioned complexity of the greenhouse environment, the architectural design of the localization subsystem contemplates two differentiated layers for the positioning solution: Absolute and Relative localizations (see Fig. 1).

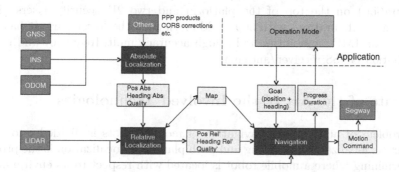

Fig. 1. Greenpatrol software architecture diagram

Absolute localization exploits the benefits of new GNSS signals introduced by the Galileo constellations (E5 AltBOC), precise positioning techniques and data fusion with dead reckoning sensors to provide the best instantaneous estimation of the robot position. Relative localization takes the robot global position solution in combination with the observations from its range sensors to estimate its location inside a model of the environment using a probabilistic approach. In this paper, the design relative layer is described, including the selection of the algorithm and its justification (by means of simulation). Verification of the performance of the selected algorithms is carried out using datasets gathered in real operative conditions in a significant testing environment (i.e. a greenhouse devoted to tomato crops, see Fig. 2). For the verification of the relative localization part of the solution, measurements processed by the absolute localization algorithm are used as inputs.

Fig. 2. Robot platform in a plants row at greenhouse test scenario

The robot platform used is a Segway® Flex OMNI, a true holonomic mobile robot platform that has been equipped with and a 3D LiDAR (60 m max range configuration) on the top of the platform and two 2D security lasers (20 m max range configuration) with 360° field of view on the lower part. It has also odometry an IMU capabilities and a high accuracy multi-frequency and multi-constellation GNSS receiver/antenna.

2   State of the Art of the Involved Technologies

The problem of autonomous navigation of mobile robots is divided into three main areas: localization, mapping and path planning. Localization is the process of determining where a mobile robot is located with respect to its environment. There is a great number of techniques that address the problem of efficiently estimating the robot position given its sensors readings and a representation of the environment like Markov Localization [7], Adaptive Monte Carlo Localization (AMCL) [6] or Gaussian Filters [19]. Mapping integrates the partial observations of the surroundings into a single consistent model and path planning determines the best route in the map to navigate through the environment. Initially, these areas were studied separately but they soon realized how the robot needs somewhere to be localized (the map) and in order to build a realistic map of the environment the robot must know its position and orientation all along. Currently, this problem is known as Simultaneous Localization And Mapping (SLAM) [2].

The main techniques used to solve the SLAM problem are the ones based on probabilistic filters, with which the system maintains a probabilistic representation of both the pose of the robot and the location of the landmarks in the environment. The use of probabilistic methods for robot navigation has been subject to extensive studies for the past decade as it provides a good mathematical framework to deal with uncertainty and noisy conditions, more specifically the Kalman filter algorithm [10]. It tries to reduce the inaccuracy of the data obtained from the sensors and for linear systems and white Gaussian errors, Kalman filter gives the best estimate based on all previous measurements. But, to make state estimation on nonlinear systems, input data must be linearized and the Extended Kalman Filter (EKF) [5] is an extension of the algorithm to overcome that limitation, but has some drawbacks related with the process of linearizion and Unscented Kalman Filter (UKF) [9] can solve some limitations.

According to the source of the input data given to the filter, many popular SLAM implementations use laser range information as input to simplify the estimation process to a pure localization and registration. Information about the current orientation changes, relative to a previous estimate, can be calculated from the encoder information in the odometry on the robot until a localization update becomes available again. But as odometry can be affected by bounces tilts in an unexpected way, an inertial system becomes necessary to deal with these alterations. The resulting estimation is susceptible to errors due to offsets and noise in the measurements so an external system of localization should give accurate information for this purpose.

GNSS positioning techniques provide real-time measurements that can be used in some scenarios as the primary sensor in agricultural robot navigation systems [15]. An indoor greenhouse scenario implies problems when using GNSS technology in the same line as an urban canyon environment, where the number of suitable satellites decreases and it is changing over time due to blockages and signal is seriously affected by the multi-path effect [23]. Signals provided by Galileo (i.e. E5 AltBOC) [22] is a valuable tool to tackle this challenge. Since the errors of GNSS and dead- reckoning (DR) techniques are complementary in nature, the integration of GNSS with inertial sensors and odometry can reduce the errors accumulated by the incremental sensors and improve the accuracy and availability of the solution in adverse conditions. Precise Point Positioning (PPP) removes the need for a local reference station, nevertheless, the main limitation of the PPP technique is its requirement of a relatively long convergence time for precise positioning.

SLAM is a process of building and updating a map of an unknown environment based on data collected by range sensors [1]. There are several SLAM methods, but the LiDAR-based SLAM has been used and tested in a large number of cases [12].

Most SLAM research studies are for indoor environments with a large number of characteristics and where GNSS is denied. Similarly, several SLAM studies have been conducted in forests [16,18,21]. Although indoor and forest environments are in some ways very different, they do share the degraded behavior of GNSS technology. In the case of study that concerns us, in a greenhouse environment, we have a scenario with characteristics of both indoor environments and forest environments. The environmental characteristics of a greenhouse are of two main types, on the one hand, those belonging to the contour of the infrastructure (walls, corridors, etc.), and on the other hand those due to the vegetation in its interior; that is why these characteristics of the greenhouse are not going to be continuous or stable. This produces gross errors of the SLAM technology, errors of scanning and drift [21]. The main cause of these errors is the incorrect estimation of the heading angle, in addition the drift errors accumulate rapidly with time. In the same way, serious errors are introduced in the relative positions between adjacent epochs [16]. Although a greenhouse may produce occlusions in the GNSS signal of indoor environments such as in environments with vegetation and, consequently, the positioning accuracy of GNSS-DR is restricted, GNSS-DR can provide some valuable navigation information. For example, the heading and velocity can be estimated with high accuracy [20] even with great occlusion of the GNSS signal. The heading angle provided by GNSS-DR can help correct drift problems, as well as GNSS-DR velocities can help control gross errors in relative positioning [16]. This is why the problems and errors derived from GNSS-DR and SLAM technologies in greenhouse environments can take advantage of their qualities and strong complementarity through GNSS-DR/SLAM fusion techniques.

Consequently, with the information mentioned above, the SLAM system makes use of the navigation information used by the GNSS-DR system. Several methodologies have been used [3,11,16] with the intention of achieving a good GNSS-DR/SLAM integration. These GNSS-DR/SLAM methodologies can be differentiated by the way in which they perform the integration; on the one hand, those that use a separate integration; and on the other hand those that perform a tightly coupled integration of all the sensors.

The methodologies that perform the GNSS-DR/SLAM integration separately, focus on using the navigation information of GNSS-DR, specifically the parameters of heading and velocity to improve the accuracy and integrity of the SLAM positioning solution. They can be divided into: Heading angle aided SLAM method; and heading angle and velocity aided SLAM method. These methodologies are based on the maximum posterior probability criterion, based on the application of brute force search methods. SLAM makes use of the GNSS-DR heading angle to reduce the size of the search space and restrict it by using relative displacements. Once obtained estimates of heading and velocity from the GNSS-DR data processing, the SLAM scan data is matched in each epoch, setting the heading angle as a known parameter in the brute force search process.

On the other hand, the previously mentioned tightly coupled integration with GNSS-DR and SLAM methods try to incorporate the benefits of both systems while saving their respective drawbacks. Unlike a loosely coupled integration, all external information is used for localization, thus combining the raw GNSS-DR measurements with the observation of the SLAM system, while the prediction process remains the same. The structure of this tightly coupled GNSS-DR/SLAM integration system can be developed from the use of KF, EKF or CEKF type filters (Compressed Kalman Filter) [3].

3   Absolute Localization High Level Description

This module combines GNSS, inertial and odometer data in order to generate real-time precise position and heading information. The GNSS processing uses the PPP approach to obtain the required absolute position performance, and the odometer and IMU data is combined with the PPP solution in DR type approach for those situations where GNSS measurements are blocked or have larger errors (e.g. due to increased multipath), and also to allow the computation of robot platform heading rather than the motion heading.

4   Relative Localization Overview

The relative localization module is integrated in the robot platform and runs over ROS [17], Robot Operating System.

The default ROS algorithm for SLAM is GMapping, that implements Fast-SLAM [8,13], and for localization AMCL [4]. Both algorithms are a good choice for the majority of cases, in particular for robots operating in a 2D office environment and they are implemented to take the odometry as input. The algorithms are mature and well tested, and are being used by most ROS users so there is a lot of information available on how to tune them for different purposes. On the other hand, a greenhouse is much more challenging than an office, both for localization and for mapping, so algorithms must be carefully adjusted in order to adapt their behavior to the greenhouse. Figure 1 depicts the block diagram of the software architecture for the complete localization and navigation subsystem. From the ROS perspective, the relative localization module in GreenPatrol receives the solution from the absolute localization module via an FTP connection. This input solution contains the absolute position of the robot, its heading and an indicator of the quality of the solution.

The proposed approach uses GMapping to generate an a-priori map from a first stage of the experiment in which the robot wonders the environment while all of its sensors are being logged and the precise absolute solution is generated off-line. From this map the real time sensor readings and absolute solution, the relative (position and heading) solution is established using AMCL.

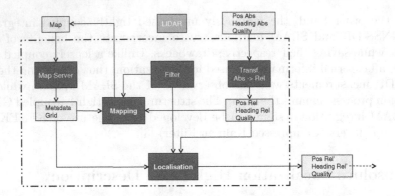

Fig. 3. Relative localization architecture diagram

5   Test

Data logs collected in real scenario of a greenhouse have been used for the verification of the Absolute Localization algorithms. A real time test has been performed inside the greenhouse using the robotic platform along with other sensors (GNSS+IMU+Odometer). During the experiment, the robot performed different movements doing the main corridor and the plants rows (Fig. 3).

6   Results

6.1   Absolute Localization Position and Heading

The absolute localization solution is generated using a PPP+DR approach. Figure 4 (left) shows the position track of the robot.

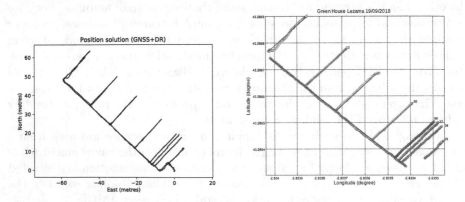

Fig. 4. Position solution from PPP+DR method (left) and schematic of true heading and measured heading (right)

In order to validate the heading from the absolute solution, a reference heading for comparison is required. Within these greenhouse tests there was not a true heading from an alternative source that can be used, and so instead a sense check is provided on the results rather than a formal validation. The first way to do is to assume that when the robot is moving along the corridors it does so in a straight line and pointing in the direction of travel. Therefore for these parts of the route where the robot was traveling up and down the corridors, a reference heading is computed using the coordinates at the start and end of the corridor. The instantaneous heading output each epoch is then compared with this reference value for those parts of the route. This is then taken to be the heading 'error' and can be used to identify places with poor heading, and to get an overall idea of the instantaneous quality of the heading.

Figure 4 (right) shows the schematic of measured heading and the reference heading. The line shows the path for which heading is calculated between starting point to end point. Whereas, circles show the track of Robot obtained by absolute position solution.

However, there are several limitations with generating a reference heading in this way, which need to be accounted for in the results. Firstly, this only covers those periods where the robot is traveling in a straight line and does not give us an indication of performance when the robot is turning. However, this is analyzed in a different way later on. Also, the generation of the reference heading assumes that the robot has kept the same heading and not changed direction at all on that part of the route. It can be seen in the figure above that in some places that is not necessarily the case (e.g. row 1, row 39 and also the long main corridor). Therefore results from those areas are not presented as the robot certainly did exhibit small turns and changes of direction. Finally, even in the other rows where space is limited, studying the motion of the robot shows that it is not always completely straight and so we do not expect from this analysis to perfectly see 5° heading performance at 95% level, but at least this will indicate the general level of performance.

The heading error has been separately calculated (compared to the reference) for each track, and listed in Table 1. The table shows the percentage of time when heading error is less than 5°, 6° and 7° respectively.

Table 1. Percentage of heading error

H.Err./Percentage (%)	<5°	<6°	<7°
12th row	87.5	89.29	**91.07**
20th row	86.79	92.45	**100.00**
30th row	96.35	97.01	**97.67**
36th row	92.30	96.15	**96.15**
37th row	91.80	100.00	**100.00**
38th row	92.00	92.00	**92.00**

The results show that in general the heading error (compared to the reference) is usually around 5° (approx. 90% of the time or more). Although this is not a formal validation, it gives some confidence that the instantaneous heading values are at the sort of level that is required.

An alternative to try to assess the heading performance is to look at the change in heading when in is updated with PPP. In the solution the PPP position estimates over a short distance will be used to estimate absolute heading, and the DR will propagate the heading in between updates. This is particularly the case when the robot is turning. If we look at the difference between the last DR heading at the end of propagation and the updated PPP heading each time this happens then we can get an idea of how much the estimated heading has drifted during the propagation, which gives us some idea of the error that would have been experienced during the turn. Again, this is not a true reference so does not give the true error, but it is a reflection of the quality of the solution. It has been verified that 85% of the values are below 5° (0.087 rad) which is encouraging. The remaining differences are less than 8°, and so this shows that the heading remains with good performance during the DR propagation when the robot is turning.

6.2 Relative Localization Position and Heading

The range sensors data form the robot platform previously logged has been fused with the absolute localization solution replacing the original odometry data and the result is used to generate a map with GMapping. After this, the data are taken as input of a simulation with AMCL and the output with the estimated position and heading is compared with the absolute position and a reference heading.

Mapping. For the GMapping SLAM algorithm several tests have been carried out using different configuration of its laser range sensors as the source of information for the robot perception of the environment. As already mentioned, each type of sensor has some advantages over the other depending on the features that need to be registered and the intended outcome. Regarding mapping generation, the quality and granularity of the map is an important issue, but it is also important that the result is not too dependent on the growth stages of the plants or other elements in the greenhouse that may change position or shape with time.

The models generated using the 3D laser are more detailed, at least in the sense that the algorithm is able to map smaller objects due to the better sensor resolution but contain more information relative to the middle and upper regions of the plants, that are more susceptible to experience changes during the plants lifetime than the lower parts, which are precisely the ones registered by the 2D lasers. Another issue with regard to the 3D laser information is that, due to the sensor disposition, there is a significant obstruction towards the rear part of the sensor. The arm and GNSS antenna mount cause obstructions that bound the field of view of the robot to its front and sides. On the contrary, 2D laser sensors provide a full 360° of perception. And finally, by using 3D, due to the minimum range of the sensor (1 m, so a 2 m diameter around it is not perceivable), very close obstacles are sensed further than they actually are. For localization and mapping, this difference in range near the robot results in a distorted perception of the rows widths, significantly lower than the blind area. For all the aforementioned advantages and disadvantages of each of the approaches, the selected configuration for mapping and localization is finally the one using the 2D safety lasers as the main source of information for the perception of the environment.

To obtain a map, GMapping is used taking as inputs relative position, heading and range sensors. The absolute localization subsystem provides absolute position and heading in terms of latitude, longitude and yaw, so a conversion is needed. The greenhouse corner near to the main door is selected as origin of the relative coordinates system and the absolute coordinates are converted to East, North, Up (ENU) coordinates. Over the data obtained several transforms are applied in order to establish the relations between the different reference frames of the robot platform needed for the mapping module like the range sensors, the odometry or the robot base frame. From these transforms and the laser scan data a map can be obtained.

Using the default configuration of the algorithm in the robot platform the resulting map is not capable of reflecting features as straight lines in the main corridor or the plants rows, right angles between them or is not able to maintain isolated the three last rows, mixing them in a single one. The default configuration considers 100 particles, a sigma for the greedy endpoint matching of algorithm 0.05 and odometry errors with 0.075 rho/rho & theta/rho, and 0.15 rho/theta & theta/theta.

To obtain a configuration that lacks these flaws an iterative process is followed, first reducing the number of particles (down to 1) since it has been observed that this reduces the faults mentioned, then reducing the parameters related with the odometry errors (down to 0), taking into account that these errors with a PPP+DR solution are significantly lower. Also the sigma has been reduced (down to 0). Once the values that meet the requirements have been found, the values were raised while the criteria is satisfied. The final configuration considers 200 particles, a sigma for greedy endpoint matching 0.05 and odometry errors with 0.000075 rho/rho & theta/rho, and 0.00015 rho/theta & theta/theta.

In Fig. 5 the difference between the maps obtained using the default robot configuration for GMapping and the selected "optimal" one (for the aforementioned criteria) is shown. Ten maps with each configuration have been generated and every map in each group shares the same strength and weaknesses. After the configuration tunning both the main corridor and plants rows are straight lines, there are right angles between them and the three last rows maintain the expected parallelism. Notice than in order to get the desired characteristics a loose of details has occurred. Also the dimensions for the second map have been checked against the real dimensions of the greenhouse (123 × 27 m).

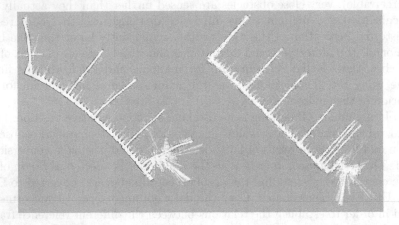

Fig. 5. Maps of the greenhouse with original and tunned configuration. Generated with 2D safety lasers

It should be noted in the results that the mapping process does not start at the greenhouse entrance, but after traversing the first row and reaching the main corridor. This is done intentionally because the absolute localization subsystem yields a poor heading solution during the first instants of the experiments. The reason is that the absolute localization algorithm requires the robot to travel a short distance (approx. 5 m) in a nice straight line in order to get a proper estimation of the robot heading but, unfortunately, the robot did not move that way during the greenhouse tests (because it was too close to the greenhouse entrance and because that conclusion was determined afterwards during the algorithm development).

Localization. An estimation of position and heading is obtained running the fusion between range sensors and absolute solution against AMCL. The configuration selected uses a number of particles between 20 K and 40 K and 2.0 expected noise in odometry SST, 0.1 for SRT, 0.1 for SRR, 0.5 for SRT and 0.4 for translation-relation noise.

Regarding localization it must be taken into account that position results in Fig. 6 have been obtained using the best available solution for the robot absolute localization as input. Therefore there is not much margin for improvement for the relative localization sub-system and, in case there were, it is very difficult to assess due to the lack of a ground truth for the robot trajectories during the greenhouse tests. It can be seen that in general the algorithm is able to get a good estimation of the robot position inside the greenhouse, but there is an average error around 0.35 m (using the absolute localization solution as reference). The maximum error (not considering the transitory peak which is near 1.75 m) is produced around the middle part of the rows, where there is more ambiguity in the robot translation because the constant references of the greenhouse walls are further. In these situations the maximum error is around 0.5–0.75 m (against the absolute position). When the robot travels back to the main corridor its position estimation is better and the error goes down below 0.25 m.

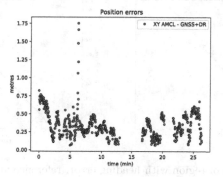

Fig. 6. Position error. AMCL solution error against absolute localization solution as a reference

For the heading error estimation the references used in the absolute localization solution is used with the same criteria of Subsect. 6.1: as no true heading reference is available, the greenhouse headings for its corridor and rows are defined using the initial and final PPP solution given by the absolute localization subsystem. The Fig. 7 represents the relative heading computed by the relative localization subsystem and the one obtained by the absolute localization (dotted line). A detail of the heading obtained by the two methods is depicted on the left for one of the corridors where the reference heading is 42.754°.

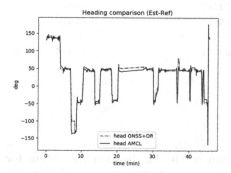
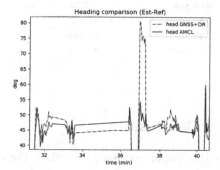

Fig. 7. Heading comparison detail of errors corrected by the rel. loc. module. Detail on the left.

It can be seen in Fig. 8 that the heading generated by the relative subsystem is able to maintain a solution within the specification in some cases where the absolute subsystem's is providing a heading with a poorer quality (row 1). The algorithm takes advantage of the information provided by the quality indicator of the absolute subsystem.

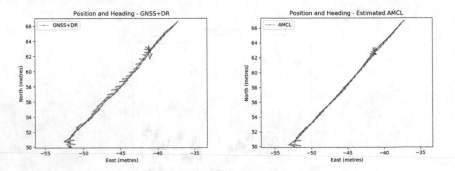

Fig. 8. Detail of region with heading error, reference and estimated

Analyzing the heading solution provided by the two subsystems for each straight portion of the robot path in the greenhouse, it can be checked in Table 2 that for all the cases the relative module is able to improve the solution provided by the absolute subsystem.

Table 2. Heading error analysis.

H.Err./Percentage (%)	Absolute H.Err. STD	Relative H.Err. reduction (°)	Err. reduction
Main corridor	4.0023	2.8115	29.75%
12th row	3.1747	2.2047	30.55%
20th row	2.0053	1.8406	8.21%
30th row	2.6772	2.1214	20.76%
36th row	2.6862	2.0617	23.25%
37th row	2.0841	2.0728	0.54%
38th row	3.2315	2.9155	10.84%

7   Conclusions

In this paper we have described the design of the localization subsystem for the Greenpatrol autonomous system, taking special attention to the Relative localization module within it, built with well known ROS implementations. The Absolute localization is also presented to give an overview of the data input to the relative part, as well as the test and verifications carried out to asses the performance of heading information. Regarding the relative localization solution, described in Sect. 4, the results of the tests show that the accuracy of the position estimation obtained by the subsystem does not improve significantly the absolute solution. The reason is that in the middle of the rows, in such a symmetric environment as the greenhouse, there are few references of the walls and the error in the position estimation grows in the direction of the row. The heading, however, can be improved thanks to the information provided by the rows of plants at both sides of the robot, by finding a match between the range sensor readings and the map. It is decided not to use the relative position solution in the sense that it was firstly intended (i.e. to improve the position of the robot) and limit its use in combination with the model of the environment to navigate and avoid obstacles. The final position that will be used to register the pest detections will be the one obtained by the absolute localization but the obtained by the relative one could be used as alternative when the quality indicators show that there is severe and prolonged performance degradation. On the other hand, the results regarding the heading estimated by the relative localization algorithm have proven to fulfill the specification and will be used to correct the ones provided by the absolute localization submodule. With all this information it has also been demonstrated the capabilities of the system to generate accurate maps of the environment, that will be used both to navigate and plan actions in the greenhouse, and to register the precise location of pests. Finally, the most suitable range sensor configuration has been obtained and tested.

Future work will try to focus on the quality of the maps by running again the map generation phase using as input the improved heading obtained by the AMCL module and a better range sensor data fusion that takes advantage of the longer available readings of the 3D lasers. The improvement in both map and localization qualities will be assessed in a later stage of the system development together with the navigation capabilities of the platform in the intended environment.

Financial Support

The presented results have been achieved within the GREENPATROL project (http://greenpatrol-robot.eu). The project has received funding from the European Union's Horizon 2020 research and innovation programme under grant agreement No 776324.

References

1. Bailey, T., Durrant-Whyte, H.: Simultaneous localization and mapping (SLAM): part II. IEEE Robot. Autom. Mag. **13**(3), 108–117 (2006)
2. Berns, K., von Puttkamer, E.: Simultaneous localization and mapping (SLAM). In: Berns, K., von Puttkamer, E. (eds.) Autonomous Land Vehicles, pp. 146–172. Springer, Heidelberg (2009). https://doi.org/10.1007/978-3-8348-9334-5_6

3. Cheng, J., Kim, J., Jiang, Z., Zhang, W.: Tightly coupled SLAM/GNSS for land vehicle navigation. In: Sun, J., Jiao, W., Wu, H., Lu, M. (eds.) China Satellite Navigation Conference (CSNC) 2014 Proceedings: Volume III. LNEE, vol. 305, pp. 721–733. Springer, Heidelberg (2014). https://doi.org/10.1007/978-3-642-54740-9_64

4. Dellaert, F., Fox, D., Burgard, W., Thrun, S.: Monte Carlo localization for mobile robots. ICRA **2**, 1322–1328 (1999)

5. Einicke, G.A., White, L.B.: Robust extended Kalman filtering. IEEE Trans. Sign. Process. **47**(9), 2596–2599 (1999)

6. Fox, D., Burgard, W., Dellaert, F., Thrun, S.: Monte Carlo localization: efficient position estimation for mobile robots. AAAI/IAAI **1999**(343–349), 2–2 (1999)

7. Fox, D., Burgard, W., Thrun, S.: Markov localization for mobile robots in dynamic environments. J. Artif. Intell. Res. **11**, 391–427 (1999)

8. Gerkey, B.P., Konolige, K.: Planning and control in unstructured terrain. In: ICRA Workshop on Path Planning on Costmaps (2008)

9. Julier, S.J., Uhlmann, J.K.: Unscented filtering and nonlinear estimation. Proc. IEEE **92**(3), 401–422 (2004)

10. Kalman, R.E.: A new approach to linear filtering and prediction problems. J. Basic Eng. **82**(1), 35–45 (1960)

11. Kim, J., Sukkarieh, S.: 6DoF SLAM aided GNSS/INS navigation in GNSS denied and unknown environments. Positioning **1**(09), 0 (2005)

12. Li, L., Yao, J., Xie, R., Tu, J., Chen, F.: Laser-based SLAM with efficient occupancy likelihood map learning for dynamic indoor scenes. ISPRS Ann. Photogrammetry Remote Sens. Spat. Inf. Sci. **3**, 119 (2016)

13. Montemerlo, M., Thrun, S., Koller, D., Wegbreit, B., et al.: FastSLAM: a factored solution to the simultaneous localization and mapping problem. AAAI/IAAI **593598** (2002)

14. Pattinson, S., et al.: GNSS precise point positioning for autonomous robot navigation in greenhouse environment for integrated pest monitoring. In: 12th Annual BaÅ¡ka GNSS Conference (2019)

15. Pérez Ruiz, M., Upadhyaya, S.: GNSS in Precision Agricultural Operations. Intech (2012)

16. Qian, C., et al.: An integrated GNSS/INS/LiDAR-SLAM positioning method for highly accurate forest stem mapping. Rem. Sens. **9**(1), 3 (2017)

17. Quigley, M., et al.: ROS: an open-source robot operating system. In: ICRA Workshop on Open Source Software, Kobe, Japan, vol. 3, p. 5 (2009)

18. Ryding, J., Williams, E., Smith, M., Eichhorn, M.: Assessing handheld mobile laser scanners for forest surveys. Rem. Sens. **7**(1), 1095–1111 (2015)

19. Schiele, B., Crowley, J.L.: A comparison of position estimation techniques using occupancy grids. Robot. Auton. Syst. **12**(3–4), 163–171 (1994)

20. Tachiki, Y., Yoshimura, T., Hasegawa, H., Mita, T., Sakai, T., Nakamura, F.: Effects of polyline simplification of dynamic GPS data under forest canopy on area and perimeter estimations. J. For. Res. **10**(6), 419–427 (2005)

21. Tang, J., et al.: SLAM-aided stem mapping for forest inventory with small-footprint mobile LiDAR. Forests **6**(12), 4588–4606 (2015)

22. Tawk, Y., Botteron, C., Jovanovic, A., Farine, P.A.: Analysis of Galileo E5 and E5AB code tracking. GPS Solutions **16**(2), 243–258 (2012)

23. Wang, Y., Chen, X., Liu, P.: Statistical multipath model based on experimental GNSS data in static urban canyon environment. Sensors **18**(4), 1149 (2018)

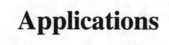

Applications

Gesture Control Wearables
for Human-Machine Interaction
in Industry 4.0

Luis Roda-Sanchez[1]([✉]), Teresa Olivares[1,2], Celia Garrido-Hidalgo[1],
and Antonio Fernández-Caballero[1,2]

[1] Instituto de Investigación en Informática de Albacete,
Universidad de Castilla-La Mancha,
02071 Albacete, Spain
luis.roda@alu.uclm.es
[2] Departamento de Sistemas Informáticos, Universidad de Castilla-La Mancha,
02071 Albacete, Spain

Abstract. The deployment of Industry 4.0 will achieve great aims
regarding production rate, control, data analysis, cost, energy consumption and flexibility. However, one of the most significant aspects is the
human factor. Robots, machinery and knowledge needed could lead to
a social problem for those operators who are not prepared to face such
big technology challenges. This could cause a technological gap resulting
in a rejection or disapproval of beneficial technology. To preserve this
emerging paradigm's balance, researchers and developers must consider
using intelligent human-machine interaction capabilities before building
novel industry deployments. This paper introduces a smart gesture control system that facilitates movements of a robotic arm with the aid of
two wearables devices. By using this kind of control system, any worker
should fit into the new paradigm where some precise, hazardous or heavy
tasks incorporate robots. Furthermore, this proposal is suited to industry scenarios, since it fulfills fundamental requirements regarding success
rate and real-time control as well as high flexibility and scalability, which
are key factors in Industry 4.0.

Keywords: Internet of Things · Industry 4.0 · Gesture control ·
Wearables · Human-machine interaction

1 Introduction

As a consequence of Industry 4.0 arrival some works are being replaced by robots
or collaboration with them is becoming essential to perform many industrial
tasks. Unfortunately, this could lead to social instability and result into the
rejection of useful technology, since many workers are not prepared to operate
complex industrial robots. In this article, a smart gesture control system using

© Springer Nature Switzerland AG 2019
J. M. Ferrández Vicente et al. (Eds.): IWINAC 2019, LNCS 11487, pp. 99–108, 2019.
https://doi.org/10.1007/978-3-030-19651-6_10

cost-effective devices is introduced. Its main objective is to develop of natural Human-Machine Interaction (HMI) systems focused on industrial scenarios based on Internet of Things (IoT). In the near future, robots will play a fundamental role in industrial routine tasks, such as movement of heavy or dangerous materials, exposure to hazardous environments or high precision operations. Sections 2 and 3 will describe in detail the designed system and their components.

There is an increasing number of articles about the contribution of IoT in industry. Our proper research team has developed two algorithms oriented to movement recognition and heart rate measurement, where the aim was to digitize industrial facilities focused on power-aware algorithms to enhance workers' conditions [1]. Another paper [2] proposed a smart factory scenario which leverages different wireless communication technologies and wearables. These are transparent to workers for the sake of avoiding social disruption, thus fulfilling the major challenges of Industry 4.0. Regarding IoT and robots, agent-oriented software engineering enables modeling behaviors and communications (e.g. [3,4]).

There are many other interesting works using gesture recognition for HMI (e.g. [5–7]). Although HMI is important itself, the manner the interaction is performed is equally important. Significant aspects such as natural interaction, easier and faster development are addressed properly by researchers trying to find improved HMI (e.g. [8–10]).

2   Gesture Control System Description

This section describes the general operation and the principal ideas behind the performed research. Figure 1 offers a state machine that shows different conditions involved in the system, which will be useful for a better understanding of the subsequent explanation. In order to avoid dangerous situations, the system starts at *Inactive* state (1) and remains in this state until a different command is sent from wearable named ControlaBLE. The control wearable provides five possible commands through five instinctive positions obtained by using accelerometer data. The operation of the whole system depends on this device, since processing takes not place until the operator selects a valid mode via ControlaBLE, as can be observed in Table 1. When an operator selects *Active* state (2), the robot can be operated with three different velocities to adjust the precision required for each task. Therefore, any of these three modes leads the system to active state.

Table 1. Commands associated with each control position in ControlaBLE

Control disabled	Low velocity	Medium velocity	High velocity	Emergency

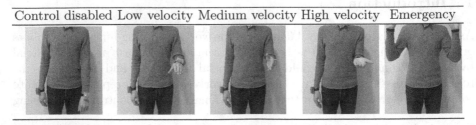

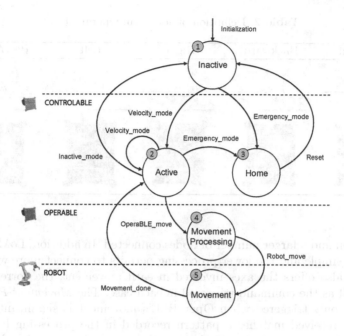

Fig. 1. System's state machine

Moreover, there are two additional commands programmed to disable movement processing from OperaBLE. This feature is needed to permit a natural performance. *Inactive* state (1) can be set from any other ControlaBLE state with the exception of *Home* (3). This is a special condition produced by an emergency stop. It is added to provide a fast manner to place the robot in its fail-safe position in case of alarm, which is mandatory in any industrial system. The emergency command is endowed with high priority, which provides rapid action independently from the current state.

The other IoT wristband (wearable) is named OperaBLE. It is used to switch among different tasks of the robot. Table 2 shows the five movements defined so far. OperaBLE sends raw movement data, while ControlaBLE performs a different preprocessing and directly transmits a command to the processing device. Once the mode selected by ControlaBLE is active, there are five predefined movements to trigger different commands. Nevertheless, LoMoCA, our proper low movement characterization algorithm [1], is prepared to recognize more movements.

LoMoCA is based on dynamic time warping and was developed to achieve a movement recognition algorithm able to work with low sample frequencies, around 10 Hz (10 times lower than usual). In fact, regarding industry requirements, in applications that involve human control, the response time should be lower than 100 ms to consider a real-time control (e.g., [11–13]). Thus, LoMoCA provides advantages such as the increase of fluency, reduction of power

Table 2. Definition of actions in OperaBLE

Forward	Backward	Right	Left	Pick/Drop

consumption and a larger number of nodes connected. In addition, LoMoCA can be built on simple and the lower processing permits to connect more wearables.

Table 2 also offers the axes involved in each movement, the corresponding path as well as the command triggered in each case. The *Movement Processing* state (4) is only triggered when OperaBLE's movement is significant enough. When data received matches a pattern recorded in the processing board, the corresponding command is sent to the robot controller represented as *Movement* state (5). Finally, after movement of the robot, the current position of the robot is sent back to enable a new processing.

3   Gesture Control System Implementation

3.1   System Architecture

The global architecture of the entire system based on five stages is shown in Fig. 2. Firstly, there are two different intelligent wearables composed of the same hardware configuration in stage (1). In this case, a microcontroller board (Light-Blue Bean) with Bluetooth Low Energy (BLE) connectivity and an inertial measurement unit conform the data acquisition stage, which is used to obtain acceleration and angular velocity. The cover was built with a 3D printer (BQ Witbox 2) using Fusion 360 as design software.

The processing stage (2) is implemented in a Raspberry Pi 2 model B single board computer (SBC). This device is responsible for managing data provided by both wearables and sent via BLE. In this case, there is a master-slave connection between wearables and SBC, being the last one the master. If ControlaBLE selects an active command (any velocity selected), the movement is processed by LoMoCA.

Once the movement is recognized, the corresponding command is remotely routed to the robot controller board via Message Queuing Telemetry Transport (MQTT). The processing device is also used to integrate a MQTT broker (3) for creating topics and managing connections to establish remote communication.

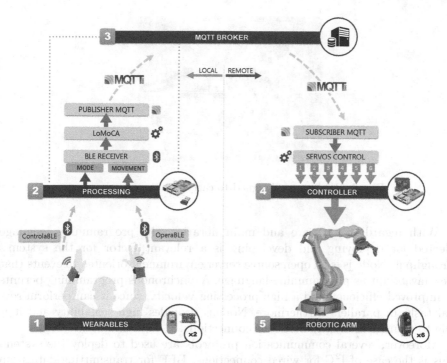

Fig. 2. System architecture showing hardware and communication stages

For this purpose, three topics are created in the broker where the MQTT publisher can send commands: robot movement, robot controller and emergency. Priorities have been established, starting from the low-priority topic which is used to send commands related to movements performed by OperaBLE. The robot controller topic shares information about control commands from ControlaBLE. Finally, the high-priority topic is the so-called emergency, where alarm commands are published. Furthermore, an extra topic is created to obtain feedback information from the robot such as its current position.

The last part of the system is attached to the robot and includes another Raspberry Pi 2, a controller board (4) to manage six servos via pulse width modulation, and the robotic arm structure (5) which carries out the action defined by the operator in each case. The subscriber MQTT is programmed in the SBC of stage (4), where the subscription to topics is done.

3.2 Hardware and Software

As shown in Sect. 2, concerning specific materials and resources used in each stage, most hardware elements have been mentioned previously. However, a brief comment on wearables' components seems adequate. Although each one runs a different program, both are composed of the same parts: microcontroller, accelerometer, gyroscope and battery. The reason of this shared use of components is that it promotes reduction in acquisition and maintenance costs.

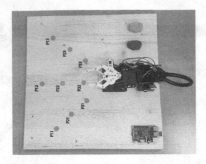

Fig. 3. Work space designed to carry out the experiments

With regard to software and main libraries, the programming language selected for deploying and developing is a relevant factor for the system's throughput. Node.js is an open source server environment oriented to events that uses JavaScript as programming language. Asynchronous programming permits an improved efficiency and a high processing velocity, since it can perform several tasks in parallel. Furthermore, Node.js provides high scalability and it is able to manage many simultaneous connections.

Moreover, several communication protocols are used to deploy the system. This is the case of I^2C for wired connections, BLE for transmitting data from intelligent wearables to the processing board, and MQTT to achieve remote communications between processing node and robot controller. MQTT has a client/server model where the server is usually known as broker. It is a lightweight machine-to-machine protocol which uses a publish-subscribe method based on Transmission Control Protocol (TCP). It is suitable for constrained systems with high reliability requirements and it is up to 90 times faster than Hypertext Transfer Protocol (HTTP) messaging [14].

4   Experimentation

4.1   Experimental Setup

The robot used to test our proposal is a six-joint robot, equipped with a gripper to pick and drop objects. It is a self-mounted, low-cost robot. On the other hand, it is important to define the work space of the robot (see Fig. 3). A 3×3 matrix is used as work space so that nine positions are defined as possible locations of the robot (named from P11 to P33). With regard to possible movements, the robot performs the following five ones: forward, backward, left, right and pick/drop. The first test is a visual example of the operation. After that, an experiment about reliability can be observed. Finally, the procedure and results of a latency times experiment are shown.

Figure 4 offers some sequences related to a complex operation test. In this experiment, all system resources are used to perform the task, simulating a real operation in an industry scenario. For this purpose, two objects are introduced

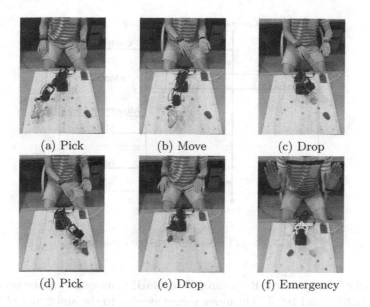

(a) Pick   (b) Move   (c) Drop

(d) Pick   (e) Drop   (f) Emergency

Fig. 4. Complex operation: pieces transportation example through the matrix

into the experiment matrix to relocate them in other places inside the work space. The movements from one point to another are performed using *High velocity* mode, whilst for *Pick* and *Drop Low velocity* is used with the aim of achieving higher accuracy. At the end, an *Emergency* movement is done, as shown in Fig. 4f. Straightaway, the robot addresses the rest position and the system switches to standby mode waiting for a manual reset.

4.2   Reliability Experiment

A reliability study is carried out to calculate the accuracy of the system. In particular, we want to know the precision of LoMoCA when recognizing movements. In order to achieve realistic accuracy results, the experiment consists in randomly executing the defined movements, considering both OperaBLE and ControlaBLE. Each movement is performed 30 times, the results are shown in Table 3.

Table 3. Results of LoMoCA Reliability

OperaBLE					ControlaBLE				
Forward	Backward	Left	Right	Pick/Drop	Inactive	Low	Medium	High	Emergency
96.67%	96.67%	90%	96.67%	100%	100%	100%	86.67%	90%	100%

As can be observed, OperaBLE movements are above 90% success in all cases. The worst are *Left* movements, which could be a problem related to a

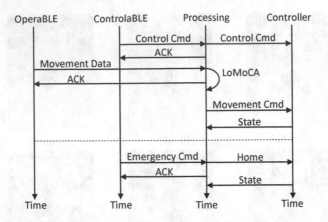

Fig. 5. Steps followed in latency experiment

bad record of this pattern. Regarding ControlaBLE movements, the accuracy is between 86.67% and 100%. The lower values are due to the ambiguity of *Medium* and *High*, which are positions that can be performed with different angles, thus reducing the movement recognition. The total average success obtained for OperaBLE is 96% while ControlaBLE reaches 95.33%.

4.3 Latency Times Experiment

The aim of this experiment is to obtain the latency times between stages and the overall time employed in the whole process. Figure 5 shows a sequence diagram of the steps followed in this test to properly understand the reported results. It consists of two parts. At the top, the sequence related to any normal movement is described. First, ControlaBLE sends a control command, which is processed and forwarded to the controller board. Then, movement data from OperaBLE is processed by LoMoCA and a movement command is sent to the controller board. Finally, this board reports the current state of the robot.

At the bottom part, the steps are shown when emergency stop is triggered. ControlaBLE transmits the command (3 times to avoid possible failures) and the processing board sends a home command to the robot controller, which reports the final state. In order to be able to measure the time spent in the process, an acknowledge message (ACK) is sent back to the wearable device.

Technically speaking, there are two significant factors in this kind of systems: reliability and latency. The precision was shown in previous experiments and, regarding latency, Table 4 shows a compendium of average response times (in milliseconds). The time at each stage of the system has been calculated performing each movement 10 times. The procedure followed to measure these intervals consist in sending an ACK back to the transmitting device after completing each stage, computing half of the time obtained.

In the first column (*Wearables-Processing*), the time elapsed between BLE sending and processing board reception is measured. In this case, for both wear-

Table 4. Average latency time for each stage in ms

	Wearables - Processing	Processing	Processing - Controller	Total time
OperaBLE	21.21	38.62	6.93	66.76
ControlaBLE	21.48	1.48	8.10	31.05

ables the time is quite similar, around 21 ms. Once all data is received, different procedures are applied depending on the source of data. Regarding OperaBLE, LoMoCA is applied to identify the movement performed. The average time obtained is 39 ms approximately with maximum value of 53 ms and minimum of 27 ms among all tests. The time invested in computing the action of ControlaBLE is totally different. The result is 1.48 ms on average to prepare the corresponding command to be sent immediately afterwards. The maximum time spent is 7 ms while the minimum is absolutely negligible.

The communication between processing and controller boards via MQTT is the last stage. Values of time spent in the transmission are quite similar for both types of data (from OperaBLE and ControlaBLE), achieving an average around 7 to 8 ms. There are few maximum values ranging from 20 to 27 ms, however, most of them are between 4 and 7 ms. Values related to the robot movement are excluded from this evaluation, since the robot used cannot cope with high operating speed. Thus, the final average time obtained for OperaBLE is 66.76 ms, whilst the control branch longs 31.05 ms. In view of the results obtained and in accordance with studies related to response time requirements, the system proposed is found to be appropriate for real-time industry environments.

5 Conclusions

This paper has introduced a system composed of two intelligent wearables, called ControlaBLE and OperaBLE, which provide control commands and movement data, respectively. Data are sent via BLE to the processing board where, so as to achieve low frequency movement recognition we developed our own algorithm, LoMoCA. It provides great benefits, since it enables the use of cost-effective, lightweight, low-power devices in addition to a reduction of processing time. Finally, MQTT provides remote control of the robotic arm. Due to the capability of processing multiple devices at the same time, thanks to the implementation of LoMoCA, and MQTT operation, the system achieves high flexibility and scalability. Thus, operators can control several robots simultaneously or each operator can perform different tasks if needed.

To sum up, the proposed gesture control system provides a natural, straightforward and flexible manner of controlling robots. It has been developed and tested, obtaining an average success in movements recognition above 95%. Regarding latency, the system achieves values for OperaBLE movement processing around 67 ms, while control commands take about 31 ms. Therefore, according to bibliography, since the response is below 100 ms, due to LoMoCA implementation this is a real-time system suitable for industry scenarios.

Acknowledgments. This work was partially supported by Spanish Ministerio de Ciencia, Innovación y Universidades, Agencia Estatal de Investigación (AEI)/European Regional Development Fund (FEDER, UE) under DPI2016-80894-R grant.

References

1. Roda-Sanchez, L., Garrido-Hidalgo, C., Hortelano, D., Olivares, T., Ruiz, M.C.: OperaBLE: an IoT-based wearable to improve efficiency and smart worker care services in Industry 4.0. J. Sens. **2018**, 6272793 (2018)
2. Garrido-Hidalgo, C., Hortelano, D., Roda-Sanchez, L., Olivares, T., Ruiz, M.C., López, V.: IoT heterogeneous mesh network deployment for human-in-the-loop challenges towards a social and sustainable Industry 4.0. IEEE Access **6**, 28417–28437 (2018)
3. Martinez-Gomez, J., Fernández-Caballero, A., Garcia-Varea, I., Rodriguez, L., Romero-Gonzalez, C.: A taxonomy of vision systems for ground mobile robots. Int. J. Adv. Robot. Syst. **11**, 111 (2014)
4. Gascueña, J.M., Fernández-Caballero, A.: Agent-oriented modeling and development of a person-following mobile robot. Expert Syst. Appl. **38**(4), 4280–4290 (2011)
5. Dajun, Z., et al.: Use of human gestures for controlling a mobile robot via adaptive CMAC network and fuzzy logic controller. Neurocomputing **282**, 218–231 (2018)
6. Mendes, N., Ferrer, J., Vitorino, J., Safeea, M., Neto, P.: Human behavior and hand gesture classification for smart human-robot interaction. Procedia Manuf. **11**, 91–98 (2017)
7. Neto, P., Pires, J.N., Moreira, A.P.: Accelerometer-based control of an industrial robotic arm. In: RO-MAN 2009 - The 18th IEEE International Symposium on Robot and Human Interactive Communication, vol. 11, pp. 1192–1197 (2009)
8. Almagro, M., Fresno, V., de la Paz, F.: Speech gestural interpretation by applying word representations in robotics. Integr. Comput.-Aided Eng. **26**(1), 97–109 (2019)
9. Sabri, L., Bouznad, S., Rama Fiorini, S., Chibani, A., Prestes, E., Amirat, Y.: An integrated semantic framework for designing context-aware Internet of Robotic Things systems. Integr. Comput.-Aided Eng. **25**(2), 137–156 (2018)
10. Daw-Tung, L., De-Cheng, P.: Integrating a mixed-feature model and multiclass support vector machine for facial expression recognition. Integr. Comput.-Aided Eng. **16**(1), 61–74 (2009)
11. Rondón, R., Gidlund, M., Landerns, K.: Evaluating bluetooth low energy suitability for time-critical industrial IoT applications. Int. J. Wirel. Inf. Netw. **24**, 278290 (2017)
12. PubNub: How fast is realtime human perception and technology. PubNub Realtime Applications. Accessed 15 Nov 2018
13. Felser, M.: Real-time ethernet - industry prospective. Proc. IEEE **93**, 1118–1129 (2005)
14. MQTT vs HTTP by IBM. IBM developer. Accessed 15 Nov 2018

Computing the Missing Lexicon
in Students Using Bayesian Networks

Pedro Salcedo L.[1], M. Angélica Pinninghoff J.[2], and Ricardo Contreras A.[2(✉)]

[1] Educational Informatics Department, University of Concepción, Concepción, Chile
psalcedo@udec.cl
[2] Computer Science Department, University of Concepción, Concepción, Chile
{mpinning,rcontrer}@udec.cl

Abstract. The available lexicon for a person usually increases according to their needs through their live evolution. It is especially important during the early stages in students formation; in every class one of the objectives is to get students capable of using an extensive vocabulary according to different topics in which they are involved. We use an online platform, Lexmath, which contains data (latent lexicon) of a significant number of students in a specific geographic region in Chile. This work introduces a software application which uses data from Lexmath to determine the missing lexicon in students, by using Bayesian networks. The goal of this development is to make available to teachers the lexical weaknesses of students, to generate recommendations to improve the available lexicon.

Keywords: Lexical availability · Bayesian networks ·
Lexicon prediction

1 Introduction

It is a common fact that native speakers do not manage completely the lexicon (all the words used in a particular language or subject), and it may produce some difficulties for communication among individuals. However, it is normal to improve the lexicon of an individual through educational processes continuously. It is expectable that students develop their lexicon according to contents to which they are exposed. Unfortunately, to acquire new words does not guarantee an accordingly understanding of the concepts involved. To determine which are the concepts about which an individual has better management the available lexicon can be used, considering the first words an individual remember when asked to think about a particular field of knowledge. These opening words represent the concepts an individual understand well.

The development of Lexmath [5,6] allows teachers to study the student's lexicon, as a mechanism for identifying those topics that did not achieve a good understanding. The platform helps to describe and quantify student's lexicon in different mathematical subjects (arithmetic, algebra, statistics, geometry, and

© Springer Nature Switzerland AG 2019
J. M. Ferrández Vicente et al. (Eds.): IWINAC 2019, LNCS 11487, pp. 109–116, 2019.
https://doi.org/10.1007/978-3-030-19651-6_11

probabilities). The platform is easily extended to deal with various topics like home, transport, city, and so on.

The objective of the present proposal is to develop a software system for using the lexicon information present in the platform to determine, through the use of Bayesian networks, the missing lexicon for a specific subset of students. In doing so, the system will generate a set of probabilistic indexes for every word in the lexicon that the student does not know. The set of collected (unknown or forgotten) words, will help teachers to identify the concepts that require additional work.

Lexmath is a platform for studying the lexicon through a set of diverse tools. The platform collects data from students using a set of lexical availability tests. The set of experiments aimed to determine the words that a specific group of students could remember when a particular interest center (the topic under consideration) is mentioned, in a reduced space of time.

This paper is structured as follows; Sect. 1 consists of the current introduction, Sect. 2 presents the theoretical frame. Section 3 describes the problem to be solved. Experiments and results are detailed in Sect. 4 and, finally, Sect. 5 highlight the conclusions derived of the work.

2   Theoretical Frame

This work is supported by two significant issues taken into account, the lexical availability, as a measure for detecting weaknesses in the group of students under study, and Bayesian network [2], as a tool for obtaining an answer to the problem.

2.1   Available Lexicon and Lexical Availability

The lexicon is usually defined as the way of expression in a language bounded to a specific social group. However, a more specific meaning is used in this work: *lexicon is the vocabulary associated with a field of knowledge (interest center)*. It is accepted that the high is the lexicon, in a particular domain, the higher is the understanding on that domain.

A fundamental concept is the *available lexicon*, which refers to the set of words that speakers have learned during their interaction with other speakers, and may use under the context of a specific topic with which they are dealing. The difference with the basic lexicon is that the later is composed more usual words in a language, and does not depend on the particular topic.

The lexical availability study allows identifying the lexicon used by a group of people about a specific topic, helping to understand the way in which concepts and issues are related.

Studies on lexical availability include the work of Echeverría, [1], which presents a quantitative and a qualitative approach to lexical availability in mathematics for a specific group of students.

2.2   Bayesian Networks

A Bayesian network is a probabilistic graphical model that represents a set of variables and their conditional dependencies via a directed acyclic graph [3], [4]. For example, a Bayesian network could represent the probabilistic relationships between diseases and symptoms. Given symptoms, the network can be used to compute the probabilities of the presence of various diseases.

In this work, the Bayesian model is used to compute the probability of the presence of a particular word, given different variables: words previously said, type of school of a student and sex of an individual. This particular word exists in the lexicon of a specific population.

For testing the model, a test was applied to 1500 students in three different types of school in the city of Concepción, Chile. During the tests, students are asked to write, in two minutes, all the words they could remember associated with a particular interest center. Then data was computationally processed for discarding non-relevant terms (nodes in a graph).

3   The Problem

Lexmath contains different lexical availability tests which correspond to individual tests of students for a specific interest center. By using Lexmath, it is possible to infer the probabilistic order in which different words should appear in the student lexicon. In doing so, it is necessary to take into account the frequency in which words appear and their semantic relationship with the other words.

For modeling the set of lexical availability tests, it is necessary to manage some indexes for correctly relate the group of students under study and the different Bayesian networks to be generated. The indexes are NDW (number of different words), and RF (relative frequency), which describes the frequency index of words. RF is computed dividing the number of times a word appears into the number of students, as indicated in Eq. 1. n_i is the number of times the same word appears in a sample, and N is the size of the sample (number of students considered).

$$RF = \frac{n_i}{N} \tag{1}$$

Other indexes are NUW, number of unknown words, i.e., the number of words the student did not remember during the test, in other words, the number of different words in the group of students minus the number of different words for the student.

Another important index is TCP, which denotes the number of tables of conditional probability. We use the name *father* to indicate every word that precedes another word, taking into account the complete set of tests in a specific class. A word can have many *fathers* or eventually no one. These tables are required to generate the *a priori* probabilities, which depend on their parents.

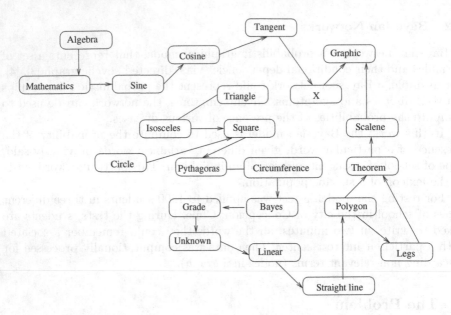

Fig. 1. Example of global graph

This index allows knowing in advance the number of conditional probability tables to assign to every word. This index is computed as shown in Eq. 2.

$$TCP(node_i) = 2^{n+1} \tag{2}$$

3.1 Global Graph Generation

The collected data is represented in a graph which takes into account every word a student in a class has remembered for a specific interest center. Graphs are a set of nodes which are connected through edges representing relationships among nodes. Every node represents a word, and every edge represents a sequence of two words, the first one of them mentioned in position i and the other one mentioned in position $i + 1$.

The global graph denotes the graph generated by considering every word mentioned in every lexical availability test in a specific class and for a particular interest center. The global graph is the basis for building the Bayesian networks for every word a student does not know. Figure 1 shows a global graph generated taking into account a set of four tests.

3.2 Bayesian Network Generation

The Bayesian network for every word a student does not know is based on the global graph. Each one of these words is a node in the graph, and their parents are iteratively considered giving birth to a subgraph in which cycles are removed

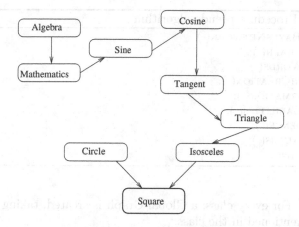

Fig. 2. Bayesian network for the word *Square*

(according to their relevance and order). Figure 2 shows an example of Bayesian network for the word *square*.

Every node holds two values, *present*, which indicates the probability that the corresponding word is mentioned; and *not present*, which indicates the probability that the corresponding word is not mentioned. Based on the values (present and not present) and the parents for every node, probability tables are fulfilled as a previous step for the *a priori* Bayesian network.

To compute the *a priori* probability, for nodes which do not have parents, it is necessary to know the relative frequency for the node in the set which contains all the words mentioned in the class. However, to compute the conditional probability for nodes which have a parent, it is necessary to know, additionally, how many times appears the parent. For example, if A is the father of B, the probability that B occurs is the number of (A, B) relationships, divided into the number of times that B in mentioned in the whole sample (Table 1).

Table 1. Conditional table for node B with parent A

	A present	A not present
B present	$P(B|A)$: $|(A, B)|/|B|$	$P(B|\text{not } A)$: $|\text{not}(A, B)|/|B|$
B not present	1 - $P(B|A)$	1 - $P(B|\text{not } A)$

For building the *a priori* bayesian network, it is necessary to add evidence. The evidence is the set of words the student mention; hence every test is a set of evidence, and every student will probably have different pieces of evidence. Algorithm 1 shows the general structure of the procedure.

Algorithm 1. Procedure pseudo algorithm

```
1: procedure BAYESNETWORK( )
2:     GLOBALGRAPH( );
3:     MISSINGWORDS( );
4:     SUBGRAPHCREATION( );
5:     TRANSFORMATION( );
6:     ADDPROBABILITIES( );
7:     ADDEVIDENCE( );
8:     NODEANALYSIS( );
9: end procedure
```

GlobalGraph. For every class, a Global Graph is created, taking into account all the words mentioned in the class.

GlobalGraph. For every student, it is created a list containing all the words the student did not mention. It corresponds to the difference between the words in the global graph and the words mentioned by the student.

SubgraphCreation. It is built a subgraph, based on the global graph, considering each word the student did not mention.

Transformation. Every subgraph is converted to a network removing edges which belong to cycles, taking into account the frequency and order for each node.

AddProbabilities. *A priori* probabilities are assigned to every network, obtaining an *a priori* Bayesian network.

AddEvidence. The evidence added, to every *a priori* Bayesian network. Evidence corresponds to a word the student mentioned during the test.

NodeAnalysis. The specific node is analyzed. If the network has been created starting with node B, the B node is analyzed, and the probability that B occurs is stored. In the end, nodes are ordered in decreasing probability of appearance, and the result is informed as a group taking into account the ID of the student.

4 Experiments and Results

Different experiments were conducted for testing the prediction capability of the system. It means, the ability to predict which terms (concepts) are not familiar to the students. A set of 60 tests was realized with coverage of fifteen different schools, considering last four year of a high school level. The selected center of interest is *Geometry* and there is not a gender classification.

The software uses a three-layered structure because it simplifies the understanding and organization of complex systems. The term *layer* refers to the strategy for segmenting a solution from a logical point of view. Every one of the three layers into which this architecture pattern is divided holds a set of clearly defined interfaces (see Fig. 3).

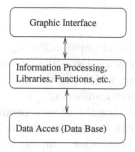

Fig. 3. Three layers architecture

On the execution time, it depends on the number of words and students involved, as expected. It is normal if we consider that every word mentioned implies the creation and processing of a Bayesian network. When execution time increases, it is possible to pre-process the set of data by removing those words which appear in less than 1% of cases.

The experiments are grouped in the four following families:

- Class with a high number of students. This test family considered classes from 35 to 45 students. Additionally, this group is divided into two subgroups, one of them containing students which answered from 1 to six words, and the other one, with students who answered seven or more words.
- Tests with a high number of words. This test family remarks the fact that students with a high number of answers generally corresponded with reduced and well-known concepts; i.e., words predicted by the software correspond to the same concepts to which students answers belong.
- Tests with a reduced number of words. In this case, results have a low probability of occurrence, and therefore, coherence is low (weak correspondence between words and a specific concept).

Table 2 summarizes results obtained.

Table 2. Relationships among number of students and number of words

	Low number of students	High number of students
High number of words	Important number of evidences and coherent results	Slow propagation probability, acceptable results
Low number of words	Low number of evidences, in general result present a low coherence	Slow propagation probability, results are poor

5   Conclusions

The software developed works as planned, allowing the teacher to obtain the set of words a student should know in a specific center of interest. By using this software, it is possible to detect which are the concepts the student knows and which is the topic which requires reinforcing.

Although the software was thought of as a product for helping students to improve their performance, it can be used in other fields. As an example, it could be used to hire personnel in a particular company to obtain information on how high is the degree of knowledge of an applicant about the central topics of the position to be filled.

References

1. Echeverría, M., Urzúa, P., Sáez, K.: Lexical availability in mathematics. A quantitative and qualitative analysis. J. Appl. Theor. Linguist. (2006). (in Spanish)
2. Heckerman, D., Mamdani, A., Wellman, M.P.: Real-world applications of Bayesian networks. ACM Commun. Assoc. Comput. Mach. **38**, 24–26 (1995)
3. Narayanan, S., Jurafsky, D.: Bayesian Models of Human Sentence Processing. Lawrence Erlbaum (1998)
4. Narayanan, S., Jurafsky, D.: A Bayesian model predicts human parse preference and reading time in sentence processing. Adv. Neural Inf. Process. Syst. **14**, 59 (2002)
5. Salcedo Lagos, P., del Valle, M., Contreras Arriagada, R., Pinninghoff, M.A.: LEX-MATH - a tool for the study of available lexicon in mathematics. In: Ferrández Vicente, J.M., Álvarez-Sánchez, J.R., de la Paz López, F., Toledo-Moreo, F.J., Adeli, H. (eds.) IWINAC 2015. LNCS, vol. 9108, pp. 11–19. Springer, Cham (2015). https://doi.org/10.1007/978-3-319-18833-1_2
6. Salcedo, P., Pinninghoff, M.A., Contreras, R., Figueroa, J.: An adaptive hypermedia model based on student's lexicon. Expert Syst. **34**(4), e12222 (2017)

Control of Transitory Take-Off Regime in the Transportation of a Pendulum by a Quadrotor

Julián Estévez[(✉)] and Jose Manuel López-Guede

Computational Intelligence Group, University of the Basque Country, UPV/EHU,
San Sebastian, Spain
julian.estevez@ehu.es

Abstract. In this article, a q-learning control strategy is proposed for a system consisting of a UAV lifting a damped pendulum from the ground. This dynamic system is highly nonlinear and thereafter, it represents a challenging task to get a smooth and precise behaviour. Aerial transportation of a pendulum in a stable way is a step forward in the state of art, which permits to study the delivery of different deformable linear objects.

Keywords: UAV · Pendulum · Reinforcement learning

1 Introduction

Transportation is a challenging task for Unmanned Aerial Vehicles (UAV), and even more if the payload is a deformable-linear object (DLO). This kind of objects includes cables, wires or hoses like solids, whose dynamic, graphic, kinematic behaviour poses specific challenges. The deep analysis of the effects that a DLO transportation generate on a quadrotor is required for the achievement of transportation tasks in unstructured and unexplored environments, or for the automation of expensive and slow industrial tasks.

Modeling DLO kinematics is a complex task due to the several material properties that can be represented. Computing its reaction to external forces involves careful modeling and optimization techniques. The DLO acts as a passive object that links otherwise isolated and independent quadrotors, introducing dynamic interactions among the robots in the form of non-linear constraints.

However, solution of the control of a team of quadrotors subject to non-linear interactions induced by a DLO hanging from them is far from being solved. The works initiated in the Computational Intelligence Group of the UPV-EHU [3–5] open a new venue of research, directly related to efforts of control of cooperative teams of aerial robots under the non-linear dynamical interactions introduced by the DLO linking. Nevertheless, the achieved dynamic model for

© Springer Nature Switzerland AG 2019
J. M. Ferrández Vicente et al. (Eds.): IWINAC 2019, LNCS 11487, pp. 117–126, 2019.
https://doi.org/10.1007/978-3-030-19651-6_12

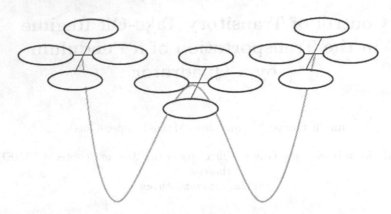

Fig. 1. Transportation of DLO with drones

aerial transportation was limited to stationary state transportation of DLO with drones Fig. 1, where the DLO is represented by two sections of catenaries and/or parabolic functions.

The present work aims to go further in the study of a team of quadrotors transporting a DLO and propose a dynamic model for representing the DLO in transient regime and to study the efforts and constraints that generate on the UAV. This transient regime goes from the lift of the DLO from the floor till it loses the contact with the surface.

The effects of this state are coped by a quadrotor with a cascade close-loop control configuration. Particle-swarm optimization and fuzzy logic are used to tune the PIDs that rule the quadrotors behaviour. This tuning and control have proved to perform in an efficient way for non-stationary regimes and aggresive maneouvres.

DLO model in contact with surfaces has been dealt with in robotic surgery research. However, most of models neglect some of the properties of the materials to get a simulation of this kind of solid. However, not all these models fit into our transportation task, as the cost of computation of the model is a critical aspect for the simulations developed in current work. Election of DLO model will constraint the kind of control of the quadrotor [1] and its navigation strategy [2].

The article is structured as follows: Sect. 2 presents a review of the different cable towing models, and based on current problem boundary conditions, a DLO model for cable towing is proposed. Section 3 recalls description of the physical and control system of the quadrotor already presented in previous works. Q-learning algorithm and its application is described in Sect. 4. Section 5 gives the experimental design, reporting results DLO model for the transient take-off phase, which are presented in Sect. 6. Finally, Sect. 7 gives some conclusions about the present work.

2   Cable Modeling

2.1   Introduction

In the past decades, towed cable systems have been studied in various applications since the 70s. Such applications include payload delivery, kites, aerostats, towing bodies, terrain following and aerial refueling systems [6]. Later, cable towing models have also been applied to quadrotors [7,8] although most of cases the problem was reduced to a taut-cable quadrotor control [9–11]. However, cable towing has also been widely applied to submervise cable systems and mooring lines study.

The central problem in modeling for towing cable systems is how the cable is treated. Basically, methods of mathematical modeling for cables can be classified into two categories: continuous methods and discrete methods. Each modeling class has subsets and the choice of which approach to utilize depends on various factors [12]. As proposed in [13], an easy, simple method that can solve any unsteady-state problem to a good accuracy and yet require only small amount of computation time is a need.

Continuous Models
The mathematical modelling of a tether from a continuous perspective considers a differential element of the tether in space. The objective of such a model is to determine the motion of the entire tether as a continuous structure and as a function of time by applying appropriate boundary conditions. Cable dynamics are theoretically more accurately represented because they consider each material point within the tether separately and usually need to be solved with a system of partial differential equations [15].

Discrete Models
The problem is approximated in physical terms by breaking the structure down into a number of simpler rod elements of finite length. Each element can then be treated individually by writing force and moment equations to represent its motion and this model can represent the phenomena of varying cable types, attached loads and mass discontinuities. Naturally, appropriate modifications are required to deal with each element's boundary conditions. These models tend to be solved by sets of ordinary differential equations.

Among discrete methods, finite segments method and lumped-mass method are the most used methods. Finite segments method divides the cable into small elements, where each of them might considered rigid, straight or curved. Lumped-mass method, on the other hand, concentrates the mass of each element of the cable at the end of each respective segment, so that each mass can be considered as a particle and avoids inter-element coupling [14]. The drogue point to the vehicle is considered as a point mass, which is the last joint of the cable. It is the most used method according to Choo and Casarella [13].

In the literature, researchers developed the equations of motion for towed cable systems using Lagrange's method [7], Newtonian mechanics [16] and Kane's equations [12] or Gauss's principle. Most of these models require that the internal and external forces are described explicitly, and thus do not scale well to a large number of links. These methods resulted in dynamic models that are complicated and difficult to use for the purposes of simulation and control law design [13,17].

Catenaries are widely accepted as cable modeling systems, and have been used in mooring cable simulations [18,19]. However, catenaries usage for aerial towing is not deeply studied, although the promising results presented in previous works [16,18,20]. Catenaries can be discrete or continuous model.

2.2   Our Cable Proposal

The main aim of this article is to proof the validity of a dynamic model to lift from the floor in a stable manner a deformable linear object. And so, this operation requires solid and wall interaction, which is not widely studied in this kind of applications [21].

Although the operation will be limited to the lifting of the DLO some few cm above the ground, it is advisable to choose a cable model which is extensible to future applications, as cooperative lifting with two UAVs, for instance.

This is the reason why as a first approach, the DLO is going to be modelled as a pendulum. Eventually, the work developed by the research group mentioned in Sect. 1 could be expanded by the replacement of the catenaries by the chain of pendulums, which is a promising approach [20].

The parameters used in the pendulum will be a formed by a massed particle and a perfectly taut massless link. The joint point between the quadrotor and the pendulum will be attached to the gravity center of the robot, as shown in Fig. 2.

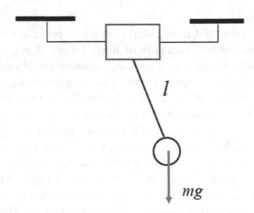

Fig. 2. Pendulum and UAV modelling

The pendulum particle will have no friction with any contact and the interaction with the walls will be perfectly non-elastic.

3   Quadrotor Control Strategy

This section recalls the equations and parameters of quadrotor control. The basic quadrotor movements are related to the propellers' squared speed, assuming that rotors are set in a cross configuration. They are given by the following equations:

$$U_1 = b \left(\Omega_1^2 + \Omega_2^2 + \Omega_3^2 + \Omega_4^2 \right),$$
$$U_2 = l \left(-\Omega_2^2 + \Omega_4^2 \right),$$
$$U_3 = l \left(-\Omega_1^2 - \Omega_3^2 \right),$$
$$U_4 = d \left(-\Omega_1^2 + \Omega_2^2 - \Omega_3^2 + \Omega_4^2 \right), \tag{1}$$

where U_2, U_3 and U_4 are, respectively, roll, pitch and yaw torques, and Ω_i^2 is the squared speed of the i-th propeller, and U_1 is the total thrust of the quadrotor.

The parameter b is the propeller thrust coefficient, while parameter d is its drag.

Angles ϕ, θ, and ψ represent the Euler angles referring the Earth inertial frame with respect to the body-fixed frame (ϕ, θ, and ψ represent the rotation along axis Y, X and Z respectively).

Equation 2 provides necessary modifications for angular and linear accelerations, where d_{GC} is the quadrotor height from its gravity center to the joining point, and T_H and T_V are the horizontal and vertical tensions of the pendulum respectively [5].

$$\ddot{z} = -g - \frac{T_V}{m} + (\cos\theta \cos\phi)\frac{U_1}{m},$$
$$\ddot{\phi} = \frac{U_2}{I_{xx}},$$
$$\ddot{\theta} = \frac{U_3}{I_{yy}} + \frac{(T_H)\cdot d_{GC}}{I_{yy}},$$
$$\ddot{\psi} = \frac{U_4}{I_{zz}}. \tag{2}$$

The block diagrams specifying the control of the degrees of freedom of each quadrotor is shown in Fig. 3.

In the four cases, the aim is that the real value of the degree of freedom reaches the desired value, denoted by a d subindex. K_P, K_I, and K_D are the three PID control parameters to be tuned. Finally, I_{XX}, I_{YY}, I_{ZZ} $[Nms^2]$ are the body rotational moment of inertia around the X, Y and Z axis. Tuning the PDI parameters to reach the vertical equilibrium state was reported in [5,22], and need not to be reproduced here. The control system is scalable and can work with a multiple combination of drones. Moreover, our approach does not need the Integral term in the control, hence we work with PD controllers.

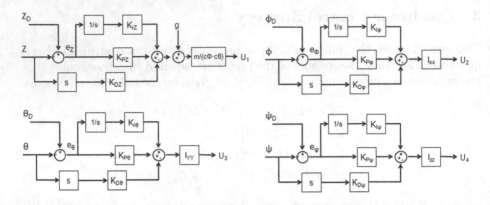

Fig. 3. PID control blocks

4   Reinforcement Learning Model

An alternative approach in controlling unmanned aerial vehicles is to design a learning controller [23]. Many real world control problems, particularly in robotics, require actions of a continuous nature, in response to continuous state measurements. Therefore, a robot control system should be capable of producing actions that vary smoothly in response to smooth changes in state. The real world is continuously valued; positions, forces, and velocities rarely have a discrete range of possible values. Robotics problems often involve mapping, accurate positioning, manipulation, or trajectory tracking.

The emphasis is on Q-learning systems since they support off-policy learning.

- For each state-action pair (s, a), initialize the table entry $Q(s, a)$ to zero
- Observe the current state s
- Do forever:
  - Select an action a and execute it
  - Receive immediate reward r
  - Observe the new state s'
  - Update the table entry for $Q(s, a)$ as follows:

$$Q(s, a) = Q(s', a') + \alpha \cdot [r + \gamma \cdot (Q_{Max} - Q(s', a'))] \tag{3}$$

In this case, the $Q(s, a)$ function is the dynamic ascending model of UAV + Pendulum, while the reward is to achieve the minimum pendulum oscillation and reach to the desired height smoothly (no overshot).

5   Experiment

An experiment will be implemented, in which a quadrotor will lift a pendulum from the ground till a height of 10 cm and a final speed of approximately 0 cm/s.

As previously stated, the pendulum will be laid on the ground, perfectly taut and will have no friction with the ground.

The ascension of the quadrotor will have just a vertical component, and so, no angles rotations will exist. Its mass is 1 kg.

The pendulum will have a damping factor of $k = 0.5$ and its weight will be 0.25 kg. The length of the link is 5 cm.

About the reinforcement learning algorithm, $\alpha = 0.5$ and $\gamma = 0.5$ the reward is modelled as $r = A_1 A_2$, where:

$$\begin{cases} A1 = e^{\frac{-|(InstantHeight-Finalheight|}{(0.1\cdot25)}}; \\ A2 = e^{\frac{-|(InstantVel-FinalVel|}{(0.1\cdot10)}}; \end{cases} \qquad (4)$$

where 25 and 10 are the full range of states and speeds respectively. The states (heights) are discretized is 1/10 of cm and the speed is discretised in units of cm/s. Two actions are used for the quadrotor: $a = [10\ 9.6]$ in Newtons (one force overcomes the mass of pendulum+UAV, while the other doesn't). The Q matrix is initialized with ones.

The dynamic parameters of the UAV are specified next (Table 1):

Table 1. Dynamic parameters of the quadrotor

Parameter	Value
Mass, m	0.5 kg
Arm length, l	25 cm
Inertia moments, $I_{xx} = I_{yy}$	$5 \cdot 10^{-3} [\mathrm{Nms^2}]$
Inertia moment, I_{zz}	$1 \cdot 10^{-2} [\mathrm{Nms^2}]$
Propeller thrust coefficient, b	$3 \cdot 10^{-6} [\mathrm{Ns^2}]$
Drag, d	$1 \cdot 10^{-7} [\mathrm{Nms^2}]$

6   Results

After approximately 15.000 iterations of the algorithm, the Q matrix converges and the quadrotor reaches the desired point and speed. The results of the experiment are shown next:

The pendulum particle trajectory is shown in Fig. 4:

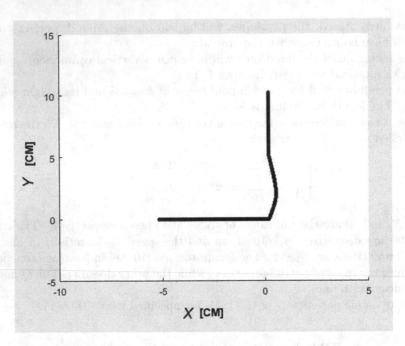

Fig. 4. Pendulum trajectory

The thrust along the time is shown next in Fig. 5:

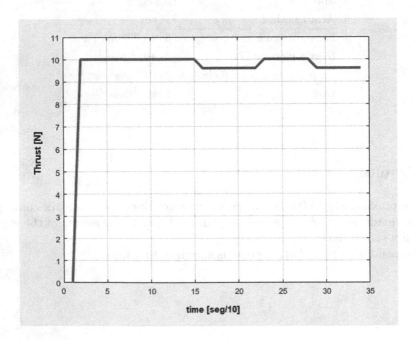

Fig. 5. Thrust of the UAV along the time

7   Conclusions

In this experiment, we proved the feasibility and robustness of the lifting of a pendulum with a UAV implemented with a reinforcement learning control strategy. Future work involves the modelling of a chain of pendulums, and eventually, the transport of that chain with a team of UAVs.

References

1. Khan, M.J., Hong, K.S.: Hybrid EEG-fNIRS-based eight-command decoding for BCI: application to quadcopter control. Front. Neurorobotics **11**, 6 (2017)
2. Kinjo, K., Uchibe, E., Doya, K.: Evaluation of linearly solvable Markov decision process with dynamic model learning in a mobile robot navigation task. Front. Neurorobotics **7**, 7 (2013)
3. Estevez, J., Graña, M., Lopez-Guede, J.M.: Online fuzzy modulated adaptive PD control for cooperative aerial transportation of deformable linear objects. Integr. Comput. Aided Eng. **24**(1), 41–55 (2017)
4. Lopez-Guede, J.M., Fernandez-Gauna, B., Graña, M.: State-action value function modeled by ELM in reinforcement learning for hose control problems. Int. J. Uncertainty Fuzziness Knowl. Based Syst. **21**(supp02), 99–116 (2013)
5. Estevez, J., Lopez-Guede, J.M., Graña, M.: Particle swarm optimization quadrotor control for cooperative aerial transportation of deformable linear objects. Cybern. Syst. **47**(1–2), 4–16 (2016)
6. Sun, L., Castagno, J.D., Hedengren, J.D., Beard, R.W.: Parameter estimation for towed cable systems using moving horizon estimation. IEEE Trans. Aerosp. Electron. Syst. **51**(2), 1432–1446 (2015)
7. Goodarzi, F.A., Lee, D., Lee, T.: Geometric control of a quadrotor UAV transporting a payload connected via flexible cable. Int. J. Control Autom. Syst. **13**(6), 1486–1498 (2015)
8. Lee, T.: Geometric controls for a tethered quadrotor UAV. In: 2015 IEEE 54th Annual Conference on Decision and Control (CDC), pp. 2749–2754. IEEE, December 2015
9. Michael, N., Fink, J., Kumar, V.: Cooperative manipulation and transportation with aerial robots. Auton. Robots **30**(1), 73–86 (2011)
10. Wang, C., Song, B., Huang, P., Tang, C.: Trajectory tracking control for quadrotor robot subject to payload variation and wind gust disturbance. J. Intell. Robot. Syst. **83**(2), 315–333 (2016)
11. Lupashin, S., D'Andrea, R.: Stabilization of a flying vehicle on a taut tether using inertial sensing. In: 2013 IEEE/RSJ International Conference on Intelligent Robots and Systems (IROS), pp. 2432–2438. IEEE, November 2013
12. Williams, P., Lapthorne, P., Trivailo, P.: Circularly-towed lumped mass cable model validation from experimental data. In: AIAA Modeling and Simulation Technologies Conference and Exhibit, p. 6817 (2006)
13. Choo, Y.I., Casarella, M.J.: A survey of analytical methods for dynamic simulation of cable-body systems. J. Hydronaut. **7**(4), 137–144 (1973)
14. Murray, R.M.: Trajectory generation for a towed cable system using differential flatness. In: IFAC world Congress, pp. 395–400, July 1996
15. Skop, R.A., Choo, Y.I.: The configuration of a cable towed in a circular path. J. Aircr. **8**(11), 856–862 (1971)

16. Clifton, J.M., Schmidt, L.V., Stuart, T.D.: Dynamic modeling of a trailing wire towed by an orbiting aircraft. J. Guidance Control Dyn. **18**(4), 875–881 (1995)
17. Sun, L.: Dynamic modeling, trajectory generation and tracking for towed cable systems. Ph.D. dissertation (2012)
18. Chatjigeorgiou, I.K.: A finite differences formulation for the linear and nonlinear dynamics of 2D catenary risers. Ocean Eng. **35**(7), 616–636 (2008)
19. Gobat, J.I., Grosenbaugh, M.A.: Dynamics in the touchdown region of catenary moorings. Int. J. Offshore Polar Eng. **11**(04) (2001)
20. Doroudgar, S.: Static and dynamic modeling and simulation of the umbilical cable in a tethered unmanned aerial system. Doctoral dissertation, Applied Sciences: School of Mechatronic Systems Engineering (2016)
21. Cruz, P.J., Fierro, R.: Cable-suspended load lifting by a quadrotor UAV: hybrid model, trajectory generation, and control. Auton. Robots **41**(8), 1629–1643 (2017)
22. Estevez, J., Graña, M.: Robust control tuning by PSO of aerial robots hose transportation. In: Ferrández Vicente, J.M., Álvarez-Sánchez, J.R., de la Paz López, F., Toledo-Moreo, F.J., Adeli, H. (eds.) IWINAC 2015. LNCS, vol. 9108, pp. 291–300. Springer, Cham (2015). https://doi.org/10.1007/978-3-319-18833-1_31
23. Bou-Ammar, H., Voos, H., Ertel, W.: Controller design for quadrotor UAVs using reinforcement learning. In: 2010 IEEE International Conference on Control Applications (CCA), pp. 2130–2135. IEEE, September 2010

Improving Scheduling Performance of a Real-Time System by Incorporation of an Artificial Intelligence Planner

Jesus Fernandez-Conde[1]([✉]), Pedro Cuenca-Jimenez[1], and Rafael Toledo-Moreo[2]

[1] GSyC Department, ETSIT, Universidad Rey Juan Carlos, Madrid, Spain
{jesus.fernandez,pedro.cuenca}@urjc.es
[2] Space Science and Engineering Laboratory, Univ. Politecnica de Cartagena, Cartagena, Spain
rafael.toledo@upct.es

Abstract. Scheduling is one of the classic problems in real-time systems. In real-time adaptive applications, the implementation of some sort of run-time intelligence is required, in order to build real-time intelligent systems capable of operating adequately in dynamic and complex environments. The incorporation of artificial intelligence planning techniques in a real-time architecture allows the on-line reaction to external and internal unexpected events. In this work a layered architecture integrating real-time scheduling and artificial intelligence planning techniques has been designed, in order to implement a real-time scheduler with capability to perform effectively in these scenarios. This multi-level scheduler has been implemented and evaluated in a simulated information access system destined to broadcast information to mobile users. Results show that incorporation of artificial intelligence to the real-time scheduler improves the performance, adaptiveness and responsiveness of the system.

Keywords: Real-time scheduling · AI planner · Mobile computing

1 Introduction

In the domain of complex real-time systems, Artificial Intelligence (AI) techniques appear as an effective approach to cope with real-time decision making, as a component of real-time architectures [1,2]. By complex we understand those systems which need to be modeled as a number of loosely-coupled agents which work concurrently under the same environment, and communicate and cooperate in solving a problem.

One of the classic problems in real-time systems engineering is task scheduling. Several AI techniques have been proposed in order to produce the best possible results, guaranteeing that time and resource requirements are met. Some of these techniques [3,4] are expected to be the backbone on which complex

© Springer Nature Switzerland AG 2019
J. M. Ferrández Vicente et al. (Eds.): IWINAC 2019, LNCS 11487, pp. 127–136, 2019.
https://doi.org/10.1007/978-3-030-19651-6_13

real-time systems expected to work in dynamic environments must be built in order to achieve the required performance.

The integration of the two different approaches in a layered architecture, using a hard real-time scheduler at the base and AI techniques at higher levels, seems to be the adequate approach. An architecture model that includes a high level AI planner, a low level real-time scheduler and an appropriate interface between the scheduler and the AI planner [2,5] appear to be suitable if we want to achieve real-time predictability and the ability to cope with complex problem solving (e.g., serving multimedia information under dynamic environments).

This work focuses in the evaluation of the incorporation of AI planning techniques in a real-time scheduling scenario, in order to confer the system the capability to react to environmental changes under complex situations while dealing with temporal constraints.

The real-time scenario chosen for this evaluation is based on the Adaptive Hybrid Broadcast (AHB) model [6–8], where an information access server is devoted to schedule requests from clients (with associated deadlines) and broadcast the information accordingly to minimize the number of deadlines missed and the average data access latency, in a mobile computing environment. The incorporation of AI in the AHB server scheduler is bound to improve performance, reducing the number of deadline misses, minimizing data access latency and making better use of the server resources, thus conferring the system some performance improvement.

The remainder of this paper is organized as follows: In Sect. 2, we discuss in more detail the characteristics of the AHB model. The Sect. 3 describes the scheduling approach taken to incorporate AI planning techniques in the AHB server. The simulation framework used for the evaluation of the different broadcast server scheduling policies is described in Sect. 4. Section 5 presents the results obtained and their interpretation. Finally, Sect. 6 draws the main conclusions and points out future lines of work.

2   The Adaptive Hybrid Broadcast Model

In the rapidly evolving field of mobile computing, there is a growing concern to provide mobile users with timely and low power access to large amounts of information. Examples of such services include weather reports, highway conditions, traffic directions, news and stock quotes. Due to the intrinsic constraints of mobility such as bandwidth restrictions, asymmetry in the communication channel (cost in the up-link direction is higher than that of the down-link direction), power consumption, etc., the design of an efficient, scalable and cost-effective mobile information access system is a challenging task.

Data broadcasting has become a very convenient way of providing the information required by mobile users, because bandwidth is a limited resource in this scenario. Most work on data broadcasting has focused either on pure push [9] or pull-based approaches. The AHB model proposed in [6–8] combines the best of both worlds, taking into account downlink and uplink available bandwidth and timing constraints associated with user requests.

Under the AHB model, mobile users have the capability of requesting information to the broadcast server. In addition, the broadcast server has a certain degree of flexibility in the scheduling of the response to a particular request. AHB takes advantage of the benefits of broadcast disks (high bandwidth utilization, high scalability, etc.) and the interactive/on-demand model, thus allowing a mobile client to access any data item under temporal constraints.

2.1 Scheduling Information in the AHB Server

AHB considers two different information transmission modes: *periodic*, in which information is broadcast periodically according to a broadcast program (this is supposed to be the "hot" data, information that a large number of users want to listen, so it is broadcast automatically and is not related to requests of users), and *on-demand*, devoted to broadcasting information explicitly requested by users via the uplink channel.

In AHB, the amount of downlink bandwidth assigned to each mode changes dynamically to adapt to the actual user access pattern, in order to minimize the total number of deadlines missed. The periodic broadcast program is computed on a per-cycle basis, and the server includes in it only the items that are expected to produce bandwidth savings when broadcast periodically.

The method used for multiplexing periodic and on-demand information from a single server is based on time-division broadcasting. The broadcast server dynamically assigns a fraction of the total available bandwidth for the periodic broadcast, and the rest of the bandwidth is assigned for on-demand broadcast. Broadcasting of each mode is interleaved with a granularity of a transmission data unit. We can think of the AHB broadcasting server as two separate logical servers, the first dedicated to broadcast the periodic data items and the second serving the requests made by mobile clients.

Periodic Broadcast. For periodic broadcast, the AHB model makes use of the multi-disk broadcast paradigm developed in [9]. In this paradigm the inter-arrival times of subsequent copies of a data item are fixed and there exists a well-defined unit of broadcast, after which the broadcast repeats itself. The unit of broadcast is referred to as the "period" and it is set to the Least Common Multiple (LCM) of the different periods of the data items.

Data organization for a period of the broadcast is predetermined before the period begins. The data is organized using the LCM of all data items selected to be broadcast in the next period. This schedule can be changed (periodic broadcast data can change its content, grow or shrink) between successive broadcast periods if indexing is incorporated in the multi-disk broadcast scheme.

Some indexing methods multiplex index and data in an efficient way with respect to access time and tuning time, with the objective of lowering power consumption at the client and maintaining the data access latency low. This multi-disk structure allows the broadcasting of periodic data items with different frequencies, matching high/low frequencies with hot/cold data for a determined client population.

On-Demand Broadcast. For data items requested by mobile clients, the server needs to schedule their broadcasting within a certain deadline, using the fraction of bandwidth allocated to on-demand broadcast. It is assumed that the deadline is provided in the request and it represents the maximum delay that the mobile client is willing to wait for a particular data item.

3 Incorporation of AI Planning: Multi-level Scheduling

For on-demand broadcast, a multi-level scheduler that integrates a real-time policy and AI planning techniques is needed if we demand the capability to serve effectively complex requests (e.g., multimedia information) and adapt to the conditions of the environment. In order for the server to make better use of its resources, that is, to maximize performance regarding number of deadlines missed, data access latency and bandwidth utilization, we consider a model that uses different scheduling levels and policies depending on the type of data that is to be broadcast.

We can conceptually divide the incorporated multi-level scheduling in:

1. **High-level scheduler (HLS):** responsible for determining the requests that are going to be serviced from all the requests received, and the specific data units that are going to be transmitted for each request (e.g. quality of service for a determined request) to mobile clients, depending on its perception of the state of the system.
2. **Low-level scheduler (LLS):** responsible for generation of a schedule for all the data units that are going to be broadcast. An appropriate scheduling policy for these data units is Earliest Deadline First (EDF), in order to satisfy as many temporal constraints as possible.

The layered architecture of the AHB server scheduler proposed and evaluated in this paper is shown in Fig. 1. This architecture uses a real-time scheduler at the lower level and an AI expert system planner at a higher level. In this way, the performance and flexibility of the system are improved.

Although AI methods have traditionally not been used in real-time systems because of their inability to define a worst-case behavior, in our case HLS is intended to deal with large time ranges (as opposed to LLS), and therefore the incorporation of AI techniques in HLS does not prevent the system from performing adequately under temporal constraints.

The architecture described above works as follows: requests arrive to HLS from mobile clients. If a request is composed of more than one data item and there exists a given relationship among its data items (e.g. a movie with a specified minimum quality of service), HLS will decide if the request is going to be serviced or not, and which data items of the request are going to be broadcast and which are not, for those requests being serviced. We will refer to this type of requests as complex requests. As opposed to these, a simple request will be composed of a single data item (or several data items without a relationship among them).

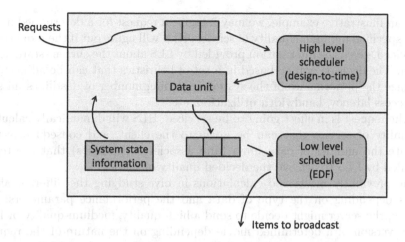

Fig. 1. Layered architecture of an AHB server scheduler.

In order to determine if a request can be serviced entirely, HLS consults its model of the environment, which includes the current bandwidth utilization, the number of deadlines missed and the average data access latency. HLS decides if the request is going to be serviced and, if the request is complex, which data units are/are not going to be passed to LLS (e.g. the quality of service of a determined movie), calculating also the corresponding deadlines associated to each data unit. If HLS decides to service a request, the corresponding data units are passed to LLS. LLS tries to schedule all the data units passed to it using the EDF scheduling algorithm.

HLS is based in part on Design-to-Time real-time scheduling [3], which is applicable in environments in which complex task interrelationships exist and can be exploited by the scheduling process. The decisions made by HLS, based on its perception of the current state of the system, include whether to immediately reject an order from a mobile client because the current state of the system indicates that it is not worth the effort or there are too many requests to be scheduled, when to submit a data unit to LLS, and calculation of the adequate deadline for every data unit passed to LLS.

HLS reasons independently of the mechanisms used by LLS to schedule the data items to be broadcast. HLS performs its job using heuristics to schedule complex requests. These heuristics are used to represent the HLS current knowledge of the state of the system. By manipulating the heuristics as a result of information provided by LLS and as a result of the arrival of new requests, HLS determines which requests (and which data units of each request, with associated deadlines) are worth to be scheduled, using a design-to-time scheduling algorithm similar to the one presented in [3]. In our case, the tasks to be scheduled are the requests made by mobile users, and they are divided into subtasks corresponding to the different data units to be broadcast for each request.

As an illustrative example, we may imagine a request for a determined movie with a specified minimum quality of service. HLS will figure out if the request can be serviced, given the information provided by LLS about the current state of the system. The decision will be based in a set of heuristics that can be adjusted to maximize the performance of the system regarding number of deadlines missed, data access latency, bandwidth utilization, etc.

If the request is in effect going to be serviced, HLS will dynamically calculate the quality of service that can be given to the client, and consequently will calculate the number of data units (and associated deadlines) that are to be scheduled by LLS to achieve the decided quality of service.

The previously mentioned calculations involve studying the different alternatives depending on the type of data and the performance parameters. For example, the server might decide to send a high-quality, medium-quality or low-quality version of a determined movie depending on the nature of the request and the state of the system. This would cause an improvement in the number of requests that could be serviced. Another example of performance improvement could be the minimization of data access latency, where HLS would have to modify (make shorter) the deadlines of each data unit in order to send the information at a higher rate.

Summarizing, the multi-level scheduling AHB server will schedule the broadcasting of information as follows:

1. Divide the available bandwidth into two partitions. The first partition is used for periodic broadcast, as the second one handles the on-demand requests. Relative sizes of partitions are calculated depending on the system state.
2. Periodic broadcast: Build a layout for periodic broadcasting of data items, including indexing. This allows different broadcasting frequencies for hot/cold data, using the broadcast disk paradigm.
3. On-demand broadcast: for each request made by a mobile user, decide if the request is going to be serviced, and which data units are going to be transmitted for each request to be serviced, basing these decisions on the perception of the current state of the system and the relative importance of the performance parameters to be maximized/minimized (e.g. data access latency, number of deadlines missed).
4. Use the EDF scheduling policy for scheduling and broadcasting the data units selected in the previous point.

4 Simulation of the AHB Communication Environment

In order to understand and evaluate the properties of the AHB, a simulation model of an asymmetric communication environment has been implemented. The simulator models a single server that continuously broadcasts periodic data, and also on-demand broadcast corresponding to the requests of mobile clients. The simulator is time-driven, the time being measured in broadcasting units (the time required to transmit a single data unit). Periodic broadcast and on-demand broadcast is interleaved with a granularity of a single data unit. The data items in each logical sub-channel are scheduled using the following policies:

- *Periodic broadcast:* The periodic broadcast program is computed on a per-cycle basis, and the server includes in it only the items that are expected to produce bandwidth savings when broadcast periodically. The broadcast frequency of an item is the minimum needed to satisfy all requests for that item. The bandwidth required corresponds to the minimum frequency needed to ensure that all deadlines corresponding to the item are met. This is accomplished by using a *pfair* method [8].
- *On-demand broadcast:* A multi-level scheduling scheme is used, in concrete using a LLS at low level that schedules data units (EDF scheduling algorithm) and a HLS at high level that schedules requests (design-to-time scheduling algorithm).

Upon arrival of a request, HLS decides if the request is going to be serviced or not, and if in fact it is, HLS uses a set of heuristics in order to select the data units that are going to be scheduled by LLS. HLS bases its decisions in its perception of the current state of the system provided by LLS and the performance goals. For example, a performance goal can be the minimization of deadlines missed.

In the actual implementation of the simulator, the information provided by LLS includes the number of deadlines missed, the data access latency and the bandwidth utilization. HLS uses this information to estimate the evolution of the system high load and decide whether to submit more requests or not and which data units and associated deadlines are passed to LLS, depending on the performance parameter(s) to be minimized/maximized.

5   Experiments and Results Obtained

We developed an off-line generator which creates the data set and workload for each of the experiments. The workload corresponds to the on-demand requests of a group of mobile users. Among the parameters used to generate the data set and workload, the following ones are the most relevant:

- bandwidth of the down-link and uplink channels
- number of data items available to the clients
- size of the data items (in data units)
- range of possible values of deadlines (random variable, uniform distribution)
- mean inter-arrival rate of the requests (exponential distribution), used to control the load imposed to the system

The experiments have been performed varying the mean inter-arrival time of the requests (that is, the system load). The rest of the parameters are fixed. Figures 2 and 3 below show the results of the experiments. There are 4 different curves in each figure, corresponding to different scheduling alternatives in the AHB server:

- **Unmodified AHB:** in this case, there is only one scheduling level. Complex requests are scheduled in the same way as simple ones.
- **Period only:** HLS varies the deadline (associated to the frequency of a sequence for multimedia information) of complex requests depending on the state of the system provided by LLS (data access latency).
- **Size only:** HLS varies the size of data units of complex requests (this is equivalent to vary the quality of different frames in multimedia information) depending on the state of the system provided by LLS (number of deadlines missed).
- **Combined:** HLS varies the deadline and the size of data units of complex request depending on the state of the system provided by LLS (parameter that combines heuristically data access latency and number of deadlines missed).

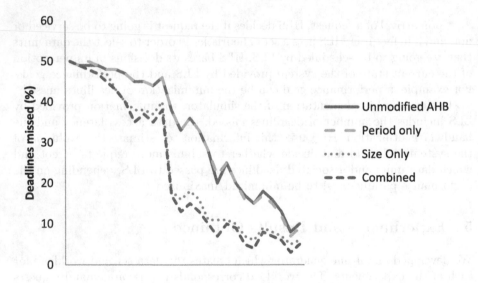

Fig. 2. Percentage of deadlines missed as a function of mean time between requests.

Regarding the perception of the system state by HLS, the evolution of the data access latency and the ratio *deadlines_missed/total_deadlines* are evaluated to make every scheduling decision, using a temporal window. Variations in data access latency are weighted adequately, as a little variation may imply a large variation in the system load. In the combined alternative, the state of the system is extracted from a single parameter that combines the evolution of latency and deadlines missed. Interpretation of results leads to the following facts:

1. The combined method outperforms the others in the number of deadlines missed (see Fig. 2), although the average latency seems to be higher than unmodified AHB and period-only for some ranges of the system load (see Fig. 3). The reason is that the combined method is missing less deadlines than

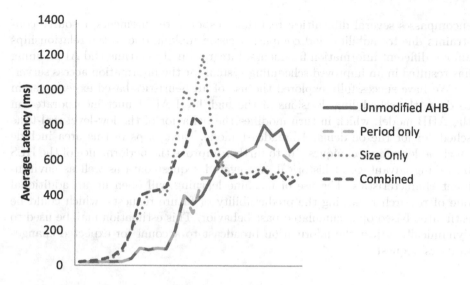

Fig. 3. Average latency as a function of mean time between requests.

the others, and consequently it is servicing more requests. If the system load is high, the average data access latency will be higher for the alternative that is servicing more requests. Nevertheless, we observe that in low load situations, the combined method outperforms the others in number of deadlines missed and data access latency, although it is servicing more requests.

2. The period-only alternative seems to have little effect in the overall behavior of the system, although the average latency shown in Fig. 3 seems to be slightly reduced compared to the unmodified AHB alternative in low workload situations.

6   Conclusions and Further Work

In this paper we have proposed, described, implemented and evaluated an architectural model intended to satisfy real-time performance requirements, being efficient and possessing some kind of run-time intelligence by the incorporation of AI planning techniques, in order to adapt and react to a changing environment when complex requests are present. The results obtained in the experiments suggest that multi-level scheduling is a convenient approach for the system to be effective, adaptive and responsive.

The integration of a Design-to-Time based high-level AI planner and a low-level scheduler that uses a real-time scheduling algorithm in a single architecture makes it possible to implement a real-time system with improved performance, due to its adaptation capabilities. In such a system the communication between the different scheduling levels plays a key role for performance improvement.

A real-time scheduling scenario based on the AHB model has been presented, illustrating the concepts previously exposed. The scheduling problem reported encompasses several difficulties: real-time response requirements, resource constraints due to mobility, and complex decision making due to the relationships among different information fragments. Integration of real-time and AI planning has resulted in an improved scheduling system for the information access server.

We have successfully explored the use of an heuristics-based expert system to drive the scheduling decisions of the high-level AI planner incorporated in the AHB model, which in turn modifies the behavior of the low-level real-time scheduler for the on-demand broadcast mode. Next steps in this area include machine-learning techniques [10] to further improve the performance of the HLS by taking advantage of historical, aggregated request data as well as environment characteristics. The use of machine learning will open up an additional line of research regarding the predictability of future requests, which could be estimated based on accumulated past behavior. This estimation may be used to dynamically adjust the information broadcast to account for expected changes in users' requests.

References

1. Garvey, A., Lesser, V.: A survey of research in deliberative real-time artificial intelligence. Real-Time Syst. **6**(3), 317–347 (1994)
2. Musliner, D., Durfee, E., Shin, K.: CIRCA: a cooperative intelligent real-time control architecture. IEEE Trans. Syst. Man Cybern. **23**(6), 1561–1574 (1993)
3. Garvey, A., Lesser, V.: Design-to-time real-time scheduling. IEEE Trans. Syst. Man Cybern. **23**(6), 1491–1502 (1993)
4. Zilberstein, S.: Operational rationality through compilation of anytime algorithms. Ph.D. dissertation, Computer Science Department, Berkeley (1993)
5. Stankovic, J.: The many faces of multi-level real-time scheduling. In: Proceedings of 2nd International Workshop on Real-Time Computing Systems and Applications RTCSA, Tokyo, Japan (1995)
6. Fernandez-Conde, J., Mozos, D.: Pull vs. hybrid: comparing scheduling algorithms for asymmetric time-constrained environments. In: Proceedings of 2008 International Conference on Wireless Networks, Las Vegas, USA, pp. 222–228 (2008)
7. Fernandez-Conde, J., Mozos, D.: Efficient scheduling for mobile time-constrained environments. IET Electron. Lett. J. **43**(22), 1214–1215 (2007)
8. Fernandez-Conde, J., Ramamritham, K.: Adaptive dissemination of data in time-critical asymmetric communication environments. Mob. Netw. Appl. **9**(5), 491–505 (2004)
9. Acharya, S., Alonso, R., Franklin, M., and Zdonik, S.: Broadcast disk data management for asymmetric communication environments. In: Proceedings of ACM SIGMOD Conference, San Jose, California, USA (1995)
10. Abroyan, N. and Hakobyan, R.: A review of the usage of machine learning in real-time systems. In: Proceedings of NPUA Information Technologies, Electronics, Radio, Engineering (2016)

Convolutional Neural Networks for Olive Oil Classification

Belén Vega-Márquez[1](✉), Andrea Carminati[1], Natividad Jurado-Campos[2],
Andrés Martín-Gómez[2], Lourdes Arce-Jiménez[2], Cristina Rubio-Escudero[1],
and Isabel A. Nepomuceno-Chamorro[1]

[1] Department of Computer Languages and Systems,
University of Sevilla, Sevilla, Spain
bvega@us.es

[2] Institute of Fine Chemistry and Nanochemistry,
Department of Analytical Chemistry,
University of Córdoba, Córdoba, Spain
qa1arjil@uco.es

Abstract. The analysis of the quality of olive oil is a task that is having a lot of impact nowadays due to the large frauds that have been observed in the olive oil market. To solve this problem we have trained a Convolutional Neural Network (CNN) to classify 701 images obtained using GC-IMS methodology (gas chromatography coupled to ion mobility spectrometry). The aim of this study is to show that Deep Learning techniques can be a great alternative to traditional oil classification methods based on the subjectivity of the standardized sensory analysis according to the panel test method, and also to novel techniques provided by the chemical field, such as chemometric markers. This technique is quite expensive since the markers are manually extracted by an expert.

The analyzed data includes instances belonging to two different crops, the first covers the years 2014–2015 and the second 2015–2016. Both harvests have instances classified in the three categories of existing oil, extra virgin olive oil (EVOO), virgin olive oil (VOO) and lampante olive oil (LOO). The aim of this study is to demonstrate that Deep Learning techniques in combination with chemical techniques are a good alternative to the panel test method, implying even better accuracy than results obtained in previous work.

Keywords: Convolutional Neural Network · Olive oil classification · GC-IMS method

1 Introduction

Olive oil is a fatty vegetable oil obtained from the fruit of the Olive tree, a traditional tree crop of the Mediterranean area. For more than six centuries [6], olive oil has been used in different daily areas: making cosmetics, medicines and

© Springer Nature Switzerland AG 2019
J. M. Ferrández Vicente et al. (Eds.): IWINAC 2019, LNCS 11487, pp. 137–145, 2019.
https://doi.org/10.1007/978-3-030-19651-6_14

soaps, used for fuel, and most famous of all, the use of olive oil in gastronomy. The increasing use in recent years of this oil has led to the search for the best quality for its use.

The current European Union Regulation [4] classifies olive oil into three classes that in descending order of quality are named as extra virgin olive oil (EVOO), virgin olive oil (VOO) and *lampante* olive oil (LOO). The difference among the three categories resides in their levels of free fatty acid, a condition that correlates with the condition of the olives when they are crushed. Damaged or old olives are high in oleic acid content, which makes a lower quality oil. It is important to clearly discriminate the types of oil that are commercialized due to two fundamental reasons: in the first place it is necessary to take into account that depending on the type of oil it can be suitable for consumption or not: extra virgin olive oil (EVOO) and virgin (VOO) are suitable, lampante (LOO) is not. In second place, the price of this product changes a lot depending on the category, including cases of fraud in which oil that was not of good quality has been sold as if it was. For this reason, the importation and exportation of this product is increasingly being controlled, with even more exhaustive quality controls.

The most common form of oil classification is currently carried out by means of a tasting by experts who identify the quality of the oil being studied via sensory attributes. This technique, although it can be considered reliable, is manual and not objective. Therefore, the development of techniques to automatically classify olive oil samples from gas chromatography coupled to ion mobility spectrometry is necessary. In this work we use deep learning as a good alternative to consider to advise these experts and the community behind the world of olive oil.

Previous studies have addressed this problem from a number of different perspectives. The first of them carried out by [2] takes the image obtained by GC-IMS analysis and applies several techniques, such as Principal Component Analysis (PCA), Linear Discriminant Analysis (LDA) and finally the K Nearest Neighbor (k-NN) algorithm to perform the classification. Secondly, in our previous study [12] we carried out the classification by extracting interesting areas as preprocessing phase from the images, called markers to which we then applied Deep Learning techniques. Although this approach was quite accurate, the marker extraction phase is made by an expert and it was very expensive and subjective, as it was the expert who pointed at them by eye.

The main problem of the previous studies is that the classification phase was not direct, but before there were a preprocessing phase to perform, assuming a higher cost. The aim of our study is to provide a standard technique that reduces time and complexity in the classification of olive oils, eliminating the need for an expert to extract markers from images.

The article is organized as follows, Sect. 2 describes the data used in the study and the algorithm and methodologies used to the classification task. Section 3 shows the results obtained with the techniques explained in the Methodology section. Finally, Sect. 4 provides some conclusions obtained after the study.

2   Methodology

The goal of this study is to use Deep Learning techniques in combination with chemical methods to provide, on the one hand, an alternative to the standardized sensory analysis according to the panel test method for the classification of olive oil samples and, on the other hand, to provide a simpler and quicker technique for carrying out this task, trying to improve the results obtained in previous investigations.

2.1   Olive Oil Samples

A total of 701 olive oil samples were chosen to constitute the final sample of this study. The samples were taken from olives from two separate harvests. The first harvest covered the years 2014–2015 and the second the years 2015–2016. Figure 1 shows the proportion of classes of the two harvests in the study. In the first one there are a total of 292 instances of which 35 were LOO, 98 EVOO and the remaining 159 VOO. Secondly, the harvest covering the years 2015–2016 included a total of 409 examples, 121 LOO, 92 EVOO and 196 VOO.

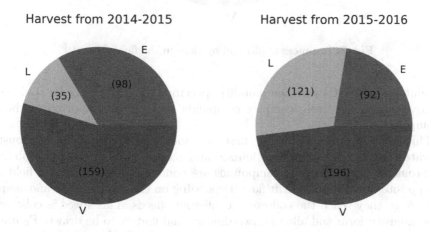

Fig. 1. Instances of oilive oil by class in the two harvests of the study

As you can see the number of instances for each of the harvests is relatively small, therefore, since the two harvests had been extracted in the same way we decided to merge them into a single set of data. Figure 2 illustrates the final proportion of classes in the dataset. We have a total of 701 samples where 156 are LOO, 190 EVOO and 355 VOO.

2.2   Chemical Methods for Data Acquisition

GC-IMS method was used for data acquisition. The GC-IMS method for olive oil analysis was obtained from a previous work by [2]. This method combines gas

Harvest from 2014-2016

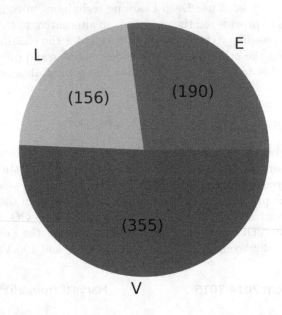

Fig. 2. Instances of olive oil by class in the final dataset

chromatography (GC) with ion mobility spectrometry (IMS) in order to detect sensitively and selectively complex compunds that can be vaporized without decomposition [8].

This method works as follows: first, compounds that have been previously separated into a GC column are ionized and passed through the Ion Mobility Spectrometer (IMS). Ionized compounds are conducted by a magnetic field in the opposite direction to a drift flow. Depending on the charge, mass and shape of the ions, they reach the collector at different speeds. This speed is collected in an intensity form and allows a two-dimensional matrix to be drawn. Figure 3 shows an example of olive oil image obtained with GC-IMS method.

2.3   Deep Learning Approach

The use of Deep Learning techniques is not something new in the field of gastronomy or agriculture, for example, it has already been used to detect the quality of wine using taste sensors and neural networks [10], in the detection of plant diseases with leaf images and computer vision [5] and in food classification [3].

The case of study for a classification task has been performed with a convolutional neural network (CNN). Convolutional neural networks are computational systems inspired by the human nervous system [13]. The fundamental structure of any neural network is formed by interconnected nodes that simulate the neurons of the brain. These nodes can be combined in layers that will be trained

Fig. 3. Example of image obtained from olive oil instance with GC-IMS method

after an iterative process to learn from the input data and be able to give the desired output.

2.4   Software and Experimental Setting

The CNN used in this study has been implemented with the Keras library [1] running on top of Tensorflow and written in Python code. The data visualization of the images has been made with Python. The train test split method has been carried out with scikit-learn library [9]. Due to the amount of data available, the runnings of the code were performed on an Intel machine, specifically Intel(R) Core(TM) i7-8700 CPU @ 3.20 Ghz, with 64 GB of RAM and 12 cores.

3   Results

3.1   Architecture of the Model

The architecture of a neural network is the determinant of the precision and accuracy of the model, therefore, defining a good architecture beforehand is the fundamental part in the learning process.

The network used for oil classification is a convolutional neural network. These networks have proved to be the pioneers in image classification tasks, with the best in world image classification competitions [7]. CNNs are comprised of four types of layers. Firstly, the input layer that holds the pixel values of the input image. Secondly, the convolutional layer which determines the output of neurons which are connected to local regions of the input through the calculation of the scalar product between their weights and the region connected to the input. In the third case, pooling layers reduce the dimensionality of the representation to reduce the number of parameters to assist the learning process by significantly reducing the number of parameters and the complexity of the model. Finally, the fully-connected layers that perform the classification task with class scores, these scores indicate the probability that the input data belongs to one class or another.

The combination of layers gives rise to a neural network. The one used consists of three convolutional layers which in turn consist of pooling layers, a flatten layer and four dense layers which will determine the predicted class as can be seen in Fig. 4.

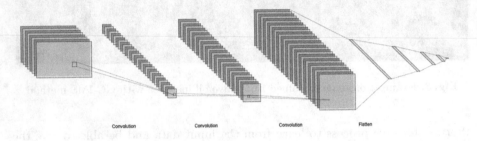

Fig. 4. Convolutional Neural Network used in this study

3.2 Training the Model

The training step in a neural network needs some parameters that will indicate the way the model is going to be trained, such as the optimizer to be used, the loss function to be taken into account, the number of epochs or the learning rate.

Table 1 shows the parameters chosen in the training step after hyperparameter tunning.

Table 1. Parameters used in the training step

Parameter	Value
Optimizer	SGD
Loss	Sparse categorical crossentropy
Metrics	Accuracy
Learning rate	0.01
Momentum	0.4
Epochs	125

We can see in Fig. 5 that with a momentum of 0.4 and 125 epochs the minimum loss is reached with a learning rate of 0.01. We have also noticed that with this methodology the training time is very fast, less than ten minutes for the full data set.

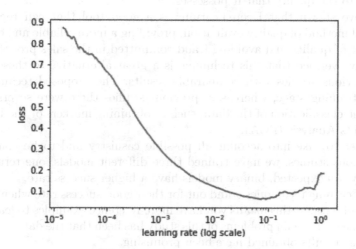

Fig. 5. Learning rate tunning

3.3   Classification Performance

A train-test split method was used for the validation of the CNN model. In order to be able to compare our work with the previous results obtained by [2], we have chosen for the set of train and test the same instances that they chose in their study, implying 80% of examples of each of the harvests for train and the remaining 20% for test. The performance of the CNN was measured by the accuracy score. A total of three experiments were made, one of them classified between the three existing classes (EVOO/LOO/VOO), and the other two classified distinguishing one class against the others (EVOO/non-EVOO, LOO/non-LOO), i.e. a ternary model and two binary models were trained. Table 2 compares the results obtained with our model to those obtained by [2] with the spectral fingerprint, i.e. the full image and those obtained with the Deep Learning techniques applied to the specific markers [12].

Table 2. Comparison of our results with previous results

	Spectral fingerprint	Specific markers	Convolutional neural net
EVOO/VOO/LOO	79.40	74.29	82.86
EVOO/non-EVOO	85.10	85.72	87.85
LOO/non-LOO	92.90	90.71	94.57

144 B. Vega-Márquez et al.

4 Discussion

In this paper we present a Convolutional Neural Network (CNN) that classifies olive oil chemical data obtained from GC-IMS method in their respective classes according to the quality that it possesses.

We have shown that Deep Learning is a good tool that can replace the traditional method of quality evaluation, providing a more reliable and objective assessment of quality and avoiding fraud committed in the sales process.

We have verified that this technique is a great alternative to those carried out in previous studies with comparable results. The proposed technique has only one training stage, whereas in previous studies there were several stages prior to the classification of the data, such as obtaining markers or the Principal Components Analysis (PCA).

In order to take into account all possible casuistry and to be comparable with previous studies, we have trained three different models, one ternary and two binary. As expected, binary models have a higher success rate.

Deep Learning techniques stand out for their good success rate when working with a lot of data, as this means you have more reference examples to learn from. Perhaps one of the main problems of this study has been that the data was scarce, even so, the results obtained have been promising.

As future work, we study two alternative ways, on the one hand to train the developed model with more data. On the other hand, we carry out a pre-processing of the images, such as the Super-Pixel segmentation technique [11], in order to obtain the best results.

References

1. Chollet, F., et al.: Keras (2015). https://keras.io
2. Contreras, M.D.M., Jurado-Campos, N., Arce, L., Arroyo-Manzanares, N.: A robustness study of calibration models for olive oil classification: target and untargeted fingerprint approaches based on GC-IMS (2019, in press)
3. Debska, B., Guzowska-Świder, B.: Application of artificial neural network infood classification. Analytica Chimica Acta **705**(1), 283–291 (2011). A selection of papers presented at the 12th International Conference on Chemometrics in Analytical Chemistry. https://doi.org/10.1016/j.aca.2011.06.033. http://www.sciencedirect.com/science/article/pii/S0003267011008622
4. EEC: European Commission Regulation (EEC). European Commission Regulation EEC/2568/91 of 11 July on the characteristics of olive and pomace oils and on their analytical methods. Off. J. Eur. Communities **L248**(640), 1–82 (1991)
5. Ferentinos, K.P.: Deep learning models for plant disease detection and diagnosis. Comput. Electron. Agric. **145**, 311–318 (2018). https://doi.org/10.1016/j.compag.2018.01.009. http://www.sciencedirect.com/science/article/pii/S0168169917311742
6. Galili, E., Stanley, D.J., Sharvit, J., Weinstein-Evron, M.: Evidence for earliest olive-oil production in submerged settlements off the Carmel coast, Israel. J. Archaeol. Sci. **24**(12), 1141–1150 (1997). https://doi.org/10.1006/jasc.1997.0193. http://www.sciencedirect.com/science/article/pii/S030544039790193X

7. Hussain, M., Bird, J.J., Faria, D.R.: A study on CNN transfer learning for image classification. In: Lotfi, A., Bouchachia, H., Gegov, A., Langensiepen, C., McGinnity, M. (eds.) UKCI 2018. AISC, vol. 840, pp. 191–202. Springer, Cham (2019). https://doi.org/10.1007/978-3-319-97982-3_16

8. Kanu, A.B., Hill, H.H.: Ion mobility spectrometry detection for gas chromatography. J. Chromatogr. A **1177**(1), 12–27 (2008). https://doi.org/10.1016/j.chroma.2007.10.110

9. Pedregosa, F., et al.: Scikit-learn: machine learning in python. J. Mach. Learn. Res. **12**, 2825–2830 (2011)

10. Riul, A., et al.: Wine classification by taste sensors made from ultra-thin films and using neural networks. Sens. Actuators B: Chem. **98**(1), 77–82 (2004). https://doi.org/10.1016/j.snb.2003.09.025. http://www.sciencedirect.com/science/article/pii/S0925400503007512

11. Soomro, N., Wang, M.: Superpixel segmentation: a benchmark. Sig. Process. Image Commun. **56** (2017). https://doi.org/10.1016/j.image.2017.04.007

12. Vega-Márquez, B., Nepomuceno-Chamorro, I., Jurado-Campos, N., Martín-Gómez, A., Arce, L., Rubio-Escudero, C.: Deep Learning Techniques to Improve the Performance of Olive Oil Classification (2019, in press)

13. Wu, J.: Introduction to convolutional neural networks. Technical report (2017). https://doi.org/10.1007/978-3-642-28661-2-5

An Indoor Illuminance Prediction Model Based on Neural Networks for Visual Comfort and Energy Efficiency Optimization Purposes

M. Martell, M. Castilla$^{(\boxtimes)}$ (iD), F. Rodríguez (iD), and M. Berenguel (iD)

Dpto. de Informática, University of Almería, CIESOL-ceiA3, 04120 Almería, Spain
mariamrtll@gmail.com, {mcastilla,frrodrig,beren}@ual.es

Abstract. Energy and comfort management are becoming increasingly relevant topics into buildings operation, for example, looking for trade-off solutions to maintain adequate comfort conditions within an efficient energy use framework by means of appropriate control and optimization techniques. Moreover, these strategies can take advantage from predictions of the involved variables. In this regard, visual comfort conditions are a key aspect to consider. Hence, in this paper an indoor illuminance prediction model based on a divide-and-rule strategy which makes use of Artificial Neural Networks and polynomial interpolation is proposed. This model has been trained, validated and tested using real data gathered in a bioclimatic building. As a result, an acceptable forecast of indoor illuminance level was obtained with a mean absolute error equals to 8.9 lx and a relative error lower than 2%.

Keywords: Indoor illuminance prediction · Neural networks ·
Prediction model · System identification · Comfort control

1 Introduction

From the beginning, human beings have been bounded to the necessity of energy both to survive and to satisfy their own needs. This trend has been increasing according to world population growth and the discovery of new technologies. Nevertheless, as non-renewable energy sources, such as oil and coal, are more and more exhausted [4] the integration and use of different energy sources, just as renewable and non-renewable ones, is taking on special relevance. Furthermore, a model can be defined as *sustainable* if it is able "to satisfy the actual needs without compromising the ability of future generations to satisfy their own needs" [12]. Hence, it can be stated that, at present, the global energetic model is unsustainable from social, economic and environmental points of view [10].

This work has been funded by the National R+D+i Plan Project DPI2017-85007-R of the Spanish Ministry of Science, Innovation and Universities and ERDF funds.

© Springer Nature Switzerland AG 2019
J. M. Ferrández Vicente et al. (Eds.): IWINAC 2019, LNCS 11487, pp. 146–156, 2019.
https://doi.org/10.1007/978-3-030-19651-6_15

Therefore, energy efficiency is becoming an increasingly relevant topic which has caused the appearance of several regulations which try to reduce global energy consumption and non-renewable energy sources dependency within main economic sectors [13].

Buildings sector is currently a major energy consumer. According to the information provided by Eurostat [14], energy consumption of building sector represents 38% of global energy consumption. Besides, the most part of it is originated fundamentally by the use of HVAC (Heating, Ventilation and Air-Conditioning) and lighting systems. The use of those systems allows to guarantee users' comfort from thermal and visual points of view [3]. Moreover, assuring a certain comfort degree has a direct impact on performance, productivity and users' health. Thus, energy efficiency and users' comfort management are raising great interest in researchers and companies. In fact, some control architectures are able to manage both objectives [3]. For that reason, it is needed to predict environmental conditions, that is, indoor temperature, illuminance level, air quality, etc.

This paper is focused on the development of an indoor illuminance prediction model for an office-room located inside a bioclimatic building, the CIESOL building. Multiple approaches have been presented in literature for this purpose. Moreover, it is worthy to highlight these ones: (i) based on scale models; (ii) based on computer simulations and (iii) based on analytical equations. However, illuminance level in a room is difficult to be modelled either by analytical equations, since a lot of variables are involved, or by a scale model mainly due to the fact that some elements cannot be identically reproduced, such as the main characteristics of construction materials. In addition, model integration into a control architecture is a relevant factor to take into account. In this regard, software for illuminance level simulation is not feasible, and thus, those methods become unattractive for addressing this problem.

More in detail, the indoor illuminance prediction model presented in this paper has been developed following a divide-and-rule strategy, and thus, a prediction model based on Artificial Neural Networks (ANN) has been developed [7,8] to counteract the contributions of daylight into indoor illuminance. In addition, a polynomial interpolation has been implemented in order to consider the contribution of adjustable artificial lights into indoor illuminance. Besides, this prediction model has been used to support the upper layer, that is a set-points optimizer, of a multilevel hierarchical control system [9]. The complete illuminance prediction model has been tested using real data from a bioclimatic building and promising results have been obtained with a relative error lower than 2%.

The rest of the paper is organised as follows. In Sect. 2, a description of visual comfort concept and the facilities where the study has been conducted are presented. In Sect. 3, a model for illuminance level estimation is defined, while in Sect. 4, results for model validation are shown and discussed. Lastly, in Sect. 5, main conclusions and future works are summarised.

2   Scope of the Research: Visual Comfort and CIESOL

Visual comfort can be defined as *"A subjective condition of visual well-being induced by the visual environment"* [6]. Therefore, to reach an appropriate visual comfort sensation it is needed to consider the properties of the visual environment, such as: illuminance level and its distribution, colour of light, glare, etc. The most recommendable values for these properties can be determined from international standards [6]. In this paper, it has been considered that a visual comfort condition can be achieved by means of an appropriate indoor illuminance level. Therefore, three key elements must be taken into account: natural light, artificial lighting and shading devices.

On the other hand, The CIESOL (http://www.ciesol.es) is a research centre on solar energy located inside the Campus of University of Almería, in the South East of Spain. Furthermore, this centre was built under some bioclimatic criteria (such as specific insulation depending on the orientation or HVAC systems based on solar cooling). The building itself has a total surface of 1071.91 m^2 distributed into two floors. Moreover, every room is monitored by a network of sensors, whose data is stored through an acquisition system, and controlled by means of some actuators, e.g HVAC systems, automated windows or shading devices. Data related to meteorological conditions, such as solar radiation, temperature or humidity, is collected and stored as well.

The model proposed in this paper has been obtained for a characteristic room of CIESOL building, where all the data were gathered, henceforth called L6. This room, with a total surface of 76.8 m^3 (4.96 m × 5.53 m × 2.8 m), is located in the first floor of the building and faces north, a moreover, it is delimited by two similar laboratories. It has a single window located at north wall covering 4.49 m^2 (2.15 m × 2.09 m). L6 is fully equipped with sensors and actuators which make possible an effective comfort control [3]. More in detail, L6 is equipped with automatic window and blind which can be operated from a remote computer. In addition, as artificial lights it counts with fluorescent lamps whose intensity can be regulated by applying a voltage between $[0, 10]$ V.

3   A Neural Network Model for Indoor Illuminance of an Office-Room

To estimate users' visual comfort inside a room, it is required to use a prediction model of indoor illuminance. To do that, it is worthy to mention that indoor illuminance is influenced by two main factors: (i) Natural light through window, which depends on global, diffuse or direct radiation, outdoor illuminance and window's parameters, and (ii) Artificial lighting which can be obtained as a function of indoor lights and lamps. Furthermore, to obtain an accurate illuminance prediction model, it is needed to take into account the geometry of the room and its main constructive characteristics. Nevertheless, the procedure to determine these parameters is a very complex task and, sometimes, even impossible. Therefore, an indoor illuminance prediction model in a room could be highly inaccurate if those parameters are not well characterised. For this reason, in this paper a black-box prediction model based on ANN has been obtained. The election of ANN approach has been motivated by the complexity of the problem and the principal features of ANNs: self-adaptive, fault tolerance, learning, flexibility and real time response [1,2,5].

More in detail, the black-box model presented in this paper has been defined using a divide-and-rule strategy by considering that artificial and natural lighting are unrelated, but an additive phenomena. Besides, artificial lighting can easily be modelled by means of a polynomial interpolation since they depend only from the input voltage applied to the regulate their intensity. On the contrary, contributions due to natural light depends on a huge variety of factors that can handily be managed by an ANN. The architecture proposed for the black-box model can be observed in Fig. 1.

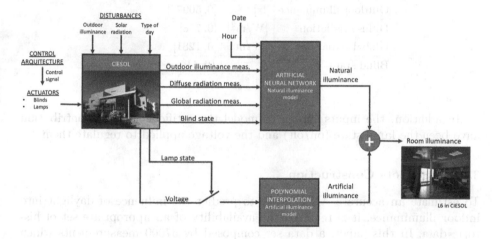

Fig. 1. Model architecture based on a divide-and-rule strategy.

The procedure to obtain the ANN forecasting model could be summarized as follows: (i) selection of inputs for the indoor illuminance prediction model; (ii) construction of the training, validation and testing data sets; (iii) establishment of ANN paradigms, that is, its architecture and structure; and (iv) training, implementation and evaluation of the indoor illuminance prediction model.

3.1   ANN Inputs and Size

Firstly, it is required to determine which are the key parameters that affect the model distinguishing between daylight and artificial lighting contributions. More concretely, the inputs selected for the model which represent the natural light contribution have been: date, hour, outdoor illuminance, diffuse and global radiation, blind state (open/close). Date and hour variables are significant since they provide to the ANN information about how solar path changes along the year.

In addition, outdoor illuminance and diffuse and global radiation also provide information about the outdoor environmental conditions. To simplify the ANN model, an static model is assumed, that is, the current output does not depend on past outputs. In addition, the geometrical characteristics of the room have been also neglected, so an average workplace in L6 has been selected for data gathering. Finally, in order to achieve an appropriate performance, some limits have been established over these inputs, see Table 1.

Table 1. List of input variables for the ANN model

Variable	Unit	Measurement range
Date	–	$[1, 366]$
Hour	–	$[0, 1]$
Outdoor illuminance	[lx]	$[0, 56977]$
Diffuse radiation	$[W/m^2]$	$[0, 758]$
Global radiation	$[W/m^2]$	$[0, 1281]$
Blind state	–	$\{0, 1\}$

In addition, the inputs chosen to model the artificial lighting contribution have been the lamp state (on/off) and the voltage applied to regulate them.

3.2 Data-Sets Construction

To estimate an accurate ANN model to predict the influence of daylight into indoor illuminance, it is required the availability of an appropriate set of historic data. In this paper, a data set composed by 57000 measurements which encompasses from March to July has been used. To obtain this data set, several tests using the available actuators in L6 have been performed in order to gather all the dynamics needed to determine an ANN with a good performance. More information about the instrumentation used to acquire them can be found in [3]. Furthermore, this data set has been divided into three different data subsets which have been used to train, validate and test the ANN model. The first data subset which can be denoted as *Training Data Set* encompasses 75% of total measurements and it is used to estimate ANN parameters through the Levenberg-Marquardt optimization algorithm [11]. The second data subset, *Validation Data Set*, includes 20% of total data points and it is employed to measure ANN generalization, and thus, to prevent *over-training*. Finally, the *Testing Data Set* utilizes 5% of total measurements and it is an independent data subset used to determine the ANN performance after training process. Concretely, the *Testing Data Set* is composed of data selected in order to encompass different types of environmental conditions and situations which can appear in an office room, see Table 2.

Table 2. Description of the Testing Data Set

Samples	Date	Type of day	Test
1–650	March, 31st	Clear day	Blind test
651–825	April, 5th	Clear day	Blind test
826–1080	April, 11th	Clear day	Blind and variable lamps' voltage test
1081–1220	July, 10th	Clear day	Variable lamps' voltage test
1221–1420	July, 14th	Clear day	Constant lamps' voltage test

3.3   Architecture and Structure Selection

As it has been mentioned previously, an ANN model acts as a black-box model, and thus, it is not necessary to acquire a deep knowledge about the modelled system since ANN approach is able to determine the existing relationship among inputs and outputs by using historical data. As it is well known, an ANN is composed of an input layer, one or more hidden layers and one output layer [10].

In this paper, to establish the appropriate number of hidden layers and neurons a sensitivity analysis and an optimization process considering time of training and results accurateness have been performed. At the end, this paper proposes an ANN indoor illuminance prediction model based on daylight contribution with two hidden layers, each of which is composed by 12 neurons and a sigmoid activation function.

4   Results and Discussion

The proposed indoor illuminance prediction model has been validated using real data from L6 room in CIESOL building. As it was emphasized before, this model is composed of an ANN used to predict the contribution of natural light and a polynomial interpolation in order to deal with artificial lighting contribution. Firstly, an overview of the results obtained for the ANN illuminance prediction model is presented. Afterwards, the validation of the polynomial interpolation developed to counteract the effect of artificial lights into indoor illuminance model has been included. At the end, reader can find validation results for the complete illuminance prediction model presented in Sect. 3. For goodness-of-fit evaluation, Mean Absolute Error (MAE) index has been used, see Eq. (1), where y_i represents the real data gathered at L6 and $\hat{y}_i$ shows the results provided by the ANN model.

$$MAE = \frac{1}{n} \sum_{i=1}^{n} |y_i - \hat{y}_i| \qquad (1)$$

Figure 2 presents the results obtained for the ANN illuminance prediction model to counteract daylight effect using the *Validation Data Set*. As it can be observed, error is primarily distributed on a range of ± 2 lx with an average of 0.2 lx, revealing a good behaviour of the ANN. Besides, a MAE index equals to 1.2 lx, that is 0.4%, and a standard deviation of 2.1 lx have been obtained. In addition, Fig. 3 depicts a regression analysis, that is, a representation of the existing relation between real and estimated data. Ideally, a $y = x$ line represents the best performance of the ANN (regression coefficient, $R = 1$). Hence, a regression coefficient $R = 0.999$ proves a reasonably acceptable ANN prediction model.

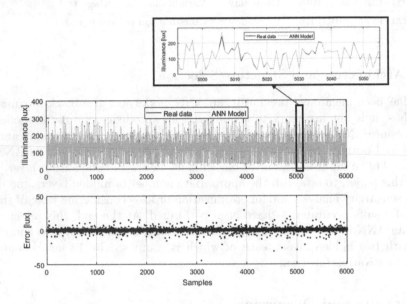

Fig. 2. Validation of the ANN model to counteract natural light effect

In Fig. 4, a validation of the polynomial interpolation for artificial illuminance and its maximum absolute error for voltages comprised between $[0, 10]$ V is shown. As can be observed, error becomes bigger at lower voltages as there are some non-linearities. Even so, these errors can be considered tolerable mainly due to the following reasons: (i) normal operating conditions imply high voltages as an input because of selected set-points; (ii) MAE index is equal to 6.2 lx (2.2%) with a standard deviation of 3.7 lx.

Finally, regarding the validation of the complete illuminance prediction model, the model's output has been calculated as an aggregation of natural and artificial illuminance predictions. Figure 5 shows the validation results obtained by using the *Testing Data Set* presented in Sect. 3.2. The upper graph in Fig. 5 depicts the evolution of indoor illuminance for both real data gathered in L6 (in blue) and the results provided by the complete model (in red). Besides, the lower graph shows the error. It can be observed that the error is primarily concentrated in a ±20 lx range with an average error equals to −4.1 lx is observed, pointing out some negative trend. In addition, MAE index is equal to 8.9 lx and standard deviation of 7.6 lx. These values can be considered negligible since the total

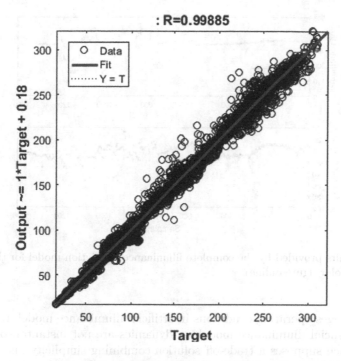

Fig. 3. Regression analysis for ANN model

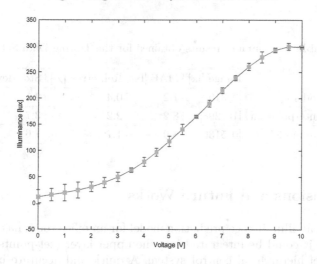

Fig. 4. Validation of the polynomial interpolation to counteract artificial lights effect

range of the *Testing Data Set* is equal to 513 lx, that is, a relative error equals to 1.73%. In this concern, the performance of the proposed prediction model is considered to be suitable for the addressed problem, as two main phenomena were neglected and have become the main source of error: (i) non-linearities observed

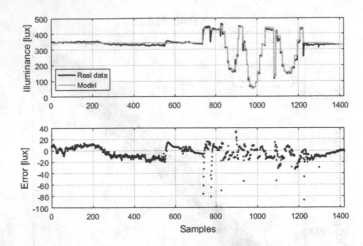

Fig. 5. Results provided by the complete illuminance prediction model for the Testing Data Set (Color figure online)

for low voltages operating conditions in artificial illuminance model, (ii) settling time in artificial illuminance model, as dynamics are not instantaneous. Thus, this approach supposes a trade-off solution combining simplicity and speed for modelling. Table 3 shows a summary of the results obtained and discussed in this section.

Table 3. Summary results obtained for the Testing Data Set

Model	Range [lx]	MAE [lx]	Rel. error [%]	Std. dev. [lx]
ANN model	[0, 310]	1.2	0.4	2.1
Polyn. interpolation	[10, 298]	8.2	2.2	3.7
Complete model	[0, 513]	8.9	1.7	7.6

5   Conclusions and Future Works

In this paper, an illuminance prediction model for an office room has been developed, so that it could be integrated into the upper layer (set-points optimizer) of a multilevel hierarchical control system. A quick and accurate implementation of such estimator was needed. For that, an innovative approach - following divide-and-rule strategy - has been presented as a methodology for constructing an illuminance model composed by two main inputs: natural light model, based on ANN, and artificial lighting model, based on polynomial interpolation. This approach enables to simplify ANN inputs, in order to optimize ANN training, both from time and necessary data points of view.

Illuminance modelling can become a huge challenge as lots of variables are involved. In this regard, this paper presents a simple, fast and potentially adaptable methodology, that allows to work from a black-box model perspective, making these variables transparent for the user. However, some information is missed, concretely differences between workplaces in the office, as geometrical parameters are neglected.

The performance of the proposed model has been tested along different days from March to July and, as it was shown within Sect. 4, the obtained results are promising. More in detail, the model is able to estimate illuminance level with a relative error of 1.7% for the studied range ([0,513] lx). These results show that ANN models are flexible and versatile options to consider when dealing with such kind of dynamics.

However, the model is currently able to accurately estimate illuminance for the period of the year from March to July, it should be capable to make whole-year predictions though. As future works, a 12-month period training has to be accomplished.

References

1. Basheer, I.A., Hajmeer, M.: Artificial neural networks: fundamentals, computing, design and application. J. Microbiol. Methods **43**, 3–31 (2000)
2. Castilla, M., Álvarez, J.D., Ortega, M.G., Arahal, M.R.: Neural network and polynomial approximated thermal comfort models for HVAC systems. Build. Environ. **59**, 107–115 (2013)
3. Castilla, M., Álvarez, J.D., Rodríguez, F., Berenguel, M.: Comfort Control in Buildings. Advances in Industrial Control. Springer, London (2014). https://doi.org/10.1007/978-1-4471-6347-3. ISBN 978-1-4471-6346-6
4. Castilla, M., Bordons, C.: Optimal management of a microgrid to guarantee users' thermal comfort. In: International Conference on Smart Energy Systems and Technologies (SEST 2018), Sevilla, Spain (2018)
5. Chen, S., Billings, S.A.: Neural networks for nonlinear dynamic system modelling and identification. Int. J. Control **56**, 319–346 (1992)
6. EN-12665: Light and lighting: basic terms and criteria for specifying lighting requirements. European Committee for Standardization, Brussels (2018)
7. Kazanasmaz, Z.T., Gnaydin, M., Binol, S.: Artificial neural networks to predict daylight illuminance in office buildings. Build. Environ. **44**(8), 1751–1757 (2009)
8. Logar, V., Kristl, Z., Škrjanc, I.: Using a fuzzy black-box model to estimate the indoor illuminance in buildings. Energy Build. **70**, 343–351 (2014)
9. Martell, M.: Multiobjective optimization of comfort and energy efficiency in sustainable buildings (in Spanish). Diploma thesis, University of Almería (2017)
10. Mena, R., Rodríguez, F., Castilla, M., Arahal, M.R.: A prediction model based on neural networks for the energy consumption of a bioclimatic buildings. Energy Build. **82**, 142–155 (2014). https://doi.org/10.1016/j.enbuild.2014.06.052
11. Moré, J.J.: The Levenberg-Marquardt algorithm: implementation and theory. In: Watson, G.A. (ed.) Numerical Analysis. LNM, vol. 630, pp. 105–116. Springer, Heidelberg (1978). https://doi.org/10.1007/BFb0067700
12. W.E.C. United Nations Department of Economic & Social Affairs, World Energy Assessment. Energy and the Challenge of Sustainability, United Nations Development Programme (2000)

13. https://ec.europa.eu/info/business-economy-euro/economic-and-fiscal-policy-coordination/eu-economic-governance-monitoring-prevention-correction/european-semester/framework/europe-2020-strategy_en . Accessed 22 Feb 2019
14. Eurostat. Final energy consumption by sector. https://ec.europa.eu/eurostat. Accessed 22 Feb 2019

Using Probabilistic Context Awareness in a Deliberative Planner System

Jonatan Gines Clavero[1]([✉]), Francisco J. Rodriguez[2], Francisco Martín Rico[1],
Angel Manuel Guerrero[2], and Vicente Matellán[2]

[1] Robotics Lab, Universidad Rey Juan Carlos, Madrid, Spain
j.gines@alumnos.urjc.es, franscisco.rico@urjc.es
[2] Robotics Group, Department of Mechanical, Computer and Aerospace Engineering,
University of Leon, 24071 León, Spain
{fjrodl,am.guerrero,vicente.matellang}@unileon.es

Abstract. When a Social Robot is deployed in a service environment it has to manage a highly dynamic scenarios that provide a set of unknown circumstances: objects in different places and humans walking around. These conditions are challenging for an autonomous robot that needs to accomplish assistive tasks. These partially known scenarios has negative effects on hybrid architectures with deliberative planning systems adding extra sub-tasks to main goal or continuous re-planing with deadlocks. This paper proposes the use of a probabilistic Context Awareness System that provides a set of belief states of the environment to a symbolic planner enabling PDDL metrics. The Context Awareness System is composed by a Deep Learning classifier to process audio input from the environment, and an inference probabilistic module for generating symbolic knowledge. This approach delivers a method to generate correct plans efficiently. The solution presented in this paper is being successfully applied in a robot running Robot Operating System (ROS) on two experimental scenarios that illustrates the utility of the technique showing a reduction on execution time.

Keywords: Context Awareness · Deliberative · PDDL

1 Introduction

An autonomous social robot requires to analyze multiple alternative tasks every time that a goal is decided. The evaluation and consequent tasks execution has a negative effect in terms of time and the decision making performance.

The goal of this research is to offer a time optimization to a classic deliberative process based on classic planners and PDDL. Particularly, the idea is to deal with it from a bio-inspired perspective. The robot has to proceed with a set of behaviors to reach a goal, thus, authors as Gómez [7] defines the behavior concept from

This work has been supported by the Spanish Government TIN2016-76515-R Grant, supported with Feder funds.

biological perspective, as those egocentric and allocentric actions performed in an organized temporal sequence due to internal and external reasons. Although we are already managing the internal reasons using a motivational architecture [9], the variability of the environment continues adding difficulties when facing long-term and complex tasks. As Gómez pointed out, three main features define an animal behavior, however, we consider that these three properties can be easily transferred to a robot system: (1) relational, it interacts with the environment, (2) dynamic, it presents changes along the time, and (3) highly dimensional, that presents the behavior as something complex and unpredictable.

In order to facilitate the generation of behaviors in a Human-Robot inter-action scenario, thus producing accurate and natural responses to human behaviours, a robot should understand user's context. In this way to recognize and label the user activity is a corner stone for any autonomous Social Robot providing services at home [11]. For years, the activity context identification has been used for enhancing robot performance and particularly the deliberative system [8].

Under these circumstances, this research proposes a hybrid approach combining reactive and deliberative elements. It deals the robot behavior generation and selection based on four elements: (1) A hierarchy of needs associated with Elder-fer's need levels [1]. (2) A set of motivational variables given a *robot role*. Understanding motivation as the desire to do things, these variables provide a mechanism to influence robot behavior to act differently. This approach is inspired by motivational proposals such as [2,3] and closer to the anthropomorphic-based architectures [4]. (3) A pool of finite state machines (FSM) defining the robot behaviors available per robot role. These behaviors will have a level of complexity that favors reusing those behaviors with low complexity when a high-complexity behavior is generated. (4) A context awareness component that combines localization information, objects identification, human interaction, human bracelets and smartphones. These sources of information provide crucial information for recognizing human activities and accurately calculate human properties proposed by Gómez in a home-like scenario.

1.1   Contribution

Previous phases of this research added the ability to identify the context to autonomous robots running in home-like environments. Using Acoustic Recognition solutions and adding a Context Awareness Component (CAC) [10] for enhancing the decision making process.

The first contribution of this research is to calculate human position in the home-like environment in partially-known environments using the CAC. The outcome generated in this case is a set of symbolic predicates with a probability associated which will be used for the Deliberative subsystem, which is based on ROSPlan and PDDL v2.1.

In addition, this contribution assess the real impact that CAC factor has over a symbolic component such as a Planner, presenting the differences when the CAC is disables, when it provides binary information (a context or nothing) and when it is providing probabilistic states.

Based on the above, we will present the hypothesis on which we will work and we will validate with the results obtained in the experiments Sect. 3. This hypothesis is: *A mobile robot performs tasks more efficiently if it can obtain and classify the acoustic stimulus that is generated in its environment.*

1.2 Paper Organization

The work presented here presents and discuss both contributions. Section 2 defines the architecture in which is embedded the symbolic decision making, the behavior generation and the Context Awareness Component description and how it provides probabilistic predicates. Section 3 describes the performance of the CAC when offers symbolic predicates. Finally, conclusions are presented in Sect. 4.

2   Framework Description

On our previous research, we proposed a hybrid framework (Reactive-Deliberative) that integrated components that extracted knowledge of the environment, through the use of deep learning networks and planning components. The previous research was focus on recognition of sounds and activities through acoustic signals, likes the ones shown in Fig. 1, using a convolutional neuronal network, which model architecture is shown in Fig. 2, but in this contribution we will focus on deliberative and planning components, offering an optimal planning approach and comparing it with a classic planning approach. Figure 3 shows a graphic description of the full framework. Sensors get the data of the environment, we will focus on the microphone, and Preprocessing & Fusion module classifies and labels sounds through a convolutional deep neural network. It has been developed to identify 14 different relevant sounds grouped into classes:

- General: Door bell, Entry Door, Exit Door, Silence, Window.
- Bathroom: Cistern, tap.
- Kitchen: Induction, Fridge, Kettle, Microwave, Oven Alarm.
- Room: TV, Radio.

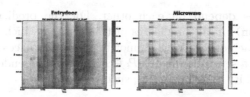

Fig. 1. Examples of normalized and log-scaled spectrograms (from [10]).

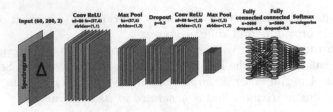

Fig. 2. Convolutional neuronal network topology (from [10]).

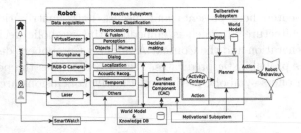

Fig. 3. The design of our hybrid cognitive architecture integrating a context-awareness component and a planner to take decisions (from [10]).

The framework is enriched with two new contributions. First, a probabilistic inference module that takes as input all the available context information. This module includes both the perceptual stimuli detected by the convolutional neuronal network and the time of day or any available information. This module includes in the knowledge base of a planner predicates with its probability. Secondly, we will show how to optimize the plans generated by the planner using the probabilistic modeling of the predicates that are part of the knowledge base.

2.1 Probabilistic Inference Module

The probabilistic inference module takes as inputs all the perceptual and contextual stimuli available to the robot, and as outputs will be a set of predicates with an associated probability. A predicate $p_i \in P$ describes symbolic information in PDDL [6] format, for example:

```
(person_at Anna kitchen)
(object_in apple kitchen)
```

Some predicates depend on each other. For the predicate (person at? ?person ?location), in all predicates of this type in which ?Person is Anna, are dependent on each other. Anna cannot be in all the places at once and must be somewhere. For a set of predicates $P_i \in P$ that are dependent on each other, we define a probability distribution F_i, such that:

$$F_i(x) = Prob(X \le x) = \sum_{k=-\infty}^{x} f_i(x) \tag{1}$$

$$\sum^{x} f_i(x) = 1 \tag{2}$$

The set O contains the input stimuli to the probabilistic inference module. Each stimulus $o \in O$ has a function q associated (a function from P to the distribution of probability on O), where $q(o|p)$ is the probability of observing o if predicate p is true. For example:

$$q(microwave|AnnaInKitchen) = 0.9$$
$$q(microwave|AnnaInOutdoor) = 0.001 \tag{3}$$

where $AnnaInKitchen$ is (person_at Anna kitchen) and $AnnaInOutdoor$ is (person_at Anna outdoor). We model q as a $P \times O$ function built with prior expert knowledge. The stimulus o, in this case, is to be perceiving the sound of the microwave, and q defines the probability that Anna is in the kitchen or outside the house if the robot perceives this stimulus. We update each predicate $p \in P$ according the Principle of Markov, where $F(x)$ in time $t + 1$ only depends on $F(x)$ in time t, and the observation o:

$$F_i^{t+1}(p) = \frac{1}{scale} q(o|p) F_i^t(p), p \in P, o \in O \tag{4}$$

Where $scale$ is a normalization constant that ensures that Eq. 2 is satisfied for each subset $P_i \in P$ of dependent predicates.

Finally, to illustrate this explanation, we will show a real example in which we want to determine the probability that two people, Anna and Jack, are in each of the rooms of a house. The stimuli that we will take into account in this example are the sound of microwave and the sound of the radio, which is in Anna's room. There are two probability distributions in this case: those that contain Jack as the subject of the predicate and those that include Anna. At any given time, Anna's discrete distribution, already shown as PDDL functions, could be:

```
(= (person_at Anna kitchen) 0.9)
(= (person_at Anna Anna's_room) 0.1)
(= (person_at Anna Jack's_room) 0.015)
(= (person_at Anna outdoor) 0.0005)
```

In Fig. 4 we show the part of the function q with Jack and Anna as subjects, and the microwave and the radio as observation.

2.2   Probabilistic Planning

The planner is shown in detail in Fig. 5. In our case, it follows the PDDL 2.1 [5] standard, which allows us to use durative actions and functions. Durative actions are non-atomic actions that will enable you to specify when your requirements are evaluated (at the beginning, at the end or during the entire execution). Also, the functions allow us to associate a numeric value to an existing predicate, as we have done in the previous section.

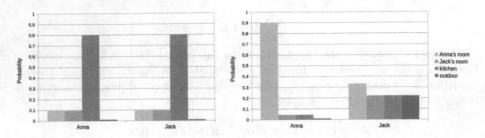

Fig. 4. The function q(ojp) value when microwave ring (left) and when the radio its run (right).

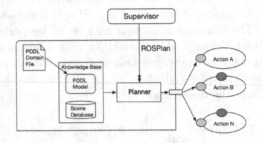

Fig. 5. The planning system.

Both the PDDL model (where data types are defined, the types of predicates and actions) and the current state (the problem) are stored in the knowledge base. Each time a plan is required, the plan is generated based on the content of the knowledge base.

We use metric for using the output of the probabilistic inference module. Metrics in PDDL let us generate un plan improving the value of a function that takes part as the result of actions. In the next example, we make plans improving the value of function `total-prob`, that is a predicate that returns a value:

```
add_metric("maximize", "total-prob")
```

An action that uses an output of the probabilistic inference module accumulates this value as a result of its application. Next example would find a person in his most probable location:

```
(:durative-action find_person
    :parameters (?r - robot ?p - person ?l - location)
    :duration ( = ?duration n)
    :condition (and
        ...
    )
    :effect (and
        (at end(increase (person-total-prob) (person_at ?p ?l)))
        ...
    )
)
```

3   Experimentation

Use Case: Our experiments to validate the proposed algorithm aims the use case of a service robot in a home must notify one of the tenants that he or she will receive a package. First, the robot has to be in the same room that the receiver of the notify, because of this it should search the whole house, and once there give him the message using a voice command.

Scenario: The domestic scenario, simulated with Gazebo, it is composed of 3 rooms, kitchen, Jack's room, and Anna's room. Also, it's possible that the people aren't in the house. The auditory stimuli that the robot receives will be simulated. Table 1 shows the relation between the sound producer's objects and their location.

Table 1. Stimuli producers and their location.

Object	Location
TV	Jack's room
Radio	Anna's room
Microwave	Kitchen
Entrance door	
Exit door	

PDDL Domain: The actions and functions that we use during the experiments and that are involved in the proposed solution are shown below.

```
(:predicates                                          :parameters (?r - robot ?p - person ?from - room)
    (heard ?o - object)                               :duration ( = ?duration 1)
    (person_at_room ?p - person ?room - room)         :condition (and
    (person_not_founded ?p - person)                     (at start(robot_at_room ?r ?from))
    (robot_at_room ?r - robot ?room - room)              (at start(person_not_founded ?p))
)                                                     )
                                                      :effect (and
(:functions                                              (at end(not(person_not_founded ?p)))
    (person_at_prob ?p - person ?from - room)            (at end(person_at_room ?p ?from))
    (total-prob)                                         (at end(increase (total-prob) (person_at_prob ?p ?from)))
)                                                     )
                                                  )
(:durative-action look_for_person
```

3.1   Evolution of the Location Probability

In this experiment, we will simulate two domestic situations and we will show how the probabilities of each subject evolve as the system is receiving new stimuli and these are integrated into the knowledge base. In Fig. 6 we show the evolution of the probability for a simple sequence of stimuli. The sequence is: at first the exit door sounds since Jack leaves the house, and then the radio sounds. We observe that at the begging of the experiment all locations have the same probability of occurrence, 0.25, and how at the end of the experiment most likely Anna is in her room and Jack is out of the house. Figure 7 shows another simple experiment that exemplifies the evolution of the probability for short sequences of stimuli.

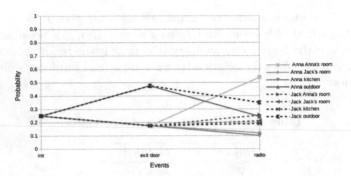

Fig. 6. Evolution of the probability when the robot perceives the exit door sound and the radio starts to run.

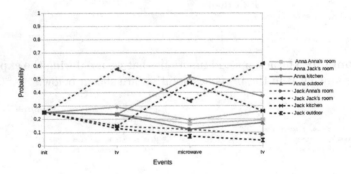

Fig. 7. Evolution of the probability when the sequence of events is tv, microwave, and tv.

After these experiments, we will simulate a situation of greater duration. Suppose that Jack is watching television in his room and Anna comes home from work. Jack goes to the kitchen to prepare his dinner and then Anna does. Figure 8 shows how changes the probability based on the stimuli that the robot receives, showing at the end of the sequence that most likely Jack is in his room watching tv and Anna is in the kitchen preparing her dinner.

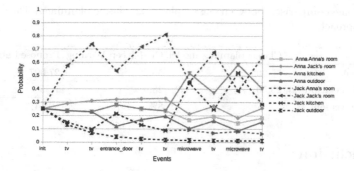

Fig. 8. Evolution of the probability for a greater duration sequences of stimuli.

3.2 Comparison with Baseline

We will now analyze the time it takes the robot to execute the same task, it have to notifies the arrive of a packages to a certain person, based on the running modules.

- Firstly, we will do an experiment using classic planning, consequently, the robot has not got information about the environment. During the experiment, the robot will navigate to a room and check if the person is in there. If it is in there the robot will give the notification, if not it has to go to the next room to search the receiver. This process will be executed until the receiver will be found.
- Secondly, we will activate the Deep Learning classifier to process audio of the environment although the CAC module will remain inactive. Under these circumstances, the robot will navigate to the room where it is the object that sounded by the last time. If the person is not there the robot has to navigate the rest of the rooms until the receiver will be found. This approach would be correct if there could not be more than one person in the house, a very unlikely scenario for an assistive robot.
- Finally, we will do the experiment using full system, activating the Deep Learning classifier to process audio and the CAC module to knowledge inference. In this case, the robot has the knowledge of the sound events over time and it knows the probability of where is each person, consequently, the robot will navigate directly to the most likely room.

Table 2 shows the comparison in time between the three approaches exposed previously. As you can see the proposed algorithm reduce the time to deliver a message of more than 50%, taking an average of 27,05 s versus the 55 s of the classic planning model and the 50 s of the classic planing model combined with the Deep Learning classifier.

Table 2. Time comparison between classic planning, classic planning + Deep learning, and our approach.

	Classic planning model	CP + Deep learning	Proposed algorithm
Average (s)	55,009	50,6	27,097
Standard deviation (s)	25,50	28,0	1,25
% of improvement		8%	50,74%

4   Conclusions

It is not enough to have a classic planning system or to have a deep neural network that recognizes sounds, it is necessary to have a system that interprets all the information and generates knowledge that can be used by the robot. A probabilistic knowledge inference algorithm based on Markov has been proposed that improves the planning, reducing the number of replannings, and the total time of execution of the tasks in a 50%.

For the future work, we also wish to evaluate reinforcement learning approaches and their relationship to the plan refinement.

References

1. Alderfer, C.P.: An empirical test of a new theory of human needs. Organ. Behav. Hum. Perform. **4**(2), 142–175 (1969)
2. Arkin, R.C., Fujita, M., Hasegawa, R., Takagi, T.: Ethological modeling and architecture for an entertainment robot (2001)
3. Breazeal, C., et al.: A motivational system for regulating human-robot interaction. In: AAAI/IAAI, pp. 54–61 (1998)
4. Duffy, B.R.: Anthropomorphism and the social robot. Robot. Auton. Syst. **42**(3), 177–190 (2003)
5. Fox, M., Long, D.: PDDL2.1: an extension to PDDL for expressing temporal planning domains. CoRR abs/1106.4561 (2011). http://arxiv.org/abs/1106.4561
6. Ghallab, M., et al.: PDDL–The Planning Domain Definition Language (1998). http://citeseerx.ist.psu.edu/viewdoc/summary?doi=10.1.1.37.212
7. Gomez-Marin, A., Paton, J.J., Kampff, A.R., Costa, R.M., Mainen, Z.F.: Big behavioral data: psychology, ethology and the foundations of neuroscience. Nat. Neurosci. **17**(11), 1455–1462 (2014)
8. Liao, L., Fox, D., Kautz, H.: Location-based activity recognition. In: Advances in Neural Information Processing Systems, vol. 18, p. 787 (2006)
9. Rodríguez-Lera, F.J., Matellán-Olivera, V., Conde-González, M.Á., Martín-Rico, F.: HiMoP: a three-component architecture to create more human-acceptable social-assistive robots. Cogn. Process. **19**(2), 233–244 (2018)
10. Rodriguez Lera, F.J., Martín Rico, F., Matellán Olivera, V.: Context awareness in shared human-robot environments: benefits of environment acoustic recognition for user activity classification. In: 8th International Conference of Pattern Recognition Systems (ICPRS 2017), Madrid (Spain), 11–13 July 2017, p. 24. Institution of Engineering and Technology (2017)
11. Zhu, C., Sheng, W.: Motion-and location-based online human daily activity recognition. Pervasive Mob. Comput. **7**(2), 256–269 (2011)

Combining Data-Driven and Domain Knowledge Components in an Intelligent Assistant to Build Personalized Menus

Miquel Sànchez-Marrè[1,3]([⊠]), Karina Gibert[2,3], and Beatriz Sevilla-Villaneva[2,3]

[1] Computer Science Department, Universitat Politècnica
de Catalunya - BarcelonaTech, Jordi Girona 1-3, 08034 Barcelona, Spain
miquel@cs.upc.edu
[2] Statistics and Operations Research Department, Universitat Politècnica de
Catalunya - BarcelonaTech, Jordi Girona 1-3, 08034 Barcelona, Spain
[3] Knowledge Engineering and Machine Learning Group (KEMLG) at Intelligent
Data Science and Artificial Intelligence Research Center (IDEAI), Universitat
Politècnica de Catalunya - BarcelonaTech, Jordi Girona 1-3, 08034 Barcelona, Spain

Abstract. In this paper, some new components that have been integrated in the Diet4You system for the generation of nutritional plans are introduced. Negative user preferences have been modelled and introduced in the system. Furthermore, the cultural eating styles originated from the location where the user lives have been taken into account dividing the original menu plan in sub-plans. Each sub-plan is in charge to optimize one of the meals of one day in the personal menu of the user. The main latent reasoning mechanism used is case-based reasoning, which reuses previous menu configurations according to the nutritional plan and the corresponding hard constraints and the user preferences to meet a personalized recommendation menu for a given user. It uses the cognitive analogical reasoning technique in addition to ontologies, nutritional databases and expert knowledge. The preliminary results with some examples of application to test the new contextual components have been very satisfactory according to the evaluation of the experts.

Keywords: Personalized recommendation ·
Nutritional plan prescription · Case-Based Reasoning ·
Knowledge management · Contextual information · Healthy life-styles

1 Introduction

Nowadays, it is widely accepted that many of modern lifestyle habits such as diet and exercise, together with genetics, play an important role in the development of many diseases such as cardiovascular diseases, diabetes, cancer, obesity and so on. Thanks to the great advances in genetics in recent years, nutritional genomics science has emerged to personalize diet, at individual level, based on the particular needs of each person. The concept of personalized diet has become

© Springer Nature Switzerland AG 2019
J. M. Ferrández Vicente et al. (Eds.): IWINAC 2019, LNCS 11487, pp. 167–179, 2019.
https://doi.org/10.1007/978-3-030-19651-6_17

very popular in the recent years. Although there is no complete knowledge yet about all the effects of nutrients on all existing organisms, personalized menus can significantly contribute to the maintenance of healthy lifestyles and prevention. The project Diet4You aims at building a personalized menu planner that recommends a specific menu depending on the person and his/her personal characteristics and context. Diet4You is an Intelligent Decision Support System providing strategies to achieve an optimal diet at individual level. The system takes into account the nutritional goals to be achieved, the characteristics of the person and his/her health status and context, which includes habits of the individual and his/her food preferences as well. Through a complex combination of Knowledge Engineering, Case-Based Reasoning (CBR), and Data Analysis based on advanced data mining techniques, the system proposes nutritional plans, by recommending the nutritional characteristics of the convenient diet for a certain person and for a certain period of time. It uses previous learnt successful experiences and knowledge extracted from previous databases or provided directly by experts. In a second phase, a proposal of complete menus for the full nutritional plan prescribed (either by the system itself or the nutritionist) and for the full target period will be elaborated, taking into account the desired restrictions and expected effects given by the nutritionist, as well as the food preferences of the individual.

The paper is structured as follows: Sect. 2 outlines the related work, Sect. 3 describes an overview of the Diet4You project, and the formalization of a basic nutritional plan is described in Sect. 4. In Sect. 5, the innovative components of Diet4You and their interaction are explained. Section 6 describes an example of application, and finally in Sect. 7 some conclusions and future work are outlined.

2   Related Work

The system deployed within the Diet4You project is an Intelligent Decision Support System, which proposes a personalized nutritional plan for a concrete person in a determined period of time. It integrates nutrigenomic knowledge, health expert knowledge, ontologies and food databases, and a historical experiential knowledge, including cultural context, as well as the data related to the individual at different levels. Currently, there is not a well-established methodology to design a complete nutritional plan simultaneously taking into account nutrition, genetics, metabolism of people, health considerations, life style habits, cultural context and personal preferences Some nutritional applications have been deployed in the literature like The Automatic Meal Planner - Eat This Much [1], which is an automatic menu planner that given a number of Kcal, it prepares a menu trying to maintain the proportions of macronutrients. Even respecting the specifications of the final diet for an isolated meal, it does not take into account the special characteristics of the person. The USDA (United States Department of Agriculture) offers an application for health professionals to compute the DRIs (Dietary Reference Intake) based on the person's gender, age, height, weight, and physical activity [2]. There are other systems that allow creating a menu interactively, such as the application Menu planner, created by NHL organization [3] where a person can manually combine dishes. This system does not control the balance of the final diet. It only indicates the total amount of Kcal, carbohydrates and fat that the menu contains. From the 70's [10] the field of Decision Support Systems (DSS) is responsible for the generation of software that can analyse data and provide answers to pertinent and relevant questions in decision making of a specific organization. By the late 90s, Intelligent Decision Support Systems (IDSS) [12] begin to include specific domain knowledge and the ability of automatic reasoning. Research to establish a stable infrastructure to the rapid development of IDSS [15] is intense, but there are still many open challenges. However, it seems clear that the IDSS have to combine data-driven models, analytical models, model-driven techniques, specific domain knowledge and some capacity of reasoning to provide a relevant end-user support [14]. Although some efforts have been done to determine a general purpose architecture for IDSS [5], we are still far from general IDSS frameworks for real systems, and specific IDSS should be built for each particular application. One of the main components of an IDSS is the use of data-driven decision methods, which may include methods from the data mining (DM) field, both ma-chine learning or multivariate statistics methods [8]. These modules explore the available data to extract the information that will become knowledge for the sup-port of the posterior decisions. On the other hand, several model-driven techniques, like expert-based models are integrated in IDSS to get more reliable systems for supporting the end users.

As it has been said, the present proposal aims to use advanced semantic comparisons [7], reasoning and statistics to catch the complex structure of the target data, for supporting further decision-making for successful dietary interventions. The proposed IDSS browses the data contained in food databases containing prepared dishes to build nutritional plans according to nutritional prescriptions. This system encompasses several components, some data-driven, some knowledge-driven and some based on a Case-Based Reasoning (CBR) approach. CBR is a methodology that simulates the natural reasoning model of human beings, reasoning by analogy, to solve new problems using similar previous experiences [11]. This is a stable and efficient methodology that has been used in many applications and domains. CBR has been used in the construction of menus such as in the systems MIKAS [9] or CAMPER [13], using this later system rules as well.

3   Overview of Diet4You

As depicted in Fig. 1, the Diet4You system is composed of two main blocks:

1. *A Nutritional Plan Generator (NPG).* This part of the system is designed to return a nutritional plan given personal specifications. The generator receives the following pieces of information as input:
   - *Dietary profiles* that can be prescribed to certain types of persons with certain genetic characteristics and lifestyle habits, and the pattern of expected diet effects in those scenarios.

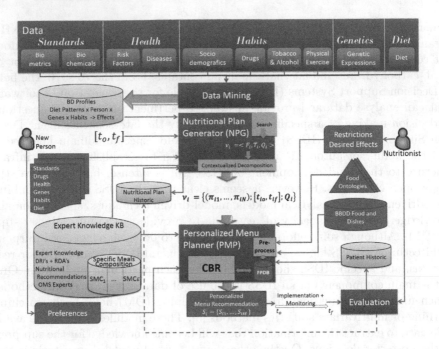

Fig. 1. Flowchart of the Diet4You system

- *Expert knowledge* including Daily Reference Intakes (DRIs) of micronu-trients and trace elements; the Recommended Daily Allowance (RDA) of macronutrients; and nutritional and institutional recommendations, such as those provided by the OMS.
- *History of Nutritional Plans*, which contains a case base made of all the personalized nutritional plans generated by the system in past experi-ences and feed the CBR that builds the nutritional plans. The nutritional plan may be accompanied by the nutritionist's evaluation of the outcome observed in past applications of the plan.
- *Characteristics of the person* who wants to follow a nutritional plan. This means standard information of the health status of the person including biometrics and biochemical characteristics. Also, drugs intakes, medical history including current, past, and risk factors. Context data such as socio-demographic and habits such as tobacco, alcohol, physical exercise and diet. It can include genetic information when available.

With all these inputs the NPG provides a recommended nutritional plan for a given person to be followed along a certain period.

2. *Personalized Menu Planner (PMP)*. Given a nutritional plan, either coming from the previous subsystem or directly provided by a nutritionist, this sub-system search on food databases for the menus better combining to fit the target nutritional plan. The result is a personalized menu for a given period of time. In Diet4You project, this system is also based on CBR. The system

retrieves and adapts dishes to be included in the menu until it is considered that the plan is satisfied. This subsystem includes several components as well:

- *Cultural styles*: Is a knowledge-based component that can manage the different cultural eating styles regarding how meals distribute along day (Mediterranean, British, ...)
- *Restrictions*: Is a knowledge-based component that permits nutritionists to express nutritional restrictions (like no sugars for diabetic patients), specific allergies of the person that cannot be included in the proposal of dishes of the recommended nutritional plan
- *Preferences*: Including user limitations based on personal criteria that will be taken into account as far as possible, trying to avoid proposed menus containing the ingredients excluded by the user.

Thus, the Diet4You system is composed of two subsystems NPG and PMP both combined to give the person guidelines on how to eat for a certain period of time to achieve certain given goals (reduce cholesterol, feed better, improve healthy lifestyle, etc.).

4 Formalization of the Nutritional Plan

A nutritional plan contains the specification of the proportions of families of foods to be taken during a certain period of time. A nutritional plan is defined as the triplet:

$$\mathcal{N} = <F, T, Q>$$

where,

- $F = (\pi_1, ..., \pi_N)$ is a vector containing the recommended balance of food families to be taken along a certain period of time.
- $\pi_{f, f \in \{1: N\}}$ is the proportion of food family F_f recommended, such that $(\sum_{f=1: N} \pi_f = 1)$, given a set of N foods families $\mathcal{F} = \{F_1, ..., F_N\}$ (i.e., fruits, proteins, etc.)
- $T = [t_0, t_f]$ is the period of time where the diet must be followed
- Q indicates the total quantity of food in Kcal to be intaken along the whole diet.

The quantity Q is needed due to the fact that food proportions are different for children, young or elderly people.

5 Innovative Components of Diet4You

The goal of PMP system is to search in a background database, entitled Food Proportion Data Base (FPDB), a combination of food and dishes appropriate for breakfast, lunch or dinner that fits Q in a time period T and balanced according to F distribution. The system retrieves from FPDB (the reference food database used as background in Diet4You) the dishes whose global composition aggregates to the balance of foods prescribed in the nutritional plan. Indeed, every single dish might contain more or less percentage of a certain food family than the one specified in the nutritional plan. Thus, the possible menus generated at this step propose combinations of the different family of foods in the proportion specified by the nutritional plan, structured in several prepared dishes (like roasted chicken or cheesecake).

5.1 Hard Nutritional Restrictions Management

The Personalized Menu Planner must deal with additional restrictions to be satisfied by the final recommendation. Restrictions specify that some foods or families are not allowed for a certain person. According to *health conditions* due to *medical reasons*, the nutritionist may impose some restrictions in the design of the menu. For example, for diabetic patients, avoiding sugars, or refined flours might be mandatory, as avoiding saturated fats might be mandatory for persons with cholesterol.

In addition, known *allergies* of the person, like some nuts in determined people, can be managed as well by declaring the ingredients that must be avoided in the proposed menu.

Finally, some *cultural features* of the person, like avoiding meat for a vegetarian person, avoiding pork meat for a Muslim, can be managed as well, by using same mechanisms.

Diet4You is behaving very respectfully with all kinds of hard restriction and guarantees that the proposed menu will not include a single dish containing restricted ingredients or food families. This strategy is implemented by filtering the food database and building the personalized menu over the remaining dishes.

5.2 User Preferences

Another interesting feature of the system is the management of the user preferences. A *user preference* expresses that a person likes or dislikes some kind of food. For example, some person could dislike the fish or the chicken. The system takes into account the negative preferences declared by the person, by minimizing the probability that dishes containing these ingredients are selected for the PMP component to compose the final menu. In this case there is no guarantee that the disliked food is completely eliminated from the dishes in the proposed menu, because the final DRIs of the food must be ensured, but the dishes containing these ingredients will be avoided as much as possible in the solution. This will be internally managed by introducing penalization of associated dishes.

5.3 Cultural Eating Styles

There is a *cultural factor* in the nutrition habits of a person according to where the person lives. For instance, in a Mediterranean country, the breakfast usually contains calories and few proteins, the lunch is usually basically concentrating proteins, and the dinner has less proteins and more vegetables or fruits. However, a person living in an Anglo-Saxon-style country, will have more proteinous breakfast, a light lunch with vegetables and not much calories, and finally a dinner with more proteins.

The nutritional plan is divided into sub-plans for each one of the meals during a day: breakfast, lunch and dinner in Mediterranean or Anglo-Saxon styles, but it could contain 5 or 2 meals a day according to the cultural context. The percentages of family foods in each sub-plan concentrate the nutrients in particular sub-plans according to the cultural habits definition. The personal menu planer is optimized at the local level of each sub-plan and the whole resulting menu fits the global nutritional plan originally prescribed.

5.4   Personal Menu Planner

The personal menu planner (PMP) is mainly implemented following the cycle of Case-Based Reasoning.

Given a nutritional plan for a certain individual $i : \nu_i = <F_i, T_i, Q_i>$, and considering that the F_i vector contains the N families of food resulting from a certain level of granularity determined in the reference food ontology:

1. *Pre-processing step.* Pre-process the DB in order that all food families have equivalent units in Kcal, the standard unit most commonly used to specify diets. Usually, the database uses different measurement units for each food family like Kcal for sugars or grams for vegetables. Equivalences are first of all used to transform the database into vectors of proportions of Kcal per food family and the quantity of a portion in Kcal as well. Thus, all p_{d_f} will express the proportion of Kcal. From now on, we will refer to this transformed data base as Food Proportions Data Base (FPDB). The FPDB contains a set of prepared dishes or simple foods, with the quantities considered as a standard portion and their decomposition in F families. FPDB provides the following information of a given dish d:
   - $p_d = (p_{d_1}, \ldots, p_{d_N})$ where p_{d_f} is the proportion of food family F_f contained in one standard portion of dish d $(f = 1{:}N)$.
   - q_d is the quantity associated to one standard portion of dish d, in grams or cups or the corresponding measurement unit.
2. *Retrieval step.* After the previous step, p_d is a vector of proportions and thus, it is directly comparable with F_i. Determine a suitable distance for comparison. Since both are vectors of proportions, the Euclidean distance is suitable to that purpose. Use the FPDB as the case base to identify candidate dishes with their corresponding p_d close to F_i required in the nutritional plan. Sort the elements in FPDB into $FPDB^* = \{d_{(k)} \mid d_{(k)} \in FPDB \land d(p_{d_{(k)}}, F_i) \leq d(p_{d_{(k+1)}}, F_i)\}$. Candidates will be in the first positions of $FPDB^*$.
3. *Reuse step.* Implement the reuse step of CBR by adapting the candidate solutions contained in $FPDB^*$ to the recommendation to be presented to the end-user in form of complete menus for the period T_i. As a first trial, a simple version of this mechanism is presented, building complete menus

for $T_i = 1$, *i.e.*, a single day, as a first step to the general solution where larger periods will be considered. Solving the problem along one single day, the extension to several days is not difficult. Q_i is the total quantity of kcal to be ingested during T_i. Given the candidate solutions $d \in FPDB^*$, it will hold that $q_d < Q_i$ and some adaptation strategy is required to combine the first elements in $FPDB^*$ in such a way that S (the resulting solution menu) contains the first elements in $FPDB^*$ and $\sum_{\forall d \in S} q_d = Q_i$. Elaboration of menus requires no repetition of dishes along same day. For achieving this goal an iterative process of retrieving and adapting is computed until the nutritional plan is satisfied. At each iteration, the candidate solutions $d \in FPDB^*$ are sequentially included in the menu, and the corresponding q_d are subtracted from the Q_i associated to the nutritional plan. The plan is satisfied when $card(S)$ is such that the $Q_i - \sum_{\forall d \in S} q_d$ is minimum. In previous works [16,17] three strategies were proposed: the Single Candidates Generation (SCG), the iterative Candidates Generation (ICG) and the Decomposed Nutritional Plans (DNP), which is a refinement of iCG. From the preliminary evaluation of all strategies, the iCG strategy obtained the best results, and hence, it is the one used.

The iCG strategy retrieves d and updates F_i and Q_i at every iteration according to the quantities of food families consumed with the selected dish d incorporated into the menu and it re-computes $FPDB^*$ accordingly before subsequent iteration. The process is as follows:

1. Include the first dish d from $FPDB^*$ into the resulting menu S.
2. Compute $E = Q_i - q_d$.
3. if $E \geq 0$, eliminate d from $FPDB^*$, update $Q_i = E$, and compute the quantity of food families corresponding to one portion of d : $(q_1 \ldots q_N)$, being $q_f = q_d \times p_{d_f}$, compute the quantities of food families required in the nutritional plan $(Q_1 \ldots Q_N)$, with $Q_f = Q_i \times \pi_{f_i}$, build the residual quantities: $(R_1 \ldots R_N)$, with $R_f = Q_f - q_f$, and update F_i with $F_{f_i} = R_f / Q_i$, recompute $FPDB^*$ and repeat (go to step 1).
4. If $E < 0$, reduce the portion of d to be included into the menu: $q_d = Q_i$ and stop.

5.5 Human and Artificial Intelligence Components Interaction

The system Diet4You currently provides an interaction of several components and elements originated from the interplay between humans and artificial intelligence. In the proposed system, the knowledge and cognitive reasoning from nutritionists is provided for the specification of the *nutritional plan*, the *hard nutritional restrictions*, and the different *cultural eating styles*.

On the other hand, the end user of the system provides his/her personal *soft constraints*, *i.e.*, *preferences*, for some type of foods, that the system will try to satisfy as much as possible in the final configured menu.

The reasoning process takes into account this interplay, and it is implemented by the menu planner. The menu planner is using a *cognitive approach* resembling the human reasoning in an artificial system by mimicking the *analogical reasoning* of humans. Similar menu plans are retrieved from the case base (collection of experienced menus), and then are adapted to fit the *personalized menu* according to the preferences and cultural eating styles of the final user. The sub-plan manager combines the information from the different sub-plans (for each meal of the day) to generate the final menu plan for a full day.

6   An Example of Application

Currently, the FNDDS and FPED databases offered by USDA [18] are used as the source knowledge for the nutritional prescription, as it was in the previous work [16,17]. FPED (Food Patterns Equivalents Database) [4] is a DB that maps the food and drinks of the FNDDS into 38 food patterns indicating the corresponding recommended quantity of each pattern. In these 38 food patterns, there are 8 main patterns and the rest are subdivisions so as to facilitate detailed data analysis.

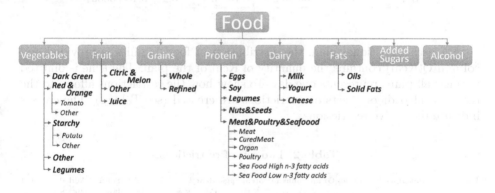

Fig. 2. Food family ontology

This classification into food families (see Fig. 2) is used as the reference ontology to group foods and dishes from a nutritional point of view. The $\mathcal{F}$ set of food families, is determined from the reference ontology, by selecting the appropriate horizontal cut of the concepts network. In this work, experts suggested to consider the first level categories shown in Fig. 2 and $\mathcal{F} = \{Fruit, Vegetables, Grains, Proteins, Dairy, Fats, Sugars\}$. Alcohol is discarded as it is considered in a non-healthy diet.

A pre-processing step, including some reasoning on the food ontology, is needed in order to specify all the measurements in the same unit and impute missing recommended quantities (see more details in [16,17]). In this case, the selected unit to express total energy of a dish is Kcal. After that, the foods are transformed into proportion of Kcal per each food family, becoming the Food Proportion Database (FPDB). The quantities and energy associated to a portion of each food or dish to be included in the menu are provided from FNDDS database. Let $\mathcal{F} = \{$ *Vegetables, Fruit, Grains, Proteins, Dairy, Fats, Sugars* $\}$ be the reference food families extracted from the food ontology. Four nutritional plans and two types of restrictions are used. The first plan Nutritionist is a general nutritional plan defined by an expert of nutrition. Other plans come from an adaptation of the data presented by National Geographic [6] regarding data from FAO (Food and Agriculture Organization of United Nations). The plans, World, Spain and USA represent the mean of what the world, Spain and USA citizens eat daily. The four plans are shown in Table 1.

Table 1. Average balance of food families in standard diets of different countries

Plan	Fruit	Veg.	Grain	Prot	Dairy	Fat	Sug.	Q(Kcal)
Nutritionist	0.15	0.15	0.15	0.25	0.05	0.2	0.05	2300
World	0.1	0.15	0.25	0.2	0.05	0.2	0.05	3000
Spain	0.05	0.1	0.2	0.2	0.1	0.3	0.05	3000
USA	0.03	0.06	0.22	0.16	0.1	0.25	0.18	3500

For each nutritional plan, the distribution of food families is provided and column Q(Kcal) contains the quantity of Kcal of the plan. The time is omitted because all plans represents one day. To show how the restrictions affects to the recommended diets, 2 sets of restrictions are created (see Table 2). The crosses indicate the active restrictions.

Table 2. Two sets of restrictions

Diet	Fruit	Juice	Vegetables	Grain	Refined	Protein	Eggs	Meat & Poultry & Seafood	Dairy	Fats	Solid fats	Added sugars	Alcohol
Diabetic				×							×	×	×
Vegetarian							×	×	×				×

Note that the restrictions can be defined in any food family even if they are from different granularity and a restriction of a food family directly affects all its subfamilies. The first set of restrictions called *diabetic* contains restrictions for persons that have problems related with insulin in their metabolism and they need to restrict the raise of glucose in blood. Therefore, the restriction is affecting the *added sugars* food family and the resulting recommendations limits the foods with high level of sugar (added sugars), simple carbohydrates as the *refined grains* and *saturated fats* represented in the solid fats family. The second set represents a personal choice related with both a life style and cultural issues like being *vegetarian* and therefore, the menu cannot contain any animal product: *protein* and *dairy* are the most affected food families. In *protein* family,

Table 3. Generated menus by the application of the nutritional plans with different sets of restrictions and different cultural eating styles

Plan	No Restrictions	Diabetic	Vegetarian
Nutritionist Original Plan: <[0.15; 0.15; 0.15; 0.25, 0.05, 0.2 ; 0.05]; [2300]> Diabetic Adapted Plan: <[0.158; 0.158; 0.263; 0.053; 0.21; 0]; [2300]> Vegetarian Adapted Plan: <[0.158; 0.158; 0.263; 0; 0.21 ; 0.053]; [2300]>	Sweet&sour chicken or turkey 252 Chicken patty/nuggets (breaded), pasta & 193 tomato sauce, fruit, dessert (frozen meal) Double cheeseburger (1/4lb each), mayon- 300 naise/ salad dressing, bun Pie,tofu&fruit 216 Nut mixture & dried fruit & seeds 9.6 <[0.14; 0.16; 0.16; 0.24; 0.02; 0.21; 0.06]; [2300]>	Rice,brown&beans 239 Shrimp salad 182 Oriental party mix: peanuts, sesame, rice, 112 green peas Fruit salad, salad dressing/mayonnaise 188 Chicken & vegetables in cream/white sauce 255 Marinated fish(Ceviche) 226 Mixed fruit juice & yogurt, babyfood 128 Salty snacks,corn 16 <[0.16; 0.16; 0.16; 0.24; 0.05; 0.21; 0]; [2300]>	Rice,brown,&beans 239 Bean cake 32 Rice&beans 239 Barley soup, sweet, Asian 300 Pie,raspberry cream 216 Sandwich spread, meat substitute type 60 Hummus 120 Banana, chocolate-covered with nuts 145 Luncheon slice,meatless 56 Loaf, lentil 47 Brown nut gravy, meatless 56.7 <[0.17; 0.15; 0.15; 0.25; 0 ; 0.21; 0.07]; [2300]>
World Original Plan: <[0.1; 0.15; 0.25; 0.2 ; 0.05; 0.2 ; 0.05]; [3000]> Diabetic Adapted Plan: <[0.11; 0.158; 0.263; 0.21; 0.053; 0.21; 0.0]; [3000]> Vegetarian Adapted Plan: <[0.11; 0.158; 0.263; 0.21; 0; 0.21; 0.053]; [3000]>	Tuna melt sandwich 150 Chicken patty sandwich & cheese, bun, let- 300 tuce, tomato and spread Sweet&sour chicken or turkey 252 Cake,raisin-nut 118 Nachos & meat,cheese & sour cream 300 Nut mixture & dried fruit & seeds 24.3 <[0.08; 0.16; 0.25; 0.20; 0.05; 0.23; 0.04]; [3000]>	Oriental party mix: peanuts, sesame, rice, 112 green peas 239 Rice,brown,with beans 182 Shrimp salad 160 Tabbouleh 189 Rice,brown,& dark green vegetables 208 Crab salad 234 Oat meal & fruit,cooked 128 Mixed fruit juice &yogurt, babyfood 71 Salty snacks,corn 244.8 Chicken & vegetables in cream / white sauce <[0.07; 0.20; 0.28; 0.21; 0.04; 0.20; 0]; [3000]>	Rice dessert bar, non dairy,carob covered 113 Oriental party mix: peanuts, sesame, rice, 112 green peas 239 Rice, brown & beans 182 Granola, homemade 239 Rice & beans 239 Barley soup, sweet, Asian 300 Cranberry salad,congealed 252 Rice, white,&lentils 207 Pie or tart 22.3 <[0.10; 0.16; 0.26; 0.21; 0 ; 0.21; 0.06]; [3000]>
Spain Original Plan: <[0.05; 0.1 ; 0.2 ; 0.2 ; 0.1 ; 0.3 ; 0.05]; [3000]> Diabetic Adapted Plan: <[0.053; 0.11; 0.21; 0.21 0.11; 0.32; 0]; [3000]> Vegetarian Adapted Plan: <[0.055; 0.11 ; 0.22 ; 0 ; 0.33 ; 0.055]; [3000]>	Corn meal dressing w/ chicken/turkey w/ 160 vegetables Spaghetti w/corned beef, Puerto Rican 215 Egg,cheese&sausage griddle cake sandwich 199 Cake,raisin-nut 118 Vegetables&cheese in pizza 103 Topping from meat pizza 164 Kellogg's Nutri-Grain Fruit & Nut Bar 32 Nut mixture &dried fruit&seeds 5.4 <[0.05; 0.12; 0.20; 0.20; 0.10; 0.30; 0.04]; [3000]>	Oriental party mix: peanuts, sesame, rice, 112 green peas Shrimp salad 182 Rice,brown &beans 239 Crab salad 208 Salty snacks,corn 71 Fruit salad, salad dressing/mayonnaise 188 Chicken&vegetables in cream/white sauce 255 Milk, dry, reconstituted 244 Imitation cheese 42 Milk, evaporated, skim 13.8 <[0.10; 0.14; 0.19; 0.23; 0.06; 0.29; 0]; [3000]>	Rice dessert bar,non dairy,carob covered 113 Bean cake 32 Luncheon slice, meatless 56 Granola, homemade 122 Brown nut gravy, meatless 90 Rice,brown & beans 239 Cookie, peanut butter, chocolate-coated 63 Rice&beans 239 Rice pudding with coconut milk, Puerto Ri- 256 can Bean dip 21.2 <[0.10; 0.16; 0.26; 0.21; 0 ; 0.21; 0.06]; [3000]>
USA Original Plan: <[0.03; 0.06; 0.22; 0.16; 0.1 ; 0.25 ; 0.18]; [3500]> Diabetic Adapted Plan: <[0.034; 0.068; 0.25; 0.18; 0.11 ; 0.284; 0]; [3500]> Vegetarian Adapted Plan: <[0.033; 0.066; 0.244; 0.17; 0 ; 0.277; 0.2]; [3500]>	Cake,nut 84 TWIX Peanut Butter Cookie Bars 42 Bread,fruit 57 Bean cake 32 Cake,allfruits 242 Double cheeseburger,tomato & catsup, bun 171 Sausage griddle cake sandwich 135 Cake,peanut butter 210.3 <[0.03; 0.02; 0.23; 0.14; 0.10; 0.29; 0.19]; [3500]>	Oriental party mix: peanuts, sesame, rice, 112 green peas 239 Rice,brown& beans 208 Crab salad 71 Salty snacks,corn 188 Chicken & vegetables in cream/white sauce 8 Fruit salad & salad dressing/mayonnaise 190 Rice,brown, corn, babyfood 244 Crunchy snacks,corn, babyfood 114 Milk,dry,reconstituted, NFS Clam 32 sauce,white NFS 128 Milk,evaporated,skim 38.5 Rice,brow & dark green veg. <[0.10; 0.14; 0.23; 0.22; 0.07; 0.24; 0]; [3500]>	Bean cake 32 NatureValley Crunchy Granola Bar 42 Granola bar,NFS 43 Cookie,peanut butter,chocolate-coated 63 Kashi GOLEAN Crunchy Bars 46 Granola,homemade 122 Boost,nutritional drink,ready-to-drink 256 Sweet bread dough, bean paste, meatless, 103 steamed Ensure,nutritional shake,ready-to-drink 252 Nature Valley Chewy Trail Mix Granola 35 Bar Rice dessert bar,non dairy,carob covered 113 Fresh corn custard, Puerto Rican 116.8 <[0.04; 0.09; 0.22; 0.16; 0 ; 0.29; 0.19]; [3500]>

those subfamilies that refer to an animal source are restricted (meat, poultry, organ, seafood, cured meat and eggs).

Table 3 shows the twelve generated menus for the four nutritional plans using the different restrictions and the different cultural eating styles. This table contains the dishes and foods recommended by PMP listed together with their quantity equivalent to a portion of the dish to be included into the menu, expressed in grams. For each complete menu suggested by the system, the total Kcal and percentages of whole diet are shown. First column represents the recommended menus when no restrictions are applied and the second and third using the *diabetic* and *vegetarian* restrictions.

The recommended menus for *diabetics* have in common more proteins from poultry, fish, legumes and vegetables while with no restrictions the presence of fish and legumes was practically non-existent. The *vegetarian* menus have an increment of beans and nuts as protein source. The nutritionist plan is quite rich in protein and the resulting menu without restrictions is plenty of meat. When the restrictions are included, in the diabetic case where the solid fats are restricted, the meat is substituted by fish and in the vegetarian case are substituted with legumes, and meat-substitute types. The vegetarian from the USA plan is plenty of cereal bars containing cereals, sugars and fats that are the main percentages of food families.

7   Conclusions

In this work, we have introduced the user preferences, and the cultural eating styles components, which modify the usual operation of the menu planner. To implement the cultural. Eating styles, the different plans are sliced in sub-plans, which are optimised according to the cultural eating styles, which means that the different type of food are distributed in a particular and cultural way.

In addition, the system takes into account the negative preferences declared by the person, by minimizing the probability that dishes containing these ingredients are selected for the PMP component to compose the final menu.

Through the preliminary evaluation with the nutritionists, it seems that the results of the system are quite accurate and provide reasonable nutritional plans which satisfies the different constraints and other personal characteristics.

To the best of our knowledge the current Diet4You systems is the first complete system integrating all these restrictions, user preferences, and cultural eating styles in the recommendation of personalized nutritional plans in the literature.

One the future lines of the work will be the integration of profile nutritional plans defined by the nutritionists in the system. The nutritional profiles are defined upon profile-diets which have been identified through the application of previous data-driven components.

Acknowledgements. This work has been partially supported by the project Diet4You (TIN2014-60557-R), the Spanish Thematic Network MAPAS [TIN2017-90567-REDT (MINECO/FEDER EU)], and the Consolidated Research Group Grant from AGAUR (Generalitat de Catalunya) IDEAI-UPC (AGAUR SGR2017-574).

References

1. The automatic meal planner-eat this much homepage. http://www.eatthismuch.com. Accessed Feb 2019
2. Dri calculator for healthcare professionals homepage. https://fnic.nal.usda.gov/fnic/dri-calculator/. Accessed Feb 2019
3. Menu planner homepage. http://hp2010.nhlbihin.net/menuplanner/menu.cgi. Accessed Feb 2019
4. Bowman, S., Clemens, J., et al.: Food patterns equivalents database 2011–12: methodology and user guide. Food Surveys Research Group. Agricultural Research Service, USDA (2014)
5. Cortés, U., Sànchez-Marrà, M., Ceccaroni, L., R-Roda, I., Poch, M.: Artificial intelligence and environmental decision support systems. Appl. Intell. **13**, 77–91 (2000)
6. National Geographic: What the world eats. https://www.nationalgeographic.com/what-the-world-eats/. Accessed 14 May 2018
7. Gibert, K., Valls, A., Batet, M.: Introducing semantic variables in mixed distance measures: impact on hierarchical clustering. Knowl. Inf. Syst. **40**(3), 559–593 (2014)
8. Han, J., Kamber, M., Pei, J.: Data Mining: Concepts and Techniques. Elsevier (2011)
9. Khan, A., Hoffmann, A.: An advanced artificial intelligence tool for menu design. Nutr. Health **17**(1), 43–53 (2003)
10. Little, J.: Models and managers: the concept of a decision calculus. Manag. Sci. **50**(Suppl. 12), 1841–1853 (2004)
11. De Mantaras, R.L., McSherry, D., Bridge, D., et al.: Retrieval, reuse, revision and retention in case-based reasoning. Knowl. Eng. Rev. **20**(03), 215–240 (2005)
12. Marakas, G.: Decision Support Systems in the 21st Century, vol. 134. Prentice Hall (2003)
13. Marling, C., Petot, G., Sterling, L.: Integrating case-based and rule-based reasoning to meet multiple design constraints. Comput. Intell. **15**(3), 308–332 (1999)
14. Poch, M., Comas, J., et al.: Designing and building real environmental decision support systems. Environ. Model. Softw. **19**(9), 857–873 (2004)
15. Power, D.: Decision support systems: a historical overview. In: Burstein, F., Holsapple, C.W. (eds.) Handbook on Decision Support Systems 1, pp. 121–140. Springer, Heidelberg (2008). https://doi.org/10.1007/978-3-540-48713-5_7
16. Sevilla-Villanueva, B., Gibert, K., Sànchez-Marrè, M.: Generating complete menus from nutritional prescriptions by using advanced CBR and real food databases. Front. Artif. Intell. Appl. Ser. **300**, 166–175 (2017)
17. Sevilla-Villanueva, B., Gibert, K., Sànchez-Marrè, M.: Including hard restrictions into Diet4You menu planner. Front. Artif. Intell. Appl. Ser. **308**, 190 (2018)
18. USDA: USDA department of agriculture, agricultural research service, nutrient data laboratory. http://www.ars.usda.gov/ba/bhnrc/ndl. Accessed Feb 2019

Robust Heading Estimation in Mobile Phones

Fernando E. Casado[1](✉)(iD), Adrián Nieto[2], Roberto Iglesias[1](iD),
Carlos V. Regueiro[3](iD), and Senén Barro[1](iD)

[1] CiTIUS (Centro Singular de Investigación en Tecnoloxías da Información),
Universidade de Santiago de Compostela, 15782 Santiago de Compostela, Spain
{fernando.estevez.casado,roberto.iglesias.rodriguez,senen.barro}@usc.es
[2] Situm Technologies S.L., 15782 Santiago de Compostela, Spain
adrian.nieto@situm.es
[3] Department of Computer Engineering, Universidade da Coruña,
15071 A Coruña, Spain
carlos.vazquez.regueiro@udc.es

Abstract. Nowadays, mobile phones are used more and more for purposes that have nothing to do with phone calls or simple data transfers. One example is indoor inertial navigation. Within this task, a central problem is to obtain a good estimation of the user heading, robust to magnetic interference and changes in the position of the mobile device with respect to the user. In this paper we propose a method able to provide a robust user heading as a result of detecting the relative position of the mobile phone with respect to the user, together with a heuristic computation of the heading from different Euler representations. We have performed an experimental validation of our proposal comparing it with the Android default compass. The results confirm the good performance of our method.

Keywords: Heading estimation · Mobile phones · Indoor navigation ·
Inertial sensor fusion · Pattern classification · Attitude estimation

1 Introduction

The progressive incorporation of sensors on mobile phones opens important opportunities towards the development of applications that use these sensors in an increasing number of domains: healthcare, leisure, education, sport, etc. One example of this is pedestrian indoor localization using the inertial sensors of the smartphone (accelerometer, gyroscope and magnetometer) [6,9].

One popular way of dealing with indoor positioning with mobile phones is Pedestrian Dead Reckoning (PDR). PDR works by estimating successive positions starting from a known location, based on a rough calculation of the heading and the distance walked. The total distance walked can be obtained by counting the number of steps and then multiplying them by the individual step length [6].

© Springer Nature Switzerland AG 2019
J. M. Ferrández Vicente et al. (Eds.): IWINAC 2019, LNCS 11487, pp. 180–190, 2019.
https://doi.org/10.1007/978-3-030-19651-6_18

However, giving an accurate estimation of the user heading is not straightforward. Existing heading estimation proposals do not face the problem of how to deal with the change of the relative position of the phone with respect to the user. Thus, moving the phone changing its orientation would be automatically considered a change of the user's walking direction. Besides this problem, the use of the inertial sensors to estimate the heading is not except from other issues, such as noisy readings, drifts, etc. Thus, in the case of the magnetometer, the magnetic field is strongly perturbed by surrounding artificial fields [5].

In this work we propose a novel heading estimation method which combines the processing of the inertial sensor signals with machine learning techniques and quaternion algebra. We use quaternions in order to project the sensor readings into an inertial reference system (Earth frame) and get the device attitude. In this way, we avoid Euler angles limitations and minimize noise distortions from inertial sensors. We also recognize the relative position of the device with respect to the user applying machine learning techniques. Finally, our approach also introduce several filters in order to improve the quality of the estimations. One of them detects magnetic field interferences, thus excluding the magnetic field information from the attitude calculation when the field is distorted. Another important filter smooths the final heading output by applying moving averages, thus minimizing the oscillations produced when walking in non-ideal situations.

This paper is organized as follows. Section 2 describes the process of obtaining the device attitude. Section 3 explains the how we recognize the relative position of the mobile phone with respects to the user. Section 4 describes how final heading is obtained. Section 5 presents an experimental analysis of our proposal. Finally, Sect. 6 gives some conclusions of our work.

2 Attitude Estimation

The attitude of the phone is obtained from the 9-dimensional time series composed by the outputs of its three tri-axis inertial sensors: accelerometer ($^S\mathbf{a}_t$), gyroscope ($^S\boldsymbol{\omega}_t$) and magnetometer ($^S\mathbf{m}_t$), which respectively measure the acceleration, the angular velocity and the magnetic field experienced by the device:

$$\mathbf{s}_t = \begin{bmatrix} ^S\mathbf{a}_t & ^S\boldsymbol{\omega}_t & ^S\mathbf{m}_t \end{bmatrix}, \tag{1}$$

where t is the temporal index. We work with a sampling frequency of 50 Hz.

2.1 Quaternion Calculation

We work with two reference systems: (1) the sensor/local one, S (device frame), relative to the screen of the phone, and (2) the inertial reference system, E (Earth frame). The readings of the sensors are provided in the local frame and we want to obtain the attitude of the device in the inertial-Earth frame. This inertial frame is the East North Up (ENU) coordinate system. We use quaternions to represent this attitude. A quaternion is a four-dimensional vector that represents the transformation amongst two reference systems, A and B, as a rotation of an angle θ around a three-dimensional axis $\mathbf{u} = [u_x\ u_y\ u_z]$, such that:

$$
{}_B^A\mathbf{q} = [q_0\ \ q_1\ \ q_2\ \ q_3] = \left[\cos\theta \quad -u_x\sin\frac{\theta}{2} \quad -u_y\sin\frac{\theta}{2} \quad -u_z\sin\frac{\theta}{2}\right], \quad (2)
$$

being ${}_B^A\mathbf{q}$ the normalized quaternion that represents the orientation of frame B relative to frame A. Following this notation we will use ${}_E^S\mathbf{q}_t$ to refer to the current value of the quaternion that represents the orientation of the inertial/Earth frame E, relative to the sensor/local frame S. Applying Madgwick's method [2], we can obtain that quaternion at each instant t applying the following expression:

$$
{}_E^S\mathbf{q}_t = {}_E^S\mathbf{q}_{t-1} + \gamma\left(-\mu\frac{\nabla f}{\|\nabla f\|}\right) + (1-\gamma)\left(\frac{1}{2}{}_E^S\mathbf{q}_{t-1} \otimes {}^S\tilde{\boldsymbol{\omega}}_t\right) \times \Delta t, \quad (3)
$$

where $\otimes$ is the quaternion product, $\tilde{\boldsymbol{\omega}}_t = [0\ \ {}^S\boldsymbol{\omega}_t] \in \mathbb{R}^4$ and f is a function to optimize such that:

$$
f = \alpha\left[\left({}_E^S\mathbf{q}^* \otimes {}^E\mathbf{g} \otimes {}_E^S\mathbf{q}\right) - {}^S\tilde{\mathbf{a}}\right] + \beta\left[\left({}_E^S\mathbf{q}^* \otimes {}^E\mathbf{b} \otimes {}_E^S\mathbf{q}\right) - {}^S\tilde{\mathbf{m}}\right], \quad (4)
$$

being ${}^E\mathbf{g}$ the unit gravity vector in the Earth frame (${}^E\mathbf{g} = [0\ \ 0\ \ 0\ \ 1]$), ${}^E\mathbf{m}$ the Earth's magnetic field (${}^E\mathbf{b} = [0\ \ b_x\ \ 0\ \ b_z]$), ${}^S\tilde{\mathbf{a}} = [0\ \ {}^S\mathbf{a}]$ and ${}^S\tilde{\mathbf{m}} = [0\ \ {}^S\mathbf{m}]$.

2.2   Magnetometer Calibration

Magnetometer measurements ${}^S\mathbf{m}$ can be represented as follows:

$$
{}^S\mathbf{m} = \mathbf{w} \cdot \left({}_E^S\mathbf{q}^* \otimes {}^E\mathbf{b} \otimes {}_E^S\mathbf{q}\right) + \mathbf{v} + \mathbf{u}, \quad (5)
$$

where $\mathbf{v}$ and $\mathbf{w}$ are, respectively, additive and multiplicative interference [7] and $\mathbf{u}$ is the sensor's random noise. Additive interference $\mathbf{v}$ consists of hard-iron effect and sensor offset, while multiplicative interference $\mathbf{w}$ consists of soft-iron effect, magnetometer non-orthogonality and unequal gains. Random noise $\mathbf{u}$ consists of random fluctuations, including excitation current, feedback circuit from inside the sensor and currents within coils outside the sensor. Considering all possible device frames, the universal set of geomagnetic fields in device frames can be illustrated as the blue sphere in Fig. 1. Multiplicative interference $\mathbf{w}$ makes the magnetic field gain different along different axis, turning the universal set into an ellipsoid, while noise $\mathbf{u}$ and additive interference $\mathbf{v}$ makes the universal set ellipsoid leave the original phone frame, as yellow ellipsoid shows. In other words, one magnetometer measurement ${}^S\mathbf{m}$ is one vector from the origin to a point of the yellow ellipsoid in Fig. 1. Thus, the correction of $\mathbf{w}$ and $\mathbf{v}$ distortions is equivalent to obtaining the yellow ellipsoid centre and parameters (radii and eigenvectors), and then recover the original sphere from the ellipsoid.

Any Android mobile phone that has a magnetometer provide a magnetic field calibration which corrects both additive and multiplicative distortions. However, it presents several problems. On the one hand, the Android calibration process

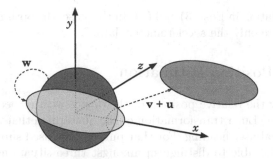

Fig. 1. Existing distortions in geomagnetic field measurement. (Color figure online)

runs in background assuming that the user is moving the phone enough to record omnidirectional data but, if it is not the case, the precision in estimating the calibration parameters decreases. On the other hand, the periodic calibration produces discontinuities in the data stream with high frequency. For these reasons, we decided to perform our own calibration process, which consists of three stages: First, omnidirectional data is collected in a fixed location, moving the phone in all directions during 1 min and recording at 50 Hz. Then, the ellipsoid is fitted using the algorithm proposed in [3], obtaining its centre ($\mathbf{v}$) and its parameters (from which we can obtain $\mathbf{w}^{-1}$) from the recorded data. Finally, any magnetometer reading $^S\mathbf{m}_t$ can be calibrated applying the following expression:

$$^S\tilde{\mathbf{m}}_t = \mathbf{w}^{-1} \cdot (^S\mathbf{m}_t - \mathbf{v}). \qquad (6)$$

2.3 Opportunistic Updates

Even though we calibrate the magnetometer readings, that does not prevent the natural magnetic distortions caused by the presence of pillars, escalators, computers, etc., in the environment, and which will alter the sensor readings. Our proposal to deal with this problem is to detect when large distortions occur and, in that case, ignore the magnetometer readings during the quaternion calculation. For that purpose, we study the variance of the norm of the magnetic field, $\left\|^S\mathbf{m}\right\|$, in time windows, comparing it with a threshold [4]:

$$\frac{1}{M+1} \sum_{k=t-M}^{t} \left(\left\|^S\mathbf{m}_k\right\| - \xi_{ref} \right)^2 < \gamma \qquad (7)$$

where M is the length of the time window, ξ_{ref} is the reference norm for the current window and γ is a threshold. The threshold γ is defined as the maximum deviation of the field during a static and undisturbed window. We use $\gamma = 15\ \mu T$ and $M = 50$, which is equivalent to 2.5 s when working at 50 Hz. The reference norm is defined at the beginning of the window as the mean of the M_{first} values of the static period. In our case, we consider $M_{first} = 15$. When a distortion is detected, the magnetometer readings are suppressed from the quaternion calculation in Eqs. (3) and (4). In this case, the optimization function f, Eq. (4), will use only the accelerometer data.

3   Relative Position Estimation

We need to know the relative position of the device with respect to the user in order to choose the Euler transformation of the quaternion that is the most suitable to get the real user heading. For that purpose, we used supervised learning to train a classifier able to distinguish amongst three situations: (1) mobile in hand, (2) mobile in the pocket or (3) unknown situation.

The classifier is built from the most representative features of the 9-dimensional time-series data s, Eq. (1). First, the time series is filtered and centred for noise reduction. Since most of the energy captured by the inertial sensors associated to human walking is bellow 3 Hz [10], we can apply a low-pass filter over the components in Eq. (1) to minimize the signal noise. Specifically, we use a 10th order Butterworth filter with a 3 Hz cut-off frequency. In this way, we remove the high-frequency components of the noise. The presence of a non-zero DC component can hide important information, especially in the frequency domain. To solve this issue, we apply a DC-bias filter to centre the signal. Features are calculated over the time window that comprises the last 100 sensor measurements: $\tilde{s}_t, \tilde{s}_{t-1}, \ldots, \tilde{s}_{t-99}$. We use an overlap of 50% between consecutive windows. Since we sample at 50 Hz, 100 samples correspond to 2 s. We chose this way of partitioning based on previous results [5,8].

Based on previous works [6,8], we collected a total of 46 features and applied feature selection, suppressing those redundant or irrelevant. The final subset is made up of just 4 variables: (a) the energy of the angular velocity norm [8], (b) the standard deviation of the angular velocity on the x-axis, (c) the standard deviation of the angular velocity on the y-axis, and (d) the standard deviation of the acceleration on the y-axis. The chosen classifier is a Support Vector Machine (SVM) trained with data of the mobile phone being carried in hand and in the pocket. The classifier provide probabilistic predictions, so that when the probability of the output is under 0.9, the system acts conservatively and considers it an unknown situation.

A last step is to distinguish whether the mobile phone is facing inwards or outwards when it is in the pocket. For that purpose, we analyse the acceleration in the z-axis in the last time window by simply computing its mean and looking at its sign. The sign is an unequivocal indicator of whether the device is placed with the screen facing inwards (negative sign) or outwards (positive sign) when the user is walking.

4   Heading Estimation

Combining the information obtained in Sects. 2 and 3, we are able to determine the user heading. Basically, the idea is to obtain the Euler angles ($\theta = [\theta_1, \theta_2, \theta_3]$) from the last value of the quaternion, Eq. (3). One of these angles will be the heading of the device. However, several representations of Euler angles can be obtained from the same quaternion depending on which of the twelve possible rotation sequences is assumed (xyz, xzy, yxz...) [1]. We have to select the best rotation sequence depending on the relative position of the mobile with respect to the user. Moreover, as we have explained in Sect. 1, the device heading will not always match the user heading. Therefore, we must apply a number of correction criteria in order to give a good user heading.

Given the quaternion q, its equivalent transformation matrix M can be expressed as [1]:

$$M = \begin{pmatrix} q_0{}^2 + q_1{}^2 - q_2{}^2 - q_3{}^2 & 2(q_1q_2 - q_0q_3) & 2(q_1q_3 + q_0q_2) \\ 2(q_1q_2 + q_0q_3) & q_0{}^2 - q_1{}^2 + q_2{}^2 - q_3{}^2 & 2(q_2q_3 - q_0q_1) \\ 2(q_1q_3 - q_0q_2) & 2(q_2q_3 + q_0q_1) & q_0{}^2 - q_1{}^2 - q_2{}^2 + q_3{}^2 \end{pmatrix}. \tag{8}$$

Any of the twelve rotation sequences can be obtained form M. In this work, we use three of these sequences: (1) zyx, (2) zxy and (3) zxz. For the first one, zyx, the three Euler angles $\Theta_{zyx} = [\theta_{1,zyx}, \theta_{2,zyx}, \theta_{3,zyx}]$ are defined as follows:

$$\Theta_{zyx} = \left[\tan^{-1}\left(\frac{m_{2,1}}{m_{1,1}}\right), \ \tan^{-1}\left(\frac{-m_{3,1}}{\sqrt{1-m_{3,1}{}^2}}\right), \ \tan^{-1}\left(\frac{m_{3,2}}{m_{3,3}}\right) \right], \tag{9}$$

where $m_{i,j}$ is the element in the ith row and the jth column of matrix M. For the second one, zxy, the three Euler angles are calculated as:

$$\Theta_{zxy} = \left[\tan^{-1}\left(\frac{-m_{1,2}}{m_{2,2}}\right), \ \tan^{-1}\left(\frac{m_{3,2}}{\sqrt{1-m_{3,2}{}^2}}\right), \ \tan^{-1}\left(\frac{-m_{3,1}}{m_{3,3}}\right) \right]. \tag{10}$$

Finally, for the third one, zxz, the three Euler angles are obtained as:

$$\Theta_{zxz} = \left[\tan^{-1}\left(\frac{m_{1,3}}{-m_{2,3}}\right), \ \tan^{-1}\left(\frac{\sqrt{1-m_{3,3}{}^2}}{m_{3,3}}\right), \ \tan^{-1}\left(\frac{m_{3,1}}{m_{3,2}}\right) \right]. \tag{11}$$

Euler angles from Eqs. (9) to (11) are given in radians, so we need to convert them to degrees (π rad $= 180°$). Once we know the Euler angles for the three rotation sequences, we can obtain the user heading, θ_u, by applying the set of rules from lines 7 to 18 in Algorithm 1.

If the device is in the pocket, the best rotation sequence we can use is zxz. We assume that the mobile is in an upright position and, therefore, we only need to differ whether it is facing inwards or outwards. With this aim, we check the sign of the acceleration in the z-axis (lines 8 to 11 in Algorithm 1). In the first case (facing inwards, negative sign), the device heading provided by $\theta_{1,zxz}$ match the user heading, whilst in the second case (facing outwards, positive sign) the device heading is exactly the opposite of the user heading.

When the device is in the hand, we distinguish three situations:

- If $\theta_{1,zyx}$ and $\theta_{1,zxy}$ match (giving a tolerance threshold γ_1), then the mobile is in the palm of the hand of user (line 13 in Algorithm 1). In this situation, the user heading matches the device heading.

Algorithm 1. User heading estimation.

---

1 $\theta_u = 0$
2 **while** *process is running* **do**
3   **get** last inertial data values s_t, Eq. (1)
4   **calibrate** magnetometer readings, Section 2.2
5   **get** relative position of the mobile using the SVM classifier, Section 3
6   **calculate** Euler angles from transformation matrix, Eq. (8)
7   **if** *smartphone in the pocket* **then**
8   **if** *sign of acceleration in z-axis < 0* **then**
9              $\theta_u = \theta_{1,zxz}$
10   **else**
11             $\theta_u = \theta_{1,zxz} + 180$
12   **else if** *smartphone in the hand* **then**
13   **if** $|\theta_{1,zyx} - \theta_{1,zxy}| < \gamma_1$ **or** $|\theta_{1,zxy} - \theta_{1,zyx}| < \gamma_1$ **then**
14             $\theta_u = \theta_{1,zyx}$
15   **else if** $|\theta_{1,zyx} - \theta_{1,zxy}| > (180 - \gamma_1)$ **or** $|\theta_{1,zxy} - \theta_{1,zyx}| > (180 - \gamma_1)$
        then
16             $\theta_u = \theta_u + \min(\Delta\theta_{1,zyx}, \Delta\theta_{1,zxy})$
17   **else if** $|\theta_{3,zyx} - 90| < \gamma_2$ **or** $|\theta_{3,zyx} - 270| < \gamma_2$ **then**
18             $\theta_u = \theta_u + \Delta\theta_{1,zxz}$
19   **smooth out** θ_u using moving averages and **save** the current value
20   **update** quaternion, Eq. (3)
21 **end**

- If $\theta_{1,zyx}$ and $\theta_{1,zxy}$ are the opposite (line 15 in Algorithm 1), then the phone is facing down. This situation is totally ambiguous, thus, we update θ_u by adding the minimum of the increases produced in $\theta_{1,zyx}$ and $\theta_{1,zxy}$ since the last iteration. We denote those increases as $\Delta\theta_{1,zyx}$ and $\Delta\theta_{1,zxy}$, respectively.
- If the mobile is in the hand but in a vertical position (line 17 in Algorithm 1), then we update the value of θ_u by adding the increase produced in $\theta_{1,zxz}$.

Any other situation is considered unknown, which means that the user heading will not be updated, thus maintaining its last value and assuming that the user is walking straight. In our experiments, we used $\gamma_1 = 2$ and $\gamma_2 = 15$. When the device is placed in the pocket, the fluctuation in the heading is much higher than if it is carried in the hand. In order to reduce that fluctuation, we apply a moving averages filter as a final step (line 26 in Algorithm 1) considering the last 100 values of θ_u, which is equivalent to 2 s iterating at 50 Hz.

5   Experimental Evaluation

To analyse the performance of our proposal, we carried out 12 different tests in which two different people have participated. We asked them to walk randomly carrying the mobile in several conditions: in the palm of their hands horizontally and vertically, in the front/back pockets with the screen facing inwards/outwards

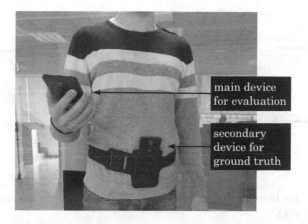

Fig. 2. Illustration of the two mobile devices used during the experimental evaluation.

and in the hand moving it randomly. We developed an Android application in order to record the inertial sensor data and process them to obtain the user heading. The smartphone used in all the experiments was a Nokia 6.1 with Android 9.0. The application performs all the processing stages in real time, working at 50 Hz. We also recorded the Android's compass for comparison purposes. Finally, in order to obtain a ground truth, we placed another phone in the trunk of the volunteer (Fig. 2) to get the real user heading using Google's ARCore. This technology is a visual inertial odometry framework that combines the inertial data with the information provided by the camera of the device.

Table 1 shows the root mean square error (RMSE) obtained in the experiments. As we can see, the Android compass deviates from ground truth more than double our approach does. The error committed by our proposal is due to artefacts such as differences (shift) in the sensor readings, owing to the specific position of the mobile phone in the pocket (right or left leg, the mobile is not perfectly vertical, etc.). This error is usually between 30 and 45 degrees. On the other hand, the fact of using moving averages to smooth the output causes a slight delay on the detection of sudden changes of heading. Figure 3 shows a visual representation of the performance of our proposal compared to the Android compass and the ground truth in three different scenarios.

Table 1. Root mean square error (RMSE) obtained in the experiments (in degrees).

	User 1	User 2	Total
Android compass	87.19	98.22	88.48
Our proposal	35.79	49.00	37.49

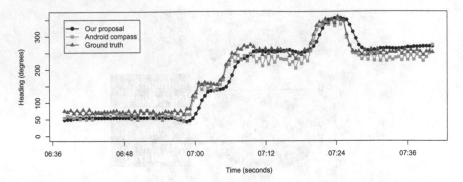

(a) The user walks through the corridors changing his heading when the mobile is in his hand (vertically).

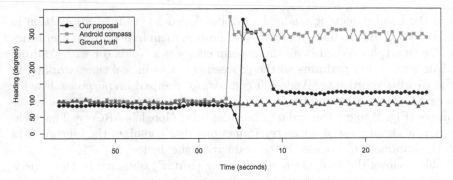

(b) The user walks straight with the mobile in the palm of the hand and, in the middle of the test, he puts it in his pocket.

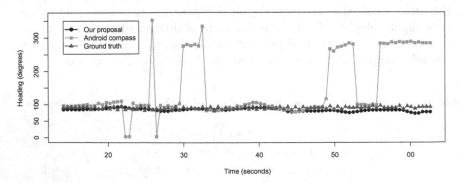

(c) The user walks straight with the mobile in hand moving it randomly.

Fig. 3. Performance of our proposal in three different tests.

6   Conclusions

The use of the inertial information in mobile phones to estimate the user heading is an important issue in indoor navigation, in particular, in Pedestrian Dead Reckoning techniques. Nevertheless, knowing the user heading is challenging due to sensor noise, magnetic interferences, attitude parametrization and the diversity of positions in which the mobile phone can be carried. In this paper we have developed a new method robust to the problems we just mentioned. Our method combines the processing of the inertial sensor data with machine learning techniques and quaternion algebra. We use quaternions to project the sensor readings into an inertial reference system (Earth frame). In this way, we obtain a robust attitude representation minimizing noise distortions from inertial sensors. We also recognize the relative position of the device with respect to the user (when the phone is carried in the hand or in the pocket) applying machine learning. In this way, we can give an accurate user heading by choosing the best Euler transformation from the quaternion representation and making opportunistic corrections in the device heading for each situation. Our approach also introduce filters in order to improve the quality of the estimations. The experimental results show the high performance achieved with our method.

Acknowledgment. This research has received financial support from AEI/FEDER (EU) grant number TIN2017-90135-R, as well as the *Consellería de Cultura, Educación e Ordenación Universitaria* and the European Regional Development Fund (ERDF) (accreditation 2016–2019, ED431G/01 and ED431G/08 and reference competitive group ED431C 2018/29). It has also been supported by the *Ministerio de Economa, Industria y Competitividad* in the *Industrial PhD* 2015 program.

References

1. Henderson, D.: Euler angles, quaternions, and transformation matricesworking relationships. NASA TM-74839, JSC-12960 (1977)
2. Madgwick, S.O., Harrison, A.J., Vaidyanathan, R.: Estimation of IMU and MARG orientation using a gradient descent algorithm. In: Proceedings of the IEEE International Conference on Rehabilitation Robotics (ICORR), pp. 1–7. IEEE (2011)
3. Petrov, Y.: Ellipsoid fit. MATLAB Central File Exchange. https://es.mathworks. com/matlabcentral/fileexchange/24693-ellipsoid-fit
4. Renaudin, V., Combettes, C.: Magnetic, acceleration fields and gyroscope quaternion (MAGYQ)-based attitude estimation with smartphone sensors for indoor pedestrian navigation. Sensors 14(12), 22864–22890 (2014)
5. Renaudin, V., Susi, M., Lachapelle, G.: Step length estimation using handheld inertial sensors. Sensors 12(7), 8507–8525 (2012)
6. Rodríguez, G., Casado, F.E., Iglesias, R., Regueiro, C.V., Nieto, A.: Robust step counting for inertial navigation with mobile phones. Sensors 18(9), 3157 (2018)
7. Shao, W., et al.: Location fingerprint extraction for magnetic field magnitude based indoor positioning. J. Sens. 2016, 1–16 (2016)

8. Susi, M., Renaudin, V., Lachapelle, G.: Motion mode recognition and step detection algorithms for mobile phone users. Sensors **13**(2), 1539–1562 (2013)
9. Yan, H., Shan, Q., Furukawa, Y.: RIDI: robust IMU double integration. In: Proceedings of the European Conference on Computer Vision (ECCV), pp. 621–636 (2018)
10. Zijlstra, W., Hof, A.L.: Displacement of the pelvis during human walking: experimental data and model predictions. Gait Posture **6**(3), 249–262 (1997)

Bioinspired Systems

Crowding Differential Evolution for Protein Structure Prediction

Daniel Varela and José Santos[✉]

Computer Science Department, University of A Coruña, A Coruña, Spain
{daniel.varela,jose.santos}@udc.es

Abstract. A hybrid combination between differential evolution and a local refinement of protein structures provided by fragment replacements was performed for protein structure prediction. The coarse-grained protein conformation representation of the Rosetta environment was used. Given the deceptiveness of the Rosetta energy model, an evolutionary computing niching method, crowding, was incorporated in the evolutionary algorithm with the aim to obtain optimized solutions that at the same time provide a set of diverse protein folds. Thus, the probability to obtain optimized conformations close to the native structure is increased.

1 Introduction

Protein Structure Prediction (PSP) remains as one of the major challenges in computational biology, since the protein native structure is related with its biological function. There are PSP methods that rely on the knowledge of resolved structures (3D structure is known), stored in databases like Protein Data Bank [7]. For example, when predicting the structure of a protein sequence, a common method is the search of proteins with homologous primary structure (amino acid sequence) in the databases, assuming that similar sequences have similar 3D structure. However, there is an increasing gap between the number (millions) of known protein sequences (result of multiple genome sequencing projects), and the limited number of proteins with resolved structure (hundreds of thousands). This is because wet-lab methods for resolving the location of protein atoms, like X-ray crystallography and NMR spectroscopy, are expensive, laborious and slow.

The "sequence/structure gap" is the reason of the importance of computational "ab initio" methods, that use only the protein primary sequence of amino acids to directly determine the final native structure. In fact, the final structure is assumed to be the one that minimizes the Gibbs free energy and it is also assumed that is determined only with the sequence of the primary structure [1].

Protein representation models typically use different simplifications with respect to real proteins, for example locating the amino acids in the pre-specified points of a grid (lattice models) or with models that can locate the amino acids and their atoms without such a restriction (off-lattice models). In simple lattice models, like the commonly used HP model [3], amino acids are categorized in only two classes depending on their hydrophobicity (H-hydrophobic, P-polar).

© Springer Nature Switzerland AG 2019
J. M. Ferrández Vicente et al. (Eds.): IWINAC 2019, LNCS 11487, pp. 193–203, 2019.
https://doi.org/10.1007/978-3-030-19651-6_19

On the other hand, atomic models use off-lattice representations, but even in this case these models can also use simplifications that lower the level of the protein conformation resolution, such as considering only the main atoms of the protein backbone chain, as in "coarse-grained representations" [6]. As detailed later, one of these last models is used in this work.

Moreover, the energy models associated with protein conformations are full of local minima and usually are referred as funnel-like [18]. Thus, PSP turns into a search of the energy minimum that corresponds with the native structure. Given the high dimensional spaces associated with protein models, the use of different metaheuristics was continuously considered [15,18]. It should be noted that even in the simplest case of the HP model, the problem is NP-complete [18]. In fact, there has been an ample research using many optimization methods, with the combination of different metaheuristics (especially evolutionary algorithms - EAs) for PSP with simple and detailed lattice models [12,15,17,18].

In addition, in atomic models another problem appears when the energy model does not guarantee that the energy minimum corresponds with the native structure. This is what happens with the Rosetta model [10], one of the most successful environments for protein design. The reason is the combination in the energy model of physics energy terms (such as force fields) and "knowledge-based" terms derived from the statistics of resolved protein structures (implying less computational time). This introduces a level of "deceptiveness" in the energy landscape, since the search of the global minimum in the high dimensional space does not guarantee the success in finding the native structure. The strategy in this case turns into a search of local minima associated with different conformations. For example, Rosetta's strategy implies the use of multiple (thousands) Monte Carlo (MC) searches (using a coarse-grained representation), starting with different seeds, to obtain a set of protein "decoys", some of which (after a clustering process) can be refined in a posterior phase with a full atomic model.

Given the previous problem with the deceptive energy models, previous research was focused on trying to obtain a diverse set of protein conformations that minimize the energy [5] (e.g., in local minima), and consequently adopt a conformation "native-like", since those can be close to the real native structure. The use of Evolutionary Computing (EC) methods, as done in previous works [5,11,16], incorporates the advantage of their global search, with respect to a MC local search as used in Rosetta. In the EC search, an additional aim is that the conformations obtained should be diverse in their respective folds, with the hope that one corresponds (or is very close) to the real native structure [5,11].

However, there is a possibility in EC that was not directly considered in this problem, which is the use of niching methods in a multimodal energy landscape, methods that can locate the individuals of the population in the most promising areas (niches) of the fitness landscape. That is the current problem, since our objective is the use of an evolutionary algorithm (combined with local search) to sample the energy landscape, in combination with a classical niching method (crowding [2]), in order to directly obtain protein conformations that correspond to decoys in different niches with different folds.

2   Methods

2.1   Main Aspects of PSP with Rosetta

The low level coarse-grained representation of Rosetta [10] was used. This cen-troid mode considers the location of the main backbone atoms, whereas each amino acid side chain is represented by a united pseudo-atom located at the side-chain center of mass (Fig. 1). Thus, protein conformation can be described with the dihedral angles (ϕ, ψ and ω) between the atoms of the backbone chain.

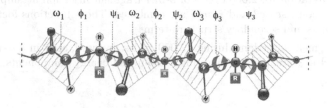

Fig. 1. Low level coarse-grained representation of Rosetta. Only the main backbone atoms are considered, while the lateral chains (R) are represented with a pseudo-atom. Each protein conformation is encoded with the dihedral angles of the amino acids.

Rosetta defines an energy associated with a protein conformation, energy function that is a weighted sum of physics and knowledge-based energy terms. Knowledge-based potential [13] refers to the empirical energy terms derived from the statistics of the solved structures deposited in PDB [7]. Common physics-based energy terms are associated with bond lengths, torsion angles, Van der Waals and electrostatic interactions. The combined energy function is used dur-ing the conformational search, combined by assembling small protein fragments (3-mers and 9-mers) taken from the PDB library to narrow the search.

Rosetta ab initio protocol [9] starts with the coarse-grained representation. To search through the conformational space a Metropolis Monte Carlo search is performed. It generates trial conformations using fragment replacements (in random positions of the target protein). The selection of those fragments (for each target protein) is based on the sequence similarity between the fragment and the region (window of amino acids) of the target sequence where it is going to be inserted. That "library of fragments" is defined from a set of non-redundant PDB resolved proteins [7] and it is generated previously to the ab initio run.

The number of fragment attempts can be modified with a Rosetta parameter, called *increase_cycles*, which multiplies the default values of cycles in the different stages (Table 1). The Metropolis criterion is used to determine the acceptance of a fragment insertion attempt by calculating the energy difference between the new conformation (after the insertion) and the previous one, following a Boltzmann energy distribution for a given temperature (a fixed temperature of 2 is used). The ab initio protocol is divided in 4 stages, which basically change the weight set of the energy terms and the number of fragment attempts (Table 1).

Table 1. Main aspects of Rosetta stages.

S1	Begins with a fully extended chain and inserts 9-mer fragments until all the backbone angles were modified at least once and with a maximum of 2,000 cycles (fragment insertion attempts). The energy function (*score0*) only considers the steric-clash term to prevent overlapping between backbone atoms and side-chain centroids
S2	Employs 9-mer fragment insertions during 2,000 cycles, using *score1*, which adds terms such as hydrophobic burial and specific pair interactions, as well as secondary structure scores
S3	Runs 10 iterations of 2,000 cycles of 9-mer fragment insertion attempts. Two score functions, *score2* and *score5* are combined. Those functions focus on compactness and secondary structure terms
S4	3-mer fragment insertions during 12,000 cycles are used, split in 3 iterations of 4,000 cycles. *score3*, which takes into account all energy components, is used

This ab initio procedure, with the four stages, is repeated thousands of times due to the stochasticity of the process. Some of the final conformations ("decoys") of this phase can be subjected to a refinement, with the side chain reconstruction and all-atom energy minimization, in a second "Ab initio relax" procedure, a high time-consuming refinement using an all-atom representation.

2.2 Crowding-Based Differential Evolution

The integration of the classical crowding niching method [2] of evolutionary computing with the Differential Evolution (DE) algorithm [8] used, for example, by Thomsen [14], was employed here. DE [8] is a population-based search method. DE creates new candidate solutions by combining existing ones according to a simple formula of vector crossover and mutation, and then keeping whichever candidate solution has the best score or fitness on the optimization problem at hand. The central idea of the algorithm is the use of difference vectors for generating perturbations in a population of vectors.

Differential Evolution needs a reduced number of parameters to define its implementation. Apart from the population size, the parameters are F or differential weight and CR or crossover probability. The weight factor F (usually in $[0, 2]$) is applied over the vector resulting from the difference between pairs of vectors (x'_2 and x'_3 in Algorithm 1). CR is the probability of crossing over a given vector of the population (target vector x) and a "mutant" vector created from the weighted difference of two vectors ($x'_1 + F(x'_2 - x'_3)$) (line 13). The "binomial" crossover (specified in Algorithm 1) was used for defining the value of the "trial" vector (y) in each vector component or position i. The index R guarantees that at least one of the parameters (genes) will be changed in the generation of the trial solution (line 12).

Algorithm 1. CrowdingDE Algorithm

1: Initialize protein conformations - Rosetta Stage 1
   {DE with three stages, using the score and replacement cycles of the corresponding Rosetta stages (Table 1)}
2: **for** $s = 2$ to 4 **do**
3:   **for** $x = 1$ to *Population Size* **do**
4:     Let $x' \leftarrow$ *Rosetta Stage s* (x) {Rosetta stage s applied to all individuals in generation 1}
5:   **end for**
6:   **for** $g = 2$ to MAX_GEN **do**
7:     **for** $x' = 1$ to *Population Size* **do**
8:       Let $x'_1, x'_2, x'_3 \in$ population, randomly obtained $\{x'_1, x'_2, x'_3, x'$ different from each other}
9:       Let $R \in \{1, ..., n\}$, randomly obtained {n is the dimension of the search space}
10:       **for** $i = 1$ to n **do**
11:         Pick $r_i \in U(0, 1)$ uniformly from the open range (0,1).
12:         **if** $(i = R) \vee (r_i < CR)$ **then**
13:           $y_i \leftarrow x'_{1i} + F(x'_{2i} - x'_{3i})$ {mutant vector}
14:         **else**
15:           $y_i = x'_i$
16:         **end if**
17:       **end for**{$y = [y_1, y_2...y_n]$ is a new generated candidate or trial individual}
18:       Let $y' \leftarrow$ *Rosetta Stage s* (y) {trial y is refined with Rosetta stage s to generate y'}
19:       **if** $f(y') \leq f(x')$ **then**
20:         Replace individual x' by y'
          {In CrowdingDE, the refined trial vector y' is compared with its most similar vector in the subset defined by parameter CF}
21:       **end if**
22:     **end for** {individual x'}
23:   **end for** {generation g}
24: **end for** {stage s}
25: **return** $z \in$ population$\backslash \forall t \in$ population, $f(z) \leq f(t)$

When defining the "mutant" vector, the DE scheme that chooses the base vector x'_1 randomly was basically used (variant $DE/rand/1/bin$, where 1 denotes the number of differences involved in the construction of the mutant vector and *bin* denotes the crossover type), which provides the lowest selective pressure. Note that the fundamental idea of DE is to adapt the step length ($F(x'_2 - x'_3)$) intrinsically along the evolutionary process [4]. At the beginning of generations the step length is large, because individuals are far away from each other. As the evolution goes on, the population converges and the step length becomes smaller and smaller, providing this way an automatic balance in the search.

Crowding, introduced by De Jong [2], is one of the most used niching methods for dealing with multimodal optimization problems in EC. The goal of niching methods is to simultaneously search in the most promising areas of the multi-modal fitness landscape. The simple idea behind crowding is the preservation of genetic diversity, where an offspring individual replaces the most similar one in the population if it has a better fitness. That (most similar) individual is selected among a randomly chosen subset of the population, where the subset size is determined by a parameter called Crowding Factor (CF). The integration with DE (CrowdingDE) is simple [14], extending DE with the classical crowding scheme. The only modification is that now each trial individual is compared against its nearest neighbor (most similar) among that subset CF of the population. If the trial vector is fitter, then it replaces the closest one from the subset.

Phases of CrowdingDE. The same combination between an evolutionary algorithm and the Rosetta ab initio search of Garza-Fabre et al. [5] was used. The pseudo-code of Algorithm 1 summarizes the procedure of the hybrid DE. The difference with respect to the procedure of Garza-Fabre et al. [5], in addition to the incorporation of niching, is that those authors used a classical genetic algorithm (GA) as evolutionary framework, with the usual GA operators of crossover and mutation, and these were applied only in the residues located at loop regions.

The individuals code different protein conformations, that are encoded with their dihedral angles. The initialization of the population is defined with Stage 1 of Rosetta (using *score0* as energy), that is, applying fragment replacements over the initial extended conformation in order to provide a diversified set of structures. Afterwards, the hybrid DE version employs 3 sequential stages (S1, S2 and S4) with the same number of evolutionary generations (MAX_GEN), using in each stage the corresponding Rosetta score functions (Sect. 2.1).

In the first generation of each stage, no trial individuals are generated. In generation 1, all the individuals are refined with the Rosetta replacement procedure of the corresponding stage, that is, with the corresponding score function, number of fragment attempts and fragment lengths (Sect. 2.1). Each individual x is therefore refined to an individual x' (line 4). The next generations are standard DE generations since, for each target individual x', a trial individual y is defined after the mutation and crossover DE operators. Now, the Rosetta replacements are applied only to the trial individuals y, generating refined trial individuals y' (line 18). As in standard DE, the fitness of the final trial individual y' is compared with the fitness of the corresponding target individual x' (line 19), to determine which one enters the population in the next generation. However, if crowding is considered (CrowdingDE), the fitness of the refined trial individual ($f(y')$) is compared with its nearest neighbor in order to decide which one enters the next generation (comment in line 20).

2.3   Structural Diversity Measure

The protein structural diversity measure defined by Garza-Fabre et al. [5] was used. This structural measure defined by the authors describes (coarsely) the relative position of each pair of protein secondary structure elements (SSEs, e.g. helix and strand) with respect to each other. Distances are computed between the C_α atoms of the amino acid residues at the center of the SSEs (Fig. 2). For a given protein conformation with E SSEs, the set of interdistances between each pair of SSEs is calculated (The number of

Fig. 2. Interdistances between pairs of secondary structure elements in a hypothetical protein (2 strands and 1 helix). The interdistance set coarsely describes the protein conformational fold.

interdistances is $\binom{E}{2}$ for a protein with E SSEs). Each interdistance is normalized considering half of its maximum distance when the conformation is fully extended (as indicated by the authors practically all the explored conformations correspond to values within 50% of that upper bound [5]). Such SSEs are determined, for a given protein sequence, with a SSE predictor, process which is previous to the evolutionary search.

Finally, to measure the structural difference between two protein folds, the Root Mean Square Error (RMSE) between the sets of interdistances of the two proteins is calculated. This simple procedure is appropriate for the purpose of comparison in the folds of two proteins, and does not have the problems of calculating the best superposition or alignment between two proteins when the RMSD between the atom positions of the two proteins is considered as measure of structural difference.

3   Results

Figure 3 shows a comparison of the results of Rosetta against the results of crowdingDE, using two values for the parameter CF. DE strategy $DE/rand/1/bin$ was used, which selects the base vector x_1 randomly and which implies the lowest selective pressure. DE parameters were: $CR = 0.99$ whereas $F = 0.025$. The low F value generates small perturbations in the dihedral angles of the mutant vectors whereas the high CR value ensures few changes in the final trial vector with respect to the mutant vector (Sect. 2.2). 6 different PDB proteins were used in the experiments. Figure 3 shows the normalized energy value (*score3*) in axis y, whereas in axis x the RMSD value is shown (from the native structure).

The settings for the comparison of approaches are the following: For each target protein, Rosetta was run to generate a set of 1,000 candidate conformations. That is, the Rosetta ab initio protocol was run 1,000 times, where each run produced a single final conformation. Rosetta recommended parameter settings [10] were considered in all runs. Moreover, as in [5], Rosetta parameter *increase_cycles* was set to 10, that is, the default values of cycles (fragment attempts) in the different Rosetta stages are multiplied by that value.

The comparison of final results must imply that the different approaches use the same number of fragment attempts (and corresponding energy tests). In crowdingDE, a population of 100 individuals was used (as in [5] with a hybrid GA). However, the parameter *increase_cycles* was set to 0.1, since now the DE operators and corresponding fragment attempts act over a number of generations (100) in the three sequential stages (Algorithm 1). Given the stochastic nature of crowdingDE runs, 10 independent runs of the EA were considered, which generate 1,000 final solutions for comparison with the same number of Rosetta solutions. Note that the fragment attempts are the same in both approaches, since Rosetta used *increase_cycles* $= 10$, and the EA used *increase_cycles* $= 0.1$, but with 100 individuals and during 100 generations working with the same Rosetta stages, evolutionary process that was repeated 10 times.

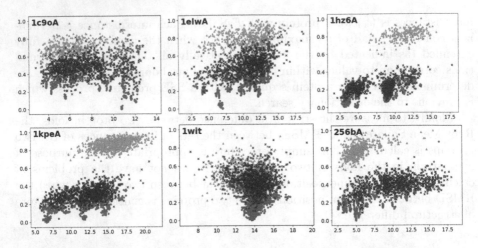

Fig. 3. Scaled energy vs. RMSD (from the native structure) for six PDB proteins. Gray: Rosetta results, Red: CrowdingDE (CF = 100%), Blue: CrowdingDE (CF = 10%). (Color figure online)

In Fig. 3 the *score3* energy values were normalized between 0 and 1, taking into account the lowest and highest values obtained by the 3 considered approaches. Clearly, crowdingDE improves the energy values of the solutions obtained in all proteins, while maintaining a diverse set of folds in the final populations, even with the energy improvement in most solutions with respect to the Rosetta solutions (a high improvement in proteins like *1kpeA*). The lowest RMSD values are similar in both approaches (crowdingDE and Rosetta), except in proteins *1hz6A* and *1kpeA*. The main difference between the two approaches with crowdingDE is that, with $CF = 100\%$, the dispersion of solutions tends to be higher with respect to the use of a lower crowding factor ($CF = 10\%$). This is logical since, in the latter case, several solutions can fall in the same landscape area, which also contributes to a better exploitation and to obtain slightly better energy results.

Given that the RMSD values of the obtained decoys (final conformations) is one of the most important aspects to minimize, Table 2 shows the best RMSD values obtained with the different approaches. Even with the clear energy improvement in the conformations obtained with crowdingDE, the RMSD results are not necessarily better with respect to the final Rosetta solutions with worse energies. However, crowdingDE

Table 2. RMSD values obtained with proteins of Fig. 3. First columns: PDB Id, amino acid number and native fold topology. 4th and 5th columns: lowest RMSD obtained with crowdingDE with $CF = 100\%$ and $CF = 10\%$ in 10 independent runs. 6th column: best RMSD value in 1,000 Rosetta ab initio runs.

PDB id	Size	Fold topol.	Lowest RMSD CrowdingDE (CF = 100%)	Lowest RMSD CrowdingDE (CF = 10%)	Lowest RMSD Rosetta
1c9oA	66	β	2.81	3.52	2.98
1elwA	117	α	1.56	2.75	2.14
1hz6A	61	α-β	1.73	2.69	2.64
1kpeA	108	α-β	5.31	5.86	7.22
1wit	93	β	7.26	8.13	6.74
256bA	106	α	2.62	2.54	2.57

improves the energy without focusing on a particular area of the conformational space, as the RMSD dispersions in Fig. 3 show. Protein *1wit* is a clear example of the deceptiveness of the Rosetta energy landscape, where the area of low energy values does not correspond with the closer conformations to the native structure. The comparison with the values reported in [5] is difficult, since the authors used different fragment libraries in their Rosetta ab initio runs. Nevertheless, crowdingDE obtains wider RMSD distributions. For example, with protein *1hz6A* the RMSD standard deviation values reported in [5], with 3 strategies/GA variants, are 0.34, 2.02 and 2.76, whereas the standard deviations of the final solutions with crowdingDE are 2.69 ($CF = 100\%$) and 3.47 ($CF = 10\%$). With protein *1kpeA*, crowdingDE RMSD standard deviations are 2.58 ($CF = 100\%$) and 3.02 ($CF = 10\%$), while the values in [5] are 1.03, 2.30 and 2.74.

Finally, Fig. 4 shows a comparison of results with different selective pressures. The left subfigure corresponds with the results produced by 10 independent runs of crowdingDE with an intermediate $CF = 50\%$, using the strategy $DE/rand/1/bin$ 100% of times. The results in the central subfigure correspond to an increase of the selective pressure since now the strategy $DE/best/1/bin$ (which selects the best current base vector, Sect. 2.2) is selected 50% of times in the generation of mutant vectors. The right subfigure corresponds with 10 hybrid DE runs but without using crowding (the trial vector is compared with its corresponding target as in standard DE, Algorithm 1), and using the lowest selective pressure ($DE/rand/1/bin$ 100% of times). With a higher selective pressure in the central subfigure, slightly better energy values are obtained, without losing the RMSD dispersion in final solutions. On the contrary, without crowding (right subfigure), even with the low selective pressure, hybrid DE generates worse values in terms of RMSD dispersion. The reason is the fast loss of variability in the DE population with the fast convergence to suboptimal energy values in the DE runs, contrary to the maintained variability imposed by crowding.

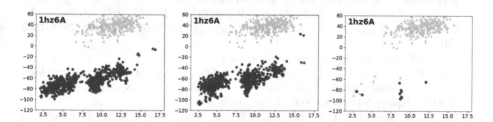

Fig. 4. Energy (*score3*) vs. RMSD for protein 1hz6A with 3 strategies. CrowdingDE (CF = 50%) with $DE/rand$ 100% (Left) and with $DE/rand$ 50% - $DE/best$ 50% (Center). Right: DE (without crowding) and $DE/rand$ 100%. Gray: Rosetta results.

4   Conclusions

The combination of the global search provided by DE with the local refinement procedure using protein fragments clearly samples the energy/fitness landscape more efficiently than the widely used Rosetta ab initio protocol, obtaining better protein conformations in terms of energy. However, given the deceptiveness of the Rosetta energy landscape, the required strategy is to obtain solutions with a diverse set of folds. The incorporation of the crowding niching method in the hybrid DE algorithm allows to straightforwardly obtain such a diverse set of folds, at the same time that the conformations minimize the energy. Therefore, a set of solutions "native-like" are easily obtained, solutions that can be subjected to a posterior refinement with the Rosetta full atom procedure.

Acknowledgments. This work was funded by Xunta de Galicia ("Centro singular de investigación de Galicia" accreditation 2016-2019 ED431G/01) and the European Regional Development Fund (ERDF). D. Varela grant has received financial support from the Xunta de Galicia and the European Union (European Social Fund - ESF).

References

1. Anfinsen, C.B.: Principles that govern the folding of proteins. Science **181**(96), 223–230 (1973)
2. De Jong, K.A.: An analysis of the behavior of a class of genetic adaptive systems. Doctoral dissertation, University of Michigan, Ann Arbor, MI (1975)
3. Dill, K.A.: Dominant forces in protein folding. Biochemestry **29**, 7133–7155 (1990)
4. Feoktistov, V.: Differential Evolution: In Search of Solutions. Springer, New York (2006). https://doi.org/10.1007/978-0-387-36896-2
5. Garza-Fabre, M., Kandathil, S.M., Handl, J., Knowles, J., Lovell, S.C.: Generating, maintaining, and exploiting diversity in a memetic algorithm for protein structure prediction. Evol. Comput. **24**(4), 577–607 (2016)
6. Kmiecik, S., Gront, D., Kolinski, M., Wieteska, L., Dawid, A.E., Kolinski, A.: Coarse-grained protein models and their applications. Chem. Rev. **116**, 7898–7936 (2016)
7. Protein Data Bank. http://www.wwpdb.org
8. Price, K.V., Storn, R.M., Lampinen, J.A.: Differential Evolution. A Practical Approach to Global Optimization. Natural Computing Series. Springer, Heidelberg (2005). https://doi.org/10.1007/3-540-31306-0
9. Rohl, C.A., Strauss, C.E.M., Misura, K.M., Baker, D.: Protein structure prediction using Rosetta. Methods Enzym. **383**, 66–93 (2004)
10. Rosetta system. http://www.rosettacommons.org
11. Saleh, S., Olson, B., Shehu, A.: A population-based evolutionary search approach to the multiple minima problem in de novo protein structure prediction. BMC Struct. Biol. **13**(1), S4 (2013)
12. Santos, J., Diéguez, M.: Differential evolution for protein structure prediction using the HP model. In: Ferrández, J.M., Álvarez Sánchez, J.R., de la Paz, F., Toledo, F.J. (eds.) IWINAC 2011. LNCS, vol. 6686, pp. 323–333. Springer, Heidelberg (2011). https://doi.org/10.1007/978-3-642-21344-1_34

13. Sippl, M.J.: Knowledge-based potentials for proteins. Curr. Opin. Struct. Biol. **5**(2), 229–235 (1995)
14. Thomsen, R.: Multimodal optimization using crowding-based differential evolution. In: Proceedings of the IEEE Congress on Evolutionary Computation, pp. 1382–1389 (2004)
15. Unger, R.: The genetic algorithm approach to protein structure prediction. Struct. Bond. **110**, 153–175 (2004)
16. Varela, D., Santos, J.: Combination of differential evolution and fragment-based replacements for protein structure prediction. In: GECCO 2015 Proceedings Companion, pp. 911–914 (2015)
17. Varela, D., Santos, J.: A hybrid evolutionary algorithm for protein structure prediction using the face-centered cubic lattice model. In: Liu, D., Xie, S., Li, Y., Zhao, D., El-Alfy, E.S. (eds.) ICONIP 2017. LNCS, vol. 10634, pp. 628–638. Springer, Cham (2017). https://doi.org/10.1007/978-3-319-70087-8_65
18. Zhao, X.: Advances on protein folding simulations based on the lattice HP models with natural computing. Appl. Soft Comput. **8**, 1029–1040 (2008)

Bacterial Resistance Algorithm.
An Application to CVRP

M. Angélica Pinninghoff J., José Orellana M., and Ricardo Contreras A.[✉]

Computer Science Department, Engineering Faculty,
University of Concepción, Concepción, Chile
rcontrer@udec.cl

Abstract. This work considers an approach called Bacterial Antibiotic Resistance Algorithm (BARA) in which a bacteria colony represents a set of candidates solutions subjected to the presence of an antibiotic as a pressure factor for separating good and wrong answers. In our terms, the classification allows us to have two groups: resistant and non-resistant bacteria. Then, by using genetic variation mechanisms (conjugation, transformation, and mutation), it is expected that non-resistant bacteria may improve their defense capability to enhance their probability of survival. The proposed algorithm implements and evaluates instances of the Capacitated Vehicle Routing Problem (CVRP). Results are comparable to those obtained in similar approaches.

Keywords: Bacteria · Antibiotic resistance algorithm

1   Introduction

There are some hard problems for which it is not possible to write an algorithm that, in polynomial time, solve them. The complexity of this class of problems lies in the fact that the space of solutions grows exponentially according to the size of the problem. In this situation, a brute force algorithm is not a feasible alternative.

Different approaches have been used to deal with these problems; Ant Colony Optimization (ACO) [1], Simulated Annealing (SA) [2].

A classical approach used to deal with highly combinatorial problems is Genetic Algorithms (GA) [3,7].

Antibiotic resistance is a phenomenon where infectious bacteria are no longer susceptible to previously effective antibiotics. Antibiotics are typically used to treat bacterial infections.

In this work, a natural phenomenon acts as an inspiration to develop a method which can solve difficult problems. The phenomenon is bacteria behavior; in particular, how bacteria share or modify their genetic material to deal with a common enemy, such as an antibiotic. Bacteria exhibit a great adaptation capability on their surrounding environment, and this fact allows to bacteria the survival under hostile conditions.

© Springer Nature Switzerland AG 2019
J. M. Ferrández Vicente et al. (Eds.): IWINAC 2019, LNCS 11487, pp. 204–211, 2019.
https://doi.org/10.1007/978-3-030-19651-6_20

The proposal represents a set of solutions through a bacteria colony, in which every bacteria collaborates with the others to strengthen their collective resistance, for instance, to antibiotics. To reinforce the bacteria behavior means to have better solutions as times goes by. The hypothesis is that a collaborative approach allows obtaining results as good as those obtained by using classical metaheuristics like Genetic Algorithms.

Bacteria are microscopic single-celled organisms that thrive in diverse environments. They can live within the soil, in the ocean, and inside the human gut. Humans' relationship with bacteria is complex. Sometimes they lend a helping hand, by curdling milk into yogurt or helping with our digestion. At other times they are destructive, causing diseases like pneumonia and MRSA.

Chemotaxis is the directed motion of an organism toward environmental conditions it deems attractive and away from surroundings it finds repellent. In [5], a chemotaxis-based bacterial colony algorithm is used to guide the bacterium to fine-tune the solution enhancing the local exploitation ability of the algorithm. Authors claim that experiments show the effectiveness and efficiency of the proposed algorithm in terms of both quality solution and computational time.

The objective of this work is to propose a collaborative method based on bacteria behavior, to show that collaborative approaches are as good as are competitive classical proposals. It includes to understand the genetic material transference among bacteria, showing results obtained when dealing with a known problem as the Capacitated Vehicle Routing Problem (CVRP).

This article is structured as follows; the first section is this current introduction, the second section introduces the biological inspiration for the proposed algorithm; the third section presents the algorithm, and the fourth section describes how the proposal applies to the CVRP problem. Section five shows some results obtained, and finally section six exhibits the conclusions.

2   Bacterial Antibiotic Resistance Algorithm

The proposal is inspired by how a bacteria population evolves and becomes resistant when faced with antibiotics attack.

One key issue in bacteria behavior is collaboration among individuals in a bacteria population. Stronger bacteria, which can survive to the application of antibiotics, may transfer part of their DNA information to the weakest bacteria, to make them, also, antibiotic resistant. It is interesting to note that, even being simple organisms, having only one chromosome, the weakest bacteria are capable of resist when facing an antibiotic attack. The critical element for this survival characteristic is how bacteria share their genetic information.

A relevant difference between bacteria and superior organisms is that bacteria share genetic material with other individuals in the same individual's generation. The bacteria reproduce using cell division. It implies that individuals are created with identical genetic material [6]. Genetic diversity is achieved through mutations and three different mechanisms for genetic material transference among individuals in the same population.

Mutation is a change in the genetic information of an organism. It occurs with a certain probability, and it is typically produced by mistake in the DNA replication process. Sometimes, a mutation may give to the mutant an advantage over the original organism and may present a better behavior, in terms of survival and resistance, and therefore the new mutant is capable of replacing the original one by a different, improved individual.

Genetic transference, on the other side, uses three mechanisms:

- Conjugation. There is a transference of genetic material from one bacterium to another.
- Transformation. Bacteria are capable of capturing some genetic material present in their environment (typically, part of the genetic material of a died bacterium).
- Transduction. Transference of genetic material supported by a bacteriophage, for example, a virus.

By using these different alternatives of genetic transference, bacteria develop the capability of turning resistant to an antibiotic. A resistant bacterium becomes dominant and shares genetic information with their neighbors making them resistant too. In doing so, the probability for a bacteria population of surviving in a hostile environment increases.

This work emphasizes the collaborative bacteria behavior and considers the following biologic issues as an inspiration source to develop the proposed mechanism:

- The capability of creating antibiotic resistance by using a collaborative strategy. This issue takes into account the genetic transference through conjugation and transformation.
- The horizontal genetic transference; i.e., the process of sharing genetic material with their neighborhood, with the neighbors that belong to the same generation.

Hence, it is possible to see that bacteria behavior represents a new paradigm for dealing with an evolving population of individuals, a common strategy for solving optimization problems. The use of genetic algorithms for known optimization problems presents an exciting benchmark to evaluate the performance of this proposal.

3   The Algorithmic Proposal

The algorithm uses a variable called Antibiotic, which exerts selective pressure on the population, to stimulate improvement of the individuals in terms of survival. The algorithm exhibits a collaborative performance in the sense that, when faced to the presence of an antibiotic, the most resistant bacteria, through the conjugation mechanism, will try to strengthen the non-resistant individuals to make them improve and increase their survival probability. Bacteria do it by transferring part of their genetic code.

On the other side, bacteria that do not improve die, spreading part of their genetic material into the environment? This genetic material which can be captured by other bacteria, in the process called transformation.

The main components of the algorithm are:

- A bacteria population. Every bacteria holds a chromosome which represents a solution for the problem under consideration (in this case, a set of n routes).
- An antibiotic, which pressures the population and divides it into two groups: the resistant bacteria and the non-resistant bacteria.
- Three genetic variation mechanisms: conjugation, transformation, and mutation.

The genetic variation mechanisms allow increasing the number of resistant bacteria (improving the quality of solutions).

Conjugation is a process which involves a resistant bacterium and a non-resistant one. The resistant bacteria transfer part of their genetic material (a copy) to the non-resistant bacteria. This step permits to intensify the search for good solutions. Only resistant bacteria may realize mutation and transformation. These processes are used to increase diversity in the exploration of the space of solutions. The mutation can occur in a resistant bacterium, but only when it improves their quality. In this last case, the mechanism plays the role of intensifying the search of solutions.

If every bacterium converges to the same solution, there is a loss of genetic variability. In this case, each bacterium can perform mutation and transformation, independently of whether this improves the quality of the answers (the fitness); to recover the genetic variability of the population. This stage does not have a correspondence with the biological reality, but it is essential for the improvement of solutions the algorithm produces.

The general structure of the Bacterial Antibiotic Resistance Algorithm (BARA) is shown in Algorithm 1.

Initialization. Is in charge of generating an initial bacteria population. The size of the population is a parameter, which remains constant during the iteration of the algorithm.

Antibiotic Formulation. The antibiotic is a solution arbitrarily chosen from the initial population. The fitness value of the antibiotic is an intermediate value which acts as a threshold for separating the resistant bacteria from the non-resistant bacteria.

Classification. Every bacterium having a fitness value higher than the antibiotic is classified as antibiotic resistant. On the other side, every bacterium having a fitness value lower than the antibiotic become a non-resistant bacteria.

Genetic Variation. In this stage, individuals in the population are modified, trying to increase the number of resistant bacteria for improving the quality of solutions. Three different mechanisms are used:

Algorithm 1. BARA pseudo-algorithm

```
 1: procedure BARA( )
 2:     INITIALIZATION( );
 3:     while Stop condition not achieved do
 4:         ANTIBIOTIC FORMULATION( );
 5:         CLASSIFICATION( );
 6:         GENETIC VARIATION( );
 7:         RE-CLASSIFICATION( );
 8:         ANTIBIOTIC APPLICATION( );
 9:         POPULATION REGENERATION( );
10:         repeat
11:             Free Genetic Variation
12:         until Population variability recovered
13:     end while
14: end procedure
```

- **Conjugation.** A donor resistant bacterium transfers part of their genetic material to a recipient non-resistant bacterium, through a procedure similar to the OX crossover mechanism [4] used in genetic algorithms.
- **Transformation.** A non-resistant bacterium may, with a probability p_{tr}, recombine their genetic material with material available in the environment, which comes from died bacteria. This process is as follow: (i) a piece of genetic material remaining in the environment is randomly chosen, (ii) a point x randomly chosen in the chromosome which belongs to the recipient bacterium, and y, and a y point computed according to the length of the genetic material from the environment, (iii) the new genetic material is inserted between points x and y and then the remaining genes are sorted as in Conjugation. This step makes it possible to recover good segments of a discarded solution.
- **Mutation.** A non-resistant bacterium has a probability p_m of change, increasing the likelihood of evolving to a resistant condition. Mutation is achieved by randomly selecting two genes in the chromosome and swapping the corresponding values. Mutation in resistant bacteria only is allowed if it improves their fitness value.
- **Re-classification.** Individuals in the population are re-evaluated, because of the changes generated in previous steps.
- **Antibiotic application.** In this stage, every non-resistant bacteria dies to leave, with a probability p_A, part of their genetic material in the environment. It is accomplished by randomly selecting two points in the chromosome, x and y, and putting into the environment the genetic material bounded by x and y.
- **Population regeneration.** In this stage, the antibiotic replaces every died bacteria.
- **Free Genetic Variation.** When the set of solutions arrives at a steady state (best and worst solution are the same), free changes are realized to recover the genetic variability of the population. These changes are accomplished through *Conjugation*, *Transformation* and *Mutation*.

4   BARA Algorithm Applied to the CVRP

The key issues for applying the algorithm to the CVRP are to establish a solutions representation and an evaluation function.

4.1   Solutions Representation

The representation of a solution consists of a permutation of integer values, which denotes the order for visiting customers. When a customer demand exceeds the capacity of a vehicle, a zero value (which represents the depot) is inserted into the chromosome, and a new vehicle is considered, from that point, for adding the new demands until the capacity of the vehicle is again exceeded.

Figure 1 shows the evolution of a solution starting with a chromosome which considers the customers, but not considered the depot yet. The final solution introduces a zero value, for representing the depot.

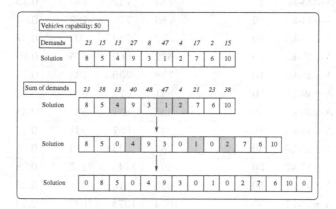

Fig. 1. Evolution of a solution

4.2   Solutions Evaluation

To evaluate the quality of a solution, we use a function which computes the total distance involved in a solution; see Eq. 1.

$$F = \sum_{(i,j) \in E} (c_{ij} \cdot x_{ij}) \cdot cv^2 \tag{1}$$

where E is the set of edges considered, c_{ij} is the distance between customers i and j. x_{ij} is a binary variable which takes value one if the edge (i, j) belongs to the evaluated solution and takes the value zero otherwise. cv represents the number of vehicles used, and it serves as a penalization factor when the number of vehicles increases.

5   Results

To evaluate the BARA algorithm, it was computed the relative deviation percentage (RDP) concerning a known set of instances proposed by Augerat[1]. The RDP is computed as indicated in Eq. 2. A set of 1395 test instances were considered for population sizes of 10, 50, 100 and 200 bacteria.

$$RDP = \frac{Sol_{BARA} - Sol_{Opt}}{Sol_{Opt}} \cdot 100 \qquad (2)$$

Table 1. Numerical results

Instance	Population size	Sol_{GA}	Sol_{Opt}	Sol_{BARA}	RDP
A-n32-k5	10	797	784	798	1.78
A-n33-k5	10	662	661	662	0.15
A-n33-k6	10	743	742	743	0.13
A-n34-k5	10	786	778	783	0.64
A-n36-k5	10	802	799	802	0.37
A-n37-k5	10	672	669	675	0.89
A-n38-k5	10	738	730	734	0.54
A-n39-k5	50	831	822	830	0.97
A-n39-k6	10	835	831	835	0.48
A-n44-k6	10	947	937	941	0.42
A-n45-k6	50	981	944	953	0.95
A-n45-k7	50	1164	1146	1155	0.78
A-n46-k7	50	925	914	918	0.43
A-n48-k7	50	1074	1073	1097	2.23
A-n53-k7	50	1038	1010	1038	2.77
A-n54-k7	50	1190	1167	1182	1.28
A-n55-k9	50	1098	1073	1081	0.74
A-n60-k9	50	1387	1354	1375	1.55
A-n61-k9	100	1053	1034	1076	4.06
A-n62-k8	50	1333	1288	1327	3.02
A-n63-k9	50	1700	1616	1647	1.91
A-n63-k10	50	1348	1314	1335	1.59
A-n64-k9	50	1463	1401	1436	2.49
A-n65-k9	50	1221	1174	1220	3.91
A-n69-k9	100	1211	1159	1193	2.93
A-n80-k10	100	1864	1763	1839	4.31

[1] http://neo.lcc.uma.es/vrp/vrp-instances/capacitated-vrp-instances/.

Sol_{BARA} is the solution found by BARA algorithm, and Sol_{Opt} is the known optimum value. Table 1 shows the best values obtained for BARA and GA, which correspond to different population sizes. Instances denoted by $A - nx - ky$, indicates a random distribution for customers (A), while x represents the number of customers and y represents the number of vehicles for the optimum solution.

The set of parameters considered for testing are Conjugation probability, Mutation probability, Transformation probability, and Population size.

6   Conclusions

The proposed algorithm uses for testing the benchmark proposed by Augerat. Previous results using genetic algorithms were also used to compare with this proposal; in the average, results are similar. However, the results improve clearly when the number of customer increases.

However, an important fact is that, with this proposal, the solution always gives the optimum (minimum) number of vehicles. It is not the usual situation when using genetic algorithms. In this sense, we can say BARA is a competitive algorithm, at least in the case of CVRP. Future work should consider a broad family of combinatorial optimization problems.

References

1. Dorigo, M., Stuetzle, T.: Ant Colony Optimization, 5th edn. A Bradford Book, Cambridge (2004)
2. Du, K.-L., Swamy, M.N.S.: Search and Optimization by Metaheuristics. Birkhauser, Basel (2016)
3. Kramer, O.: Genetic Algorithm Essentials. Springer, Cham (2017). https://doi.org/10.1007/978-3-319-52156-5
4. Michalewicz, Z., Fogel, D.: How to Solve It: Modern Heuristics, 2nd edn. Springer, Heidelberg (2004). https://doi.org/10.1007/978-3-662-07807-5
5. Niu, B., Chan, F.T.S., Xie, T., Liu, Y.: Guided chemotaxis-based bacterial colony algorithm for three-echelon supply chain optimisation. Int. J. Comput. Integr. Manuf. **30**(2–3), 305–319 (2017)
6. Snyder, L., Peters, J.E., Henken, T.M., Champness, W.: Molecular Genetics of Bacteria, 4th edn. ASM Press, Washington, D.C. (2013)
7. Talbi, E.G.: Metaheuristics: From Design to Implementation. Wiley, New York (2009)

Conceptual Description
of Nature-Inspired Cognitive Cities:
Properties and Challenges

Juvenal Machin(iD) and Agusti Solanas$^{(\boxtimes)}$(iD)

Universitat Rovira i Virgili, Tarragona, Spain
{juvenal.machin,agusti.solanas}@urv.cat

Abstract. Smart cities result from the wide adoption of information and communication technologies aimed at addressing challenges arising from overpopulation and resources shortage. Despite their important and fundamental contributions, ICT alone can hardly cope with all the challenges posed by growing demands of overpopulated cities. Hence, novel approaches based on innovative paradigms are needed.

In this article we revise the concept of *Cognitive City* founded on Siemens' *Connectivism* and understood as the evolution of current smart cities augmented with artificial intelligence, internet of things, and ubiquitous computing. We present the concept of cognitive city as a complex system of systems resembling complex adaptive systems with natural resilient capabilities. We build and propose our model upon the principles of decentralized control, stigmergy and locality, multi-directional networking, randomness, specialization and redundancy. Also, we show a realistic application of our model.

With the aim to set the ground for further research, we summarize the main challenges that remain open, both from a societal and technical perspective. Hence, the goal of this article is not to provide a solution to those challenges but, to raise awareness on the problem, and foster further research in the multiple lines that remain open.

Keywords: Cognitive city · Smart city · Artificial intelligence ·
Natural computing · Learning strategies · Human-machine interaction

1 Introduction

Population is growing, and it is steadily shifting towards urban areas. By 2030, 60% of the world's population is expected to reside in cities, with 30% living in large cities with more than half a million citizens. This urbanization process will create mega-cities, with at least ten million citizens, in which 9% of the world's population will dwell [1]. Such mega-cities will benefit from costs reductions due to economies of scale, but they will face serious problems in terms of efficiency, sustainability, security, public health, well-being and resiliency.

© Springer Nature Switzerland AG 2019
J. M. Ferrández Vicente et al. (Eds.): IWINAC 2019, LNCS 11487, pp. 212–222, 2019.
https://doi.org/10.1007/978-3-030-19651-6_21

Information and Communication Technologies (ICT) are fundamental allies against the challenges posed by unbridled urbanization. Introducing ICT in cities helps to gather lots of data, process them and obtain knowledge that—theoretically—could lead to make better decisions. In this sense, by using ICT, cities aim at improving (and ideally optimizing) their use of resources, fostering citizens participation, increasing the quality of life and well-being of citizens [2], protecting them [3], and becoming sustainable and environmentally-friendly.

Although the smart city concept is not unique, fully stable, or well-established yet, the aforementioned challenges foster the emergence of novel augmented concepts for cities. In recent years, the term *Cognitive City* has been proposed as an evolution of the smart city concept, to address these future threats. It results from the raise of Artificial Intelligence (AI), the generalization of the Internet of Things (IoT), and the wide development of Ubiquitous Computing (UC).

2   The Cognitive City

According to Machin and Solanas [4], the cognitive city concept comes from the fields of urban planning and human-computer interaction, and it was first conceptualized in the ICT context by Mostashari *et al.*, as an evolution of the smart city idea, focusing on the issue of intelligent urban governance. As stated by Mostashari, a cognitive city is *"one that learns and adapts its behavior based on past experiences and is able to sense, understand and respond to changes in its environment"* [5, p. 4]. A cognitive city is, thus, a learning and resilient city.

Cognitive cities accomplish these goals by means of an intelligent amplification loop [6] between the city and the citizens, to build a composite aggregated intelligence that can overcome the challenges of future cities. This is done by a hyper-connected, continuous, bidirectional, communication flow between city infrastructures and citizens, leveraging the idea of *citizens as sensors* [7].

The concept was further developed by Kaltenrieder *et al.* by including distributed knowledge, as posited by *Connectivism* [8], to fully integrate the collective learning process of the city as a whole. This cognitive city vision would allow to empower every citizen with collective intelligence learning resources to address individual efficiency and resiliency on their everyday's life in the city [9,10]. Also, an evolutionary cognitive city view was presented in [11]. According to the authors, the emergent socio-technical system would be able to learn, and adapt to shocks from its environment, thanks to the collaborative intelligence of the cognitive actors in the city. This last evolutionary step towards resiliency—the authors claim—will be achieved by means of *"new forms of machine intelligence involving human-machine interactions"* [11, p. 5], and *a network of autonomous cognitive actors with learning capabilities, that will allow the city to evolve* [11, p. 8].

3   The City as a Complex System

While the map is not the territory, a city cannot be reduced to its infrastructures. A city is the emergent phenomenon that derives from a complex system [12], which includes space, infrastructures, people and human organizations, cars, and so on and so forth, but also intangible cultural, socio-economical, and political dimensions. Moreover, cities include the dynamics established by all those building blocks, in a multi-layered, network-aggregated, hyper-connected structure. This structure consists of different levels of organization: family, neighborhood, street, etc, which obey to their own set of rules. While there are hierarchical layers of aggregation, there is not a top-down centralized mechanism for governing or coordinating the system as a whole. As a result, the interaction among city agents might result in emergent patterns of bottom-up self-organization [13].

This kind of self-organized, emergent, and collective behavior appears frequently in nature (*e.g.*, collective behavior of social insects such as ants colonies, flocks of birds, schools of fishes, and neural circuits are well-known examples of self-organization). From this point of view, the city is a complex system of systems and it cannot be explained by merely understanding its components individually. On the contrary, what characterizes a complex system (such as a city) are its patterns: how their components relate to each other, and how patterns persist even after their generating components change or disappear.

4   Natural Resilient Systems

Complex adaptive systems (CAS) are systems *"that have a large numbers of components, often called agents, that interact and adapt or learn"* [14, p. 1]. Resilience is an emergent property of CAS, which are frequently seen in nature showing a self-organizing behavior. Examples of such resilient systems include: living organisms, ecosystems, social insects colonies, the immune system, the brain, bacterial colonies, etc. [15,16]. Ant colonies are well-known examples of resilient systems. Colonies perform a distributed computation that creates a collective intelligence, greater than the intelligence of any of its individual members [17]. Colony computation is adaptive, robust and scalable, and can perform complex operations like collective decision making, and task allocation with no central control [18]. This emerging intelligence has driven them to become exceptionally successful foragers: on average, ants constitute 20% of the overall terrestrial animals biomass [19], and have inspired solutions to problems in computer science, like the *Ant Colony Optimization* Algorithm [20], as well as many other successful applications in telecommunications, and robotics [21].

Moreover, specialization of the components is a requirement for complexity (*e.g.*, ant societies have division of labour). Furthermore, in a CAS, roles can mutate, for instance: in the species *Harpegnathos saltator*, once the queen dies, worker daughters battle to chose a small group of reproductive individuals, hence, making the colony virtually *immortal* [22, pp. 339–340].

5   Our Nature-Inspired Cognitive City Model

In a cognitive city there must be a cognitive interplay among the components of the city, *e.g.*, between humans and computer systems, among computer systems, and among humans. Although artificial intelligence is steadily growing in complexity and capabilities, it is still people, with their cognitive capabilities, those that make a city a complex cognitive system. We are, in fact, complex systems ourselves [23]. Urban computer-empowered components – humans and machines – should be integrated, becoming part of an emergent cognitive set of processes. With their interaction, the city (understood from a holistic perspective) could learn and become resilient through a process of continuous adaptation.

In this line, we suggest a unifying cognitive city model that aims to set the ground for further research and for the development of the concept in practical scenarios. Our model is inspired by nature, and stresses the importance of distributed knowledge (*i.e.,* as suggested by *Connectivism*) and by an autonomous co-operative multi-agent network linked to the city space. Hence, we focus our model of cognitive city on the intelligent agents (*e.g.,* humans or machines) that live within the space of the city, and we define the properties that such agents should fulfill in order to enable the creation of a cognitive city.

5.1 Decentralized Control

One of the most important characteristics of a resilient system is its ability to keep functioning – as a whole – in the event of failure of one or more of its components. This functional ability does not reside in a selected group of components but, on the contrary, it lies within the global and inter-connected structure of the very system. For the system to be resilient, its components must be autonomous (or, at least, have a basic degree of autonomy that allows them to keep functioning under failure conditions). In fact, self-organization and the components' interaction with their neighbors through feedback loops, leads to the emergence of adaptation patterns that enable innovative responses to failures and, thus, the adaptation to changing environments [12,24].

Urban components with computation capabilities (*i.e.,* both humans and machines) should be integrated, and become part of an emergent cognitive process. With their interaction, the city can learn and become resilient, understanding resiliency as a process of continuous adaptation. Computational paradigms like swarm intelligence [25] can be used to implement the core functions of our model, as it is based on decentralized control, autonomy and emergence.

5.2 Locality and Stigmergy

Following the above principle of decentralization, city agents should be able to interact and coordinate primarily with their neighbors. The definition of "neighbor" and "neighborhood" depends on many factors associated with city agents, *e.g.,* their physical distance, their behaviour similarity, or the relations among their activities, are examples of criteria to determine agents neighborhoods. In cities, the physical environment is paramount and agents should be considered in this spacial contextual environment. Hence, instead of a general/global knowledge of the state of the city, agents need local context-awareness. This can be achieved by direct interaction or by using the environment as an intermediate communication media, thus, following the stigmergy principle.

5.3   Networking and Feedback Loops

Although agents must follow the principles of decentralization and locality, they should be integrated and have access to the information flows of the city. This implies the possibility of establishing connections with – and learning from – other agents, not only locally but globally in a city network. The network has to enable the interaction among agents, both humans and machines, in a meaningful way.

Additionally, the interaction between two or among several agents should be bidirectional or multi-directional respectively, so as to allow the creation of feedback loops among agents. By creating feedback loops, agents can learn from peers and provide information to other agents, hence, promoting their learning and improving their adaptability.

5.4   Specialization and Redundancy

Building upon the specialization of labour, agents will have one or a pool of specialized functions. Current agent roles would depend on those of their neighbors and the perceived conditions from their surrounding environment. Human specialization and adaptation to changes is well-known, however, non-human specialization and adaptation is far more difficult to achieve and might be based on response thresholds mechanisms with learning [21].

Although specialization is fundamental for the functional optimization of a cognitive city, for the sake of resilience no function/task will be developed by a unique agent. There is a need for redundant agents within a given area of the city (both physically and logically) to avoid catastrophic failures.

5.5   Randomness

Agents should allow random interactions, meaning that potential interacting agents will not be restricted by default or hardwired. Random interactions are a well-known generator of new patterns and emergent behavior [12, p. 72].

5.6   Governance

Managing complexity in city governance is challenging. Although prediction-based models can be used to perform simulations that help in the decision making process, it is still difficult to link them to automatic decisions on the city as a whole. We suggest to use the streams of data provided by citizens and non-human agents to generate hypotheses and expose hidden urban patterns.

Policies can be implemented by using positive or negative feedback over clusters of self-organized agents. In this line, the government of a city should foster and provide the necessary resources to develop virtual communities that mimic the organizational structure of the city, neighborhood, street, cultural associations, etc., including humans and non-human agents. Furthermore, it will also enable a participative government, that can be developed using self-regulated collective intelligence mechanisms, like the ones exhibited by well-known Internet forums that base their operation on a *karma* system [12, pp. 139–140].

6   Example: A Cognitive City Scenario

Our nature-inspired model is, indeed, theoretic and describes the properties that agents comprising a cognitive city should have. However, it is possible to identify practical cognitive cities examples following those theoretic principles and transform theory into practice. In order to illustrate the practicability of our model, we describe a simple example of a situation that might happen in a cognitive city and how its agents could behave according to the properties of our model:

Consider a cognitive city CC geographically divided in a set of quarters $Q = \{q_1, q_2, \ldots, q_l\}$, a set of agents $A^{q_j} = \{V^{q_j}, P^{q_j}, TL^{q_j}\}$ located in a given quarter q_j, where $V^{q_j} = \{v_1^{q_j}, v_2^{q_j}, \ldots, v_n^{q_j}\}$ is a set of intelligent vehicles in q_j, $P^{q_j} = \{p_1^{q_j}, p_2^{q_j}, \ldots, p_m^{q_j}\}$ is a set of pedestrians in q_j, and $TL^{q_j} = \{tl_1^{q_j}, tl_2^{q_j}, \ldots, tl_k^{q_j}\}$ is a set of traffic lights in q_j.

An intelligent vehicle $v_i^{q_j} \in V^{q_j}$ has a blowout, due to the poor state of the road, and remains stopped blocking a lane. The vehicle tries to communicate the situation to nearby agents (*e.g.*, other vehicles, pedestrians) *[locality: the vehicle interacts with nearby agents]* but it also has an electric problem and the communication system malfunctions. However, a pedestrian $p_i^{q_j} \in P^{q_j}$ sees the incident and reports the problem with a mobile phone to the nearby agents *[redundancy: the citizen acting as a sensor transmits the alert that the vehicle could not send]*, thus, nearby vehicles in V^{q_j} could try to avoid the blocked lane *[stigmergy: agents communicate and react through changes in the environment]*.

The closest traffic light $tl_f^{q_j}$, equipped with smart cameras and speed sensors, adapts its role to evaluate the incident *[specialization: Agents have a set of specialized roles, in this case, "control traffic lights" and "evaluate traffic incidents"]*. $tl_f^{q_j}$ detects and confirms the incident, performs an overall evaluation of the status of the occupants of the vehicle, and sends an alert to the road emergency teams (located in another quarter q_v of the city). *[networking: Despite the importance of the locality principle, agents have access to the information flows of the city and can communicate information to agents in other quarters of the city]*. Also, $tl_f^{q_j}$ informs nearby traffic lights and exchanges congestion information, thus, allowing the rearrangement of their green/red patterns to adapt to the event, so that traffic keeps flowing without major disturbances. *[feedback loops: agents (e.g., traffic lights) exchange information in a multi-directional way and create feedback loops that allow them to gradually adapt to changes in the environment]*. Traffic lights in TL^{q_j} learn from their interactions and behave proactively by sending alerts to nearby vehicles and pedestrians.

In the midterm, and after several incidents in the same place, a collective report from TL^{q_j} agents is sent to local authorities, so that they can be aware of the problems in this area, evaluate the risks, and plan the proper actions to mitigate accidents (in this case, repaving the road would be a solution) *[governance: Agents proactively collaborate to generate knowledge and share it with local authorities to help them make better decisions]*. Note that the whole situation has been managed without a central authority controlling the procedure, on the contrary, each agent acts autonomously and collaborates with the others to adapt and address situations *[decentralized control]*.

7 Open Challenges

In previous sections we have justified the need for new paradigms of cities and proposed our model of cognitive city along with a practical example of its applicability. However, cognitive cities can only become a reality in the near future if the proper decisions are made. Many challenges have to be addressed in order to achieve this goal. Next, we identify and explain some of the main challenges, classified under two categories: namely societal and technical.

7.1 Societal Challenges

Under this category we list challenges that affect citizens, their rights and duties, their liberties, and their interactions.

Citizens Participation and Usability: Citizens engagement and participation are essential. Involving citizens in decision-making processes is a fundamental premise to build cognitive cities. Although this is a difficult task, gamification strategies with incentives could help in increasing citizens engagement. Moreover, usability and educational issues should be also taken into account so as to avoid *uncanny valley*-like effects, in which users feel that their interactions with AI systems are unpleasant.

Disruption, Inequality and Discrimination: As a result of the adoption of the Cognitive City paradigm, it is expected that new business models based on cognitive urban technologies will appear. They will be disruptive and will pose societal, regulatory, and economic challenges, which could lead to inequalities. The digital divide should be prevented specially for those citizens with limited technological background. These inequalities would lead to a biased city cognition, thus, missing contributions and needs of minorities, which could be discriminated. On the other hand, avoiding the digital divide and considering the needs of minorities is an opportunity to assist them, and to increase their quality of lives in the cognitive city.

Social Codes and Liability: Societies operate on social codes to which we all agree upon. With the dawn of cognitive cities, these social codes may suffer from a transformation that would require an educational effort to teach citizens these new communication codes. Also, since decisions are decentralized by nature, it is not clear how to behave when something goes wrong: who takes responsibility for the damages? There is a significant amount of work to be done so as to address legal and regulatory concerns.

Data Ownership and Open Data: Data ownership will need to be carefully defined. Who is the owner of the data and the created knowledge? The citizen? The city government? The service provider? The infrastructure provider? Also, transparency is a key factor that could be addressed by putting in place open data policies, but data protection regulations must be carefully considered.

7.2   Technical Challenges

Under this category we list those challenges that affect information and communication technologies, supporting infrastructure, and algorithms.

Data Volume, Heterogeneity and Quality: Processing huge data volumes at agents' side requires to further develop and standardize computing paradigms such as edge and fog computing, and to reduce latency and dependency of communication links. Also, lightweight machine learning algorithms will be needed to circumvent the limitations of IoT regarding computational power and storage.

Not only volume but heterogeneity poses significant problems: Standardization across heterogeneous systems will require new protocols and ontologies to integrate architectures from multiple vendors and service providers. Moreover, massive processing of incomplete (missing values), imprecise, and untagged data will require robust machine learning approaches.

Autonomy: To achieve real autonomy, agents will need to reach high levels of self-optimization, self-diagnosis, and self-healing. However, total autonomy is costly in terms of computational power. Hence, a trade-off between autonomy and emergent collaborative behavior among agents can help to mitigate the problem, especially in large multi-agent networks.

Security and Privacy: Security is important everywhere but, in a cognitive environment, it becomes paramount. For instance, the injection of tampered data into a cognitive system could lead to serious unwanted consequences, which could put in danger the very system and people lives. Assuring the trustworthiness and accuracy of communications among agents becomes essential. Moreover, the massive collection of citizen data raises serious privacy concerns. Every component of the cognitive systems should be implemented with a privacy-by-design approach in mind, and the appropriate safeguards for the existing risks should be implemented and managed. Open data policies, needed to achieve citizens' involvement, will have to be balanced with strong privacy-preserving mechanisms.

The Control Problem: While self-organization and feedback loops are preconditions for the emergence of new adaptive patterns and, thus, to resiliency, not all feedback loops are beneficial (*e.g.*, stock market panic episodes). The detection of these unwanted effects must be addressed, and new methods should be developed and implemented to fight them. Furthermore, uncontrolled positive feedback loops could endanger the system, since they tend to drain resources.

Research in nonlinear systems theory and agent-based control can be used to detect emergent undesirable behaviors [26], and interaction tuning techniques can be used to reward those individual behaviors that maximize collective benefit [18]. Other radical mechanisms, like kill switches, could be implemented by manufacturers to stop uncontrollable feedback effects.

8   Conclusions

Cities needs are progressively growing as a result of the urbanization process. With the aim to lessen the problems of overpopulation in cities, ICT technologies were put in place and the paradigm of Smart Cities generalized. However, the smart city idea has limitations in its very fundamentals, namely lack of decentralized control, lack of proactivity, lack of learning and adaptation abilities, and so on. Despite their limitations, smart cities provide the basic ICT ground for the creation of a more powerful and sustainable approach: Cognitive cities.

In this article, we have recalled the concept of cognitive city and we have justified its need. Also, we have proposed our model of cognitive city inspired in complex adaptive systems with natural resiliency capabilities, and we have defined the fundamental properties of the agents that form these cities of the future, namely decentralized control, locality and stigmergy, global networking, use of feedback loops, specialization, redundancy, randomness and proactive governance. Although our model is mainly theoretic, we showed an example to illustrate the practical applicability of our model, and its usefulness as well.

Being this a seminal article, there remain many open issues that require further discussion and analysis. In fact, probably the main contribution of this article is to set the ground for the discussion of the challenges that Cognitive Cities have ahead. To that end, we have summarized some of the most relevant challenges to be addressed in future cognitive cities. In the near future, we plan to focus on some of the aforementioned challenges, specially those related to security, privacy, and healthcare [27]. Also, we will pay special attention to the ethical issues emerging from the use of artificial intelligence.

References

1. United Nations Population Division, Department of Economic and Social Affairs: The World's Cities in 2016 - Data Booklet (ST/ESA/ SER.A/392) (2016)
2. Solanas, A., et al.: Smart health: a context-aware health paradigm within smart cities. IEEE Commun. Mag. **52**(8), 74–81 (2014)
3. Martinez-Balleste, A., Perez-Martinez, P.A., Solanas, A.: The pursuit of citizens' privacy: a privacy-aware smart city is possible. IEEE Commun. Mag. **51**(69), 136–141 (2013)
4. Machin, J., Solanas, A.: A review on the meaning of cognitive cities. In: 2018 9th International Conference on Information, Intelligence, Systems and Applications (IISA), Zakynthos, Greece, July 2018
5. Mostashari, A., Arnold, F., Mansouri, M., Finger, M.: Cognitive cities and intelligent urban governance. Netw. Ind. Q. **13**(3), 4–7 (2011)
6. Ashby, W.R.: An Introduction to Cybernetics. Chapman & Hall Ltd., London (1961)
7. Mostashari, A., Arnold, F., Maurer, M., Wade, J.: Citizens as sensors: the cognitive city paradigm. In: 2011 8th International Conference & Expo on Emerging Technologies for a Smarter World, November, pp. 1–5 (2011). https://doi.org/10.1109/CEWIT.2011.6135861
8. Siemens, G.: Connectivism: a learning theory for the digital age. Int. J. Instr. Technol. Distance Learn. **2**(1), 3–10 (2005)
9. Kaltenrieder, P., Portmann, E., Myrach, T.: Fuzzy knowledge representation in cognitive cities. In: 2015 IEEE International Conference on Fuzzy Systems (FUZZ-IEEE), August, pp. 1–8 (2015). https://doi.org/10.1109/FUZZ-IEEE.2015.7337951
10. Kaltenrieder, P., Portmann, E., D'onofrio, S.: Enhancing multidirectional communication for cognitive cities. In: 2015 Second International Conference on eDemocracy & eGovernment (ICEDEG), pp. 38–43. IEEE (2015)
11. Finger, M., Portmann, E.: What are cognitive cities? In: Portmann, E., Finger, M. (eds.) Towards Cognitive Cities. SSDC, vol. 63, pp. 1–11. Springer, Cham (2016). https://doi.org/10.1007/978-3-319-33798-2_1
12. Johnson, S.: Emergence: The Connected Lives of Ants, Brains, Cities and Software. Scribner, New York (2001)
13. Krugman, P.R.: The Self-organizing Economy. Blackwell, Oxford (1996)
14. Holland, J.H.: Studying complex adaptive systems. J. Syst. Sci. Complex. **19**(1), 1–8 (2006). https://doi.org/10.1007/s11424-006-0001-z
15. Holland, J.: Complex adaptive systems. Daedalus **121**(1), 17–30 (1992)
16. Cunha, D., Xavier, R., de Castro, L.N.: Bacterial colonies as complex adaptive systems. Nat. Comput. **17**(4), 781–798 (2018). https://doi.org/10.1007/s11047-018-9689-7
17. Li, L., Peng, H., Kurths, J., Yang, Y., Schellnhuber, H.J.: Chaos-order transition in foraging behavior of ants. Proc. Nat. Acad. Sci. (2014). https://doi.org/10.1073/pnas.1407083111
18. Moses, M., Flanagan, T., Letendre, K., Fricke, M.: Ant colonies as a model of human computation. In: Michelucci, P. (ed.) Handbook of Human Computation, pp. 25–37. Springer, New York (2013). https://doi.org/10.1007/978-1-4614-8806-4_4
19. Schultz, T.: In search of ant ancestors. Proc. Nat. Acad. Sci. U.S.A. **97**(26), 14028–14029 (2000). https://doi.org/10.1073/pnas.011513798

20. Dorigo, M., Caro, G.D.: Ant colony optimization: a new meta-heuristic. In: Proceedings of the 1999 Congress on Evolutionary Computation-CEC99 (Cat. No. 99TH8406), July, vol. 2, pp. 1470–1477 (1999). https://doi.org/10.1109/CEC.1999.782657

21. Bonabeau, E., Dorigo, M., Theraulaz, G.: From Natural to Artificial Swarm Intelligence. Oxford University Press Inc., New York (1999)

22. Holldobler, B., Wilson, E.: The Superorganism: The Beauty, Elegance, and Strangeness of Insect Societies. W.W. Norton & Company, New York (2008)

23. Portugali, J.: What makes cities complex? In: Portugali, J., Stolk, E. (eds.) Complexity, Cognition, Urban Planning and Design, pp. 3–19. Springer, Cham (2016). https://doi.org/10.1007/978-3-319-32653-5_1

24. Wiener, N.: The Human Use of Human Beings: Cybernetics and Society. Houghton Mifflin, Boston (1950)

25. Beni, G., Wang, J.: Swarm intelligence in cellular robotic systems. In: Dario, P., Sandini, G., Aebischer, P. (eds.) Robots and Biological Systems: Towards a New Bionics?, vol. 102, pp. 703–712. Springer, Berlin (1993). https://doi.org/10.1007/978-3-642-58069-7_38

26. Van Dyke Parunak, H., VanderBok, R.S.: Managing emergent behavior in distributed control systems. In: ISA TECH/EXPO Technology Update Conference Proceedings, vol. 1, pp. 59–66 (1997)

27. Solanas, A.: The evolution of healthcare: First steps towards cognitive healthcare. In: Invited Talk in Advances and Applications of Data Science and Engineering. Royal Academy of Engineering, Madrid, June 2016

Genetic Algorithm to Evolve Ensembles of Rules for On-Line Scheduling on Single Machine with Variable Capacity

Francisco J. Gil-Gala and Ramiro Varela[✉]

Department of Computer Science, University of Oviedo,
Campus of Gijón, 33204 Gijón, Spain
{giljavier,ramiro}@uniovi.es,
http://www.di.uniovi.es/iscop

Abstract. On-line scheduling is often required in real life situations. This is the case of the one machine scheduling with variable capacity and tardiness minimization problem, denoted $(1, Cap(t)|| \sum T_i)$. This problem arose from a charging station where the charging periods for large fleets of electric vehicles (EV) must be scheduled under limited power and other technological constraints. The control system of the charging station requires solving many instances of this problem on-line. The characteristics of these instances being strongly dependent on the load and restrictions of the charging station at a given time. In this paper, the goal is to evolve small ensembles of priority rules such that for any instance of the problem at least one of the rules in the ensemble has high chance to produce a good solution. To do that, we propose a Genetic Algorithm (GA) that evolves ensembles of rules from a large set of rules previously calculated by a Genetic Program (GP). We conducted an experimental study showing that the GA is able to evolve ensembles or rules covering instances with different characteristics and so they outperform ensembles of both classic priority rules and the best rules obtained by GP.

Keywords: One machine scheduling · Priority rules ·
Ensembles of rules · Genetic Algorithm · Hyperheuristics ·
Electric Vehicle Charging Scheduling

1 Introduction

This paper tackles the one machine scheduling problem with variable capacity, denoted $(1, Cap(t)|| \sum T_i)$. In this problem, a number of jobs must be scheduled on a single machine, whose capacity varies over time, with the objective of minimizing the total tardiness objective function. This problem arose from the Electric Vehicle Charging Scheduling (EVCS) problem confronted in [5]. Indeed, solving this problem requires solving many instances of the $(1, Cap(t)|| \sum T_i)$ problem on-line.

© Springer Nature Switzerland AG 2019
J. M. Ferrández Vicente et al. (Eds.): IWINAC 2019, LNCS 11487, pp. 223–233, 2019.
https://doi.org/10.1007/978-3-030-19651-6_22

Priority rules are of common use in on-line scheduling. For example, in [5], the $(1, Cap(t) || \sum T_i)$ problem is solved by means of the *Apparent Tardiness Cost* (ATC) priority rule. Priority rules can be defined manually by experts on the problem domain, as it is the case of the ATC rule [8], although it is clear that automatic methods could capture some characteristics of the scheduling problem that are not clear to human experts. For this purpose, hyper-heuristics as Genetic Programming (GP) are a good choice.

As it may be expected, a single rule, even being very good in average for a large set of instances, may not be good for a number of them. For this reason, some researchers focus in calculating sets of rules that collaboratively solve the problem. This may be done in different ways. For example, in [4] the authors propose GP to obtain a set of rules that are applied in turn to schedule a single operation. In this paper, we take an alternative approach. Given the low time required to compute a solution to the instances of the $(1, Cap(t) || \sum T_i)$ problem generated when solving the EVSC in [5], we propose to use a set of priority rules in parallel to obtain a number of solutions. Our working hypotheses is that if these rules are trained to solve instances with different characteristics, any of the rules will produce a good solution for each particular instance.

So, it is our goal to devise ensembles of rules from a large pool of rules obtained by other method; in our study, we will consider rules evolved by the GP proposed in [3]. To this end, we propose to use a Genetic Algorithm (GA). The results produced by the evolved ensembles are compared with those from the best on-line and off-line methods in the literature to solve the $(1, Cap(t) || \sum T_i)$ problem. As far as we known, these methods are the GP proposed in [3] and the genetic algorithm proposed in [9]. The results of the experimental study show that the solutions obtained from the evolved ensembles are better that those produced by the sets of best rules obtained in [3] and that these solutions are actually close to those obtained off-line in [9].

The remainder of the paper is organized as follows. In the next section we give a formal definition of the $(1, Cap(t) || \sum T_i)$ problem. Section 2 introduces the solving method used for the $(1, Cap(t) || \sum T_i)$ problem on-line, which consists of two main components: schedule builder and priority rules. In Sect. 3 we present the GA devised to evolve ensembles of rules. In Sect. 4 we report the results of the experimental study. Finally, in Sect. 5 we summarize the main conclusions and outline some ideas for future work.

1.1   Problem Definition

The $(1, Cap(t) || \sum T_i)$ problem may be defined as follows. We are given a number of n jobs $\{1, \ldots, n\}$, available at time $t = 0$, which have to be scheduled on a machine whose capacity varies over time, such that $Cap(t) \geq 0, t \geq 0$, is the capacity of the machine in the interval $[t, t+1)$. Job i has duration p_i and due date d_i. The goal is to allocate starting times $st_i, 1 \leq i \leq n$ to the jobs on the machine such that the following constraints are satisfied:

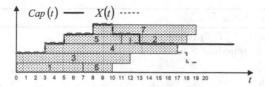

Fig. 1. One schedule for an instance of the $(1, Cap(t) || \sum T_i)$ problem with 7 tasks and a machine with capacity varying between 2 and 5.

i. At any time $t \geq 0$ the number of jobs that are processed in parallel on the machine, $X(t)$, cannot exceed the capacity of the machine; i.e.,

$$X(t) \leq Cap(t). \tag{1}$$

ii. The processing of jobs on the machine cannot be preempted; i.e.,

$$C_i = st_i + p_i, \tag{2}$$

where C_i is the completion time of job i.

The objective function is the total tardiness, defined as:

$$\sum_{i=1,...,n} \max(0, C_i - d_i) \tag{3}$$

which should be minimized.

Figure 1 shows a schedule for a problem with 7 jobs; the capacity of the machine varies between 2 and 5 over time. Due dates are not represented for the sake of clarity. As we can observe, $X(t) \leq Cap(t)$ for all $t \geq 0$.

One particular case of this problem is the parallel identical machines problem [8], denoted $(P || \sum T_i)$, which is NP-hard. Thus, the $(1, Cap(t) || \sum T_i)$ problem is NP-hard as well.

2   Solving Method

Given the real time requirements of the EVCSP, to solve the $(1, Cap(t) || \sum T_i)$ problem, we consider a schedule builder guided by priority rules.

2.1   Schedule Builder

We use here the schedule builder proposed in [9], which produces *left-shifted schedules*, a subspace of feasible schedules that includes at least one optimal solution. This schedule builder is depicted in Algorithm 1; it maintains a set US with the unscheduled jobs, as well as the consumed capacity $X(t)$ due to the jobs scheduled so far. In each iteration, the algorithm builds the subset US^* containing the jobs in US that can be scheduled at the earliest possible starting

---

Algorithm 1. Schedule Builder

Data: A $(1, Cap(t) \| \sum T_i)$ problem instance $\mathcal{P}$.
Result: A feasible schedule S for $\mathcal{P}$.
$US \leftarrow \{1, 2, ..., n\}$;
$X(t) \leftarrow 0; \forall t \geq 0$;
while $US \neq \emptyset$ **do**
    $\gamma(\alpha) = min\{t' | \exists u \in US; X(t) < Cap(t), t' \leq t < t' + p_u\}$;
    $US^* = \{u \in US | X(t) < Cap(t), \gamma(\alpha) \leq t < \gamma(\alpha) + p_u\}$;
    Non-deterministically pick job $u \in US^*$;
    Assign $st_u = \gamma(\alpha)$;
    Update $X(t) \leftarrow X(t) + 1; \forall t$ with $st_u \leq t < st_u + p_u$;
    $US \leftarrow US - \{u\}$;
end
return *The schedule* $S = (st_1, st_2, ..., st_n)$;

---

time, denoted $\gamma(\alpha)$, and selects one of these jobs non-deterministically to be scheduled. For example, the sequence of choices $(1, 3, 4, 5, 6, 7, 2)$ would lead to building the schedule in Fig. 1(b). The schedule builder may be instantiated by using any priority rule or heuristic, as we will see in the next section. Besides, it could be embedded as a decoder in a genetic algorithm, as done in [9].

2.2 Priority Rules for the $(1, Cap(t) \| \sum T_i)$

The non-deterministic choice in each iteration of Algorithm 1 may be done with a priority so that the job having the highest priority in US^* is chosen to be scheduled. In the literature there are a number of rules that could be adapted to the $(1, Cap(t) \| \sum T_i)$ problem. Among them, we may consider the *Apparent Tardiness Cost* (ATC) rule, which was used with success to solve some scheduling problems with tardiness objectives (e.g. [7,10]); with this rule, the priority of each job $j \in US^*$ is given by

$$\pi_j = \frac{1}{p_j} exp \left[\frac{-max(0, d_j - \gamma(\alpha) - p_j)}{g\bar{p}} \right] \tag{4}$$

In Eq. (4), $\bar{p}$ is the average processing time of the jobs in US and g is a look-ahead parameter to be introduced by the user. We may consider other priority rules simpler than ATC, for example *Earliest Due Date* (EDD) or *Shortest Processing Time* (SPT) rules, which calculate priorities for an eligible job j as $\pi_j = 1/d_j$ and $\pi_j = 1/p_j$ respectively.

As pointed, an alternative to the priority rules defined by experts are rules created automatically for systems as GP [1–4,6]. These systems are used to evolve priority rules that are trained to solve a set of given instances for different scheduling problem, and then evaluated over a set of unseen instances. In this way, they are able to evolve rules that are good in average on the training set, but the best of these rules may be not so good for each single instance.

Table 1. Summary of results obtained from ensembles of rules evolved by GP, an ensemble of ATC rules, the best rule evolved by GP and the best ATC rule. For each method, average tardiness values on the training and testing sets of instances considered in [3] are reported.

Set of rules	Size	Training	Testing
ATC(0.5)	1	1000.52	1011.33
ATC(0.1,...,1.0)	10	984.18	989.57
GP best rule	1	986.32	992.14
GP best rules	10	974.24	975.97

2.3   Considering Ensembles of Rules and Some Previous Results

From the above observations, it seems clear that it is not easy to evolve a rule that may generalize well over a large set of unseen instances so that it can compete with off-line algorithms such as GA introduced in [9]. Therefore, we propose considering ensembles or rules in the following way: each instance is solved by a set of rules (10 rules or so) and then the best of the 10 solutions is taken. This method would be feasible due to the execution time being still suitable for the real time requirements of the EVCSP. To estimate the viability of this method, we may analyse the results in Table 1, which shows solutions from two single rules, ATC(0.5) and the best rule evolved by GP in [3]; and two ensembles with 10 instances of the ATC rule, g varying in $0.1\ldots1.0$, and the ensemble formed by the 10 best of the 30 rules obtained by GP. We can observe that putting 10 learned rules to work together reduces significantly the average tardiness. These results strongly suggest that learning ensembles of rules is an interesting line of research.

3   Evolving Ensembles of Rules with Genetic Algorithms

We are given a large set $\mathcal{N}$ of N priority rules and the results of these rules over a set of M instances; i.e., the tardiness values obtained by Algorithm 1 guided by each one of these N rules. The goal is to obtain a small ensemble of P rules such that they cover the M instances; namely, such that the average value of the best solutions to the M instances obtained by the rules in P is minimized.

To solve this problem we propose a genetic algorithm (GA). The main elements of this algorithm are chosen as follows:

Coding Scheme. Individuals are given by variations with repetition of the N rules taken P by P; so, there are M^N different chromosomes in all. This encoding allows for efficient genetic operators and, having duplicated rules in the chromosome, the GA may keep good rules (those covering many instances) more easily after mating and mutation. Furthermore, it gives GA the chance to reach ensembles with less than P different rules.

Initial Population. Initial chromosomes are random variations of the N rules. In principle, every rule has the same probability to be chosen. However, other strategies could be better, for example giving each rule a probability proportional to the average value of the solutions obtained by that rule on the M instances; i.e., the fitness value of this rule in the GP.

Crossover. In this problem, the order of rules in the chromosome is not relevant, so it is enough to make that each offspring inherits some rules from each one of the parents. So, a simple scheme as the following may be appropriate. Given two parents, two offspring are obtained. Firstly, a binary string of length P is generated, each bit chosen uniformly in $\{0, 1\}$. Then, the first offspring includes in each position the rules from the first parent with 0 in the same position in the bit string and those with 1 in the second parent. Analogously for the second offspring swapping 0 and 1.

Mutation. Mutation plays a very important role in this GA as it is in charge of including in the population new rules from the set $\mathcal{N}$. It changes the rules in a number of positions, between 1 and $P/2$, of the chromosome by random rules chosen uniformly from $\mathcal{N}$.

Evolutionary Scheme. The main structure of the algorithm is given in Algorithm 2. It is a generational GA with random selection and replacement by tournament among every two mated parents and their two offspring, which confers the GA an implicit form of elitism.

Evaluation. For each of the M instances, the solution given by the best of the P rules in the ensemble is considered. Then the fitness value of the chromosome is the average value of the M solutions.

Algorithm 2. Genetic Algorithm.

Data: A set of M instances of the $(1, Cap(t)|| \sum T_i)$ problem. A set $\mathcal{N}$ of N priority rules and the average tardiness of the solutions to the N instances obtained by the N rules. Parameters: crossover probability p_c, mutation probability p_m, number of generations $\#gen$, population size $\#popsize$, chromosome length P (the size of the ensemble).

Result: A ensemble of P priority rules

Generate and evaluate the initial population $\mathcal{P}(0)$;

for $t=1$ to $\#gen\text{-}1$ **do**

    Selection: organize the chromosomes in $\mathcal{P}(t-1)$ into pairs at random;

    Recombination: mate each pair of chromosomes and mutate the two offsprings in accordance with p_c and p_m;

    Evaluation: evaluate the resulting chromosomes;

    Replacement: make a tournament selection among every two parents and their offsprings to complete $\mathcal{P}(t)$;

end

return *the best ensemble of P priority rules reached;*

---

4   Experimental Study

We have conducted an experimental study aimed at analysing the behaviour of the proposed GA. To this end, we implemented a prototype in Java, the target machine was Windows on top of Intel i5 @4.2 GHz. 15.5 GB RAM.

4.1   Test Bed and Previous Results

The test bed considered in this study is set $\mathcal{N}$ of $N = 10000$ different priority rules obtained by the GP proposed in [3]. The GP exploited a set of $M = 50$ instances of the $(1, Cap(t)|| \sum T_i)$ problem as training set to evolve the rules. The same M instances are considered here. It is important to remark that the N rules correspond to different generations of the GP, therefore their qualities are quite different. The set of $M = 50$ instances is a subset of the set of 1000 instances proposed in [9]. The remaining 950 instances in this set are considered here to evaluate the best evolved ensembles.

Before going to the experiments and results from GA, it is worth analysing some previous results. Table 2 shows the average results obtained by three classic priority rules, SPT, EDD and ATC, taking the parameter $g = 0.5$ that is usually the best one, and the best of the $N = 10000$ rules evolved by GP, on all the instances. As we can see, SPT is really bad as it seems natural due to the fact that it only considers processing times but not due dates. EDD is better, but it is ATC the classic rule that produces the best results of the classical rules as it considers both processing times and due dates to calculate jobs' priorities. Besides, the best rule evolved by GP is even better than ATC. As can be expected, these values are far from the results obtained by the GA proposed in [9], which of course takes much more time, about 40 s per run, versus a few ms taken by the schedule builder combined with a single priority rule. If we look at the last column of the table, we can see that the quotient of values on the training and testing sets are quite similar and closed to 1.0, showing that all rules perform similarly on both sets, what in particular means that the rules evolved by GP generalize quite well.

Table 2. Summary of results obtained by the classical rules and the best rule obtained by GP on the instances of the $(1, Cap(t)|| \sum T_i)$ problem considered in this study.

| Rule | Avg. Tardiness | | |
	Training (50 inst.)	Testing (950 inst.)	Test./Train.
SPT	5473.18	5319.81	1.03
EDD	1256.84	1291.66	0.97
ATC(0.5)	1000.52	1011.33	0.99
Best rule(GP)	988.02	997.65	0.99
GA (30 runs) Best/Avg.	950.18/950.63	959.06/959.51	0.99/0.99

Table 3. Summary of results obtained from different subsets of $\mathcal{N}$. $Better_R$ is the subset of rules of $\mathcal{N}$ that produces a result better or at least equal to the rule R.

Set of rules	#rules	Avg. Tard. (50 inst.)
All	10000	1769.50
$Better_{SPT}$	9302	1306.53
$Better_{EDD}$	7654	1108.88
$Better_{ATC(0.5)}$	784	993.63

It is also worth to consider the tardiness values obtained by some subsets of the N rules on the M instances. This provides some reference on the results one may expect from the ensembles evolved by GA. Table 3 shows results from all rules in $\mathcal{N}$ and from some subsets. $Better_R$ denotes the subset of $\mathcal{N}$ such that each rule in the subset produces better or at least equal result to R. The second column in the table shows the number of rules of the set (#*rules*) and the third one shows the average tardiness from all rules on all 50 instances (so each value is the average of #*rules*×50 single tardiness values). These results show that the rules in $\mathcal{N}$ produce quite different tardiness values and that restricting to subsets of rules that individually perform better than a given threshold, these subsets perform better and better. This is natural and suggests that varying $\mathcal{N}$ over these subsets the GA could obtain better and better ensembles as well.

4.2   Results from GA

The GA was run 30 times on each instance with the following parameters: #*popsize* $= 100$, #*gen* $= 1000$, $p_c = 0.8$, $p_m = 0.2$. Besides, four values of the ensemble size P (or chromosome size) were considered: 3, 5, 10 and 50. With these values, the time taken in each single run of GA varies between 2 s and 360 s.

Table 4. Summary of results from GA starting from different sets of rules $\mathcal{N}$ (*All*, $Better_{SPT}$, $Better_{EDD}$, $Better_{ATC(0.5)}$) and for different ensemble sizes P (3, 5, 10, 50). Values in **bold** are the best ones

P	*All*		$Better_{SPT}$		$Better_{EDD}$		$Better_{ATC(0.5)}$	
	Avg.	Best	Avg.	Best	Avg.	Best	Avg.	Best
3	978.52	**978.14**	978.46	**978.14**	978.31	**978.14**	978.14	**978.14**
5	975.64	974.70	975.66	**974.64**	975.49	**974.64**	975.32	975.20
10	972.74	971.90	972.55	971.48	972.55	**971.32**	972.89	972.66
50	968.14	967.56	968.03	967.62	967.91	**967.42**	971.86	971.86

Table 4 reports the results from GA starting from different sets of rules $\mathcal{N}$. For each value of P and set $\mathcal{N}$, the best ensemble of each of the 30 runs is recorded. Then we show the average fitness and the fitness of the best ensemble reached. Remember that to obtain the fitness of an ensemble we consider for each of the M instances the best solution from the P rules and then take the average value over the M instances. We can observe that these values clearly depend on the value of P, as expected, being better and better as long as P increases. At the same time, the results depend on the set $\mathcal{N}$ of initial solutions, even though to a lesser extent. So, the results are rather similar for the sets All, $Better_{SPT}$ and $Better_{EDD}$, showing that GA is robust. However, for values of P larger than 3, the results get worse if the candidate rules are restricted to the set $Better_{ATC(0.5)}$, which includes only about the best 10% of the 10000 rules considered. This fact shows that to obtain good ensembles it is not enough to count only on the best rules.

Table 5. Summary of results from different ensembles.

Ensemble	Size	Training	Testing
ATC(0.1,...,1.0)	10	984.18	989.57
Best rules	3	985.64	994.97
	5	985.64	994.90
	10	983.96	992.40
	50	975.58	978.56
Evolved	3	978.14	985.94
	5	974.64	981.69
	10	971.32	978.26
	50	967.42	974.68

To assess the performance of the ensembles evolved by the GA, we consider the best ensembles obtained for each value of P and other ensembles obtained from classical rules or those obtained from the best rules of the initial set. Specifically, we consider the ATC rule with 10 values of the parameter g (0.1,...,1.0), which in practice perform quite well, and the ensembles given by the 3, 5, 10 and 50 best rules of the initial set. Table 5 summarizes the results of these ensembles on the training set and also on the testing set that includes 950 unseen instances.

As we can see, the ATC(0.1,...,1.0) ensemble is better or at least similar to the ensembles of the 10 or less best rules. Only from the 50 best rules is obtained a better ensemble than ATC(0.1,...,1.0). However, the ensembles evolved by GA are clearly better than those composed by the best rules. In particular, if we take the ensembles with 10 rules, which are reasonable considering the real time requirements of the EVCSP, the evolved ensemble improves in more than 10 units the values produced by the others. This value is actually relevant if we consider that the average value of the best solutions reached to the 50 instances of the test set by all the 10000 rules is 967.28. In terms of relative error we can tell that the evolved ensemble of 10 rules reduces this value in about 75%.

Furthermore, for $P = 50$, GA almost reaches the optimal solution; i.e., the best ensemble that can be built from the initial rules.

From these results, we may conclude that the proposed GA combined with the GP proposed in [3] is a good approach to obtain ensembles of rules to solve the $(1, Cap(t) || \sum T_i)$ problem.

5 Conclusions

We have demonstrated that an ensemble of priority rules is a good option to solve scheduling problems on-line. From a large set of priority rules with different characteristics, it is possible to evolve small ensembles such that for any unseen instance of the scheduling problem any of the rules in the ensemble has a high chance of getting a good solution. We have experimented with the one machine scheduling problem with variable capacity, denoted $(1, Cap(t) || \sum T_i)$, and the pool of priority rules evolved by the genetic progam proposed in [3], which evolves rules that minimize the total tardiness on a set of instances. Clearly, the same method could be applied to other scheduling problems. Besides, pools of rules evolved by other methods could also be considered. Indeed, one of the lines of research we propose is aimed to evolve rules covering instances of the $(1, Cap(t) || \sum T_i)$ problem having quite different structure.

Acknowledgements. This research has been supported by the Spanish Government under research project TIN2016-79190-R and by Principality of Asturias under grant IDI/2018/000176.

References

1. Branke, J., Hildebrandt, T., Scholz-Reiter, B.: Hyper-heuristic evolution of dispatching rules: a comparison of rule representations. Evol. Comput. **23**(2), 249–277 (2015)
2. Durasevic, M., Jakobovi, D., Kneževi, K.: Adaptive scheduling on unrelated machines with genetic programming. Appl. Soft Comput. **48**, 419–430 (2016)
3. Gil-Gala, F., Mencía, C., Sierra, M., Varela, R.: Genetic programming to evolve priority rules for on-line scheduling on single machine with variable capacity. In: XVIII Conferencia de la Asociación Española para la Inteligencia Artificial, MAEB (2018)
4. Hart, E., Sim, K.: A hyper-heuristic ensemble method for static job-shop scheduling. Evol. Comput. **24**(4), 609–635 (2016)
5. Hernández-Arauzo, A., Puente, J., Varela, R., Sedano, J.: Electric vehicle charging under power and balance constraints as dynamic scheduling. Comput. Ind. Eng. **85**, 306–315 (2015)
6. Jakobović, D., Marasović, K.: Evolving priority scheduling heuristics with genetic programming. Appl. Soft Comput. **12**(9), 2781–2789 (2012)
7. Kaplan, S., Rabadi, G.: Exact and heuristic algorithms for the aerial refueling parallel machine scheduling problem with due date-to-deadline window and ready times. Comput. Ind. Eng. **62**(1), 276–285 (2012)

8. Koulamas, C.: The total tardiness problem: review and extensions. Oper. Res. **42**, 1025–1041 (1994)
9. Mencía, C., Sierra, M., Mencía, R., Varela, R.: Evolutionary one-machine scheduling in the context of electric vehicles charging. Integr. Comput.-Aided Eng. **26**(1), 1–15 (2019)
10. Sang-Oh Shim, S.O., Kim, Y.D.: Scheduling on parallel identical machines to minimize total tardiness. Eur. J. Oper. Res. **177**(1), 135–146 (2007)

Multivariate Approach to Alcohol Detection in Drivers by Sensors and Artificial Vision

Paul D. Rosero-Montalvo[1,2]([✉]), Vivian F. López-Batista[2],
Diego H. Peluffo-Ordóñez[3,4], Vanessa C. Erazo-Chamorro[5],
and Ricardo P. Arciniega-Rocha[5]

[1] Universidad Técnica del Norte, Ibarra, Ecuador
pdrosero@utn.edu.ec
[2] Universidad de Salamanca, Salamanca, Spain
[3] Universidad de Nariño, Pasto, Colombia
[4] SDAS Research Group, Yachay Tech University, Urcuquí, Ecuador
https://sdas-group.com/
[5] Instituto Tecnológico Superior 17 de Julio, Ibarra, Ecuador

Abstract. This work presents a system for detecting excess alcohol in drivers to reduce road traffic accidents. To do so, criteria such as alcohol concentration the environment, a facial temperature of the driver and width of the pupil are considered. To measure the corresponding variables, the data acquisition procedure uses sensors and artificial vision. Subsequently, data analysis is performed into stages for prototype selection and supervised classification algorithms. Accordingly, the acquired data can be stored and processed in a system with low-computational resources. As a remarkable result, the amount of training samples is significantly reduced, while an admissible classification performance is achieved - reaching then suitable settings regarding the given device's conditions.

Keywords: Alcohol detection · Drunk detection ·
Prototype selection · Sensors · Supervised classification

1 Introduction

The World Health Organization has reported that 40% of all road traffic accidents are caused by the drivers' drunkenness status [1]. In addition, it is the fifth main reason for deaths on the roads. As a result, 51 million people are injured or killed every year [2]. This entails a loss for expenses of approximately 500 million dollars worldwide [3]. In Ecuador, there have been registered 2100 road traffic accidents every year caused by alcohol. Unfortunately, in the last 3 years, this percentage has increased, causing a greater number of lost lives and high economic cost for society. This is because the effects of alcohol on a driver causes vision disturbances, the psychomotor function, changes in ability to react to an

© Springer Nature Switzerland AG 2019
J. M. Ferrández Vicente et al. (Eds.): IWINAC 2019, LNCS 11487, pp. 234–243, 2019.
https://doi.org/10.1007/978-3-030-19651-6_23

alert, behaviour and conduct [4]. Concerning psychomotor functions, the reaction time of the driver increases. This is mainly reflected when the driver needs to change the foot of the accelerator to the brake which normal time is 0.75 s, while for a driver in a drunken status, the reaction time can be 2 or more seconds [5]. As a result, the probability of suffering a road traffic accident increases considerably [6].

To counteract this high number of accidents, in Ecuador road checks are made to avoid drivers with alcohol effects transiting the roads. The main tests performed on drivers are based on the relationship between the psychological and physical faculties that a person has at the time of driving and the volume of ethanol in the body [7]. Which are based on balance tests (taking as a reference a straight line in which the driver must walk), coordination (properly locate the upper and lower extremities) and spatial perception (considering the environment in which it is located). However, the results of each test do not accurately determine the blood alcohol concentration (BAC) [8]. In addition, they present a manual approach with unlikely probabilities to detect most cases. As a result, this concentration percentage can affect the driver from least to greatest and will not be detected by the control entity. The possible alterations can be a sensation of relaxation, sedation and euphoria (0.03 to 0.05 BAC level) to vegetative state (over 0.40 BAC level).

Recent research in several biometric modalities, such as the face, the fingerprint, the iris and the recognition of the retinal area of the eye. Facial recognition is the most appropriate modality, since it is the natural way of identification among humans and is totally discreet [2,8]. However, one of the most challenging modalities in the field of artificial vision. Other studies seek to detect the parameters of alcohol in the blood through sensors [7]. The same ones that allow to share data and propose different solutions to a variety of suppliers. As a result, 4 types of knowledge have been defined for the detection of driver's driving status: (i) physiological (breathing, blood or urine), (ii) vehicle-based (road vehicle behaviour), (iii) in biological signals (cardiac and cerebral) and (iv) visual characteristics. During the last decade several studies have been carried out applying these forms of detection [5]. However, these principles can not meet the objective of an early warning that prevent the use of the vehicle by a person in drunkenness state is allowed. In addition, they can be intrusive in nature, causing discomfort to the driver, making it difficult to implement and scalability [2].

All approaches and papers presented, acquire data of the person who has the uncertainty of his ethyl state. However, many of them do not present a data analysis that allows them to make the appropriate decision and learn from the experience in different cases. In this context, the different recognition techniques have gained great acceptance in the different real-life areas [3,9]. In the field of detection of alcohol in the blood, an open touch-up is based on the application of these learning algorithms within a vehicle. In this sense, embedded systems, due to their great flexibility and portability, can be an optimal alternative. Since they seek to emulate the process performed by the human brain [10,11].

The proposed system is based on the implementation and comparison of three approaches for driver's data acquisition. In this connection, we propose to use a set of specific sensors, namely: a sensor to measure the alcohol concentration in the environment (a physiological-type one, a sensor to capture the temperature of some defined driver's face points (biological-type), and another sensor able to identify and recognize the thickness of the pupil (visual-characteristic-type). Given this, on the one hand our system seeks to eliminate the uncertainty of the concentration of alcohol in the blood. On the other hand, the system is implemented inside the car in a non-invasive way that allows to recognize the driver and monitor his/her different physical and biological signals to determine his/her suitableness to steering wheel. Consequently, it is necessary to perform a signal processing stage at a sensor level. Subsequently, a data analysis is implemented allowing for choosing the appropriate algorithm by taking into consideration the nature of the data. Finally, the system is evaluated with some performance criteria: (i) Error rate, (ii) system classification speed, and (iii) optimal usage of embedded system resources.

The rest of the document is structured as follows: Sect. 2 presents the materials and methods for the system's software and hardware. Section 3 shows the results obtained in the tests of the data analysis and the overall system operation. Finally, Sect. 4 gathers the conclusions and future work.

2 Materials and Methods

The present system is designed for the stages: (a) Design and requirements of the system, (b) The data storage scheme and (c) Data analysis.

2.1 Electronic Design

The body eliminates alcohol approximately 10 h after its intake. For this reason, the system must monitor the driver when trying to drive the vehicle. The approaches to be taken into account are presented in the scheme of Fig. 1.

As a first approach, a gas detection sensor is implemented. The same one that seeks to reveal the presence of ethanol. The selected sensor is the MQ-3, due to its sensitivity to different gases and its rapid integration into the system. Subsequently, the signal must be coupled according to the curve of the gas to be used from the digital analogue converter and configure the electric resistance Rs/Ro to convert to mg/L.

As a second approach, we seek to determine the facial thermal change of the person. since it has been proven that the temperature increases in the face of a person in the ethyl state, due to that the arteries and blood vessels increase their activity. According to [2], there are 20 different points where there is a visible variation. The same ones are: nose, eyebrows, chin and forehead. Therefore, the MLX90621 sensor is used due to its speed and temperature resolution. In addition, it has a pixel array of 16 × 4 sensitive to thermal infrared radiation.

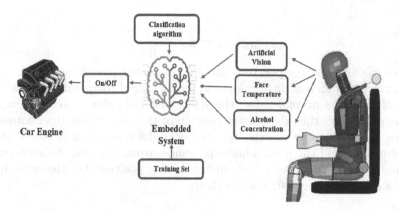

Fig. 1. Electronic system scheme

The third approach used is that of visual characteristics. Because a person who consumes alcohol the iris becomes darker, which means that its temperature compared to the sclerotic decreases. This is because the sclera is full of blood vessels that increase the temperature with alcohol consumption.

The process of acquisition of data from the pupil of the eye needs to fulfill some phases for its correct implementation. These are: (i) acquisition of images, (ii) preprocessing, (iii) segmentation, (iv) description and extraction of characteristics and (v) recognition and interpretation. Due to these reasons, there are different ways in face detection. In this system, the Viola-Jones detector has been chosen. This is because it is the one implemented by the OpenCv library that can be compiled within an embedded system.

Finally, the embedded systems that allow implementing the proposed approaches, on the one hand, the Arduino Uno for the use of the MQ-3 sensors (alcohol in the environment) and the MLX90621 for the facial temperature. On the other, the Raspberry Pi version 3 that allows to incorporate a camera for artificial vision. In addition, its computational capabilities allow the incorporation of machine learning algorithms through programming in Python.

2.2   Data Coupling Scheme

Under the criterion of a classification task, is necessary the appropriate training data set. For this reason, a stage of coupling of the sensors is performed for its correct operation [10].

As a first point, the MQ-3 sensor configures its electrical resistance for alcohol monitoring inside the vehicle. For this, data is taken in controlled tests of the environment. Subsequently, an exponential linear regression is carried out that allows to represent the concentration of the appropriate gas in representation of mg/L.

The equation to express in alcohol at a scale of 0.1 mg/L.

$$Alcohol = 0.4226 * \frac{Rs^{-1.448}}{Ro} \tag{1}$$

Once the ambient temperature and the conductor have been found, a conversion is created on a scale of colours at the measured temperature. Where the green colour shows normal value, the yellow and red colours are the temperature increase. With this, the correct position of the sensor that the information is trying to turn on the vehicle. As a result, data acquisition is stored at the minimum value and the maximum facial temperature. The Fig. 2 shows, on the one hand, the driver of the vehicle in the driving position. On the other hand, the data collection in colour scale is shown.

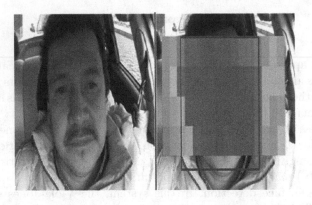

Fig. 2. Face driver temperature detection in colour scale inside at the vehicle (Color figure online)

Finally, the acquisition of images presents the following stages of prepossessing: (i) Conversion of RGB to gray scale, (ii) Equalization of the histogram (improves the contrast of a magnet and normalizes the gray scale), (iii) Detection of the face, (iv) eye detection, (v) eye pupil detection and (vi) eye pupil radius. As a result, only stage (vi) is stored for data analysis.

2.3   Data Analysis

The acquired data is stored in a matrix $Y \in \mathbb{R}^{m \times n}$, where: m is the number of samples and n represents the quantity of data acquired by the sensors and the camera. Meanwhile $L \in \mathbb{R}^{m \times 1}$ represents the vector of the labeling of the samples. In this case $m = 312$ and $n = 4$. These data were obtained from 10 controlled experiments. On the one hand, the driver of the vehicle ingested different amounts of alcohol. Subsequently, an analysis of alcohol in the blood was made through the transit entity. On the other hand, the user did not ingest any kind of alcohol for data collection.

By having embedded systems of limited computational resources, the training set of classification algorithms is crucial for the response time in the detection of the assigned task. For this, the techniques of prototype selection (PS) are based on the concept that not all data provide relevant information to the classifier. There are three changes at the time of applying the prototype selection: (i) Condensation,(ii) Editions and (iii) Hybrid [9,12].

Based in a debugged training, the main task of the system is the identification of a person with alcohol in the blood through supervised classification. Due to this, the classification criteria have been taken: (i) by distances, (ii) by probabilities (iii) based on models and (iv) based on heuristics, in order to determine the appropriate one.

3   Results

This section shows the data analysis results and system implementation.

3.1   Prototype Selection

The algorithms used are in relation to the 3 approximations of PS. For this reason, the most representatives and used algorithms of each of them are chosen. **condensation:** Condensed Nearest Neighbor (CNN), Reduced Nearest Neighbor (RNN) and Selective Nearest Neighbor (SNN). **Edition:** Edited Nearest Neighbor (ENN), All-k Edited Nearest Neighbors (AENN), Iterative Partitioning Filter (IPF) and **Hybrid:** Decremental Reduction Optimization Procedures 2 (DROP 2), Decremental Reduction Optimization Procedures 3 (DROP3) and Iterative Noise Filter based on the Fusion of Classifiers (INFFC). The algorithms are executed on an I7 processor computer and 16 gigs of RAM. As a result, the result of its execution time, the reduction of instances and its percentage of elimination is shown in Table 1.

Table 1. PS data analysis

PS algorithm	Proc. time (s)	Remv. inst	% of remv. inst
CNN and RNN	6.01	290	92.94
SNN	261.15	222	71.15
DROP2	444.91	224	73.7
DROP3	399.45	292	93.58
AENN	2.66	14	4.48
ENN	0.77	10	3.2
INFFC	13.5	5	1.60
IPF	0.86	2	0.64
RNN	4.31	275	88.14

3.2   Classification Algorithms

The distance-based algorithm is considered k Nearest Neighbor (k-NN). According to the literature, the best results are obtained with k = 3 and with k = 5. A Bayesian classifier (criterion by probabilities), obtains the posterior probability of each class, C_i, using the Bayes rule, as the product of the probability *apriori* of the class by the conditional probability of attributes (E) of each class, divided by the probability of the attributes: $P(C_i|E) = P(C_i)P(E|C_i)/P(E)$. Under the model-based criteria, it uses the decision support machine (SVM) method. In this sense, the polynomial kernel function has been used: $k_P(x, y) = ((x, y) + gamma)$. Finally, as a heuristic criterion, the classification tree algorithm is used. Since a classifier can be defined as a function $d(x)$ defined in the classification space **X** in **M** different subsets $A_1, A_2, ..., A_M$, being **X** the union of all of them for all x belonging to A_m to the predicted class C_m.

In order to define the classification criteria, the all databases within the PS section have worked. Table 2 shows the performance of each classifier with its most optimal variants and its classification average.

Table 2. PS classification performance

PS algorithm	k-NN	Clas. Bayes	Tree Dec.	SVM sigmoid
Complex data	95.15	80	97.43	96.15
CNN	80.76	45.5	79.48	94.87
SNN	79.48	55.12	97.43	93.58
DROP2	84.61	55.12	97.43	93.58
DROP3	79.48	45.5	97.43	96.15
AENN	96.15	61.15	96.15	94.87
ENN, INFFC	96.15	61.15	96.15	97.43
IPF	96.15	61.15	97.43	97.43
RNN	80.76	55.12	79.48	93.58
Average	88.58	50.06	93.58	95.12

As a result, algorithms with criteria based on heuristics and models have a high classification performance. In order to know their decision edges, the bases of greater reduction of instances were used through the reduction of dimensionality for their visualization. In Fig. 3 Decision Tree is shown.

As a result, due to the computational cost that DROP3 needs, the base to be implemented is CNN called X *in* $\mathbb{R}^{p \times n}$, where **p** is less than **m**. In this case, $p = 22$ and $n = 4$. In addition, the algorithm chosen by its edges is suitable for execution and its high performance is SVM. However, when performing the decision tree algorithm, it was possible to know the weighting of the variables for the classification. As a result, the concentration of ethanol with the MQ3 sensor provides more information to the classifier.

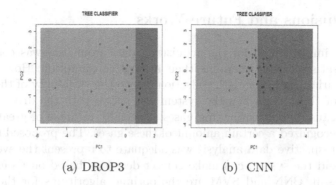

(a) DROP3   (b) CNN

Fig. 3. Decision tree algorithm

3.3 Implementation

Once the developed electronic system and the selected classification algorithms are done, the system is installed on a particular vehicle for validation. The relay module allows activating the fuel chamber of the vehicle that performs the ignition process. As a result, the system allows you to start the vehicle. In the Fig. 4 the implemented system is shown.

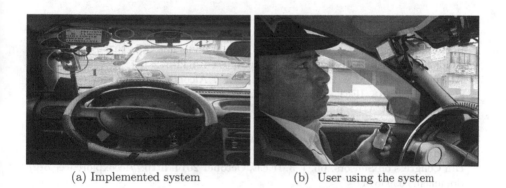

(a) Implemented system   (b) User using the system

Fig. 4. Real test of the embedded system inside the car

Subsequently, the system is tested by the drivers of the vehicle for proper operation. In addition, an SVM algorithm is implemented in each data collection, a compiled CNN is included to improve the training matrix in each iteration.

There were 31 tests with different drivers and different drunkenness state. The system had a yield of 93.54% with a sensitivity of 100%. A specificity of 85% and a presicion of 89%. At the end of the system and with CNN's interaction in the next 20 tests, a yield of 95% was obtained. This is because the training matrix increased in value with two more instances improving the ranking algorithm.

4   Conclusions and Future Works

The criteria implemented for the acquisition data from user was correct as it allowed to satisfactorily determine their alcohol consumption. However, there were some variations in the data collection due to the variability of the environment. One of them was when the system was active with the driver's window open. This caused the surrounding gases, especially in areas of greater traffic, the sensor recognized a certain amount of these gases. The proposed methodology for the respective data analysis was adequate to represent the event in real conditions and the system can make correct decisions based on its experience. For this reason, CNN and SVM are the optimal algorithms for the acquired data set. Finally, the proposed system was not invasive to the driver and can be implemented in other types of vehicles without major inconveniences.

As future work, a phase of facial recognition of the driver is proposed to be oriented to public transport entities and mitigate more accidents on the roads in vehicles with larger numbers of passengers.

Acknowledgment. This work is supported by the "Smart Data Analysis Systems - SDAS" group (http://sdas-group.com).

References

1. Assailly, J.-P.: Young people drunk-driving: process and outcome evaluation of preventive actions. In: von Holst, H., Nygren, Å., Andersson, Å.E. (eds.) Transportation, Traffic Safety and Health - Human Behavior, pp. 297–326. Springer, Heidelberg (2000). https://doi.org/10.1007/978-3-642-57266-1_18
2. Al-Youif, S., Ali, M.A.M., Mohammed, M.N.: Alcohol detection for car locking system. In: 2018 IEEE Symposium on Computer Applications and Industrial Electronics (ISCAIE), pp. 230–233. IEEE, April 2018. https://ieeexplore.ieee.org/document/8405475/
3. Paredes-Doig, A.L., del Rosario Sun-Kou, M., Comina, G.: Alcohols detection based on Pd-doped SnO_2 sensors. In: 2014 IEEE 9th IberoAmerican Congress on Sensors, pp. 1–3. IEEE, October 2014. http://ieeexplore.ieee.org/document/6995514/
4. Drunk driving detection based on classification of multivariate time series. J. Saf. Res. **54**, 61.e29–64 (2015)
5. Nair, V., Charniya, N.: Drunk driving and drowsiness detection alert system. In: Pandian, D., Fernando, X., Baig, Z., Shi, F. (eds.) ISMAC 2018. LNCVB, vol. 30, pp. 1191–1207. Springer, Cham (2019). https://doi.org/10.1007/978-3-030-00665-5_113
6. Klajner, F., Sobell, L.C., Sobell, M.B.: Prevention of drunk driving. In: Nirenberg, T.D. (ed.) Prevention of Alcohol Abuse, pp. 441–468. Springer, Boston (1984). https://doi.org/10.1007/978-1-4613-2657-1_21
7. Koukiou, G., Anastassopoulos, V.: Local difference patterns for drunk person identification. Multimed. Tools Appl. **77**(8), 9293–9305 (2018). https://doi.org/10.1007/s11042-017-4892-6

8. Wu, Y., Xia, Y., Xie, P., Ji, X.: The design of an automotive anti-drunk driving system to guarantee the uniqueness of driver. In: 2009 International Conference on Information Engineering and Computer Science, pp. 1–4. IEEE, December 2009. http://ieeexplore.ieee.org/document/5364823/
9. Rosero-Montalvo, P., et al.: Neighborhood criterion analysis for prototype selection applied in WSN data. In: 2017 International Conference on Information Systems and Computer Science (INCISCOS), pp. 128–132. IEEE, November 2017. http://ieeexplore.ieee.org/document/8328096/
10. Rosero-Montalvo, P., Peluffo-Ordonez, D.H., Batista, V.F.L., Serrano, J., Rosero, E.: Intelligent system for identification of wheelchair user's posture using machine learning techniques. IEEE Sens. J. 1 (2018). https://ieeexplore.ieee.org/document/8565996/
11. Rosero-Montalvo, P.D., et al.: Intelligence in embedded systems: overview and applications. In: Arai, K., Bhatia, R., Kapoor, S. (eds.) FTC 2018. AISC, vol. 880, pp. 874–883. Springer, Cham (2019). https://doi.org/10.1007/978-3-030-02686-8_65
12. Rosero-Montalvo, P., et al.: Prototype reduction algorithms comparison in nearest neighbor classification for sensor data: Empirical study. In: 2017 IEEE Second Ecuador Technical Chapters Meeting (ETCM), pp. 1–5. IEEE, October 2017. http://ieeexplore.ieee.org/document/8247530/

Optimization of Bridges Reinforcements with Tied-Arch Using Moth Search Algorithm

Óscar Carrasco[1], Broderick Crawford[1], Ricardo Soto[1],
José Lemus-Romani[1(✉)], Gino Astorga[2], and Agustín Salas-Fernández[1]

[1] Pontificia Universidad Católica de Valparaíso, Valparaíso, Chile
{oscar.carrasco,jose.lemus.r,juan.salas.f}@mail.pucv.cl,
{broderick.crawford,ricardo.soto}@pucv.cl
[2] Universidad de Valparaíso, Valparaíso, Chile
gino.astorga@uv.cl

Abstract. The deterioration in the bridges that cross the watercourses is a situation that must be resolved in a timely manner to avoid the collapse of its structure. Its repair can mean a high cost, road and environmental alteration. An effective solution, which minimizes this impact, is the installation of a superstructure in the form of an arch that covers the entire length of the bridge and which, by means of a hook anchored to the deck of the bridge, allows the arch to support the weight. This structure must try to maintain the original properties of the bridge, so the calculation of the magnitude of tension of the hangers and the order in which it is applied should not cause damage to the structure. In this document, we propose to optimize the process of calculating the hanger magnitudes and the order in which they must be applied using the moth search algorithm, in order to obtain one or several satisfactory solutions. Finally, we present the results obtained for an arch bridge and three hangers and, thus, evaluate the efficiency and effectiveness in the process of obtaining results in comparison with the Black Hole Algorithm.

Keywords: Reinforcement of bridges · Metaheuristics ·
Moth search algorithm · Combinatorial optimization

1 Introduction

Computer science is a transversal discipline for many areas of study and human activities. One of them is the construction area. Many constructive designs are based on models that predict how the behavior of the design will be, in order to avoid risks or unexpected results. The more data representative of reality is able to capture the model, it will be possible to generate information to make better decisions. However, the quality of the information depends on the quality of the data and the accuracy in them is a fundamental requirement. This is where

© Springer Nature Switzerland AG 2019
J. M. Ferrández Vicente et al. (Eds.): IWINAC 2019, LNCS 11487, pp. 244–253, 2019.
https://doi.org/10.1007/978-3-030-19651-6_24

computing comes into play, by processing data more accurately and quickly, delivering timely, useful and error-free information.

A bridge is a structure built with the purpose of saving a geographical accident, road, water course or other obstacle that comes before it. Its design depends on its function and the nature of the terrain on which it rests. They are usually built on the basis of metallic structures, reinforced concrete, wood or a combination of these. Basically, the forms that the bridges adopt are three, being directly related to the efforts that support their constructive elements. These are: beam bridges, arches and pendants. The present paper will address the reinforcement of a beam bridge through an arch with tension hangers.

Every structure created by the human being has a useful life. In the case of bridges vary depending on various causes. In the case of beam bridges, the undermining of the piers is one of the most frequent causes and damage to these structures can be very serious, such as collapse. Repairing them has a high impact on cost, time and use, so a suitable solution alternative is one that has the least impact. The design of a cable-stayed bridge with a lower deck is a viable solution. This consists of an arc that covers the longitudinal extension of the bridge from which hangings hang anchored to the board, supporting the weight of the structure, in this way it is possible to do without the piers where it rested.

This paper is organized in the following way, in Sect. 2 the problem to be solved is presented, in Sect. 3 Moth Search algorithm is explained, in Sect. 4 the integration of metaheuristics to the bridges problem, and in Sect. 5 the results obtained with their respective statistical tests to evaluate performance, ending with the conclusion and future work.

2 Problem

The problem to solve was proposed by Valenzuela [10–12] using Algorithm Genetic [4] and then by Black Hole [3] in order to determine which of the algorithms achieved better results. The best of both turned out to be Black Hole. Now we will use Moth Search (MS) [13] to determine if it achieves better results than Black Hole [7].

The structure of the bridge is modeled in a CAD application called SAP2000 [1], which provides an API that allows it to be operated externally by our algorithm. Thanks to this, the application will perform many complex structural calculations, so that our algorithm will provide the necessary data to perform these calculations and, thus, obtain a solution.

2.1 Objective Function

The objective function is defined as the sum of the tense difference between the original and the modified bridge for each of K cuts in each of the beams, minimizing this difference.

$$min \sum_{i=1}^{2} \sum_{k=1}^{K} |\sigma o_{i,k} - \sigma m_{i,k}| \; ; \; i \in \{1,2\}, \; k \in \{1,2,\ldots,k\} \tag{1}$$

Minimize the difference between the stresses of the original bridge and the modified arch bridge of the hangers. As long as the optimum result tends to zero, it means that the stress calculations will tend to equal the stresses of the models of both bridges (original and modified), preserving the original properties of the bridge. The tensions are obtained through the following formulas.

$$\sigma o_{i,k} = \frac{Mo_{i,k} \cdot v_i}{Io_i}; \qquad i \in \{1,2\}, \; k \in \{1,2,\ldots,k\} \tag{2}$$

$$\sigma m_{i,k} = \frac{P}{A} + \frac{P \cdot e \cdot v_i}{Im_{TOTAL}} + \frac{Mm_{i,k} \cdot v_i}{Im_i}; \qquad i \in \{1,2\}, \; k \in \{1,2,\ldots,k\} \tag{3}$$

2.2 Decision Variable

For a bridge of three hanging will be 6 decision variables, three to indicate the order of tension and the other three to determine the magnitude of tension of each hanger.

$$ord_1, ord_2, \ldots, ord_n \; \in \{1,2,\ldots,n\} \quad (Orders) \tag{4}$$

$$mag_1, mag_2, \ldots, mag_n \; \in [T_{min}, T_{max}] \quad (Magnitudes) \tag{5}$$

2.3 Constraints

The problem have two constraints that must be met to satisfy the objective function.

– The hangers cannot be jacking simultaneously.

$$ord_w \neq ord_j \; ; \; \forall w, j \quad con \; w \neq j \quad w, j \in \{1,2,\ldots,n\} \tag{6}$$

– The effort of the modified bridge deck should not pass the limits of the BAM:

$$\sigma m_{i,k} \geq \sigma o \tag{7}$$

$$\sigma m_{i,k} \geq f_{ct} \tag{8}$$

$$\sigma m_{i,k} \leq f_{cmax2} \quad (in \; internmediate \; stages) \tag{9}$$

$$\sigma m_{i,k} \leq f_{cmax} \quad (in \; final \; stages) \tag{10}$$

$\sigma m_{i,k}$: Tension (top or bottom) in the beams of the cable-stayed bridge.
f_{ct}: Maximum tension of admissible traction by the concrete.
f_{cmax}: Maximum compressive stress admissible by the concrete.
f_{cmax2}: Maximum compressive stress admissible for expanded concrete.

3   Moth Search

Moth Search is a bio-inspired metaheuristic algorithm to respond to global optimization problems. It was created by Wang [13].

Moths are a type of insects that belong to the order Lepidoptera. Among the various characteristics of moths, phototaxis and Levy flights are the most representative characteristics described below.

Phototaxis is the orientation reaction of free cellular organisms in response to a luminous stimulus. In general, moths tend to fly around the light source, in the form of Lévy flights.

3.1   Lévy Flights

Lévy flights are one of the most important flight patterns in nature. Many species move following a flight pattern of Lévy and describe a type of random walks, whose length steps are taken from the distribution of Lévy. The distribution of Lévy can be expressed mathematically in the form of a power law formula.

$$L(s) \sim |s|^{-\beta} \tag{11}$$

where $1 < \beta <= 3$

Lévy flights can maximize the efficiency of finding resources in uncertain environments. Therefore, $\beta = 1.5$ is used to optimize benchmarks and engineering cases.

The moths, which have a smaller distance than the best, will fly around it in the form of Lévy flights. In other words, their positions are updated by Lévy flights.

For moth i in each variable, it can be updated as:

$$x_i^{t+1} = x_i^t + \alpha L(S) \tag{12}$$

$$x_i^{t+1} = x_i^t + \alpha \left(\frac{(\beta - 1)\Gamma(\beta - 1)sin(\frac{\pi(\beta - 1)}{2})}{\pi S^\beta} \right) \tag{13}$$

Where x_i^{t+1} and x_i^t are respectively the updated original position in generation t, and t is the current generation. L(s) is the passage of Lévy flights. The parameter is the scale factor related to the problem of interest. In our current work, it can be given as:

$$\alpha = \frac{S_{max}}{t^2} \tag{14}$$

Where S_{max} is the maximum walking step and its value is established according to the given problem. Lévy distribution L(s) in equation can be formulated as follows:

$$L(s) = \frac{(\beta - 1)\Gamma(\beta - 1)sin(\frac{\pi(\beta - 1)}{2})}{\pi S^\beta} \tag{15}$$

Where s is greater than 0, $\Gamma(s)$ it is the gamma function.

3.2 Straight Flight

Certain moths that are far from the source of light will fly towards that source of light in line. This process can be described below.

For moth i in each variable, its flights can be formulated as:

$$x_i^{t+1} = \lambda(x_i^t + \phi(x_{best}^t - x_i^t)) \tag{16}$$

where x_{best}^t is the best moth in generation t, and ϕ is an acceleration factor established in golden relation in our current work. λ is a scale factor. On the other hand, the moth can fly towards the final position that is beyond the light source. For this case, the final position for moth i can be formulated as:

$$x_i^{t+1} = \lambda(x_i^t + \frac{1}{\phi}(x_{best}^t - x_i^t)) \tag{17}$$

For simplicity, for moth i, its position will be updated by Eqs. 16 or 17 with the possibility of 50%. In addition, these two update processes mentioned above can be represented in (Fig. 1a, b) respectively. In Fig. 1, x_{best}, x_i and $x_{i,new}$ are respectively the best, original and updated position for moth i, and are considered as a light source, start point and end point. λ is a scale factor that can control the speed of convergence of the algorithm and improve the diversity of the population. In our current work, the scale factor is set to a random number drawn by the standard uniform distribution.

4 Integration

In the MS method, for simplicity, the entire population of moths is divided into two equal subpopulations (Subpopulation 1 and Subpopulation 2) according to their suitability, and they are updated according to the Lévy flights or in a straight line, respectively. This is equivalent to saying that the moths in Subpopulation 1 are much closer to the better than Subpopulation 2. In addition, like many other metaheuristic algorithms, an elitism strategy is incorporated in order to accelerate the convergence of the MS method. *MaxIterations* is the initial maximum generation that can be considered as the term condition.Algorithm 1 describes this process.

In synthesis, two models will be used: one of the original bridge and another with the modifications to compare it with the first one. Therefore, the metaheuristic will provide the voltage magnitudes for SAP2000 to perform and thus obtain a solution. The communication between metaheuristics and SAP2000 will be made through the API provided by the latter.

Algorithm 1. Integration between SAP2000 and Moth Search algorithmic.

1: Establish bridge models to evaluate (Instance).
2: **for all** Instance **do**
3:     SAP2000.Open
4:     SAP2000.Load(Original Bridge Model)
5:     Randomly initialize the population P of NP moths randomly
6:     Set MaxIterations, MaxWalkStep S_{max}, β, φ
7:     **for** Iteration $\leq$ MaxIterations **do**
8:         SAP2000.Load(Modified Bridge Model)
9:         SAP2000.ApplyTension()
10:        SAP2000.GetFitness()
11:        Sort all the moth individuals as per their fitness and Save BesthMoth.
12:        Save Best Moth
13:        **for** $i = 1$ to $NP/2$ (for all moth individuals in Subpopulation 1) **do**
14:            **for** $j = 1$ to D **do**
15:                Generate x_{ij}^{t+1} by (15) performing Lévy flights.
16:            **end for**
17:        **end for**
18:        **for** $i = NP/2 + 1$ to NP **do**
19:            **for** $j = 1$ to D **do**
20:                **if** $rand > 0.5$ **then**
21:                    Generate x_{ij}^{t+1} by (16)
22:                **else**
23:                    Generate x_{ij}^{t+1} by (17)
24:                **end if**
25:            **end for**
26:        **end for**
27:    **end for**
28:    SAP2000.Close()
29: **end for**

The configuration was parameters used for the execution, it was obtained through parametric sweep are shown in the Table 1 [5].

Table 1. Parameters for execution.

Population	Executions	Iterations	Alpha
48	15	200	0.000001

5   Experimental Results

The Tables 2, 3 and 4 summarize the best solutions achieved in each of the 15 executions for instance.

Table 2. Fitness comparation (a)

	PV-TCV		HW-TCV		PT-TCV		AB-TCV	
	BH	MS	BH	MS	BH	MS	BH	MS
1	525788,701	524139,528	522992,527	520707,516	520560,471	522709,168	520152,444	529824,623
2	524362,167	527337,192	518566,592	521467,410	520610,728	523656,669	520848,212	529462,056
3	523983,245	526024,026	520271,778	521921,189	523880,059	523871,984	519373,561	529358,722
4	523941,247	522720,317	517752,373	522429,087	518340,350	520855,130	520872,273	534472,795
5	523427,989	522383,486	518554,722	522249,702	519411,917	523411,190	524023,770	529321,548
6	523381,036	523860,029	521443,876	521619,530	525110,874	521199,953	524821,681	529332,343
7	522809,147	522924,479	523204,076	522837,239	520863,041	525332,737	524246,509	529154,644
8	522648,276	522267,417	520515,557	522237,042	522029,399	523449,317	523785,395	538118,512
9	522138,965	524027,438	520214,641	525463,179	521966,778	522385,429	521241,888	528748,384
10	521950,827	523160,081	518227,336	522954,810	526676,105	523310,390	517068,779	528751,098
11	521351,709	521923,453	519526,112	522385,494	522617,218	521627,024	520203,824	528794,300
12	521114,467	522200,113	519225,675	525625,865	525204,201	521776,053	523623,834	528710,845
13	520927,571	522624,045	516990,684	522918,025	524252,033	526735,660	520622,784	528653,496
14	520202,016	522023,396	521974,260	520395,044	518891,310	524878,383	522447,219	528455,727
15	518788,669	522492,710	522006,562	521272,424	523880,059	525725,692	517564,071	527881,264

Table 3. Fitness comparation (b)

	WR-TCV		VC-TCV		CC-TCV		TC-TCV	
	BH	MS	BH	MS	BH	MS	BH	MS
1	523896,152	529477,706	521676,411	519846,831	518616,048	527953,566	522834,907	520217,120
2	519204,810	531663,354	523586,259	521680,027	524706,864	529698,713	521301,708	524967,128
3	522236,031	531239,237	520710,801	522635,853	522562,147	530439,770	522591,311	524796,056
4	525384,947	531139,511	521939,460	521775,646	517694,832	536831,146	525268,020	522572,121
5	519448,379	529715,769	516764,747	523607,474	520212,174	531236,044	519571,134	523143,451
6	519880,227	528671,041	526420,203	523382,604	520538,000	532152,376	524103,151	523030,723
7	518685,865	529270,895	520958,228	522720,927	515930,442	530039,302	521634,820	521806,946
8	521471,347	529918,358	522523,255	522645,384	520447,927	530745,301	523052,417	523451,586
9	521745,606	530487,258	520900,604	527274,068	520404,149	531022,389	521994,378	524235,633
10	521210,450	533216,584	517454,836	534720,702	520682,197	529892,495	519824,404	522523,995
11	523417,258	530490,245	521104,325	536159,250	523472,335	537619,557	524988,999	523543,682
12	522611,368	528807,423	524091,123	529433,687	524143,332	529270,743	519926,614	523253,590
13	526646,976	528620,138	517878,923	530675,662	522918,409	531145,877	522386,876	523829,050
14	522051,315	529381,392	520548,389	527051,075	515608,056	531853,565	519598,167	523178,525
15	519162,739	530263,611	515963,267	530497,598	519413,560	530729,770	522191,193	523907,308

5.1   Comparing Results

To determine which algorithm achieves the best results, the best solutions of the 15 executions made to each instance have been collected.

This allows obtaining 2 sets of data to be compared for each instance: those obtained with BH and those obtained with MS. These two samples are subjected to two statistical tests. The first allows to determine if both samples are independent, which would clear the doubt if the samples are reliable to compare, and the second to verify the veracity of the hypothesis formulated with respect to the best result obtained.

Table 4. Fitness comparation (c)

	RD-AA10		RC-AA10		CR-AA10	
	BH	MS	BH	MS	BH	MS
1	517200,649	524066,303	514508,111	520920,138	511024,809	521705,173
2	512678,644	521738,302	517790,493	521047,167	517088,897	522055,256
3	511107,489	521460,585	515619,911	522175,344	515740,371	522952,922
4	508556,024	521818,123	514564,776	520969,151	514210,370	521523,765
5	519226,401	521090,646	514605,633	521769,704	514470,308	521105,522
6	513572,503	521829,232	517856,008	522029,575	517102,869	520597,009
7	514930,924	522007,048	513847,138	521218,138	512584,970	521202,212
8	509176,298	521473,608	514603,894	523063,544	517126,961	522001,367
9	514299,205	521996,533	514367,665	522363,607	514913,049	522064,221
10	517038,968	520935,668	514019,852	521063,580	517761,806	521254,353
11	512632,111	520250,193	513776,522	520626,463	516430,949	526959,437
12	516494,402	523463,306	514272,046	520083,744	512943,624	520758,016
13	511665,241	520327,645	514457,070	524280,148	514502,449	520874,602
14	513408,640	521210,740	513593,241	520569,576	512808,821	520048,010
15	515799,785	520597,995	510072,744	520109,998	516154,932	520660,141

The Kolmogorov-Smirnov test, with Lilliefors correction [6], is used to test if a data set fits a normal distribution or not, in our the test concluded that the samples are independent.

Then, the Mann-Whitney-Wilcoxon test [2] will be applied to the same group of data to determine the veracity of the hypothesis with respect to which algorithm of the comparators presents the best results, based on the following hypotheses:

H_0 : MS is better than BH
H_1 : BH is better tha MS

If the p-value of a hypothesis of one sample with respect to the other is less than 0.05, it can not be assumed to be true.

When applying this test, the results presented in Table 5 were obtained.

5.2   Distribution Comparison

The best solutions obtained in each execution are presented in the following graphs, where you can see a comparison between Black Hole and Moth Search. The boxes of blue color represent the solutions given by BH, the red ones correspond to those of MS.

In all situations, the results obtained by MS do not surpass BH. This is due to a number of insufficient iterations, a small population and parameter settings that allow greater precision (progress at a smaller step).

Table 5. p-value Mann-Whitney-Wilcoxon test

Instance	BH better than MS	MS better than BH
PV-TCV	0,864152	0,13584722
HW-TCV	0,998273	0,00172669
PT-TCV	0,873017	0,12698204
AB-TCV	0,999998	0,00000153
WR-TCV	0,999998	0,00000153
VC-TCV	0,999346	0,00065324
CC-TCV	0,999998	0,00000153
TC-TCV	0,979971	0,02002832
RD-AA10	0,999998	0,00000153
RC-AA10	0,999998	0,00000153
CR-AA10	0,999998	0,00000153

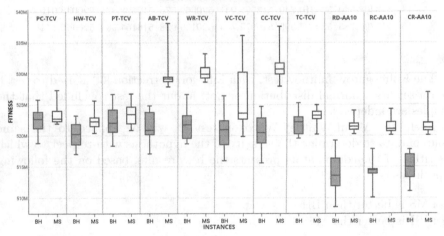

Fig. 1. Best fitness instances

6   Conclusions

The use of optimization techniques, present great advantages when solving problems of great complexity [8,9]. The solutions given by Moth Search in the vast majority of cases do not exceed those achieved by Black Hole. However, in some situations the proximity has been close, so it is possible to infer that by making the necessary adjustments to the algorithm, results such as Black Hole can be achieved.

In two of the eleven instances it is not concluded that Moth Search is unable to achieve results like those of Black Hole, which would lead to promising results if improvements are applied to the algorithm and execution parameters.

In conclusion, it is proposed to make improvements in the parameters such as Population Size, Number of Iterations, Acceleration Factors, Disturbance Operators and in the algorithm as Elitist Strategies, Convergence Acceleration Strategies, Selective Population, Population Grouping, others.

Acknowledgements. Broderick Crawford is supported by Grant CONICYT/ FONDECYT/REGULAR/1171243, Ricardo Soto is supported by Grant CONI-CYT/FONDECYT/REGULAR/1190129, Gino Astorga is supported by Postgraduate Grant Pontificia Universidad Católica de Valparaíso 2015, José Lemus is Beneficiario Beca Postgrado PUCV 2018. This work was funded by the CONICYT PFCHA/DOCTORADO BECAS NACIONAL/2019 - 21191692.

References

1. SAP2000. http://www.csiespana.com/software/2/sap2000
2. Mann, H.B., Whitney, D.R.: On a test of whether one of two random variables is stochastically larger than the other. Ann. Math. Stat. 50–60 (1947)
3. Hatamlou, A.: Black hole: a new heuristic optimization approach for data clustering. Inf. Sci. **222**, 175–184 (2013)
4. Holland, J.H., et al.: Adaptation in Natural and Artificial Systems: An Introductory Analysis with Applications to Biology, Control, and Artificial Intelligence. MIT Press, Cambridge (1992)
5. Lanza-Gutierrez, J.M., Crawford, B., Soto, R., Berrios, N., Gomez-Pulido, J.A., Paredes, F.: Analyzing the effects of binarization techniques when solving the set covering problem through swarm optimization. Expert Syst. Appl. **70**, 67–82 (2017)
6. Lilliefors, H.: On the Kolmogorov-Smirnov test for normality with mean and variance unknown. J. Am. Stat. Assoc. **62**(318), 399–402 (1967)
7. Matus, S., Soto, R., Crawford, B.: Optimización del refuerzo de puentes mediante arco atirantado con black hole algorithm. Master's thesis, Escuela de Ingeniería Informática, Pontificia Universidad Católica de Valparaíso, Valparaíso, Chile (2018)
8. Soto, R., et al.: Solving the non-unicost set covering problem by using cuckoo search and black hole optimization. Nat. Comput. **16**(2), 213–229 (2017)
9. Soto, R., Crawford, B., Olivares, R., Barraza, J., Johnson, F., Paredes, F.: A binary cuckoo search algorithm for solving the set covering problem. In: Ferrández Vicente, J.M., Álvarez-Sánchez, J.R., de la Paz López, F., Toledo-Moreo, F.J., Adeli, H. (eds.) IWINAC 2015. LNCS, vol. 9108, pp. 88–97. Springer, Cham (2015). https://doi.org/10.1007/978-3-319-18833-1_10
10. Valenzuela, M., Casas, J.: Bridge strengthening by conversion to network arch: design criteria and economic validation. Struct. Infrastruct. Eng. **12**(10), 1310–1322 (2015)
11. Valenzuela, M.A., Casas Rius, J.R.: Bridge strengthening by structural change: optimization via genetic algorithm. In: IABSE-IASS 2011 Symposium (2011)
12. Valenzuela, M.A., Casas Rius, J.R., et al.: Structural behavior and design criteria for bridge strengthening by tied arch. Comparison with network arch bridges. In: ARCH 2013 Proceedings of the 7th International Conference on Arch Bridges, pp. 829–836 (2013)
13. Wang, G.-G.: Moth search algorithm: a bio-inspired metaheuristic algorithm for global optimization problems. Memetic Comput. **10**, 1–14 (2018)

Repairing Infeasibility in Scheduling via Genetic Algorithms

Raúl Mencía$^{(\boxtimes)}$, Carlos Mencía, and Ramiro Varela

Department of Computer Science, University of Oviedo, Campus of Gijón,
33204 Gijón, Spain
{menciaraul,menciacarlos,ramiro}@uniovi.es
http://www.di.uniovi.es/iscop

Abstract. Scheduling problems arise in an ever increasing number of application domains. Although efficient algorithms exist for a variety of such problems, sometimes it is necessary to satisfy hard constraints that make the problem unfeasible. In this situation, identifying possible ways of repairing infeasibility represents a task of utmost interest. We consider this scenario in the context of job shop scheduling with a hard makespan constraint and address the problem of finding the largest possible subset of the jobs that can be scheduled within such constraint. To this aim, we develop a genetic algorithm that looks for solutions in the search space defined by an efficient solution builder, also proposed in the paper. Experimental results show the suitability of our approach.

1 Introduction

The practical relevance of scheduling cannot be overstated, as it constitutes an essential task in many different areas. When facing a scheduling problem, users are often interested in finding a schedule optimizing a given objective function. However, in some cases there can be hard constraints that make the problem unfeasible. In this scenario, beyond detecting infeasibility, it may be useful to identify possible ways of repairing it so that *solving* the problem to some extent.

In this paper we study the task of repairing infeasibility in the context of job shop scheduling with a hard makespan constraint, that imposes that all the jobs must be completed within a given time limit. Such constraint appears naturally in practice and some variants of scheduling problems with a limit on the makespan have been studied in the literature (e.g. [1,4,5]). We consider a setting in which the problem can be relaxed by dropping some of the jobs, which enables repairing infeasibility by identifying feasible subsets of the jobs and gives rise to the optimization problem of finding the largest of such subsets.

For solving this problem, we first propose a solution builder that aims at approximating set-wise maximal feasible subsets of jobs, defining a suitable search space. The solution builder is then used as a decoder by a genetic algorithm that searches over the subset space of the jobs and the space of schedules for any subset of jobs at the same time. The results from an experimental study show that the genetic algorithm is successful at solving the problem.

J. M. Ferrández Vicente et al. (Eds.): IWINAC 2019, LNCS 11487, pp. 254–263, 2019.
https://doi.org/10.1007/978-3-030-19651-6_25

The remainder of the paper is organized as follows. In Sect. 2 we give a formal definition of the problem. Section 3 describes the proposed solution builder, which is integrated in the genetic algorithm presented in Sect. 4. The results of an experimental study are reported in Sect. 5. Finally, the paper concludes in Sect. 6.

2   Definition of the Problem

The job shop scheduling problem (JSP) consists in scheduling a set of n jobs $\mathcal{J} = \{J_1, \ldots, J_n\}$ on a set of m resources or machines $\mathcal{M} = \{M_1, \ldots, M_m\}$. Each job $J_i \in \mathcal{J}$ consists of a sequence of m tasks or operations $(\theta_{i1}, \ldots, \theta_{im})$, each requiring a particular machine $M(\theta_{ij})$ during a processing time $p_{\theta_{ij}}$.

A schedule S is an assignment of a starting time $st_{\theta_{ij}}$ to each of the operations such that the following constraints are satisfied:

i. The operations in a job must be scheduled in the order they appear in the job, i.e., $st_{\theta_{ij}} + p_{\theta_{ij}} \leq st_{\theta_{i(j+1)}}$ with $i = 1, \ldots, n$ and $j = 1, \ldots, m - 1$.
ii. No machine can process more than one operation at a time, which translates in disjunctive constraints of the form $(st_u + p_u \leq st_v) \vee (st_v + p_v \leq st_u)$ for all operations u, v with $u \neq v$ and $M(u) = M(v)$.
iii. Preemption is not allowed, i.e., $C_u = st_u + p_u$ for all u, where C_u denotes the completion time of operation u.

The makespan of a schedule S, denoted $C_{max}(S)$, is defined as the maximum completion time of the operations in S.

The decision version of the JSP is the problem of deciding whether there exists a schedule S such that $C_{max}(S) \leq C$, where C is a fixed limit on the maximum makespan allowed. If such a schedule S exists, the problem instance is said to be *feasible*, whereas it is *unfeasible* otherwise.

In this paper we focus on the latter case, where a hard makespan constraint makes the problem unfeasible and, more concretely, on the task of repairing such infeasibility in the best possible manner. In a job shop setting, a natural way of addressing this task is to relax the problem by dropping some of the jobs, so that the remaining ones can be scheduled within the makespan limit. To this respect, the following definitions introduce useful notions for coping with infeasibility. Throughout, we refer to an unfeasible problem instance by a pair $\mathcal{I} = (\mathcal{J}, C)$, consisting in scheduling the set of jobs $\mathcal{J}$ within a maximum makespan of C.

Definition 1 (FSJ). *Given an unfeasible instance $\mathcal{I} = (\mathcal{J}, C)$, $\mathcal{S} \subsetneq \mathcal{J}$ is a feasible subset of jobs (FSJ) of $\mathcal{J}$ iff $(\mathcal{S}, C)$ is feasible.*

Definition 2 (MFSJ). *Given an unfeasible instance $\mathcal{I} = (\mathcal{J}, C)$, $\mathcal{S} \subsetneq \mathcal{J}$ is a maximal feasible subset of jobs (MFSJ) of $\mathcal{J}$ iff $(\mathcal{S}, C)$ is feasible and for all $\mathcal{S}' \subseteq \mathcal{J}$ with $\mathcal{S} \subsetneq \mathcal{S}'$, $(\mathcal{S}', C)$ is unfeasible.*

Definition 3 (maxFSJ). *Given an unfeasible instance $\mathcal{I} = (\mathcal{J}, C)$, $\mathcal{S}^* \subseteq \mathcal{J}$ is a maximum feasible subset of jobs (maxFSJ) iff $(\mathcal{S}^*, C)$ is feasible and for all FSJs $\mathcal{S}'$ of $\mathcal{J}$, $|\mathcal{S}'| \leq |\mathcal{S}^*|$.*

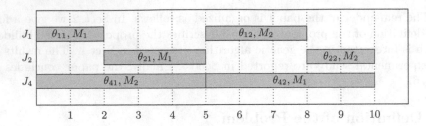

Fig. 1. Gantt chart of a schedule for the maxFSJ $\{J_1, J_2, J_4\}$ in Example 1.

FSJs constitute subsets of the jobs that can be scheduled within the makespan limit. On the other hand, MFSJs and maxMFSJs represent different notions of maximality. MFSJs are maximal w.r.t. set inclusion, i.e., no superset of an MFSJ is an FSJ, while maxFSJs are maximal w.r.t. set cardinality, that is, these are the largest possible FSJs. Clearly, maxFSJs are MFSJs as well, but the opposite does not necessarily hold. The definitions above build on related concepts in the field of unsatisfiablity analysis of propositional formulas, such as *maximal satisfiable subformula* (MSS) or *maximum satisfiability* (maxSAT) [7].

Example 1. Consider a job shop with four jobs $\mathcal{J} = \{J_1, J_2, J_3, J_4\}$ and two machines $\mathcal{M} = \{M_1, M_2\}$. Each job J_i consists of a sequence of two operations $(\theta_{i1}, \theta_{i2})$, with processing times and required machine as shown in Table 1:

Table 1. Instance data.

	J_1	J_2	J_3	J_4
θ_{i1}	2 (M_1)	3 (M_1)	6 (M_2)	5 (M_2)
θ_{i2}	3 (M_2)	2 (M_2)	4 (M_1)	5 (M_1)

With a hard constraint limiting the makespan to $C = 10$ the instance $(\mathcal{J}, C)$ is unfeasible. There are 11 FSJs of $\mathcal{J}$: $\emptyset$, $\{J_1\}$, $\{J_2\}$, $\{J_3\}$, $\{J_4\}$, $\{J_1, J_2\}$, $\{J_1, J_3\}$, $\{J_1, J_4\}$, $\{J_2, J_3\}$, $\{J_2, J_4\}$ and $\{J_1, J_2, J_4\}$ as there exists a schedule with makespan less than or equal to 10 for each of them. Out of these sets, three are MFSJs: $\{J_1, J_3\}$, $\{J_2, J_3\}$ and $\{J_1, J_2, J_4\}$; and only the last one is a maxFSJ. Figure 1 shows a schedule for the maxFSJ with makespan 10, which does not exceed the limit C.

In this paper, we address the problem of approximating maxFSJs for a given unfeasible instance $(\mathcal{J}, C)$, that is finding feasible subsets of jobs with the largest size. It is therefore a maximization problem. This problem is related to the problem considered in [5], where the goal is to find a feasible subset of jobs in a two-stage flow shop maximizing a weighted sum of the jobs.

3   Solution Builder

Due to their high computational complexity, solving scheduling problems usually requires *searching* over a (possibly large) space of schedules. As a consequence, efficient scheduling algorithms typically rely on so-called *schedule builders*, which enable the computation and enumeration of a subset of all the schedules for a given problem instance, and so define a search space (e.g. [6,9,10]). However, for the problem of approximating maxFSJs, computing schedules does not suffice, since it is also necessary to identify feasible subsets of the initial set of jobs. As a consequence, defining a search space for this problem requires different mechanisms than a classical schedule builder.

In this section, we describe a *solution builder* for approximating maxFSJs. The solution builder aims at producing MFSJs for a given unfeasible problem instance. Focusing on MFSJs instead of on arbitrary FSJs comes with the benefit of defining a (much) smaller search space. At the same time, the set of all MFSJs is dominant for any given problem instance, that is, it contains at least one optimal solution. This follows from the fact that all maxFSJs are MFSJs as well. The solution builder exploits the following monotonicity property of FSJs, that all subsets of an FSJ are also FSJs:

Proposition 1. *Let* $\mathcal{I} = (\mathcal{J}, C)$ *be an unfeasible problem instance and* $\mathcal{S} \subsetneq \mathcal{J}$ *an FSJ of* $\mathcal{J}$. *Then, for all* $\mathcal{S}' \subseteq \mathcal{S}$, $\mathcal{S}'$ *is an FSJ of* $\mathcal{J}$.

Proof. Since $\mathcal{S}$ is an FSJ of $\mathcal{J}$, there exists a schedule S for the jobs in $\mathcal{S}$ with $C_{max}(S) \leq C$. Given $\mathcal{S}' \subsetneq \mathcal{S}$, we can build a schedule S' by assigning each task in $\mathcal{S}'$ the same starting time as in S. S' would be a schedule for the jobs in $\mathcal{S}'$ and, by definition, $C_{max}(S') \leq C_{max}(S) \leq C$. Thus, $\mathcal{S}'$ would be an FSJ of $\mathcal{J}$.

Notice that the proof above relies on the nature of the makespan, and hence this result may not hold for some variants of the problem where a metric other than the makespan is used. The contrapositive of Proposition 1 establishes that any superset of an unfeasible set of jobs is also unfeasible. This observation allows for an alternative definition of MFSJs:

Proposition 2. *Let* $\mathcal{I} = (\mathcal{J}, C)$ *be an unfeasible problem instance.* $\mathcal{S} \subsetneq \mathcal{J}$ *is an MFSJ of* $\mathcal{J}$ *iff* $(\mathcal{S}, C)$ *is feasible and for all* $j \in \mathcal{J} \setminus \mathcal{S}$, $(\mathcal{S} \cup \{j\}, C)$ *is unfeasible.*

Proof. (If) $(\mathcal{S}, C)$ is feasible, so $\mathcal{S}$ is an FSJ of $\mathcal{J}$. Let's suppose $\mathcal{S}$ is not maximal. Then, there exists an FSJ $\mathcal{S}' \subsetneq \mathcal{J}$ such that $\mathcal{S} \subsetneq \mathcal{S}'$. As $\mathcal{S}'$ is a strict superset of $\mathcal{S}$, $\mathcal{S}'$ must contain some element $j \in \mathcal{J} \setminus \mathcal{S}$. By the contrapositive of Proposition 1, any superset of an unfeasible set of jobs is unfeasible and, since $(\mathcal{S} \cup \{j\}, C)$ is unfeasible for all $j \in \mathcal{J} \setminus \mathcal{S}$, $(\mathcal{S}', C)$ is necessarily unfeasible. A contradiction.

(Only if) $\mathcal{S}$ is an MFSJ of $\mathcal{J}$ so, by definition, for all $\mathcal{S}' \subseteq \mathcal{J}$ such that $\mathcal{S} \subsetneq \mathcal{S}'$, $(\mathcal{S}', C)$ is unfeasible. Hence, for all $j \in \mathcal{J} \setminus \mathcal{S}$, $(\mathcal{S} \cup \{j\}, C)$ is unfeasible.

Proposition 2 enables computing an MFSJ by testing the feasibility of $|\mathcal{J}|$ subsets, which constitutes a remarkable saving w.r.t. considering all the $2^{|\mathcal{J}|}$ subsets of $\mathcal{J}$.

Algorithm 1. Solution Builder.

Data: Set of jobs $\mathcal{J}$, makespan limit C
Result: $\mathcal{S} \subsetneq \mathcal{J}$ an MFSJ of $\mathcal{J}$
$\mathcal{R} \leftarrow \mathcal{J}$ // Initialize reference set to the set of all jobs;
$\mathcal{S} \leftarrow \emptyset$; // Initialize $\mathcal{S}$ to the empty set;
while $\mathcal{R} \neq \emptyset$ **do**
    Pick $j \in \mathcal{R}$; //Non-deterministically;
    $\mathcal{R} \leftarrow \mathcal{R} \setminus \{j\}$;
    if $Feasible(\mathcal{S} \cup \{j\}, C)$ **then**
        $\mathcal{S} \leftarrow \mathcal{S} \cup \{j\}$;
    end
end
return $\mathcal{S}$;

The proposed solution builder is depicted in Algorithm 1. This algorithm uses a decision procedure *Feasible* that decides whether a given set of jobs $\mathcal{S} \subseteq \mathcal{J}$ is feasible under the given makespan constraint. It maintains two sets of jobs: a reference set $\mathcal{R}$ containing all the jobs that remain to be tested and a set $\mathcal{S}$ representing an underapproximation of the MSFJ under construction. Through the course of the algorithm, the set $\mathcal{S}$ will grow until representing an MFSJ of $\mathcal{J}$. Initially, $\mathcal{R} = \mathcal{J}$ and $\mathcal{S}$ is the empty set. At each iteration, the algorithm picks a job $j \in \mathcal{R}$, and tests whether the instance $(\mathcal{S} \cup \{j\}, C)$ is feasible. If it is, $\mathcal{S}$ is extended with j. In either case, j is removed from $\mathcal{R}$. The algorithm terminates when $\mathcal{R}$ becomes empty, in which case $\mathcal{S}$ represents an MFSJ of $\mathcal{J}$.

The correctness of Algorithm 1 follows from Proposition 2, provided that *Feasible* is a complete decision procedure. Also, note that the selection of the job j in each iteration is non-deterministic. For example, considering the instance from Example 1, the sequence of choices (J_1, J_2, J_3, J_4) would result in the MFSJ $\{J_1, J_2, J_4\}$. Alternatively, the sequence of choices (J_1, J_3, J_2, J_4) would yield the MFSJ $\{J_1, J_3\}$. In addition, considering all possible sequences of choices (permutations of the jobs) results in the definition of a search space that contains all MFSJs of a given problem instance, including all the maxFSJs.

Each feasibility test requires solving an NP-complete problem, so using a complete decision procedure for this purpose may be impractical. As an alternative one could use an incomplete procedure, at the expense of losing the guarantee that the computed subset represents a maximal FSJ. In this case, given a feasibility test on a set $(\mathcal{S} \cup \{j\}, C)$, the incomplete procedure would look for a schedule for the set of jobs in $\mathcal{S} \cup \{j\}$ with makespan not exceeding C. If it finds such a schedule, the set of jobs would be declared feasible. Otherwise, there would not be the guarantee that the set is unfeasible, although the algorithm would treat it as such (not extending the set $\mathcal{S}$ with j).

To this respect, our approach uses the well-known G&T schedule builder [6]. Given a JSP instance, this algorithm schedules one operation at a time in an iterative fashion. Its pseudocode is shown in Algorithm 2, where for an operation u,

---

Algorithm 2. Schedule builder $G\&T$.

Data: A JSP problem instance $\mathcal{P}$
Result: A feasible schedule S for $\mathcal{P}$
$A \leftarrow \{t_{i1}; J_i \in \mathcal{J}\}$;
$SC \leftarrow \emptyset$;
while $A \neq \emptyset$ **do**
  $v^* \leftarrow argmin\{r_v + p_v; v \in A\}$;
  $B \leftarrow \{u \in A; M(u) = M(v^*), r_u < r_{v^*} + p_{v^*}\}$;
  Pick $u \in B$ non deterministically;
  Set $st_u \leftarrow r_u$ in S;
  Add u to SC and update r_v for all $v \notin SC$;
  $A \leftarrow \{v; v \notin SC, P(v) \subseteq SC\}$;
end
return *the built schedule S*;

$P(u)$ denotes its immediate predecessor in its job and r_u denotes its earliest possible starting time, referred to as the *head* of u. The algorithm maintains a set SC with the operations scheduled so far as well as the set A containing all the unscheduled operations that are either the first one in their job or whose immediate predecessor in their job has been already scheduled. At each iteration, the algorithm identifies the operation $v^* \in A$ with the earliest possible completion time and builds a set B with all the operations $v \in A$ that require the same machine as v^* and can be scheduled before the earliest possible completion time of v^*. At this point, one operation in B is selected and scheduled at its earliest possible starting time, updating SC, A and the heads of the operations that remain to be scheduled.

Upon termination, the G&T algorithm is guaranteed to return an *active* schedule, in which no operation can be scheduled earlier without delaying the starting time of some other operation. The selection of the job $j \in B$ to be scheduled at a given iteration is non-deterministic. This way, the G&T schedule builder defines a search space, particularly that formed by the set of all active schedules, which is dominant for the makespan, i.e. it always contains at least one schedule with the minimum makespan.

4   Genetic Algorithm

In this section, we review the main components of the GA proposed in this work for approximating maxFSJs. Algorithm 3 shows its main structure: it is a generational genetic algorithm with random selection and replacement by tournament among parents and offsprings, which confers the GA an implicit form of elitism. The algorithm requires five parameters: crossover and mutation probabilities (P_c and P_m), number of generations ($\#gen$) and population size ($\#popsize$). We describe the main components of the GA:

Algorithm 3. Genetic Algorithm.

Data: A problem instance $\mathcal{P}$ and a set of parameters $(P_c, P_m, \#gen, \#popsize)$
Result: A solution for $\mathcal{P}$
Generate and evaluate the initial population $P(0)$;
for $t=1$ to $\#gen-1$ **do**

> **Selection:** organize the chromosomes in $P(t-1)$ into pairs at random ;
> **Recombination:** mate each pair of chromosomes and mutate the two offsprings in accordance with P_c and P_m;
> **Evaluation:** evaluate the resulting chromosomes;
> **Replacement:** make a tournament selection among every two parents and their offsprings to generate $P(t)$;

end
return *the best solution built so far*;

Coding Schema. The GA exploits a coding schema of common use in the context of job shop scheduling, in which chromosomes are permutations with repetitions [3]. In particular, for an instance with n jobs and m machines, a chromosome is a permutation of the job indices where each job appears m times.

A permutation represents a tentative ordering of the operations, that we refer to as *operation sequence*: in a chromosome the jth occurrence of job J_i (from left to right) corresponds to the operation θ_{ij}. For example, the chromosome (4, 1, 1, 3, 2, 4, 2, 3) represents the operation sequence $(\theta_{41}, \theta_{11}, \theta_{12}, \theta_{31}, \theta_{21}, \theta_{42}, \theta_{22}, \theta_{32})$ for an instance with 4 jobs and 2 machines. This sequence can be used to guide a schedule builder, in the search of a schedule for a given problem instance.

In addition, this representation can be exploited to guide the construction of an (approximate) MSFJ as it establishes a total order of the jobs, that we refer to as *job sequence*. Concretely, given a chromosome the job sequence it represents would be defined by the order of the jobs w.r.t. their first occurrence in the chromosome. For instance, the chromosome (4, 1, 1, 3, 2, 4, 2, 3) represents the job ordering (J_4, J_1, J_3, J_2). As a result, the coding schema, in combinanion with decoding algorithm presented below allows the GA to search in both the subset space of the set of jobs and in the space of schedules for any given subset of jobs *at the same time*.

Decoding Algorithm. The GA uses the solution builder described in Sect. 3 as a decoder. Given a chromosome, the decoder builds an (approximate) MFSJ using Algorithm 1, selecting the jobs in the order they appear in the job sequence extracted from the chromosome. In other words, at the ith iteration of the algorithm, it picks the job appearing in the ith position of the job sequence.

The procedure *Feasible* in Algorithm 1 is implemented by an invocation to the G&T schedule builder described in Algorithm 2, which is guided by the operation sequence extracted from the chromosome. At a given iteration, the operation in the set $\mathcal{B}$ that appears first in the operation sequence is chosen to be scheduled. If the makespan of the built schedule satisfies the hard makespan constraint the subset of jobs is declared feasible, and unfeasible otherwise. Since this does not constitute a complete decision procedure, there is no guarantee that an MFSJ would be computed, but an approximation instead. Nevertheless, as the search space defined by the G&T algorithm is dominant, there always exists the *possibility* of finding an actual MFSJ.

After the execution of the solution builder, the cardinality of the computed set is taken as the fitness of the chromosome.

Crossover and Mutation. As the crossover operator, we use *Job-based Order Crossover* (JOX) [3] for permutations with repetitions. Given a pair of chromosomes, JOX selects a random subset of the jobs and copies their genes to the offspring in the same positions as they are in the first chromosome; then the remaining genes are taken from the second chromosome maintaining their relative order. For producing the second offspring the parents switch roles.

On the other hand, the mutation operator implements a simple procedure, which randomly swaps two consecutive positions of the chromosome.

5   Experimental Study

In order to evaluate the performance of the genetic algorithm (GA) proposed in Sect. 4, we conducted a series of experiments over a set of unfeasible instances derived from classical JSP instances [2].

Concretely, the benchmark set consists of instances with a different number of jobs $n \in \{10, 15, 20\}$ and machines $m \in \{5, 10\}$. For each JSP instance, we built three unfeasible instances by imposing different values for the makespan limit C to be 70%, 80% and 90% of the optimal makespan C_{opt}. Among the JSP instances considered, there are 21 instances with $n = 10$: LA01-05 ($m = 5$), FT10, ORB01-10 and LA16-20 ($m = 10$); 10 instances with $n = 15$: LA06-10 ($m = 5$) and LA21-25 ($m = 10$); and 11 instances with $n = 20$: LA11-15, FT20 ($m = 5$) and LA26-30 ($m = 10$). So, there are 126 instances in all.

Our prototype was coded in C++ and all the experiments were run on a Linux cluster (Intel Xeon 2.26 GHz, 128 GB RAM).

The experimental study is divided in two parts. Firstly, we evaluate the quality of the search space defined by the solution builder presented in Sect. 3. Then, we analyze the GA in terms of its efficiency and the quality of the solutions it obtains.

Assessment of the Solution Builder. The first series of experiments are aimed at evaluating the quality of the search space defined by the solution builder (SB) presented in Algorithm 1. For this purpose, we compare it with a *naive* version of this algorithm, that we refer to as NSB (for *Naive Solution Builder*), in which the construction of an MFSJ stops whenever the procedure *Feasible* declares a subset as unfeasible. This way, NSB is expected to yield worse approximations of MFSJs.

Table 2. Summary of results

n	$\%C_{opt}$	SB		NSB		GA			
		Best	Avg.	Best	Avg.	Best	Avg.	SD	Time (s)
10	70	5.33	3.64	5.24	2.06	5.43	5.35	0.04	2.83
	80	6.81	4.62	6.48	3.11	7.00	6.91	0.08	3.66
	90	7.71	5.57	7.57	4.22	8.24	8.08	0.13	4.28
15	70	9.70	6.99	9.10	4.78	10.00	9.82	0.12	8.58
	80	11.10	8.43	10.70	6.39	11.70	11.38	0.26	10.04
	90	12.50	9.86	11.90	8.10	13.10	12.84	0.20	11.37
20	70	13.09	10.05	12.45	7.82	13.73	13.61	0.14	18.62
	80	15.09	11.92	14.45	9.95	15.82	15.51	0.21	21.34
	90	16.64	13.80	16.36	12.12	17.27	17.10	0.12	23.47

A total of 125000 random solutions were computed for each instance with both SB and NSB. The results are shown in Table 2 which reports the best and average size of the feasible subset of jobs obtained by each method, averaged for groups of instances with the same number of jobs n and percentage of the optimal makespan ($\%C_{opt}$) considered. Table 2 also shows the results from GA, which are discussed below. As we can observe, in all cases SB finds larger feasible subsets of jobs than NSB. The difference is sharper if we look at the quality of the average solutions, which confirms that searching over tighter approximations of MFSJs is beneficial.

Assessment of the Genetic Algorithm. The second series of experiments was conducted with the goal of evaluating the performance of GA. In all the experiments, GA evolves a population of 250 individuals over 500 generations with mutation probability of 0.2 and crossover probability of 0.9. The algorithm was run 20 times on each instance, recording the size of the best and average solutions found, as well as the standard deviation.

Table 2 shows a summary of the results, including the computation time of GA, averaged for each group of instances. As we can observe, GA reaches (much) better solutions than the random ones computed with both SB and NSB. Indeed, the average solutions produced by GA are better than the best random solutions, which indicates that GA is able to conduct the search effectively. The small differences between the best and average solutions computed by GA, along with the low values of the standard deviation (SD) show that GA is also stable. Finally, regarding the time taken by GA to tackle each set of instances, we can observe that, as expected, it grows with n, but also, with $\%C_{opt}$. This could be explained by the fact that, with a larger value of the limit on the makespan C, the decoder would have to build larger schedules; that take longer for $G\&T$ to build. In any case, the largest instances were solved in less than 25 seconds, which shows that GA is very efficient.

Bearing these results in mind, we can draw the conclusion that GA and the solution builder work well together, combining their strengths to create a powerful solver.

6   Conclusions

We study the task of repairing unfeasible scheduling problems, focusing on job shops with a hard makespan constraint. Particularly, we consider a setting in which the problem can be relaxed by dropping some of the jobs, so that the remaining ones can be scheduled within the makespan limit. In this context, we face the problem of finding the largest possible feasible subset of the jobs, and propose an efficient genetic algorithm for this purpose. The genetic algorithm relies on a solution builder also proposed in the paper. The results from an experimental study show that our approach is successful at solving the problem.

As future work, we plan to study alternative solution builders for the problem. Besides, considering hard constraints on metrics different from the makespan, such as the total tardiness [8] seems a promising line of research.

Acknowledgements. This research is supported by the Spanish Government under project TIN2016-79190-R and by the Principality of Asturias under grant IDI/2018/000176.

References

1. Allahverdi, A., Aydilek, H.: Total completion time with makespan constraint in no-wait flowshops with setup times. Eur. J. Oper. Res. **238**(3), 724–734 (2014)
2. Beasley, J.E.: Or-library: distributing test problems by electronic mail. J. Oper. Res. Soc. **41**(11), 1069–1072 (1990)
3. Bierwirth, C.: A generalized permutation approach to job shop scheduling with genetic algorithms. OR Spectr. **17**, 87–92 (1995)
4. Choi, J.Y.: Minimizing total weighted completion time under makespan constraint for two-agent scheduling with job-dependent aging effects. Comput. Ind. Eng. **83**, 237–243 (2015)
5. Dawande, M., Gavirneni, S., Rachamadugu, R.: Scheduling a two-stage flowshop under makespan constraint. Math. Comput. Model. **44**(1), 73–84 (2006)
6. Giffler, B., Thompson, G.L.: Algorithms for solving production scheduling problems. Oper. Res. **8**, 487–503 (1960)
7. Marques-Silva, J., Janota, M., Mencía, C.: Minimal sets on propositional formulae. Problems and reductions. Artif. Intell. **252**, 22–50 (2017)
8. Mencía, C., Sierra, M.R., Mencía, R., Varela, R.: Evolutionary one-machine scheduling in the context of electric vehicles charging. Integr. Comput.-Aided Eng. **26**, 49–63 (2019). https://doi.org/10.3233/ICA-180582
9. Mencía, R., Sierra, M.R., Mencía, C., Varela, R.: Schedule generation schemes and genetic algorithm for the scheduling problem with skilled operators and arbitrary precedence relations. In: Proceedings of ICAPS, pp. 165–173. AAAI Press (2015)
10. Palacios, J.J., Vela, C.R., Rodríguez, I.G., Puente, J.: Schedule generation schemes for job shop problems with fuzziness. In: Proceedings of ECAI, pp. 687–692 (2014)

Application of Koniocortex-Like Networks to Cardiac Arrhythmias Classification

Santiago Torres-Alegre[1(✉)], Yasmine Benchaib[2],
José Manuel Ferrández Vicente[3], and Diego Andina[1] (iD)

[1] Group for Automation in Signals and Communications,
Universidad Politécnica de Madrid, 28040 Madrid, Spain
{santiago.torres,d.andina}@upm.es
[2] Biomedical Engineering Laboratory, University of Abou Bakr Belkaid,
Tlemcen, Algeria
yasmine.benchaib@univ-tlemcen.dz
[3] Universidad Politécnica de Cartegena, Campus Muralla del Mar,
30202 Cartagena, Spain
jm.ferrandez@upct.es

Abstract. KLN (Koniocortex Like Network) is a novel Bioinspired Artificial Neural Network that models relevant biological properties of neurons as Synaptic Directionality, Long Term Potenciation, Long Term Depression, Metaplasticity and Intrinsic plasticity, together with natural normalization of sensory inputs and Winner-Take-All competitive learning. As a result, KLN performs a Deeper Learning on DataSets showing several high order properties of biological brains as: associative memory, scalability and even continuous learning. KLN learning is originally unsupervised and its architecture is inspired in the koniocortex, the first cortical layer receiving sensory inputs where map reorganization and feature extraction have been identified, as is the case of the visual cortex. This new model has shown big potential on synthetic inputs and research is now on application performance in complex problems involving real data in comparison with state-of-art supervised and unsupervised techniques. In this paper we apply KLN to explore its capabilities on one of the biggest problem of nowadays society and medical community, as it is the early detection of cardiovascular disease. The world's number one killer, with 17,9 million deaths every year. Results of KLN on the classification of Cardiac arrhythmias from the well-known MIT-BIH cardiac arrhythmias database are reported.

Keywords: Metaplasticity · Koniocortex · KLN · ECGs ·
Arrhythmias · Unsupervised neural networks

1 Introduction

The koniocortex is a common denomination for all regions of the cerebral cortex containing a granular layer (layer IV). The granular (grainy) texture of this layer

J. M. Ferrández Vicente et al. (Eds.): IWINAC 2019, LNCS 11487, pp. 264–273, 2019.
https://doi.org/10.1007/978-3-030-19651-6_26

is due to the abundance of spiny stellate neurons that directly receive neural projections from the thalamus. The thalamus, at the center of the brain, is the main relay station from the senses to the cortex.

The Koniocortex-like networks (KLN) are neural models that possess at least two layers: one layer containing neurons that are similar to the thalamo-cortical neurons of the thalamus, and another layer whose neurons resemble the spiny biological neurons, in addition to this they usually have a sensory or input layer and an inhibitory layer to carry out the whole classification process.

According to [1] the real koniocortex can be considered as a competitive system because only a small number of spiny neurons spiny stellate neurons are active in the presence of sensory stimuli. This behavior resembles the Winner-Take-All (WTA) process of competitive artificial networks. In WTA, the most active neuron remains active while the other neurons are set to zero.

The difference between conventional competitive networks and the biologically inspired KLN is that, while conventional competitive neurons find the most active neuron through calculation, in the case of the KLNs, the winning neuron emerges naturally from the interaction between the neurons being ones of them exciting neurons an others inhibiting ones. In addition, non-winning neurons become silent due to the activity of its neighbour neurons, not because they are algorithmically reset.

Previous works also studied the neural dynamics leading to emergent competition in terms of the different properties potentially involved in the process, like the strength and range of lateral inhibition [2–4], the value of the firing threshold [2], and the steepness of the activation function [5].

The main properties involved in competitive learning carried out in the KLN model are synaptic metaplasticity and intrinsic plasticity. Intrinsic plasticity adjusts the global excitability of the neuron so that highly excited neurons will be less excitable in the future, and vice versa while metaplasticity adjust the evolution of the weights of the network.

In this paper, we continue the research started in previous works [6–10] applying KLN networks to classify arrythmia patterns contained in the MIT BIH Data base.

For assessing the classification performance of this algorithm, we used the most common performance measures: specificity, sensitivity and accuracy. The results obtained were validated using the 10-fold cross-validation method. The paper is organized as follows. Section 2 presents a brief summary on the problem on cardiac diseases. In Sect. 3 the database, data preparation and the KLN algorithms are shown. In Sect. 4 we present the experimental results obtained. A brief discussion of these results is commented in Sect. 5 and, finally, in Sect. 6 we summarize the main conclusions of this work.

2 Application of KLN to Cardiac Arrhythmias Classification

Cardiovascular Diseases (CVDs) are still one of the most important diseases in the world causing one death out of three as stated by the World Health

Organization [11]. Each year, there are an estimated of seven million deaths around the world due to cardiac arrhythmias [12].

To prevent these cardiac diseases ECGs are very widely used as an inexpensive and non-invasive method to diagnose heart disease, identify irregular cardiac rhythms (arrhythmias) and evaluate the effects of drugs and monitor surgical procedures. The ECG signal measures the electrical activity of specialised heart cells that generate repetitive self-induced action potential. Each action potential generated leads to a contraction of the heart muscle and thus the heartbeat. The magnitude, conduction and duration of these potentials are detected by placing electrodes on the patient's skin. The ECG signal allows for the analysis of anatomic and physiologic aspects of the whole cardiac muscle [13]. The ability to identify arrhythmias from Electrocardiogram (ECG) recordings automatically is important for clinical diagnosis and treatment because changes in the normal rhythm of a human heartbeat may result in different cardiac arrhythmias, which may be immediately fatal or may cause irreparable damage to the heart sustained over long periods of time.

Recent studies show that generally there are significant cardiovascular abnormal symptoms such as palpitations, faints, chest pain and shortness of breath, which appear before the sudden occurrence of a heart attack. If these abnormal symptoms could be detected and diagnosed early, time would be saved to prevent the occurrence of heart attack or to provide an efficient treatment on time. Therefore, to reduce the number of disabilities and deceases caused by heart attack, it is necessary to have an effective method for early detection. Medical diagnosis is a promising domain where we use intelligent automated systems to enable detection of diseases. This detection may be used to assist doctors in more efficient and fast decision-making.

Computer-assisted ECG interpretation and automatic classification have received great attention from the biomedical engineering community in the last years. In this sense, The KLN model considered in this work is a novel bio-inspired structure that resemble several characteristics which make it suitable for this purpose as it is an autonomous system with no need of external supervision and can be applied to different biomedical problems.

The bio-inspired systems have the potential to provide a more efficient and effective use of explicit and implicit knowledge present in the data to be evaluated. The characteristics of the neural connections included in the KLN are believed to be crucial in achieving the biological Deep Learning which allows biological brains to successfully deal with real-world complex problems like the classification of the cardiac arrhythmias.

3   Materials and Methods

3.1   MIT-BIH Dataset

The MIT-BIH Arrhythmia Database was the first generally available set of ECGs test material for evaluation of arrhythmia detectors [14]. Database contains 48 half-hour excerpts of two-channel, 24-h, studied by the BIH Arrhythmia Labo-ratory. 1000 annotated ECG beats which contain 4 different waveforms related to cardiac arrhythmias target, Normal beat (N); Premature ventricular contrac-tion (PVC); Right bundle branch block (RBBB) and Left bundle branch block (LBBB) has been used in this research. The last three of them are abnormalities of cardiac system function.

In Table 1 the eleven feature descriptors for characterizing the cardiac arrhythmias are presented. Components P, QRS, T and U of an ECG beat can be seen in Fig. 1.

Table 1. Feature descriptors.

Attributes	Meaning
Duration P	The width of the P wave
PR interval	The distance between the beginning of the P wave and the beginning of QRS
QRS complex	The distance between the beginning of the Q wave and the end of the S wave
Duration T	The width of the T wave
ST segment	The distance between the end of the S wave or R and the beginning of the T wave
QT interval	The distance between the beginning of QRS and the end of the T wave
RR previous: RRp	The distance between the R peak of the present beat and the R peak of the previous beat
RR next: RRn	RRn: the distance between the R peak of the present beat and the R peak of the following beat
RDI (delay of the deflexion)	From the beginning of QRS to the top of the latest wave of positivity R peak
Beat duration	The distance between the beginning of the P wave and the end of the T wave
RRp/RRn.	The ratio RRp/RRn

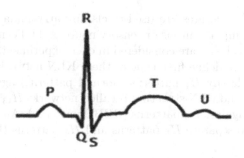

Fig. 1. ECG components.

3.2   Data Preparation

The data set formed by 1000 patterns is divided equally in four classes with 250 patterns each (N, PVC, RBBB and LBBB). We denominate respectively these classes as H_1, H_2, H_3, and H_4.

To obtain results statistically independent of the distribution of the patterns a 10 fold cross validation evaluation method has been considered. Using this method the possible dependence of the results with the distribution of the input patterns in the training and performance evaluation phases is eliminated cause all the patterns are used to train and evaluate the performance of the networks in different executions of the experiments for the same initial neural networks. Mean values are calculated to establish the final performance results.

3.3   Koniocortex-Like Network Model

By a combination of biologically plausible models of neurons found in some relevant parts of the neo-cortex that process signals, as it is the visual cortex, KLN learning models relevant biological properties of neurons as synaptic directionality, Long Term Potentiation (LTP), Long Term Depression (LTD), Metaplasticity and Intrinsic plasticity, together with normalization and Winner-Take-All competitive learning. As a result, KLN performs a Deeper Learning on DataSets showing several high order properties of biological brains as:

- Memory, by acting as an Associative Network.
- Scalability. Size of the network can be increased to perform as Deep Network
- Continuous Learning (adapting to changes in training set while continuously training).

A detailed description and discussion of KLN can be found in seminal papers [9,15].

4   Results

4.1   Network Characteristics

Three parallel KLN structures are used to classify arrythmia patterns. Each of this networks has 11 input neurons or sensory neurons, 11 TC neurons, 2 neurons in the S layer as two classes are considered in each experiment, and 2 neurons in the upper B layer. We define first type of these KLN network as networks H_{12} which are used to classify H_1 patterns (normal patterns) against H_2 patterns (PVC patterns). Second KLN structure is called networks H_{13} which are used to classify H_1 pattern against H_3 patterns (RBBB patterns). And finally H_{14} KLN networks are used to separate H_1 patterns and H_4 patterns (LBBB patterns).

Twenty H_{12}, H_{13} and H_{14} networks are used to obtain final results. In each of them WTA process occurs naturally as an emergent consequence of the individual computation of each neuron without the need of externally monitoring the network. Once the input is fed to the network, its activation is "propagated" until all layers are activated. At the end of the process one of the neurons presents a higher output than the other one, so it is possible to classify the patterns taking into account which output is activated and which one is inhibited.

Parameters of KLN networks are obtained by simulations until adequate results are obtained and the networks are able to learn without external supervision. The final values used in this simulation are v set to 0.025 and ξ to 0.001, the curve-compressing factor k is set to 25.00, the initial sigmoid shift was 0.5, initial weights from TC to S neurons were negligible and random, and non-modifiable weights were set to $W_{S_S} = 0.85$, $W_{S_B} = 0.98$, $W_{I_{TC}} = 1.0$ and $W_{B_S} = 0.5$.

4.2 Evaluation Method

For each type of networks H_{12}, H_{13} and H_{14}, 20 different networks have been trained. 10 fold cross validation method is used to validate the results are not dependent of the concrete patterns used for training performance evaluation. Besides, using these 20 different initial networks and calculating mean values we assure that the results are independent of the initial random values in the creation of the networks. From the results obtained for the same network with each one of the folders the mean confusion matrix is obtained for each network. Once we have these 20 mean values an additional calculation is made and the final mean value is obtained as the final result of the experiment.

The following hypothesis are defined for classify arrythmia patterns:

- H_1: The pattern corresponds to a Normal beat.
- H_2: The pattern corresponds to a PVC beat.
- H_3: The pattern corresponds to a RBBB beat.
- H_4: The pattern corresponds to a LBBB beat.

To evaluate the KLN structure performances the well known concepts of Specificity (SP), Sensitivity (SE), Accuracy (AC)are used. The most important figure in these experiments is in the sensitivity considered as true positive percentage, cause it is much more important to detect all the malicious patterns than classifying as malicious a benign one.

4.3 Classification Results

As mentioned in Sect. 4.1 we had use three types of KLN structures, networks H_{12}, networks H_{13}, and networks H_{14} to separate normal patterns from one of each cardiac abnormalities. Different experiments have been performed with 20 different networks for each type and best results have been obtained for 20 training epochs. We have performed different experiments with different number of epochs in each experiment (considering one epoch like presenting the full set of input patterns once to the network). The output of the network is integrated by two neurons, depending on which one presents the higher level at the output we have considered that one of the classes, normal or abnormality pattern, is selected by the network.

Best results obtained after 20 training epochs are provided in Table 2.

Table 2. Performance results after 20 training epochs.

Networks	SP	SE	AC
H_{12}	98.16	98.28	98.21
H_{13}	95.96	96.1	96.03
H_{14}	96.81	96.68	96.75
Average	96.98	97.02	97.01

It can be seen that better results are obtained by networks types H_{12}, these are the ones that separate normal patters from PVC patterns, while worst results are obtained for H_{13} and H_{14} networks the ones dedicated to separate normal beats from RBBB and LBBB beats respectively. Results for H_{13} and H_{14} networks are worst than for H_{12} networks no matter the number of epochs.

Regarding to the evolution with the number of epochs in the training phases we present in Table 3 the average value for 20 H_{12}, H_{13}, and H_{14} networks for 10, 20 and 30 epochs.

Table 3. Performance results tables.

Epochs	SP	SE	AC
10	76,78	75,61	76,19
20	96.98	97.02	97.01
30	94.73	87.85	91.29

For comparison purpose in Table 4 results of proposed KLN are showed among other classifiers

5   Discussion

– Simulations performed show that the proposed prototype performance is comparable with some of the state-of the-art learning algorithms. If we compare it with other unsupervised methods results are similar to those obtained with Kohonen SOM neural networks studied by the authors in previous works [26]. However performance is lower than the AMSOM (Artificial Metaplasticity Self-Organizing Maps) which is another unsupervised neural network classifier presented in [26].

Table 4. Classification accuracies obtained with our method and other classifiers from the literature.

Authors (year)	Method	Accuracy
Minami et al. [16] (1999)	Fourier-NN	98.00
Owis et al. [17] (2002)	Blind Source Separation	96.79
Yu et al. [18] (2008)	ICA-NN	98.71
Ghorbanian et al. [19] (2011)	CWT-NN	99.17
Benchaib et al. [20] (2013)	AMMLP1	98.25
Alonso et al. [21] (2014)	SVM	99.10
Torres et al. [22] (2015)	AMMLP2	98.70
Elhaj et al. [23] (2016)	SVM-RBF	98.91
Kyranyaz et al. [24] (2016)	1D-CNNs	99.00
Shansan et al. [25] (2017)	FE-SVM	98.41
Torres-Alegre et al. [26] (2018)	SOM	97.50
Torres-Alegre et al. [26] (2018)	AMSOM	99.0
In this study	**KLN**	**97.01**

- It is important to mention the importance of KLN parameters values. Slight variations in these parameters like k or v, can affect significatively the performance so the KLN prototype is not totally stable nor fully optimized. Also we notice that the number of epochs affect significatively the performance of the network. It can be seen that the results improve to the maximum performance in only 20 epochs. After that the evolution is similar to the one presented in [10], where in less of 20 epochs, overtraining (network specialization on training patterns) degrades generalization capabilities.
- The strategy of establishing three parallel KLNs let us see the difference in classification while separating Normal patterns from PVC patterns or separating Normal patterns from RBBB or LBBB patterns where performance is lower.
- Results are quite promising taking into account that is an unsupervised learning algorithm and it is a novel prototype not totally optimized which encourage the authors to continue with this research.

6   Conclusions

In this paper a prototype of a KLN network is applied to a real data set of ECG beats. Results obtained show that the proposed prototype is comparable with several advanced state-of the-art learning algorithms. Results are quite promising taking into account that is an unsupervised learning algorithm and the prototype is not totally optimized. These results allow having an initial idea of the possibilities of this new structure in terms of performance and adaptation capabilities to several kinds of input patterns.

References

1. Miller, K.D.: Synaptic economics: competition and cooperation in synaptic plasticity. Neuron **17**, 371–374 (1996)
2. Kaski, S., Kohonen, T.: Winner-take-all networks for physiological models of competitive learning. Neural Netw. **7**(6/7), 973–984 (1994)
3. Fukai, T., Tanaka, S.: A simple neural network exhibiting selective activation of neuronal ensembles: from winner-take-all to winners-share-all. Neural Comput. **9**(1), 77–97 (1997)
4. Mao, Z.H., Massaquoi, S.G.: Dynamics of winner-take-all competition in recurrent neural networks with lateral inhibition. IEEE Trans. Neural Netw. **18**, 55–69 (2007)
5. Yang, J.F., Chen, C.M.: Winner-take-all neural network using the highest threshold. IEEE Trans. Neural Netw. **11**, 194–199 (2000)
6. Andina, D., Alvarez-Vellisco, A., Aleksandar, J., Fombellida, J.: Artificial metaplasticity can improve artificial neural network learning. Intell. Autom. Soft Comput.; Spec. Issue Signal Process. Soft Comput. **15**(4), 681–694 (2009)
7. Andina, D., Ropero-Pelaez, J.: On the biological plausibility of artificial metaplasticity learning algorithm. Neurocomputing (2012). https://doi.org/10.1016/j.neucom.2012.09.028
8. Ropero-Peláez, F.J., Andina, D.: Do biological synapses perform probabilistic computations? Neurocomputing (2012). https://doi.org/10.1016/j.neucom.2012.08.042
9. Ropero-Peláez, F.J., Aguiar-Furucho, M.A., Andina, D.: Intrinsic plasticity for natural competition in koniocortex-like neural networks. Int. J. Neural Syst. 16(5) (2016)
10. Fombellida, J., Martin-Rubio, I., Romera-Zarza, A., Andina, D.: KLN, a new biological koniocortex based unsupervised neural network: competitive results on credit scoring. Natural Comput. (2018). https://doi.org/10.1007/s11047-018-9698-6
11. World Health Organization: Global status report on noncommunicable diseases, Geneva (2010)
12. World Health Organization: Global Atlas on Cardiovascular Disease Prevention and Control, Geneva (2010)
13. Dey, N., Prasad Dash, T., Dash, S.: ECG signal denoising by functional link artificial neural network (FLANN). Int. J. Biomed. Eng. Technol. **7**(4), 377–389 (2011)
14. Moody, G.B., Mark, R.G.: The impact of the MIT-BIH arrhythmia database. IEEE Eng. Med. Biol. Mag. **20**(3), 45–50 (2001)
15. Peláez, F.J.R., Andina, D.: The koniocortex-like network: a new biologically plausible unsupervised neural network. In: Ferrández Vicente, J.M., Álvarez-Sánchez, J.R., de la Paz López, F., Toledo-Moreo, F.J., Adeli, H. (eds.) IWINAC 2015. LNCS, vol. 9107, pp. 163–174. Springer, Cham (2015). https://doi.org/10.1007/978-3-319-18914-7_17
16. Minami, K., Nakajima, H., Toyoshima, T.: Real-time discrimination of ventricular tachyarrhythmia with Fourier-transform neural network. IEEE Trans. Biomed. Eng. **46**(2), 179–185 (1999)
17. Owis, M.I., Youssef, A.B.M., Kadah, Y.M.: Characterization of ECG signals based on blind source separation. Med. Biol. Eng. Comput. **40**(5), 557–564 (2002)
18. Yu, S.N., Chou, K.T.: Integration of independent component analysis and neural networks for ECG beat classification. Expert Syst. Appl. **34**(4), 2841–2846 (2008)
19. Ghorbanian, P., Jalali, A., Ghaffari, A., Nataraji, A.: An improved procedure for detection of heart arrhythmias with novel pre-processing techniques. Expert Syst. **29**(5), 478–491 (2009)

20. Benchaib, Y., Marcano-Cedeño, A., Torres-Alegre, S., Andina, D.: Application of artificial metaplasticity neural networks to cardiac arrhythmias classification. In: Ferrández Vicente, J.M., Álvarez Sánchez, J.R., de la Paz López, F., Toledo Moreo, F.J. (eds.) IWINAC 2013. LNCS, vol. 7930, pp. 181–190. Springer, Heidelberg (2013). https://doi.org/10.1007/978-3-642-38637-4_19

21. Alonso-Atienza, F., Morgado, E., Fernandez-Martinez, L., Garcia-Alberola, A., Rojo-Alvarez, J.: Detection of life-threatening arrhythmias using feature selection and support vector machines. IEEE Trans. Biomed. Eng. **61**(3), 832–840 (2014)

22. Torres-Alegre, S., Fombellida, J., Piñuela-Izquierdo, J.A., Andina, D.: Artificial metaplasticity: application to MIT-BIH arrhythmias database. In: Ferrández Vicente, J.M., Álvarez-Sánchez, J.R., de la Paz López, F., Toledo-Moreo, F.J., Adeli, H. (eds.) IWINAC 2015. LNCS, vol. 9107, pp. 133–142. Springer, Cham (2015). https://doi.org/10.1007/978-3-319-18914-7_14

23. Elhaj, F., Salim, N., Harris, A., Swee, T., Ahmed, T.: Arrhythmia recognition and classification using combined linear and nonlinear features of ECG signals. Comput. Methods Programs Biomed. **127**, 52–63 (2016)

24. Kiranyaz, S., Ince, T., Gabbouj, M.: Real-time patient-specific ECG classification by 1-D convolutional neural networks. IEEE Trans. Biomed. Eng. **63**, 664–675 (2016)

25. Shanshan, C., Wei, H., Zhi, L., Jian, L., Xingjiao, G.: Heartbeat classification using projected and dynamic features of ECG signal. Biomed. Signal Process. Control **31**, 165–173 (2017)

26. Torres-Alegre, S., Fombellida, J., Piñuela-Izquierdo, J.A., Andina, D.: AMSOM: artificial metaplasticity in SOM neural networks. Application to MIT-BIH arrhythmias data base. Neural Comput. Appl. (2018). https://doi.org/10.1007/s00521-018-3576-0

Machine Learning for Big Data and Visualization

Content Based Image Retrieval
by Convolutional Neural Networks

Safa Hamreras[1], Rafaela Benítez-Rochel[2], Bachir Boucheham[1],
Miguel A. Molina-Cabello[2(✉)], and Ezequiel López-Rubio[2]

[1] Department of Computer Science,
University of 20 August 1955,
BP 26, Route El Hadaiek, 21000 Skikda, Algeria
safahamreras@gmail.com,bachir.boucheham@hotmail.com
[2] Department of Computer Languages and Computer Science,
University of Málaga, Bulevar Louis Pasteur, 35,
29071 Málaga, Spain
{benitez,miguelangel,ezeqlr}@lcc.uma.es,
http://www.lcc.uma.es/~ezeqlr/index-en.html

Abstract. In this paper, we present a Convolutional Neural Network
(CNN) for feature extraction in Content Based Image Retrieval (CBIR).
The proposed CNN aims at reducing the semantic gap between low-
level and high-level features. Thus, improving retrieval results. Our CNN
is the result of a transfer learning technique using Alexnet pretrained
network. It learns how to extract representative features from a learning database and then uses this knowledge in query feature extraction.
Experimentations performed on Wang (Corel 1K) database show a significant improvement in terms of precision over the state of the art classic
approaches.

Keywords: Content based image retrieval ·
Convolutional neural networks · Feature extraction

1 Introduction

The increased use of digital computers, multimedia, and storage systems over
recent years has result in large image and multimedia content repositories. This
huge amount of multimedia data is being used in many fields like medical treatment, satellite data, electronic games, archaeology, video and still images repository, and digital forensics and surveillance systems. That rapid growing has
created an ongoing demand of retrieval images systems operating on a large
scale.

Content Based Image Retrieval (CBIR) is the procedure of automatically
retrieving images by the extraction of their low-level visual features, like color,
texture, shape properties or any other features being derived from the image
itself. The performance of a CBIR system mainly depends on these selected

J. M. Ferrández Vicente et al. (Eds.): IWINAC 2019, LNCS 11487, pp. 277–286, 2019.
https://doi.org/10.1007/978-3-030-19651-6_27

features [14]. Thus, it can be said that through navigation, browsing, query-by-example etc, we can calculate the similarity between the low-level image contents which can be used for the retrieval of relevant images. The most challenging issue associated with CBIR systems is reducing the semantic gap. It is the information lost by representing an image in terms of its features i.e., from high level semantics to low level features [7]. This gap exists between the visual information captured by the imaging device and the visual information perceived by the human vision system (HVS) and it can be reduced either by embedding domain specific knowledge or by using some machine learning technique to develop intelligent systems that can be trained to act like HVS.

There has been a significant growth in machine learning research but mainly deep learning has already demonstrated its potential in large-scale visual recognition [1]. The main reasons behind its success are the availability of large annotated data sets, and the GPUs computational power and affordability.

Deep learning is a subset of machine learning which uses a hierarchical level of artificial neural networks to carry out the process of machine learning. The term Deep Neural Network (DNN) refers to describe any network that has more than three layers of non-linear information stages in its architecture and Deep Learning (DL) is a collection of algorithms for learning in Deep Neural Networks, used to model high-level abstractions in data [15]. Thus, deep learning techniques gives a direct way to get feature representations by allowing the system (deep network) to learn complex features from raw images without using hand crafted features [4].

Deep learning has been successfully applied to many problems e.g., computer vision and pattern recognition [16], computer games, robots and self-driving cars [9], voice recognition and generation [3] and natural language processing [11].

Due the success of deep leaning, and the importance of feature extraction in CBIR systems, in this work we propose a CNN for learning feature representation in CBIR. The proposed CNN learns how to extract relevant features from a given images database and then applies this information in image retrieval process. The rest of this paper is organized as follows: Sect. 2 reviews the state of the art approaches in CBIR, Sect. 3 presents the adopted methodology, Sect. 4 reports the obtained results, and Sect. 5 concludes this paper.

2   State of the Art

The used features and similarity measure are the two critical choices to make when building a CBIR system. Therefore most researches in CBIR focus on these topics to enhance these systems. In this section we discuss the major contributions that treat these points as well as a recent approach adopted in CBIR which is Deep Learning.

In feature representation level, recent traditional approaches focus on efficient representation of images by improving visual descriptors and combining them in order to improve retrieval results. Walia et al. [2] proposed a CBIR framework where they used late fusion techniques in order to improve the accuracy, the techniques used were: Borda Count, Min-Max normalization and Z-Score normalization. The fusion was performed on two descriptors: Modified Color Difference Histogram (CDH) which was improved by using filtering on lab color space images and modified edge orientation, and The Angular Radial Transform (ART). Guo et al. [5] designed a framework that generates an efficient feature vector using low complexity-Dither Block Truncation Coding (ODBTC). The result feature vector is composed of color co-occcurence feature (CCF) and bit pattern features (BPF). Similar images are then sorted based on the relative distance measure between query image and all database images. In another similar work, Guo et al. [6] used Dot-Diffused Block Truncation Coding Features to create a feature vector composed of Color Histogram Feature (CHF) and Bit Pattern Feature (BPF). For similarity measure they used: L1 distance, x2 distance, Fu distance, and Modified Canberra Distance. Charles et al. [13] used Local Mesh Texture Color Pattern descriptor to represent an image. In this work, there is a merge of three color spaces: l1l2l3, YIQ, YcbCr, where the three components: l1, Cb, Q are extracted from these color spaces in order to create three opponent texture patterns: l1Cb, CbQ, and l1Q. Finally, the three opponent patterns are fused in order to create one feature vector. Moreover they used four distance functions for similarity measurement: Manhattan, Euclidian, Canberra, and d1 distance measure. Wang et al. [12] proposed a system that combines color and texture features including: Pseudo-Zernike chromacity distribution moments in opponent chromacity space for color representation, and rotation-invariant and scale-invariant descriptor in steerable pyramid domain for texture representation.

Some other recent approaches are interested in similarity measurement. For example, ELALMI [10] proposed a model for CBIR where he injected a matching strategy to measure similarity between images, the proposed model extracts color and texture features from images, and then reduces this set by selecting relevant and non-redundant features. After that, ANN network is used to classify images so that the retrieved images are from the same class as the query image. For retrieval step, the model uses a matching strategy by calculating the area between image query features vectors and all database images features vectors.

Recently, researchers are using CNNs to learn image representation and similarity measure. One of the most interesting contributions belongs to Lin et al. [8]. The authors proposed a framework for image retrieval using CNNs where they use binary hash codes for less time consuming. Moreover, the binary hash codes are learned simultaneously while fine-tuning the network. For similarity measure, they first use Hamming distance in order to compare query image binary hash code and database images binary hash codes. The result set of similar images is then filtered and sorted so the most k similar images are extracted, for that they use the euclidean distance to measure similarity between features extracted from F7 layer.

In this paper, we focus on image representation in CBIR by learning efficient feature representation. In order to achieve this we use a CNN to carry out feature extraction process. The used method is described in the following sections.

3   Methodology

In order to design a Content Based Image Retrieval (CBIR) system based on a Convolutional Neural Network (CNN), we propose to employ a neural architecture which has an output layer with one output neuron for each object class in the training image database. Let D be the number of object classes. The CNN has to be trained on the images of the training database, where the desired output for each image is a unit vector of size C with a one at the component associated to the class of the object which is depicted in the training image, and zeros at the rest of the components. Given this configuration, the CNN learns to estimate the probabilities that an image represents an object class:

$$f\left(\mathbf{X}\right) = \left(P\left(C_1|\mathbf{X}\right), ..., P\left(C_D|\mathbf{X}\right)\right) \in [0,1]^D \tag{1}$$

where $\mathbf{X}$ is an input image, and C_i is the i-th object class, with $i \in \{1, ..., D\}$.

After the CNN is trained in this way, the system is ready to accept user queries. Let us note $\mathbf{X}_{Query}$ the query image, and $\mathbf{X}_j$ the training database images, where $j \in \{1, ..., N\}$ and N is the number of images in the database. Then the database images are ranked according to the Euclidean distances between the probability vector $f\left(\mathbf{X}_{Query}\right)$ associated to the query image, and the probability vectors $f\left(\mathbf{X}_j\right)$ associated to the database images. For example, the most similar image in the database can be obtained as follows:

$$s = \arg \min_{j \in \{1, ..., N\}} \|f\left(\mathbf{X}_{Query}\right) - f\left(\mathbf{X}_j\right)\| \tag{2}$$

It is then possible to obtain the k most similar images in the database, as ranked by $\|f\left(\mathbf{X}_{Query}\right) - f\left(\mathbf{X}_j\right)\|$. Alternatively, a similarity threshold τ can be defined so that all images in the database with $\|f\left(\mathbf{X}_{Query}\right) - f\left(\mathbf{X}_j\right)\| < \tau$ are declared to be similar to the query image.

4   Experimental Results

In this section, we report the obtained results by our approach, which uses Convolutional Neural Networks, and compare them with other state of the art traditional approaches.

4.1   Methods

In this work, the transfer learning technique using Alexnet pretrained network has been applied. The advantage of this technique is the use of an existing neural network without the need to build it from scratch. This network is adapted to the image classification task and it can learn an efficient feature representation. Our work consists of fine-tuning this network to adapt it to our used database by replacing the final layers, we can then train the network so that it learns feature representation for our new task. As a result, we will have database images with the probability of belonging to each class. This information can be deployed

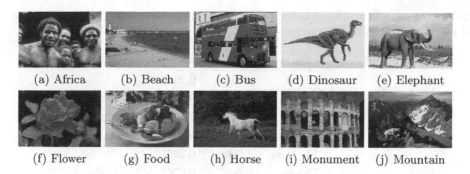

| (a) Africa | (b) Beach | (c) Bus | (d) Dinosaur | (e) Elephant |

| (f) Flower | (g) Food | (h) Horse | (i) Monument | (j) Mountain |

Fig. 1. Some samples representing the 10 semantic classes of Wang database.

later in image retrieval task: similarity between images is calculated based on the distance between class membership probabilities of query image and database images.

The selected methods to compare the results of our proposal are *Walia et al.* (noted as Walia) [2], *Elalami* [10], *ODBTC* [5], *DDBTC* [6] and *LMCTP* [13]. Walia method is based on a combination of color, texture, and shape features using different fusion techniques. The Elalami method introduces an effective matching strategy in order to measure similarity between images. Both of ODBTC and DDBTC consist in generating a feature vector derived respectively from low complexity-Dither Block Truncation and Dot-Diffused Block Truncation Coding. Finally, a merged color space is created in LMCTP, from which local mesh color features are extracted.

4.2 Hardware and Software

The experiments have been established on a machine with Ubuntu 64 bits operating system, 2,9 GiB RAM, Intel Core 2 QUAD CPU with a frequency of 2,40 GHz and NVIDIA Graphic card. The used programming language is MAT-LAB R2018a.

4.3 Images Database

In this paper, we use Wang (Corel 1k) database which is available in its website[1]. This database contains 1000 images grouped into 10 semantic classes: Africa, Beach, Bus, Dinosaur, Elephant, Flower, Food, Horse, Monument, Mountain. 70% of images are used to train the neural network, where 30% are left for the test phase. Figure 1 shows some samples of this database.

4.4 Results

We have employed several well known measures to measure the performance of each approach in order to establish a comparison between the different competitor methods from a quantitative point of view. The selected measures are the

---

[1] http://wang.ist.psu.edu/docs/related/.

Table 1. Precision and recall performances of our approach by using a k fixed number of retrieved images. In this case, $k = 20$.

Classes	Precision	Recall
Africa	0.9333	0.2667
Beach	0.9000	0.2571
Bus	1.0000	0.2857
Dinosaur	1.0000	0.2857
Elephant	1.0000	0.2857
Flower	0.9667	0.2767
Food	0.9683	0.2767
Horse	1.0000	0.2857
Monument	0.9667	0.2762
Mountain	0.8383	0.2395
Overall	0.95733	0.2735

precision (P) and the recall (R). These measures provide a real number between 0 and 1, where higher is better, and they are given by the following equations:

$$P = \frac{Number\ of\ relevant\ images\ retrieved}{Total\ number\ of\ retrieved\ images} \tag{3}$$

$$R = \frac{Number\ of\ relevant\ images\ retrieved}{Total\ number\ of\ relevant\ images} \tag{4}$$

In order to check the goodness of our proposal, our approach has been compared to other CBIR classic approaches and the retrieval process has been established using two different comparisons. A first comparison, that we note as *Fixed number of retrieved images*, has been carried out. In this comparison the number of images to retrieve is fixed previously. The parameter k represents this number and we have considered $k = 20$ in this comparison. The most k similar images are selected based on their distances with the query image. So that, according to the lowest distances belong to the most similar images.

The performance measures of our proposal are reported in Table 1, where precision and recall values are shown for each class. As it can be observed the proposal achieves a high precision, although the recall is low.

On the other hand, Table 2 shows the comparison with other CBIR classic approaches. As it is shown, our convolutional neural network approach outperforms significantly these approaches in terms of precision.

Moreover, our experiments have shown that the number of images retrieved affects significantly the recall, which is not the case for precision. Figure 2 shows variation of precision and recall values in terms of the number of images retrieved. This number varies between 10 to 70 which is the maximum number of relevant images that can be retrieved (Number of instances in each class in learning

Table 2. Comparison between our approach and other traditional approaches in terms of precision. A k fixed number of retrieved images has been used. In this case, $k = 20$. The best result is highlighted in **bold**.

Approach	Precision
Walia [2]	0.783
Elalami [10]	0.761
ODBTC [5]	0.779
DDBTC [6]	0.792
LMCTP [13]	0.765
Our method	**0.957**

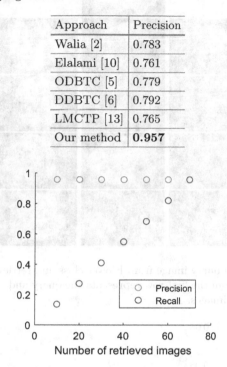

Fig. 2. Precision and recall performance of our proposal depending on the number of retrieved images parameter k.

database). We can see that precision keeps almost the same value even with a higher number of retrieved images which reflects the effectiveness of our approach. However recall is increasing notably which means that more relevant images are being retrieved. Precision and recall are equal when the number of retrieved images is 70 which is the same as the number of relevant images.

Furthermore, the obtained results can be observed from a qualitative point of view. Figure 3 illustrates a user query with the relevant images returned by our system. In this figure, the image from the first row represents the query and the remaining images represent the retrieved images. For this query the obtained precision by our approach is perfect (so that, 1).

In addition, a second comparison, noted as *Defined threshold for the distance*, has been performed. In this case, for each query image, the number of retrieved images is determined based on a threshold τ. The distance between the query and all database images is calculated and then relevant images are selected. So that, the distance between a selected image and the query must be less than the defined threshold.

Fig. 3. An example of a query image from Flower class and retrieved images using our approach. The image from the first row represents the query and the remaining images represent the retrieved images.

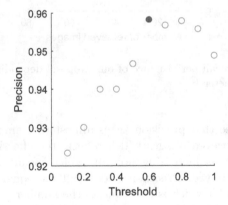

Fig. 4. Precision in terms of some experimented threshold values t. The red circle indicates the maximum reached precision which equals 0.9583 where the corresponding threshold value τ is $\tau = 0.6$. (Color figure online)

In this comparison, the definition of the threshold value is based on the precision, where the chosen threshold is the one that maximizes it. Figure 4 shows obtained precision values in terms of the used threshold.

After that, the precision and recall performances of our approach are reported in Table 3. Compared to the first comparison, it can be observed that the pre-

Table 3. Precision and recall values using a defined threshold. Precision and recall performances of our approach by using a defined threshold τ for the distance. In this case, $\tau = 0.6$.

Classes	Precision	Recall
Africa	0.9333	0.9010
Beach	0.9000	0.9000
Bus	1.0000	1.0000
Dinosaur	1.0000	1.0000
Elephant	1.0000	1.0000
Flower	0.9667	0.9667
Food	0.9667	0.9667
Horse	1.0000	1.0000
Monument	0.9662	0.9667
Mountain	0.8500	0.8338
Overall	0.9583	0.9535

cision is practically the same but the recall has increased in a remarkable way. Thus, the used threshold allows our system to retrieve most of relevant images in the database.

5   Conclusion

A new content based image retrieval method by employing convolutional neural networks has been presented in this work. It uses a trained neural network in order to obtain the probabilities that an image represents an object class. Given a query image, two ways can be defined to provide the most similar images. In the first proposal, the output system is the k most similar images in the database, while in the second proposal the system supplies images which have a probability vector distance lower than a threshold τ.

The retrieval capabilities of the proposal have been tested in the experimental section. Well-known state-of-art methods, dataset and measures have been chosen to compare the performance. Quantitative results exhibit the goodness of the approach.

Acknowledgments. This work is partially supported by the Ministry of Economy and Competitiveness of Spain under grant TIN2014-53465-R, project name Video surveillance by active search of anomalous events. It is also partially supported by the Autonomous Government of Andalusia (Spain) under projects TIC-6213, project name Development of Self-Organizing Neural Networks for Information Technologies; and TIC-657, project name Self-organizing systems and robust estimators for video surveillance. All of them include funds from the European Regional Development Fund (ERDF). The authors thankfully acknowledge the computer resources, technical expertise and assistance provided by the SCBI (Supercomputing and Bioinformatics) center of the University of Málaga. They also gratefully acknowledge the support of NVIDIA Corporation with the donation of two Titan X GPU. Authors are also immensely grateful for ERASMUS+ program, CEI.MAR (Campus de Excelencia International del Mar), and University of 20 August 1955 for making this collaborative work possible.

References

1. Krizhevsky, A., Sutskever, I., Hinton, G.E.: Imagenet classification with deep convolutional neural networks. In: Advances in Neural Information Processing Systems (2012)
2. Walia, E., Pal, A.: Fusion framework for effective color image retrieval. J. Vis. Commun. Image Represent. **25**(6), 1335–1348 (2014)
3. Hinton, G., et al.: Deep neural networks for acoustic modeling in speech recognition: the shared views of four research groups. IEEE Signal Process. Mag. **29**(6), 82–97 (2012)
4. Wan, J., et al.: Deep learning for content-based image retrieval: a comprehensive study. In: Proceedings of the ACM International Conference on Multimedia (2014)
5. Guo, J.-M., Prasetyo, H.: Content-based image retrieval using features extracted from halftoning-based block truncation coding. IEEE Trans. Image Process. **24**(3), 1010–1024 (2015)
6. Guo, J.-M., Prasetyo, H., Wang, N.-J.: Effective image retrieval system using dot-diffused block truncation coding features. IEEE Trans. Multimed. **17**(9), 1576–1590 (2015)
7. Kranthi Kumar, K., Venu Gopal, T.: A novel approach to self order feature reweighting in CBIR to reduce semantic gap using relevance feedback. In: International Conference on Circuits, Power and Computing Technologies (2014)
8. Lin, K., Yang, H.-F., Hsiao, J.-H., Chen, C.-S.: Deep learning of binary hash codes for fast image retrieval. In: The IEEE Conference on Computer Vision and Pattern Recognition (CVPR) Workshops (2015)
9. Bojarski, M., et al.: End to end learning for self-driving cars. In: Computer Vision and Pattern Recognition (2016)
10. ElAlami, M.E.: A new matching strategy for content based image retrieval system. Appl. Soft Comput. **14**, 407–418 (2014)
11. Zhou, S., Chen, Q., Wang, X.: Active deep networks for semi-supervised sentiment classification. In: Neurocomputing (2013)
12. Wang, X.-Y., Zhang, B.-B., Yang, H.-Y.: Content-based image retrieval by integrating color and texture features. Multimed. Tools Appl. **68**(3), 545–569 (2014)
13. Charles, Y.R., Ramraj, R.: A novel local mesh color texture pattern for image retrieval system. Int. J. Electron. Commun. **70**(3), 225–233 (2016)
14. Liu, Y., Zhang, D., Lu, G., Ma, W.-Y.: A survey of content-based image retrieval with high-level semantics. Pattern Recogn. **40**(1), 262–282 (2007)
15. Bengio, Y., Courville, A., Vincent, P.: Unsupervised feature learning and deep learning: a review and new perspectives. CoRR, abs/1206.5538 (2012)
16. Cao, Z., Simon, T., Wei, S.-E., Sheikh, Y.: Realtime multi-person 2D pose estimation using part affinity fields. In: Computer Vision and Pattern Recognition Proceeding (2017)

Deep Learning Networks with p-norm Loss Layers for Spatial Resolution Enhancement of 3D Medical Images

Karl Thurnhofer-Hemsi[1]([✉])[iD], Ezequiel López-Rubio[1][iD], Núria Roé-Vellvé[2], and Miguel A. Molina-Cabello[1][iD]

[1] Department of Computer Languages and Computer Science, Institute of Biomedical Research of Málaga (IBIMA), University of Málaga, Bulevar Louis Pasteur, 35, 29071 Málaga, Spain
{karlkhader,ezeqlr,miguelangel}@lcc.uma.es
[2] Biomedical Research Networking Center in Bioengineering, Biomaterials and Nanomedicine (CIBER-BBN), Barcelona, Spain
nuriaroe@gmail.com

Abstract. Nowadays, obtaining high-quality magnetic resonance (MR) images is a complex problem due to several acquisition factors, but is crucial in order to perform good diagnostics. The enhancement of the resolution is a typical procedure applied after the image generation. State-of-the-art works gather a large variety of methods for super-resolution (SR), among which deep learning has become very popular during the last years. Most of the SR deep-learning methods are based on the minimization of the residuals by the use of Euclidean loss layers. In this paper, we propose an SR model based on the use of a p-norm loss layer to improve the learning process and obtain a better high-resolution (HR) image. This method was implemented using a three-dimensional convolutional neural network (CNN), and tested for several norms in order to determine the most robust fit. The proposed methodology was trained and tested with sets of MR structural T1-weighted images and showed better outcomes quantitatively, in terms of Peak Signal-to-Noise Ratio (PSNR) and Structural Similarity Index (SSIM), and the restored and the calculated residual images showed better CNN outputs.

Keywords: Super resolution · Magnetic resonance images · Convolutional neural networks

1 Introduction

Obtaining high quality, high resolution images is critical for medical diagnosis, due to the impact of the subsequent clinical decisions. Even though acquisition techniques for MR imaging are continuously being improved, resolution is always limited by a variety of factors. This calls for the application of post-processing

© Springer Nature Switzerland AG 2019
J. M. Ferrández Vicente et al. (Eds.): IWINAC 2019, LNCS 11487, pp. 287–296, 2019.
https://doi.org/10.1007/978-3-030-19651-6_28

algorithms to optimize image quality. Resolution enhancement is of particular interest, and the improvement of super-resolution (SR) algorithms is also a subject of constant interest. Many different approaches have been applied to obtain resolution-enhanced images in the recent years, and, among them, deep learning has been gaining increasing popularity. Most of these methods are based on the minimization of the residuals using Euclidean loss layers.

In recent times, the use of p-norm methods in optimization algorithms has drawn attention for various applications. They have been used for machine learning binary classifiers [4,5], and in the framework of optimal control [2]. Due to the properties of the p-norm when dealing with sparse vectors and matrices [1,3,8,14], it has also been applied for feature selection [13].

One of the advantages of using a p-norm, with $p < 2$, is that it can allow reducing the effect of outliers in a minimization problem. Noise and artifacts in the images of the training set for MR superresolution are outliers that have to be avoided so that a SR algorithm provides realistic high quality solutions. In this work, the p-norm with $p < 2$ is proposed as the loss function for neural layers of super resolution convolutional neural networks, and the most suitable values of p are studied.

The rest of paper is organized as follows: Sect. 2 contains the theoretical background of our model. Then, in Sect. 3 the experiments carried out and the outcomes are described. Finally, the conclusions and future works are presented in Sect. 4.

2 The Model

In this section we present the learning rule for neural layers with p-norm loss function. The rationale behind our proposal is that the classic quadratic loss function, which corresponds to $p = 2$, may be outperformed by loss functions based on the p-th power of the absolute value of the error. For $p < 2$, this increases the robustness of the learning rule against outliers, i.e. training samples with extremely large values of the error.

The p-norm of a D-dimensional vector $\mathbf{v} \in \mathbb{R}^D$ is defined as:

$$\|\mathbf{v}\|_p = \sum_{j=1}^{D} |v_j|^p \tag{1}$$

For deep learning neural networks, the standard loss function is the square of the Euclidean (2-norm) of the difference between the desired output vector and the output vector obtained from the network, averaged for all available training samples. While this choice yields excellent results for many applications, there is room for improvement, since the exponent p in (1) determines the importance that the loss function gives to those training samples which have components with higher absolute values $|v_j|$. The higher p, the more importance that is given to extreme values of $|v_j|$. It must be considered that maybe those extreme values of $|v_j|$ correspond to badly measured training samples, or irrelevant observations.

Therefore, a loss function which does not get too influenced by those extreme errors might obtain better values than the 2-norm. The most promising values of p are those for which the p-norm fulfills the mathematical definition of norm, i.e. $1 \leq p \leq 2$.

Given the above considerations, we propose to employ neural layers with a p-norm loss function. The loss function is defined as follows, for N samples of dimension D:

$$E = \sum_{i=1}^{N} \sum_{j=1}^{D} |y_{ij} - z_{ij}|^p \tag{2}$$

where y_{ij} is the j-th component of the i-th obtained output vector from the network and z_{ij} is the desired output.

The derivative of the loss function with respect to a synaptic weight w is:

$$\frac{\partial E}{\partial w} = \sum_{i=1}^{N} \sum_{j=1}^{D} p |y_{ij} - z_{ij}|^{p-1} \operatorname{sign}(y_{ij} - z_{ij}) \frac{\partial y_{ij}}{\partial w} \tag{3}$$

where the sign function is defined as follows:

$$\operatorname{sign}(x) = \begin{cases} -1 & \text{if } x < 0 \\ 1 & \text{if } x \geq 0 \end{cases} \tag{4}$$

Stochastic gradient methods can be applied to the gradient of the loss function (3), in order to train a p-norm neural layer within a deep neural network.

3   Experimental Results

This section describes the experiments we carried on. First, Subsect. 3.2 explains the low-resolution image generation, as well as the software and hardware employed, and the selected performance metrics for comparison between p-norms. The input datasets are described in Subsect. 3.1. Finally, we report the findings of the experiments in Subsect. 3.3.

3.1   Datasets

Six different T1-weighted MR images are considered for the evaluation of the p-norms:

- 2 images of the Kirby 21 (images 10 and 11) [7]. These data were acquired using a 3-T MR scanner with a $1.0 \times 1.0 \times 1.2 \, \text{mm}^3$ voxel resolution over an field-of-view (FOV) of $240 \times 204 \times 256 \, \text{mm}$ acquired in the sagittal plane.
- 2 images of the OASIS dataset (images 1 and 2 of the cross-sectional data) [9]. Data were acquired on a 1.5-T Vision scanner with a $1.0 \times 1.0 \times 1.25 \, \text{mm}^3$ voxel resolution over an FOV of $256 \times 256 \, \text{mm}$.
- 1 image of the IBSR public dataset [12]. It is named IBSR_07, it has image size $256 \times 256 \times 128$, with $1.5 \times 1.0 \times 1.0 \, \text{mm}^3$ voxel resolution.

- 1 T1-weighted image from CIMES[1] using a 3-T MR scanner with a $0.93 \times 0.93 \times 1.0 \, \text{mm}^3$ voxel resolution over an FOV of $256 \times 256 \, \text{mm}$.

3.2 Methods

The deep network used to evaluate our proposal was the SRCNN3D method [10], which is a super-resolution convolutional neural network for three-dimensional MR images. The convolutional network have been developed using Caffe package [6] on a Python framework. One of the motivations of selecting this network is its simplicity to understand and modify the source code to create our customized p-norm loss layer.

Given an image $\mathbf{Y}$ and its respective LR one $\mathbf{X}$, this CNN is based on the application of three blocks of convolutional Rectified Linear Unit (ReLU) layers successively, to a pre-interpolated image $\mathbf{Z} = I(\mathbf{X})$. This step is internal to the method. Thus, the net computes a super-resoluted HR image by the minimization of the Euclidean loss between the output of the CNN, $s(\mathbf{Z})$, and the original HR image $\mathbf{Y}$.

$$f = arg\,min_s \sum ||\mathbf{Y} - s(\mathbf{Z})||^2 \tag{5}$$

This network is trained using overlapping patches that are extracted from a set of HR reference images. A down-sampling and up-sampling is applied to each patch and a set of pairs input-target is created in order to learn an end-to-end function between low and high resolution images. Specific details of the implementation of this network can be found in the literature.

We carried out a training over 50000 iterations for each p-norm, using momentum of 0.9, learning rate of 0.0001 and batch size of 256. Stochastic Gradient Descent (SGD) was used for model optimization (all are default parameters). Images 33–42 from Kirby dataset were used for training. Furthermore, zoom factors 2 and 3 were employed in our analysis. Figure 1 shows the training loss curves for each value of p. We used a fixed number of iterations for every training to make a fair comparison, and the selected number of iterations assess the convergence of all the trainings. We have also tested $1 \leq p < 1.5$ but no convergence was achieved. The comparison experiments have been carried out on a 64-bit Personal Computer with an six-core Intel i7 3.50 GHz CPU, 64 GB RAM, with a GPU Nvidia GTX Titan.

On the other hand, LR images were created applying the following algorithm to the HR images:

1. Crop HR image dimensions to make divisible by the scale factor.
2. Apply a 3D Gaussian filter with standard deviation equal to 1.
3. Use an bi-cubic interpolation method to generate LR image.

---

[1] https://fguma.es/unidad-imagen-molecular/.

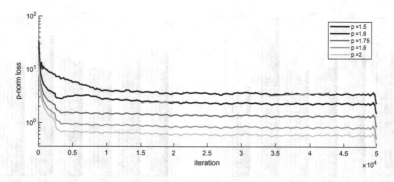

Fig. 1. Training loss for the p-norms ($p \in \{1.5, 1.6, 1.75, 1.9, 2\}$) during 50000 iterations, smoothed using a sliding window of 50.

In this work, Matlab functions were used with default parameters.

Three quality measures were used to evaluate the proposed method:

– *Peak Signal-to-Noise Ratio (PSNR)*, measured in (decibels) dB, and the more high value, the better is the likeness.

$$PSNR = 10 \log_{10} \left(\frac{peakval^2}{MSE} \right) \qquad (6)$$

where *peakval* is maximum possible value of the image and *MSE* refers to the Mean Squared Error.

– *Structural Similarity index (SSIM)* [11], which focuses on structural similarities between images, returning a value between 0 and 1 (higher is better):

$$SSIM(x, y) = \frac{(2\mu_x\mu_y)(2\sigma_{xy} + c_2)}{(\mu_x^2 + \mu_y^2 + c_1)(\sigma_x^2 + \sigma_y^2 + c_2)} \qquad (7)$$

where μ_x and μ_y are the mean value of images x and y, σ_x and σ_y are the standard deviation of images x and y, σ_{xy} is the covariance of x and y, $c_1 = (k_1 L)^2$ and $c_2 = (k_2 L)^2$ (default values were used: $L = 1$ is the dynamic range, $k_1 = 0.01$ and $k_2 = 0.03$).

Besides, we used residual images to analyze the results from a qualitative point of view:

$$residual = h - s \qquad (8)$$

where h represents the original HR image and s the output of the CNN. The best performance is such that the residual image is the zero matrix. As it is difficult to distinguish dark values, we subtracted the constant 0.5 to the residual images in order to see the performance differences. Thus, the residual images appear in gray.

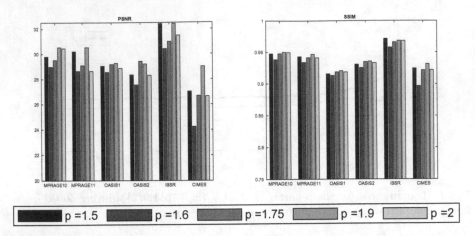

Fig. 2. Comparison of the PSNR and SSIM for the p-norms ($p \in \{1.5, 1.6, 1.75, 1.9, 2\}$) and the six tested images, using a scale factor equal to 2.

3.3   Results

First, we evaluate each convolutional neural network from a quantitative point of view. Performance results in terms of PSNR and SSIM for each image applying a zoom factor of 2, are depicted in Fig. 2. Each color bar represents one value of p. The higher is the bar, the better is the network. In both metrics, for five of the six tested images the "winner" is the 1.9-norm. If we focus on the difference with respect to the euclidean norm, there are great improvements for MPRAGE11 and CIMES images. $p = 1.5$ also shows good performance in PSNR compared to $p = 2$, so it is shown that it is not always the best and we can get better results with a different minimization. However, there are irregularities for $p = 1.6$ and $p = 1.75$, as for some images performs better but for others worse. This analysis can be extrapolated to the SSIM metric too, where the differences between nets are smaller but similar.

Figure 3 shows the results for zoom factor 3. In general, the performance is worse because we are trying to infer more information from the LR image, and difference between images is greater. Here again the pattern is the same. The networks based on the 1.5-norm and the 1.9-norm carried out a better prediction of most of the images, being $p = 1.9$ the best one in both PSNR and SSIM.

The general behaviour of each neural network across all images is summarized in Fig. 4. We computed a ranking sorting each p-norm according to its performance with respect each image and we assigned points from 1 to 5. The less punctuation the better is the network. For scale 2, shown in Fig. 4a, the best method is that one based on the 1.9-norm loss layer. The performance of $p = 1.6$ in terms of both PSNR and SSIM is clearly the worst, followed by the 2-norm, specially in PSNR. For the similarity metric there are not great differences between 2, 1.5 and 1.75. Rank of zoom 3 is depicted in Fig. 4b. Here the differences with respect to zoom 2 go in favour of $p = 2$, which is situated in the

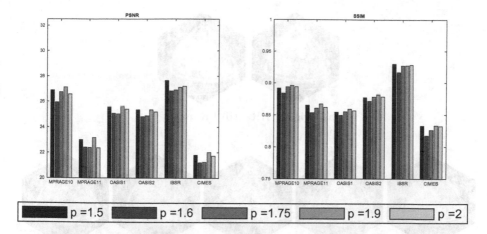

Fig. 3. Comparison of the PSNR and SSIM for the p-norms ($p \in \{1.5, 1.6, 1.75, 1.9, 2\}$) and the six tested images, using a scale factor equal to 3.

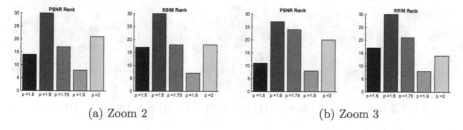

(a) Zoom 2   (b) Zoom 3

Fig. 4. Rank of the PSNR and SSIM for the p-norms for scale factors 2 and 3, taking into account all the images.

second place of our SSIM rank. Nevertheless, $p = 1.9$ is still the best method, followed closely by $p = 1.5$ in PSNR.

On the other hand, we compare the output of the networks from a qualitative point of view in Figs. 5 and 6. Residual images are also displayed to have a better discrimination between methods.

Firstly, in Fig. 5 is shown a three-dimensional perspective of the CNN's outcome of image 11 of the Kirby dataset. The differences can be seen on the third row, where the intensity of gray varies from one p-norm to other. The darkest images are the ones corresponding to $p = 1.6$ and $p = 2$, which indicates that the difference between the output of the net and the ground truth is greater. On the other hand, the image where less structures are removed, that is, the most gray uniform one, corresponds to $p = 1.9$. This results matches with the previous quantitative analysis, where its values of PSNR and SSIM are the best.

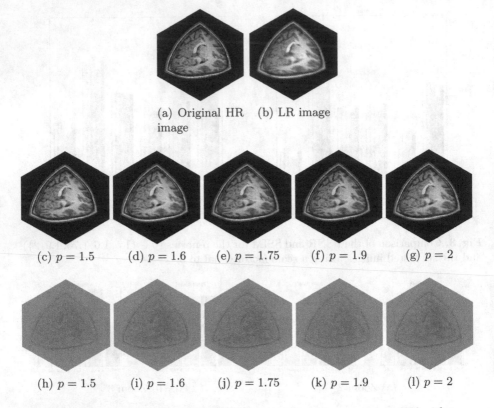

(a) Original HR   (b) LR image
image

(c) $p = 1.5$ (d) $p = 1.6$ (e) $p = 1.75$ (f) $p = 1.9$ (g) $p = 2$

(h) $p = 1.5$ (i) $p = 1.6$ (j) $p = 1.75$ (k) $p = 1.9$ (l) $p = 2$

Fig. 5. Qualitative results for $MPRAGE11$ image for each p-norm, applied with zoom factor 2. Second row shows the reconstructed image by each algorithm and third row shows residual images between the reconstructed and the original HR image.

An axial section of the image 1 of the OASIS dataset is compared in Fig. 6. In this case, a zoom factor of 3 is used. The main differences can be seen in the borders of the lateral ventricle (the uniform centered region). The output with less dark border is the one produced using $p = 1.9$, followed by $p = 2$ and $p = 1.5$. This can indicates that the structural surcus of the cerebrum are restored in a proper way. Moreover, some dark spots are conserved better since they appear clearer in the residual image of our proposed method, which is fundamental to not carry on a bad diagnostic.

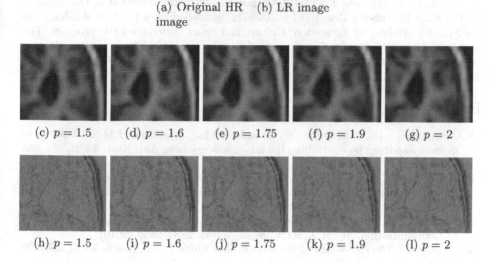

(a) Original HR   (b) LR image
image

(c) $p = 1.5$ (d) $p = 1.6$ (e) $p = 1.75$ (f) $p = 1.9$ (g) $p = 2$

(h) $p = 1.5$ (i) $p = 1.6$ (j) $p = 1.75$ (k) $p = 1.9$ (l) $p = 2$

Fig. 6. Qualitative results for a section of the axial view of the $OASIS1$ image for each p-norm, applied with zoom factor 3. Second row shows the reconstructed image by each algorithm and third row shows residual images between the reconstructed and the original HR image.

4   Conclusion

This work presents a robust three-dimensional super-resolution method for magnetic resonance images. It is based on the use of a p-norm loss layer instead of the usual Euclidean formulation. High-resolution images are obtained by learning a map between an interpolated low-resolution image and the ground truth, where the optimization function is defined as the p-norm to reduce the overall error in the training. T1 structural images from different origins were used to evaluate the efficiency of each variant of the network, achieving better performance. Results show that the Euclidean loss layer is not always the best norm, since PSNR and SSIM have increased for most images and zoom factors. Qualitatively, restored images look more refined and with less structural degradation. The proposed approach could be extended to another neural networks in order to improve the quality of the outputs.

Acknowledgements. This work is partially supported by the Ministry of Economy and Competitiveness of Spain under grant TIN2014-53465-R, project name Video surveillance by active search of anomalous events. It is also partially supported by the Autonomous Government of Andalusia (Spain) under project P12-TIC-657, project name Self-organizing systems and robust estimators for video surveillance. Both of them include funds from the European Regional Development Fund (ERDF). The authors thankfully the grant of the University of Málaga and acknowledge the computer resources, technical expertise and assistance provided by the SCBI (Supercomputing and Bioinformatics) center of the University of Málaga. They also gratefully acknowledge the support of NVIDIA Corporation with the donation of two Titan X GPUs. Karl Thurnhofer-Hemsi (FPU15/06512) is funded by a PhD scholarship from the Spanish Ministry of Education, Culture and Sport under the FPU program. The authors acknowledge the funding from the following grants, which was used to develop the OASIS database by its creators: P50 AG05681, P01 AG03991, R01 AG021910, P50 MH071616, U24 RR021382, R01 MH56584.

References

1. Abramovich, F., Benjamini, Y., Donoho, D.L., Johnstone, I.M.: Adapting to unknown sparsity by controlling the false discovery rate. Ann. Stat. **34**(2), 584–653 (2006)
2. Blueschke, D., Savin, I.: No such thing as a perfect hammer: comparing different objective function specifications for optimal control. Cent. Eur. J. Oper. Res. **25**(2), 377–392 (2017)
3. Chen, X., Xu, F., Ye, Y.: Lower bound theory of nonzero entries in solutions of l_2-l_p minimization. SIAM J. Sci. Comput. **32**(5), 2832–2852 (2010)
4. Gentile, C.: The robustness of the p-norm algorithms. Mach. Learn. **53**(3), 265–299 (2003)
5. Grove, A.J., Littlestone, N., Schuurmans, D.: General convergence results for linear discriminant updates. Mach. Learn. **43**(3), 173–210 (2001)
6. Jia, Y., et al.: Caffe: convolutional architecture for fast feature embedding. arXiv preprint arXiv:1408.5093 (2014)
7. Landman, B.A., et al.: Multi-parametric neuroimaging reproducibility: a 3-T resource study. Neuroimage **54**(4), 2854–2866 (2011)
8. Li, Z., Tang, J., He, X.: Robust structured nonnegative matrix factorization for image representation. IEEE Trans. Neural Netw. Learn. Syst. **29**(5), 1947–1960 (2018)
9. Marcus, D.S., Wang, T.H., Parker, J., Csernansky, J.G., Morris, J.C., Buckner, R.L.: Open access series of imaging studies (OASIS): cross-sectional MRI data in young, middle aged, nondemented, and demented older adults. J. Cogn. Neurosci. **19**(9), 1498–1507 (2007). https://doi.org/10.1162/jocn.2007.19.9.1498
10. Pham, C.H., Ducournau, A., Fablet, R., Rousseau, F.: Brain MRI super-resolution using deep 3D convolutional networks. In: 2017 IEEE 14th International Symposium on Biomedical Imaging (ISBI 2017), pp. 197–200, April 2017. https://doi.org/10.1109/ISBI.2017.7950500
11. Wang, Z., Bovik, A.C., Sheikh, H.R., Simoncelli, E.P.: Image quality assessment: from error visibility to structural similarity. IEEE Trans. Image Process. **13**(4), 600–612 (2004)
12. Worth, A.J.: MGH CMA internet brain segmentation repository (IBSR) (2010). http://www.cma.mgh.harvard.edu/ibsr/
13. Ye, Y.F., Shao, Y.H., Deng, N.Y., Li, C.N., Hua, X.Y.: Robust Lp-norm least squares support vector regression with feature selection. Appl. Math. Comput. **305**, 32–52 (2017)
14. Zhang, C., Li, D., Tan, J.: The support vector regression with adaptive norms. Procedia Comput. Sci. **18**, 1730–1736 (2013)

Analysis of Dogs's Abandonment Problem Using Georeferenced Multi-agent Systems

Zoila Ruiz-Chavez$^{(\boxtimes)}$, Jaime Salvador-Meneses, Cristina Mejía-Astudillo, and Soledad Diaz-Quilachamin

Universidad Central del Ecuador, Ciudadela Universitaria, Quito, Ecuador
{zruiz,jsalvador,acmejia,msdiazq}@uce.edu.ec

Abstract. This paper evaluates the social and public health impact of the abandonment of dogs in one of the tourist sectors of the city of Quito, "El Panecillo". Some of the consequences of this abandonment are analyzed: overpopulation, traffic accidents, spread of diseases, among others. Through the georeferenced multi-agents modeling, different factors that intervene in this problematic are analyzed and a simulation that allows to visualize the growth of the canine population in condition of abandonment and the consequences that this generates over time is generated. The GIS layers based environment allows a real analysis of terrain conditions and geographical limitations, this gives greater simulation realism with a complex systems approach.

Keywords: Agents · Multi-agents · GIS · Complex systems

1 Introduction

In addressing the behavior of society, a culture has been identified based on the indifference of the vast majority of people to other living beings, which allows us to see the social problem that stems from the indolence of the community in general towards the abandonment of dogs. In the city of Quito, there is illicit dogs trade, purchase, sale, abandonment and uncontrolled reproduction, without any regulation sanctioning these activities. The abandonment of dogs can be due to economic or housing issues of the owners, there are also cases of lost pets or puppies born to a dog in a situation of abandonment [1].

The most representative figures of dogs in street situation are found in urban public spaces such as squares and parks. *El Panecillo* is one of the points with the highest number of cases [2], so the simulation is developed in this sector. El Panecillo has great historical importance in the city.

Irresponsible dog abandonment leads to a wide range of problems in the health sector, as well as a lack of sensitivity, awareness and responsibility on the part of the authorities and society with respect to this issue [3]. In order to overcome this problem, the Quito Metropolitan District Health Secretariat offers free sterilization [1]. According to Urbanimal, street dogs overpopulation

J. M. Ferrández Vicente et al. (Eds.): IWINAC 2019, LNCS 11487, pp. 297–306, 2019.
https://doi.org/10.1007/978-3-030-19651-6_29

has become a public health problem. Due to the large number of dogs, there could be a proliferation of diseases and contamination of the spaces they occupy, in addition to the dogs in search of food, scatter the waste from garbage containers and their own, making the collection process difficult [4]. Traffic accidents caused by dogs can also cause human losses, this is another factor that allows the development of infectious agents for public health, causing deaths of dogs that enter a process of decomposition that could last several weeks. In addition, cases of mistreatment by citizens who have not received any sanction have been identified; dogs are exposed to innumerable dangers every day due to the scarcity of food and care. It is the duty of the community to maintain a dignified environment for all those who live within the city.

This paper is organized as follows: Sect. 2 summarizes the work carried out in the area, Sect. 3 describes the problem and gives a brief description of basic concepts associated with simulation with georeferenced multi-agents, in Sect. 4 the simulation model is proposed to address the specific problem of Sect. 3, and finally, Sects. 5 and 6 presents some conclusions and proposals for future work.

2   Related Work

The current technological evolution allows the development of tools that allow the simulation of social phenomena through models based on multi-agent systems [5], which have an extensive number of applications in different research areas.

The Cociba project, of the Universidad San Francisco de Quito, performs a census of abandoned dogs using a methodology that consists of capture and recapture of georeferenced photographs to obtain the location of abandoned dogs [3]. The results of the First Citizen Census of Abandoned Dogs in Quito reveal the existence of accelerated growth between 2013 and 2018 [6].

In order to extract useful results between the relationship of *Vehicle* and *Can* agents, a mobility analysis can be carried out, as the environment refers to a tourist site located within a residential area, where there are numerous factors that influence the simulation, as reflected in the Camacho study, which presents a traffic simulation using multi-agents to find new solutions that benefit a populated area [7].

An agents based system can intervene in multiple subjects, but it is not exempt from making mistakes in an investigation that aims to assess the quality of service in public transport [8]. According to Saeed, control systems can be used to prevent accidents in urban areas using proximity sensors [9], thus detecting certain *agents* and alerting drivers through luminous traffic signs.

There are several research works that broaden the subject matter addressed, and propose possible solutions, for example, Revelo presents an investigation that addresses the abandonment of dogs in the streets of Quito from the cultural point of view. It is based on the study of consumer behavior, and presents a reflective point of view through social marketing [10]. In addition to the above, Delgado's work presents an analysis of the factors that influence abandonment and its impact on the city of Guayaquil, and proposes that its results be evaluated and contribute to reducing the abandonment rate [11].

3 Problem Statement

In Ecuador, there are a number of rules and regulations that attempt to control abandonment rates, including: Municipal Ordinance N048 on Tenure, Protection and Control of Urban Fauna passed in 2001, which aims to regulate urban fauna in accordance with the agreement to the public health law [12], to generate balance and security to urban ecosystems [10]. The analysis of applicability and enforcement of laws, conducted by several national entities, gives unfavorable results [10], because in 10 years the canine population has grown by 85%, compared to 23.5% growth in the human population [11].

According to the reports of several Ecuadorian newspapers, Fig. 1 shows the dare related to abandoned animals in the city of Quito.

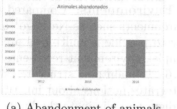
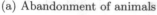
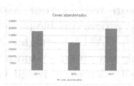

(a) Abandonment of animals

(b) Canine Growth

Fig. 1. Statistics in the city of Quito

The canine population is concentrated in the southeastern, southwestern, central-eastern and northwestern suburbs of Quito [2], people are more likely to abandon females dogs due to the possibility of future offspring, the number of offspring they can have in a litter depends on factors such as: age, size, breed, body weight or health, and can vary from 1 to 14 puppies in each oestrus [11].

To create this simulation, certain general concepts were taken into account.

Geographic Information Systems: The automation of georeferenced spatial data management allows the production of maps with agile and dynamic digital processing of information [13].

Multi-agent Systems: A multi-agent based system is autonomous, proactive and flexible, which is why they constitute a valuable advance in the improvement of software tools [14].

Multi-agent Architectures: The internal structure of each agent and the organization of an entire multi-agent system are determined by an architecture; this architecture controls the mechanisms that an agent uses to react to stimuli with other agents [15]. Multi-agent architectures allow to manage a complex system, coordinating to the intelligence of its subsystems and integrating particular objectives in a single common objective. Architectures can be structured in hierarchical layers, generally with three levels: reactive, knowledge and social. The overall behavior of the agent is defined by the interaction between these levels.

GAMA Platform: The Gis & Agent-based Modeling Architecture (GAMA) platform is based on a meta-model dedicated to the representation of complex environments and multilevel models [16]. It has been developed to address certain problems of a social nature, such as traffic, migration, evacuations among others; using agent based models, which allows us to build, combine and reuse complex models.

Comparison with Other Modeling Environments: Compared to other multi-agent programmable modeling environments such as NetLogo[1] or Repast Symphony[2], GAMA highlights its ability to provide a multi-level architecture (expandable via plug-ins) and a very complex environment representation that can be easily defined through GAML [16]. It maintains structures similar to those obtained in Netlogo, to which it integrates notions about inheritance and security to extend the agents based paradigm and eliminate the limits between the model domain.

4   Simulation Model

The proposed simulation model concentrates its analysis in the El Panecillo sector in the Metropolitan District of Quito. The study area was delimited according to the parameters established by the map of the Metropolitan District of Quito using GIS layers.

– Georeferenced multi-agent simulations: The amount of information that is broken down from communication between agents, demands the use of large computer resources, due to the continuous communication that agents maintain within the environment [14].

4.1   Simulation Specifications and Features

In the agents creation, stimuli can be implemented to identify the change between states within the simulation, that is, the agent will act according to the guidelines specified within its coded structure when it identifies the action it will perform. The agent determines the path to follow from the behaviors performed by the group of agents that coexist with him. Such is the case of the agent *Vehicle*, which changes its color taking into account whether it has had contact with an

---

[1] https://ccl.northwestern.edu/netlogo/.
[2] https://repast.github.io/.

agent *Can* or not; or the agent *Can* which can change its state each time it is reached by an agent *Vehicle*. In addition there are two types of agent *Can*, so it is necessary to adapt extra parameters to females type, because they can have puppies every certain period of time, and these puppies in turn have the ability to grow and become an adult agent *Can* and perform all their skills.

Agent Modeling. Agents implement states, movements, abilities and reactions to stimuli (*reflex*). To provide movement to the agents, each agent has been defined with *skills:[moving]* to parameterize certain necessary conditions.

Figure 2 shows the three types of agents.

(a)
Vehicle
Agent

(b) Can
Agent

(c)
Person
Agent

Fig. 2. Agents involved

- *Person* agent: this type of agent can move through *Blocks* and *Streets* layers all the day, it has been assigned the *icon* aspect type and a purple base color; people can move or return home. The reflex *staying* and reflex *move* allow for the movement of the agent and offer the opportunity to be created in random locations within the environment.
- *Can* agent: can move through the *streets* layer, there are females and males, each has the reflex that allows it to die (impact vehicle or starvation), which can simulate the death of dogs. The females also have a reproduction reflex through *create_groups*, which implements the ability to procreate puppies from lists and offers them the ability to stay together while it is puppy, this allows to simulate the increase of dogs, according to the time that each female takes to procreate a new litter. At the same time each puppy can grow after a certain time and become an agent *Can* and inherit all its characteristics, through the reflex *merge_nearby_groups* and the action *disaggregate*; that allows to continue with this repetitive cycle during all the time of existence of an agent can in the simulation.
- *Vehicle* agent: the agent can move through the *streets* layer around the whole environment, it has been defined with black base color and an *icon* aspect type. It has the ability to deteriorate the life of an agent *Can* through a reflection that allows to diminish the value of the vital variable of the can, in this way you can simulate the death or bad state of a can in traffic accidents. The agent *Vehicle* has the capacity to move all day and night, simulating the presence of traffic in this tourist sector. Each time an agent runs over a dog, it changes its color to blue to obtain the numbers of vehicles that cause the dog death.

4.2   Analysis and Definition of the Environment

An environment has been defined based on the *Blocks* and *streets* GIS layers, delimited by a geometric type layer based on the *Blocks* layer, this layer represents the area of study. Figure 3 shows a brief description of each used layer.

Fig. 3. GIS layers that form the environment

- Streets *calles_corte.shp*: This layer is part of the environment. The agents *Can* can move through it and interact with *Vehicle* agents. It has been specified as the communication route between each of the agents of the different species and GIS layers. We get information about its attributes to set some restrictions.
- Blocks *manzanas_corte.shp*: This layer covers existing households and commercial premises within the area, where inhabitants and street dogs can move around.

The layers were created in the QGIS software and later declared as species within the GAMA platform to allow the manipulation of the attributes of each of them as evidenced in the implementation of the layers.

4.3   Simulation Structure and Behavior

The initialization of the variables corresponds to data obtained in the first sections of this article. Lists have been used to store information and facilitate data integration and a color code has been established to evaluate the results. The behavior between dogs, food, vehicles and people is determined by proximity detection between any of them.

The *Blocks* GIS layer is part of the dog environment, and is divided into 3 types. The first type is *LIVING*, with more dogs, due to the existence of waste they generate. The second type *FOREST*, which are used as shelter by the dogs. The third type are the areas near the monument of the Virgen del Panecillo, the most visited attraction in the sector, with the largest amount of waste. Finally, the area called *OTHER* refers to museums, churches, shelters, cemeteries, lounges, among other historical and cultural sites existing in the sector, which are of great tourist importance.

People and vehicles move at different speeds using the equation $vel\_min + rnd(vel\_max - vel\_min)$. The *Persona* species has the ability to move, in addition, it was assigned a target, which is determined by the operator *any_location_in*, to specify the random displacement in a point of the *Blocks* layer.

In addition, using *state follow_nearest_dog* you search for the closest element to start the cycle by referring to the agent that executes the current declaration. The direction in which the *Can* species moves is determined through another state called *chaos*, in which the option to change the color of the new puppies is also implemented. Additionally, the reflex *create_groups* is defined, which establishes the possibility that one can follow another, in order to provide the ability to form packs. Finally, the possibility of feeding is specified, in a new *reflex* that allows adding a unit to the capacity variable, which refers to the feeding of the dog; in the same way, the capacity to disappear within the environment is implemented when an agent *Vehicle* touches it. For the creation of puppies, it is required that they relate, therefore, in order for a new litter to be born, a female and male must coincide.

4.4   Environment and Agents Interactions

The *Can* and *Puppy* agents have been grouped within a *group* species, which is responsible for managing the decision making of all the variants that can defrost these agents. According to the above, the speed with which the activities visualized in the simulation is defined, in such a way that the computational cost is directly proportional to the growth of the number of agents.

In order to determine the variation in the operation of the simulation, two cases have been specified. The first one establishes initial parameters of the simulation that present average data during a day without too much vehicle load and with a reduced number of passers-by. In the second case, the results of a particularly busy day are evaluated.

The results obtained in the first case are explained below. In average there are 10 vehicles circulating with an approximate speed of 8 km/h, and 10 people that transit through the sector, in addition there is an average of 20 dogs. Figure 4 shows the results obtained.

In this case, a considerable increase in the number of dogs can be observed, from the two months, it could also be verified that the survival of puppies depends on the feeding that they can or not receive, this is the reason that not all puppies can become a *Can* agent. A large number of vehicles have had some kind of dog accident.

The dogs can survive if they interact with food residues, this fact has been specified within the simulation. According to this result, it is possible to verify the importance of proceeding to a massive sterilization, in addition to a process of location and responsible handling of each one of the dogs to separate them from the streets and to provide a plausible improvement in their lifestyle.

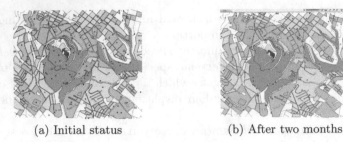

(a) Initial status   (b) After two months

Fig. 4. Average results

The second case is presented below, where the parameters were modified in the simulation to present average data during a day with a high vehicle load and a considerable number of passers-by. In average, there are 30 vehicles circulating with an approximate speed of 10 km/h, and 30 people that transit through the sector, in addition there is an average of 20 dogs. Figure 5 shows the results obtained.

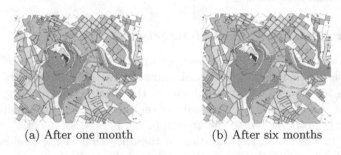

(a) After one month   (b) After six months

Fig. 5. Simulation results in concurrent periods

In this case, a similarity with the previous results can be observed, since there is an exponential increase in the number of dogs, from the second month and with respect to the analysis carried out after two and six months.

The general results can be compared with those obtained by Barros in 2015 (see left side of Table 1). The Canina population had a significant increase according to Grijalva in 2013 and Cociba in 2018, we can see on the right side of Table 1, where:

- P.I: Percentages from Investigations
- P.S: Percentages from Simulation
- P.S.D: Population of Street dogs Equivalence

Table 1. Real vs obtained percentages/growth abandoned dogs

Indicators	P.I	P.S	Year	P.S.D	Equivalence
Puppy mortality rate	80	82	2013	41676	1 dog/59 people
Likelihood of reaching adulthood	50	48	2018	122280	1 dog/22 people
Chance of procreation	-	56			
Mortality rate after childbirth	-	20			
Adult mortality rate	65	53			

5 Conclusions

The abandonment of dogs is a topic widely covered in research documents, but has not been put into practice; it is a social responsibility to contribute to the solution of this problem due to the magnitude of the effects, not only related with the environment or health, but also in the social impact generated by the precarious level of laws and statutes that promote social awareness of the suffering of these creatures, therefore, it is the duty of human beings to find a solution that integrates bipartite benefits between human beings and dogs.

Integrating software to determine the impact of the situation was beneficial to study the levels of affectation, and by implementing GIS in a model through multi-agent systems, an approach can be obtained that can be adjusted quickly and easily to obtain a broad spectrum of results.

The architecture initially defined in the document rigorously encompasses all the details of the simulation. Therefore, it has allowed the modeling of a simulated environment that offers the appropriate characteristics for the case study. The hybrid architecture made it possible to integrate various stimuli to the agents, and to determine the possible consequences derived from the rapid growth of dogs in the area.

6 Future Work

Based on the results, an in-depth study could be considered on the culture, customs and habits of the population of the sector to determine possible solutions to the problem; in the same way, the study area could be expanded and other factors such as climate, number of inhabitants or visitors could be taken into account in order to contemplate more broadly the variability of the problem.

References

1. Alejandra Monroy, E.T.: En quito el abandono de perros y gatos aún no se controla (2018). Accedido el 16 June 2018
2. Gabriela Castellanos, E.C.: Los lugares donde se abandonan más perros en quito (2016). Accedido el 28 June 2018
3. Coello, C.: Censo cuantificará los perros abandonados en quito (2018). Accedido el 12 June 2018
4. Ariana Almeida, E.E.: Sobrepoblación de perros callejeros pone en riesgo a los quiteños (2016). Accedido el 16 June 2018
5. Ziervogel, G., Bithell, M., Washington, R., Downing, T.: Agent-based social simulation: a method for assessing the impact of seasonal climate forecast applications among smallholder farmers. Agric. Syst. **83**(1), 1–26 (2005)
6. Díaz, V., Landeta, D.: Por cada 22 habitantes hay un perro abandonado en quito, según un censo (2018). Accedido el 08 Oct 2018
7. Camacho, J., Medina, S., Terán, O.: Simulación del tráfico de autos en una intersección: desde la perspectiva de una plataforma multiagente. Ciencia e Ingeniería **33**(2), 85–93 (2012)
8. Callejas-Cuervo, M., Valero-Bustos, H., Alarcón-Aldana, A., et al.: Agentes de software como herramienta para medir la calidad de servicio prestado en un sistema de transporte público colectivo urbano. Información tecnológica **25**(5), 147–154 (2014)
9. Saeed, Y., Khan, M.S., Ahmed, K., Mubashar, A.S.: A multi-agent based autonomous traffic lights control system using fuzzy control. Int. J. Sci. Eng. Res. **2**(6), 1 (2011)
10. Revelo Revelo, G.A.: Propuesta de marketing social fundamentada en un estudio del comportamiento del consumidor en la ciudad de quito caso: perros abandonados para el año 2012. B.S. thesis, Quito/PUCE (2013)
11. Delgado Jorán, E.P.: Análisis de los factores que inciden en el abandono de mascotas (perros) y su impacto social en el sector Fertisa de la coop "AHORA LE TOCA AL PUEBLO", de la ciudad de Guayaquil. Ph.D. thesis, Universidad de Guayaquil (2017)
12. General, S.: Ordenanza municipal 0048 (2011). Accedido el 28 June 2018
13. García, C.C.: Áreas de aplicac ó medioambiental de los 'sig'. modelización y avances recientes. Papeles de Geografía (23–24), 101–115 (1996)
14. Hurtado Terán, A.E., Chamba, L., Javier, J.: Interfaz gráfica para la visualización de una red de grafos georeferenciados de las principales calles del centro de la ciudad de quito. B.S. thesis (2017)
15. Corchado, J.M.: Modelos y arquitecturas de agente. Univerisdad de Salamanca, Espana (1999)
16. Drogoul, A., et al.: GAMA: a spatially explicit, multi-level, agent-based modeling and simulation platform. In: Demazeau, Y., Ishida, T., Corchado, J.M., Bajo, J. (eds.) PAAMS 2013. LNCS (LNAI), vol. 7879, pp. 271–274. Springer, Heidelberg (2013). https://doi.org/10.1007/978-3-642-38073-0_25

Background Modeling by Shifted Tilings of Stacked Denoising Autoencoders

Jorge García-González[✉], Juan M. Ortiz-de-Lazcano-Lobato,
Rafael M. Luque-Baena, and Ezequiel López-Rubio

Department of Computer Languages and Computer Sciences,
University of Málaga, Bulevar Louis Pasteur, 35, 29071 Málaga, Spain
{jorgegarcia,jmortiz,rmluque,ezeqlr}@lcc.uma.es

Abstract. The effective processing of visual data without interruption is currently of supreme importance. For that purpose, the analysis system must adapt to events that may affect the data quality and maintain its performance level over time. A methodology for background modeling and foreground detection, whose main characteristic is its robustness against stationary noise, is presented in the paper. The system is based on a stacked denoising autoencoder which extracts a set of significant features for each patch of several shifted tilings of the video frame. A probabilistic model for each patch is learned. The distinct patches which include a particular pixel are considered for that pixel classification. The experiments show that classical methods existing in the literature experience drastic performance drops when noise is present in the video sequences, whereas the proposed one seems to be slightly affected. This fact corroborates the idea of robustness of our proposal, in addition to its usefulness for the processing and analysis of continuous data during uninterrupted periods of time.

Keywords: Background modeling · Deep learning · Autoencoders

1 Introduction

Visual pieces of information such as images or video sequences are massively generated and used nowadays. Therefore, reliable and efficient ways to process that kind of data are needed more than ever. Video surveillance remains a very active field in the area of artificial vision, due to the fact that some demanding tasks have not been addressed adequately yet, as it is the case of background modeling, which consists of deciding whether an object of an image belongs to the scene foreground or background.

Robustness is a key feature which foreground detection algorithms must present. They should work continuously and they have to be prepared to cope with events which make the background characteristics vary. A change in the weather conditions in outdoor environments or lightning variations in indoor

© Springer Nature Switzerland AG 2019
J. M. Ferrández Vicente et al. (Eds.): IWINAC 2019, LNCS 11487, pp. 307–316, 2019.
https://doi.org/10.1007/978-3-030-19651-6_30

environments may compromise the reliability of moving object detection. Therefore, the algorithm performance must be kept at an acceptable level not only for the initial video frames but also for the entire sequence. This goal is hard to achieve and many published methods stop working properly when changes in the environment occur.

Most of the foreground detection algorithms work at pixel level. They attempt to learn a model per pixel in order to compute the likelihood of each pixel to belong to one of the two possible classes: foreground or background. The main differences among the most referenced proposals reside in the underlying model that represents each pixel intensity of color over time. Wren et al. [14] defines pixel models based on a Gaussian distribution, whereas the GMM model [10] uses K distributions to manage multimodal funds. An intermediate approach can be found in Zivkovic [16], where as many Gaussians as necessary up to a maximum value (K) are considered. On the other hand, Elgammal et al. [2] uses kernel distributions to obtain non parametric probabilistic models. Finally, it must be cited SOBS [5] and FSOM [3], whose models are based on self-organizing maps, which are unsupervised neural networks in which a topology is defined. Model robustness is provided by combining each pixel output (probability of belonging to a moving object) with their neighbor ones.

In this work a foreground detection algorithm that attenuates the impact of noise in scene background modeling is presented. Each image will be divided into patches that are part of distinct shifted tilings of the video frame. As a consequence, each pixel will belong to different tiling patches. The noise that is present in the patches will be removed by a previously trained stacked autoencoder, which is an unsupervised deep learning neural network well suited to information representation, due to its ability to provide relevant data features [12]. Single layer autoencoders are proved to span the same subspace as a Principal Components Analysis technique [1]. The reduced patch information will be inputted to a mixture of Gaussian probabilistic model. Finally, each pixel classification will combine the classification outputs of the patches to which it belongs.

The paper is divided in the following sections: Sect. 2 presents the object detection methodology based on the analysis of image patches to obtain a foreground mask from an input frame; Sect. 3 reports the experimental results over several public surveillance sequences and Sect. 4 concludes the article.

2   Methodology

Most previous approaches to background modeling in video sequences represent each pixel of the video frame separately. Our method intends to model patches of size $N \times N$ pixels, so that for each incoming video frame an estimation is made in order to know whether each patch belongs to the background of the scene. Furthermore, M shifted tilings of the video frame are considered, so that a particular pixel is classified by M background models. These M classifications are subsequently combined to yield a single classification output. The process is

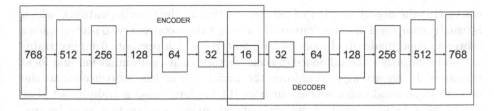

Fig. 1. Complete autoencoder structure with layers sizes.

divided in two stages: firstly, a condensed representation of the patch, composed of significant features, is obtained by means of a previously trained Stacked Denoising Autoencoder (SDA) [12]; secondly, a probabilistic model classifies the patch according to their computed set of relevant features. Once all the patches have been classified the pixels are labelled accordingly.

2.1 Patch Feature Extraction

It turns out that stacked denoising autoencoders might find difficulties in modeling too small patches. Here we propose to overcome this limitation by using big $N \times N$ pixel patches, where N is big enough that the autoencoder models the patches adequately. Then we have M tilings of the video frame, so that each tiling is composed by $N \times N$ patches. The i-th tiling, where $i \in \{1, ..., M\}$ is characterized by a unique shift vector $\mathbf{s}_i \in \{0, ..., N-1\} \times \{0, ..., N-1\}$, which makes it different from all the other tilings. Please note that the upper left corner of a $N \times N$ patch of the i-th tiling must be located at position $\mathbf{s}_i$ in the video frame. The video frame is extended as required by symmetric (mirror) padding, so that all patches are complete with their $N \times N$ pixels irrespective of the shifts.

Let $\mathbf{X} \in \mathbb{R}^H$ be a patch of size $H = N^2$, where tristimulus pixel color values are assumed. A single stacked denoising autoencoder processes all the patches of all the tilings:

$$\tilde{\mathbf{X}} = g\left(f\left(\mathbf{X}\right)\right) \tag{1}$$

$$f \: : \: \mathbb{R}^H \to \mathbb{R}^L \tag{2}$$

$$g \: : \: \mathbb{R}^L \to \mathbb{R}^H \tag{3}$$

where $\tilde{\mathbf{X}} \in \mathbb{R}^H$ is the reconstructed version of the input patch $\mathbf{X}$, f is the encoding part of the autoencoder, g is the decoding part of the autoencoder, and L is the number of neurons of the innermost layer of the neural architecture, i.e. the autoencoder reduces the high dimensional input of size H to a a low dimensional set of features of size L with $L < H$.

The autoencoder is trained to minimize the reconstruction error $\mathcal{E}_{train}$:

$$\mathcal{E}_{train} = \sum_{i=1}^{R} \left\| \mathbf{X} - \tilde{\mathbf{X}} \right\|^2 \tag{4}$$

where R is the overall number of patches existing in the training data set, which is usually composed of video frames. Denoising autoencoders try to learn a robust representation made up of more general features which prevents from overtraining and diminishes the influence of scene factors such as illumination and local variation. In an attempt to enforce the invariance of the autoencoder to the diverse scene conditions, several authors [13,15] have used a training set that comprises a huge amount of generic natural image patches that may be corrupted instead of patches extracted from the frames corresponding to the video to process. This approach is followed in our proposal, where the training set for our single autoencoder (Fig. 1) is generated from the Tiny Images dataset [11].

2.2 Patch Classification

As the video sequence progresses, the features which are discovered by the autoencoder are extracted, and a probabilistic model is learned for each patch of each tiling. This model aims to capture the main characteristics of the probability distribution of the feature vector $\mathbf{v} \in \mathbb{R}^L$:

$$\mathbf{v} = f(\mathbf{X}) \tag{5}$$

To this end, the mean $\mu_j = E[v_j]$ and the variance $\sigma_j^2 = E\left[(v_j - \mu_j)^2\right]$ of each component of $\mathbf{v}$ are approximated by the Robbins-Monro stochastic approximation algorithm [7]. Initially, μ_j is set to the median reduced feature vector of the first video frames, while the initial value for σ_j^2 is obtained from the autoencoder training image set. During the training phase each probabilistic model characteristics are updated only if the patch j is classified as background:

$$\mu_{j,t+1} = (1 - \alpha)\mu_{j,t} + \alpha v_{j,t} \tag{6}$$

$$\sigma_{j,t+1}^2 = (1 - \alpha)\sigma_{j,t}^2 + \alpha (v_{j,t} - \mu_{j,t})^2 \tag{7}$$

where t is the time instant (the frame index) and α is the step size.

Each patch is declared to belong to the foreground whenever the number of components of the feature vector which are far from its estimated mean, as measured with respect to the estimated variance, is higher than a given threshold:

$$C < \sum_{j=1}^{L} \mathbb{I}\left(|v_{j,t} - \mu_{j,t}| > K\sigma_{j,t}\right) \tag{8}$$

where $\mathbb{I}$ stands for the indicator function, C is a tunable parameter which specifies the number of components which must be far from its estimated mean to declare that the small patch belongs to the foreground, and K is another tunable parameter which specifies how many standard deviations an observation must depart from its estimated mean to be considered to be far away.

Each pixel of the video frame belongs to M patches, one per tiling. The fraction of these patches which have been declared as foreground is computed. Then the pixel is declared to belong to the foreground whenever the fraction is higher than a prespecified threshold τ, where $\tau \in [0, 1]$.

Table 1. Final parameter selection for each video. $\tau = 0.5$ in any case.

Canoe	Fountain01	Fountain02
$C = 2$, $K = 1$, $\alpha = 0.001$	$C = 2$, $K = 2$, $\alpha = 0.01$	$C = 6$, $K = 0.5$, $\alpha = 0.001$
Boats	Pedestrians	Overpass
$C = 6$, $K = 2$, $\alpha = 0.001$	$C = 10$, $K = 0.5$, $\alpha = 0.001$	$C = 3$, $K = 3$, $\alpha = 0.005$

3 Experimental Results

3.1 Methods

Seven methods have been selected in order to make a performance comparison with our proposal: WrenGA [14], ZivkovicGMM [16], ElgammalKDE [2], SuB-SENSE [9], SC-SOBS [6], CL-VID [4] and FSOM [3].

The first four of these methods are available on BGS library [8][1]. SC-SOBS executable has been obtained from CVPRLAB web[2]. FSOM and CL-VID code have been obtained from their authors' websites. The different method parameters are set to the default values indicated by the authors.

Our proposed approach has been implemented using Python. The neural network implementation makes use of the high-level application programming interface Keras[3] which is based on TensorFlow[4].

A thousand random images from Tiny Images dataset [11][5] have been used to train and test our autoencoder implementation. Total amount of autoencoder training data is 400,000 since each image has 32×32 pixels and we have divided each one to obtain four 16×16 images.

Input video sequences with added Gaussian noise have been generated once so all studied methods process the same sequences in order to be as fair as possible when comparing them. We do not use any additional post processing in any of the methods.

3.2 Sequences

A set of video sequences have been selected from the 2014 dataset of the ChangeDetection.net website[6]. Five of the selected scenes are from Dynamic Background category, and another one from the Baseline one. *Fountain01* shows a road next to vertical water springs (432×288 pixels and 1184 frames), while in *Fountain02* a road next to a fountain spitting water out can be seen. (432×288 pixels and 1499 frames). *Canoe* presents a canoe going across a river with water

---

[1] https://github.com/andrewssobral/bgslibrary.
[2] http://cvprlab.uniparthenope.it/index.php/code/moving-object-detection-software-2.html.
[3] https://keras.io/.
[4] https://www.tensorflow.org/.
[5] http://groups.csail.mit.edu/vision/TinyImages/.
[6] http://changedetection.net/.

and forest background (320×240 pixels and 1189 frames). *Boats* shows a river and a road. Various vehicles move on the road and various boats cross through the river. (320×240 pixels and 7999 frames). In *Overpass*, a road behind a bridge traversed by a man and a river is displayed (320×240 pixels and 3000 frames). Finally, *Pedestrians* is a baseline video where pedestrians walk over from one end of the screen to the other (360×240 pixels and 1099 frames).

3.3 Parameter Selection

Five parameters must be fixed in order for our method to work properly (τ, M, C, K and α). τ has been set to 0.5 for all experiments, thus, a pixel is segmented as foreground if at least half of the M tiles where it belongs are considered as foreground. $M \in \{1, 4, 16, 64\}$ has been tested to study parameter M influence and Fig. 3 on page 8 shows that comparison without noise and with it. Our experiments reveal the greater M, the better performance. However we have selected $M = 16$ as our method version to compare with competitor methods so that a reasonable execution time is maintained. C, K, and α have been selected empirically based on our previous experience an preliminary experiments. Table 1 on page 5 shows final parameter selection for each video. The same configuration has been used for each noise and M value in experiments.

3.4 Evaluation

As a measure to perform a quantitative comparison among methods, the well-known *F-score* (also noted as *F-measure* or F_1 score) is used. It is defined as a balanced harmonic mean of precision and recall. This measure provides values in the interval $[0, 1]$, where values close to one mean better performance.

F-score has been calculated for each binary frame in Region of Interest (specified by ChangeDetection.net) generated using each previously mentioned method and we have obtained the mean for all frames with $TP + FN$ greater than zero.

Comparison among methods for videos with different Gaussian noise levels can be observed on Table 2 on page 8. The table shows how the proposed method is able to deal with greater amount of noise than its contenders. While some of those methods can deal with Gaussian noise with $\sigma = 0.1$ (SUBSENSE, CL-VID and SC-SOBS, for example), their performance drops significantly in most tests where $\sigma = 0.2$. In Fig. 2 on page 7, it can be observed that our method copes with noise increasing faintly the number of FN pixels instead of increasing FP pixels.

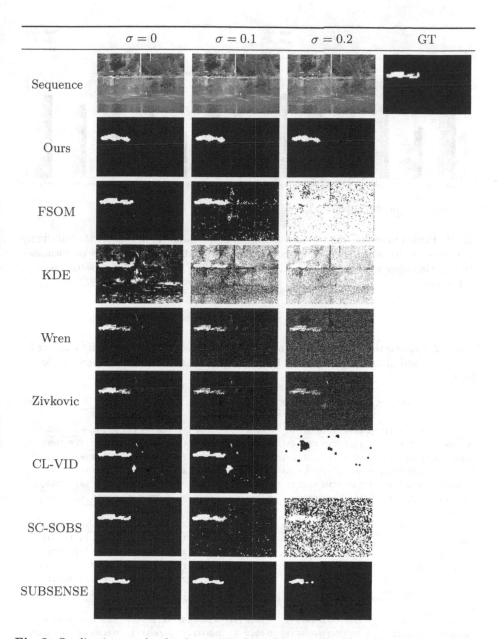

Fig. 2. Qualitative results for frame 742 from fountain02 video. From left to right: images with different amount of Gaussian noise with mean 0. First row is original dataset input image with different amounts of Gaussian noise and ground-truth. Other rows correspond to foreground segmentation performed for various methods for each input image.

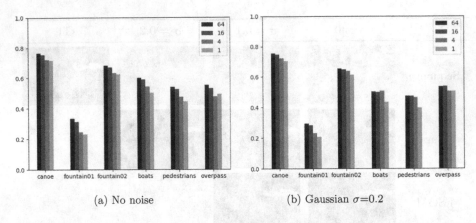

(a) No noise   (b) Gaussian $\sigma=0.2$

Fig. 3. Performance of our method using different number of tilings M. Sub-figure (a) shows results when there is no noise in videos. Sub-figure (b) shows performance when a Gaussian noise with $\sigma = 0.2$ is present. The greater M, the better average performance.

Table 2. Quantitative results. Each method *F1-Score* is showed next to its ranking for each video and Gaussian noise level. Last row is the sum of all ranks where the lower, the better.

	oursM = 16	WREN	ZIVKOVIC	SC-SOBS	CL-VID	FSOM	KDE	SUBSENSE
$\sigma = 0$								
Canoe	0.7526 (4)	0.4584 (7)	0.6097 (6)	0.8178 (2)	0.8020 (3)	**0.8234 (1)**	0.2196 (8)	0.7142 (5)
Fountain01	0.3124 (3)	0.1325 (7)	0.1767 (6)	0.3067 (4)	0.1823 (5)	0.4333 (2)	0.0429 (8)	**0.7083 (1)**
Fountain02	0.6677 (4)	0.6053 (7)	0.6533 (6)	**0.7886 (1)**	0.6596 (5)	0.7516 (3)	0.1114 (8)	0.7777 (2)
Boats	0.5870 (4)	0.3871 (7)	0.4803 (6)	**0.7582 (1)**	0.6910 (2)	0.6239 (3)	0.1359 (8)	0.5619 (5)
Pedestrians	0.5250 (7)	0.7031 (3)	0.6813 (4)	**0.7250 (1)**	0.6748 (5)	0.6623 (6)	0.3557 (8)	0.7235 (2)
Overpass	0.5320 (6)	0.4012 (7)	0.5470 (5)	0.6889 (3)	0.7237 (2)	**0.7786 (1)**	0.1595 (8)	0.6761 (4)
$\sigma = 0.1$								
Canoe	**0.7567 (1)**	0.3600 (7)	0.5174 (5)	0.5868 (2)	0.5846 (3)	0.3828 (6)	0.1385 (8)	0.5420 (4)
Fountain01	0.3214 (2)	0.0621 (7)	0.0811 (6)	0.1410 (3)	0.1192 (4)	0.1017 (5)	0.0114 (8)	**0.5097 (1)**
Fountain02	0.6705 (2)	0.2376 (7)	0.3620 (6)	0.4595 (4)	0.5046 (3)	0.4043 (5)	0.0313 (8)	**0.7724 (1)**
Boats	0.5836 (4)	0.2266 (7)	0.3897 (6)	0.5857 (3)	**0.7771 (1)**	0.6849 (2)	0.1072 (8)	0.4521 (5)
Pedestrians	0.5104 (5)	0.4820 (6)	0.5984 (4)	0.6731 (3)	0.7013 (2)	0.4420 (7)	0.0995 (8)	**0.7417 (1)**
Overpass	0.6048 (2)	0.3002 (6)	0.4723 (5)	0.4916 (4)	**0.6823 (1)**	0.5478 (3)	0.1024 (8)	0.2577 (7)
$\sigma = 0.2$								
Canoe	**0.7460 (1)**	0.2285 (3)	0.3504 (2)	0.1826 (5)	0.1451 (6)	0.1293 (7)	0.1176 (8)	0.2004 (4)
Fountain01	**0.2825 (1)**	0.0169 (4)	0.0254 (3)	0.0115 (5)	0.0093 (7)	0.0093 (7)	0.0089 (8)	0.0352 (2)
Fountain02	**0.6485 (1)**	0.0538 (4)	0.0864 (3)	0.0306 (5)	0.0222 (8)	0.0234 (6)	0.0232 (7)	0.4946 (2)
Boats	**0.4983 (1)**	0.1086 (4)	0.1685 (2)	0.0741 (5)	0.0737 (6)	0.1106 (3)	0.0732 (7)	0.0057 (8)
Pedestrians	0.4737 (2)	0.1166 (4)	0.1766 (3)	0.0782 (5)	0.0466 (6)	0.0381 (8)	0.0454 (7)	**0.7174 (1)**
Overpass	**0.5383 (1)**	0.1528 (3)	0.2559 (2)	0.1040 (6)	0.1228 (5)	0.1235 (4)	0.0848 (7)	0.0777 (8)
Σ rank	**51**	100	80	62	74	79	140	63

4   Conclusions

A methodology for detecting the foreground in video sequences has been presented. It combines M tilings of $N \times N$ patches of the video frame and a previously trained stacked autoencoder which attempts to discover significant features of the patches even in presence of noise. The reduced representation of each patch is provided to a multidimensional probabilistic model which determines the likelihood of a patch to belong to background or foreground.

The influence of the tilings in the model capability is clearly manifest. The higher the number of them, the better the performance. In the case of using two or more, they allow the model, which works at region level, to provide a particular pixel classification output which may differ from the classification output of the pixels of the same patch, because those pixels are also part of different patches in the remaining tilings. However, the computational cost inherent to the processing of patches of a new tiling must be taken into account. A trade-off between accuracy and computing time is needed and $M = 16$ is the recommended value according to the experiments.

Several heterogeneous scenes, with and without noise, have been processed and the results yielded by our method and other seven background modeling methods have been compared. According to those results, the method robustness must be highlighted. Not only is it able to keep a good performance even though noise appears but it is also the method that best works with very noisy sequences, which make the performance of the other methods fall drastically whereas the proposed method one is slightly diminished.

Acknowledgements. This work is partially supported by the Ministry of Economy and Competitiveness of Spain under grant TIN2014-53465-R, project name Video surveillance by active search of anomalous events, besides for the projects with codes TIN2016-75097-P and PPIT.UMA.B1.2017. It is also partially supported by the Autonomous Government of Andalusia (Spain) under grant TIC-657, project name Self-organizing systems and robust estimators for video surveillance. All of them include funds from the European Regional Development Fund (ERDF). The authors thankfully acknowledge the computer resources, technical expertise and assistance provided by the SCBI (Supercomputing and Bioinformatics) center of the University of Málaga. They also gratefully acknowledge the support of NVIDIA Corporation with the donation of two Titan X GPUs used for this research. The authors would like to thank the grant of the Universidad de Malaga.

References

1. Baldi, P., Hornik, K.: Neural networks and principal component analysis: learning from examples without local minima. Neural Netw. **2**(1), 53–58 (1989)
2. Elgammal, A., Harwood, D., Davis, L.: Non-parametric model for background subtraction. In: Vernon, D. (ed.) ECCV 2000. LNCS, vol. 1843, pp. 751–767. Springer, Heidelberg (2000). https://doi.org/10.1007/3-540-45053-X_48
3. López-Rubio, E., Luque-Baena, R., Domínguez, E.: Foreground detection in video sequences with probabilistic self-organizing maps. Int. J. Neural Syst. **21**(3), 225–246 (2011)

4. López-Rubio, E., Molina-Cabello, M.A., Luque-Baena, R.M., Domínguez, E.: Foreground detection by competitive learning for varying input distributions. Int. J. Neural Syst. **28**(05), 1750056 (2018). https://doi.org/10.1142/S0129065717500563

5. Maddalena, L., Petrosino, A.: A self-organizing approach to background subtraction for visual surveillance applications. IEEE Trans. Image Process. **17**(7), 1168–1177 (2008)

6. Maddalena, L., Petrosino, A.: The SOBS algorithm: what are the limits? pp. 21–26, June 2012

7. Robbins, H., Monro, S.: A stochastic approximation method. Ann. Math. Stat. **22**(3), 400–407 (1951)

8. Sobral, A., Bouwmans, T.: BGS library: a library framework for algorithm's evaluation in foreground/background segmentation. In: Background Modeling and Foreground Detection for Video Surveillance. CRC Press, Taylor and Francis (2014)

9. St-Charles, P., Bilodeau, G., Bergevin, R.: SuBSENSE: a universal change detection method with local adaptive sensitivity. IEEE Trans. Image Process. **24**(1), 359–373 (2015). https://doi.org/10.1109/TIP.2014.2378053

10. Stauffer, C., Grimson, W.: Adaptive background mixture models for real-time tracking, vol. 2, pp. 246–252 (1999)

11. Torralba, A., Fergus, R., Freeman, W.: 80 million tiny images: a large data set for nonparametric object and scene recognition. IEEE Trans. Pattern Anal. Mach. Intell. **30**(11), 1958–1970 (2008)

12. Vincent, P., Larochelle, H., Lajoie, I., Bengio, Y., Manzagol, P.: Stacked denoising autoencoders: learning useful representations in a deep network with a local denoising criterion. J. Mach. Learn. Res. **11**, 3371–3408 (2010)

13. Wang, N., Yeung, D.: Learning a deep compact image representation for visual tracking. In: Advances in Neural Information Processing Systems 26, pp. 809–817 (2013)

14. Wren, C., Azarbayejani, A., Darrell, T., Pentl, A.: Pfinder: real-time tracking of the human body. IEEE Trans. Pattern Anal. Mach. Intell. **19**(7), 780–785 (1997)

15. Zhang, Y., Li, X., Zhang, Z., Wu, F., Zhao, L.: Deep learning driven blockwise moving object detection with binary scene modeling. Neurocomputing **168**, 454–463 (2015)

16. Zivkovic, Z., van der Heijden, F.: Efficient adaptive density estimation per image pixel for the task of background subtraction. Pattern Recognit. Lett. **27**(7), 773–780 (2006)

Deep Learning-Based Security System Powered by Low Cost Hardware and Panoramic Cameras

Jesus Benito-Picazo(✉)(iD), Enrique Domínguez(iD), Esteban J. Palomo(iD), and Ezequiel López-Rubio(iD)

Department of Computer Languages and Computer Science, University of Málaga, Boulevar Louis Pasteur 35, 29071 Málaga, Spain
{jpicazo,enriqued,epalomo,ezeqlr}@lcc.uma.es

Abstract. Automatic video surveillance systems are usually designed to detect anomalous objects being present in a scene or behaving dangerously. In order to perform adequately, they must incorporate models able to achieve accurate pattern recognition in an image, and deep learning neural networks excel at this task. However, exhaustive scan of the full image results in multiple image blocks or windows to analyze, which could make the time performance of the system very poor when implemented on low cost devices. This paper presents a system which attempts to detect abnormal moving objects within an area covered by a 360° camera. The decision about the block of the image to analyze is based on a mixture distribution composed of two components: a uniform probability distribution, which represents a blind random selection, and a mixture of Gaussian probability distributions. Gaussian distributions represent windows in the image where anomalous objects were detected previously and contribute to generate the next window to analyze close to those windows of interest. The system is implemented on a Raspberry Pi microcontroller-based board, which enables the design and implementation of a low-cost monitoring system that is able to perform image processing.

Keywords: Foreground detection · Feed forward neural network · Panoramic camera · Convolutional neural network

1 Introduction

More and more public awareness about security issues is increasing due to the numerous social conflicts present in media. Thus, video surveillance systems have become an active research area, where more robust and precise systems are sought. These video surveillance systems need to process and analyze a source of data, which is commonly obtained from fixed and pan-tilt-zoom (PTZ) cameras [4,11,18]. Real time operation is also essential for the successful deployment of these systems [12,15].

© Springer Nature Switzerland AG 2019
J. M. Ferrández Vicente et al. (Eds.): IWINAC 2019, LNCS 11487, pp. 317–326, 2019.
https://doi.org/10.1007/978-3-030-19651-6_31

Although the use of PTZ cameras is a common practice in computer vision research [3,5,6,16,21], there is a lack of a comprehensive theory which sets the foundations for the development of practical systems. Also, PTZ and other conventional cameras are limited in their field of view. Hence in this work we focus on the use of panoramic (360°) cameras for the detection of anomalous objects in the scene, in order to take into account as much area as possible for the video surveillance process. This kind of cameras have been successfully applied to different computer vision applications over years [10,19,20,23].

Moreover, computer vision systems have been widely using deep neural networks to carry out many different tasks such as object recognition and image classification [13,14]. These systems based on deep learning need the help of GPU-accelerated computing techniques, which requires a high power consumption due to the use of high performance and expensive hardware. However, microcontroller boards can be used in motion detection systems due to their low energy consumption and reduced cost since they constitute economic, small and flexible hardware [2,8,22]. There are different proposals that use microcontrollers to estimate motion and proximity [7,9]. They are also used for energy-saving street lighting in smart cities [1]. Recently, a motion detection algorithm based on Self-Organizing Maps (SOMs) was developed in an Arduino DUE board [17]. The implementation of the SOM algorithm was employed as a motion detector for static cameras in a video surveillance system.

In this paper, a deep-learning based surveillance system for detection of moving anomalous objects is proposed. This system is powered by microcontrollers and panoramic (360°) cameras, so that a low energy and low cost system is achieved.

2   Methodology

Given an environment of the kind that we have considered before, an object is defined as anomalous whenever it does not correspond to usually observed objects in the scene, i.e. whenever it should trigger an alarm in the video surveillance system.

In what follows, we present the anomaly detection model which is proposed for the above mentioned purpose. The core of the model is a set of active detections, which corresponds to the set of objects that have been detected recently by the system. We define a detection as a vector of four components (π_i, x_1, x_2, x_3) where:

- π_i is the *a priori* probability of observing the object
- x_1 is the vertical coordinate of the detected object, as expressed in the panoramic coordinate system of the video frame.
- x_2 is the horizontal coordinate of the detected object, as expressed in the panoramic coordinate system of the video frame.
- x_3 is the length in pixels of the window which defines the detected object.

It is necessary to transform the frame coordinates of the detections from the current video frame to the next one, as a new frame is acquired. The transformation rules are as follows:

$$\pi_i(t) = \alpha \pi_i(t-1) \tag{1}$$

$$x_1(t) = x_1(t-1) \tag{2}$$

$$x_2(t) = x_2(t-1) \tag{3}$$

$$x_3(t) = x_3(t-1) \tag{4}$$

where α stands for a forgetting rate, $0 < \alpha < 1$. If a detected object departs from the field of view of the camera, the associated detection becomes inactive.

For the sake of simplicity, we will note $\mathbf{x} = (x_1, x_2, x_3)$. With this shorthand definition, we can express the valid ranges for $\mathbf{x}$ as follows:

$$V = [1, N_{rows}] \times [1, N_{cols}] \times [S_{min}, S_{max}] \subset \mathbb{R}^3 \tag{5}$$

where $N_{rows} \times N_{cols}$ is the height and width of the incoming frame in pixels, and the possible sizes of the detections are assumed to be lower and upper bounded by are S_{min} and S_{max}, respectively.

Now it is time to define a probabilistic model to account for the possible positions of the objects to be detected:

$$p(\mathbf{x}) = qU_V(\mathbf{x}) + (1-q)\frac{1}{N_{detections}} \sum_{i=1}^{N_{detections}} \pi_i Gauss(\mathbf{x}_i, \sigma) \tag{6}$$

where $U_V(\mathbf{x})$ stands for the uniform probability distribution on V, $Gauss(\mu, \sigma)$ denotes a multivariate homoscedastic Gaussian distribution with mean vector μ and variance σ^2, $N_{detections}$ is the count of active detected objects, $q \in (0,1)$ is a mixing weight (which is tunable) and σ is a standard deviation (which is also tunable). The overall goal is to look for objects in those regions of the incoming frame where previous detections have been attained. Nevertheless, the rest of the frame must also be scanned, although at a smaller rate.

Given the above cnsiderations, it is possible to define an algorithm in order to detect anomalous objects for panoramic cameras, which is given by the following steps:

1. Initialize the set of current detected objects $\mathcal{A}$ to the empty set.
2. Acquire the next panoramic frame from the camera.
3. Update the active detected objects by using Eqs. (1)–(4). The updated objects which are out of view, i.e. they are not in V are removed because they are no longer active.
4. Draw a set of M samples from the probability distribution (6). Find the frame window associated to each sample, and resize it to the size that the convolutional neural network (CNN) employs. After that, the resized window is provided to CNN. If the output vector indicates a high likelihood that an object has been detected, then insert the sample into $\mathcal{A}$, and associate the sample with a the probability that the detection is real.
5. Go to step 2.

Next a possible implementation of the described algorithm on microcontroller hardware with low energy requirements is proposed.

3   System Architecture

In a regular basis this is a task that would comprehend a big amount of data and bandwidth consumption. For this reason, in-motion object detection and classification from images supplied by a 360° camera would be considered as a high computing power consuming task. However, it would be desirable to design a system which performs the same job but at a small fraction of the price and power consumption a conventional system would do. For these purposes, a system architecture has been proposed which consists on a convolutional neural network-based object detection and classification software, specially designed and optimized to achieve acceptable results when deployed in a microcontroller-based system. The choice of the neural network that will be used in the detection and categorization of the anomalous objects is critical as it has to present a balance between speed and classification accuracy. These reasons led the authors of this research to select a particular CNN designed by the Microsoft Embedded Learning Library team which architecture can be seen in the Fig. 2.

3.1   Software Architecture

The software architecture of the system can be checked in Fig. 1. The first part consists of a program developed in c++ that accepts a continuous stream of images supplied by a *Point Grey Ladybug 3 Spherical camera.*

The second part of the software architecture is the object detection and characterisation engine consisting of a convolutional neural network which will be in charge of processing the information found in each one of the windows generated by the window generator in each frame.

Working with CNNs can be difficult unless a Deep Learning framework is used to implement those networks. Simultaneously, it is convenient to have in mind the limited computing power of the hardware we are employing, so an optimized library for deploying CNNs in microcontrollers is needed. These reasons led us to select the *Microsoft Cognitive Toolkit* (CNTK) combined with the *Embedded Learning Library* (ELL) also developed by Microsoft. The first one is a framework intended for designing and training Convolutional Neural Networks and the second one is a special library mainly used to optimize the code so it extracts the highest performance level of the mentioned microcontroller-based hardware architectures.

The last part of the software architecture is a program that implements the mathematical model explained in Sect. 2. As it can be seen in Fig. 1, this program is designed to receive a video frame from the 360° camera and generate a fixed number of potential detections whose coordinates in the panoramic frame will be determined by the result of the gaussian-uniform mixture function proposed in Sect. 2, or a random function. Next, the area of the main frame enclosed by

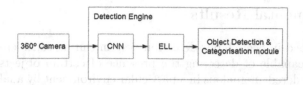

Fig. 1. Overview of the proposed implementation

the cited windows will be supplied to the CNN who will determine whether the potential detection contains any object appearing in the list of anomalous objects. If this would be the case, the new detection would be added to the detections set (A) and the possible detection will become a real detection that will be drawn in the main frame.

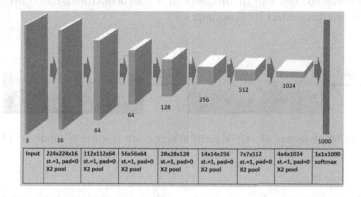

Fig. 2. Architecture of the CNN

3.2   Hardware Architecture

Hardware selection is critical when it comes to microcontroller-powered Deep Learning applications. The main reason is the balance between performance and power consumption that must be achieved when designing systems with a high level of autonomy. Thus, because of its computing power, low power consumption and low price, a raspberry Pi microcontroller-based board has been considered to be used in this project.

More precisely, the platform used is a raspberry Pi 3 Model B presenting a Broadcom BCM2837 microcontroller, featuring a CortexV8 Quad Core CPU running at 1200 Mhz from ARM, 1 GB of RAM memory and a microSD data storage card. It can be powered by a 5.1 V power source and its max power consumption is up to 2.5 A approximately at max operating load using plenty of USB external devices.

4   Experimental Results

As it is described in Sect. 2, our detection system can be considered as an algorithm that is capable of detecting the presence of certain objects whose categories are considered anomalous in a particular environment by analyzing a video stream of it, supplied by a 360° static camera. This video stream is supplied, in the form of separate frames, to a potential detections generation module that will formulate a certain number of possible predictions consisting of various areas of the frame. These predictions will be fed to a convolutional neural network that will identify the objects framed by the cited areas.

As stated in Sect. 3, because of its speed and ease of use, we have selected a CNN designed and trained using the convolutional neural networks implementation from Microsoft Cognitive Toolkit (Microsoft CNTK)[1] combined with the Embedded Learning Library[2], also from Microsoft, whose mission is to optimize neural networks so they can fit properly in a microcontroller-based architecture such as the one presented by Raspberry Pi.

Fig. 3. Working diagram of the algorithm's regular operation mode. (Color figure online)

Once the software tools used by the project are explained, the operating of the program can be checked in Fig. 3. In first place, a new frame is acquired from the 360° camera. Next, the potential detection generation engine scatters certain amount of windows representing potential object detections over the frame. Those would be localized in the coordinates determined by the p function expressed in Eq. 6 or a random function. Then, the areas of the frame enclosed by each one of those possible detections are fed to a pre-trained CNN which will state whether the frame section delimited by certain window contains any of the objects appearing in the anomalous object category list. When the CNN finds some anomalous object in a certain window, this window will be drawn in the original input image in different colors, using green for confidence value above 70%, yellow for a value between 40% and 70% and red for a value under 40%.

In order to test the accuracy and performance of the system described, a series of experiments has been performed by using two different probability distribution-based functions that will be used as the basis of the possible detection window generator. Aiming to make the experiments as rigorous as possible, it is very important to test the methods in the same conditions. To achieve this,

---

[1] https://www.microsoft.com/en-us/cognitive-toolkit/.
[2] https://microsoft.github.io/ELL/.

a controlled scenario has been used where a certain video supplied by the 360°
camera has been modified by introducing, using a video edition software, 11
random moving objects to be detected: Aegyptian cat, Golden Retriever, soccer
ball, sunglasses, laptop, hat, bird, banana, wall clock, backpack and chainsaw.
Experiments consisted of counting the number of objects detected by the system by performing 10 recognition passes to 100 panoramic modified frames taken
consecutively from a video previously supplied by the 360° camera. The tests
were performed for a number of random windows that goes from 1 to 10 and all
these operations were performed for each potential detections generation methods considered in this document: A gaussian-uniform mixture and a uniform
distribution.

When it comes to test execution, it is very convenient to reduce the amount
of the possible values that the variables can have, so the amount of cases to
test is manageable. With this purpose, according to the mathematical model
described in Sect. 2, we have fixed some values leaning on our empirical observations. Therefore, the damping factor, α, will be set to 0.1. The standard deviation, σ, will be assigned with the value of 0.5 and q will also be fixed to 0.5.

As for the dataset, it has been used the Large Scale Visual Recognition
Challenge 2012 (ILSVRC2012). It is important to remark that due to efficiency
reasons, only the detection and classification stage is performed on-the-fly by
the raspberry Pi. The training of the network has been achieved offline using a
NVIDIA TITAN X GPU.

Under these conditions, the mean number of objects detected by the two
methods can be checked in the Fig. 4.

This figure illustrates how the gaussian-uniform mixture potential detection generator designed for this investigation achieves a higher mean number
of anomalous object detections for a small number of potential detections, while
the uniform distribution seems to perform better for a higher number of potential detections. In the opinion of the authors, this makes the mixture method
more adequate for its deployment in a raspberry Pi, where the generation and
classification of a high number of potential detections drastically reduces the
performance of the system.

Time performance is a critical matter when facing the design of an deep
learning-based moving object detection and categorisation software, more specially when this software is going to be deployed in a low computing capability
hardware such as the one described in Sect. 3. Hence, several time performance
tests have been performed after deploying the described system in the raspberry
Pi microcontroller. Just as it was done with the previously illustrated accuracy
tests, experiments consisted of counting the number of objects detected by the
system by performing 10 recognition passes to the mentioned 100 360° video
frames for a number of random windows that goes from 1 to 10. These operations were performed for each one of the gaussian-uniform mixture and the
uniform distribution. Results obtained can be checked in the Table 1.

According to them, it can be observed that even though it is not capable
of real-time object detection, is capable of detecting foreground objects which

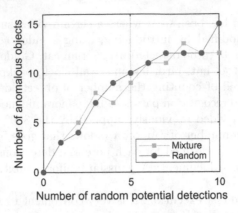

Fig. 4. Number of objects detected from the scene for each method versus number of random windows generated in each frame

Table 1. System performance expressed in mean frames per second versus number of potential detection generations for mixture model and uniform model.

# Windows	1	2	3	4	5	6	7	8	9	10
Mixture (fps)	2.0586	1.0275	0.679421	0.520843	0.417071	0.348473	0.298591	0.259482	0.231173	0.208052
Uniform (fps)	2.06798	1.0467	0.694499	0.523141	0.420252	0.347659	0.29877	0.262332	0.234082	0.210444

are in motion in a non-controlled environment in half a second approximately. For this reasons we think our proposal is justified in terms of autonomy and price/performance relation, as it can be deployed in a hardware that costs approximately 25$. When it comes to time performance comparison, the mixture model speed seems to be slightly higher than the model involving the uniform distribution potential detection generator. Hence, the accuracy improvement illustrated in the figures and tables also justifies the use of the mixture model suggested in this document.

5   Conclusions

In this paper, an anomalous object detection system powered by microcontrollers using panoramic cameras is proposed. This system is based on a Convolutional Neural Network (CNN) for detecting and characterizing objects present in the scene. Furthermore, a mathematical model has been proposed to generate a fixed number of potential detections in the frame, which will be used to detect and track anomalous objects. On the other hand, images supplied by a panoramic camera can be high computing power consuming. However, our proposal is a low energy and low cost system since it has been optimized for a raspberry Pi microcontroller. Experimental results confirm the good performance of our low-cost proposal.

Acknowledgment. This work is partially supported by the Ministry of Economy and Competitiveness of Spain under grant TIN2014-53465-R, project name Video surveillance by active search of anomalous events. It is also partially supported by the Autonomous Government of Andalusia (Spain) under project P12-TIC-657, project name Self-organizing systems and robust estimators for video surveillance. All of them include funds from the European Regional Development Fund (ERDF). The authors thankfully acknowledge the computer resources, technical expertise and assistance provided by the SCBI (Supercomputing and Bioinformatics) center of the University of Málaga. They also gratefully acknowledge the support of NVIDIA Corporation with the donation of two Titan X GPUs used for this research.

References

1. Adnan, L., Yussoff, Y., Johar, H., Baki, S.: Energy-saving street lighting system based on the waspmote mote. Jurnal Teknologi **76**(4), 55–58 (2015)
2. Angelov, P., Sadeghi-Tehran, P., Clarke, C.: AURORA: autonomous real-time onboard video analytics. Neural Comput. Appl. **28**(5), 855–865 (2017)
3. Boult, T., Gao, X., Micheals, R., Eckmann, M.: Omni-directional visual survcillance. Image Vis. Comput. **22**(7), 515–534 (2004)
4. Chen, C., Li, S., Qin, H., Hao, A.: Robust salient motion detection in nonstationary videos via novel integrated strategies of spatio-temporal coherency clues and low-rank analysis. Pattern Recognit. **52**, 410–432 (2016)
5. Ding, C., Bappy, J.H., Farrell, J.A., Roy-Chowdhury, A.K.: Opportunistic image acquisition of individual and group activities in a distributed camera network. IEEE Trans. Circ. Syst. Video Technol. **27**(3), 664–672 (2017)
6. Ding, C., Song, B., Morye, A., Farrell, J., Roy-Chowdhury, A.: Collaborative sensing in a distributed PTZ camera network. IEEE Trans. Image Process. **21**(7), 3282–3295 (2012)
7. Dobrzynski, M.K., Pericet-Camara, R., Floreano, D.: Vision tape-a flexible compound vision sensor for motion detection and proximity estimation. IEEE Sens. J. **12**(5), 1131–1139 (2012)
8. Dziri, A., Duranton, M., Chapuis, R.: Real-time multiple objects tracking on raspberry-Pi-based smart embedded camera. J. Electron. Imaging **25**, 041005 (2016)
9. Fung, V., Bosch, J.L., Roberts, S.W., Kleissl, J.: Cloud shadow speed sensor. Atmos. Meas. Tech. **7**(6), 1693–1700 (2014)
10. Gandhi, T., Trivedi, M.M.: Motion analysis for event detection and tracking with a mobile omnidirectional camera. Multimedia Syst. **10**(2), 131–143 (2004)
11. Huo, J., Gao, Y., Yang, W., Yin, H.: Multi-instance dictionary learning for detecting abnormal events in surveillance videos. Int. J. Neural Syst. **24**(03), 1430010 (2014)
12. Lacabex, B., Cuesta-Infante, A., Montemayor, A.S., Pantrigo, J.J.: Lightweight tracking-by-detection system for multiple pedestrian targets. Integr. Comput.-Aided Eng. **23**(3), 299–311 (2016)
13. Liu, W., Wang, Z., Liu, X., Zeng, N., Liu, Y., Alsaadi, F.E.: A survey of deep neural network architectures and their applications. Neurocomputing **234**(November 2016), 11–26 (2017)
14. McCann, M.T., Jin, K.H., Unser, M.: Convolutional neural networks for inverse problems in imaging: a review. IEEE Sig. Process. Mag. **34**(6), 85–95 (2017)

15. Mesquita, R., Mello, C.: Object recognition using saliency guided searching. Integr. Comput.-Aided Eng. **23**(4), 385–400 (2016)
16. Micheloni, C., Rinner, B., Foresti, G.: Video analysis in pan-tilt-zoom camera networks. IEEE Sig. Process. Mag. **27**(5), 78–90 (2010)
17. Ortega-Zamorano, F., Molina-Cabello, M.A., López-Rubio, E., Palomo, E.J.: Smart motion detection sensor based on video processing using self-organizing maps. Expert Syst. Appl. **64**, 476–489 (2016)
18. Sajid, H., Cheung, S.C.S., Jacobs, N.: Appearance based background subtraction for PTZ cameras. Sig. Process.: Image Commun. **47**, 417–425 (2016)
19. Sato, Y., Hashimoto, K., Shibata, Y.: A new networked surveillance video system by combination of omni-directional and network controlled cameras. In: Takizawa, M., Barolli, L., Enokido, T. (eds.) NBiS 2008. LNCS, vol. 5186, pp. 313–322. Springer, Heidelberg (2008). https://doi.org/10.1007/978-3-540-85693-1_33
20. Scotti, G., Marcenaro, L., Coelho, C., Selvaggi, F., Regazzoni, C.S.: Dual camera intelligent sensor for high definition 360 degrees surveillance. IEE Proc. Vis. Image Sig. Process. **152**(2), 250–257 (2005)
21. Song, K.T., Tai, J.C.: Dynamic calibration of pan-tilt-zoom cameras for traffic monitoring. IEEE Trans. Syst. Man Cybern. Part B: Cybern. **36**(5), 1091–1103 (2006)
22. Tong, L., Dai, F., Zhang, D., Wang, D., Zhang, Y.: Encoder combined video moving object detection. Neurocomputing **139**, 150–162 (2014)
23. Yagi, Y.: Omnidirectional sensing and its applications. IEICE Trans. Inf. Syst. **82**(3), 568–579 (1999)

Biomedical Applications

Neuroacoustical Stimulation of Parkinson's Disease Patients: A Case Study

Gerardo Gálvez-García[1] ⓘ, Andrés Gómez-Rodellar[2] ⓘ,
Daniel Palacios-Alonso[2,3] ⓘ, Guillermo de Arcas-Castro[1] ⓘ,
and Pedro Gómez-Vilda[2(✉)] ⓘ

[1] Instrumentation and Applied Acoustic Research Group (I2A2),
Universidad Politécnica de Madrid, Campus Sur,
Ctra. de Valencia km. 7, 28031 Madrid, Spain
[2] Neuromorphic Speech Processing Lab, Center for Biomedical Technology,
Universidad Politécnica de Madrid, Campus de Montegancedo,
28223 Pozuelo de Alarcón, Madrid, Spain
andres.gomez@ctb.upm.es, pedro@fi.upm.es
[3] Escuela Técnica Superior de Ingeniería Informática,
Universidad Rey Juan Carlos, Campus de Móstoles,
Tulipán, s/n, 28933 Móstoles, Madrid, Spain

Abstract. It is a well-known fact that Parkinson's Disease (PD) patients present important alterations in speech and phonation. Recent studies have shown that neuroestimulation using binaural beats have an effect on the neuromotor and cognitive conditions of patients suffering from PD, at least temporarily after stimulation. The present study aims to test if this phenomenon has any observable effect on phonation as a manifestation of the patient's neuromotor conditions. With this aim in mind, an experimental framework has been set up, consisting in the stimulation of PD patients with two types of signals, the first consists in a supposedly active signal (binaural beats and pink noise) and the second an inert signal (consisting only of pink noise), recording specific sustained vowels and reading text before and after each stimulation process. The sustained vowels were analyzed in further depth to estimate phonation features associated with instability (jitter, shimmer, biomechanical unbalances, and tremor in different bands). A specific study case is presented, for which the analysis shows statistically significant changes in phonation before and after active neurostimulation, whereas these changes were not detected when inert neurostimulation was used. This effect could open the possibility for the development of neuroacoustic rehabilitative therapies, based on low-cost portable acoustical stimulation devices.

Keywords: Parkinson's Disease · Neuroacoustical stimulation · Neuromechanics · Speech processing

J. M. Ferrández Vicente et al. (Eds.): IWINAC 2019, LNCS 11487, pp. 329–339, 2019.
https://doi.org/10.1007/978-3-030-19651-6_32

1   Introduction

The effects of neurodegenerative diseases on speech are well known, both in phonation, articulation, prosody and fluency. Parkinson's Disease (PD) is among the most prevalent neurodegenerative diseases, affecting an estimate of 5 million people over the age of 50 in the 15 world most populated countries in 2005; this estimation is expected to double by 2030, as a consequence of the progressive population aging [5]. The typical symptoms associated to PD are bradykinesia, rigidity, freezing of gait, frozen facial mask (hypomimia), postural sway, and distal limb resting tremor, among others [13]. It is well known that speech is strongly related to axial symptoms [4,20]. On the one hand, phonation, articulation, prosody and fluency are speech characteristics strongly affected by PD. Phonation symptoms (musculus vocalis hypotonia), vocal fold unbalance and tremor (altered neuromotor feedback) are some ways in which the neurodegeneration manifests. Articulatory instability is observed mainly as reduced vowel space and vowel centralization distortion [22]. Dysprosody and dysfluency are also common symptoms having received attention [9,21]. A view of the most comprehensive studies in the field can be found in [3,14]. On the other hand, it is well known that neuroacustical stimulation based on the acoustic effect known as binaural beats may modify the brain activity measured in the cortex by electroencephalography (EEG) as a frequency following response (FFR) [12], influencing cognition, mental states and motor performance. Binaural beats stimulation is a perceptual phenomenon where two sine waves (pure tones) are presented to a subject in a dichotic way, i.e., separately through each ear [19]. In the present study the neuroacoustic stimulation will be composed by a sine wave of 154 Hz to the left ear, and as 168 Hz to the right ear, resulting in a binaural tone of 14 Hz derived from the difference between both tones. With this previous information in mind, the objective of this study is to test to what extent neuroacoustical stimulation is able of modifying the behavioral condition of PD patients by means of pre-stimulation and post-stimulation estimations of phonation features derived from the acoustic analysis of patients' voice. The working hypothesis assumes that listening a binaural beat stimulation will induce a normalization of brain activity, which will show an improvement in phonation features resulting from the phonation neuromotor activity. It is expected that this improvement will be statistically significant with respect to another acoustic stimulation with similar acoustic properties, but not containing binaural beats (supposedly inert not being able of showing statistically significant effects).

2   Fundamentals

Neuroacoustical stimulation based on binaural beats is of great interest in neurological studies because of its non-invasiveness, simplicity, low cost and clinical potential. Nevertheless, the review of state-of-the-art literature shows contradictory information, as some studies report positive effects, whereas others do not report significant changes in cognitive or neuroelectrical activity. In this sense, a recent review presents a meta-analysis based on 32 studies, concluding that these stimulations are effective means for cognitive behavior modification in PD [8], therefore, this seems to be an open research field that requires further exploration. The neuroacoustical stimulation seems to show effects also in neuromotor behavior of PD, improving the stability and step cadence of patients [2]. Consequently, the present work is devoted to analyze the effects of neuroacoustical stimulation in cognition and brain activity from the acoustic analysis of phonation from previous work data [7].

Phonation theory is founded on the well known source-filter model proposed by Gunnar Fant almost six decades ago [6]. This model considers that voice is produced by the vibrations of the vocal folds, which result in strong pressure changes in the supraglottal side of the vocal folds in larynx, this pressure signal being known as the glottal source. This signal is composed of a train of pulses or glottal arches, showing a sharp negative spike known as the Maximum Flow Declination Ratio (MFDR) responsible of exciting the pharyngeal, oral and nasal cavities, whose resonances would enhance or attenuate certain frequencies present in the wide-band spectrum of the glottal source. The resulting acoustic pressure is radiated mainly by the oral and nasal cavities producing voice. The stability of voice, also known as phonation, is the biomarker used in the present study to avail the effectiveness of neuroacoustical stimulation. This quality is usually estimated by certain types of features, which may be classified under the groups of distortion, biomechanical unstability and tremor. The distortion features are usually jitter and shimmer. Both are seen as relative fluctuations of the periodicity and amplitude of the glottal source, given as:

$$J_k = 2\frac{T_k - T_{k-1}}{T_k + T_{k-1}}; S_k = 2\frac{A_k - A_{k-1}}{A_k + A_{k-1}} \tag{1}$$

where J_k and S_k are the jitter and shimmer and T_k and T_{k-1}, A_k and A_{k-1} are respectively the periods and amplitudes of the k and k-1 glottal cycles. The biomechanical instability features are based on the indirect estimation of the mass and stiffness associated to the vocal folds when seen as parameters of a two-mass biomechanical model [10]. To obtain these estimates, the following steps apply:

- The voice signal is radiation–compensated by pre-emphasis to remove the effects of lip radiation.
- Inverse filtering by lattice-ladder adaptive filtering is used to remove the effects of the vocal tract, generating a filtering residual signal.
- The residual signal is integrated to produce an estimate of the glottal source.
- The spectrum of the glottal source is used to generate an estimate of the distributed mass M_b of the vocal fold body (musculus vocalis), and the transversal tension Q_b applied to the vocal fold body (stiffness).
- A residual of the glottal source, known as the mucosal wave correlate is produced after removing the biomechanical effects of the vocal fold body.
- The mucosal wave correlate spectrum is used to estimate the distributed mass M_c and stiffness Q_c of the vocal fold cover (epithelial layer).

Similarly to the case of jitter and shimmer, estimates of the two-mass model parameters M_b, M_c, Q_b, Q_c are obtained per each glottal cycle, and from these, their corresponding unbalances are defined as:

$$U_{Mbk} = 2\frac{M_{bk} - M_{bk-1}}{M_{bk} + M_{bk-1}}; U_{Qbk} = 2\frac{Q_{bk} - Q_{bk-1}}{Q_{bk} + Q_{bk-1}}; \qquad (2)$$

$$U_{Mck} = 2\frac{M_{ck} - M_{ck-1}}{M_{ck} + M_{ck-1}}; U_{Qck} = 2\frac{Q_{ck} - Q_{ck-1}}{Q_{ck} + Q_{ck-1}}; \qquad (3)$$

Finally, other important correlates of phonation instability are tremors. Classically tremor in voice [15] has been divided into three bands, known as physiological (between 2–4 Hz), neurological (5–8 Hz) and flutter (9–12 Hz). All these are semantic under the point of view of neuromotor disorders. Tremor may be derived from the distributed body stiffness [11]. As the vocal fold body (musculus vocalis) is directly activated by the retrolaryngeal and thyro-aritenoid nerves, this correlate is a direct indicator of neuromotor activity producing phonation. The most semantic tremor features are the amplitudes associated to each of the three bands and a feature summarizing the presence of these bands and other possible higher-frequency perturbations, known as the root-mean square value of tremor. These are defined as:

$$Z_{Pk} = \frac{\|\Delta Q_{Pk}\|}{\bar{Q}_b}; Z_{Nk} = \frac{\|\Delta Q_{Nk}\|}{\bar{Q}_b}; Z_{Fk} = \frac{\|\Delta Q_{Fk}\|}{\bar{Q}_b}; R_{msk} = \frac{\|\Delta Q_{bk}\|}{\bar{Q}_b}; \qquad (4)$$

where $\bar{Q}_b$ is the average stiffness of the vocal fold body for the time window considered, and $\{\|\Delta Q_{Pk}, \|\Delta Q_{Nk}, \|\Delta Q_{Fk}\|\}$ are the estimates of the absolute values of the physiological, neurological and flutter band amplitudes, evaluated for each phonation cycle on the time window considered (see [11]). The next issue to deal with is the adequate time windows of interest for the estimation of tremor on maintained vowels. The production of a vowel may be an exhausting exercise for a PD patient in advanced stages of disease. It cannot be expected that an open vowel as [a:] could be sustained more than 2–3 s. The first part of the vowel (onset) is usually more energetic and intense, with a duration not lasting more than half a second. The vowel nucleus may be a bit longer (around a second). The trailing decay may last also around half a second, phonation being weak, rough and airy. Therefore, estimations of phonation behavior should be taken at least in three different points. As the minimum band to be estimated (physiological) may be within 2–4 Hz, at least 500 ms long windows should be used. This gives an idea on where estimation windows are to be defined. At least three estimations per vowel should be produced (onset, nucleus, decay), equally spaced, and if the vowel is not long enough, some overlapping would be unavoidable. The vowel insertion (first 200 ms) should be avoided, as well as the last 200 ms of decay.

3   Methods and Materials

The working hypothesis establishes the possibility of improving cognition and neuromotor behavior by modifying brain activity through neuroacoustic stimulation using binaural beats. This hypothesis is assessed in the present study by acoustic analysis of phonation of PD patients before (pre) and after (post) stimulation. It is well known that PD patients suffer speech degradation with the progression of the disease, which is highly notorious in late stages, but this deterioration starts quite early, and may go unnoticed by patients and caretakers. The intention of the study is to show that this deterioration may be reverted using neuroacoustical stimulation. The extent and duration of the reversal is one of the hot issues in the study. A cohort of 14 volunteer speakers in stages 1 and 2 of Hoehn & Young scale (2.14 ± 0.66) were recruited among patients of the Parkinson's Disease Association of Madrid. The study was approved by the Ethical Committee of Universidad Politécnica de Madrid. A written informed consent was signed by all participants prior to inclusion in the study. The principles of the Declaration of Helsinki were strictly followed. The speakers' conditions are given in Table 1.

Table 1. Descriptions of the participating speakers' conditions

Code	Gender	Age	Time since 1st diagnostic (y)	H&Y
P01	M	57.92	7	2
P02	F	66.47	9	2
P03	F	65.40	10	2
P04	M	59.79	4	2
P07	F	59.27	5	3
P08	M	46.40	4	1
P10	F	70.73	19	3
P11	F	68.85	15	3
P12	M	64.66	5	3
P18	M	60.16	1	1
P20	F	63.29	10	2
P22	F	56.22	5	2
P23	M	64.43	3	2
P34	F	64.93	5	2

Each patient was submitted to two neuroacoustical stimulations with a minimum separation of seven days (see Fig. 1, top). In each session a different signal was used. The signals consisted in pink noise (inert) and in pink noise to which a combination of rhythmic binaural beats was added (active). The binaural beats were generated as a pair of sine waves of 154 and 168 Hz, applied to the left and right ears, respectively accompanied by pink noise, to generate a perceptual beat of 14 Hz, as this frequency is supposed to be associated to the EEG activity decay detected in PD [16,23]. Binaural beats are presented at a rate of 120 per minute, because this is a typical rate described by PD patients as beneficial to keep their

pace rhythm [17,18]. The signals used in the active stimulation set at 77.0 dB
(55.4 dBA) and 78.4 dB (61.0 dBA) for the left and right channels, respectively,
where dBA refers to sound levels corrected accordingly to the perception curve
A, as described in the standard ANSI S1.4 acknowledged by ISO (International
Organization for Standardization), see [1]. The inert stimulation was set to 75.1
dB (50.4 dBA) and 75.8 dB (54.6 dBA) for the left and right ears. These levels
were measured on a Head and Torso Simulator (HATS, model 4100) connected
to the platform PULSE®from Brüel&Kjaer®. These levels were subjectively
adjusted attending to conditions reported by five subjects, above of what is considered a hearing loss (20 dB) and under 85 dB, which is the level of dis-comfort.
Voice and speech recordings were conducted before and after each stimulation
session, as described also in Fig. 1 (bottom). Recordings consisted of sustained
phonations during around two-seconds of the vowels [aː, iː, uː] and a one-minute
reading in Spanish.

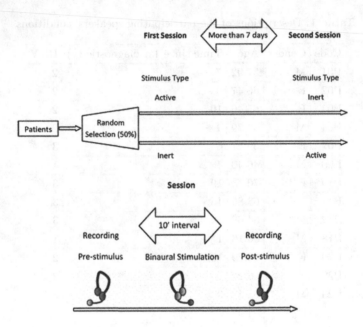

Fig. 1. Top: Description of the neurostimulation sessions. Bottom: Timing of a session.

The instrumentation used in the recordings was a high quality open-field
electret microphone (CRL-MV 181A) connected to an MSI GE60 2PE Apache
Pro computer with codec PCM S16 LE by an oxygen-free copper cable, at 16-bits
and 44100 Hz sampling rate. The phonation analysis is based on the description
and study of the results derived from patient P23 (a sixty four and a half years
old male patient, having been diagnosed for the first time three years prior to
the recording, scored stage 2 in H&Y scale). Four recordings, corresponding
to session 1 emission of vowel [aː] with the active stimulation signal (pre and

post), and to session 2 with the inert stimulation signal (pre and post), labeled respectively as reg-S1-a-pre, reg-S1-a-post, reg-S2-a-pre and reg-S2-a-post were analyzed following the phonation feature extraction described in Sect. 4. The signals from session 1 (S1) were analyzed in three different time instants: at the vowel onset, nucleus and trailing decay. The signals from session 2 (S2) were analyzed at the vowel nucleus.

4   Results and Discussion

The features corresponding to the analysis of the maintained vowel [a:] from the two sessions (S1 pre- and post- with the response to active stimulation examined at three instants; and S2 pre- and post- with the response to inert stimulation examined at a single instant) are given in Table 2. Its graphical representation is given as well in Fig. 2. For a fast and easy visual comparison, results have been normalized with feature averages derived from a database of 50 male and 50 female normative speakers, validated by the ENT services of University Hospital Gregorio Marañón, Madrid, Spain. It may be seen that from the case of the analysis of the pre-stimulation in S1 there is a clear differentiation among the three analysis instants as far as the biome-chanical distortion features are concerned $(2 - J_k, 3 - S_k, 38 - M_{bk}, 40 - S_{bk}, 44 - M_{ck}, 46 - S_{ck})$, the most stable part corresponding to the vowel onset section (pre-0.6, producing the smallest normalized values) than to vowel nucleus (pre-1.2) or decay (pre-2.0). The situation with the tremor features $(69 - Z_{Nk}, 71 - Z_{Fk}, 72 - R_{msk})$ is the opposite, as they show larger instability in the vowel nucleus (pre-1.2) than in the vowel onset (pre-0.6) or decay (pre-2.0). The behavior of feature 67 (physiological tremor: Z_{Pk}) is a bit different, as it is stronger on the onset (pre-0.6). The values of the features in the post-stimulus part of S1 (post-0.3, post-0.6 and post-0.9) are clearly lower than the pre-stimulus ones, indicating that a reduction of instability has been observed after neuroacoustical stimulation. This situation is more clearly seen in the nucleus than in the onset or decay. Finally, in S2, the situation is the opposite, as generally the values of the normalized instability features in the vowel nuclei are smaller in the pre-stimulus record (pre-0.7) than in the post-stimulus (post-0.7), possibly pointing to an inert action, or even to an aggravation in the neuromotor instability. The statistical relevance of the effect observed (possibly due to neuroacoustical stimulation) is evaluated by means of t-Student tests involving the different sets of features derived from the acoustical analysis, as given in Table 3. Confronting the pre- and post-stimulus features in S1, the null hypothesis (equivalent generating distributions on the means) is rejected with a p-value of 9.10^{-6}, thus indicating that there is a significant change observed in the phonation behavior based on these estimates. If the same test is conducted on the pre- and post-stimulus features for S2 a rejection of the null hypothesis is granted with a p-value of 0.005228, pointing also to a different phonation behavior in pre- and post-stimulus with a supposedly inert signal, although in the reverse sense, i.e., pointing to a worsening in the instability of phonation. If a test is conducted to compare the pre-stimulus recordings of S1 with respect to

Table 2. Feature values of the segments analyzed from vowel [a:]

Features/Samples	r23-S1-a-pre-0.6	r23-S1-a-pre-1.2	r23-S1-a-pre-2.0	r23-S1-a-pst-0.3	r23-S1-a-pst-0.6	r23-S1-a-pst-0.9	r23-S2-a-pre-0.7	r23-S2-a-pst-0.7
Abs. Norm. Jitter	0.0204	0.0517	0.0884	0.0167	0.0061	0.0191	0.0044	0.0295
Abs. Norm. Ar. Shimmer	0.0212	0.0243	0.0433	0.0154	0.0189	0.0151	0.0176	0.0403
Body Mass Unbalance	0.1113	0.3352	0.5315	0.0339	0.0028	0.0741	0.0009	0.0990
Body Stiffness Unbalance	0.1424	0.4189	0.6376	0.0705	0.0143	0.1057	0.0090	0.1573
Cover Mass Unbalance	0.0728	0.1185	0.1078	0.1407	0.0548	0.0722	0.0472	0.1208
Cover Stiffness Unbalance	0.1313	0.2772	0.2627	0.2894	0.0533	0.0810	0.0400	0.1923
PhysTremor Est. Amplitude	0.6882	0.2248	0.0811	0.0039	0.0111	0.0663	0.0015	0.0382
NeurTremor Est. Amplitude	0.1329	0.3016	0.0733	0.0026	0.0044	0.0140	0.0010	0.0180
FlutTremor Est. Amplitude	0.0987	0.3019	0.0934	0.0027	0.0034	0.0164	0.0005	0.0122
Global Tremor (rMSA)	0.6868	0.7306	0.3011	0.0142	0.0172	0.0762	0.0042	0.0732

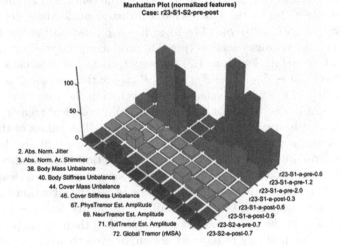

Fig. 2. Plot of the normalized phonation features used in the study for the 3-pre and 3-post tests with active stimulation, and the pre- and post-tests with inert stimulation.

Table 3. Statistical relevance of the differentiation tests (t-Student)

p-value(S1-pre-post)	p-value(S2-pre-post)	p-value(S1-S2-pre)	p-value (S1-S2-post)
0.000009	0.005228	0.002471	0.001316

S2, the null hypothesis is also rejected, with a p-value of 0.002471, pointing to a different phonation behavior in both cases (the S1 pre-stimulus is much worse than the S2 pre-stimulus, indicating that possibly the active stimulus is still 'remembered' after the inter-session time interval). Finally, a test between the post-stimulus effects in S1 with respect to S2, rejects the null hypothesis with a p-value of 0.001316, showing a different behavior in both sessions of post-stimulus effects, as the S1 post-stimulus shows an improvement in phonation stability, but the S2 post-stimulus shows a worsening of stability. The results shown point out to a statistically relevant change of the neuromotor stability of phonation in the post-stimulus recording, with respect to the pre-stimulus one when the supposedly active neuroacoustic stimulation has been used (session S1). This does not seem to be the case when the supposedly inert stimulation has been used (S2). This differentiation may imply that the phonation behavior may be the result of the neuroacoustical stimulation, although many questions still remain unsolved. On the one hand, there is not a validated and optimal neuroacoustical stimulation or a signal composition with larger effects, other combinations having to be explored and contrasted. On the other hand, it is also unclear if the control signal (inert) has null or even worse stimulation effects on neuromotor behavior. Besides, it has to be established to which extent a better neuromotor phonation behavior must necessarily mean an improvement in the cognitive and general neuromotor condition of the PD patient. In this sense, the present work has to be considered as a pilot study pointing to the way in which further patient studies have to be analyzed. More comparisons using the complete set of patients, and possibly new recordings under the same conditions would allow generalizing the present results. Besides, a similar study including not only phonation stability, but also articulation features, could help in determining the relevance of this methodology.

5   Conclusions

From the present work, although subject to the limitations discussed previously, important and relevant consequences have to be derived, these being the most prominent ones:

- It seems clear that a certain 'positive' effect is produced by neuroacoustical stimulation in the phonation neuromotor stability of the patient subject to the specified conditions. It has to be better established if this effect is permanent or transitory, and in this second case, during what period of time.
- It seems that the stimulation considered as 'active' produces a measurable effect, although a deeper study on other stimulation combinations is still pending.
- The same may be said of the 'inert' stimulation, as it seems that it does not induce more phonation stability, although other 'inert' combinations should be sought.

In any case, although this study requires further validation for its generalization, it seems that results point out to a possible way of mitigating or relieving PD neuromotor symptoms by way of simple and costless non-invasive methods, thus opening a new line of rehabilitative care for this painful disease.

Acknowledgments. This work is being funded by TEC2016-77791-C4-4-R (MINECO, Spain) and CENIE_TECA-PARK_55_02 INTERREG V-A Spain-Portugal (POCTEP). The authors would like to thank "Asociación de Parkinson de Madrid", and Dr. J. C. Martínez-Castrillo from Hospital Universitario Ramón y Cajal of Madrid for their help and advice, and especially to the Foundation for the Promotion of Industrial Innovation (F2I2) as the funding body in part of this research.

References

1. ANSI   S1.4.   https://law.resource.org/pub/us/cfr/ibr/002/ansi.s1.4.1983.pdf. Accessed 4 Jan 2019
2. Arias, P., Cudeiro, J.: Effect of rhythmic auditory stimulation on gait in Parkinsonian patients with and without freezing of gait. PLoS ONE **5**(3), e9675 (2010)
3. Brabenec, L., Mekyska, J., Galaz, Z., Rektorova, I.: Speech disorders in Parkinson's disease: early diagnostics and effects of medication and brain stimulation. J. Neural Transm. **124**(3), 303–334 (2017)
4. Cantiniaux, S., et al.: Comparative analysis of gait and speech in Parkinson's disease: hypokinetic or dysrhythmic disorders? J. Neurol. Neurosurg. Psychiatry **81**(2), 177–184 (2010)
5. Dorsey, E., et al.: Projected number of people with Parkinson disease in the most populous nations, 2005 through 2030. Neurology **68**(5), 384–386 (2007)
6. Fant, G.: Acoustic theory of speech production. The Hague-Paris (1960)
7. Gálvez, G., Recuero, M., Canuet, L., Del-Pozo, F.: Short-term effects of binaural beats on eeg power, functional connectivity, cognition, gait and anxiety in Parkinson's disease. Int. J. Neural Syst. **28**(05), 1750055 (2018)
8. Garcia-Argibay, M., Santed, M.A., Reales, J.M.: Efficacy of binaural auditory beats in cognition, anxiety, and pain perception: a meta-analysis. Psychol. Res. **83**(2), 357–372 (2019)
9. Goberman, A.M., Blomgren, M., Metzger, E.: Characteristics of speech disfluency in Parkinson disease. J. Neurolinguistics **23**(5), 470–478 (2010)
10. Gómez-Vilda, P., et al.: Glottal source biometrical signature for voice pathology detection. Speech Commun. **51**(9), 759–781 (2009)
11. Gómez-Vilda, P., Palacios-Alonso, D., Rodellar-Biarge, V., Álvarez-Marquina, A., Nieto-Lluis, V., Martínez-Olalla, R.: Parkinson's disease monitoring by biomechanical instability of phonation. Neurocomputing **255**, 3–16 (2017)
12. Hink, R.F., Kodera, K., Yamada, O., Kaga, K., Suzuki, J.: Binaural interaction of a beating frequency-following response. Audiology **19**(1), 36–43 (1980)
13. Jankovic, J.: Parkinson's disease: clinical features and diagnosis. J. Neurol. Neurosurg. Psychiatry **79**(4), 368–376 (2008)
14. Mekyska, J., et al.: Robust and complex approach of pathological speech signal analysis. Neurocomputing **167**, 94–111 (2015)
15. Mertens, C., Grenez, F., Viallet, F., Ghio, A., Skodda, S., Schoentgen, J.: Vocal tremor analysis via AM-FM decomposition of empirical modes of the glottal cycle length time series. In: 16th Annual Conference of the International Speech Communication Association (Interspeech 2015), pp. 766–770 (2015)
16. Neufeld, M., Blumen, S., Aitkin, I., Parmet, Y., Korczyn, A.: EEG frequency analysis in demented and nondemented Parkinsonian patients. Dement. Geriatr. Cogn. Disord. **5**(1), 23–28 (1994)
17. Nombela, C., Hughes, L.E., Owen, A.M., Grahn, J.A.: Into the groove: can rhythm influence Parkinson's disease? Neurosci. Biobehav. Rev. **37**(10), 2564–2570 (2013)

18. del Olmo, M.F., Cudeiro, J.: Temporal variability of gait in Parkinson disease: effectsof a rehabilitation programme based on rhythmic sound cues. Parkinsonism Relat. Disord. **11**(1), 25–33 (2005)
19. Oster, G.: Auditory beats in the brain. Sci. Am. **229**(4), 94–103 (1973)
20. Ricciardi, L., et al.: Speech and gait in Parkinson's disease: when rhythm matters. Parkinsonism Relat. Disord. **32**, 42–47 (2016)
21. Rusz, J., et al.: Imprecise vowel articulation as a potential early marker of Parkinson's disease: effect of speaking task. J. Acoust. Soc. Am. **134**(3), 2171–2181 (2013)
22. Sapir, S., Ramig, L.O., Spielman, J.L., Fox, C.: Formant centralization ratio: a proposal for a new acoustic measure of dysarthric speech. J. Speech Lang. Hear. Res. **53**(1), 114–125 (2010)
23. Soikkeli, R., Partanen, J., Soininen, H., Pääkkönen, A., Riekkinen Sr., P.: Slowing of eeg in Parkinson's disease. Electroencephalogr. Clin. Neurophysiol. **79**(3), 159–165 (1991)

Evaluating Instability on Phonation in Parkinson's Disease and Aging Speech

Andrés Gómez-Rodellar[1] , Daniel Palacios-Alonso[1,2] ,
José Manuel Ferrández Vicente[3] , J. Mekyska[4] ,
Agustín Álvarez Marquina[1,2,3,4] , and Pedro Gómez-Vilda[1(✉)]

[1] Neuromorphic Speech Processing Lab, Center for Biomedical Technology,
Universidad Politécnica de Madrid, Campus de Montegancedo,
28223 Pozuelo de Alarcón, Madrid, Spain
pedro@fi.upm.es
[2] Escuela Técnica Superior de Ingeniería Informática, Universidad Rey Juan Carlos,
Campus de Móstoles, Tulipán, s/n, 28933 Móstoles, Madrid, Spain
[3] Universidad Politécnica de Cartagena,
Campus Universitario Muralla del Mar Pza. Hospital 1, 30202 Cartagena, Spain
[4] Department of Telecommunications, Brno University of Technology, Technicka 10,
61600 Brno, Czech Republic

Abstract. Speech is controlled by axial neuromotor systems, highly sensible to certain neurodegenerative illnesses as Parkinson's Disease (PD). Patients suffering PD present important alterations in speech, which manifest in phonation, articulation, prosody and fluency. Usually phonation and articulation alterations are estimated using different statistical frameworks and methods. The present study introduces a new paradigm based on Information Theory fundamentals to use common statistical tools to differentiate and score PD speech on phonation and articulation estimates. A study describing the performance of a methodology based on this common framework on a database including 16 PD patients, 16 age-paired healthy controls (HC) and 16 mid-age normative subjects (NS) is presented. The results point out to the clear separation between PD patients and HC subjects with respect to NS, but an unclear differentiation between PD and HC. The most important conclusion is that special effort is needed to establish differentiating features between PD, and organic laryngeal, from aging speech.

Keywords: Parkinson's disease · Phonation distortion ·
Aging speech · Speech neuromechanics

1 Introduction

The effects of neurodegenerative diseases on speech are well known, both in phonation, articulation, prosody and fluency. Parkinson's Disease (PD) is among the most prevalent neurodegenerative diseases, affecting an estimate of 5 million people over the age of 50 in the 15 world most populated countries in

© Springer Nature Switzerland AG 2019
J. M. Ferrández Vicente et al. (Eds.): IWINAC 2019, LNCS 11487, pp. 340–351, 2019.
https://doi.org/10.1007/978-3-030-19651-6_33

2005; this estimation is expected to double by 2030, as a consequence of the progressive population aging [2]. The typical symptoms associated to PD are bradykinesia, rigidity, freezing of gait, frozen facial mask (hypomimia), postural sway, and distal limb resting tremor, among others [7]. It is well known that speech is strongly related to axial symptoms [11]. On the one hand, phonation, articulation, prosody and fluency are speech characteristics strongly affected by PD [1,9]. Phonation symptoms (musculus vocalis hypotonia), vocal fold unbalance and tremor (altered neuromotor feedback) are some ways in which the neurodegeneration manifests [6]. With this previous information in mind, the objective of this study is to describe phonation by means of features derived from the acoustic analysis of patients' voice. The working hypothesis assumes that the regularity of phonation may be detected from the statistical distribution of phonation correlates, as the glottal source or flow. Information Theory may be used to evaluate distances between amplitude distributions from PD patients, aging subjects and normative subjects. The paper is structured as follows: Sect. 2 is devoted to introduce the phonation fundamentals used in the study. Section 3 describes the materials and methods employed. Section 4 exposes and discusses the results, and Sect. 5 summarizes the most important conclusions.

2   Phonation Fundamentals

The human voice production system (HVPS) is divided in a chain of subsystems involved in respiration, phonation, articulation and sound radiation. Phonation may be explained by Rothenberg's model [12], described in Fig. 1.

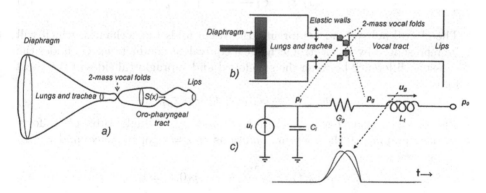

Fig. 1. Rothenberg's model. (a) Simplified representation of its uni-axial rectified cylindrical equivalent model. (b) Reduced HVPS. (c) Electromechanical equivalent model, where G_g is the glottal aperture and u_g is the glottal flow.

The HVPs is composed of different cavities (lungs, bronchi, trachea, larynx, pharynx, nasopharynx and oral and nasal cavities), ending at the lips. In the present study the following hypotheses will be considered:

- The system of cavities may be modeled by their equivalent cylindrical section as a chain of tubes of varying section along a single axial line (see Fig. 1a).
- The axial line in the sagittal plane may be straightened to an axis normal to the mouth radiation plane (medial). The distances along this rectified axis will be denoted by x. The origin $x = 0$ will be taken at the lips, pointing to the glottis $(x = x_g)$.
- Only pure oral or nasal articulations will be considered, in order for the HVPS to be modeled as a single tube with no lateral derivations, This condition will exclude the production of phonations related with [m, n, η] and nasalized vowels (symbolically [ṽ], produced with open an velo-pharyngeal switch).

The idealized HVPS will assume that plane wave propagation is to be considered along the transversal section of the equivalent cylindrical model $S(x)$. It will be possible to divide the HVPS into three main subsystems described by the following models:

- The respiratory subsystem, comprising the diaphragm, lungs, bronchi and trachea, may be described as a flow injection electromechanical equivalent, where C_l is the mechanical compliance of the respiratory cavities, and $u(x = x_l, t)$ and $u(x = x_g, t)$ are the airflows at the subglottal $(x = x_l)$ and supraglottal $(x = x_g)$ sides of the vocal folds

$$u(x_l, t) = C_l \frac{\delta p(x_l, t)}{\delta t} + u(x_g, t) \tag{1}$$

- The glottal subsystem, comprising the vocal folds biomechanics, which will be represented by its electromechanical equivalent conductance G_g under the pressure difference between the subglottal and supraglottal sides of the vocal folds

$$u(x_g, t) = G_g(p(x_l, t) - p(x_g, t)) \tag{2}$$

- The oro-naso-pharyngeal tract, represented by a single tube of uniform section, simplifying the contour conditions at $x = 0$ (open space) and $x = x_g$

$$p(x_g, t) = L_t \frac{\delta u(x_g, t)}{\delta t}; (p(0, t) = 0 \tag{3}$$

This model considers that voice is produced by the vibrations of the vocal folds, which result in strong pressure changes in the supraglottal side of the vocal folds in larynx. This pressure signal $p(x_g, t)$ is known as the glottal source (see Fig. 2c).

The glottal source is composed of a train of glottal cycles, showing a sharp negative spike known as the Maximum Flow Declination Ratio (MFDR, signaled by red stars) responsible of exciting the pharyngeal, oral and nasal cavities, whose resonances would enhance or attenuate certain frequencies present in the spectrum of the glottal source. The resulting acoustic pressure is radiated mainly by the oral and nasal cavities producing voice. The stability of phonation, estimated as the glottal flow probability density function (GFpdf) is the biomarker used in the present study to characterize voice quality, which is usually estimated by certain types of features, classified under the groups of distortion, biomechanical instability and tremor [8].

3 Materials and Methods

The phonation stability in a maintained [a:] has been used to assess the capability of this simple method in PD patients from healthy controls within the same age range, with respect to a normative reference set considered the golden standard regarding maintained phonation. Therefore, a three-band mutual information study has been carried out between GFpdf's from PD patients and healthy controls, using data from normative speakers, confronting the three sets of speakers in terms of Jensen-Shannon Distance (JSD). Vowel utterances of [a:] from 8 male and 8 female PD patients randomly selected from male and female databases within an age range of 66.3 ± 8.6 and 69 ± 7.7 years (respectively) have been processed to produce a PD database (MPD from male subjects, and FPD for female ones). Similar utterances from another set of 8 male and 8 female control subjects randomly selected within an age of 65.6 ± 8.9 and 61.8 ± 9.1 years old (respectively) have also been processed to a healthy control database (MHC from male subjects and FHC from female ones). The database (PARCZ) was collected at St. Anne's University Hospital in Brno (Czech Republic), including also demographic and clinical information from each patient as gender, age, time since first diagnosis, scores of the Unified Parkinson's Disease Rating Scale, part III (UPDRS-III: motor examination), and part IV (UPDRS-IV: complications of therapy), freezing of gait questionnaire (FOG-Q), non-motor symptoms scale (NMSS), REM sleep disorders (RBDSQ), mini-mental state examination (MMSE), Addenbrooke's cognitive evaluation revised (ACE-R), Beck depression inventory (BDI), faciokinesis and phonorespiratory competence. Recordings were taken at 48 kHz and 16 bits. All patients signed an informed consent form that was approved by the local ethics committee. The study was also approved by the Ethical Committee of Universidad Politécnica de Madrid. The PD patients are labelled as P1xxx (females) and P2xxx (males), and the paired healthy controls are labelled as K1xxx (females) and K2xxx (males), as described in Table 1.

Finally, 8 male and 8 female subjects have been randomly selected from a normative database recorded at Hospital Gregorio Marañón, of Madrid, Spain, within an age range of 32 ± 8 and 37 ± 13 (years) respectively, as given in Table 2.

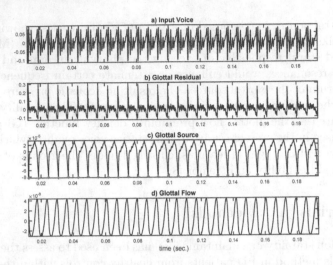

Fig. 2. Glottal signals from a segment of a maintained [a:] from a male speaker: (a) segment of vowel under analysis; (b) filtering residual; (c) glottal source $p(x_g, t)$; (d) glottal flow $u(x_g, t)$.

Table 1. PD patient and HC subject set lists (PD: PD patient subject; HC: healthy control subject; UIII: evaluation according to UPDRS-III scale).

Code	Gend	Age	Cond	UIII	Code	Gend	Age	Cond	UIII
P1006-a	F	59	PD	24	P2005-a	M	46	PD	25
P1007-a	F	76	PD	55	P2009-a	M	66	PD	14
P1008-a	F	78	PD	23	P2010-a	M	66	PD	39
P1020-a	F	64	PD	8	P2012-a	M	71	PD	35
P1021-a	F	65	PD	5	P2017-a	M	63	PD	19
P1022-a	F	72	PD	6	P2018-a	M	63	PD	32
P1025-a	F	64	PD	8	P2019-a	M	73	PD	12
P1026-a	F	76	PD	12	P2023-a	M	73	PD	13
K1003-a	F	63	HC	-	K2001-a	M	59	HC	-
K1004-a	F	65	HC	-	K2002-a	M	68	HC	-
K1005-a	F	59	HC	-	K2008-a	M	70	HC	-
K1006-a	F	64	HC	-	K2009-a	M	68	HC	-
K1007-a	F	59	HC	-	K2010-a	M	83	HC	-
K1012-a	F	67	HC	-	K2011-a	M	55	HC	-
K1017-a	F	61	HC	-	K2013-a	M	54	HC	-
K1018-a	F	45	HC	-	K2014-a	M	62	HC	-

Table 2. Normative subject set (NS).

Code	Gender/age	Code	Gender/Age
N1005-a	M/21	N1105-a	F/43
N1018-a	M/29	N1108-a	F/22
N1027-a	M/34	N1112-a	F/20
N1028-a	M/28	N1116-a	F/45
N1030-a	M/25	N1117-a	F/25
N1032-a	M/48	N1120-a	F/33
N1033-a	M/42	N1121-a	F/57
N1034-a	M/30	N1125-a	F/38

The study is based on the mutual information between two given probability density functions, p(x) and q(x) estimated as a Jensen-Shannon Divergence (JSD) [3]:

$$D_{JS} = \frac{D_{KL}(p|m) + D_{KL}(m|p)}{2} \qquad (4)$$

where DKL is a modified version of Kulback-Leibler's Divergence [4,13] given by:

$$D_{KL}(p|q) = \int_0^\infty p(x)|log\frac{p(x)}{q(x)}|dx \qquad (5)$$

and $m(x)$ is the average of $p(x)$ and $q(x)$. The probability density functions $p(x)$ and $q(x)$ are defined in the positive part of the real axis ($x \geq 0$), as the glottal flow is a positively definite function. Jensen-Shannon's Divergence is symmetrical with respect to $p(x)$ and $q(x)$, and it is normalized to the interval $[0,1]$. The JSD's between the PD set, the HC set and the NS set using their GFpdf's is estimated as follows:

- Recordings of vowel set [a:] are downsampled to 16 kHz.
- The ONPT transfer function is evaluated by a 20-pole adaptive inverse lattice-ladder filter [10]. A complete description of the adaptive filtering details can be found in Gómez et al. [5].
- The integrals of the inverse residual are the glottal source and flow ($p(x_g, t)$, $u(x_g, t)$).
- The GFpdf is estimated from the normalized amplitude histogram.
- The histograms are used to estimate probability density functions by Kolmogorov - Smirnov approximations [14].
- Six average pdf's, one for each subset are estimated: avMNS, avFNS, avMHC, avFHC, avMPD and avFPD.
- The JSD between each patient's histogram-derived distribution vs that of the control subject are estimated as by (5).

4 Results and Discussion

The JSD's between avMNS, avMHC and avMPD (male sets), and avFNS, avFHC and avFPD (female sets) were estimated. The divergences of the MPD vs MNS and MHC averages are shown in Table 3.

Table 3. JSD between male and female subset averages.

Datasets	JSD
avMPD vs avMNS	0.259
avMHC vs avMNS	0.270
avMPD vs avMHC	0.092
avFPD vs avFNS	0.244
avFHC vs avFNS	0.393
avFPD vs avFHC	0.253

The top template in Fig. 3 shows the actual appearance of the PD male sample GFpdf's in dash-red, whereas the NS male GFpdf's are given in full-blue. It may be easily seen that the NS set is more concentrated towards both extremes of abscise, whereas the PD set is more concentrated in the center part. The upper-right legend gives the codes of the speaker samples included in the tests.

The GFpdf's from the male and female subsets have been compared against the respective normative and control subset averages (avMNS, avMHC, for male samples, and avFNS and avFHC, for female samples). Table 4 gives the JSD for each sample.

Surprisingly, it may be seen that distances from healthy controls to their respective normative sets (MHC and FHC vs MNS and FNS) are in many cases larger than the pathological distributions to normative ones (MPD and FPD vs MNS and FNS). This observation may indicate that the healthy controls are farther away from normative sets than expected in terms of glottal source stability. This brings to light the difficulty of separating subsets which are much closer themselves than with respect to a golden standard set as NS. The JSD between each sample in the study and the normative and control subset averages (avMNS and avMHC) represented graphically in the plots shown in Fig. 4 may help in understanding better the relationships involved.

In agreement with the contents of Table 4 it may be seen that the distance of the normative set NS with respect to its centroid avNS is small, but it is significantly large with respect to the healthy control centroid avHC, both for male and female samples. On its turn, the situation of samples from healthy

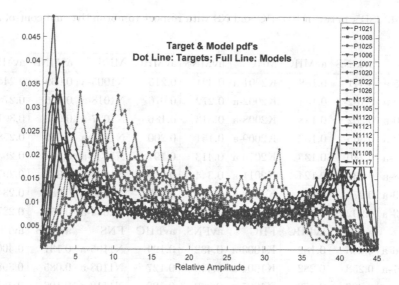

Fig. 3. Glottal flow pdf's of the PD (dash-red lines) and the NS (full-blue lines) male subsets. The normative subset is distributed to more extreme values than the PD subset. (Color figure online)

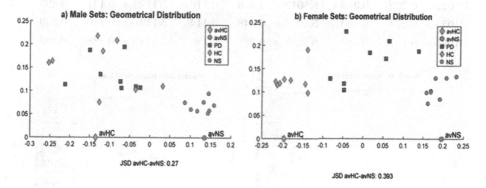

Fig. 4. Distribution of each male sample with respect to the male HC and NS averages. (a) Biplot in terms of JSD respect to the centroids avHC and avNH. (b) Idem for the female sets. Red squares: PD samples. Blue diamonds: HC samples. Green bullets: NS samples. (Color figure online)

controls and PD patients is the reverse, they are far from the normative centroid avNS, not that far from the healthy control average avHC. This reflects the difficulty in separating both sets of samples as far as sustained vowel phonation is concerned. This situation is also illustrated by hierarchical clustering in terms of each sample JSD with respect to their respective average normative sets (avMNS and avFNS), as reflected in Fig. 5.

Table 4. JSD's between PD, HC and NS with respect to normative and control averages.

MPD	avMNS	avMHC	MHC	avMNS	avMHC	MNS	avMNS	avMHC
P2005-a	0.341	0.188	K2001-a	0.301	0.215	N1005-a	0.069	0.244
P2009-a	0.192	0.154	K2002-a	0.272	0.076	N1018-a	0.076	0.278
P2010-a	0.202	0.148	K2008-a	0.313	0.186	N1027-a	0.073	0.301
P2012-a	0.365	0.137	K2009-a	0.151	0.200	N1028-a	0.060	0.258
P2017-a	0.240	0.135	K2010-a	0.413	0.197	N1030-a	0.053	0.283
P2018-a	0.231	0.124	K2011-a	0.344	0.218	N1032-a	0.095	0.295
P2019-a	0.278	0.207	K2013-a	0.199	0.143	N1033-a	0.089	0.234
P2023-a	0.292	0.136	K2014-a	0.420	0.199	N1034-a	0.059	0.287
FPD	avFNS	avFHC	FHC	avFNS	avFHC	FNS	avFNS	avFHC
P1006-a	0.265	0.182	K1003-a	0.432	0.124	N1105-a	0.131	0.400
P1007-a	0.258	0.282	K1004-a	0.413	0.127	N1108-a	0.085	0.398
P1008-a	0.307	0.172	K1005-a	0.360	0.128	N1112-a	0.106	0.381
P1020-a	0.248	0.335	K1006-a	0.421	0.119	N1116-a	0.104	0.380
P1021-a	0.332	0.277	K1007-a	0.397	0.126	N1117-a	0.083	0.367
P1022-a	0.222	0.306	K1012-a	0.426	0.116	N1120-a	0.131	0.425
P1025-a	0.271	0.190	K1017-a	0.348	0.114	N1121-a	0.106	0.369
P1026-a	0.197	0.384	K1018-a	0.385	0.199	N1125-a	0.138	0.449

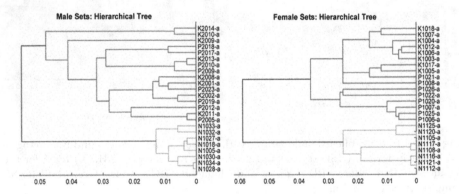

Fig. 5. Hierarchical clustering of speaker samples by JSD to their respective average normative distribution. Left: male subsets. Right: female subsets.

The male datasets are separated in two clusters, one including the normative samples, and the second one grouping the intermixed PD and HC samples. The female datasets are also separated in two clusters, but the differentiation between PD and HC is clearer, although as mentioned before, HC are more distant than PD with respect to the normative set. The question now is if this distance is statistically significant to assume different information contents among pathologic, control and normative subsets. This is confirmed by t-Student, Kolmogorov-Smirnov (considering equal-means) and Mann-Whitney tests (considering equal-distributions) as null hypothesis conditions. As it may be seen in Table 5, the tests including healthy controls and PD samples reject the null hypothesis, both for males and females, pointing to strong differences with respect to normative speakers as far as vowel phonation is concerned. But the situation is completely different when PD sets are compared with healthy controls. Whereas for female sets t-Student, Kolmogorov-Smirnov and Mann-Whitney tests reject the null hypothesis, in the case of male sets, all the mentioned tests fail in rejecting the null hypothesis, pointing to more similarities than expected between healthy controls and PD patients. Aging could be the cause behind this fact.

Table 5. Estimated p-values from inter-subset tests. t-St: t-Student; KS: Kolmogorov-Smirnov; MW: Mann-Whitney. The cases not rejecting null hypothesis a 5% level are printed in bold.

Datasets	t-St	KS	MW
MPD vs MNS	8.84.10-6	0.000156	0.000155
MHC vs MNS	8.45.10-5	0.000156	0.000155
MPD vs MHC	**0.181**	**0.188**	**0.130**
FPD vs FNS	4.79.10-7	0.000158	0.000155
FHC vs FNS	6.98.10-11	0.000156	0.000155
FPD vs FHC	0.001250	0.001430	0.001090

These results show that PD and HC datasets are clearly separable from normative controls at highly significant levels, both in the case of male and female subsets. HC are also significantly different than normative sets. But separability between PD and age-paired HC is not granted under acceptable standards, possibly due to the aging characteristics of HC phonation deterioration due to age. This is not clear in the female set, where the three tests (t-Student, Kolmogorov-Smirnov and Mann-Whitney) avail separability. But in the male case, the three tests fail in rejecting the null hypothesis, pointing to the difficulty in distinguishing both sets on the basis of phonation stability, a fact which is also observable in Fig. 4. HC shows a closer phonation characteristic with respect to PD, which results in some confusion and separation difficulties. Maybe this similarity is of aging nature, i.e., healthiness of healthy controls cannot be assimilated to normative phonation. On the one hand, age-paired HC show certain similarities with PD patients due to the effects of aging in phonation, although this assumption must be proven. On the other hand, studies based on phonation features subject to these three-band tests ensure that they are sensitive to this separability problem. These considerations raise immediate methodological concerns regarding tests including PD patients and healthy controls paired in age. It is unclear if this separability problem is due to aging voice in healthy controls, and in that case, if distortions found in PD samples could be due also to aging, and not only to pathology. The conclusion is that more tests with larger number of samples should be conducted to confirm or reject this observation, and that sharper methods should be designed for studies involving phonation, classically based on distortion correlates as jitter, shimmer, signal-to-noise ratios and non-linear features. Special care should be observed regarding MFCC's (mel-frequency cepstral coefficients), as these features are sensitive both to dysphonia and to dysarthria. In this sense, resolutive features are to be sought and tested using three-band benchmarks in the way shown in the present study.

5   Conclusions

Although the present work is subject to limitations as the short number of samples used, some relevant consequences can be derived, as the following ones:

- It seems clear that certain degree of phonation instability may be captured by the glottal flow probability density function.
- A clear separation between PD and aging HC and normative subjects is a well established fact.
- A clear separation between PD and paired aging HC is not always possible.
- It seems that aging phonation presents stronger instability than PD, at least for the datasets included.

In any case, this study requires further validation for its generalization, possibly including the effects of laryngeal pathology cases, which is known to strongly alter the phonation profile. This points out to the need to include not only paired healthy controls, but also organic larynx and neuromotor pathological databases in the analysis, and to search for differentiation features capable of differentiating among them.

Acknowledgments. This work is being funded by TEC2016-77791-C4-4-R (MINECO, Spain) and CENIE_TECA-PARK_55_02 INTERREG V-A Spain - Portugal (POCTEP), 16-30805A, LO1401, and SIX Research Center (Czech Republic).

References

1. Brabenec, L., Mekyska, J., Galaz, Z., Rektorova, I.: Speech disorders in Parkinson's disease: early diagnostics and effects of medication and brain stimulation. J. Neural Transm. **124**(3), 303–334 (2017)
2. Dorsey, E., et al.: Projected number of people with Parkinson disease in the most populous nations, 2005 through 2030. Neurology **68**(5), 384–386 (2007)
3. Endres, D.M., Schindelin, J.E.: A new metric for probability distributions. IEEE Trans. Inf. Theor. **49**(7), 1858–1860 (2003)
4. Georgiou, T.T., Lindquist, A.: Kullback-Leibler approximation of spectral density functions. IEEE Trans. Inf. Theory **49**(11), 2910–2917 (2003)
5. Gómez-Vilda, P., et al.: Glottal source biometrical signature for voice pathology detection. Speech Commun. **51**(9), 759–781 (2009)

6. Gómez-Vilda, P., Palacios-Alonso, D., Rodellar-Biarge, V., Álvarez-Marquina, A., Nieto-Lluis, V., Martínez-Olalla, R.: Parkinson's disease monitoring by biomechanical instability of phonation. Neurocomputing **255**, 3–16 (2017)
7. Jankovic, J.: Parkinson's disease: clinical features and diagnosis. J. Neurol., Neurosurg. Psychiatry **79**(4), 368–376 (2008)
8. Kreiman, J., et al.: Variability in the relationships among voice quality, harmonic amplitudes, open quotient, and glottal area waveform shape in sustained phonation. J. Acoust. Soc. Am. **132**(4), 2625–2632 (2012)
9. Mekyska, J., et al.: Robust and complex approach of pathological speech signal analysis. Neurocomputing **167**, 94–111 (2015)
10. Proakis, J., Deller, J., Hansen, J.: Discrete-time Processing of Speech Signals. Macrnillan Pub. Co., New York (1993)
11. Ricciardi, L., et al.: Speech and gait in Parkinson's disease: when rhythm matters. Park. Relat. Disord. **32**, 42–47 (2016)
12. Rothenberg, M.: A new inverse-filtering technique for deriving the glottal air flow waveform during voicing. J. Acoust. Soc. Am. **53**(6), 1632–1645 (1973)
13. Salicrú, M., Morales, D., Menéndez, M., Pardo, L.: On the applications of divergence type measures in testing statistical hypotheses. J. Multivar. Anal. **51**(2), 372–391 (1994)
14. Webb, A.R.: Statistical Pattern Recognition. Wiley, Hoboken (2003)

Differentiation Between Ischemic and Heart Rate Related Events Using the Continuous Wavelet Transform

Carolina Fernández Biscay[1,2], Pedro David Arini[1,2],
Anderson Iván Rincón Soler[1,2], and María Paula Bonomini[1,2(✉)]

[1] Instituto de Ingeniería Biomédica, Facultad de Ingeniería,
Universidad de Buenos Aires, Buenos Aires, Argentina
[2] Instituto Argentino de Matemática, 'Alberto P. Calderón', CONICET,
Buenos Aires, Argentina
paula.bonomini@conicet.gov.ar

Abstract. Cardiovascular diseases are one of the main causes of death in the world, as a result much efforts have been made to detect early ischemia. Traditionally changes produced in the ST or STT segments of the heartbeat were analyzed. The main difficulty relies on alterations produced in the ST or STT segment because of non ischemic events, such as changes in the heart rate, the ventricular conduction or the cardiac electrical axis. The aim of this work is to differentiate between ischemic and heart rate related events using the information provided by the continuous wavelet transform of the electrocardiogram. To evaluate the performance of the classifier, the Long Term ST Database was used, with ischemic and non ischemic differentiated events annotated by specialists. The analysis was performed over 77 events (52 ischemic and 25 heart rate related), obtaining a sensitivity and positive predictivity of 86.64% for both indicators.

Keywords: Cardiac ischemia · Continuous wavelet transform · Classification analysis

1 Introduction

Silent ischemia is a common cardiac disease defined as a reduction or lack of blood flow to myocardial cells. When this is prolonged in time it is formed a necrosis or infarct zone. To prevent this, it is necessary to detect early ischemia by analyzing the changes that this condition produces on the electrocardiogram. These changes are manifested as modifications in the amplitude, time and duration of the STT complex (see Fig. 1). The ST segment represents the period of time from the end of ventricular depolarization to the beginning of ventricular repolarization (T wave). Under normal conditions this segment is isoelectric compared to the PR segment. However, in the presence of myocardial ischemia, the ST segment is elevated or depressed with respect to the PR segment (see

© Springer Nature Switzerland AG 2019
J. M. Ferrández Vicente et al. (Eds.): IWINAC 2019, LNCS 11487, pp. 352–360, 2019.
https://doi.org/10.1007/978-3-030-19651-6_34

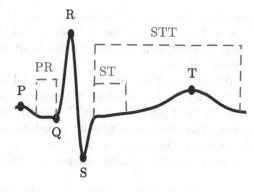

Fig. 1. A normal heart beat with its components

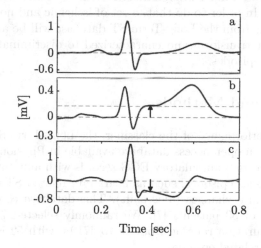

Fig. 2. In (a) a normal heart beat is plotted, in (b) and (c) ischemic beats with an elevation and depression of the ST segment are plotted, respectively.

Fig. 2). This phenomenon is due to the reduction of blood supply to cardiac muscle tissue, which causes depolarization of membrane potentials at rest.

Its diagnosis consists of continuous monitoring of ischemia episodes and automated algorithms for detection, more specifically, automatic ST segment and T-wave (STT) analysis. Since it is crucial not to miss an ischemic event, these algorithms were developed intentionally to obtain a high sensitivity at the expense of the specificity. Then, the amount of false positive events is the reason why this automated results must still be checked by a professional.

The major difficulty of automatic ST analysis lies in the effects of non-ischemic ST drifts due to changes in the heart rate, the ventricular conduction or the cardiac electrical axis [5,8]. The latter were acceptably resolved by modeling the cardiac axis shifts arisen from postural changes by a step function in the Karhunen-Love transform coefficients of the QRS and STT complexes [9]. However, the STT changes due to increase of the heart rate are the most important source of over-detection and still remains the Achilles heel of these methods [6]. In fact, most works usually treat ischemic events and heart rate STT changes jointly, as ischemic episodes [1,11].

Traditionally, time domain analysis are carried out for STT analysis. In general, a time series is constructed with two-lead ST levels [12] or the root mean squared difference from the STT and a pattern [3]. Nevertheless, some recent approaches have employed the continuous wavelet transform to detect ischemic events, either from the heart rate variability series [2] or the ECG signal [10], but no attempts have been made to differentiate ischemic from non-ischemic (heart rate induced) events.

The aim of this work is to test if the continuous wavelet transform can solve the issue of heart rate induced non-ischemic events by differentiating them from ischemic episodes. In order to do that, a set of ischemic and non-ischemic heart rate induced events from the Long-Term ST database will be analyzed with the continuous wavelet transform and characterized to discriminate ischemic from heart rate related episodes.

2   Materials and Methods

To evaluate the performance of the classifier, the Long Term ST Database was used (LTST DB), an open access database available in Physionet [4]. LTST DB consists of 24 h duration ambulatory ECG records with annotated ischemic and non ischemic episodes episodes, such as heart rate related ST episodes and ST drifts due to postural changes (axis shift). This database contains 86 records with 2 or 3 leads of 80 patients [7]. We randomly selected 77 episodes of 35 patients, with a duration ranging from 48 to 4710 s, with 52 ischemic episodes and 25 heart rate related episodes.

Figure 3 is a flow chart that shows the proposed ischemic detector. It is separated in three stages. In stage 1, implemented in this work, a time series of the root mean squared difference from the STT and a pattern is constructed. First, the ECG signal is preprocessed by: ECG delineation (QRS detector), filtering (the baseline is removed and the ECG is low pass filtered) and segmentation (ST or STT segmentation). Then an ST or STT segment template is obtained by averaging 100 normal heart beats. With this template, the root mean square (RMS) difference series is calculated for each beat of the record as proposed in the literature [3,8]. This series are then filtered (median and exponential filter) so that an adaptative threshold can be used to detect the ischemic episodes. With these results, stage 2, implemented by Mincholé et al. [9], differentiates episodes related with axis shifts by modeling them with a step function in the Karhunen-Loeve transform coefficients of the QRS and STT complexes.

This work proposes a novel procedure, stage 3, to differentiate between ischemic and heart rate related episodes. This stage analyzes the information given by the Continuous Wavelet Transform (CWT), which gives frequency as well as time information of the series. Often used to characterize singularities

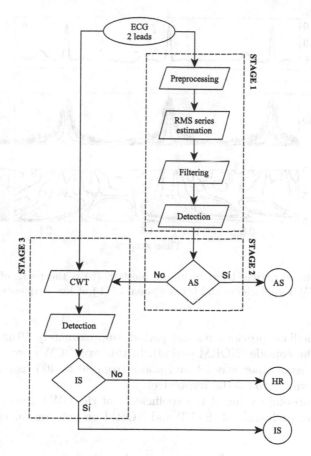

Fig. 3. Flow chart of the proposed ischemic detector.

in functions, the CWT ($W_n(s)$) of a discrete time series x_n is defined as the convolution of x_n with a scaled and translated version of $\psi(\eta)$ [13]:

$$W_n(s) = \sum_{n'=0}^{N-1} x_{n'} \psi^* \frac{(n-n')\delta t}{s} \tag{1}$$

where $\psi(\eta)$ is a function called the mother wavelet, which is scaled with parameter s and translated along the localized time index n. The (*) indicates the complex conjugate and N is the size of the time series. The scales give the frequency information in a particular moment in time given by the translation. An example can be seen in Fig. 4, a contourn plot of an example of the absolute value of the coefficients given by the CWT of three normal beats. Figure 4c is a zoom of Fig. 4b at low frequencies, where it is the main information given by the ST and STT segment (generally between 0,5 and 2,5 Hz).

The CWT is applied to an interval of the original ECG given by the duration, between 48 to 4710 s, of the episode detected in stage 1 (EP period) together

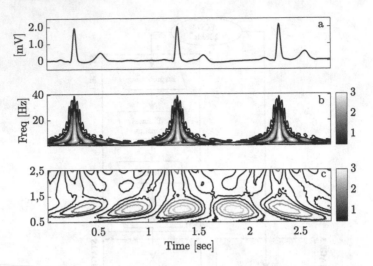

Fig. 4. In (a) three normal heart beats are plotted. (b) is the result of the absolute values of the CWT coefficients and (c) is a zoom of (b) at low frequencies.

with the immediate previous normal period, approximately 10 min before the detection of the episode (NORM period). In this work, CWT was implemented using the Morlet mother wavelet and scales from 80 to 400 (corresponding to frequencies from 2.5 to 0.5 Hz, respectively).

Once the absolute value of the coefficients of the CWT are computed, the sum in time for each scale of the EP and NORM periods are calculated:

$$S_{CWT}(s) = \sum_{n=0}^{N} |W_n(s)| \qquad (2)$$

where N is the length of each period, EP and NORM.

From this time sum, 4 parameters are obtained: the scales/frequencies for which the maximun of $S_{CWT}(s)$ for the EP and NORM periods is reached (namely s_{EP} and s_{NORM} or their equivalent in frequencies f_{EP} and f_{NORM}, respectively), and the maximum of $|W_{s_{EP}}(n)|$ and $|W_{s_{NORM}}(n)|$ (namely a_{EP} and a_{NORM}, respectively). With this parameters, two differential coefficients are calculated as:

$$\Delta f = f_{EP} - f_{NORM} \qquad (3)$$

$$\Delta a = a_{EP} - a_{NORM} \qquad (4)$$

The information given by Δf and Δa is used to decide whether the episode is ischemic or heart rate related. By an empirical exploration of the variation in the sensitivity and positive predictivity values of Δf and Δa, constant thresholds were selected to separate ischemic from heart rate related episodes.

3   Results

Stage 3 was tested with 77 episodes that were detected in stage 1 (by the RMS series) as ischemic episodes, where actually 52 were ischemic and 25 were heart rate related episodes. In a first approach, using only a fixed threshold of $\Delta f <$ 0,45 Hz a sensitivity of 84,62% and positive predictivity of 86,27% was reached. When applying the thresholds of Table 1 obtained empirically, sensitivity an positive predictivity increased slightly to 86,64% for both indicators, where 45 of the 52 events were detected as ischemic and 18 of the 25 events were detected as heart rate related events. When both criteria were considered simultaneously, sensitivity was increased at the expense of positive predictivity (90.38% and 82,46% respectively).

Table 1. Thresholds set empirically for detection of ischemic events

Δa	Δf
<0.3	>0
(0.3; 0.45)	>0.5
(0.45; 1)	>2.25
>1	>3

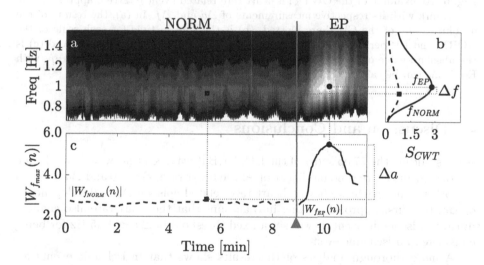

Fig. 5. An example of the CWT of an ischemic event (starting approximately at 9 min), with its respective measurements of Δa and Δf. In (a), the results of the absolute value of the CWT are plotted. (b) is the sum in time for each scale of the NORM and EP periods, calculated with Eq. 2, Δf is obtained with Eq. 3. And (c) is the absolute value of the CWT coefficients for $s_{max} = s_{NORM}$ and $s_{max} = s_{EP}$, with Eq. 4, Δa can be calculated.

Examples of the results obtained for ischemic and heart rate related episode can be seen in Figs. 5 and 6, respectively. Results obtained for Δf and Δa can be compared: in Fig. 5 (corresponding to an ischemic events) a smaller Δf and greater Δa is obtained compared to the results in Fig. 6, of a heart rate related event.

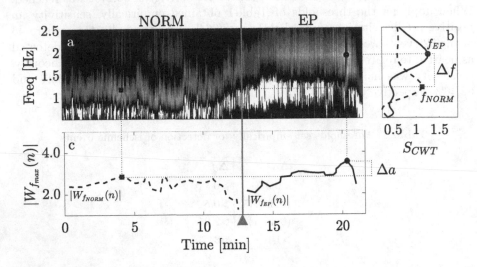

Fig. 6. An example of the CWT of a heart rate related event (starting approximately at 13 min), with its respective measurements of Δa and Δf. In (a), the results of the absolute value of the CWT are plotted. (b) is the sum in time for each scale of the NORM and EP periods, calculated with Eq. 2, Δf is obtained with Eq. 3. And (c) is the absolute value of the CWT coefficients for $s_{max} = s_{NORM}$ and $s_{max} = s_{EP}$, with Eq. 4, Δa can be calculated.

4   Discussion and Conclusions

After studding the 77 episodes of the LTST DB it was seen that when an ischemic episode occurs there is no modification of the heart rate, $\Delta f = 0$ and $\Delta a > 0$. On the other hand, when we have a heart rate related episode $\Delta f > 0$ independent of Δa. In a first approach, taking into account that the heart rate also changes during an ischemic event, it was set a fixed threshold in $\Delta f < 0,45$ Hz for being considered an ischemic event.

A more thorough analysis of the results shows that in ischemic events for larger Δf, there were larger Δa compared with heart rate related events of similar Δf. Thus, it was possible to empirically set some thresholds for detecting ischemic events (see Table 1), where it requires higher Δa for higher Δf to be considered as an ischemic event. This empirical assumption is a limitation of this work and further efforts should be made towards an automatic detection.

These are the first results obtained by analyzing the database with the CWT and a deeper analysis of the results will hopefully give more accurate and automatic results. It is expected also that other ST episodes, such as axis shift might also be detected with the CWT.

In [2] the CWT is also used for ischemic detection. In this work it is calculated the CWT of the heart rate variability and it is tested over the European ST-T Database (ESC DB). This database contains annotations done by specialist only of ischemic episodes and not of other type of events. Also, the ESC DB does not include a sufficient number of non ischaemic episodes adequately to test the specificity of automated ischemia detectors [7].

Another work that uses CWT for ischemic detection is [10], where the CWT is analyzed also in high frequencies, but no database was used to test the results.

Mincholé et al. [8] separate ischemic with heart rate events by obtaining ECG indices such as heart rate-based indices, correlation between the absolute ST segment deviation and heart rate series, T wave amplitude, the signal-to-noise ratio and changes in the upward/downward slopes of the QRS complex, and then performed a discrimination analysis between the different types of events. The results of sensitivity and specificity for separating ischemic of heart rate related events were 84.5% and 86.6%. In a future work some of this indices might be used together with the results obtained with the CWT to improve sensitivity and positive predictivity.

References

1. Dranca, L., Goñi, A., Illarramendi, A.: Real-time detection of transient cardiac ischemic episodes from ECG signals. Physiol. Meas. **30**(9), 983–998 (2009). https://doi.org/10.1088/0967-3334/30/9/009. http://stacks.iop.org/0967-3334/30/i=9/a=009?key=crossref.1157bd7b62f6b629cd7c959dbbe0f186

2. Gamero, L.G., Vila, J., Palacios, F.: Wavelet transform analysis of heart rate variability during myocardial ischaemia. Med. Biol. Eng. Comput. **40**(1), 72–78 (2002). https://doi.org/10.1007/BF02347698

3. García, J., Sörnmo, L., Olmos, S., Laguna, P.: Automatic detection of ST-T complex changes on the ECG using filtered RMS difference series: application to ambulatory ischemia monitoring. IEEE Transact. Biomed. Eng. **47**(9), 1195–1201 (2000). https://doi.org/10.1109/10.867943

4. Goldberger, A., et al.: PhysioBank, PhysioToolkit, and PhysioNet: components of a new research resource for complex physiologic signals. Circulation **23**, e215–e220 (2000)

5. Jager, F., Moody, G.B., Mark, R.G.: Detection of transient ST segment episodes during ambulatory ECG monitoring. Comput. Biomed. Res. Int. J. **31**(5), 305–322 (1998). https://doi.org/10.1006/cbmr.1998.1483

6. Jager, F.: ST analysis. In: Advanced Methods and Tools for ECG Data Analysis, chap. 10, pp. 269–290. Artech House (2006)

7. Jager, F., et al.: Long-term ST database: a reference for the development and evaluation of automated ischaemia detectors and for the study of the dynamics of myocardial ischaemia. Med. Biol. Eng. Comput. **41**(2), 172–182 (2003). https://doi.org/10.1007/BF02344885

8. Mincholé, A., Jager, F., Laguna, P.: Discrimination between ischemic and artifactual ST segment events in Holter recordings. Biomed. Signal Process. Control 5(1), 21–31 (2010). https://doi.org/10.1016/j.bspc.2009.09.001
9. Mincholé, A., Sörnmo, L., Laguna, P.: Detection of body position changes from the ECG using a Laplacian noise model. Biomed. Signal Process. Control 14(1), 189–196 (2014). https://doi.org/10.1016/j.bspc.2014.08.002. http://dx.doi.org/10.1016/j.bspc.2014.08.002
10. Provazník, I.: Wavelet analysis for signal detection - applications to experimental cardiology research. Ph.D. thesis, Brno University of Technology (2002)
11. Smrdel, A., Jager, F.: Automated detection of transient ST-segment episodes in 24h electrocardiograms. Med. Biol. Eng. Comput. 42(3), 303–311 (2004)
12. Taddei, A., Costantino, G., Silipo, R., Emdin, M., Marchesi, C.: A system for the detection of ischemic episodes in ambulatory ECG. In: Computers in Cardiology, pp. 705–708 (1995). https://doi.org/10.1109/CIC.1995.482762
13. Torrence, C., Compo, G.P.: A practical guide to wavelet analysis. Bull. Am. Meteorol. Soc. 79(1), 61–78 (1998). https://doi.org/10.1175/1520-0477(1998)079⟨0061:APGTWA⟩2.0.CO;2

Automatic Measurement of ISNT and CDR on Retinal Images by Means of a Fast and Efficient Method Based on Mathematical Morphology and Active Contours

Rafael Verdú-Monedero[1]([✉]), Juan Morales-Sánchez[1], Rafael Berenguer-Vidal[2], Inmaculada Sellés-Navarro[3], and Ana Palazón-Cabanes[3]

[1] Universidad Politécnica de Cartagena, 30202 Cartagena, Spain
`rafael.verdu@upct.es`
[2] Universidad Católica San Antonio, 30107 Murcia, Spain
[3] Hospital Universitario Reina Sofía, 30003 Murcia, Spain

Abstract. This paper describes a fast and efficient method to automatically measure the ISNT and CDR in retinal images. The method is based on a robust detection of the optic disk and excavation in a enhanced retinal image by means of morphological operators. Using this coarse segmentation as initialization, two parametric active contours implemented in the frequency domain perform a fine segmentation of the optic disk and excavation. The resulting curves allow the automatic calculation of the ISNT and CDR values, which are important features to consider in the early detection of glaucoma. The accuracy and precision of the method has been tested and compared with the evaluation of two ophthalmologists in a preliminary set of images.

Keywords: Glaucoma · ISNT · CDR · Image processing ·
Mathematical morphology · Active contours

1 Introduction

The development of computer applications for the anatomical evaluation of the optic nerve in digital images represents an important aid in the detection of optic neuropathies. Among them, glaucoma is undoubtedly the most prevalent disease. Without adequate treatment, this clinically silent ocular disease can lead to a progressive deterioration of the visual field causing eventually total blindness. For this reason, the development of techniques of early detection of glaucoma is crucial, given that it can help maintain eye health and minimize healthcare costs.

It is known that ocular anatomical alterations appear several years before the characteristic and irreversible lesions in the visual field, as a consequence of the death of the retina ganglion cells [20]. Initial clinical explorations that may lead to suspected glaucoma are intraocular pressure levels and the appearance

J. M. Ferrández Vicente et al. (Eds.): IWINAC 2019, LNCS 11487, pp. 361–370, 2019.
https://doi.org/10.1007/978-3-030-19651-6_35

of the optic nerve. In these cases, other complementary test as the assessment of the retinal fibers layer and the study of the visual field should confirm the diagnosis.

One of the drawbacks of establishing suggestive values of the optic nerve in early stages of the disease is the variability in size and appearance of the papilla in the normal population [10]. Some anatomical parameters of the papilla can be indicators of the onset of neuronal lesions and can be used as reference indices in the early detection of glaucoma [2,4]. This set of indicators includes the analysis of the size and shape of the optic nerve, the relationship between the size of the papillary excavation and the neuroretinal ring, the configuration of the excavation depth, the exit position of the papillary vessels, the presence of peripapillary hemorrhages, the nerve fiber defect or the chorioretinal atrophy, among others [11].

As shown in [10], in normal optic nerves the neural ring measured in the vertical and horizontal poles of the papilla follows a rule which states that the amplitude of the inferior neuroretinal ring (I) is the greatest, followed by the superior (S) and nasal (N), the temporal (T) being the smallest. This pattern is known as the ISNT rule, which has been confirmed by other authors [1,9,24]. Many studies relate the violation of this rule as a characteristic of nerves with glaucomatous damage. However, the predictability of this rule improves when it is complemented with other measurements and exploration data, such as, i.e., the disc-excavation relationship [12].

It has also been observed that the presence of asymmetries in the papillary excavation between both eyes is a suggestive factor of suffering from glaucoma [3, 22]. Although other authors [15] do not consider it useful as an isolated parameter to identify patients suffering from simple chronic glaucoma.

In recent years medical equipment has evolved so that it is capable of providing images as well as a quantitative analysis of the papilla, see e.g., confocal laser ophthalmoscopy (Heildeberg Retinal Tomograph, HRT) or optical coherence tomography (OCT). However, clinical studies indicate that it is necessary more than one determination and/or screening method to obtain evidence with high sensitivity and specificity in the early diagnosis of glaucoma [21]. On the other hand, the association of more than one diagnostic test entails more exploration time, which compromises the usefulness and effectiveness of early detection programs in a large population group. For this reason, research into methods of comprehensive analysis of optic nerve morphology that allow early detection of the disease is a priority.

2   Method

This section briefly describes the steps of the proposed approach. Initially, the acquired images are preprocessed by enhancing the dynamic range and by a slight correction of the illumination. In the second step, both the optical disk and excavation are automatically located in the image by means of morphological operations. In the next step, two active contours are employed to accurately delineate the optical disk and the excavation and provide the curves of each one. Two measurements are performed with these curves, ISNT and CDR, which are important features to help in the diagnostic of glaucoma.

2.1   Image Acquisition and Enhancement

The fundus images were acquired by the Ophthalmology Service of the *Hospital General Universitario Reina Sofía* (Murcia, Spain) by means of a Topcon TRC-NW400 non-mydriatic retinal camera. This work uses a preliminary set of images while the whole database with healthy and unhealthy eyes (glaucomatous optic neuropathy) is compiled.

These color images (RGB and 8 bit/channel) are in DICOM format, with a picture angle of 30° and a resolution of 1934×2576 pixels. Since this resolution is too high for the objective pursued, the images have been downsampled to 600×800 pixels before processing (see Fig. 1(a)), thus keeping enough resolution while allowing the minimization of the computational cost as well as preserving the image aspect ratio.

Next, two common preprocessing operations were also performed: (1) a contrast stretching for a full widening of the dynamic range, and (2) a smooth local and adaptive histogram equalization for homogenizing the illumination of the images. Such preprocessing steps alleviate the parameters variability in the processing stage, and thereby allow us to reach a robust adjustment of the algorithm.

2.2   Mathematical Morphology

Mathematical morphology is an important field of image processing based on the shape of the objects [17,18]. It is fundamentally based on the set theory, in the consecutive application of mathematical morphology operators. These functions allow to simplify the image data while maintaining its shape characteristics and minimizing artefacts or uninteresting elements. Most of morphology operations are based on testing the data with a binary image with a simple shape called structuring element. Depending on both the element and the morphological operation chosen, different results are obtained [19]. In the proposed approach, the following morphological operations are used: dilation, opening and closing, denoted, respectively with the symbols $\oplus$, $\circ$ and $\bullet$.

In order to locate the optical disk, the red channel of the image, I_{R0}, is usually considered [14] (see Fig. 1(c)). In I_{R0} a closing and an opening are performed,

$$I_{R1} = ((I_{R0} \bullet D_{11}) \circ D_{11}),\tag{1}$$

where D_{11} is a flat disk-shaped structuring element with radius $R = 11$. These operations erase bright and dark elements smaller than the structuring element. As a result, as shown in Fig. 1(f), the veins are removed from the image. An opening is then applied and the result is subtracted from the previous one,

$$I_{R2} = (I_{R1} - (I_{R1} \circ D_{99})),\tag{2}$$

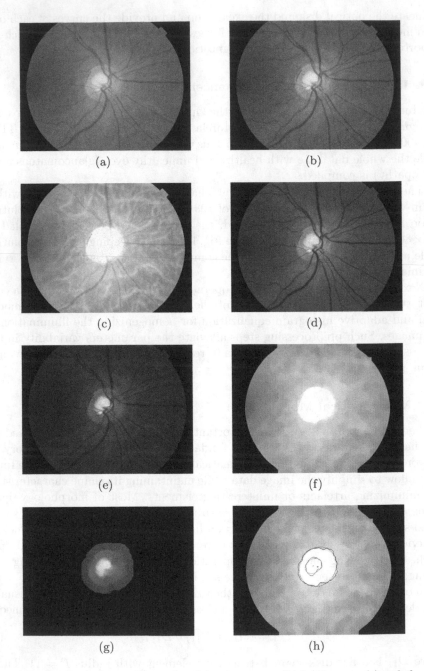

Fig. 1. Images involved in the process: (a) color image, (b) luminance, (c) red channel I_{R0}, (d) green channel I_{G0}, (e) blue channel I_{B0}, (f) red channel without veins I_{R2}, (g) blue channel without veins I_{B2}, (h) automatic location of optical disc and excavation and their ellipse fitting. (Color figure online)

being D_{99} a $R = 99$ disk-shaped structuring element. By applying a threshold to I_{R2}, elements smaller than D_{11} and larger than D_{99} are removed from the image,

$$M_{OD} = \text{thres}(I_{R2}). \tag{3}$$

As a result of these operations, only the area corresponding to the optical disc remains in the image.

The location of the excavation follows a process similar to the optical disk, but starting from the blue channel of the image, I_{B0}, (see Fig. 1(e)). Firstly, the area outside the optical disc is removed considering a binary mask with the optical disk previously detected and a dilation with a disk-shaped structuring element with radius $R = 31$, resulting in I_{B1}. Next, a closing and an opening with the structuring element D_{11} are executed,

$$I_{B2} = ((I_{B1} \bullet D_{11}) \circ D_{11}). \tag{4}$$

Again veins and small elements are removed from the data (see Fig. 1(g)). Similar operations to the case of the optical disc are then applied,

$$M_E = \text{thres}(I_{B2} - (I_{B2} \circ D_{51})), \tag{5}$$

with the only difference that D_{51}, a $R = 51$ disk-shaped structuring element, is now used.

The results of these steps, M_{OD} and M_E, i.e., the coarse segmentation of the optical disk and the excavation, are shown in Fig. 1(h) in blue and red line, respectively. Figure 1(h) also shows the approximation of M_{OD} and M_E by least-squares ellipse fitting. These ellipses are the initialization of the active contours used in next section to further refine the segmentations.

2.3   Parametric Active Contours

Parametric active contours or snakes are time-varying curves widely used in image processing for describing boundaries of objects [13]. Usual applications are segmentation and tracking of structures of interest within the image [5, 8].

An active contour is described by a parametric curve $\mathbf{v}(s,t) = [v_1(s,t), v_2(s,t)]$ defined in $\mathbb{R}^2$, where t denotes the time, $v_i(s,t)$ represents the coordinate function for dimension i and s is the parametric variable. The shape and position of the curve is governed by the influence of internal and external forces. The internal ones emulate the physical characteristics of the objects in the image, such as the elasticity or stiffness. By contrast, the external forces lead the model to fit the shape of the region to be segmented. The final shape of the curve is usually determined from the minimization of an energy functional defined by a second-order partial differential equation system, which incorporates both internal and external forces [13].

The proposed approach uses an efficient frequency-based implementation described in [6]. First, a spatial discretization is applied to the curve by means of finite elements,

$$v_i(s,t) = \mathbf{N}(s)\mathbf{u}_i(t), \tag{6}$$

where $\mathbf{N}(s)$ is the shape function and $\mathbf{u}_i(t)$ are the nodal variables of the i-th coordinate. Second, time is discretized $t = \xi \Delta t$, where Δt is the time step and $\xi \in \mathbb{N}$ the iteration index. Finally the model formulation is translated into the frequency domain, being the spatial variable s translated accordingly into the frequency variable ω. This leads to an iterative equation which rules the adaptation of the curve to the data within the image,

$$
U_\xi(\omega) = H(\omega) \left(a_1 U_{\xi-1}(\omega) + a_2 U_{\xi-2}(\omega) + \frac{Q_{\xi-1}(\omega)}{\eta F(\omega)} \right), \tag{7}
$$

where $U(\omega)$ and $F(\omega)$ are the Fourier transforms of the nodal variables of the model and the shape functions of the spatial discretization respectively. Internal forces due to physical characteristics of the curve are imposed by the filter $H(\omega)$, whereas external forces provided by the image are gathered in $Q(\omega)$. The first and second order coefficients of the iterative system a_1 and a_2 depends on the parameters η and γ which control the inertia of the model. The optimum value of these parameters to improve the convergence of the active contour can be found in [7,23].

The segmentation of the optical disk and the excavation are performed by applying two active contours in the green channel without veins. B-spline are chosen as shape function of the models because of their capability to minimize noise and data artefacts. In addition, the external forces $Q(\omega)$ of the models are obtained by applying two successive gradient operations to these images. As a result, two parametric curves are obtained outlining the two regions of interest, as depicted in Fig. 2.

3   Results

This section is devoted to the results obtained with the proposed approach and the preliminary set of images. The main features considered in the early detection of glaucoma are ISNT and CDR, which are briefly described below. The measurements computed automatically by the proposed method are complemented with the CDR provided by two expert ophthalmologists.

3.1   ISNT

In order to differentiate normal from glaucomatous eyes in the clinical evaluation of the optic nerve head, the ISNT rule states that normal eyes show a characteristic configuration for disc rim thickness of inferior (I) greater or equal than superior (S), greater or equal than nasal (N), greater or equal than temporal (T), i.e., $I \geq S \geq N \geq T$ [9]. Eyes that deviate from the ISNT rule may need close monitoring for glaucoma. However, the utility of this rule as a standalone criterion is not demonstrated for the early diagnosis of glaucoma [16].

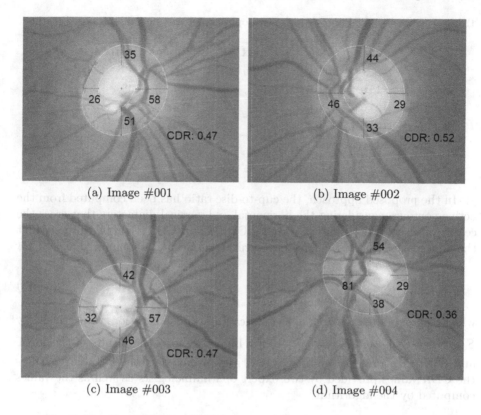

(a) Image #001

(b) Image #002

(c) Image #003

(d) Image #004

Fig. 2. Results of ISNT and CDR computed with the proposed approach.

3.2 Cup to Disc Ratio

The cup-to-disc ratio (CDR) is commonly used in ophthalmology as a measurement to evaluate the evolution of glaucoma. The optic disc is the area where the optic nerve and blood vessels enter the retina, becoming the blind spot of the eye. The pink rim of the disc contains nerve fibers whereas the white cup is a pit with no nerve fibers. The CDR compares the diameter of the cup portion of the optic disc with the total diameter of the optic disc. Normal values of cup-to-disc ratio are 0.3–0.4.

Glaucoma, which is in most cases associated with an increase in intraocular pressure, often produces additional pathological cupping of the optic disc. As glaucoma advances, the cup enlarges until it occupies most of the disc area. Then, a large cup-to-disc ratio may imply glaucoma or other pathology. However, cupping by itself is not indicative of glaucoma. Rather, an indicator of glaucoma is an increase in cupping as the patient ages. Deep but stable cupping can occur due to hereditary factors without glaucoma.

Table 1. Values of CDR provided by two ophthalmologist and the proposed method.

	Expert #1		Expert #2		Proposed method		
	CDR_H	CDR_V	CDR_H	CDR_V	CDR_H	CDR_V	CDR_S
Image #1	0.4	0.5	0.4	0.4	0.45	0.48	0.47
Image #2	0.6	0.6	0.5	0.5	0.52	0.53	0.52
Image #3	0.4	0.4	0.4	0.3	0.45	0.46	0.45
Image #4	0.2	0.1	0.3	0.2	0.29	0.39	0.36

In the proposed approach, the cup-to-disc ratio has been computed from the active contours considering the horizontal and vertical diameters that cross the center of mass of both curves. Besides CDR_H and CDR_V, taking into account the area of each curve, the cup-to-disc ratio has been also computed as:

$$CDR_S = \sqrt{\frac{S_{cup}}{S_{OD}}}, \tag{8}$$

which approximates the area of the optical disk and excavation, respectively, by $S_{OD} = \pi \left(\frac{d_{OD}}{2}\right)^2$ and $S_{cup} = \pi \left(\frac{d_{cup}}{2}\right)^2$. Figure 2 shows the results of the ISNT and CDR measured in the images with the proposed method. Table 1 gathers the CDR values provided by two expert ophthalmologists as well as the values computed by the algorithm.

4   Conclusions

This paper has addressed a method to automatically locate and segment the optic disk and the excavation in retinal fundus images. This fast and efficient approach is based on mathematical morphology and a frequency-based implementation of active contours. Results show the accuracy of the proposed method to provide the CDR measurements. In ongoing research, the method will be compared with other approaches using databases such as STARE[1] or ORIGA-light [25], whose performance is available.

Acknowledgments. This work has been partially supported by Spanish National projects AES2017-PI17/00771 and AES2017-PI17-00821 (Instituto de Salud Carlos III).

---

[1] http://cecas.clemson.edu/~ahoover/stare.

References

1. Alasil, T., et al.: Analysis of normal retinal nerve fiber layer thickness by age, sex, and race using spectral domain optical coherence tomography. J. Glaucoma **22**(7), 532–541 (2013)
2. Antón, A., Moreno-Montañes, J., Blázquez, F., Álvarez, A., Martín, B., Molina, B.: Usefulness of optical coherence tomography parameters of the optic disc and the retinal nerve fiber layer to differentiate glaucomatous, ocular hypertensive, and normal eyes. J. Glaucoma **16**(1), 1–8 (2007)
3. Armaly, M.F.: Genetic determination of cup/disc: ratio of the optic nerve. Arch. Ophthalmol. **78**(1), 35–43 (1967)
4. Banegas, S.A., Antón, A., Morilla-Grasa, A., Bogado, M., Ayala, E.M., Moreno-Montañes, J.: Agreement among spectral-domain optical coherence tomography, standard automated perimetry, and stereophotography in the detection of glaucoma progressionagreement for detection of glaucomatous progression. Invest. Ophthalmol. Vis. Sci. **56**(2), 1253–1260 (2015)
5. Bastida-Jumilla, M.C., Menchón-Lara, R.M., Morales-Sánchez, J., Verdú-Monedero, R., Larrey-Ruiz, J., Sancho-Gómez, J.L.: Segmentation of the common carotid artery walls based on a frequency implementation of active contours. J. Digit. Imaging **26**(1), 129–139 (2013)
6. Berenguer-Vidal, R., Verdú-Monedero, R., Morales-Sánchez, J.: Design of B-spline multidimensional deformable models in the frequency domain. Math. Comput. Model. **57**(7–8), 1942–1949 (2012)
7. Berenguer-Vidal, R., Verdú-Monedero, R., Morales-Sánchez, J.: Convergence analysis of multidimensional parametric deformable models. Comput. Vis. Image Underst. **135**, 157–177 (2015)
8. Berenguer-Vidal, R., Verdú-Monedero, R., Legaz-Aparicio, Á.-G.: Dynamic modelling of the whole heart based on a frequency formulation and implementation of parametric deformable models. In: Ferrández Vicente, J.M., Álvarez-Sánchez, J.R., de la Paz López, F., Toledo-Moreo, F.J., Adeli, H. (eds.) IWINAC 2015. LNCS, vol. 9107, pp. 330–339. Springer, Cham (2015). https://doi.org/10.1007/978-3-319-18914-7_35
9. Harizman, N., et al.: The ISNT rule and differentiation of normal from glaucomatous eyes. Arch. Ophthalmol. **124**(11), 1579–1583 (2006)
10. Jonas, J.B., Gusek, G.C., Naumann, G.O.: Optic disc, cup and neuroretinal rim size, configuration and correlations in normal eyes. Invest. Ophthalmol. Vis. Sci. **29**(7), 1151–1158 (1988)
11. Jonas, J.B., Fernández, M.C., Naumann, G.O.H.: Glaucomatous parapapillary atrophy: occurrence and correlations. Arch. Ophthalmol. **110**(2), 214–222 (1992)
12. Law, S.K., Kornmann, H.L., Nilforushan, N., Moghimi, S., Caprioli, J.: Evaluation of the "IS" rule to differentiate glaucomatous eyes from normal. J. Glaucoma **25**(1), 27–32 (2016)
13. Liang, J., McInerney, T., Terzopoulos, D.: United snakes. Med. Image Anal. **10**(2), 215–233 (2006)
14. Oktoeberza, K.Z.W., Nugroho, H.A., Adji, T.B.: Optic disc segmentation based on red channel retinal fundus images. In: Intan, R., Chi, C.-H., Palit, H.N., Santoso, L.W. (eds.) ICSIIT 2015. CCIS, vol. 516, pp. 348–359. Springer, Heidelberg (2015). https://doi.org/10.1007/978-3-662-46742-8_32
15. Ong, L.S., Mitchell, P., Healey, P.R., Cumming, R.G.: Asymmetry in optic disc parameters: the blue mountains eye study. Invest. Ophthalmol. Vis. Sci. **40**(5), 849–857 (1999)

16. Poon, L.Y.C., et al.: The ISNT rule: how often does it apply to disc photographs and retinal nerve fiber layer measurements in the normal population? Am. J. Ophthalmol. **184**, 19–27 (2017)
17. Serra, J.: Image Analysis and Mathematical Morphology, vol. I. Academic Press, London (1982)
18. Serra, J.: Image Analysis and Mathematical Morphology: Theoretical Advances, vol. II. Academic Press, London (1988)
19. Soille, P.: Morphological Image Analysis: Principles and Applications, 2nd edn. Springer, Heidelberg (2003). https://doi.org/10.1007/978-3-662-05088-0
20. Sommer, A., et al.: Clinically detectable nerve fiber atrophy precedes the onset of glaucomatous field loss. Arch. Ophthalmol. **109**(1), 77–83 (1991)
21. Tatham, A.J., Weinreb, R.N., Medeiros, F.A.: Strategies for improving early detection of glaucoma: the combined structure-function index. Clin. Ophthalmol. **8**, 611 (2014)
22. Varma, R., et al.: Race-, age-, gender-, and refractive error-related differences in the normal optic disc. Arch. Ophthalmol. **112**(8), 1068–1076 (1994)
23. Verdú-Monedero, R., Morales-Sánchez, J., Weruaga, L.: Convergence analysis of active contours. Image Vis. Comput. **26**(8), 1118–1128 (2008)
24. Wang, Y., Xu, L., Jonas, J.B.: Shape of the neuroretinal rim and its correlations with ocular and general parameters in adult chinese: the Beijing eye study. Am. J. ophthalmol. **144**(3), 462–464 (2007)
25. Zhang, Z., et al.: ORIGA-light: an online retinal fundus image database for glaucoma analysis and research. In: International Conference of the IEEE Engineering in Medicine and Biology, pp. 3065–3068 (2010)

Bihemispheric Beta Desynchronization During an Upper-Limb Motor Task in Chronic Stroke Survivors

Santiago Ezquerro[1], Juan A. Barios[1,2]([✉]), Arturo Bertomeu-Motos[1],
Jorge Diez[1], Jose M. Sanchez-Aparicio[2], Luis Donis-Barber[2],
Eduardo Fernández-Jover[1], and N. Garcia-Aracil[1]

[1] Biomedical Neuroengineering Research Group (nBio), Systems Engineering
and Automation Department, Miguel Hernández University,
Avda. de la Universidad s/n, 03202 Elche, Spain
jbarios@umh.es
[2] Fundacion Instituto San Jose, Pinar San Jose s/n, 28003 Madrid, Spain

Abstract. For severe motor paralysis patients, most rehabilitation
strategies require residual movements that, however, are lacking in up to
30–50% of stroke survivors. In these patients, motor imagery based BCI
systems might play a substantial role in rehabilitation strategies. 11
severely motor-injured stroke patients and 6 healthy participants participated in this study. During an unilateral upper-hand motor task, stroke
patients shown significant modulation of sensorimotor rhythms in both
hemispheres, shown that EEG signals of both hemispheres can be used
for control of BMI systems. Main findings were that ERD amplitude
was reduced in affected hemisphere, and that ERD when using affected
hand was lateralized to and more marked in ipsilateral (unaffected) hemisphere. Significant activation differences between healthy and affected
hemisphere were found, suggesting participation of different physiological mechanisms in both, that might be explored in future experimentation for improving the design and implementation of EEG-based BMI
systems and use of these systems in neurorehabilitation of stroke.

Keywords: EEG · Beta oscillations · Motor cortex · ERD/ERS ·
Active hand movement

1 Introduction

During voluntary movements, a well-established pattern of oscillatory responses
appears in the sensorimotor cortex. These oscillations are modulated along the
pre-movement, execution and end of voluntary movement [1–5]. Pfurtscheller
et al. described the reduction in this oscillatory power in alpha and beta bands
as event-related desynchronization (ERD). This phenomenon is related to stimulus processing or motor output and is characteristic for cortical areas that process

© Springer Nature Switzerland AG 2019
J. M. Ferrández Vicente et al. (Eds.): IWINAC 2019, LNCS 11487, pp. 371–379, 2019.
https://doi.org/10.1007/978-3-030-19651-6_36

sensory information to execute a motor command. It can be found during and before of sensory and cognitive processing and motor tasks. The opposite phenomenon, event-related synchronization (ERS), describes the phasic and regionally localized increase of alpha and beta band activity, usually at the end of the movement [6,7]. Characteristic of both phenomena - ERS and ERD - is that they can be either externally (e.g. by visual stimuli) or internally (e.g. by voluntary motor action) paced and that they have a specific topographical distribution depending upon the state of the brain.

The modulation of this physiological oscillations has been extensively used for Brain–machine interfaces (BMI). BMI systems translate electric or metabolic brain signals into control signals of computers or machines. One of the main uses of BMI systems is for neurorehabilitation, specially in stroke, one of the leading causes for severe adult long-term disability. Assistance in recovery of stroke survivors' motor function is mainly based in assistive BMIs, using brain control of robotic devices or functional electric stimulation (FES) to assist in performing daily life activities and in rehabilitative BMIs aiming at augmentation of neuroplasticity facilitating recovery of brain function [8].

Although six months to a year after stroke, the potential for recovery has substantially diminished, recent evidences suggest that stroke rehabilitation using constrained induced movement therapy (CIMT) can be effective even in the "chronic" stage of stroke [9,10], suggesting that neuroplasticity mechanisms are still active long time after stroke. However, for severe motor paralysis patients, there is currently no standardized or accepted treatment strategy, because these rehabilitation strategies require residual movements that, however, are lacking in up to 30–50% of stroke survivors. In these patients, motor imagery based BCI systems might play a substantial role in rehabilitation strategies.

Cortical oscillations of contralateral hemisphere to upper limb motor task are the usual control signal in BMI systems in healthy subjects. Both ipsilateral and contralateral signals to affected hand have been successfully used previously [11]. These signals are heavily modified after a hemispheric stroke for controlling affected hand. Thus, for increasing knowledge about EEG changes in ipsilateral and contralateral limb movements during motor control, this study seeks to evaluate differences in activation of both hemispheres in stroke survivors during a motor task usually employed for BCI control.

2   Materials and Methods

2.1   Participant Recruitment

The study sample was 11 stroke patients [8 men; mean age 59.18 years, standard deviation (SD) 13.06 years.] and 6 healthy participants [4 men; mean age 59.18 years, SD 8.3 years]. Table 1 shown the demographic and stroke typology of patients. The inclusion criteria for the patients were as follows. Male or female stroke volunteers, in the age group 18–85 years, with only one stroke episode, occurred between 2 months and 1 year, with unilateral affectation. They should be able to follow verbal and visual commands and communicate with researchers

Table 1. Description patients characteristics.

Patient	Age	Clinical Cause	Daniel's Muscular Test	Asworth	Craniotomy
1	77	Ischemic Stroke, MCA	0/5	0	No
2	24	Hemorrhagic Frontoparietal Stroke	3/5	0	Yes
3	69	Hemorrhagic Ganglia Basal	0/5	0	No
4	53	Head Injury	2/5	0	Yes
5	59	Hemorrhagic Ganglia Basal	3/5	0	No
6	65	Ischemic Stroke, MCA	0/5	0	No
7	65	Ischemic Stroke, MCA	0/5	0	No
8	56	Hemorrhagic Ganglia Basal	0/5	1	No
9	56	Hemorrhagic Ganglia Basal	0/5	1	Yes
10	69	Hemorrhagic Thalamic	0/5	0	No
11	58	Ischemic Stroke, ICA	0/5	1	No
Mean	59.18				
Median	59				
SD	13.06				

[a]Daniel's Muscular Test indicates muscular strength; Asworth Scale indicates the spasticity level of patients; MCA, middle cerebral artery; ICA, internal carotid artery.

and without severe behavioural disorders. The presence of high muscle spasticity or pain during the mobilization (EVA Scale ≤ 4) and severe visual disturbances was also set as an exclusion criteria. Occupational Therapists and Physiotherapists collected different variables of interest from the initial assessment, age, gender and functional state before stroke, stroke typology (ischemic or hemorrhagic) and stroke subtype with OCSP criteria: total anterior circulation infarcts (TACI), partial anterior circulation infarcts (PACI), lacunar infacts (LACI), and posterior circulation infarcts (POCI).

2.2 Experimental Setup

The experimentation was performed at San Jose Institute Foundation, Madrid (patients) and at the Biomedical Neuroengineering Laboratory of the Miguel Hernandez University, Elche (healthy participants). All participants gave written informed consent before the session. We had a comfortable and silent room with enough place for the wheelchair patient's. The participants sat in front of table with a screen where experimental cues were presented. During all the experimental tests, the occupational therapist stood next to them while looking at subjects and their EEG signal. Figure 1 shows the scheme of experimental setup and a time-frequency analysis of a representative recording. EEG data was acquired using a non-invasive commercial EEG system based on a wireless amplifier (BrainVision®). For synchronization of experimental cues and setting up of experimental tasks, the BCI2000 system was employed [12]. It is a open-source software which we employed to define the parameters and characteristics of each task Fig. 1(B).

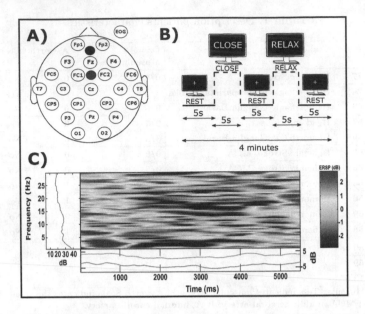

Fig. 1. (A) Electrodes placement for the experimentation. The black circle shown the ground electrode placement, and blue circle shown the reference electrode placement. (B) Overview of the task, the image shown the three cues that the participants had to follow and the time had to perform them. (C) Time-Frequency of one epoch (CLOSE) in a frequency range (0–30 Hz) and time-interval (0–5500 ms). The *upper left panel* shows the baseline mean power spectrum, and the lower part of the upper panel, the ERSP envelope (low and high mean dB values, relative to baseline, at each time in the epoch). (Color figure online)

2.3   Experimental Protocol

The experimentation was carried out in a single session. The task was divided in two different sub-tasks. First, the patients performed the grasping movement with non-paretic hand, and then executed it with paretic hand. In the case of healthy participants, first, the grasping movement with right (dominant) hand were performed, and then, with the left hand.

Each task was divided in twenty-four trials and each trial lasted for 5 s. While the occupational therapist placed the EEG cap, the participants received instructions about the experimentation and how should performed the different tasks.

The task consisted on performing a unilateral grasping hand movement, following the cues that appeared on the screen. The cues were three: CLOSE, the participants performed the grasping movement, closing the hand, aproximately 1 time per second. RELAX, the participants had to think on some image not related to the movement (e.g. a forest, beach, etc.). Finally, REST, the participants had to do nothing.

2.4   EEG Data Acquisition and Analysis

The EEG data was acquired using 24 electrodes according to 10/20 system (impedance was kept below 20 kΩ) and one electrode to acquire the EOG signal. The reference and ground placed shown in Fig. 1(A). The sample rate was 500 Hz.

The data were processed in Matlab 2017b using scripts based on EEGLAB 13.6.5, as well as a dedicated home-made code created for this study. Visible artifacts in the EEG recordings (i.e. eye movements, cardiac activity and scalp muscle contraction) were removed using an independent component analysis (ICA) procedure [13]. The EEG recordings were filtered (high band-pass 0.5 Hz, low band-pass 40 Hz). The EEG data of each cue (lasting from −3000 to 6000 ms) and the trial were divided into 24 epochs. The execution or imagery grasp movement produce ERD/ERS over the sensorimotor area at alpha (8–12 Hz) and beta (13–30 Hz) frequency ranges were analyzed.

3   Results

3.1   EEG Topographic Analysis

During patients' affected hand movement, peak point of ERD dipole appears over ipsilateral sensorimotor area (electrode C4), although appears in a wide area including frontal and parietal regions (see Fig. 2. Interestingly, the beta power decrease (ERD) is clearly higher in the ipsilateral hemisphere (C3), than in contralateral hemisphere (C4). On the other hand, ERD only appears in the contralateral SM1 area (C4) when the unaffected hand is moved.

During controls' dominant hand movement, ERD phenomenon, that is clearly localized to a small cortical area, is shown over contralateral hemisphere (C3). Differently, the decrease in ERD is presented over both contralateral and ipsilateral SM1 areas (C3 and C4) when using the non-dominant hand. However, the power decrease is higher in contralateral SM1 area (C4) than, ipsilateral hemisphere (C3).

3.2   Time-Frequency Analysis

In Fig. 3, time-frequency analysis of EEG in stroke patients and control subjects is presented. In affected hemisphere of stroke patients, there is a significant ERD in alpha and beta bands more marked when using contralateral (affected) hand, (difference with non-affected hand was not statistically significant). Power changes were more marked in control group, although differences did not reach statistical significance. In control group, the grasping movement performed with dominant hand shown a power increase in beta band at the end of the movement (ERS) that did not appear in patient's group. However, it did not reach statistical significance ($p < 0.05$) in this hemisphere.

In unaffected hemisphere of stroke patients, time-frequency analysis of EEG shown the presence of a significant ERD in alpha and beta bands, clearly more

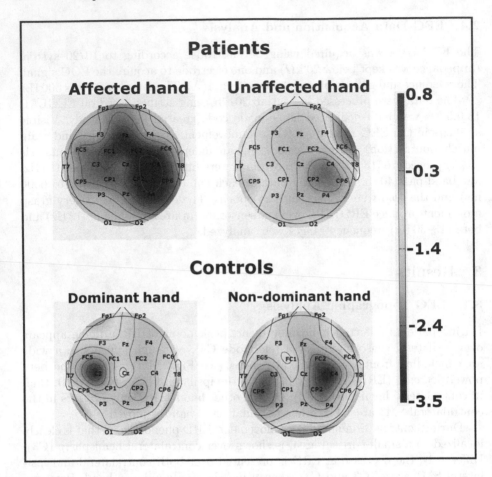

Fig. 2. Topographic map showing ERD/ERS in beta band during grasping movement task. Image shows the topographic distribution in 1200–1800 ms time-range from onset of CLOSE cue. Up image shows the task performed by stroke patients with affected and unaffected hand. Down image shows the task performed by control participant with dominant and non-dominant hand. Notice the absence of significant ERD in affected hemisphere. Blue color coding indicates maximal ERD. Grand-average of 11 stroke patients and 6 control subjects. (Color figure online)

marked than in affected hemisphere, without differences between hands. Differences vs control group were statistically significant in beta band when using affected (ipsilateral) hand. In control group, the grasping movement performed with non-dominant hand shown a power increase in beta band at the end of the movement (ERS) that did not appear in patient's group. At this point of time, differences were statistically significant (p < 0.05).

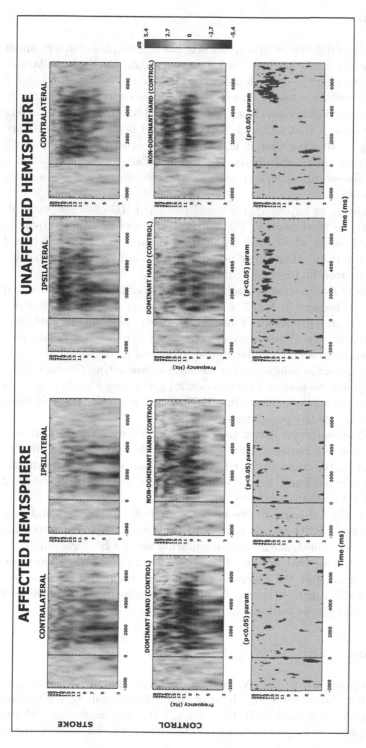

Fig. 3. Time-frequency analysis of EEG of participants, showing ERD/ERS in beta band during unilateral grasping movement task. Left half, affected hemisphere in patients, left hemisphere in controls. Right half, unaffected hemisphere in patients, right hemisphere in controls. Up image show the task performed by patient with affected and unaffected. Down image show the task performed by control participant with dominant and non-dominant hand. Blue color coding indicates maximal ERD. Notice the clear ERD in unaffected hemisphere while closing affected (ipsilateral) hand. Grand-average of 11 stroke patients and 6 control subjects. (Color figure online)

4   Discussion

We have evaluated the differences in activation of both hemispheres in a group of severely-injured motor stroke patients and a control group. Cortical oscillations of contralateral hemisphere to upper limb motor task are the usual control signal in BMI systems in healthy subjects, but these signals are expected to be heavily modified after a hemispheric stroke when using affected hand. The main finding of our experimentation is that although EEG signals of both hemispheres vary during a motor task, showing that it is possible to control BMI system with signals obtained from both hemispheres, significant differences appear between them implying different physiological mechanisms that might be relevant for BMI implementation.

In control subjects, as expected, we found cortical ERD changes predominately contralateral to movement: in Fig. 2 it is shown a clear unique dipole in contralateral motor cortex when using dominant hand and two dipoles (left and right sensorimotor cortex) when using non-dominant hand. This is compatible with previously reported findings using fMRI [14].

Hemispheric EEG modulation in stroke patients was different. When affected hand is used, as can be seen in Fig. 2, a dipole in affected hemisphere was not found, while a wide area dipole was found over healthy hemisphere, including frontal and parietal regions. When using healthy hand, in unaffected hemisphere of stroke patients a surprisingly similar dipole to control group was found, suggesting that although same compensation mechanism are acting (because ERD changes are clearly less pronounced that in control group, see Fig. 3), control of the unaffected hand of stroke patients in a BCI system might be possible using similar techniques to healthy population.

Contralesional activation of cortex has been observed with fMRI, TMS and EEG techniques in stroke patients. Involvement of ipsilateral cortex to affected hand was greatest in the more impaired patients [15]. Consistently, we report that, when using affected hand, beta desinchronization is greater in unaffected hemisphere (ipsilateral) than in affected hemisphere.

For control of affected hand in stroke patients, both ipsilesional and contralesional hemispheric EEG signals have been previously employed, reporting similar favorable results in stroke neurorehabilitation using a BMI system [8,11]. Our findings corroborate that activity from both hemispheres was modulated during the motor task, but the differences in cortical mapping representation of dipoles suggest differences between physiological mechanisms responsible of these changes that might be explored in future experimentation.

5   Conclusion

Severely motor-injured stroke patients shown significant ERD changes in both hemispheres during the motor task, showing that EEG signals of both hemispheres can be used for control of BMI systems. ERD amplitude was reduced in affected hemisphere. ERD, when using affected hand, was lateralized to and more marked in ipsilateral (unaffected) hemisphere. These are relevant facts that might be taken into account in the design and implementation of EEG-based BMI systems and use of these systems in neurorehabilitation of stroke.

References

1. Salmelin, R., Hámáaláinen, M., Kajola, M., Hari, R.: Functional segregation of movement-related rhythmic activity in the human brain. Neuroimage **2**, 237–243 (1995)
2. Pfurtscheller, G., Stancak Jr., A., Neuper, C.: Post-movement beta synchronization. A correlate of an idling motor area? Electroencephalogr. Clin. Neurophysiol. **98**, 281–293 (1996)
3. Leocani, L., Toro, C., Manganotti, P., Zhuang, P., Hallett, M.: Event-related coherence and event-related desynchronization/synchronization in the 10 hz and 20 hz eeg during self-paced movements. Electroencephalogr. Clin. Neurophysiol./Evoked Potentials Sect. **104**, 199–206 (1997)
4. Cassim, F., et al.: Does post-movement beta synchronization reflect an idling motor cortex? Neuroreport **12**, 3859–3863 (2001)
5. Parkes, L.M., Bastiaansen, M.C., Norris, D.G.: Combining EEG and fMRI to investigate the post-movement beta rebound. Neuroimage **29**, 685–696 (2006)
6. Pfurtscheller, G.: Event-related synchronization (ERS): an electrophysiological correlate of cortical areas at rest. Electroencephalogr. Clin. Neurophysiol. **83**, 62–69 (1992)
7. Pfurtscheller, G., Neuper, C.: Future prospects of erd/ers in the context of brain-computer interface (BCI) developments. Prog. Brain Res. **159**, 433–437 (2006)
8. Soekadar, S.R., Birbaumer, N., Slutzky, M.W., Cohen, L.G.: Brain-machine interfaces in neurorehabilitation of stroke. Neurobiol. Dis. **83**, 172–179 (2015)
9. Teasell, R.W., Fernandez, M.M., McIntyre, A., Mehta, S.: Rethinking the continuum of stroke rehabilitation. Arch. Phys. Med. Rehabil. **95**, 595–596 (2014)
10. Corbetta, D., Sirtori, V., Castellini, G., Moja, L., Gatti, R.: Constraint-induced movement therapy for upper extremities in people with stroke. Cochrane Database Syst. Rev. **2015**(10). https://doi.org/10.1002/14651858.CD004433.pub3. Article no. CD004433
11. Bundy, D.T., et al.: Contralesional brain-computer interface control of a powered exoskeleton for motor recovery in chronic stroke survivors. Stroke **48**, 1908–1915 (2017)
12. Schalk, G., McFarland, D.J., Hinterberger, T., Birbaumer, N., Wolpaw, J.R.: BCI: a general-purpose brain-computer interface (BCI) system. IEEE Trans. Biomed. Eng. **51**, 1034–1043 (2004)
13. Jung, T.P., et al.: Removing electroencephalographic artifacts by blind source separation. Psychophysiology **37**, 163–178 (2000)
14. Singh, L.N., et al.: Comparison of ipsilateral activation between right and left handers: a functional MR imaging study. Neuroreport **9**, 1861–1866 (1998)
15. Johansen-Berg, H., Rushworth, M.F., Bogdanovic, M.D., Kischka, U., Wimalaratna, S., Matthews, P.M.: The role of ipsilateral premotor cortex in hand movement after stroke. Proc. Nat. Acad. Sci. **99**, 14518–14523 (2002)

Modeling and Estimation
of Non-functional Properties: Leveraging
the Power of QoS Metrics

Cristina Vicente-Chicote[1(✉)], Daniel García-Pérez[1], Pablo García-Ojeda[1],
Juan F. Inglés-Romero[2], Adrián Romero-Garcés[3], and Jesús Martínez[3]

[1] Quercus Software Engineering Group,
Universidad de Extremadura, Cáceres, Spain
{cristinav,danielgp,pablogo}@unex.es
[2] Biometric Vox, S.L., Murcia, Spain
juanfran.ingles@biometricvox.com
[3] Universidad de Málaga, Málaga, Spain
{argarces,jmcruz}@uma.es

Abstract. Non-Functional Properties (e.g., safety, dependability or resource consumption, just to name a few), play a key role in most software systems. The RoQME Integrated Technical Project, funded by the EU H2020 RobMoSys Project, aims at contributing a model-driven toolchain for dealing with system-level non-functional properties through the specification of global quality-of-service (QoS) metrics. The estimation of these metrics at runtime, in terms of the available contextual information, can then be used for different purposes, such as dynamic software adaptation or benchmarking. This paper describes the advances achieved in RoQME and presents one of the pilot experiments developed to showcase the tool-chain developed as part of the project.

Keywords: Non-functional properties · QoS metrics · RoQME

1 Introduction

Component-Based Software Development (CBSD) aims at promoting software reuse for significantly reducing development time and cost. Existing solutions are encapsulated in well-defined components with clear (required and provided) interfaces that enable their connection to and interoperation with other components. Building systems out of components requires taking into account both functional and non-functional properties. Non-functional properties define *how* a system performs rather than *what* it does [16]. Examples of non-functional properties include timing, dependability, safety or resource consumption, among others. Despite the importance of non-functional properties, few component models explicitly support their specification and management throughout the

J. M. Ferrández Vicente et al. (Eds.): IWINAC 2019, LNCS 11487, pp. 380–388, 2019.
https://doi.org/10.1007/978-3-030-19651-6_37

development process. In most cases, this support is limited and, unlike the well-established solution of embodying functional properties into interfaces, no consensus has emerged on how to handle non-functional properties both at a component and at a system level [16].

RobMoSys: Composable Models and Software for Robotics[1] is a 4-year Project (2017–2020), funded by the EU H2020 Research and Innovation Program under grant agreement No. 732410. The vision of RobMoSys is to create better models, as the basis for better tools and better software, which then allow building better robotic systems. RobMoSys seeks to enable the composition of robotics applications with managed, assured, and maintained system-level properties using Model-Driven Engineering (MDE) techniques from a CBSD perspective.

RobMoSys financially supports, through a cascade funding scheme, third party contributions as means to achieve its own objectives. *RoQME: Dealing with non-functional properties through global Robot Quality-of- Service Metrics*[2] has been one of the selected Integrated Technical Project (ITP) to be funded in the context of the first RobMoSys open call.

The main intended goal of RoQME is to provide software engineers with a model-driven tool-chain allowing them to: (1) model relevant system-level non-functional properties in terms of the (internal and external) contextual information available at runtime; and (2) generate *QoS Metrics Provider* components, ready to inform other components in the architecture about how the non-functional properties, previously specified, evolve in time.

RoQME has been running for one year (March 2018–February 2019). Achieving substantial results in such a short period of time requires building on previous results. In this vein, the RoQME partners contributed solid background in Robotics, Component-Based Software Development, and Model-Driven Engineering [1,3] [6–9,13–15]. Besides, the previous collaboration among some of the RoQME and the RobMoSys partners, has undoubtedly contributed to align RoQME to the RobMoSys vision, principles and structures [5,10,11]. Some preliminary results of the RoQME Project can be found in [4,12] [18].

The rest of the paper is organized as follows. Section 2 briefly introduces the main goals and contributions of the RoQME Project. Section 3 describes one of the pilot experiments developed to showcase the benefits of RoQME in the context of an intralogistics robotic application. Finally, Sect. 4 draws some conclusions and outlines future works.

2   RoQME Overview

The RoQME Project focuses on the modeling (at design-time) and the estimation (at runtime) of system-level non-functional properties. The RoQME tool-chain[3] provides designers with a textual model editor and a number of model-to-code transformations, enabling the automatic generation of fully operational

---

[1] https://robmosys.eu.

[2] http://robmosys.eu/roqme/.

[3] https://robmosys.eu/wiki/baseline:environment_tools:roqme-plugins.

QoS Metrics Provider components, ready to be used by other components, e.g., for benchmarking or for adapting the system behavior.

The RoQME textual model editor enables the specification of relevant application-specific properties, contexts and observations (see Fig. 1, Design-Time). Each *Property* represents the degree of fulfillment of a non-functional property. The value of a property (hereinafter referred to as *QoS Metric*) changes at runtime (within the range $[0, 1]$) in response to observations collected from different context sources. Each *Context* represents a source of information either internal (e.g., available sensors) or external (e.g., other systems or Internet-based services). Finally, *Observations* specify how particular context patterns influence (*REINFORCE* or *UNDERMINE*) one or more properties, and to what extent (*VERY_HIGH, HIGH, MEDIUM*, etc.). An example model, created with the RoQME textual editor, is later introduced in Sect. 3 (see Fig. 2).

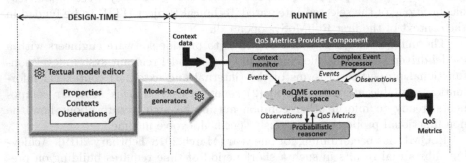

Fig. 1. Main RoQME tools and artifacts.

Each application-specific RoQME model is used as an input for generating the corresponding *QoS Metrics Provider* component (see Fig. 1, Runtime). Externally, this component provides interfaces for connecting both, the input context data providers (e.g., sensors) and the output QoS Metrics. Internally, the contextual information is sequentially processed by three modules: (1) a *Context Monitor* that receives raw context data and produces context events (e.g., changes in the battery level); (2) a *Complex-Event Processor*, aimed at detecting the context patterns specified in the RoQME model and, when found, producing the corresponding observations (e.g., battery is draining too fast); and, finally (3) a *Probabilistic Reasoner* that, based on the previous observations, computes (1) a numeric estimation for each QoS metric (i.e., the degree of fulfillment of each non-functional property); (2) a ranking of observations, according to their influence on each QoS metric; and (2) when possible, information about the degree of confidence associated to each QoS metric depending on the availability, reliability and uncertainty of the context sources [2]. The three previous modules interchange data through the so called *RoQME Com-*

mon Data Space, which is based on the Data-Distribution Service for Real-Time Systems (DDS) standard[4].

It is worth mentioning that, apart from the *QoS Metrics Provider* component, the RoQME tool-chain also generates and configures a data visualization environment. This tool connects to the RoQME common data space, enabling the real-time visualization of the raw context data, the identified events and observations, and the QoS metrics computed by the component. Furthermore, this tool stores all this information in a non-SQL database enabling the off-line reproduction of the experiments.

3 Testing RoQME in an Intralogistics Robotic Scenario

The Ulm University of Applied Sciences (HSU) is the technical lead partner of RobMoSys. HSU contributes to RobMoSys, among many other key inputs, the SmartMDSD Tool-Chain [17] (included as part of the RobMoSys baseline software) and an Intralogistics Industry 4.0 Robot Fleet Pilot[5]. HSU makes this pilot available to all the Integrated Technical Projects funded by RobMoSys as a test-bed for experimentation and showcasing. The HSU scenario counts on a fleet of robots which can collect, deliver and transport objects from/to different work stations, conveyor belts, etc. Robots can interact with each other and with human operators. This section describes how RoQME has been used to model and estimate relevant non-functional properties of an application based on the HSU intralogistics scenario.

3.1 Modeling QoS Metrics on *SAFETY* and *PERFORMANCE*

Figure 2 shows the RoQME model developed for the example scenario. Line 1 defines the name of the RoQME model, while lines 3 and 4 respectively define the following parameters: *MAX_V* defines the maximum speed allowed for the robot when there is a person in its working area, and *MAX_JOB_DONE* defines the maximum time allowed for the robot to complete each job. These two parameters need to set in the *QoS Metrics Provider* component before launching the application.

Lines 6 and 7 specify the QoS metrics on two non-functional properties: *Safety* and *Performance*. Each of these metrics takes a belief value in the range [0, 1]. It is worth mentioning that the reference value for *Safety* is 1, as the system is considered *a priory* safe. Only if there is evidence against this belief, the value of the *Safety* metric is reduced (undermined) accordingly. On the other hand, the reference value for *Performance* is 0.5, since *Performance* may be both reinforced or undermined.

Lines 9–27 specify the five contexts identified as relevant and, finally, lines 29–43 specify the observations that indicate which context patterns reinforce (or

---

[4] https://www.omg.org/dds/.
[5] https://robmosys.eu/wiki/pilots:intralogistics.

undermine) each non functional-property and to what extent. The *O1* observation strongly undermines *Safety* when a collision with the robot is detected (*Bump* event); *O2* undermines *Safety* if the robots drives faster than allowed when there is a person in the robot working area; *O3* reinforces *Performance* every time the robot successfully completes a task within the required time; and *O4* and *O5* undermine *Performance* if the robot enters into the error state or if its current task is aborted, respectively.

```
 1   roqme "IntralogisticsRoboticApplication"
 2
 3   param MAX_V              : number
 4   param MAX_JOB_DONE       : number
 5
 6   property Performance prior    0.5
 7   property Safety      prior    1
 8
 9   context Bump            : eventType
10   context Velocity        : number
11   context PersonState     : boolean
12   context JobState        : enum {
13           NOT_STARTED,
14           STARTED,
15           COMPLETED,
16           ABORTED
17   }
18   context RobotState      : enum {
19           IDLE_NOT_CHARGING,
20           IDLE_CHARGING,
21           BUSY_DRIVING_WITH_LOAD,
22           BUSY_DRIVING_EMPTY,
23           ERROR
24   }
25   context TimeJobDone  :  time :=
26           interval ( JobState::STARTED ->
27                      JobState::COMPLETED )
28
29   observation O1 : Bump
30                    undermines Safety VERY_HIGH
31
32   observation O2 : Velocity > MAX_V and PersonState
33                    undermines Safety VERY_HIGH
34
35   observation O3 : JobState::COMPLETED
36                    while ( TimeJobDone < MAX_JOB_DONE )
37                    reinforces Performance HIGH
38
39   observation O4 : RobotState::ERROR
40                    undermines Performance
41
42   observation O4 : JobState::ABORTED
43                    undermines Performance
```

Fig. 2. RoQME textual model for the intralogistics robotic application.

3.2   Execution of the Intralogistics Robotic Application

The experiment starts with the robot in an IDLE state and placed in its initial position. There is an operator ready to handover boxes to the robot.

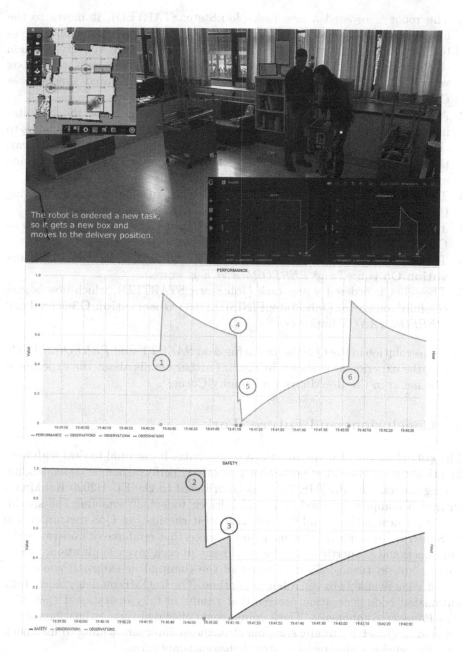

Fig. 3. Snapshot of the video recorded during the experiment (available at: https://youtu.be/fb1uLT5CNjg) and evolution of the QoS Metrics defined on *PERFOR-MANCE* and *SAFETY*. The numbers included in the two graphs refer to the six steps described in Sect. 3.2 and the corresponding observations identified during the experiment.

1. The robot is ordered a new task (Job_State::STARTED). It moves to the handover position (Robot_ State::BUSY DRIVING EMPTY). The operator puts a box on top of it and the robot moves to the delivery position (Robot_State::BUSY_DRIVING_WITH_LOAD). The robot delivers the box successfully (Job_State::FINISHED) and within the required time-slot → **Observation O3** is fired and *PERFORMANCE* improves.
2. A visitor enters the room and meets the operator (Person_State::IN). Simultaneously, the robot is ordered a new task (Job_State::STARTED) and moves to the handover position (Robot_State::BUSY_DRIVING_EMPTY). On its way, the robot moves faster than allowed when a person is in the robot working area → **Observation O2** is fired and *SAFETY* is worsen.
3. The visitor bumps into the robot (Bump) when turning around for leaving the room → **Observation O1** is fired and *SAFETY* is worsen.
4. The bumping sets the robot in the ERROR state (Robot_State::ERROR) → **Observation O4** is fired and *PERFORMANCE* is worsen.
5. The error causes the task to be aborted (Job_State::ABORTED) → **Observation O5** is fired and *PERFORMANCE* is worsen.
6. The robot is ordered a new task (Job_State::STARTED), which now is successfully completed (Job_State::FINISHED) → **Observation O3** is fired and *PERFORMANCE* improves.

The evolution of the QoS metrics defined on *SAFETY* and *PERFORMANCE* during the experiment is shown in Fig. 3. Further details about the experiment can be found in the RobMoSys Community Corner[6].

4   Conclusions and Future Work

The critical nature of many robotic systems makes it essential to deal with non-functional properties at runtime, such as safety, performance or dependability, among others. The RoQME ITP has contributed to the EU H2020 RobMoSys Project a component-based and model-driven tool-chain enabling the specification (at design-time) and the estimation (at runtime) of QoS metrics. These QoS metrics are defined in terms of observations that reinforce or undermine the non-functional properties considered relevant in each given application. Observations are, in turn, defined in terms of the (internal or external) contextual information available to the robot at runtime. The RoQME models guide a fully automated code generation process that results in fully operational *QoS Metrics Provider* components. These components offer real-time estimations of the selected QoS metrics to any component in the architecture willing to use them, e.g., for benchmarking or for system behavior adaptation.

The RoQME tool-chain has been successfully tested in an intralogistics robotic scenario, as described in Sect. 3. Currently, additional pilots for assistive robotics, smart-cities (traffic monitoring and management) or home health-care applications (e.g., Altheimer's patients monitoring and assistance) are

---

[6] https://robmosys.eu/wiki/community:roqme-intralog-scenario:start.

under development. The first one will allow us to work with a different set of non-functional properties, more focused on human-robot interaction (e.g., user engagement and satisfaction), while the second and third ones will allow us to assess RoQME outside the robotics domain, in data-intensive and highly-distributed applications.

It is worth mentioning that all the RoQME partners are fully committed to open-access and open-source policies. In this vein, all the Project results will be soon made publicly available and announced through the Project social networks (Twitter[7], LinkedIn[8], or ResearchGate[9]).

Acknowledgements. The RoQME Project has received funding from the European Union's H2020 Research and Innovation Programme under grant agreement No. 732410, in the form of financial support to third parties of the RobMoSys Project. The authors want to thank D. Stampfer, M. Lutz, A. Lotz and C. Schlegel, from the University of Applied Sciences of Ulm (Germany), for their continued support during the RoQME project and in the development of the Intralogistics Robotic pilot.

References

1. Alonso, D., Pastor, J.A., Sánchez, P., Álvarez, B., Vicente-Chicote, C.: Automatic code generation for real-time systems: a development approach based on components, models, and frameworks. Rev. Iberoamericana de Autom. Inf. Ind. (RIAI) **9**(2), 170–181 (2012). https://doi.org/10.1016/j.riai.2012.02.010
2. Cámara, J., Peng, W., Garlan, D., Schmerl, B.: Reasoning about sensing uncertainty and its reduction in decision-making for self-adaptation. Sci. Comput. Prog. **167**, 51–69 (2018). https://doi.org/10.1016/j.scico.2018.07.002
3. Gutiérrez, M.A., Romero-Garcés, A., Bustos, P.: Progress in RoboComp. J. Phys. Agents **7**(1), 39–48 (2013). https://doi.org/10.14198/JoPha.2013.7.1.06
4. Inglés-Romero, J.F., Espín, J.M., Jiménez-Andreu, R., Font, R., Vicente-Chicote, C.: Towards the use of quality-of-service metrics in reinforcement learning: a robotics example. In: Proceedings of the 5th International Workshop on Model-driven Robot Software Engineering (MORSE 2018), in Conjunction with MODELS 2018, pp. 465–474 (2018). http://ceur-ws.org/Vol-2245/morse_paper_4.pdf
5. Inglés-Romero, J.F., Lotz, A., Vicente-Chicote, C., Schlegel, C.: Dealing with runtime variability in service robotics: towards a DSL for non-functional properties. In: Proceedings of the 3rd International Workshop on Domain-Specific Languages and models for ROBotic systems (DSLRob-12) (2012). https://arxiv.org/pdf/1303.4296.pdf
6. Inglés-Romero, J.F., Romero-Garcés, A., Vicente-Chicote, C., Martínez, J.: A model-driven approach to enable adaptive QoS in DDS-based middleware. IEEE Trans. Emerg. Top. Comput. Intell. **1**(3), 176–187 (2017). https://doi.org/10.1109/TETCI.2017.2669187
7. Inglés-Romero, J.F., Vicente-Chicote, C.: Towards a formal approach for prototyping and verifying self-adaptive systems. In: Franch, X., Soffer, P. (eds.) CAiSE 2013. LNBIP, vol. 148, pp. 432–446. Springer, Heidelberg (2013). https://doi.org/10.1007/978-3-642-38490-5_39

---

[7] https://twitter.com/roqme_itp.
[8] https://www.linkedin.com/groups/12096769.
[9] https://www.researchgate.net/project/RoQME-QoS-Metrics-on-NFP.

8. Inglés-Romero, J.F., Vicente-Chicote, C., Morin, B., Barais, O.: Using models@runtime for designing adaptive robotics software: an experience report. In: Proceedings of the 1st International Workshop on Model-Based Engineering for Robotics (RoSym 2010), in Conjunction with MODELS 2010, pp. 1–11 (2010)
9. Inglés-Romero, J.F., Vicente-Chicote, C., Morin, B., Barais, O.: Towards the automatic generation of self-adaptive robotics software: an experience report. In: 2011 IEEE 20th International Workshops on Enabling Technologies: Infrastructure for Collaborative Enterprises, pp. 79–86 (2011). https://doi.org/10.1109/WETICE.2011.54
10. Lotz, A., Inglés-Romero, J.F., Stampfer, D., Lutz, M., Vicente-Chicote, C., Schlegel, C.: Towards a stepwise variability management process for complex systems: a robotics perspective. Int. J. Inf. Syst. Model. Des. **5**(3) (2014). https://doi.org/10.4018/ijismd.2014070103
11. Lotz, A., Inglés-Romero, J.F., Vicente-Chicote, C., Schlegel, C.: Managing run-time variability in robotics software by modeling functional and non-functional behavior. In: Nurcan, S., et al. (eds.) BPMDS/EMMSAD -2013. LNBIP, vol. 147, pp. 441–455. Springer, Heidelberg (2013). https://doi.org/10.1007/978-3-642-38484-4_31
12. Lutz, M., Inglés-Romero, J.F., Stampfer, D., Lotz, A., Vicente-Chicote, C., Schlegel, C.: Managing variability as a means to promote composability: a robotics perspective. In: da Cruz, A.M.R., da Cruz, M.E.F. (eds.) New Perspectives on Information Systems Modeling and Design, Chap. 12, pp. 274–295. IGI-Global (2019). https://doi.org/10.4018/978-1-5225-7271-8.ch012
13. Martínez, J., Romero-Garcés, A., Bandera, J.P., Bandera, A.: Nerve: a lightweight middleware for quality-of-service networked robotics. In: Proceedings of the 8th International Conference on Information Technology: New Generations (ITNG), pp. 655–660 (2011). https://doi.org/10.1109/ITNG.2011.116
14. Martínez, J., Romero-Garcés, A., Bandera, J.P., Marfil, R., Bandera, A.: A DDS-based middleware for quality-of-service and high-performance networked robotics. Concurrency Comput.: Pract. Exp. **24**(16), 1940–1952 (2012). https://doi.org/10.1002/cpe.2816
15. Romero-Garcés, A., Manso, L., Gutiérrez, M.A., Cintas, R., Bustos, P.: Improving the life cycle of robotics components using domain specific languages. In: Proceedings of the 2nd International Workshop on Domain-Specific Languages and models for ROBotic systems (DSLRob 11) (2011). https://arxiv.org/pdf/1301.6022.pdf
16. Sentilles, S.: Managing extra-functional properties in component-based development of embedded systems. Ph.D. thesis, Mälardalen University (2012). ISBN 978-91-7485-067-3
17. Stampfer, D., Lotz, A., Lutz, M., Schlegel, C.: The SmartMDSD Toolchain: an integrated MDSD workflow and integrated development environment (IDE) for robotics software. J. Softw. Eng. Rob.: Spec. Issue Domain-Specif. Lang. Models Rob. **7**(1), 3–19 (2016). http://joser.unibg.it/index.php/joser/article/download/91/33. ISSN 2035-3928
18. Vicente-Chicote, C., et al.: A component-based and model-driven approach to deal with non-functional properties through global QoS metrics. In: Proceedings of the 5th International Workshop on Interplay of Model-Driven and Component-Based Software Engineering (ModComp 2018), in Conjunction with MODELS 2018, pp. 40–45 (2018). http://ceur-ws.org/Vol-2245/modcomp_paper_6.pdf

Machine-Health Application Based on Machine Learning Techniques for Prediction of Valve Wear in a Manufacturing Plant

María-Elena Fernández-García[1]([✉]), Jorge Larrey-Ruiz[1], Antonio Ros-Ros[2], Aníbal R. Figueiras-Vidal[3], and José-Luis Sancho-Gómez[1]

[1] Tecnologías de la Información y las Comunicaciones, Universidad Politécnica de Cartagena, 30202 Cartagena, Spain
`elena.fdez.ga@gmail.com`
[2] Iberian Lube Base Oils Company, S.A., 30350 Cartagena, Spain
[3] Teoría de la Señal y las Comunicaciones, Universidad Carlos III de Madrid, 28911 Madrid, Spain

Abstract. The wear of mechanical components and its eventual failure in manufacturing plants, results in companies spending time and resources that, if not scheduled with predictive or preventive maintenance, can lead to production deviation or loss with dire consequences. Nonetheless, current modern plants are frequently highly monitored and automated, generating great quantities of data from a variety of sensors and actuators. Using this raw data, Machine Learning (ML) techniques can be implemented to achieve predictive maintenance. In this work, a method to predict and estimate the wear of a valve using the data related to an opening valve in Iberian Lube Base Oils Company, S.A. (ILBOC) is proposed. The dataset has been built from sensor data in the plant and formatted to use with Tensorflow package in Python. Then a Multi-Layer Perceptron (MLP) neural network is used to predict and estimate the ideal behavior of the valve without wear and a Recurrent Neural Network (RNN) to predict the real behavior of the valve with wear. Comparing both predictions an estimation of the valve wear is realized. Finally, this work closes with a discussion on an early alert system to schedule and plan the replacement of the valve, conclusions and future research.

Keywords: Recurrent networks · Machine-health · Regression · Neural networks · Prediction

1 Introduction

Nowadays, modern manufacturing plants have achieved a high level of automation parallel to their monitoring capabilities, leading to unprecedented quantities of data from sensors, actuators and other sources being stored and available for

© Springer Nature Switzerland AG 2019
J. M. Ferrández Vicente et al. (Eds.): IWINAC 2019, LNCS 11487, pp. 389–398, 2019.
https://doi.org/10.1007/978-3-030-19651-6_38

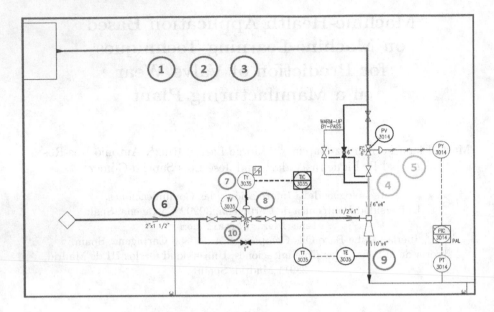

Fig. 1. Refrigeration circuit scheme of the plant.

use [1]. In this context, the correct assessment of the data plays a critical role in implementing predictive or preventive maintenance of components and pieces by the companies [2,3]. Likewise, Machine Learning (ML) techniques are evolving with these data growing times thanks to the increased process power of current computers. Taking advantage of the largely available data from manufacturing plants, ML can help achieve the implantation of predictive maintenance [4].

In this work, data from the manufacturing plant of Iberian Lube Base Oils Company, S.A. (ILBOC) located in Cartagena (Spain) is used as an example of ML techniques application in order to predict valve wear. The proposed method could similarly be applied for assessment of wear or deterioration over time in other components. The valve in question is part of a water temperature regulation system, shown in Fig. 1, from which the following signals are available for its study:

1. P_3054_1: Input water pressure
2. T_3054_2: Input water temperature
3. F_3054_3: Input water flow
4. P_3014_4: Reduced water pressure by intermediate valve 3014
5. O_3014_5: Opening of intermediate valve 3014
6. T_3052_6: Refrigerating water temperature
7. M_3035_7: Operation mode of valve 3035
8. S_3035_8: Output temperature set point
9. T_3035_9: Output water temperature
10. O_3035_10: Opening of the valve 3035.

The refrigeration system receives a certain "high pressure" steam flow (F_3054_3) from refinery with a certain temperature (T_3054_2) and pressure (P_3054_1). Afterwards, the steam pressure needs to be reduced to "medium pressure" and to a lower temperature. First, the pressure regulating valve (PV3014) reduces the output pressure (P_3014_4) by changing its opening (O_3014_5). Then, lower temperature water (T_3052_6) is injected by valve 3035, reducing the output steam temperature (T_3035_9). The flow of injected water is proportional to the opening of valve 3035 (O_3035_10) set by a Proportional Integral Derivative (PID) controller with output temperature (T_3035_9) y and set point (S_3035_8) as inputs.

In this dataset, the effects of valve wear can only be found in the opening of valve 3035 signal (O_3035_10). With time, for a set value of opening, the wear causes an increase in the flow across valve 3035, thus the PID controlling the valve orders the valve to reduce the opening to maintain a set output water temperature. The effect of valve wear is a reduced opening to keep the same water flow across the valve.

2 Methodology

In order to obtain a model to predict the wear of the valve, a prediction of the opening of valve 3035 signal (O_3035_10) is required. First, an MLP neural network (NN) is designed and trained to predict the opening of Valve 3035 in the ideal condition of no wear as described in Sect. 2.1 [5,6]. Second, an RNN model is designed and trained to predict the same opening of Valve 3035, although, this time, for real working conditions where wear is expected to increasingly affect the opening of the valve over time, as per Sect. 2.2. Both predictions are then used to predict and model valve wear in Sect. 2.3.

On assessment of the data, M_3035_7 always has the same value, thus it is discarded. The units and magnitude ranges are diverse for each variable, requiring normalization. After cleaning the dataset, removing undefined and corrupted data, all signals are transform with standard normalization to have zero mean and standard deviation of 1, as in Eq. 1.

$$X'_j = \frac{X_j - \mu_j}{\sigma_j} \tag{1}$$

where X_j is the original value of the j-th characteristic, X'_j the standardized value and μ_j and σ_j the mean and standard deviation of that characteristic respectively.

Prior to the design of the MLP and RNN, Principal Component Analysis (PCA) is performed to reduce and optimize the dimensional space of the inputs to both NN [7]. Afterwards, for each instant t_n, the input vector $\mathbf{x}(t_n)$ is built by averaging M previous time blocks of Δt duration, for each one of the N principal components, thus resulting in an input vector $\mathbf{x}(t_n)$ of length $N \cdot M$ for each instant t_n. The selected values are $M = 10$ and $\Delta t = 6$ h.

2.1   Prediction of Ideal Behavior Without Valve Wear

An MLP NN is trained to predict the opening of Valve 3035 using only data where the valve does not present wear or it is negligible, corresponding with the periods of time just after maintenance of the valve. This way, the prediction will show the opening that Valve 3035 should have under ideal conditions of no wear.

The target is opening signal O_3035_10 and the rest of the variables are inputs to the MLP, except for the discarded M_3035_7.

2.2   Prediction of Real Behavior with Valve Wear

Recurrent Neural Networks achieve good results on time series datasets, where the instant value of a variable is not only dependent on the instant values of the other variables, but it is also conditioned to previous values [8]. Of such nature is valve wear, which affects the opening of Valve 3035 increasingly over time.

The RNN is trained to predict the opening of Valve 3035 with data from the whole life cycle of the valve. This way, the output will show a prediction of the estimated opening value of Valve 3035 under real conditions of wear.

All variables, except for the discarded M_3035_7, are inputs to the RNN and opening signal O_3035_10 is the target. This time O_3035_10 is also included as input, so that the recurrent machine can learn to predict the wear effect on the opening of the valve from current opening values.

2.3   Prediction of Valve Wear

A prediction of valve wear is estimated by combining the predictions of Valve 3035 opening under ideal conditions without wear from Sect. 2.1 and under real conditions with wear from Sect. 2.2. For this purpose, valve wear is calculated as cumulative difference between both K-day predictions, where K is the number of days in the future of the prediction. In this manner, an K-day prediction of valve wear is achieved.

3   Results

The results bellow were achieved following the criteria and methods described in Sect. 2.

3.1   Prediction of Ideal Valve Opening with MLP

Performing PCA for a data variability representation over 95% results in a reduction to 6 principal components from the original 8 variables. As described in Sect. 2, the input is built using 10 previous time averages for each component and instant, producing an input vector $\mathbf{x}(t_n)$ of dimension 60 to the MLP for each sample t_n. The target output $\mathbf{d}(t_n)$ for each input sample $\mathbf{x}(t_n)$ consists of the average value of O_3035_10 during the following 24 h to instant t_n, 7 days after t_n and 14 days after t_n, so that $\mathbf{d}(t_n)$ has dimension 3. The MLP is trained with the first 2/7 of the samples from the valve life cycle, corresponding to the time when the valve wear can be considered negligible, so that the MLP predicts the opening of the valve considering no wear is present. The samples are then divided into three sets: training, validation and test randomly distributed in 60%, 20% and 20% proportions respectively.

The MLP designed has input size 60, output size 3 and a single hidden layer of size 50 selected by Cross Validation (CV) of the validation error for MLP models with hidden layer sizes from 10 to 60 nodes. The learning algorithm of the MLP is Conjugate Gradient Descend (CGD) for Backpropagation and the optimization function is Mean Square Error (MSE). Over 30 simulations, the MLP model achieves MSE of mean 0.011 and standard deviation 0.004 for the test set. The predictions after the first 2/7 of the valve life cycle start to increasingly deviate from the real opening value as expected, meaning that the valve wear increases with time. Figure 2 shows the 1, 7 and 14 day prediction of the valve opening for a full valve life cycle.

3.2 Prediction of Real Valve Opening with RNN

Similar to the design of the previous MLP NN, PCA is perform for a data variability representation over 95%, reducing to 7 the dimension from the original 9 variables. Using the same method as described in Sect. 2, the input is built using 10 previous time averages for each component and instant, producing an input vector $\mathbf{x}(t_n)$ of dimension 70 to the RNN for each sample t_n. The target output $\mathbf{d}(t_n)$ for each input sample $\mathbf{x}(t_n)$ consists of the average value of O_3035_10 during the following 24 h to instant t_n, 7 days after t_n and 14 days after t_n, so that $\mathbf{d}(t_n)$ has dimension 3. This time the training is not limited to the first samples of the valve life cycle where valve wear can be considered negligible, instead the full cycle is used dividing the samples into three sets: training, validation and test randomly distributed in 60%, 20% and 20% proportions respectively.

The RNN has input size 70, output size 3 and a single layer of 60 Gated Recurrent Units (GRU) [9]. The number of GRU has been selected by Cross Validation (CV) of the validation error on RNN models from 15 to 70 GRU. The learning algorithm used is Backpropagation with "RMSprop", a mini-batch Stochastic Gradient Descend (SGD) based algorithm [10], and the optimization function is Mean Square Error (MSE). Over 30 simulations, the RNN model achieves MSE of mean 0.013 and standard deviation 0.005 for the test set. All predictions achieve a good fit of the real opening during the valve life cycle. Figure 3 shows the 1, 7 and 14 day prediction of the valve opening for a full valve life cycle.

3.3 Prediction of Valve Wear Results

In order to achieve an K-day prediction of valve wear, a method is proposed using K-day predictions of ideal valve opening and real valve opening from Sects. 3.1

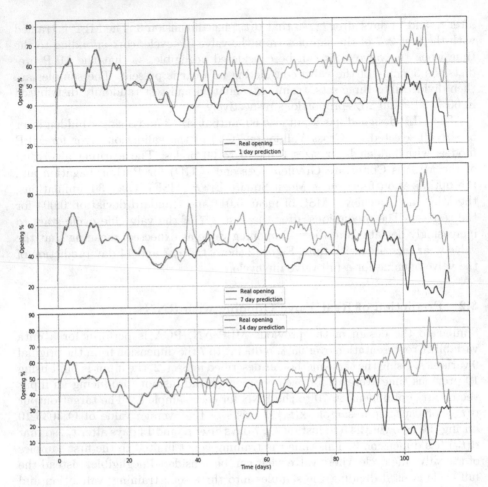

Fig. 2. Result of MLP 1, 7 and 14 day prediction (orange line) of Valve 3035 opening under ideal conditions of no wear, compared to the real opening (blue line) value at the time, for a full valve life cycle. (Color figure online)

and 3.2. Combining these results, valve wear can be expressed as the cumulative difference between ideal and real valve opening prediction calculated as in Eq. 2.

$$VW = \frac{\int_0^t \mathbf{y}'_{\mathbf{ideal}}(t) - \mathbf{y}'_{\mathbf{real}}(t)dt}{t_{end}} \qquad (2)$$

where $\mathbf{y}'_{\mathbf{ideal}}(t)$ is the prediction of ideal valve opening with no wear, $\mathbf{y}'_{\mathbf{real}}(t)$ the prediction of real valve opening, and being t_{end} a normalization term whose value is the end time of the curves.

Accordingly, Fig. 4 shows valve wear for 1, 7 and 14 day predictions where, in the last third of the cycle, the gradient of 7 and 14 day prediction curves accuse

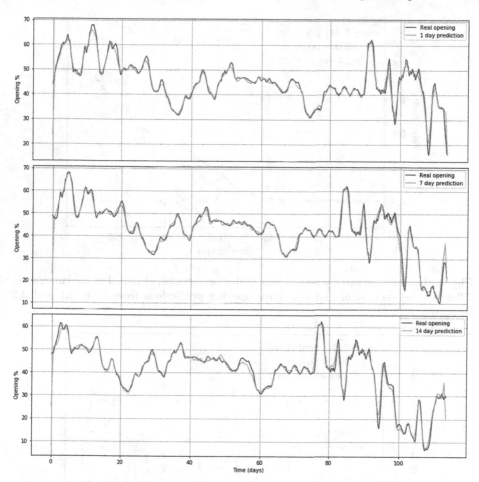

Fig. 3. Result of RNN 1, 7 and 14 day prediction (orange line) of Valve 3035 opening under real conditions of wear, compared to the real opening (blue line) value at the time, for a full valve life cycle. (Color figure online)

a strong increase. This is a clear marker of the start of severe valve wear, hence planning the maintenance of the valve should start from this moment.

Through the assessment of these predictive curves of valve wear, an idea to establish an alarm system of thresholds apprising the valve status arises, such as, if the 1-day prediction curve shows the effects of wear, yet the rest of the predictions do not show any indications of significant wear, it can be concluded that it is a false alarm. The main ideas for the design of this wear alarm system are:

1. Establishing the required time span needed for prediction of valve wear that allow to act sufficiently in advance.

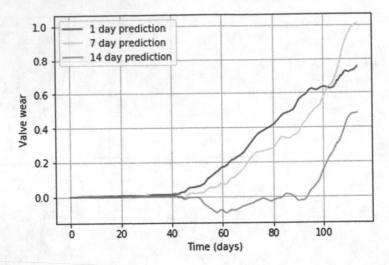

Fig. 4. Result of the valve wear 1, 7 and 14 day predictions, obtained as the cumulative difference between ideal and real valve opening predictions from Sects. 3.1 and 3.2 respectively.

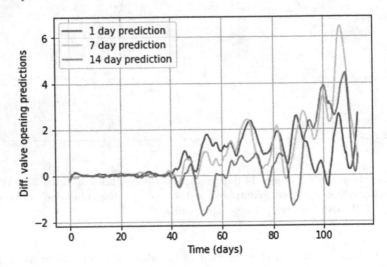

Fig. 5. Instant difference between ideal and real valve opening 1, 7 and 14 day predictions from Sects. 3.1 and 3.2 respectively.

2. Set the characteristics (absolute values, differential increases, etc.) for the alarm thresholds from each of the valve wear prediction curves.
3. Design a system that designates the probability, severity and immediacy of valve wear considering the previous points.

As mentioned before, the gradient of the longer-term valve wear prediction curves, can clearly show the effects of wear in the valve operation. Additionally, it is suggested to use the instant difference between ideal and real valve opening predictions to determine the relative severity of the wear, as represented on Fig. 5 where the difference value in the last third of the valve life cycle increase with respect to previous values, especially for 7 and 14 day longer term predictions. Instant difference and cumulative difference could be jointly studied to assess the presence and severity of the wear. Nonetheless, this idea needs of further exploration.

4   Conclusions

A method to predict wear of a valve component in ILBOC manufacturing plant has been introduced. Firstly, an MLP NN has been designed to predict the behavior of the valve under ideal conditions of negligible wear effect, training the model only with samples of periods when the valve was recently maintained. Afterwards, an RNN is trained on the whole valve life cycle to predict the real behavior of the valve with wear. Both models successfully comply with their assigned task, and their predictions are used to accomplish the prediction of valve wear itself as the cumulative difference between both ideal and real valve opening predictions. Finally, the design of an alarm system which uses thresholds to determine the presence and severity of Valve 3035 wear was proposed, based on the previous prediction of wear. This alarm system is in early stages of development and in need of further study on future works. Likewise, the prediction of valve wear could be used to predict the remaining life of the valve, in terms of percentage or number of days until total failure, for a clearer and more comprehensible way of assessing the valve wear.

Acknowledgments. Thanks to ILBOC and Fundación Séneca for supporting and funding this research work. This work has been partially supported by Spanish National projects AES2017- PI17/00771 and AES2017-PI17/00821 (Instituto de Salud Carlos III).

References

1. Obitko, M., Jirkovský, V., Bezdíček, J.: Big data challenges in industrial automation. In: Mařík, V., Lastra, J.L.M., Skobelev, P. (eds.) HoloMAS 2013. LNCS (LNAI), vol. 8062, pp. 305–316. Springer, Heidelberg (2013). https://doi.org/10.1007/978-3-642-40090-2_27
2. Swanson, L.: Linking maintenance strategies to performance. Int. J. Prod. Econ. **70**(3), 237–244 (2001). https://doi.org/10.1016/S0925-5273(00)00067-0
3. Luxhøj, J.T., Riis, J.O., Thorsteinsson, U.: Trends and perspectives in industrial maintenance management. J. Manuf. Syst. **16**(6), 437–453 (1997). https://doi.org/10.1016/S0278-6125(97)81701-3
4. Monostori, L.: AI and machine learning techniques for managing complexity, changes and uncertainties in manufacturing. Eng. Appl. Artif. Intell. - Intell. Manuf. **16**(4), 277–291 (2003). https://doi.org/10.1016/S0952-1976(03)00078-2

5. Rosenblatt, F.: Principles of Neurodynamics. Perceptrons and the theory of Brain Mechanisms. Cornell Aeronautical Lab Inc., Buffalo (1961)
6. Rumelhart, D.E., Hinton, G.E., Williams, R.J.: Learning internal representations by error propagation. CALIFORNIA University San Diego, La Jolla, Institute for Cognitive Science (1985)
7. Lovric, M. (ed.): International Encyclopedia of Statistical Science. Springer, Heidelberg (2011). https://doi.org/10.1007/978-3-642-04898-2
8. Connor, J., Atlas, L.: Recurrent neural networks and time series prediction. In: IJCNN-91-Seattle International Joint Conference on Neural Networks, vol. 1, pp. 301–306 (1991). https://doi.org/10.1109/IJCNN.1991.155194
9. Cho, K., et al.: Learning phrase representations using RNN encoder-decoder for statistical machine translation (2014). http://arxiv.org/abs/1406.1078
10. Hinton, G.E.: Lecture 6.5-RMSprop: divide the gradient by a running average of its recent magnitude (2012). https://www.cs.toronto.edu/~tijmen/csc321/slides/lecture_slides_lec6.pdf

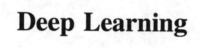

Deep Learning

Artificial Semantic Memory with Autonomous Learning Applied to Social Robots

Francisco Martin-Rico[1(✉)], Francisco Gomez-Donoso[2], Felix Escalona[2], Miguel Cazorla[2], and Jose Garcia-Rodriguez[2]

[1] University Rey Juan Carlos, Madrid, Spain
francisco.rico@urjc.es
[2] University of Alicante, Alicante, Spain
{fgomez,fescalona,miguel.cazorla,jgr}@ua.es

Abstract. Semantic memory stores knowledge about the meanings of words and the relationships between these meanings. In recent years, Artificial Intelligence, in particular Deep Learning, has successfully resolved the identification of classes of elements in images, and even instances of a class, providing a basic form of semantic memory. Unfortunately, incorporating new instances of a class requires a complex and long process of labeling and offline training. We are convinced that the combination of convolutional networks and statistical classifiers allows us to create a long-term semantic memory that is capable of learning online. To validate this hypothesis, we have implemented a long-term semantic memory in a social robot. The robot initially only recognizes people, but, after interacting with different people, is able to distinguish them from each other. The advantage of our approach is that the process of long-term memorization is done autonomously without the need for offline processing.

Keywords: People recognition · Pose estimation · Social robotics

1 Introduction

Nowadays, social assistant robots have become a way of improving people's quality of life in modern societies by performing domestic tasks. Life expectancy is in continuous growth, causing an increase in the average age of the population. For this reason, the assistance of elderly people becomes a priority for developed countries, which consider social robot assistance as a good initiative for helping dependent persons. This technological approach provides an alternative to the use of qualified human personnel, reducing economic costs in the long term.

We have come to the conclusion that memory is important for a social robot, understood as the ability of a robot to recognize objects within the same class, or a person from another. Let's focus from now on in this paper on the recognition of people, being applicable in the same way to objects. The process by

© Springer Nature Switzerland AG 2019
J. M. Ferrández Vicente et al. (Eds.): IWINAC 2019, LNCS 11487, pp. 401–411, 2019.
https://doi.org/10.1007/978-3-030-19651-6_39

which the robot acquires this knowledge is also important. Neural networks or similar classification systems have reached a level of maturity such that distinguishing people is considered solved. The problem is that the process by which this capability is acquired using these techniques requires an offline process of data collection, labeling, training of a model and deployment in the system.

In this paper we propose a memory model that learns to distinguish people during their operation. The system will initially only be able to recognize if what is in front of it is a person. Using the interaction capabilities of the robot, you can indicate to the system which person it is. The more you interact with this person, the better you will distinguish them from other people. The goal is for a robot to learn during its operation to distinguish some people from others, similar to what humans do, so that the more the robot interacts with them, the better he will recognize them. The advantage of this approach is obvious: interaction is a way of supervising fast learning by reinforcement.

An application could be a social robot that develops its activity autonomously in a residential environment. Our approach would allow the robot to customize its action on each of the patients. In the first interactions he would ask the person who he is, in the following he would ask for confirmation that he is the person recognized, and in later interactions no confirmation would be necessary. The robot could ask the patient about questions about their city, family, or show photos or play songs that could have been configured by a therapist previously for each individual.

The robotic competitions also provide a good stage to test our work. Competitions, such as RoboCup, present a problem and a common scenario where research groups from around the world apply and contrast their research. We participate in the RoboCup SSPL @ Home, in which a social robot must carry out a series of missions in a domestic environment to help a dependent person in their daily life. In one of the tests the robot must follow a person out of the house to help her unload the car. The robot must learn the person to follow in less than 15 s to a person (the referee of the test), without confusing it with any person that can detect during the follow-up. Our hope is that our system will be able to address this problem without problems, since our system is not based on recognizing its face, but its entire appearance, since the face is not visible when it is on the side during tracking.

The rest of the paper is organized as follows. Firstly, Sect. 2 analyzes the state of the art of person identification in videos based on people activity. Next, Sect. 3 provides an in-depth description of our proposal. After that, Sect. 4 is devoted to the experimentation we carried out with our system and to the corresponding discussion. Then, limitations of the system are stated in Sect. 5. At last, Sect. 6 draws conclusions about our work and presents possible future research directions.

2   Related Works

The most technical approaches to memory implementations are centered representations of the world where knowledge about the elements of the environment is maintained, together with values that indicate its reliability or accuracy. In [3] an anchoring system is presented, where each element has a reliability value associated with it, which depends on when an element has been perceived. In [22] reliability in the knowledge of an object is also associated to the time when this perception is obtained, but adding semantic relations between the elements of memory. A similar approach is presented in [16], although it focuses on the learning of elements in memory.

Biologically inspired approaches try to emulate totally or partially the mental processes that are attributed to human beings to maintain a memory. The separation between long-term, short-term, or episodic memories [5] is common in these approaches. In [10] the short-term memory focuses on the stimuli relevant to the current task, while the long-term memory contains episodic events that are derived from the interaction between a robot and a human. This type of long-term memories that remember episodes are discussed in depth in [21]. The concept of Working Memory [17,20] is applied to robots in an attempt to provide a robot with biologically inspired cognitive abilities. Our approach is among the short-term memories, being its biological approach inspired by the process of information acquisition, based on neural networks.

In the rest of the section, we present a brief analysis of the state-of-the-art methods on person re-identification based on its activity. People re-identification in videos is a challenging problem but it also promises a huge potential for a wide range of applications mainly related with security and surveillance and health care or human-machine interaction [6].

An automated re-identification mechanism takes as input either tracks or bounding boxes containing segmented images of individual persons, as generated by a localised tracking or detection process of a visual surveillance system. To automatically match people at different locations over time, a re identification process typically takes the following steps: 1. Extracting imagery features; 2. Constructing a descriptor or representation capable of both describing and discriminating individuals; 3. Matching specified probe images or tracks against a gallery of persons in another camera view by measuring the similarity between the images.

A classical taxonomy classify recognition methods as: singleshot when only one image pair is used or, Multishot when two sets of images are employed. Respect to the learning approach, they are categorized as a supervised method if prior to application, it exploits labelled samples for tuning model parameters. Otherwise a method is consider as an unsupervised approach and no training data is used to train the system.

In recent years, deep learning techniques surpassed classical methods in most of the computer vision challenges [11]. However, these models suffer from the lack of training data samples. The reason is that most of the available datasets provide only two images per each individual [7] that makes the model fail at test time due to overfitting. In this line, a number of new datasets has been proposed to solve this problem. Some of them based on images: Market1501 [24], CUHK03

[14], DukeMTMC-reID [26]. And others based on video: MARS [25], iLIDS-VID [23] or PRID2011 [9].

Some recent works using DL models include works like [1] that propose a deep convolutional architecture with layers specially designed to address the problem of re-identification. In [2] they learn multi-scale person appearance features using Convolutional Neural Networks (CNN) by aiming to jointly learn discriminative scale-specific features and maximize multi-scale feature fusion selections in image pyramid input. In [13] it is proposed a Tracklet Association Unsupervised Deep Learning (TAUDL) framework characterised by jointly learning per-camera (within-camera) tracklet association (labelling) and cross-camera tracklet correlation by maximizing the discovery of most likely tracklet relationships across camera views. Some approaches employ Graph deep neural networks like [19] that propose a novel deep learning framework, named Similarity-Guided Graph Neural Network (SGGNN). Given a probe image and several gallery images, SGGNN creates a graph to represent the pairwise relationships between pro be gallery pairs (nodes) and utilizes such relationships to update the probe gallery relation features in an end-to-end manner.

Our approach proposed combines deep learning architectures trained with our own dataset with feature extraction techniques.

Some previous work create a framework to combine different visual features [12] with a similar approach proposed in our work but our DL-based model achieve better results.

3   Person Identification Memory System Description

The aim of the proposal, which we named PIMS (Person Identification Memory System), is to provide an accurate real-time person identifier that could learn and memorize new persons on the fly for social robotics tasks. To do so, we relied on an ensemble of deep learning methods and traditional classifiers.

The deep learning based architectures provide outstanding detection and recognition capabilities. Nonetheless, these methods require high amounts of training time. On the other hand, traditional classifiers perform poorer in terms of accuracy, but they can be trained a lot faster. We used each method so we take advantage of their strengths while balancing their weaknesses.

The PIMS architecture is shown in Fig. 1. First, at training time, the user shows himself in front of the camera. For each frame, a Detector is used to locate the person. The Detector of choice in our approach is YOLO v3 [18]. This system consists in a region convolutional neural network that is able to predict the location of the persons in the image plane, namely, it returns the area of interest (AOI) of each person in the input image. Actually, it can detected several kind of objects, but as we are only interested in persons, the rest of the objects are simply ignored. Then, the AOI is cropped from the input frame and forwarded to a modified ResNet50 [8]. This architecture is a state-of-the-art convolutional neural network mainly intended for classification tasks. Nonetheless, we removed the last fully connected layer so it is no longer used classification but for Feature

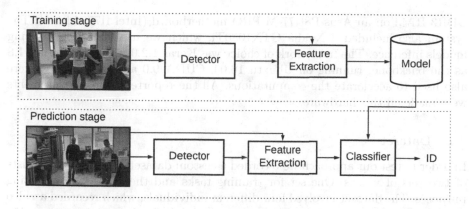

Fig. 1. Diagram of the proposal. At training stage, a model is created by gathering labeled data. At prediction stage, this model is used to perform classification. It is worth noting that this architecture is replicated in the final version of our approach: one for full body person identification and one for face-only person identification.

Extraction. Thus, the output of the network is a feature vector of 2048 values. This vector is then labeled with the identification of the person and inserted in the Model of the Classifier. The label is known as this is performed at training time.

Once the training stage is done and the model has been created, it can be used to predict the identification of the person. The pipeline is barely the same as in the training stage. An image is captured from a camera. Then, the Detector is used to infer the AOI of the persons and each AOI is forwarded through the Feature Extraction architecture. Finally, the nearest neighbor is searched in the beforehand created Model using the implementation of the approximate K-Nearest Neighbors algorithm provided by Annoy[1].

The PIMS approach is very fast to train as the training samples are inserted in a nearest neighbor model and there is no need to retrain the deep learning models. In addition, it is quite accurate as it takes advantage of deep learning architectures for detection and feature extraction. Our pipeline can also learn new classes (unforeseen person ids) without any architectural modifications. In contrast, a pure deep learning approach would require modifications on the last layer and a retraining process.

4   Experimentation

In this section, the experimentation we carried out in order to evaluate and validate our approach is described. In addition, the details of dataset we used are also reported.

It is worth noting that the experiments were carried out using the following setup: Intel Core i5-3570 with 16 GiB of Kingston HyperX 1600 MHz and CL10

---

[1] https://github.com/spotify/annoy.

DDR3 RAM on an Asus P8H77-M PRO motherboard (Intel H77 chipset). The system also included a Nvidia GTX1080Ti, which we used for deep learning models inference. The framework of choice was Keras 1.2.0 with Tensor Flow 1.8 as the backbone, running on Ubuntu 16.04. CUDA 9.0 and cuDNN v7.1 were also used to accelerate the computations. All the reported time measurements were made on this hardware.

4.1 Dataset

In order to test out approach we recorded a custom dataset. The dataset consists of two sets of videos. One set for training tasks and the other set for testing purposes. The dataset involved four different individuals, which recorded a video for training and one more for testing purposes each. In the training videos, the subjects showed themselves by turning 360° for 10 s. In the testing videos, they unconstrained and spontaneous moved around the scene. Each testing video has a duration of 20 s. The participants only received one command in this case, which was "walk around the room". An additional testing video was recorded depicting three of the individuals spontaneously walking around the scene and interacting between them. This last video was used for qualitative evaluation while the rest were used for quantitative benchmarking. In total, the dataset contained 9 different videos. It is worth noting that the dataset tries to imitate the conditions presented in the RoboCup SSPL @ Home test we mentioned before.

All the videos were recorded by a 12 MPx color camera at 1080p resolution and 30 fps. The camera also featured optical stabilization.

In the experiments, we used all four training videos to build the models. Then, these models, which can identify 4 different individuals, are used to perform inference on the test videos. As the test videos only depicts one person, it is straightforward to know if the system performed accurately or not.

4.2 Person Identification System Experiments

This set of experiments involved full body person identification. The Detector, which based on YOLO, runs a model trained on the COCO MS [15] dataset as provided by the original author. This model is able to predict AOIs of different objects but as we only are interested in persons the rest of the predictions are ignored. The feature extraction network is based on ResNet50, which we used with a model trained on the ImageNet [4] dataset as provided by the Keras framework.

For the first experiment, we sampled the training videos by performing frame skipping. We tested our approach ranging the frame skipping parameter from 0 (all frames are used) to 10 (around 30 frames remained from each training video). The results are as shown in Fig. 2.

As the results show, the accuracy is kept around 95% regardless the frame skipping parameter. Despite the model containing fewer samples as the frame skipping is increased, the accuracy is not dropping. This is because the model has

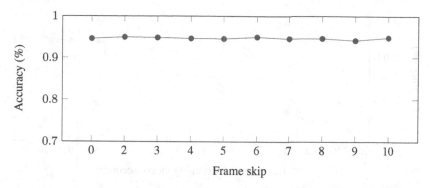

Fig. 2. Accuracy results for the testing videos by ranging the training videos frame skip from 0 to 10.

Fig. 3. Random results of our approach with the bounding box and the predicted identification of the person superimposed. Boxes and texts in green mean a hit while texts in magenta are the predictions for the frames that have no ground truth (in this case, the additional video that depicted multiple individuals interacting). The model for these results was generated using the full duration of the training videos with no frame skip. Note that the identification is accurate even in unconsidered poses. (Color figure online)

enough semantic information in every case. As mentioned earlier, the training videos consist of the individuals completely showing themselves. By sampling them at a fixed frame skipping value, the model is able to capture the features for each pose, thus leading to high accuracy rates. It is worth noting that the model generated for frame skipping equal to 10 only contains 30 samples for each individual. Random samples with the predictions superimposed are shown in Fig. 3 for qualitative evaluation.

We also tested the amount of time the training stage needs to gather images to perform accurately. This is a testing methodology nearer to a real world deployment, as the system is likely to have training time limitations. For instance, in the RoboCup SSPL @ Home test we mentioned earlier in Sect. 1, there is a limitation of 15 s. In this experiment, we simply limited the duration of the training videos from 10 s (no time limit, full duration of the videos) to 0.03 s (only the first frame for each training video). Results for this experiment are shown in Fig. 4.

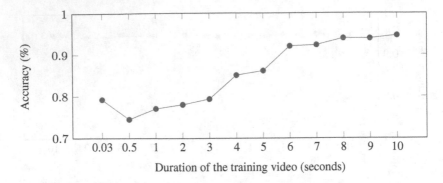

Fig. 4. Accuracy results for the testing videos by ranging the duration of the training videos from 0.03 to 10 s.

As expected, this time the accuracy drops as the number of frames contained in the model is decreased. In this case, the expressiveness of the training samples is way more reduced than in the other experiment, thus, producing an accuracy drop. As the exposure time is reduced, so is the variability of the visual features of the individuals present in the model.

Fig. 5. In both images the PIS failed due to high occlusion issues. Boxes and texts in red mean a miss while texts in magenta are the predictions for the frames that have no ground truth (in this case, the additional video that depicted multiple individuals interacting) (Color figure online)

A more in-depth analysis of the results revealed that this approach tends to fail when the body of the person is highly occluded, or the poses yielded by the users in the test stage differs significantly from those contained in the training data. In addition, the system also fails when the person is not detected at all by the person detector. Figure 5 depicts some failure cases in which the person is not correctly identified. In addition, it can be concluded that the accuracy of the model is independent of the number of samples. Instead, the accuracy is supported by a correct representation of the possibilities, so it is better to have in the model fewer samples, but with more variability than a lot of samples that are highly similar between them.

Finally, it is worth noting that a single inference step through the entire pipeline only takes 74.85 ms mean with one person, which means around 13.5 frames per second. The person detector (YOLO) takes 57.13 ms mean and is independent of the number of detections. The feature extraction (modified ResNet50) takes 16.54 ms mean and is linearly dependent of the number of persons. The rest of the time is occupied by the classifier, which is around 2 ms mean.

5   Limitations

Despite the high accuracy in the test scenario, our approach has some limitations. For instance, it is highly dependent of the visual features present in the training data. This makes that if the person is not properly represented in the model, the system is likely to fail. This reason also makes the system fail under high occlusion scenarios. Even if the AOI of the person is correctly detected, the visual features would depict the object occluding the person, leading to an eventual error.

Another limitation of the PIS is that it will produce a prediction for each person in the scene. This implies that if the input image depicts persons that are not represented in the model, the system will regardless try to identify them and assign them the label of the nearest neighbor. In some scenarios this is not a problem anyway. For instance, in the mentioned Robocup SSPL @ Home test, it is known that the referee is always on scene.

6   Conclusion and Future Works

In this work, we present PIS (Person Identification System). It consist of a deep learning-based methods and a classic classifier ensemble for person identification which is fast to train and use. First, a person detection approach is used to detect the area of interest of each person in the scene. Then, each one is cropped and forwarded to a feature extraction architecture which will describe the person. At training time, the feature vectors are inserted in a nearest neighbor model which is then used at inference stage to predict accurate person identifications. According to the experiments we carried out, our approach is able to correctly state the identification of a person in the 95% of the cases with only 10 s of training data.

As a future work, we plan to include a method to state whether the person is unknown or not considered by the model at testing time. Actually, we can currently do this by setting a nearest neighbor distance threshold, but this would be dependent of the model. We intend to accomplish this automatically, with no threshold and independently of the data and model. In addition, we plan to further improve the PIS accuracy by integrating a tracking method. For instance, if a identification in a certain moment differs from the last n predictions, it is likely a failure and it could be corrected.

Acknowledgements. This work has been funded by the Spanish Government TIN2016-76515-R grant for the COMBAHO project, supported with Feder funds. This work has also been supported by a Spanish grant for PhD studies ACIF/2017/243 and FPU16/00887. Thanks also to Nvidia for the generous donation of two Titan Xp and a Quadro P6000.

References

1. Ahmed, E., Jones, M.J., Marks, T.K.: An improved deep learning architecture for person re-identification. In: CVPR, pp. 3908–3916. IEEE Computer Society (2015). http://dblp.uni-trier.de/db/conf/cvpr/cvpr2015.html#AhmedJM15
2. Chen, Y., Zhu, X., Gong, S.: Person re-identification by deep learning multi-scale representations. In: 2017 IEEE International Conference on Computer Vision Workshops, ICCV Workshops 2017, Venice, Italy, 22–29 October 2017, pp. 2590–2600 (2017). https://doi.org/10.1109/ICCVW.2017.304
3. Coradeschi, S., Saffiotti, A.: An introduction to the anchoring problem. Robot. Auton. Syst. **43**(2), 85–96 (2003). http://www.sciencedirect.com/science/article/pii/S0921889003000216. Perceptual Anchoring: Anchoring Symbols to Sensor Data in Single and Multiple Robot Systems
4. Deng, J., Dong, W., Socher, R., Li, L.J., Li, K., Fei-Fei, L.: ImageNet: a large-scale hierarchical image database. In: CVPR 2009 (2009)
5. Dodd, W., Gutierrez, R.: The role of episodic memory and emotion in a cognitive robot. In: ROMAN 2005, IEEE International Workshop on Robot and Human Interactive Communication, pp. 692–697, August 2005
6. Gong, S., Cristani, M., Yan, S., Loy, C.C.: Person Re-Identification. Springer, London (2014). https://doi.org/10.1007/978-1-4471-6296-4
7. Gray, D., Tao, H.: Viewpoint invariant pedestrian recognition with an ensemble of localized features. In: Forsyth, D., Torr, P., Zisserman, A. (eds.) ECCV 2008. LNCS, vol. 5302, pp. 262–275. Springer, Heidelberg (2008). https://doi.org/10.1007/978-3-540-88682-2_21
8. He, K., Zhang, X., Ren, S., Sun, J.: Deep residual learning for image recognition. CoRR abs/1512.03385 (2015). http://arxiv.org/abs/1512.03385
9. Hirzer, M., Beleznai, C., Roth, P.M., Bischof, H.: Person re-identification by descriptive and discriminative classification. In: Heyden, A., Kahl, F. (eds.) SCIA 2011. LNCS, vol. 6688, pp. 91–102. Springer, Heidelberg (2011). https://doi.org/10.1007/978-3-642-21227-7_9
10. Ho, W.C., Dautenhahn, K., Lim, M.Y., Vargas, P.A., Aylett, R., Enz, S.: An initial memory model for virtual and robot companions supporting migration and long-term interaction. In: RO-MAN 2009 - The 18th IEEE International Symposium on Robot and Human Interactive Communication, pp. 277–284, September 2009
11. Lavi, B., Serj, M.F., Ullah, I.: Survey on deep learning techniques for person re-identification task. CoRR abs/1807.05284 (2018). http://arxiv.org/abs/1807.05284
12. Li, M., Shen, F., Wang, J., Guan, C., Tang, J.: Person re-identification with activity prediction based on hierarchical spatial-temporal model. Neurocomputing **275**, 1200–1207 (2018). http://www.sciencedirect.com/science/article/pii/S0925231217315837
13. Li, M., Zhu, X., Gong, S.: Unsupervised person re-identification by deep learning tracklet association. In: Ferrari, V., Hebert, M., Sminchisescu, C., Weiss, Y. (eds.) ECCV 2018. LNCS, vol. 11208, pp. 772–788. Springer, Cham (2018). https://doi.org/10.1007/978-3-030-01225-0_45

14. Li, W., Zhao, R., Xiao, T., Wang, X.: DeepReID: deep filter pairing neural network for person re-identification. In: CVPR, pp. 152–159. IEEE Computer Society (2014)
15. Lin, T., et al.: Microsoft COCO: common objects in context. CoRR abs/1405.0312 (2014). http://arxiv.org/abs/1405.0312
16. Oliveira, M., Lim, G.H., Lopes, L.S., Kasaei, S.H., Tomé, A.M., Chauhan, A.: A perceptual memory system for grounding semantic representations in intelligent service robots. In: 2014 IEEE/RSJ International Conference on Intelligent Robots and Systems, pp. 2216–2223, September 2014
17. Phillips, J., Noelle, D.: Biologically inspired working memory framework for robots. In: Proceedings of the 27th Annual Meeting of the Cognitive Science Society, pp. 1237–1383 (2005)
18. Redmon, J., Farhadi, A.: YOLOv3: an incremental improvement. arXiv (2018)
19. Shen, Y., Li, H., Yi, S., Chen, D., Wang, X.: Person re-identification with deep similarity-guided graph neural network. In: Ferrari, V., Hebert, M., Sminchisescu, C., Weiss, Y. (eds.) ECCV 2018. LNCS, vol. 11219, pp. 508–526. Springer, Cham (2018). https://doi.org/10.1007/978-3-030-01267-0_30
20. Skubic, M., Noelle, D., Wilkes, M., Kawamura, K., M Keller, J.: A biologically inspired adaptive working memory for robots, pp. 1–8, January 2004
21. Stachowicz, D., Kruijff, G.M.: Episodic-like memory for cognitive robots. IEEE Trans. Auton. Ment. Dev. 4(1), 1–16 (2012)
22. Tenorth, M., Beetz, M.: Representations for robot knowledge in the knowrob framework. Artif. Intell. 247, 151–169 (2017). http://www.sciencedirect.com/science/article/pii/S0004370215000843. Special Issue on AI and Robotics
23. Wang, T., Gong, S., Zhu, X., Wang, S.: Person re-identification by video ranking. In: Fleet, D., Pajdla, T., Schiele, B., Tuytelaars, T. (eds.) ECCV 2014. LNCS, vol. 8692, pp. 688–703. Springer, Cham (2014). https://doi.org/10.1007/978-3-319-10593-2_45
24. Zheng, L., Shen, L., Tian, L., Wang, S., Wang, J., Tian, Q.: Scalable person re-identification: a benchmark. In: 2015 IEEE International Conference on Computer Vision (ICCV), pp. 1116–1124, December 2015
25. Zheng, L., et al.: MARS: a video benchmark for large-scale person re-identification, September 2016. https://www.microsoft.com/en-us/research/publication/mars-video-benchmark-large-scale-person-re-identification/
26. Zheng, Z., Zheng, L., Yang, Y.: Unlabeled samples generated by GAN improve the person re-identification baseline in vitro. CoRR abs/1701.07717 (2017)

A Showcase of the Use of Autoencoders in Feature Learning Applications

David Charte[1]([☒]) [iD], Francisco Charte[2] [iD], María J. del Jesus[2] [iD],
and Francisco Herrera[1] [iD]

[1] Andalusian Research Institute in Data Science and Computational Intelligence,
Department of Computer Science and Artificial Intelligence, Universidad de Granada,
Periodista Daniel Saucedo Aranda, s/n, 18071 Granada, Spain
fdavidcl@ugr.es, herrera@decsai.ugr.es
[2] Andalusian Research Institute in Data Science and Computational Intelligence,
Computer Science Department, Universidad de Jaén,
Campus Las Lagunillas, s/n, 23071 Jaén, Spain
{fcharte,mjjesus}@ujaen.es

Abstract. Autoencoders are techniques for data representation learning based on artificial neural networks. Differently to other feature learning methods which may be focused on finding specific transformations of the feature space, they can be adapted to fulfill many purposes, such as data visualization, denoising, anomaly detection and semantic hashing.

This work presents these applications and provides details on how autoencoders can perform them, including code samples making use of an R package with an easy-to-use interface for autoencoder design and training, ruta. Along the way, the explanations on how each learning task has been achieved are provided with the aim to help the reader design their own autoencoders for these or other objectives.

Keywords: Autoencoders · Deep learning · Feature learning

1 Introduction

Autoencoders (AEs) [8] are versatile unsupervised learning methods. Also known as autoassociators, since their first uses their purpose has usually been to transform the input variable space into a more useful one, either one which is more compact, or whose structure is simpler or more convenient. In the last decade, deep learning methods have been gaining use since computing capabilities and optimization methods have improved. As a consequence, the topic of representation learning [2] has attained more interest, and AEs with it.

Nowadays, many variants of AEs [4] have been developed with several applications in mind. These cover from simple dimensionality reduction to instance

D. Charte is supported by the Spanish Ministry of Science, Innovation and Universities under the FPU National Program (Ref. FPU17/04069). This work is supported by the Spanish National Research Projects TIN2015-68854-R and TIN2017-89517-P.

© Springer Nature Switzerland AG 2019
J. M. Ferrández Vicente et al. (Eds.): IWINAC 2019, LNCS 11487, pp. 412–421, 2019.
https://doi.org/10.1007/978-3-030-19651-6_40

generation, data enhancement and hashing. Furthermore, they are not limited to problems with a standard (input, label) structure, but AE models have been defined for many nonstandard learning problems such as multi-view learning or multi-label learning [3,16,17].

In the following sections, AEs as a feature learning tool are described and several different applications are detailed and illustrated with examples. Each example comprises several lines of code which tackle a given task and some graphical output. The complete code samples are available at https://github.com/ari-dasci/autoencoder-showcase.

This document is structured as follows. Section 2 introduces the inner workings of AEs. Section 3.1 shows a simple visualization task, followed by an example on image denoising in Sect. 3.2. Afterwards, Sect. 3.3 describes how to detect anomalous samples with AEs and Sect. 3.4 a way to perform semantic hashing. Last, Sect. 3.5 mentions other possible applications of AEs, and Sect. 4 draws some conclusions.

2   Fundamentals of Autoencoders

AEs are artificial neural networks designed to find an alternative representation of data with some desirable properties. They are generally unsupervised techniques, that is, AEs are usually intended to complete their task without any class information. They are comprised of two distinct components: the encoder and the decoder. Both have interesting outputs: the first provides the encodings for each input instance, and the second obtains a reconstruction of the original instance. The basic objective for an AE consists in finding the parameters that allow to retrieve the most faithful reconstructions.

Figure 1 shows the architecture of a simple AE, where input data is fed into the leftmost layer and the obtained output must match it with as little error as possible. This can be interpreted as a parametrized mapping f_θ which is fitted to the data by minimizing a loss function $\mathcal{J}(\theta) = \sum_x L(x, f_\theta(x))$.

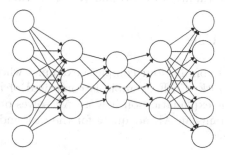

Fig. 1. Typical organization of neurons inside an autoencoder, in this case, for a 2-variable encoding.

A common application of these models is transforming the variable space into a lower-dimensional one, while keeping enough information about samples to accurately recover their values in the original variable space. In this case, AEs can be seen as a nonlinear generalization of principal components analysis [1]. However, they can show much more potential when combined with certain restrictions or modifications.

2.1 Encoded Space Structure

AEs can be altered in order for the encoded variable space to have some desirable structure, or to verify some properties. Following are some viable structures that may be applied to an AE. Among other possibilities, the encoding space can:

- be sparse, i.e. few neurons have a high value for each instance (sparse AE)
- resist distortions present in input data (denoising AE, robust AE)
- preserve local behavior and relative distances from the input space (contractive AE)
- follow a given distribution (adversarial AE)

2.2 Available Software

Any well known deep learning framework may serve as base for the construction of AEs, but very few tools facilitate the design process by abstracting common traits from usual AEs. One of them is R package `ruta` [5], which provides a variety of AE variants, allowing for easy definition, training and usage of these models. The package is available on CRAN and thus can be installed with:

```
install.packages("ruta")
```

The upcoming sections will make use of this software and other libraries in order to provide compact code listings which achieve the different tasks. Other available software packages for the purposes of autoencoder training are: `autoencoder` (R), `h2o` (multiplatform) and `yadlt` (Python).

3 Examples of Use

The following sections contain four complete examples where an AE is used to complete a learning task. Each example is comprised of a description of the tackled problem, some explanation on how an AE solves or can help solve it, a code snippet which trains an AE adequate for the task and some visual results and associated analysis.

3.1 Visualization of High-Dimensional Data

AEs can be arranged so as to produce a two-dimensional or three-dimensional code. This way, encoded instances can be directly represented in a graph. If samples are labeled with classes or target values, this can be used to provide a visual intuition on how these labels are organized.

In the following example, R packages `ruta`, `scatterplot3d` and `colorspace` are loaded. This allows to train an AE which compresses data to a three-dimensional space, extract codifications for the desired dataset and lastly plot them with colors according to their class. The chosen AE has several hidden layers in order to allow it to learn short encodings; the middle layer uses sigmoid activation which limits the codes to the $[0, 1]$ interval.

```
network <- input() + dense(12, activation = "relu") + dense(3,
  activation = "sigmoid") + dense(12, activation = "relu") + output("linear")
model <- autoencoder_sparse(network) %>% train(x_train, epochs = 40)
codes <- model %>% encode(x_train)
scatterplot3d(codes, color = rainbow_hcl(7)[class], (1:7)[class])
```

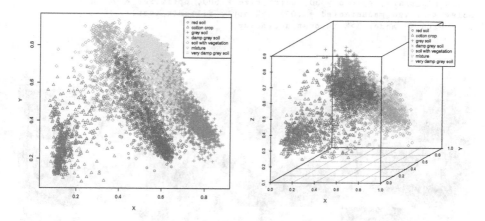

Fig. 2. Two and three-dimensional projections of the 36-variable dataset Statlog.

Figure 2 shows the result of running this code on the 36-dimensional dataset Statlog (Landsat Satellite) [6], where each instance represents a small patch of land and is labeled with the type of land associated to the central pixel. Although the graph shows some fairly separated instance clusters, it is important to remark that the AE receives no class information and thus it can be assumed that the input features also present some degree of class separation.

3.2 Image Denoising

Since AEs are not only trained to transform the variable space but also to reconstruct the original one, a specific strategy can be used so that the reconstruction process eliminates distortions or noise [18]. AEs that are trained this way are usually called denoising AEs.

For the purposes of image denoising, a convolutional AE can be used. Bidimensional convolutional layers [7] help models take advantage of the structure of images to reduce the number of parameters. The architecture of this AE does not need to reduce the dimension of the input data in the encoding layer. Instead, it is possible to increase the dimension in order for it to be able to discern useful information from noise.

In this case, a very simple architecture has been used: one convolutional layer with an upsampling operation, another one with a max-pooling operation (to decrease the dimension) and an output convolutional layer with as many filters as channels in the data. The last layer uses a sigmoid activation because the inputs are normalized to the $[0, 1]$ interval. This AE has been trained and tested with the CIFAR10 dataset included in Keras.

```
network <- input() + conv(16, 3, upsampling=2, activation="relu") + conv(16,
    3, max_pooling=2, activation="relu") + conv(3, 3, activation="sigmoid")
model <- autoencoder_denoising(network, loss = "binary_crossentropy",
  noise_type = "gaussian", sd = .05) %>%
  train(x_train, epochs = 30, batch_size = 500, optimizer = "adam")
noisy <- noise_gaussian(sd = .05) %>% apply_filter(x_test)
recovered <- model %>% reconstruct(noisy)
```

Fig. 3. Image denoising. First row shows original test samples, second row displays the noisy images fed to the AE, and third row shows reconstructed images.

The listing above also shows a way of introducing noise to the test subset and reconstructing it by means of the trained model. Figure 3 shows a sample of the obtained results drawn by means of the grid package: each test image, previously unseen by the AE, is joined by its noisy version, which is fed to the trained model, and the reconstructed version, obtained at the output of the AE.

3.3 Anomaly Detection

The encoded variable space generated by an AE usually omits information that is common to most or all instances, since the objective of an AE is to produce precise reconstructions while retaining only necessary information. Any traits present in all samples can be easily learned and recovered by the decoder, so that they do not need to be encoded. This means that, in the case that a new instance is very different from those of the training set, its reconstruction by the AE will predictably lose information and produce a high error. In these scenarios, AEs can serve as anomaly detectors [12,13]. This is especially useful when treating time series that may have abnormal regions, since detecting single examples based just on their reconstruction can be more challenging.

The following code trains a very simple denoising AE with a 16-variable encoding, and then measures the individual error made for each instance. The reason a denoising AE has been chosen in this case is that it can indirectly find lower dimensional manifolds in the data, and attempt to push instances to those when decoding. Thus, anomalous samples far from the manifold should stand out more when measuring the error.

```
model <- autoencoder_denoising(input() + dense(16, "sigmoid") + output()) %>%
    train(x_train, epochs = 50, batch_size = 32)
errors <- rowMeans((model %>% reconstruct(x_test) - x_test) ** 2)
```

The AE above has been trained with a synthetic multi-valued time series based on samples from a solution to a Lorenz system, following the experimentation in [13]. An anomalous region has been artificially introduced within the test subset. The reconstruction error has been measured for each test instance, and the results are shown in the plot in Fig. 4: anomalies present much higher errors in general, which can be used to detect that region.

3.4 Semantic Hashing

Semantic hashing [8] is a task consisting on finding short binary codes for data points so that codes with small Hamming distance correspond to similar samples, and those separated by a high Hamming distance belong to very different points.

An AE can produce encodings in the range $[0, 1]$ when the encoding layer has a sigmoid activation function. This can be joined with a high Gaussian noise at the input of that layer in order to strongly polarize its outputs [8]. The results are very close to binary, and a thresholding function can be applied to obtain exact integers.

In the following example, the network defined includes a custom Keras layer which introduces this Gaussian noise and is otherwise very standard. A basic AE is trained using this network, afterwards it encodes test instances, and the hash function applies a threshold to each encoding to find a binary hash.

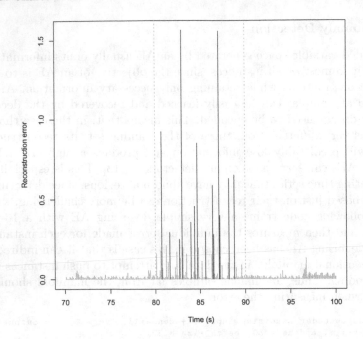

Fig. 4. Reconstruction error of a test subset of a synthetic time series. Artificially generated anomalous data is placed between the dashed lines. High reconstruction errors (above the mean error plus its standard deviation) are marked in black.

```
net <- input() + dense(256) + layer_keras("gaussian_noise", stddev = 16) +
  dense(10, activation = "sigmoid") + dense(256) + output("sigmoid")
model <- autoencoder(net, "binary_crossentropy") %>%
  train(x_train, epochs = 50)
hash <- function(model, x, threshold = 0.5) {
  t(encode(model, x) %>% apply(1, function(r) as.integer(r > threshold)))
}
hashes <- model %>% hash(x_test)
```

In order to illustrate the effectiveness of this AE, we have trained it with the training subset of the IMDB dataset available in Keras, composed of 25 000 movie reviews, from which just the 1 000 most frequent words have been used (i.e. the training subset had 1 000 variables and 25 000 samples). Then, we use the obtained model to produce hashes for each test instance.

Since the objective of semantic hashing is to obtain similar binary hashes for similar inputs, we measure the distance among instances and associate it to that among their hashes. The dataset used contains text documents, so the cosine distance is a good measure for pairs of instances in this case. Hashes will be considered distant according to their Hamming distance. Figure 5 shows that, the more different two hashes are, more distance is between the corresponding instances.

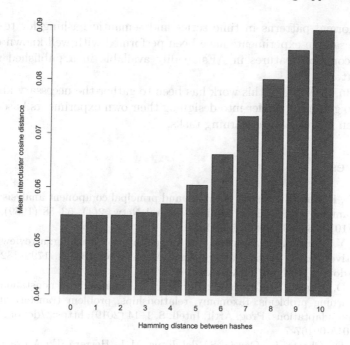

Fig. 5. Measure of average cosine distance among instances whose hash encodings differ in any Hamming distance.

3.5   Other Applications

The applications described in the examples above are only a sample of the possible purposes an AE can be used for. Another common objective for AEs is to improve classification performance [20,21]. As with image denoising, AEs can serve as enhancers for other kinds of data; particularly speech [11] and electrocardiogram signals [19].

Combinations of AEs can merge information from several sources, such as two and three-dimensional human poses [9] or pairs of image and text and other multi-view data [16]. Other AE-based models have been developed in order to improve tag recommendation [15], prediction of movement from static images [14], and translation involving sentence reordering [10].

4   Conclusions

Feature learning is a crucial task which can determine the performance of a machine learning model. In this work, AEs have been described as an adaptable basis for many different tasks which involve finding alternative representations of data.

Four example applications have been described in detail and solved using AEs: data visualization in two and three dimensions, denoising of images, detection of abnormal patterns in time series and semantic hashing for text documents. The sample experiments have been performed with well known datasets and using common features in AEs readily available in a published software package, ruta.

The main objective of this work has been to gather the necessary knowledge and ideas to guide the reader into designing their own experiments based on AE models when facing feature learning tasks.

References

1. Baldi, P., Hornik, K.: Neural networks and principal component analysis: learning from examples without local minima. Neural Netw. **2**(1), 53–58 (1989). https://doi.org/10.1016/0893-6080(89)90014-2

2. Bengio, Y., Courville, A., Vincent, P.: Representation learning: a review and new perspectives. IEEE Trans. Pattern Anal. Mach. Intell. **35**(8), 1798–1828 (2013). https://doi.org/10.1109/TPAMI.2013.50

3. Charte, D., Charte, F., García, S., Herrera, F.: A snapshot on nonstandard supervised learning problems: taxonomy, relationships, problem transformations and algorithm adaptations. Prog. Artif. Intell. **8**, 1–14 (2019). https://doi.org/10.1007/s13748-018-00167-7

4. Charte, D., Charte, F., García, S., del Jesus, M.J., Herrera, F.: A practical tutorial on autoencoders for nonlinear feature fusion: taxonomy, models, software and guidelines. Inf. Fusion **44**, 78–96 (2018). https://doi.org/10.1016/j.inffus.2017.12.007

5. Charte, D., Herrera, F., Charte, F.: Ruta: implementations of neural autoencoders in R. Knowl.-Based Syst. (in press)

6. Dheeru, D., Karra Taniskidou, E.: UCI machine learning repository (2017). http://archive.ics.uci.edu/ml

7. Goodfellow, I., Bengio, Y., Courville, A.: Convolutional Networks. In: Deep Learning, pp. 326–366. MIT Press (2016). http://www.deeplearningbook.org

8. Hinton, G.E., Salakhutdinov, R.R.: Reducing the dimensionality of data with neural networks. Science **313**(5786), 504–507 (2006). https://doi.org/10.1126/science.1127647

9. Hong, C., Yu, J., Wan, J., Tao, D., Wang, M.: Multimodal deep autoencoder for human pose recovery. IEEE Trans. Image Process. **24**(12), 5659–5670 (2015). https://doi.org/10.1109/TIP.2015.2487860

10. Li, P., Liu, Y., Sun, M.: Recursive autoencoders for ITG-based translation. In: Proceedings of the 2013 Conference on Empirical Methods in Natural Language Processing, pp. 567–577 (2013)

11. Lu, X., Tsao, Y., Matsuda, S., Hori, C.: Speech enhancement based on deep denoising autoencoder. In: Interspeech, pp. 436–440 (2013)

12. Park, S., Kim, M., Lee, S.: Anomaly detection for http using convolutional autoencoders. IEEE Access **6**, 70884–70901 (2018). https://doi.org/10.1109/ACCESS.2018.2881003

13. Sakurada, M., Yairi, T.: Anomaly detection using autoencoders with nonlinear dimensionality reduction. In: Proceedings of the MLSDA 2014 2nd Workshop on Machine Learning for Sensory Data Analysis, pp. 4–11. ACM (2014). https://doi.org/10.1145/2689746.2689747

14. Walker, J., Doersch, C., Gupta, A., Hebert, M.: An uncertain future: forecasting from static images using variational autoencoders. In: Leibe, B., Matas, J., Sebe, N., Welling, M. (eds.) ECCV 2016. LNCS, vol. 9911, pp. 835–851. Springer, Cham (2016). https://doi.org/10.1007/978-3-319-46478-7_51

15. Wang, H., Shi, X., Yeung, D.Y.: Relational stacked denoising autoencoder for tag recommendation. In: Twenty-Ninth AAAI Conference on Artificial Intelligence (2015)

16. Wang, X., Peng, D., Hu, P., Sang, Y.: Adversarial correlated autoencoder for unsupervised multi-view representation learning. Knowl.-Based Syst. (2019). https://doi.org/10.1016/j.knosys.2019.01.017

17. Wicker, J., Tyukin, A., Kramer, S.: A nonlinear label compression and transformation method for multi-label classification using autoencoders. In: Bailey, J., Khan, L., Washio, T., Dobbie, G., Huang, J.Z., Wang, R. (eds.) PAKDD 2016. LNCS (LNAI), vol. 9651, pp. 328–340. Springer, Cham (2016). https://doi.org/10.1007/978-3-319-31753-3_27

18. Xie, J., Xu, L., Chen, E.: Image denoising and inpainting with deep neural networks. In: Advances in Neural Information Processing Systems, pp. 341–349 (2012)

19. Xiong, P., Wang, H., Liu, M., Zhou, S., Hou, Z., Liu, X.: ECG signal enhancement based on improved denoising auto-encoder. Eng. Appl. Artif. Intell. **52**, 194–202 (2016). https://doi.org/10.1016/j.engappai.2016.02.015

20. Xu, J., et al.: Stacked sparse autoencoder (SSAE) for nuclei detection on breast cancer histopathology images. IEEE Trans. Med. Imaging **35**(1), 119–130 (2016). https://doi.org/10.1109/tmi.2015.2458702

21. Xu, W., Sun, H., Deng, C., Tan, Y.: Variational autoencoder for semi-supervised text classification. In: AAAI Conference on Artificial Intelligence (2017)

Automatic Image-Based Waste Classification

Victoria Ruiz[1], Ángel Sánchez[1]([✉]), José F. Vélez[1], and Bogdan Raducanu[2]

[1] ETSII - URJC, 28933 Móstoles, Madrid, Spain
{victoria.ruiz.parrado,angel.sanchez,jose.velez}@urjc.es
[2] CVC - UAB, 08193 Cerdanyola, Barcelona, Spain
bogdan@cvc.uab.es

Abstract. The management of solid waste in large urban environments has become a complex problem due to increasing amount of waste generated every day by citizens and companies. Current Computer Vision and Deep Learning techniques can help in the automatic detection and classification of waste types for further recycling tasks. In this work, we use the TrashNet dataset to train and compare different deep learning architectures for automatic classification of garbage types. In particular, several Convolutional Neural Networks (CNN) architectures were compared: VGG, Inception and ResNet. The best classification results were obtained using a combined Inception-ResNet model that achieved 88.6% of accuracy. These are the best results obtained with the considered dataset.

Keywords: Computer Vision · Deep learning ·
Convolutional neural networks · Waste classification

1 Introduction

Waste collection and recycling are essential services for modern cities, specially for the big ones. Due to a decrease of available natural resources and to environmental problems produced by the increasing amount of generated garbage, there is a need for recycling to reduce pollution and health problems for citizens. The average European generates 517 kilos of garbage per year, of which just a small percentage is recycled [1]. According to Environmental Protection Agency, 75% of waste produced by American people is recyclable, but actually only 30% is recycled. Currently, most of the garbage segregation process is done manually which creates many health problems for the workers, is time-consuming and also requires financial taxes from citizens [2]. Moreover, this waste separation must be done as soon as possible in order to reduce the contamination of waste by other materials [3].

Waste separation and recycling is necessary for a sustainable society. Currently, the application of ICT (e.g. using technologies and devices such as smart sensors, cloud platforms or Internet of Things) to smart cities in automatic

© Springer Nature Switzerland AG 2019
J. M. Ferrández Vicente et al. (Eds.): IWINAC 2019, LNCS 11487, pp. 422–431, 2019.
https://doi.org/10.1007/978-3-030-19651-6_41

garbage classification tasks can significantly improve the efficiency of these processes [1]. This classification can be made by the type of garbage [4], the biodegradable nature of the waste [2], or other aspects [5]. On the other hand, anti-littering organizations and city governments worldwide are assessing urban cleanliness by means of human audits [6]. Waste locating and quantification is an important step for improving cleanliness of cities, which could become health problem in overpopulated countries such as India [5].

These automatic garbage recycling systems can also involve Computer Vision to analyze the images or videos captured in recycling plants to determine which kind of objects are present in mixed waste. Good results in this stage will lead good results in the whole recycling process. Moreover, with recent developments of Machine Learning techniques, specially Deep Learning, very good image-based garbage classification results have been achieved [3].

In this paper, we adopt a supervised approach to effectively classify several types of waste present in images (e.g. glass, paper, cardboard, plastic and so on). For this purpose, we trained and compared several deep classification models to recognize different waste categories present in images of the TrashNet dataset [4]).

The paper is organized as follows. Section 2 reviews image-based systems for waste classification. Section 3 outlines the different deep neural architectures used or supervised classification of waste. Section 4 describes the dataset and waste classification experiments. Finally, Sect. 5 outlines the conclusions of this study.

2   Previous Work

Current Computer Vision systems for waste separation are oriented towards object detection and classification using image analysis techniques. This process could be divided in the following steps:

1. *Segmentation*: It involves separating each type of waste. First, some pre-processings on images are required to remove noise (e.g. Gaussian blur), to enhance contrast (e.g. histogram equalization) or to binarize them (e.g. Otsu algorithm). After that, diverse edge detection methods such as Canny or watershed algorithms can be applied to segment the image into homogeneous regions [1].
2. *Feature extraction*: Before the development of Deep Learning techniques, feature extraction methods (i.e. based on shape, texture or color descriptors) were required to extract useful information from segmented regions and built automatic classification models from these features. For example, statistical moments, Fourier-based, Gabor-based descriptors, Histogram Orient Gradients (HOG) are some of the used methods [1,5]. Additionally, Principal Component Analysis (PCA) was used to reduce the data dimensionality [5] prior to the classification stage.

3. *Learning and Classification*: Once the features are extracted, a classification model is trained to identify the objects in waste. For example, correlation algorithms [7], K-Nearest Neighbors (KNN) [1] or SVM [3,4]. From the emergence of Deep Learning, diverse types of deep neural architectures as AlexNet [4], Faster R-CNN [8] or GoogleNet [6] were also applied in the considered problem. Special neural architectures for this application have been recently built, such as GarbNet [5] or OscarNet [9], which are based on pretrained convolutional neural networks architectures such as AlexNet or VGG-19.

One aspect to consider in classification is image resolution. If images are large, a sliding window can be used [6]. Additionally, when the dataset size is small, data augmentation techniques can be applied as in [4]. Most of proposed systems in the bibliography are focused on localization and classification of waste types. Some of these systems have also been implemented as an Android app, as it is the case of SpotGarbage, developed by Mittal et al. [5].

However, a fair comparison of the accuracy among proposed methods is still difficult because many of them use their own datasets. So, each proposed model can be trained using different waste categories. Table 1 compares some of the current image-based deep learning systems for trash classification. As can be appreciated, some good results have been achieved in recent years. Our goal in this work is to evaluate other deep models that improve current state-of-the-art in garbage classification for the TrashNet dataset.

Table 1. Comparative of recent approaches for garbage classification

Author (Year)	Dataset (classes)	Methodology	Accuracy
Briñez et al. [7]	Own (3)	Correlation algorithm	78.00%
Mittal et al. [5]	GINI	GarbeNet (based on CNN)	87.69%
Kennedy et al. [9]	TrashNet (7)	OscarNet (based on VGG-19 pretrained)	88.42%
Sakr et al. [3]	Own (3)	SVM	94.80%
Sakr et al. [3]	Own (3)	AlexNet	83.00%
Yang et al. [4]	TrashNet (5)	SVM with SIFT features	65.00%
Yang et al. [4]	TrashNet (5)	AlexNet	22.40%
Rad et al. [6]	Own (25)	Overfeat with GoogleNet	77.35%
Awe et al. [8]	TrashNet (6)	Augmented data to train R-CNN	68.30%

3   Deep Architectures for Supervised Waste Classification

Many current neural architectures used for supervised classification of images are based on the Convolutional Neural Network (CNN) model. CNN are composed by convolutional layers where neurons are connected through a convolution function instead of a general matrix multiplication so weights are shared rather than being all connected. As a result, spatial patterns which are invariant to translations, rotations, and other transformations, are obtained.

In our experiments, we used several neural architectures, all of them based on convolutional layers. In particular:

1. **VGG**: The VGG architecture was developed for localization and classification tasks on high-resolution images [10]. VGG network is formed by many convolutional layers with increasing depth and with small kernels (i.e. 3×3) in all the convolutional layers. In this work, we have focused on two VGG models:

   (a) <u>VGG-16:</u> In VGG-16 [11], a block of 13 convolution layers and 3 fully-connected layers compose the architecture as follows. One block of two 64-depth convolutional layers with max-pooling, one block of two 128-depth convolutional layers with max-pooling, one block of three 256-depth convolutional layers with max-pooling, two block of three 512-depth convolutional layers with max-pooling, two fully-connected layers with 4096 neurons, one fully-connected layer with as many neurons as classes of the dataset and SoftMax as activation function. Figure 1(a) shows this architecture.

   (b) <u>VGG-19:</u> VGG 19 [11] is a variation of the previous model. The only difference is that the last three convolutional blocks are formed by 4 convolutional layers instead of 3. Figure 1(b) shows this architecture.

2. **ResNet**: From Deep Convolutional Networks such as AlexNet or VGG, research has been focused on increasing the depth of the architecture, but the vanishing gradient problem prevented from achieving it. ResNet introduced skip connections to avoid degrading the network performance [12]. As a result, the feature mapping achieved from a convolutional layer is combined with a feature mapping obtained by the previous layer. In our case we have used ResNet-18, which is composed by one block of three 32-depth convolutional layers and four blocks of two convolutional layers with an increasing depths of 64, 128, 256 and 512, respectively. All the convolutional layers have a 3×3 dimensional filters, except for the first two layers which have a 5×5 dimension filters. Finally, on the bottom of the network there are two fully connected or dense layers with 512 and 6 neurons. Figure 1(c) shows the ResNet-18 architecture.

3. **Inception**: Inception won the ImageNet Large-Scale Visual Recognition Challenge 2014 (ILSVRC14). Its main contribution is to increase the depth and width of the network while keeping the computational budget constant [13]. The first version of this version is the well known GoogLeNet. In Inception module, the block of convolutional layers are parallel rather than serial as in VGG. This means that, while in the VGG architecture the output of a convolutional layer was the input of the following convolutional layer in a block, in Inception architecture all, or some of the, convolutional layers in a block have the same input and they are concatenated at the end of the block. Figure 1(d) shows the Inception architecture.

4. **Inception-ResNet**: Szegedy et al. [14] combined both Inception and ResNet concepts: residual connections to avoid gradient vanishing and Inception modules to increase the network by keeping the computational cost. Figure 1(e) shows the final Inception-ResNet architecture.

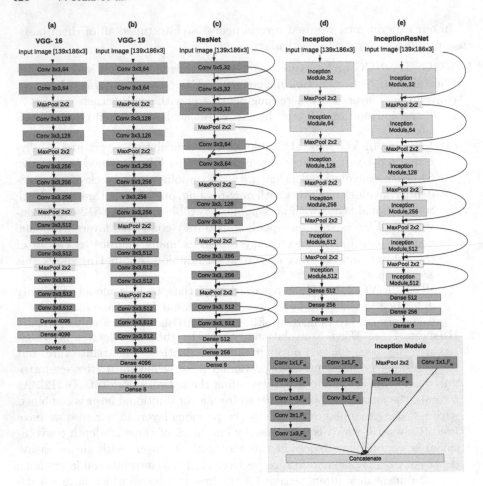

Fig. 1. Additional tested deep models: (a) VGG-16; (b) VGG-19 architectures (c) ResNet; (d) Inception; and (e) Inception-ResNet architectures

4 Classification Experiments Using TrashNet

In this section, we summarize the dataset used, the pre-processing performed on images and the experiments carried out.

4.1 The TrashNet Dataset

The TrashNet dataset [4] was created by Mindy Yang and Gary Thung at Standford University. This dataset contains RGB images of six classes of waste, where in each image only appears one type of garbage. In particular: glass, paper, cardboard, plastic, metal, and general trash, respectively. Currently, the dataset consists of 2,527 images with the following distribution of images per class: 501 of glass, 594 of paper, 403 of cardboard, 482 of plastic, 410 of metal and 137 of general trash, respectively. The images were captured by placing the object on a white posterboard and using sunlight and/or room lighting. All the pictures have been resized down to a spatial resolution of 512×384. Figure 2 illustrates the six classes present in TrashNet dataset.

As deep neural networks require larger datasets, a common practice is to augment the original collection of original images by applying a set of transformations on each of them (i.e rotations, scalings or brightness corrections, among others).

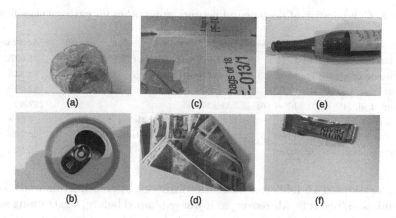

Fig. 2. Sample images of waste classes in TrashNet dataset: (a) plastic; (b) metal; (c) cardboard; (d) paper; (e) glass; and (f) general trash.

4.2   Data Pre-processing

Our first goal is to develop a deep learning model which classifies isolated garbage elements using the TrashNet dataset. For this purpose, we tried all the deep convolutional architectures explained previously. However, for all the models we needed to resize the images due to computational problems and to normalize their brightness values between 0 and 1.

Moreover, since we have a small number of images to train our models, data augmentation was used to generate a pseudo-infinite on-demand number of training samples. New images were generated at the same time the model was training, by applying combination of transformations on the original data. Transformations were chosen randomly between: rotations between 0 and $40°$, width changes between 0% and 20%, height changes between 0% and 20%, shear between 0% and 20%, zoom between 0% and 20%, and horizontal flips.

4.3   Classification Experiments and Results

We first randomly partitioned the original collection of images into three subsets: training, validation and test, respectively. All the subsets have the same rate of classes. As the number of images is small, we decided to use 80% of them for training, 10% for validation and the remaining 10% for tests. To achieve more robust

Table 2. Accuracy of tested deep neural models

Model	Mean accuracy (in %)	Std. dev. accuracy	Mean no. epochs	Std. dev. no. epochs
VGG-16	76.94	5.75	74.6	37.06
VGG-19	79.32	4.66	76.8	27.35
Inception	87.71	3.36	43.8	16.13
ResNet	88.66	1.28	45.2	5.93
Inception-Resnet	88.34	1.92	55.2	15.27

Table 3. Comparative of deep neural network approaches for garbage classification

Author (Year)	Dataset (classes)	Methodology	Accuracy
Mittal et al. [5]	GINI	GarbeNet (based on CNN)	87.69%
Kennedy et al. [9]	TrashNet (7)	OscarNet (based on VGG-19 pretrained)	88.42%
Sakr et al. [3]	Own (3)	AlexNet	83.00%
Yang et al. [4]	TrashNet (6)	AlexNet	22.40%
Rad et al. [6]	Own (25)	Overfeat with GoogleNet	77.35%
Awe et al. [8]	TrashNet (6)	Augmented data to train R-CNN	68.30%
Our proposal	TrashNet	ResNet model	88.66%

results, we adopted a 5-fold cross-validation strategy, by creating randomly 5 training/validation/test sets. Moreover, as it was explained before, the training sample is increased through data augmentation technique. The results given in this subsection correspond to the average of the 5 runs of the test datasets.

The second stage was to configure the parameters of each network. The networks' weights were in all cases initialized randomly. For all of the networks we considered in our experiments, we used a batch size of 16 samples, a Stochastic Gradient Descent (SGD) as optimization algorithm and a learning rate of 0.0002. An early stopping strategy was adopted during training. We kept the model with less validation loss and stopped the training if this result did not improve in 25 epochs time. Moreover, batch normalization layers were introduced at the end of each block of convolutional layers in all the models. The images were resized to 197×283 pixels to train the model.

Table 2 presents a comparative study in terms of mean and standard deviation accuracy results achieved using the five considered deep networks tested. Also, a comparative study of the epochs needed to train the models is shown on this Table. On one hand, best results are achieved by the ResNet model with a 88.66% of accuracy. Moreover, ResNet model is the most stable one since the standard deviation is the smallest. However, the Inception-ResNet model produced similar results. On the other hand, ResNet model is the one which needs less epochs to be trained. We can conclude that the ResNet model is the best by accuracy and speed.

Table 3 compares our best results, achieved by the ResNet model, with other deep learning models applied on waste classification. It is shown that our model wins all the other models, although is quite close to the Kennedy et al. [9] model. However, Kennedy mixed TrashNet and PASCAL data sets, with class

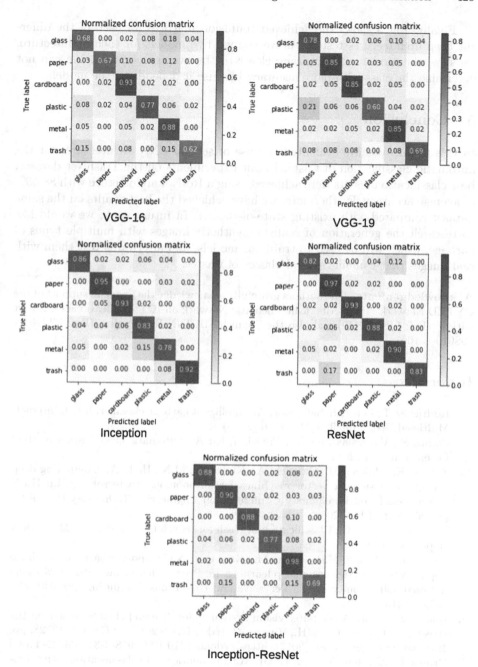

Fig. 3. Comparative of confusion matrix

7 (non waste) being the second data set. On the other hand, it is shown in his results that they overfitted the model, achieving good results in the non-waste class (PASCAL data set) but low results for the TrashNet dataset.

Finally, Fig. 3 shows the achieved confusion matrices for each of the different deep architectures tested. As we trained five models for each architecture, we show the model with accuracy closer to the average accuracy. We can not determine the class with more accuracy because it depends on the model.

5   Conclusion

In this paper, we have evaluated the use of several CNN architectures for the automatic classification of waste. In our experiments on the TrashNet dataset, best classification results were achieved using a ResNet architecture with 88.66% of average accuracy. Furthermore, we have achieved the best results on the same dataset compared with existing state-of-the-art. In future work, we would like to research the generation of realistic synthetic images with multiple types of garbage, which will be used to train our models, and afterwards test them with real images that combine several classes of wastes.

Acknowledgements. The authors gratefully acknowledge the financial support of the CYTED Network "Ibero-American Thematic Network on ICT Applications for Smart Cities" (Ref: 518RT0559) and also the Spanish MICINN RTI Project (Ref: RTI2018-098019-B-100).

References

1. Rodríguez, I., Pérez, J., Salmador, A.: Intelligent garbage classifier. Int. J. Interact. Multimed. Artif. Intell. **1**(1), 31–36 (2008)
2. Sudha, S., Vidhyalakshmi, M., Pavithra, K.: An automatic classification method for environment (2016)
3. Sakr, G.E., Mokbel, M., Darwich, A., Khneisser, M.N., Hadi, A.: Comparing deep learning and support vector machines for autonomous waste sorting. In: IEEE International Multidisciplinary Conference on Engineering Technology (IMCET), pp. 207–212. IEEE (2016)
4. Yang, M., Thung, G.: Classification of trash for recyclability status. CS229 Project Report 2016 (2016)
5. Mittal, G., Yagnik, K.B., Garg, M., Krishnan, N.C.: SpotGarbage: smartphone app to detect garbage using deep learning. In: Proceedings of the 2016 ACM International Joint Conference on Pervasive and Ubiquitous Computing, pp. 940–945. ACM (2016)
6. Rad, M.S., et al.: A computer vision system to localize and classify wastes on the streets. In: Liu, M., Chen, H., Vincze, M. (eds.) ICVS 2017. LNCS, vol. 10528, pp. 195–204. Springer, Cham (2017). https://doi.org/10.1007/978-3-319-68345-4_18
7. Briñez, L.J.C., Rengifo, A., Escobar, M.: Automatic waste classification using computer vision as an application in Colombian high schools. In: 6th Latin-American Conference on Networked and Electronic Media (LACNEM 2015), pp. 1–5. IET (2015)
8. Awe, O., Mengistu, R., Sreedhar, V.: Smart trash net: waste localization and classification (2017)
9. Kennedy, T.: OscarNet: using transfer learning to classify disposable waste (2016)

10. Simonyan, K., Zisserman, A.: Very deep convolutional networks for large-scale image recognition. arXiv preprint arXiv:1409.1556 (2014)
11. Deng, J., Dong, W., Socher, R. Li, L.-J., Li, K., Fei-Fei, L.: ImageNet: a large-scale hierarchical image database. In: 2009 IEEE Conference on Computer Vision and Pattern Recognition, CVPR 2009, pp. 248–255. IEEE (2009)
12. He, K., Zhang, X., Ren, S., Sun, J.: Deep residual learning for image recognition. In: Proceedings of the IEEE Conference on Computer Vision and Pattern Recognition, pp. 770–778 (2016)
13. Szegedy, C., et al.: Going deeper with convolutions. In: Proceedings of the IEEE Conference on Computer Vision and Pattern Recognition, pp. 1–9 (2015)
14. Szegedy, C., Ioffe, S., Vanhoucke, V., Alemi, A.A.: Inception-v4, inception-resnet and the impact of residual connections on learning. In: AAAI, vol. 4, p. 12 (2017)

Propositional Rules Generated at the Top Layers of a CNN

Guido Bologna[1,2]([✉]) [iD]

[1] University of Applied Sciences and Arts of Western Switzerland,
Rue de la Prairie 4, 1202 Geneva, Switzerland
[2] University of Geneva, Route de Drize 7, 1227 Carouge, Switzerland
Guido.Bologna@hesge.ch,Guido.Bologna@unige.ch

Abstract. So far, many rule extraction techniques have been proposed to explain the classifications of shallow Multi Layer Perceptrons (MLPs), but very few methods have been introduced for Convolutional Neural Networks (CNNs). To fill this gap, this work presents a new technique applied to a CNN architecture including two convolutional layers. This neural network is trained with the MNIST dataset, representing images of digits. Rule extraction is performed at the first fully connected layer, by means of the Discretized Interpretable Multi Layer Perceptron (DIMLP). This transparent MLP architecture allows us to generate symbolic rules, by precisely locating axis-parallel hyperplanes. The antecedents of the extracted rules represent responses of convolutional filters that makes it possible to determine for each rule the covered samples. Hence, we can visualize the centroid of each rule, which gives us some insight into how the network works. This represents a first step towards the explanation of CNN responses, since the final explanation would be obtained in a further processing by generating propositional rules with respect to the input layer. In the experiments we illustrate a generated ruleset with its characteristics in terms of accuracy, complexity and fidelity, which is the degree of matching between CNN classifications and rules classifications. Overall, rules reach very high fidelity. Finally, several examples of rules are visualized and discussed.

Keywords: Model explanation · Rule extraction · CNN

1 Introduction

Artificial neural networks learn by examining many times numerous examples. After training, it is very difficult to explain their decisions, because their knowledge is embedded within the values of the parameters and neuron activations, which are at first glance incomprehensible. Deep neural networks are at the root of the significant progress accomplished over the past five years in areas such as artificial vision, natural language processing and speech recognition. The transparency of bio-inspired models is currently an open and important research topic, as in the long term, the acceptance of these models will depend on it.

J. M. Ferrández Vicente et al. (Eds.): IWINAC 2019, LNCS 11487, pp. 432–440, 2019.
https://doi.org/10.1007/978-3-030-19651-6_42

A natural way to explain Multi Layer Perceptrons (MLPs) responses is through the use of propositional rules [5]. Andrews et al. introduced a taxonomy describing the general characteristics of all rule extraction methods [1]. Several authors proposed to interpret Convolutional Neural Networks (CNNs) in the neighbourhood of the instances. As an example, Ribeiro et al. presented *LIME* (Locally Interpretable Model Agnostic Explanations), whose purpose is to learn an interpretable model in the local region close to an input instance [10]. Similarly Turner et al. introduced the *Model Explanation System* [11]. Basically, by using a Monte Carlo technique, they derived a scoring system for finding the best explanation. Koh et al. determined the training instances that are the most important for the prediction [6]. Finally, Zhou et al. presented *CAM* whose purpose is to determine discriminative image regions using the average pooling of CNNs [13].

We propose to extract propositional rules from a CNN trained on the MNIST dataset. The generated rules at the first dense layer express in their antecedents the responses of the filters of the last convolutional layer. Thus, we can see the logic behind the network. Specifically, the wide variety of input samples with their classifications is related to the rules by a multitude of filter responses in different regions of the images. Moreover, each rule is covered by a number of samples that can be visualized as a centroid. This represents a first step towards the explanation of CNN responses, since the final explanation would be obtained in a further processing by generating propositional rules with respect to the input layer (which is not proposed here). The rules that gives some insight on the internal functioning are generated by replacing the dense layers with a transparent MLP called DIMLP [2] (Discretized Interpretable MLP). The DIMLP subnetwork from which propositional rules are generated, approximates the fully connected part of the original CNN to any desired precision. In the following paragraphs, section two describes the models, in section three we present the experiments with the MNIST dataset, followed by the conclusion.

2   Models

2.1   CNN Architecture

In this work we define a CNN architecture with:

- a two-dimensional input layer of size 28×28;
- a convolutional layer with 32 kernels of size 5×5;
- a max-pooling layer;
- a convolutional layer with 32 kernels of size 5×5;
- a max-pooling layer;
- two fully connected layers.

Two-Dimensional Convolution and Max-Pooling. Given a two-dimensional kernel $w_{p,q}$ of size $P \times Q$ and a data matrix of elements $x_{a,b}$, the calculation of an element c_{ij} of the convolutional layer is

$$c_{ij} = f(\sum_p^P \sum_q^Q w_{p,q} \cdot x_{i+p,j+q} + b_{p,q}); \tag{1}$$

with f a transfer function and $b_{p,q}$ the bias. As a transfer function we use $ReLU$ (Rectifier Linear Unit):

$$f(x) = \max(0, x). \tag{2}$$

We define S_p and S_q as the stride parameters along the horizontal and vertical axis between two successive convolutions. In this work $S_p = S_q = 1$. Moreover, we require the kernel to be completely inside the sample matrix (without zero padding).

The max-pooling layer reduces the size of a vector or a matrix by applying a "Max" operator over non-overlapping regions. In this work, the chosen reduction factor along each dimension is equal to two.

Fully Connected Layers. Two fully connected layers of weights follow the second max-pooling layer. The activation function in the first dense layer is a sigmoid function given as

$$\sigma(x) = \frac{1}{1 + \exp(-x)}. \tag{3}$$

Then, within the next dense layer we use a *Softmax* activation function. Specifically, for a number N of s_i scalars it calculates an N-dimensional vector with values between 0 and 1:

$$o_l = \frac{\exp(s_l)}{\sum_k \exp(s_k)}; \tag{4}$$

with o_l as the activation of a neuron in the output layer. In this work, the CNN architecture is summarised in Table 1. Finally, to train the network, the loss function is the cross-entropy [9].

Table 1. CNN architecture with symbols for each layer and sizes.

Input	Convolution	Max-pooling	Convolution	Max-pooling	Dense	Dense
I	C_1	M_1	C_2	M_2	D_1	D_2
28×28	$32 \times 5 \times 5$	$32 \times 2 \times 2$	$32 \times 5 \times 5$	$32 \times 2 \times 2$	$32 \times 4 \times 4 \times 256 = 512 \times 256$	256×10

2.2   The DIMLP Model

DIMLP differs from a standard MLP in the number of connections between the input layer and the first hidden layer. Specifically, any hidden neuron receives only a connection from an input neuron and the bias neuron, while all other layers are fully connected [2]. The activation function in the first hidden layer of DIMLPs is a staircase function, with Θ stairs that approximate the Identity function. With $\Theta = 1$ we obtain the step function, which is a particular case:

$$\tau(x) = \begin{cases} 1 & \text{if } x > 0 \text{ ;} \\ 0 & \text{otherwise.} \end{cases} \tag{5}$$

A typical architecture of a DIMLP includes two hidden layers, which can be designated by symbols $I - H_1 - H_2 - O$; with symbol H designating hidden layers and symbol O representing the output layer. The key idea behind rule extraction from DIMLPs is the precise localization of axis-parallel discriminative hyperplanes. In other words, the input space is split into hyper-rectangles representing propositional rules. Specifically, the first hidden layer creates for each input variable a number of axis-parallel hyperplanes that are effective or not, depending on the weight values of the neurons above the first hidden layer. More details on the rule extraction algorithm can be found in [3].

2.3 The Approximation of the CNN Architecture

The two dense layers of the CNN architecture used in this work represent an MLP with a single hidden layer h. The input layer of this MLP is represented by symbol m_2 and the output layer by o. After training, in order to generate propositional rules, a DIMLP with layers m_2-h_1-h-o replaces the MLP with layers m_2-h-o. The weight matrix between layers m_2 and h of the trained CNN is transferred to layers h_1 and h of the approximated CNN. Because of the approximation of the Identity function between m_2 and h_1, subnetwork m_2-h_1-h-o approximates subnetwork m_2-h-o to an arbitrary precision that depends to the number of stairs of the staircase activation function.

Yet, rule antecedents are related to layer m_2 representing filter values that are difficult to understand. However, from a rule is possible to determine the covered samples. Hence, we can for instance visualize the centroid of each rule, which gives us some insight into how the network works.

Generally, many rule extraction techniques generate ordered rules, which means that rules are given in a sequential order, with two consecutive rules linked by an "else" statement. A long list of ordered rules involve many implicit antecedents that makes the interpretation difficult. Rules generated from the DIMLP subnetwork are unordered. With this type of rules that in general overlap, the "else" statement is absent. Thus, each rule is considered as a single piece of knowledge that can be examined in isolation [7].

3 Experiments

The experiments were performed with the MNIST dataset [8], which includes 60000 samples from ten classes in the training set and 10000 samples in the testing set. The same CNN architecture defined in Sect. 2.1 was trained. The learning phase was performed with *Lasagne* libraries, version 0.2[1] [4]. The training parameters are:

- learning rate: 0.01;
- momentum: 0.9;
- dropout = 0.5;

The last 10000 samples of the training set were used as a tuning set for early-stopping [12]. Table 2 illustrates the results. The first row of this Table is related to the original CNN, while the second row provides results obtained by the interpretable CNN, with 50 stairs in the staircase activation function (which is a default value for DIMLPs). Columns from left to right designate:

- train accuracy;
- predictive accuracy on the testing set;
- fidelity, which is the degree of matching between generated rules and the CNN;
- predictive accuracy of the rules;
- predictive accuracy of the rules when rules and CNN agree;
- number of extracted rules and total number of rule antecedents.

Table 2. Results obtained by a CNN and its approximation with a DIMLP subnetwork in the top layers.

	Tr. Acc.	Tst. Acc.	Fid.	Rul. Acc. (1)	Rul. Acc. (2)	#Rul./#Ant.
CNN	99.79	99.49	–	–	–	–
CNN ($\Theta = 50$)	99.78	99.46	98.73	98.41	99.61	1105/11350

The predictive accuracy of 99.49% reached by the CNN represents a fairly good performance without having generated supplementary instances[2]. The CNN with a DIMLP subnetwork in the top layers approximates the original CNN very well, since accuracy values are very close: 99.79% versus 99.78% on the training set; 99.49% versus 99.46% on the testing set. Fidelity is high, with 100% on the training set and 98.73% on the testing set, respectively. The predictive accuracy of the rules is a bit lower than that obtained by the CNN (98.41% versus 99.46%). Note however that the predictive accuracy of the rules when rules and model agree is higher than that obtained by the CNN (99.61% versus 99.46%).

The obtained number of rules may seem rather large (1105), but in fact it is necessary to put them into perspective, because of the large dimensionality of the input space (784) and the number of classes (10). At the level of dense

---

[1] The Lasagne script that defines the CNN architecture is available on https://lasagne.readthedocs.io/en/latest/user/tutorial.html.

[2] See http://yann.lecun.com/exdb/mnist/ for the comparison of several models.

layers, the classification of the data is performed by using on average about ten values ($11350/1105 = 10.2$) representing filter responses in the m_2 layer. Rules are ranked according to the number of covered training samples. Since they overlap in general [3], it is therefore normal to find a certain degree of redundancy. Figure 1 illustrates the centroids of the first 49 rules. The first rule represented at the top left is of class "9"; it is activated by 4671 training samples and 800 testing samples, respectively. The 49th rule is of class "7"; it covers 1315 training samples and 207 testing samples.

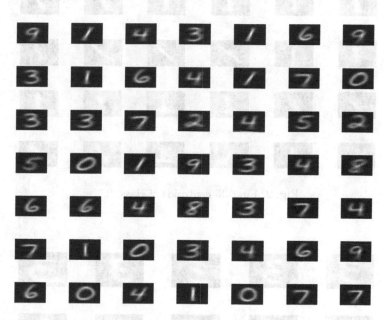

Fig. 1. Centroids representing the first 49 rules ranked according to the number of covered samples in the training set.

In Fig. 2 we focus on class "1". Again, the centroids are ranked according to the number of covered samples in the training set. The first rule represented at the top left is activated by 3402 training samples and 538 testing samples. The last rule at the bottom right covers 17 training samples and 4 testing samples. It is worth noting the different orientations, especially some in the fourth row lean very strongly to the right. In addition, a number of centroids have a small horizontal segment at the base and a small diagonal segment at the top that goes down (5th and 6th rows).

By applying a clustering algorithm to a centroid, it is possible to obtain a more detailed visualization. For instance, we executed the Kmeans algorithm with 500 iterations on the fourth centroid of class "3" represented in Fig. 1. Note that with Kmeans the number of clusters must be specified; it was set to 25 clusters. Figure 3 shows the results. It is interesting to note that some digits lean to the left, others to the right and finally some have no orientation.

Fig. 2. First 36 centroids of class "1".

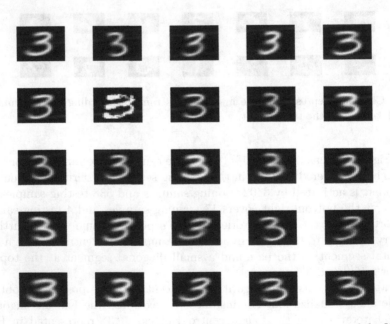

Fig. 3. Clusters of the fourth centroid of class "3" (see Fig. 1) by means of the Kmeans algorithm.

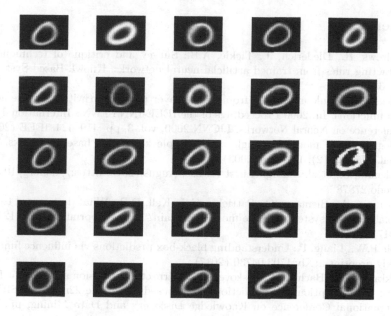

Fig. 4. Clusters of the fourteenth centroid.

The same processing was performed with the fourteenth centroid of class "0" represented in Fig. 4. Note that this centroid leans to the right, as well as the majority of the centroids obtained after the Kmeans clustering.

4   Conclusion

We trained a CNN with two convolutional layers on the MNIST dataset representing images of digits. Propositional rules were generated at the first fully connected layer, which allowed us to visualize the centroids representing the covered instances. This is a first step toward the understanding of the CNN stored knowledge, since it allows us to see how instances sharing similar characteristics in their appearance are grouped together. At this stage, we are not in a position to determine which elements are discriminatory, i.e. those that would explain why a certain classification would be chosen. Our scope in the future will be to solve this problem by propagating the propositional rules generated at the top layers backward to the input layer.

References

1. Andrews, R., Diederich, J., Tickle, A.B.: Survey and critique of techniques for extracting rules from trained artificial neural networks. Knowl.-Based Syst. **8**(6), 373–389 (1995)
2. Bologna, G.: Rule extraction from a multilayer perceptron with staircase activation functions. In: 2000 Proceedings of the IEEE-INNS-ENNS International Joint Conference on Neural Networks, IJCNN 2000, vol. 3, pp. 419–424. IEEE (2000)
3. Bologna, G.: A model for single and multiple knowledge based networks. Artif. Intell. Med. **28**(2), 141–163 (2003)
4. Dieleman, S., et al.: Lasagne: first release, August 2015. https://doi.org/10.5281/zenodo.27878
5. Holzinger, A., Biemann, C., Pattichis, C.S., Kell, D.B.: What do we need to build explainable AI systems for the medical domain? arXiv preprint arXiv:1712.09923 (2017)
6. Koh, P.W., Liang, P.: Understanding black-box predictions via influence functions. arXiv preprint arXiv:1703.04730 (2017)
7. Lakkaraju, H., Bach, S.H., Leskovec, J.: Interpretable decision sets: a joint framework for description and prediction. In: Proceedings of the 22nd ACM SIGKDD International Conference on Knowledge Discovery and Data Mining, pp. 1675–1684. ACM (2016)
8. LeCun, Y., Bottou, L., Bengio, Y., Haffner, P.: Gradient-based learning applied to document recognition. Proc. IEEE **86**(11), 2278–2324 (1998)
9. Murphy, K.P.: Machine Learning: A Probabilistic Perspective. Adaptive Computation and Machine Learning. The MIT Press, Cambridge (2012)
10. Ribeiro, M.T., Singh, S., Guestrin, C.: Why should i trust you?: explaining the predictions of any classifier. In: Proceedings of the 22nd ACM SIGKDD International Conference on Knowledge Discovery and Data Mining, pp. 1135–1144. ACM (2016)
11. Turner, R.: A model explanation system. In: 2016 IEEE 26th International Workshop on Machine Learning for Signal Processing (MLSP), pp. 1–6. IEEE (2016)
12. Yao, Y., Rosasco, L., Caponnetto, A.: On early stopping in gradient descent learning. Constr. Approx. **26**(2), 289–315 (2007)
13. Zhou, B., Bau, D., Oliva, A., Torralba, A.: Interpreting deep visual representations via network dissection. arXiv preprint arXiv:1711.05611 (2017)

Deep Ordinal Classification Based on the Proportional Odds Model

Víctor Manuel Vargas$^{(\boxtimes)}$, Pedro Antonio Gutiérrez$^{(\boxtimes)}$, and César Hervás$^{(\boxtimes)}$

Department of Computer Science and Numerical Analysis, University of Córdoba,
Córdoba, Spain
{vvargas,pagutierrez,chervas}@uco.es

Abstract. This paper proposes a deep neural network model for ordinal regression problems based on the use of a probabilistic ordinal link function in the output layer. This link function reproduces the Proportional Odds Model (POM), a statistical linear model which projects each pattern into a 1-dimensional space. In our case, the projection is estimated by a non-linear deep neural network. After that, patterns are classified using a set of ordered thresholds. In order to further improve the results, we combine this link function with a loss cost that takes the distance between classes into account, based on the weighted Kappa index. The experiments are based on two ordinal classification problems, and the statistical tests confirm that our ordinal network outperforms the nominal version and other proposals considered in the literature.

Keywords: Ordinal regression · Ordinal classification ·
Proportional odds model · Deep learning ·
Convolutional neural network

1 Introduction

Deep learning techniques were introduced by Lecun in 2015 [13]. They are a combination of multiple machine learning techniques and allow computational models that group multiple processing layers to learn representations of data with numerous levels of abstraction. The performance improvement of these methods has been proved in previous works that cover several domains, such as image classification [8] and speech recognition [9]. The weights determine the representation of each layer of the model, and they are adjusted by using the backpropagation algorithm, needing large datasets. Convolutional Neural Networks (CNN) are one type of deep learning model specially useful for images, video, speech and audio processing. CNNs can extract high-level features from the pixels of the images, through convolutional and pooling layers. These features are then used in the dense layers to classify each instance.

This work has been subsidised by the projects TIN2017-85887-C2-1-P and TIN2017-90567-REDT of the Spanish Ministry of Economy and Competitiveness (MINECO), and FEDER funds (FEDER EU).

© Springer Nature Switzerland AG 2019
J. M. Ferrández Vicente et al. (Eds.): IWINAC 2019, LNCS 11487, pp. 441–451, 2019.
https://doi.org/10.1007/978-3-030-19651-6_43

Ordinal classification is a type of classification problem in machine learning where the labels are ordered [7]. According to this order, there are different inter-classes importances for each pair of classes. They are also known as ordinal regression problems and should be treated in a particular form. The metric used to evaluate the performance of the model should take into account the order between classes. Multiple metrics for ordinal problems exist in the literature [5]. Weighted Kappa (WK) is a modified version of the Kappa index, defined by Cohen, where inter-rater weights are assigned. It measures inter-rater agreement on classifying elements into a set of categories. WK can be used in the evaluation of an ordinal model [5], considering appropriate costs for the different errors. Moreover, an ordinal weighted kappa loss was described in a previous work for deep learning models [16] (quadratic WK, QWK), based on a differentiable cost function that can improve the performance during learning.

On the other hand, the Proportional Odds Model (POM) [1,7] is a linear ordinal classification model, based on a threshold model structure. Threshold models are inspired in the concept of a latent variable which is represented by a 1-dimensional projection (in the case of POM, a linear projection) and a set of thresholds, which divide this space into the different ordered levels. The POM considers the `logit` transformation to map this projection into a set of probability estimations for the ordered categories [1], which are then used for performing maximum likelihood estimation of the model weights. In this way, the probabilistic structure of the POM could be used as an ordinal alternative to the softmax function, and, up to the authors knowledge, this possibility has not been explore in the context of deep learning.

In this way, the objective of this paper is to improve deep learning models for ordinal regression problems, based on the combination of two elements: the probabilistic ordinal link function of the POM and the aforementioned QWK loss ordinal. This combination will be compared against the nominal version (based on the standard softmax and the cross-entropy), using an appropriate statistical treatment (an approximated ANOVA III test[1] followed by a Tukey's test and a t-test). The experiments will be run using two different ordinal datasets: Diabetic Retinopathy [16], related with diabetes disease diagnostic, and Adience [2], related to age range estimation. Both age ranges and the degrees of the diabetes disease are coded as ordered categories and require an ordinal regression treatment.

This paper is organized as follows: Sect. 2 present a formal description of an ordinal problem and the POM. In Sect. 3 the QWK metric and loss functions are defined. In Sect. 4, we describe the model, the experiments and the datasets used, while, in Sect. 5, we present the results obtained and the statistical analysis. Finally, Sect. 6 includes the conclusions of this work.

---

[1] Because of computational time constraints, we will only use five executions.

2   Proportional Odds Model as the Output Layer

An ordinal classification (or ordinal regression) problem consists of predicting the label y of an input vector $\mathbf{x}$, where $\mathbf{x} \in \mathcal{X} \subseteq \mathbb{R}^K$ and $y \in \mathcal{Y} = \{\mathcal{C}_1, \mathcal{C}_2, ..., \mathcal{C}_Q\}$, i.e. $\mathbf{x}$ is in a K-dimensional input space, and y is in a label space of Q different labels. The main characteristic of ordinal problems is that labels show a natural ordering: $\mathcal{C}_1 \prec \mathcal{C}_2 \prec ... \prec \mathcal{C}_Q$. The final objective is to find a function $r : \mathcal{X} \to \mathcal{Y}$ to predict the labels or categories of new patterns, given a training set of N samples, $D = \{(\mathbf{x}_i, y_i), i = 1, ..., N\}$.

The POM arises from a statistical background and is one of the first models designed explicitly for ordinal regression. It is a member of a wider family of models recognised as Cumulative Link Models (CLM) [1]. CLMs predict probabilities of groups of contiguous categories, taking the ordinal scale into account. In this way, cumulative probabilities $P(y \preceq \mathcal{C}_q | \mathbf{x})$ are estimated as:

$$P(y \preceq \mathcal{C}_q | \mathbf{x}) = P(y = \mathcal{C}_1 | \mathbf{x}) + ... + P(y = \mathcal{C}_q | \mathbf{x}), \tag{1}$$

with $q = 2, ..., Q - 1$, and considering that $P(y = \mathcal{C}_1 | \mathbf{x}) = P(y \preceq \mathcal{C}_1 | \mathbf{x})$ and $P(y \preceq \mathcal{C}_Q | \mathbf{x}) = 1$.

The model is inspired by the notion of a latent variable, where $f(\mathbf{x})$ represents a one-dimensional mapping obtained from the pattern $\mathbf{x}$. In the case of POM, stochastic ordering of space $\mathcal{X}$ is satisfied by the following model form:

$$\text{logit}[P(y \preceq \mathcal{C}_q | \mathbf{x})] = b_q - f(\mathbf{x}), \quad q = 1, ..., Q - 1, \tag{2}$$

where logit is the logistic function, and b_q is the threshold defined for class $\mathcal{C}_q$, i.e. the projection is the same for all classes, while different biases are used for each category. Consider the latent variable $y^* = f(\mathbf{x})^* = f(\mathbf{x}) + \epsilon$, where ϵ is a random error component. In this way, the probability distribution of ϵ is modelled with the logistic function. Label $\mathcal{C}_q$ is predicted when $f(\mathbf{x}) \in [b_{q-1}, b_q]$. It is assumed that $b_0 = -\infty$ and $b_Q = +\infty$, so the real line defined by $f(\mathbf{x}), \mathbf{x} \in \mathcal{X}$, is divided into Q consecutive categories. The constraints $b_1 \leq b_2 \leq ... \leq b_{Q-1}$ ensures that $P(y \preceq \mathcal{C}_q | \mathbf{x})$ increases with q. The POM uses a linear projection for the data, in such a way that $f(\mathbf{x}) = \mathbf{w}^T \mathbf{x}$, where $\mathbf{w}$ is the projection vector. $\mathbf{w}$ and the thresholds $\mathbf{b} = (b_0, b_1, ..., b_{Q-1}, b_Q)$ are to be determined from the data.

We will consider this probabilistic structure as a link function in a deep convolutional neural network, by including a new type of output layer alternative to the standard softmax function. This output layer will transform the one-dimensional projection $f(\mathbf{x})$ into a set of probabilities. The projection, $f(\mathbf{x})$, will be estimated from a single neuron, using as input the set of features learnt by the previous layers. In this way, $f(\mathbf{x}) = l(\mathbf{x})$, where $\mathbf{x}$ is the pattern being evaluated and $l(\mathbf{x})$ is a latent representation of the pattern given by a single neuron of a deep neural network. In order to ensure the constraints of the thresholds, $b_1 \leq b_2 \leq ... \leq b_{Q-1}$, all the thresholds will be derived from the first one in the following form:

$$b_q = b_1 + \sum_{q=1}^{q-1} \alpha_q^2, \quad n = 2, ..., Q, \tag{3}$$

where b_1 and α_q are the learnable parameters, and Q is the number of classes.

3   Quadratic Weighted Kappa as the Loss Function

We will combine the POM structure in the output layer with the continuous version of the QWK loss [16] function for the optimization algorithm. Various coefficients of agreement are available to calculate classification reliability. The QWK metric can be used for evaluating an ordinal classifier:

$$QWK = \frac{\sum\limits_{i,j} \omega_{i,j} O_{i,j}}{\sum\limits_{i,j} \omega_{i,j} E_{i,j}}, \tag{4}$$

where ω is the penalization matrix (in this case, quadratic weights are considered), O is the confusion matrix and E is the normalized outer product between the prediction and the true vector.

Based on that, a continuous version of the QWK loss (QWK_l) was proposed in [16], but it was used together with a standard activation function (the $\texttt{softmax}$), which does not exploit the order of the labels. The definition of the QWK loss is given by [16]:

$$QWK_l = \frac{O}{E} = \frac{\sum\limits_{k=1}^{N} \sum\limits_{q=1}^{Q} \omega_{t_k,q} P(y = \mathcal{C}_q | \mathbf{x}_k)}{\sum\limits_{i=1}^{Q} \frac{N_i}{N} \sum\limits_{j=1}^{Q} (\omega_{i,j} \sum\limits_{k=1}^{N} P(y = \mathcal{C}_j | \mathbf{x}_k))}, \tag{5}$$

where $QWK_l \in [0, 2]$, $\mathbf{x}_k$ and t_k are the input data and the real class of the k-th sample, Q is the number of classes, N is the number of samples, N_i is the number of samples of the ith class, $P(y = \mathcal{C}_q | \mathbf{x}_k)$ is the probability[2] that the kth sample belongs to class $\mathcal{C}_q$ and $\omega_{i,j}$ are the elements of the penalization matrix. Generally, $\omega_{i,j} = \frac{|i-j|^n}{(C-1)^n}$, where $\omega_{i,j} \in [0, 1]$. In this paper, we used quadratic penalization ($n = 2$), then $\omega_{i,j} = \frac{|i-j|^2}{(C-1)^2}$. In this way, for $Q = 5$, the penalization matrix is shown in Table 1.

Table 1. Quadratic penalization matrix for $Q = 5$.

	1	2	3	4	5
1	0	0.0625	0.2500	0.5625	1
2	0.0625	0	0.0625	0.2500	0.5625
3	0.2500	0.0625	0	0.0625	0.2500
4	0.5625	0.2500	0.0625	0	0.0625
5	1	0.5625	0.2500	0.0625	0

---

[2] In this paper, $P(y = \mathcal{C}_q | \mathbf{x}_k)$ will be given by the POM probabilistic structure referred in Sect. 4.2.

According to the definition of QWK and $\omega_{i,j}$ that we have provided, the optimization of the function QWK is a minimization problem that can be solved with a gradient descent based algorithm in the following form:

$$\frac{\partial QWK_l}{\partial y_q} = \frac{\partial(\frac{O}{E})}{\partial y_q} = \frac{\frac{\partial O}{\partial y_q}E - \frac{\partial E}{\partial y_q}O}{E^2} = \frac{\partial O}{\partial y_q}\frac{1}{E} - \frac{\partial E}{\partial y_q}\frac{O}{E^2} \qquad (6)$$

where

$$\frac{\partial O}{\partial y_q(\mathbf{x}_k)} = \omega_{t_k,q} \quad \text{and} \quad \frac{\partial E}{\partial y_q(\mathbf{x}_k)} = \sum_{i=1}^{Q} \frac{N_i}{N}\omega_{i,q} \quad \text{for } q = 1, ..., Q. \qquad (7)$$

In matrix form:

$$\frac{\partial O}{\partial y_q(\mathbf{x}_k)} = \begin{pmatrix} \omega_{t_1,1} & \omega_{t_1,2} & \cdots & \omega_{t_1,Q} \\ \omega_{t_2,1} & \omega_{t_2,2} & \cdots & \omega_{t_2,Q} \\ \cdots & \cdots & \cdots & \cdots \\ \omega_{t_N,1} & \omega_{t_N,2} & \cdots & \omega_{t_N,Q} \end{pmatrix}, \frac{\partial E}{\partial y_q(\mathbf{x}_k)} = \begin{pmatrix} \sum_{i=1}^{Q}\frac{N_i}{N}\omega_{1,i} & \cdots & \cdots & \sum_{i=1}^{Q}\frac{N_i}{N}\omega_{Q,i} \\ \sum_{i=1}^{Q}\frac{N_i}{N}\omega_{1,i} & \cdots & \cdots & \sum_{i=1}^{Q}\frac{N_i}{N}\omega_{Q,i} \\ \cdots & \cdots & \cdots & \cdots \\ \sum_{i=1}^{Q}\frac{N_i}{N}\omega_{1,i} & \cdots & \cdots & \sum_{i=1}^{Q}\frac{N_i}{N}\omega_{Q,i} \end{pmatrix}.$$

$$(8)$$

4   Experiments

In this section, we describe the datasets and the models considered for the experimentation and some details about the experimental design.

4.1   Datasets

We have selected two important ordinal regression datasets:

- *Diabetic Retinopathy (DR)*[3] is a dataset containing high-resolution fundus image data. The training set consists of $17,563$ pairs of left and right eye images with five levels of the disease. DR was used in a Kaggle competition and in later works [15,16]. The validation set consists of a 10% of the training set. For our experiments, we resize the images 128×128 pixels and rescale the values to the $[0,1]$ range. Some test images are shown in Fig. 1.
- *Adience*[4]. This dataset consists of $26,580$ faces belonging to $2,284$ subjects. The dataset was preprocessed, using the methods described in a previous work [2], so that the images are 256 pixels in width and height, and pixels values follow a $(0;1)$ normal distribution. The original dataset was split into

---

[3] https://www.kaggle.com/c/diabetic-retinopathy-detection/data.
[4] http://www.openu.ac.il/home/hassner/Adience/data.html.

five folds. The training set consists of merging the first four folds which comprise a total of 15, 554 images. From this, 10% of the images are held out as part of a validation set. The last fold is reserved for test evaluation. Some images of this dataset are shown in Fig. 1 too.

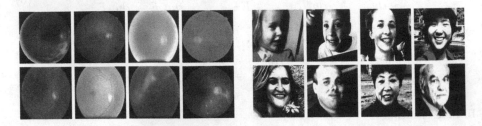

Fig. 1. Examples of the Diabetic Retinopathy (left) and Adience (right) test set.

Table 2. Description of the architectures used in the experiments. For convolutional layers, ConvWxH@FsS = F filters of size WxH and stride S. For pooling layers, Pool-WxHsS = pool size of WxH and stride S.

Diabetic Retinopathy		Adience	
Layer	Output shape	Layer	Output shape
2 x Conv3x3@32s1	252x252x32	Conv7x7@32s2	112x112x32
MaxPool2x2s2	126x126x32	MaxPool3x3s2	55x55x32
2 x Conv3x3@64s1	122x122x64	2 x ResBlock3x3@64s1	55x55x32
MaxPool2x2s2	61x61x64	1 x ResBlock3x3@128s2	28x28x64
2 x Conv3x3@128s1	57x57x128	2 x ResBlock3x3@128s1	28x28x64
MaxPool2x2s2	28x28x128	1 x ResBlock3x3@256s2	14x14x128
2 x Conv3x3@128s1	24x24x128	2 x ResBlock3x3@256s1	14x14x128
MaxPool2x2s2	12x12x128	1 x ResBlock3x3@512s2	7x7x256
Conv4x4@128s1	9x9x128	AveragePool7x7s2	1x1x256

4.2   Models Compared

CNNs have been used for both datasets. The different architectures of CNN used in these experiments are presented in Table 2. The architecture for DR is the same that was used in [16] and the network for Adience is a small Residual Network (ResNet) [8] that was used in [2]. Every convolutional layer is followed by an Exponential Linear Unit (ELU) [4] and a batch normalization [10], in this order. Dense layers also use the ELU activation function. At the output of the network, the POM is used. Also, a learnable parameter has been used to rescale the projections used as input for the POM to avoid the stagnation and to make it numerically more stable: $l(\mathbf{x}) = o(\mathbf{x})/\lambda$, where λ is also learnt from the data and $o(\mathbf{x})$ is the unscaled latent representation.

4.3   Experimental Design

The model is optimized using the Adam algorithm [11], which is a batch based first-order optimization algorithm. The learning rate parameter for this algorithm will be selected between different tested values. Also, an exponential decay will be applied to the initial learning rate to reduce it across the training epochs.

The training will be run for 100 epochs for both datasets. However, in the case of DR, the epoch size will be fixed to $100,000$ images per epoch, while, for Adience, the size will be equal to the number of images in the training set.

Data augmentation techniques were applied to both datasets [12] to get a higher number of examples and improve the capacity of generalization of the model. Different transformations were applied to each dataset: in the case of DR, augmentation was based on image cropping and zooming, horizontal and vertical flipping, brightness adjustment and random rotations. In Adience dataset, only horizontal flipping was applied.

The model was evaluated using the QWK metric described in Sect. 3. Alternative evaluation metrics have been used to ease the comparison against other works: Correct Classification Rate (CCR) and 1-off accuracy [3].

Two versions of these experiments were made: the first one used both the POM and the QWK loss (ordinal) while the second one used the softmax function and the cross-entropy loss (nominal). Every experiment was repeated five times to get more robust results, while having an affordable computational time.

In the experimentation, we considered three different factors: (1) *Learning rate* (L), where the values explored for this parameter were: $10^{-2}, 10^{-3}$ and 10^{-4}. (2) *Batch size* (B), for which we considered three separate batch sizes for each dataset. For the DR dataset, we used 5, 10 and 15, while, for the Adience dataset, 64, 128 and 256 images were used. We took the batch sizes that were used in [16] and [2] as a reference, and we expanded the range on both sides. (3) *Classification Model* (M), considering two different versions of the model: nominal (softmax and cross-entropy) and ordinal (POM and QWK loss) approaches.

5   Results

In this section, we present the results of the experiments. For each dataset, we show a table with the detailed experiments performed for training the model with each combination of parameters. As every parameter combination has been run five times, these tables show the mean value and the standard deviation (SD) of each metric across these five executions for the test set. Detailed test results are presented in Table 3. The best result for each metric is marked in bold and the second best is in italic font.

5.1   Statistical Analysis

In this section, to determine the statistical significance of the differences in mean QWK observed for each classifier, each batch size and each learning rate value,

Table 3. Mean and standard deviation (Mean$_{SD}$) of the test results for the DR dataset. M: classification Model. L: Learning rate. B: Batch size. N: Nominal. O: Ordinal.

Diabetic Retinopathy						Adience					
Factor			Evaluation metric			Factor			Evaluation metric		
M	L	B	QWK$_{(SD)}$	CCR$_{(SD)}$	1-off$_{(SD)}$	M	L	B	QWK$_{(SD)}$	CCR$_{(SD)}$	1-off$_{(SD)}$
N	10^{-2}	5	$0.205_{(0.060)}$	$0.527_{(0.035)}$	$0.673_{(0.064)}$	N	10^{-2}	64	$0.779_{(0.013)}$	$0.447_{(0.021)}$	$0.795_{(0.019)}$
N	10^{-3}	5	$0.265_{(0.118)}$	$0.525_{(0.044)}$	$0.699_{(0.103)}$	N	10^{-3}	64	$0.787_{(0.004)}$	$0.458_{(0.008)}$	$0.800_{(0.007)}$
N	10^{-4}	5	$0.445_{(0.027)}$	$0.660_{(0.038)}$	$0.836_{(0.008)}$	N	10^{-4}	64	$0.627_{(0.023)}$	$0.365_{(0.032)}$	$0.701_{(0.009)}$
N	10^{-2}	10	$0.300_{(0.050)}$	$0.569_{(0.027)}$	$0.717_{(0.054)}$	N	10^{-2}	128	$0.762_{(0.013)}$	$0.443_{(0.007)}$	$0.790_{(0.009)}$
N	10^{-3}	10	$0.399_{(0.010)}$	$0.578_{(0.026)}$	$0.798_{(0.007)}$	N	10^{-3}	128	$0.768_{(0.007)}$	$0.454_{(0.009)}$	$0.791_{(0.004)}$
N	10^{-4}	10	$0.497_{(0.011)}$	$0.692_{(0.012)}$	$0.854_{(0.006)}$	N	10^{-4}	128	$0.586_{(0.033)}$	$0.321_{(0.050)}$	$0.665_{(0.013)}$
N	10^{-2}	15	$0.368_{(0.062)}$	$0.616_{(0.032)}$	$0.775_{(0.044)}$	N	10^{-2}	256	$0.759_{(0.007)}$	$0.447_{(0.006)}$	$0.793_{(0.004)}$
N	10^{-3}	15	$0.416_{(0.029)}$	$0.600_{(0.017)}$	$0.800_{(0.025)}$	N	10^{-3}	256	$0.752_{(0.004)}$	$0.429_{(0.009)}$	$0.781_{(0.005)}$
N	10^{-4}	15	$0.486_{(0.007)}$	$0.671_{(0.022)}$	$0.854_{(0.006)}$	N	10^{-4}	256	$0.480_{(0.094)}$	$0.326_{(0.024)}$	$0.616_{(0.041)}$
O	10^{-2}	5	$0.416_{(0.041)}$	$0.563_{(0.054)}$	$0.807_{(0.029)}$	O	10^{-2}	64	$0.778_{(0.019)}$	$0.366_{(0.025)}$	$0.775_{(0.015)}$
O	10^{-3}	5	$0.554_{(0.013)}$	$0.660_{(0.008)}$	$0.853_{(0.005)}$	O	10^{-3}	64	$\mathbf{0.881}_{(0.005)}$	$\mathbf{0.518}_{(0.008)}$	$\mathbf{0.894}_{(0.005)}$
O	10^{-4}	5	$0.520_{(0.003)}$	$0.706_{(0.005)}$	$0.862_{(0.003)}$	O	10^{-4}	64	$0.784_{(0.011)}$	$0.318_{(0.026)}$	$0.731_{(0.030)}$
O	10^{-2}	10	$0.531_{(0.031)}$	$0.623_{(0.025)}$	$0.838_{(0.014)}$	O	10^{-2}	128	$0.781_{(0.041)}$	$0.398_{(0.031)}$	$0.779_{(0.020)}$
O	10^{-3}	10	$\mathbf{0.579}_{(0.009)}$	$0.686_{(0.013)}$	$0.861_{(0.002)}$	O	10^{-3}	128	$0.865_{(0.005)}$	$0.497_{(0.009)}$	$0.874_{(0.008)}$
O	10^{-4}	10	$0.539_{(0.007)}$	$0.707_{(0.010)}$	$0.858_{(0.004)}$	O	10^{-4}	128	$0.586_{(0.008)}$	$0.192_{(0.001)}$	$0.396_{(0.002)}$
O	10^{-2}	15	$0.551_{(0.020)}$	$0.654_{(0.027)}$	$0.856_{(0.015)}$	O	10^{-2}	256	$0.764_{(0.102)}$	$0.387_{(0.083)}$	$0.783_{(0.065)}$
O	10^{-3}	15	$0.551_{(0.010)}$	$0.680_{(0.019)}$	$\mathbf{0.866}_{(0.001)}$	O	10^{-3}	256	$0.851_{(0.008)}$	$0.449_{(0.015)}$	$0.850_{(0.008)}$
O	10^{-4}	15	$0.543_{(0.008)}$	$\mathbf{0.723}_{(0.004)}$	$0.862_{(0.004)}$	O	10^{-4}	256	$0.558_{(0.008)}$	$0.187_{(0.002)}$	$0.389_{(0.003)}$

we have carried out a parametric ANOVA III test. ANOVA statistical tool is applied to determine whether the influence of a change in the parameter values (classification model, M, batch size, B, and learning rate, L) is significant with respect to the obtained QWK measure (response variable) and to establish the most suitable value for these parameters to obtain good results. We did two separate tests for each dataset considered. Table 4, which contains the sum of squares (S.S.), degrees of freedom (D.F.), mean square (M.S.), test statistics (F-ratio), and significance level (Sig.), represents the analysis in a compact form.

Table 4. ANOVA III for the analysis of the main factors of the experiments.

DR dataset						Adience dataset					
Source	S.S.	D.F.	M.S.	F-ratio	Sig.	Source	S.S.	D.F.	M.S.	F-ratio	Sig.
Model	19.523	14	1.395	658.163	0.000	Model	49.107	18	2.728	1654.762	0.000
C factor	0.546	1	0.546	257.668	0.000	C factor	0.084	1	0.084	50.759	0.000
B factor	0.126	2	0.063	29.851	0.000	B factor	0.094	2	0.047	28.651	0.000
L factor	0.183	2	0.091	43.180	0.000	L factor	0.758	2	0.379	230.023	0.000
CB factors	0.017	2	0.008	3.980	0.023	CL factors	0.033	2	0.017	10.100	0.000
CL factors	0.107	2	0.054	25.303	0.000	BL factors	0.091	4	0.023	13.830	0.000
BL factors	0.036	4	0.009	4.300	0.003	CBL factors	0.031	6	0.005	3.179	0.008
Error	0.161	76	0.002			Error	0.119	72	0.002		
Total	19.684	90				Total	49.225	90			

As shown in Table 4, there are significant differences between the mean QWK. Now we analyse the magnitude of these differences to determine the order of each value associated with each factor. For this, a post-hoc HSD Tukey's multiple comparison test has been performed on the QWK means. First, the test for the DR dataset reported that the best value for the batch size is 15 (mean value 0.486) followed by 10 (mean value 0.474) and the best learning rate is 10^{-4} (0.505). Finally, we use a student t-test to determine if there are significant differences in mean associated with the type of classifier used (nominal or ordinal). A previous Levene test of equality of variances shows that they are significantly different, and the student's t-test shows that the average values obtained using the ordinal classifier are significantly higher than those of the nominal classifier. This confirms that, for this database, an ordinal classifier performs better.

The same tests were applied for Adience. The HSD Tukey's test reported that the best value for the batch size is 64 (mean value 0.817), followed by 128 (mean value 0.770), and the best learning rate is 10^{-3} (mean value 0.817). The t-test indicates that there are significant differences and the ordinal model obtains better results (i.e., for this database, it is also better to use an ordinal classifier).

5.2   Comparison with Previous Works

The best results for each dataset for the ordinal (Ord.) and nominal (Nom.) cases and the best results reported in previous works are shown in Table 5. All the results are given for the test set, except those from [16] (DR dataset), because the authors only provided validation results for 128×128 images (however, validation results are usually better than test results). The proposed ordinal model outperforms all the other alternatives in terms of QWK. The performance gain of the ordinal model over the nominal reaches 16.5% for DR and 11.9% for Adience dataset. The improvement of the ordinal method for the DR dataset is higher than that for the Adience dataset (in such a way that the performance improvement is higher when the problem is more complex).

Table 5. Comparison between the best test results of the ordinal proposal, the nominal version and previous approaches for both datasets.

	DR dataset				Adience dataset		
Method	$\overline{QWK}_{(SD)}$	$\overline{CCR}_{(SD)}$	1-off$_{(SD)}$	Method	$\overline{QWK}_{(SD)}$	$\overline{CCR}_{(SD)}$	1-off$_{(SD)}$
Ord.	$0.579_{(0.009)}$	$0.723_{(0.004)}$	$0.866_{(0.001)}$	Ord.	$0.881_{(0.005)}$	$0.518_{(0.008)}$	$0.894_{(0.005)}$
Nom.	$0.497_{(0.011)}$	$0.692_{(0.012)}$	$0.854_{(0.006)}$	Nom.	$0.787_{(0.004)}$	$0.458_{(0.008)}$	$0.800_{(0.007)}$
[16]	$0.537_{(-)}$	-	-	[6]	-	$0.451_{(0.026)}$	$0.807_{(0.011)}$
[15]	$0.555_{(-)}$	-	-	[3]	-	$0.529_{(0.060)}$	$0.885_{(0.022)}$
				[14]	-	$0.507_{(0.051)}$	$0.847_{(0.022)}$

6   Conclusions

An ordinal neural network based on the POM model has been proposed for deep learning and compared against the traditional nominal version. The results show that the ordinal version outperforms the nominal one for almost all values of the parameter configurations. Moreover, it makes the model more stable, reducing the risk of over-fitting and avoiding the stagnation. This reduces the importance of hyper-parameter adjusting compared to the nominal model. We have also checked that the optimal value for each hyper-parameter is problem-dependant, and a detailed experimental study must be performed to obtain better results. The best QWK mean for the DR dataset was obtained with the ordinal model and using a BS of 10 and a LR of 10^{-3}. In the case of Adience, the best results were obtained with a batch size of 64 and a learning rate of 10^{-3} too.

In future works, different link functions can be studied for the output layer, such as the `probit` or the complementary `log-log` function [1], instead of the `logit` link used for POM.

References

1. Agresti, A.: Analysis of Ordinal Categorical Data, vol. 656. Wiley, Hoboken (2010)
2. Beckham, C., Pal, C.: Unimodal probability distributions for deep ordinal classification. arXiv preprint arXiv:1705.05278 (2017)
3. Chen, J.C., Kumar, A., Ranjan, R., Patel, V.M., Alavi, A., Chellappa, R.: A cascaded convolutional neural network for age estimation of unconstrained faces. In: Proceedings of 8th IEEE Conference on Biometrics Theory, Applications and Systems (BTAS), pp. 1–8. IEEE (2016). https://doi.org/10.1109/BTAS.2016.7791154
4. Clevert, D.A., Unterthiner, T., Hochreiter, S.: Fast and accurate deep network learning by exponential linear units (elus). arXiv preprint arXiv:1511.07289 (2015)
5. Cruz-Ramírez, M., Hervás-Martínez, C., Sánchez-Monedero, J., Gutiérrez, P.A.: Metrics to guide a multi-objective evolutionary algorithm for ordinal classification. Neurocomputing **135**, 21–31 (2014). https://doi.org/10.1016/j.neucom.2013.05.058
6. Eidinger, E., Enbar, R., Hassner, T.: Age and gender estimation of unfiltered faces. IEEE Trans. Inf. Forensics Secur. **9**(12), 2170–2179 (2014). https://doi.org/10.1109/TIFS.2014.2359646
7. Gutierrez, P.A., Perez-Ortiz, M., Sanchez-Monedero, J., Fernandez-Navarro, F., Hervas-Martinez, C.: Ordinal regression methods: survey and experimental study. IEEE Trans. Knowl. Data Eng. **28**(1), 127–146 (2016). https://doi.org/10.1109/TKDE.2015.2457911
8. He, K., Zhang, X., Ren, S., Sun, J.: Deep residual learning for image recognition. In: Proceedings of the IEEE Conference Computer Vision and Pattern Recognition, pp. 770–778 (2016)
9. Hinton, G., et al.: Deep neural networks for acoustic modeling in speech recognition: the shared views of four research groups. IEEE Sig. Process. Mag. **29**(6), 82–97 (2012)
10. Ioffe, S., Szegedy, C.: Batch normalization: Accelerating deep network training by reducing internal covariate shift. arXiv preprint arXiv:1502.03167 (2015)
11. Kingma, D.P., Ba, J.: Adam: A method for stochastic optimization. arXiv preprint arXiv:1412.6980 (2014)
12. Krizhevsky, A., Sutskever, I., Hinton, G.E.: Imagenet classification with deep convolutional neural networks. In: Advances in Neural Information Processing System, pp. 1097–1105 (2012)

13. LeCun, Y., Bengio, Y., Hinton, G.: Deep learning. Nature **521**(7553), 436 (2015). https://doi.org/10.1038/nature14539
14. Levi, G., Hassner, T.: Age and gender classification using convolutional neural networks. In: Proceedings of the IEEE Conference Computer Vision and Pattern Recognition, pp. 34–42 (2015)
15. Nebot, À., et al.: Diabetic retinopathy detection through image analysis using deep convolutional neural networks. In: A.I. Research and Development: Proceedings of the 19th International Conference of the Catalan Association for A.I, p. 58. IOS Press (2016). https://doi.org/10.3233/978-1-61499-696-5-58
16. de la Torre, J., Puig, D., Valls, A.: Weighted kappa loss function for multi-class classification of ordinal data in deep learning. Pattern Recogn. Lett. **105**, 144–154 (2018). https://doi.org/10.1016/j.patrec.2017.05.018

Data Preprocessing for Automatic WMH Segmentation with FCNNs

P. Duque$^{(\boxtimes)}$ ⓘ, J. M. Cuadra ⓘ, E. Jiménez ⓘ,
and Mariano Rincón-Zamorano ⓘ

Departamento Inteligencia Artificial, UNED, Madrid, Spain
pablo.duque55@gmail.com, {jmcuadra,esterjimenez,mrincon}@dia.uned.es,
http://simda.uned.es/

Abstract. Automatic segmentation of brain white matter hyperintensities (WMH) is a challenging problem. Recently, the proposals based on Fully Convolutional Neural Networks (FCNN) are giving very good results, as it is demostrated by the top WMH challenge architectures. However, the problem is non completely solved yet. In this paper we analyze the influence of preprocessing stages of the input data on a fully convolutional network (FCNN) based on the U-NET architecture. Results demostrate that standarization, skull stripping and contrast enhancement significantly influence the results of segmentation.

Keywords: White matter hyperintensities ·
Fully Convolutional Neural Networks · U-NET ·
Contrast enhancement · Normalization · Standardization

1 Introduction

The presence of leukoaraiosis or white matter hyperintensities (WMH) in the brain of elderly individuals is linked to increased risk of stroke, cognitive impairment, dementia and ultimately, death. Magnetic resonance imaging (MRI) is by far the most sensitive modality for detecting WMH and MRI is consequently a very central diagnostic procedure in the elderly population. Manual WMH segmentation is very time-consuming and prone to user-bias, which has resulted in several attempts to generating automated analysis tools for WMH segmentation [1–3].

Recently, solutions based on Fully Convolutional Networks (FCNN) are giving very good results as shown by the first positions in the WMH challenge [3]. Nevertheless, there are still problems to solve such as the great inter- and intra-observer variability, so a systematic study of the phases of the problem solution is necessary. In this context, this paper focuses on the analysis of input data preprocessing and its influence on a FCNN based on the U-Net [4].

ⓒ Springer Nature Switzerland AG 2019
J. M. Ferrández Vicente et al. (Eds.): IWINAC 2019, LNCS 11487, pp. 452–460, 2019.
https://doi.org/10.1007/978-3-030-19651-6_44

2 Materials and Methods

2.1 Dataset

In all reported experiments, we relied on the publicly available dataset from the MICCAI WMH Challenge [3], organized as a joint effort of the UMC Utrecht, VU Amsterdam and NUHS Singapore for benchmarking methods for automatic WMH segmentation. It consists in 60 cases, 20 from each one of the three centres. For each subject, a 3D T1-weighted volume, and a 2D multi-slice FLAIR volume were provided. FLAIR images had the following acquisition characteristics: Utrecht (3T Philips Achieva, $0.96 \times 0.95 \times 3.00$, $240 \times 240 \times 48$), Singapore (3T Siemens TrioTim, $1.00 \times 1.00 \times 3.00$, $252 \times 232 \times 48$) and Amsterdam (3T GE Signa HDxt, $0.98 \times 0.98 \times 1.20$, $132 \times 256 \times 83$). T1 and FLAIR images were aligned using elastix [5,6] and bias correction was applied by using the SPM12 software [7]. WMH were manually segmented by experts and this masks were used for training and testing.

All slices were set to 240×240. Slices were conveniently cropped or padded to keep the center of the image. Top and bottom slices are removed to reduce noise since there is no white matter in such slices of the brain. We opted to remove the bottom 6 slices and the top 4 slices.

2.2 Preprocessing

Apart from the initial basic preprocessing performed by the WMH challenge organizers, we aimed to analyze how different transformations of the input data impact and facilitate machine learning with FCNNs.

Skull Stripping. The MRI modalities currently used to segment WMH are (1) FLAIR, where WMH appear as hyperintensities, and (2) T1, where tissues are distinguishable. In this sense, T1 gives complementary and necessary information for the segmentation task as hyperintesities in the FLAIR image may correspond also to artifacts in the GM-CSF interface, the skull or infarcted tissue. A first preprocessing step that can remove a lot of noise by focusing the analysis on the area of interest is to remove the skull using a mask. FSL-BET [8] was used to obtain the brain mask in T1, and it was applied to both input volumes afterwards.

Normalization. FLAIR and T1 images have different scales and intensity levels and are subject and machine dependent, so a normalization process is very necessary for the correct functioning of deep learning algorithms. Due to the high intersubject intensity variance, three different types of normalization were applied on a per-case basis instead of applying it directly to the entire dataset.

Generally, not normalizing images at all leads to the network not being able to converge properly, or to very unstable results. A very simple way to normalize data is to linearly move all intensities to range [0, 1] with the min-max normalization.

$$x' = \frac{x - min(x)}{max(x) - min(x)} \qquad (1)$$

As both volume inputs, FLAIR and T1, present a leptokurtic distribution with extreme outliers, a min-max normalization can squeeze the data in very low ranges as shown in Fig. 1. In order to spread the range of intensities as much as possible to allow the network to differentiate hypointense pixels from hyperintense ones we can use quantile normalization.

$$x' = \begin{cases} 0 & if \ x < P_{0.5} \\ 1 & if \ x > P_{99.7} \\ else & \frac{x - P_{0.5}}{P_{99.7} - P_{0.5}} \end{cases} \qquad (2)$$

where P_n is the percentile n. It is a non-linear transformation that cuts the ends of the distribution while preserving linearity in the central region (an example is shown in Fig. 1).

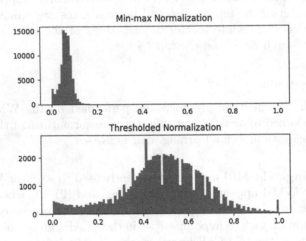

Fig. 1. FLAIR intensity distribution before and after applying quantile normalization.

Standardization. Standardization is one of the most common feature scaling techniques in machine learning. It is also widely used in fully convolutional networks as well as in similar segmentation problems. In this case, the linear transformation rescales the distribution to have zero mean and a standard deviation of one.

$$x' = \frac{x - mean(x)}{\sigma}$$

Contrast Enhancement. There exists a large inter- and intra- observer variability in the manual delineation of WMH. This makes the gold standard used for training not very precise and therefore, to obtain precise results by automatic segmentation becomes difficult [1].

In MRI brain images, several problems can lead to erroneous segmentation or pixel classification errors [9]. These problems can be: average partial volume, noise overlap and intensity of adjacent tissue classes and for WMH in FLAIR images a lower contrast may appear at the edge while in the center of the region a higher contrast [10]. To avoid these problems, a better separation between the pathology and the background of the image can be achieved using contrast enhancement techniques. A review on contrast enhancement techniques, not only subscribed to MRI, can be found in [11], for a review in MRI field see [10].

In our work we use the technique developed in [9] to improve the contrast of WMH in FLAIR images. This technique uses an estimate of the WMH edge magnitude and the intensity values combined through several transformations to highlight WMH, see Fig. 2. All the transformations are only calculated from the characteristics of each slice of the image, so they are adaptive. The technique achieves an average contrast improvement of 41.1% in the experiments performed in the original work.

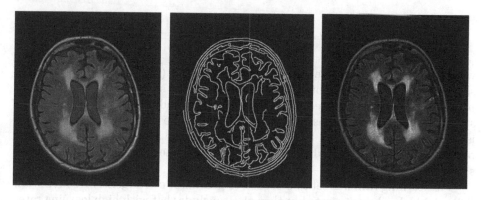

Fig. 2. Contrast enhancement: original FLAIR (left), edge map (center) and enhanced FLAIR (right).

2.3   Fully Convolutional Neural Network (adapted U-Net)

In this work we propose a deep learning approach using a FCNN that follows the U-Net architecture [4]. Due to the non-isotropic voxel size of the FLAIR volumes, we applied a two dimensional approach, analising the volume slice by slice from the axial view. The FCNN was feeded with two input channels, one corresponding to FLAIR information and the other to the T1.

In order to obtain good results, deep learning techniques usually apply data augmentation when the dataset in small batches, which allows the model to converge and generalize better. In our case, to triple the dataset, we applied affine data transformations, such as rotations on $[-30°, 30°]$ angles, shifts on both the x and y axis $[-30\%, 30\%]$ of the total width and height, respectively, zoom on both axes in the ranges $[0.9, 1.2]$ and shears in the range $[-0.2, 0.2]$. Actual values where picked randomly from a normal distribution.

The U-Net is a fully convolutional neural network. It has a contracting path on the left side and a expanding path on the right, giving it a U shape. The contracting follows a more conventional structure of two convolutions followed by a pooling layer, this process repeats four times. As the expanding path up-samples the feature maps it is concatenated with the respective level of the contracting path, then two convolutions are applied. This process is also repeated four times.

The U-Net was originally designed for multi class classification and a softmax activation layer was used in the last layer. However, here we are using a sigmoid as the final activation function due to the binary nature of the segmentation problem. On the other hand, the weighted cross entropy loss function proposed for the U-Net was not the proper choice for this problem due to how highly unbalanced our data is (only 0.17175% were WMH voxels). Instead the Dice Similarity Coefficient was used as the loss function for training the network. This metric is widely used as loss function for similar binary segmentations [12].

The loss function used was the negative Dice Similarity Coefficient:

$$DSC_{loss} = -2 \times \frac{\sum_{n=1}^{N} |p_n \circ g_n| + s}{\sum_{n=1}^{N} |p_n + g_n| + s}$$

where $\circ$ is the element-wise product of two matrices (also represented as inter-section since we are using binary matrices), $|x|$ is the sum of values of matrix x, p_n and g_n stand for predicted segmentation and ground truth, respectively, and s stands for smoothing and assures that there will be no division by 0. Generally s is set to 1.0, however it can have a big influence in the average when the number of non-zero pixels is low (which happens often in these datasets). So we lowered s to 0.01.

The learning rate was set to 0.000001 to guarantee convergence. Related work [13] set a higher learning rate but they also conclude that with high learning rates the U-Net gets stuck at a low level of DSC loss and is not able to converge in multiple trainings. For a learning rate of 0.01, the DSC value will not surpass 0.01.

All convolution kernel sizes were changed to 5×5 instead of the original 3×3, to capture richer local data. All maxpoolings are kept as 2×2 with a stride of 2×2.

The original study for the U-Net proposes initializing weights from a trun-cated Gaussian distribution centered on 0 with a standard deviation of:

$$stdv = \sqrt{\frac{2}{N}} \tag{3}$$

where N is the number of inputs from the previous layer. We used this initial-ization, which granted more stability across trainings than the Glorot uniform, also named Xavier uniform [14], which is set as default in the Keras framework.

Since the batch size and learning rate affect the gradient, we set batch size to 30 to guarantee convergence given the selected learning rate.

The number of epochs was cut to 35 to prevent the model from over-fitting. We used 81.6% of the combined datasets for training. Another 15% of the data for testing during training and evaluating our method. The 3.4% left is used for validating predictions visually and generating output images.

The network was trained on Amazon Web Services (AWS). Out of their GPU portfolio we chose the p2.xlarge EC2 instance, which suited our needs for this task. The average training time was 10 h, however this time was lower on the trainings with only one channel. We used the Keras implementation of the Adam optimizer [15] for stochastic gradient based optimization.

3   Experimental results

Table 1 shows the results, ordered by DICE, after training for the different pre-processing configurations. It can be observed that the best data normalization is given by standardization. Only one of the configurations with standardization is not found in the first ranking positions, probably due to an error during conduction of the experiment.

Secondly, the use of a brain mask and the contrast enhancement technique have a significant influence in the results.

Finally, since normalization serves to put all variables on the same scale and thus facilitate that all entries have the same influence on the solution, and that, in our case, roughly, we could say that the FLAIR image provides Information about the WMH and the T1 image on the type of tissue, it might be interesting to weight the FLAIR image more than the T1 image. To evaluate this hypothesis, three experiments with different influence of T1 were performed: (1) T1 with the same weight as FLAIR (T1 = yes), (2) T1 weighted to 0.1 w.r.t. FLAIR (weighted 10%) and (3) eliminating T1 of the input data (T1 = No). The results obtained (first three configurations of the Table 1 do not support this hypothesis, since the difference between them is not significant. It is necessary to carry out more experiments to analyze if the T1 image has any significant influence in the segmentation, since the brain mask could also be obtained from the FLAIR image.

Figure 3 shows the results obtained with the FCNN in three slices with different load of WMH. It can be observed that detection of WMH is quite consistent except for the smaller ones.

4   Discussion

Input data normalization by standardization is a determining factor in the improvement of results. This may be motivated because the distribution of intensities in each case (volume, subject) is dominated by the number of tissue voxels of WM and GM, independently of the WMH load, which approximates a normal distribution. By standardizing the intensities of voxels within each case, we are normalizing with respect to the mean and the variance and, therefore, improving the correlation of the different tissues between cases.

Table 1. Segmentation performance of the FCNN trained on the WMH challenge input data with different preprocessing. tables.

Mask	Flair	T1	Normalization	DSC
Brain	Enhanced	Yes	Standardization	81.30
Brain	Enhanced	Weighted 10%	Standardization	81.05
Brain	Enhanced	No	Standardization	81.02
No	Enhanced	Yes	Standardization	79.49
Brain	Original	Yes	Standardization	78.29
No	Original	Yes	Standardization	76.81
No	Enhanced	Yes	Min max	76.72
Brain	Enhanced	Yes	Min max	76.34
Brain	Enhanced	Yes	Quantile	74.89
No	Enhanced	Yes	Quantile	73.04
Brain	Original	Yes	Quantile	72.70
Brain	Original	Yes	Min max	69.72
No	Original	Yes	Quantile	69.12
No	Original	Yes	Min max	66.89
Brain	Original	Weighted 10%	Standardization	64.04
Brain	Original	Yes	Min max	51.80

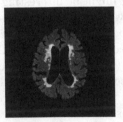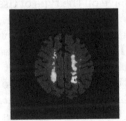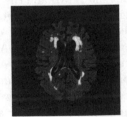

Fig. 3. Segmentation results on three slices from different subjects. True positive voxeles are shown in white or yellow colors, false positive voxels in red color and false negative voxels in green color. (Color figure online)

With the results obtained from the first three configurations of Table 1 we could conclude that the information introduced by T1 for the segmentation of the WMH is scarce, but it will be necessary to carry out more experiments to assess if the improvement is statistically significant.

5 Conclusions

In this work we analyze the use of different preprocessing techniques to improve automatic WMH segmentation based on multicontrast MRI analysis with

FCNNs. The biggest improvement is obtained by (1) using per-case standardization to normalize the data because it improves tissue intensity correlation between cases and (2) focusing the analysis in the brain removing the skull, and (3) applying a non-linear transformation that enhances WMH contrast.

The tests with FCNNs are very costly temporally and computationally (10 h on average per training), but it is demonstrated that the results obtained are competitive with the methods found in the state of the art.

In this paper we use a non-linear transformation that increases the contrast in WMH, which improves the performance of convolutional networks and at the same time poses a way of reducing the inter- and intra-observer variability. The use of more precise references would allow the system to also increase its precision.

Acknowledgements. This work is partially supported by the Autonomous Community of Madrid (PEJD-2018-PRE/TIC-8977).

References

1. Rincón, M., et al.: Improved automatic segmentation of white matter hyperintensities in MRI based on multilevel lesion features. UNED, Madrid, Spain (2017)
2. Caligiuri, M.E., Perrotta, P., Augimeri, A.: Automatic detection of white matter hyperintensities in healthy aging and pathology using magnetic resonance imaging: a review. Neuroinformatics **13**, 261 (2015). https://doi.org/10.1007/s12021-015-9260-y
3. WMH Segmentation Challenge. https://wmh.isi.uu.nl/
4. Ronneberg, O., Fischer, P., Brox, T.: U-Net: convolutional netowrks for biomedical image segmentation. University of Freiburg, Germany (2015)
5. Klein, S., Staring, M., Murphy, K., Viergever, M.A., Pluim, J.P.W.: elastix: a toolbox for intensity based medical image registration. IEEE Trans. Med. Imaging **29**(1), 196–205 (2010)
6. Shamonin, D.P., Bron, E.E., Lelieveldt, B.P.F., Smits, M., Klein, S., Staring, M.: Fast parallel image registration on CPU and GPU for diagnostic classification of Alzheimer's disease. Front. Neuroinformatics **7**(50), 1–15 (2014)
7. Ashburner, J., Barnes, G., Chen, C., Daunizeau, J., Flandin, G.: SPM12. Wellcome Trust Centre for Neuroimaging (2017)
8. Smith, S.M., et al.: Advances in functional and structural MR image analysis and implementation as FSL. NeuroImage **23**(S1), 208–19 (2004)
9. Khademi, A., Venetsanopoulos, A., Moody, A.: Automatic contrast enhancement of white matter lesions in FLAIR MRI. In: 2009 IEEE International Symposium on Biomedical Imaging, From Nano to Macro, pp. 322–325 (2009)
10. Isa, I., Sulaiman, S.N., Abdullah, M.F., Tahir, N.M., Mustapha, M., Karim, N.K.A.: New image enhancement technique for WMH segmentation of MRI FLAIR image. In: 2016 IEEE Symposium on Computer Applications Industrial Electronics (ISCAIE), pp. 30–34, May 2016
11. Huang, S.-C., Yeh, C.-H.: Image contrast enhancement for pre-serving mean brightness without losing image features. Eng. Appl. Artif. Intell. **26**(5), 1487–1492 (2013)

12. Milletari, F., Navab, N., Ahmadi, S.-A.: V-Net: fully convolutional neural networks for volumetric medical image segmentation (2016)
13. Li, H., et al.: Fully convolutional network ensembles for white matter hyperintensities segmentation in MR images (2018)
14. Glorot, X., Bengio, Y.: Understanding the difficulty of training deep feedforward neural networks. Universite de Montréal, Québec, Canada, DIRO (2010)
15. Kingma, D.P., Lei Ba, J.: ADAM, A method for stochastic optimization (2015)

FER in Primary School Children
for Affective Robot Tutors

Luis-Eduardo Imbernón Cuadrado[1](✉)(iD), Ángeles Manjarrés Riesco[2](iD),
and Félix de la Paz López[2](✉)(iD)

[1] Sopra-Steria, Madrid, Spain
imbernon@gmail.com
[2] Department of Artificial Intelligence,
Universidad Nacional de Educación a Distancia, Madrid, Spain
{amanja,delapaz}@dia.uned.es

Abstract. In the last few years, robotics has attracted much interest as a tool to support education through social interaction. Since Social- Emotional Learning (SEL) influences academic success, affective robot tutors have a great potential within education. In this article we report on our research in recognition of facial emotional expressions, aimed at improving ARTIE, an integrated environment for the development of affective robot tutors. A Full Convolutional Neural Network (FCNN) model has been trained with the Fer2013 dataset, and then validated with another dataset containing facial images of primary school children, which has been compiled during computing lab sessions. Our first prototype recognizes primary school children facial emotional expressions with 69,15% accuracy. As a future work we intend to further refine the ARTIE Emotional Component with a view to integrating the main singularities of primary school children emotional expression.

Keywords: Emotion recognition · Affective robot tutors ·
Facial emotional expression · Social emotional learning

1 Introduction

In recent years, the interest towards robotics has increased as a valuable educational tool from preschool to high school levels [4].

Conventional robots have already been quite used as pedagogical tools for Science, Technology, Engineering, and Math (STEM) education, and social robots begin to show to be effective to support education through social interaction. Social robots are not only able to interpret the student interaction with an educational content but also the social cues that indicate task engagement, confusion and attention [7].

Many studies about factors that influence the academic success of youth in schools have been carried out, concluding the advisability of SEL approaches [1]. Several educational programs involving SEL have focused on emotional expression [2].

© Springer Nature Switzerland AG 2019
J. M. Ferrández Vicente et al. (Eds.): IWINAC 2019, LNCS 11487, pp. 461–471, 2019.
https://doi.org/10.1007/978-3-030-19651-6_45

Robots are increasingly used across all sectors and for a wide range of tasks, from precision manufacturing to nursing. Thus, robotics and Artificial Intelligence (AI) are expected to leave factory floors and co-inhabit with humans. Robots acting among humans must be social [9] and a robot could not be called 'social' if the role of affect is not at least taken into account. In fact, understanding the affective state of the humans with whom social robots interact induce their engagement. Given that emotions change 'rapidly', the robot's model of the humans's emotions must be updated frequently [8]. Affective robots are effective with children as shown for example in Kindergarten Assistive Robotics (KAR) [11] and in special education Robotics, particularly in education of children with Autism Spectrum Disorder (ASD) [10].

Recognizing and reacting to cognitive and affective states is decisive to keep the learner engaged and to foster learning [12], and it is crucial in the early stages of education, hence, one of the main requirements for a robot tutor must be the ability to express and recognize emotions [4].

Our research is located in the field of affective robot tutors focused on primary school children. In particular our objective is to afford an environment for the development of affective robot tutors which will be guided by the affective state of the students, and will provide them with personalized emotional pedagogical support. In [4] we presented a first version of this environment and a simplified prototype of a tutoring robot that supervises training sessions with the educational application Scratch, identifying three basic cognitive-affective states (concentrated, distracted and inactive) on primary school children through keyboard and mouse interactions.

1.1   Affective Robot Tutors

In the affective robot tutors field, [13] suggests that an affect-aware robot can provide more affective and empathic experiences to children. This could be seen in [14] where the authors addressed teaching a second-language to children with an affective robot-child tutoring, concluding that this tutoring setup was effective in helping the children to learn new second language words.

1.2   Facial Emotion Recognition

There are a lot of ways to express emotions, but the most relevant channel to communicate them to others is the face. Focused in the best way to recognize emotions, there are over hundreds of studies devoted to facial emotion recognition (FER), described as one of the most beneficial manners to knowing how to recognize them [3]. The emotions assumed as 'basic' by the categorical emotion theory are inspired in the recognition in facial expressions of six cross-cultural emotions: anger, fear, joy, sadness, surprise and disgust [15].

Most of these studies have payed attention to adults instead of children facial expression recognition. Currently, the largest children facial expression dataset is The Child Affective Facial Expression (CAFE) set. Even this dataset, the largest with primary school children facial images, still contains a scarce amount of data to train a FER model [5]. What distinguishes our approach to affective educational robotics is the focus on primary school children, and therefore we intend that our emotional model takes into account as much as possible the idiosyncrasy of the children in this scholar stage.

Deep learning methods have achieved good results in FER, as can be seeing in [16,20,21], compared to more traditional feature extraction methods like Local Binary Patterns (LBP) [18] or Histogram of Oriented Gradients (HOG) [19].

Although some research suggests that the problem of identifying emotions from facial expressions is equivalent in adults and children [6], the fact is that there has not been much research in this field due to the aforementioned lack of repositories. Therefore, we consider essential to our research approach, starting by checking the hypothesis that algorithms designed for adults work equally well when discriminating emotions in children. Finally, we perform a preliminary analysis of the results obtained to find out if they are coherent with the research on FER in children.

The rest of the paper is structured as follows. In Sect. 2 we briefly introduce the integrated environment for the development of affective robot tutors ARTIE [4]. In Sect. 3 we present the methodology followed to develop a prototype of facial emotion expression recognition model. In Sect. 4 we analyse the results of our research. Finally, in Sect. 5 we present some conclusions and highlight some future research lines suggested by our experience.

2   ARTIE: An Integrated Environment for the Development of Affective Robot Tutors

With the aim of contributing to the rising field of affective robot tutors we have developed the Affective Robot Tutor Integrated Environment (ARTIE). In [4] we propose an architectural pattern which integrates any given educational software for primary school children with a component whose function is to identify the emotional state of the students who are interacting with the software, and with the driver of a robot tutor which provides personalized emotional pedagogical support to the students.

In order to support the development of affective robot tutors according to the proposed architecture, we also provide a methodology which incorporates a technique for eliciting pedagogical knowledge from teachers, and a generic development platform. This platform contains a component for identifying emotional states by analysing keyboard and mouse interaction data, and a generic affective pedagogical support component which specifies the affective educational interventions (including facial expressions, body language, tone of voice,...) in terms of Behavior Markup Language (BML) (a Behavior Markup Language for virtual agent specification) files which are translated into actions of a robot tutor. The platform and the methodology are both adapted to primary school students.

Finally, we have illustrated the use of this platform to build a prototype implementation of the architecture, in which the educational software was instantiated with Scratch and the robot tutor with NAO. The robot prototype interacts with its environment.

The ARTIE architecture is a reactive-deliberative robot architecture involving both the situated, the connectionist and the symbolic artificial intelligence paradigms. The robot interacts with its environment in real time, identifying the students by sensors, and communicating with them through effectors (via spoken language and body gestures, with emphasis on expressing the affective dimension), depending on its changing perceptions (with emphasis on perceiving the student emotional states), either reactively or deliberatively.

Our purpose was to demonstrate the feasibility of a general-purpose architecture of decoupled components, in which a wide range of educational software and robot tutors can be integrated and then used according to different educational criteria.

In Fig. 1 the ARTIE architectural pattern is shown.

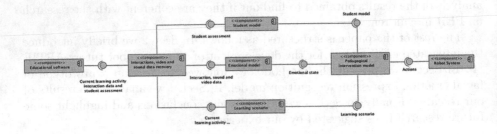

Fig. 1. ARTIE architectural pattern.

The components of this architecture are:

- **Educational Software:** In the case of this study, the educational software is Scratch.
- **Interactions, video and sound data recovery:** This component receives from the educational software all data about students and learning activities, and gathers all the student-computer interaction data, as well as the multimedia data being recorded.
- **Student Model:** This component represents the student, initially on the basis of his or her academic background and personal characteristics (learning style, skills, etc.).
- **Emotional model:** This component receives the interaction, and multimedia and returns the emotional state identified.
- **Learning scenario:** This component receives the data related to the specific learning activity being currently performed by the student and returns a specification of the learning scenario involved.
- **Pedagogical intervention model:** This component receives the dynamic student model, the current emotional state, and the current learning scenario, and returns the actions that the robot must perform.
- **Robot System:** In the frame of the reactive-deliberative paradigm, this component is responsible for ordering the movements in the effectors.

As mentioned above, this study seeks to improve the Emotional Model without using intrusive and expensive identification methods, with the aim of identifying more accurately the emotions which most affect the character of educational interventions.

3   A Facial Emotional Expression Recognition Model for Primary School Students

The objective of our research has been to generate a facial emotional expression recognition model for primary school children. Given the limited amount of facial images available for primary school children, the model has been trained using an adult facial images's dataset (FER2013). Then, the model has been validated with a dataset of facial images of primary school children, which have been collected during computer lab sessions with Scratch, and then labelled by experts. This section is divided in 3 subsections that describe, respectively: the data collection process, the manual labelling of the facial images previously collected, and the model generation.

3.1   Data Collection

Since our facial emotional expression recognition model had to be trained with an adult facial data set (FER 2013), and the purpose of this model is to detect emotions in children, we intended to test its accuracy identifying emotions in primary school children. For this reason we had to collect data of primary school children through a set of user experiences involving computer lab sessions with Scratch.

Data were collected through a software tool developed with the purpose of getting webcam images, screenshot images, keyboard and mouse interactions and student profiles.

The approval of the parents or legal tutors was necessary, as we were going to register and process personal information (facial images and the student profiles), as well as data of the tutors who supervised the sessions, due to General Data Protection Regulation (GDPR) law and the involvement of under-age students. For this purpose, an informed consent explaining what the research project was about, what data will be collected and what treatment will be given to the data was prepared. So those parents or legal tutors who wished their child to participate in the study, had to sign it.

At the time of carrying out the lab sessions, we had agreed the collaboration of Rockbotic: a company dedicated to educational robotics. The content experts and Rockbotic's tutors had designed a series of Scratch exercises that the students had to do during the data collection sessions.

The user experience took then place in a real learning environment. In Fig. 2 the data collection deployment diagram is presented.

After the data collection phase, 4 sessions of user experiences were conducted, with an average of 50 min per session. In this phase, the information was collected from 5 different participants aged between 9 and 12 years.

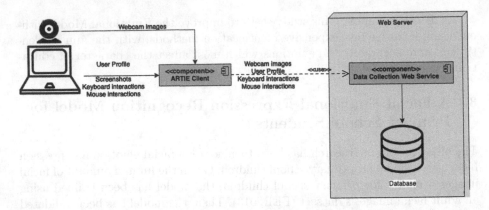

Fig. 2. ARTIE data collection deployment diagram.

The information collected could be itemized as follows:

- **4811 webcam images** (an average of 4,8 images per minute)
- **4811 screenshots** (an average of 4,8 images per minute)
- **1000 keyboard and mouse interactions sets** (an average of 1 set per minute)

3.2 Data Labelling

Once the data had been obtained, we proceeded to perform the labelling of the emotional states.

This task consisted of checking manually, the webcam images and labelling each of these images with one of the 7 emotional states (the 6 emotional states described in Sect. 1, plus a "neutral" emotional state).

For this purpose, an additional software application was developed. This application takes the images, the interaction data and the student profiles from the database and presents them in a timeline, allowing an expert to label the information with the corresponding emotional state.

Since students sometimes move from their place to interact with other classmates, some images did not include any children's face. In these cases, experts had the possibility to discard those sequences of images that did not show student's faces.

The result of the labeling is, on the one hand, the images classified by folders according to the emotional state and, on the other hand, the set of data of the keyboard and mouse interactions and the profiles of the students labelled with their emotional states.

3.3 Emotional Model Generation

As shown in [17], very good results have been obtained when using a FCNN approach. This architecture has been the most widely used in facial emotional expression recognition.

In our study, facial emotional expression recognition is based in [16], where besides getting good results in the International Conference on Machine Learning (ICML) (FER2013) dataset, the authors report having obtained good results in Toronto Face Dataset (TFD).

The model implemented is based in a FCNN composed by 3 convolutional layers and a fully connected neural network. The main function of the convolutional layers is to detect generic features like edges and shapes, and the purpose of the fully connected neural network is to detect more specific features. In all of these layers we have used the Rectified Linear Unit (ReLU) activation function except for the last layer, in which we used a softmax activation function that provides the probability of the class. Moreover, to avoid overfitting during the training phase we have added some dropout layers. Our model has been trained with Fer2013 dataset, a batch size of 64 and for 100 epochs.

In Table 1 our FCNN architecture is presented.

Table 1. ARTIE FCNN architecture for facial emotion recognition

Layers	Architecture
1	Input (48×48, 1)
2	Conv2D (32, (42×42), relu, same)
3	MaxPool 2D (32, (21×21))
4	Conv2D (32, (21×21), relu, same)
5	AvgPool 2D (32, (10×10))
6	Conv2D (64, (10×10), relu, same)
7	AvgPool 2D (64, (5×5))
8	Flatten
9	Dense (3072, relu)
10	Dropout (0.5)
11	Dense (3072, relu)
12	Dropout (0.5)
13	Softmax (7)

4 Results

For the training of our emotional recognition model we have used the Fer2013 dataset, however, because our goal is the identification of the emotional status of primary school children, this model has been validated with facial images of primary school children collected during the user experiences described in Sect. 3.1, and which have been classified by experts. Therefore, our model got two phases of validation: the first one with the validation set included in Fer2013, and the last one with the facial images of primary school children.

FER 2013 Dataset is composed by grayscale images with size of 48 × 48 pixels and classified through 7 emotional expressions (Angry (AN), Disgusted (DI), Afraid (AF), Happy (HA), Sad (SA), surprised (SU), and Neutral (NE)). These images are divided into 3 different subsets: a training set with 28709 images, a test set with 3589 images and a validation set with 3589 images. During the training phase with FER2013 dataset we have obtained an accuracy of 65,47% on the validation set and 66,15% on the test set. In Table 2 we show the Fer 2013 dataset distribution per class.

Table 2. FER 2013 distribution per class

Emotions	AN	DI	AF	HA	SA	SU	NE	Total
Training	3995	436	4097	7215	4830	3171	4965	**28709**
Test	467	56	496	895	653	415	607	**3589**
Validation	491	55	528	879	594	416	626	**3589**

During the user experiences described in Sect. 3.1, we have collected 4811 webcam images, of which those that did not show the face of the children were discarded, so finally we were left with 1328 images. In Table 3 we present the data collected through the user experiences.

Table 3. ARTIE data collection distribution per class

Emotions	AN	DI	AF	HA	SA	SU	NE	Total
ARTIE Collection	192	0	92	245	448	109	242	**1328**

In order to perform the validation with the dataset of primary school children, a web service that consults the emotional recognition model has been implemented. Through the ARTIE Labeller application, each of the images of the primary school children was sent to the web service; once the web service received the images, they were pre-processed (transforming the images in 48 × 48 px size and grayscale) and labelled by using the emotional recognition model trained before. The labels obtained from the web service's return were then compared with the experts' labelled ones. In Fig. 3 the deployment diagram of our validation system is presented.

In this validation phase, our model has obtained a 69,15% of accuracy. From the images collected we have identified 6 from 7 emotional states (Angry, Fear, Happy, Neutral, Sad and Surprise). The confusion matrix is shown below:

		Angry	Fear	Happy	Neutral	Sad	Surprise
				Actual			
Predicted	Angry	0.73	0	0.09	0.01	0	0.02
	Fear	0.01	0.99	0.01	0.03	0	0
	Happy	0.08	0	0.54	0.51	0	0.05
	Neutral	0.02	0	0.11	0.12	0	0
	Sad	0	0.01	0.12	0.05	0.99	0.16
	Surprise	0.16	0	0.13	0.28	0.01	0.77

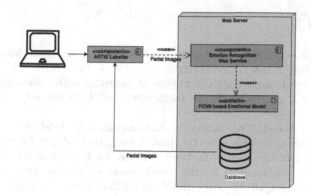

Fig. 3. ARTIE Data Labelling deployment diagram

There is a slight improvement in the identification of emotional states in the validation with children's facial images, compared to the identification of emotional states in adults in [16]. This may be due to the small amount of children's facial images, where 6 of 7 emotions were identified during user's experiences. Finally, if we compare the results obtained in our study with the results in [17] and [21]; they even reach better results, their improved results being under the 5% compared with ours.

5   Conclusions

We have developed a first prototype of emotional model capable to identify 7 emotional states, to be integrated into our ARTIE development platform. This emotional model has been based on a FCNN approach, that has been trained with the FER2013 dataset and validated with children images in a real learning environment, obtaining 69.15% of accuracy.

We consider this result is relevant because, there are few repositories that collect children's faces, and FER studies are based on adult faces datasets up to now. Recently the CAFE dataset has been compiled, but this dataset is still not big enough to train the algorithms. In addition, the models found in the literature such as [16,17,21] have only been validated in controlled scenarios, while our model has been validated in real learning scenarios.

As future work, we intend to develop a multimodal emotion recognition model, where keyboard and mouse interactions, as well as facial images data are combined. Finally, we intend to perform a refinement of the ARTIE pedagogical intervention model according to the refined emotional model, as well as to carry out user experiences using the different emotional models (the initial model based on keyboard and mouse interactions, the model based on facial emotional expressions, and a multimodal model) in order to compare the results regarding the pedagogical effectiveness of the tutor robot.

References

1. Johnson, A.: Supporting teachers through social and emotional learning. Success High-Need Sch. J. **14**(1), 26–29 (2018)
2. Van Deur, P.: Transforming the Future of Learning with Educational Research, no. May, vol. i, pp. 79–98 (2015). ISBN 9781466674950. https://doi.org/10.4018/978-1-4666-7495-0
3. Kulkarni, A., Shendge, A., Varma, V., Kimmatkar, N.V.: Intelligent emotion detection system using facial images. Int. Res. J. Eng. Technol. (2015). ISSN 2395–0072
4. Imbernón Cuadrado, L.-E., Manjarrés Riesco, Á., De la Paz López, F.: ARTIE: an integrated environment for the development of affective robot tutors. Front. Comput. Neurosci. **10**, 77 (2016). ISSN 1662–5188. https://doi.org/10.3389/fncom.2016.00077
5. LoBue, V., Thrasher, C.: The child affective facial expression (CAFE) set: validity and reliability from untrained adults. Front. Psychol. **5**(OCT), 1–8 (2014). ISBN 1664-1078 (Electronic), ISSN 16641078, pmid: 25610415. https://doi.org/10.3389/fpsyg.2014.01532
6. Wenzler, S., et al.: Beyond pleasure and pain: facial expression ambiguity in adults and children during intense situations. Emotion **16**(6), 807–814 (2016). ISBN 1528-3542, ISSN 19311516, pmid: 27337681. https://doi.org/10.1037/emo0000185
7. Scassellati, B., Kennedy, J., Belpaeme, T., Ramachandran, A., Tanaka, F.: Social robots for education: a review. Sci. Robot. **3**(21), aat5954 (2018). ISSN 2470–9476. https://doi.org/10.1126/scirobotics.aat5954
8. Skillicorn, D.B., Alsadhan, N., Billingsley, R., Williams, M.-A.: Social Robot Modelling of Human Affective State, pp. 1–32. arxiv: 1705.00786 (2017)
9. Deisenroth, M., Pantic, M., Merino, L., Schuller, B., Evers, V.: Social and Affective Robotics Tutorial, pp. 1477–1478 (2016). ISBN 9781450336031. https://doi.org/10.1145/2964284.2986914
10. Boccanfuso, L., et al.: Emotional robot to examine different play patterns and affective responses of children with and without ASD, In: ACM/IEEE International Conference on Human-Robot Interaction, vol. 2016-April, pp. 19–26 (2016). ISSN 21672148, ISBN 9781467383707. https://doi.org/10.1109/HRI.2016.7451729
11. Keren, G., Ben-David, A., Fridin, M.: Kindergarten assistive robotics (KAR) as a tool for spatial cognition development in pre-school education. In: IEEE International Conference on Intelligent Robots and Systems, pp. 1084–1089 (2012). ISSN 21530858, ISBN 9781467317375. https://doi.org/10.1109/IROS.2012.6385645

12. Schodde, T., Hoffmann, L., Kopp, S.: How to manage affective state in child-robot tutoring interactions? In: 2017 International Conference on Companion Technology, ICCT 2017, vol. 2018-February, pp. 1–6 (2018). ISBN 9781538611609. https://doi.org/10.1109/COMPANION.2017.8287073

13. Spaulding, S., Aviv, T., Breazeal, C.: Affect-aware student models for robot tutors. In: Proceedings of the 15th International Conference on Autonomous Agents and Multiagent Systems (AAMAS 2016) (2016). ISSN 15582914, ISBN 978-1-4503-4239-1

14. Gordon, G., et al.: Affective personalization of a social robot tutor for children's second language skills. In: Proceedings of the 30th Conference on Artificial Intelligence (AAAI 2016), no. 2011 (2016). ISBN 9781577357605

15. Moerland, T.M., Broekens, J., Jonker, C.M.: Emotion in reinforcement learning agents and robots: a survey. Mach. Learn. **107**(2), 443–480 (2018). ISSN 15730565, ISBN 1099401756660, pmid: 16720230. arxiv: 1705.05172. https://doi.org/10.1007/s10994-017-5666-0

16. Devries, T., Biswaranjan, K., Taylor, G.W.: Multi-task learning of facial landmarks and expression. In: Proceedings - Conference on Computer and Robot Vision, CRV 2014, pp. 98–103 (2014). ISBN 9781479943388. https://doi.org/10.1109/CRV.2014.21

17. Pramerdorfer, C., Kampel, M.: Facial Expression Recognition using Convolutional Neural Networks: State of the Art, arxiv: 1612.02903, eprint: 1612.02903 (2016)

18. Zhou, W., Ahrary, A., Kamata, S.I.: Image description with local patterns: an application to face recognition. IEICE Trans. Inf. Syst. **E95-D**(5), 1494–1505 (2012). ISSN 17451361. https://doi.org/10.1587/transinf.E95.D.1494

19. Déniz, O., Bueno, G., Salido, J., De La Torre, F.: Face recognition using histograms of oriented gradients. Pattern Recogn. Lett. **32**(12), 1598–1603 (2011). ISSN 01678655, ISBN 9789896740283. https://doi.org/10.1016/j.patrec.2011.01.004

20. Jain, N., Kumar, S., Kumar, A., Shamsolmoali, P., Zareapoor, M.: Hybrid deep neural networks for face emotion recognition. Pattern Recogn. Lett. (2018). ISSN 01678655, ISBN 978-953-51-1183-2. https://doi.org/10.1016/j.patrec.2018.04.010

21. Kim, B.K., Dong, S.Y., Roh, J., Kim, G., Lee, S.Y.: Fusing aligned and non-aligned face information for automatic affect recognition in the wild: a deep learning approach. In: IEEE Computer Society Conference on Computer Vision and Pattern Recognition Workshops, pp. 1499–1508 (2016). ISSN 21607516, ISBN 9781467388504. https://doi.org/10.1109/CVPRW.2016.187

Author Index

Printed in the United States
By Bookmasters